Kurdish Nationalism: An Analytical History of the Democratic Party of Iranian Kurdistan

Nasser Jahani Asl

Copyright ©2024 Nasser Jahani Asl
All rights reserved

Preface

I would like to address a few important issues briefly. This book, *Kurdish Nationalism: An Analytical History of the Democratic Party of Iranian Kurdistan*, is the outcome of changes that I have done in my PhD Dissertation of 2017 from the University of Victora, British Colombia, Canada. The Dissertation titled *Identity, Politics, Organization: A Historical Sociology of the Democratic Party of Iranian Kurdistan and the Kurdish Nationalist Movement*. Although the structure, essence, and content of the Dissertation significantly remain basically as it was before, the book has been grammatically profoundly edited.

Next, in the "Acknowledgment" and "Dedication" sections, to show my appreciation to the people who supported me in different ways when I was working on my dissertation, I have intentionally not changed the word "dissertation" to "book".

In addition, I greatly appreciate the Emily White, the Marketing Head of Amazon, who have professionally and kindly led the process of publication of this book. I also seriously appreciate the editor of Amazon, Anna Richard, who has profoundly, meticulously, and kindly edited and polished the book.

Moreover, since 2017, the Middle East including Greater Kurdistan and its political organizations has witnessed many changes, however, I have not included them in this book. For instance, since 21 September 2022, the Democratic Party of Iranian Kurdistan and the Kurdistan Democratic Party have seriously and practically started the process of unification, established a shared leadership, and acted under the name of the Democratic Party of Iranian Kurdistan. They are supposed to be officially unified in the 17th Congress of the PDKI. Aside from the advantages and positiveness of this unification for Kurdish nationalism, it is questionable and researchable whether this process is democratic or not.

Finally, *I dedicate this book to my beloved wife Jamileh Halabi and our lovely daughter Rojeh Jahani Asl.* As always, while writing this book, they momentously and completely supported me.

Acknowledgments

When I was working on my dissertation, some people supported me in different ways. To show my gratitude to them, I want to keep these sections almost untouched. So, I have not changed the word "dissertation" to "book".

I would like to thank my Senior Supervisor, Dr. Peyman Vahabzadeh, who accepted me as a graduate student, gave me the freedom to write as I wished, carefully reviewed, corrected, and gave me guidance to work on my dissertation. Indeed, he has guided me long before I started my PhD program at University of Victoria, when I was an undergraduate Sociology and Anthropology student and then a graduate student in Education at Simon Fraser University. I am also grateful to the members of my supervisory committee—Dr. William K. Carroll, Dr. Andrew Wender, and Dr. Behrooz Ghamari-Tabrizi—who generously accepted to read my lengthy dissertation, and provided thoughtful feedback, just as they supported me intellectually during my years in the PhD Program. I am also grateful to Sociology staff members. Carole Rains and Zoe Lu, and Aileen Chong have always assisted me kindly. I also thank Christopher Evans and Rojeh Jahani Asl for contributing their support for my writing and formatting processes.

While I sincerely grateful to all of the people who accepted to be my interviewees, I also thank the leaders, cadres, and members of the political parties including—Mustafa Hijri, Qadir Wirya, Hassan Sharafi, Khalid Azizi, Ebrahim Alizadeh, Abdullah Mohtadi, Amir Karimi, Azad Awraz, Baba Sheikh Husseini, Kamil Nuranifard, Hussein Yazdanpanah, and Rzgar Abaszadeh—who provided the opportunity for me to do my research on their organizations.

During my research, many people including my family members and friends, in different ways such as providing documents, sources, books, introducing other researchers and key informants, and offering places to stay away from my home. My special thanks go to Ata Kawian, Hassan Hatami, Mohayadin Palani, and Qadir Wirya.

In addition, during my research, my brother Karim Jahani Asl suggested a great financial help, and although I did not accept, I sincerely appreciate his offer. Others who provided various financial assistances include my dear Supervisor Peyman Vahabzadeh, and my beloved friends Sylvia Bak and Soheyla Tabai. I truly appreciate their contributions and they share my dissertation with me.

Moreover, since my arrival to Canada 20 years ago I got my BA, MA, and PhD. These achievements could not be easily done without the great comprehensive support of my beloved wife Jamileh Halabi and my cherished daughter Rojeh Jahani Asl. During this long period of study, I have lost precious time with them and neglected some of my duties as a father and a husband due to the extensive and all-consuming nature of my endeavors. Therefore, I greatly appreciate them, and what I have achieved belongs to them.

Finally, lots of family members, friends, and other people have emotionally supported my journey. I am deeply grateful to all of them although their names will not appear in the following list. Below, I have alphabetically listed the names of some other people who have assisted me: Abdul Aziz Mawloudi Sabian, Abdullah Abdali, Abdullah Mohtadi, Ahmad Labadi, Ahmad Safa, Ali Karimi, Alireza Mianali, Dr. Amir Hassanpour, Anwar Karimi, Asaad Yousefi, Ata Kawian, Azad Mohammadzadeh, Ibrahim (Braym) Choukali, Diyako Khayat, Ebrahim Alizadeh, Ebrahim Jahangiri, Ebrahim Sahafi, Fatah Kawian, Galawej Hesam, Qasim Qazi, Golaleh Sharafkandi, Halimeh Yazdanfar, Hammid Bahrami, Hassan Hatami, Hassan Azimi Kor, Hassan Ghazi, Hassan Rastgar, Hosein Bakhchi, Hussein Khalighi, Hussein Nazdar, Kamal Vafaee, Karin Dekker, Kawa Soor, Khalid Yazdanfar, Khosrow Sani, Isa Mergasori, Jafar Mofti, Jalil Gadani, Jina Totagajy, Mohammad Khizri, Morteza Paki, Omar Halabi, Parvin Sidgi, Reza Haydarlou, Saad Qazi, Salahedin Ashti, Salahaddin Hallaj, Sayyed Muhammad Samadi,

Setareh Hallaj, Shahla Rashidi, Sherko Jahani Asl, Shirin Jahanai Asl, Sirwan Qawi Panjeh, Taban Shariat, Tahir Mahmoudi, and Wahed Rahim Zadeh.

Dedication

This "Dedication" includes two parts: (1) as it is in my dissertation; and (2) for this book.

(1):

This dissertation is dedicated to:

Those who have struggled for democracy, social justice, and the freedom of the oppressed Kurdish nation.

It is also dedicated to all leaders and members of the PDKI, KDP, and other leaders of the Kurdish nationalist movement, especially to Qazi Muhammad, Mullah Mustafa Barzani, Jalal Talabani, Abdul Rahman Zabihi, Mamosta Hemin (Sayyed Mohammad Amin Shaikholislami Mukri), Mamosta Hajar (Abdul Rahman Sharafkandi), Abdul Rahman Ghassemlou, Seddiq Anjiri, Sulayman Mo'ini, Isma'il Sharifzadeh, Mullah Awara, Aziz Yousefi, Ghani Bolourian, Amir Qazi, Sadiq Sharafkandi, Abdullah Hassanzadeh, Jalil Gadani, Hassan Rastgar, Fatah Kawian, Hossein Madani, Mostafa Shalmashi, Hussein Khalighi, Khalid Azizi, Isma'il Bazyar, Qadir Wirya, Hassan Hatami, Mohayadin Palani, all women combatant from Mina Khanim Qazi to Golaleh Sharafkandi, and all members of the Democratic Women's Union of Iranian Kurdistan and the Democratic Women's Union of Kurdistan.

As well, this dissertation is also dedicated to my dear supervisor Dr. Peyman Vahabzadeh.

Above all, *I dedicate this dissertation to the loves of my life—my wife Jamileh Halabi and my daughter Rojeh Jahani Asl.*

(2):

I dedicate this book to my beloved wife Jamileh Halabi and our lovely daughter Rojeh Jahani Asl. As always, while writing this book, they momentously and completely supported me.

Translation and Transliteration

All of the English translations of the Kurdish, Persian, and Turkish books, articles, documents, and website texts which have been used for this research have been translated by the author of this book. In general, I have not translated the majority of the geographic names. However, when I have translated the names of a publication, such as a journal, magazine or a TV program, I have sometimes translated them to the English, for instance, the magazine *Nishtman* (Homeland), or the *Tishk* (Ray) TV. As for the translation of the name of the publications, such as books and article in the Bibliography, which rarely the authors have translated the titles to English, I have used those translations. However, sometimes their translations have seemed to be problematic, therefore, I have translated these titles while I have mentioned those authors' translations, too.

The non-English words, such as the Kurdish vocabularies, all appear in the English alphabet. Therefore, non-English transcriptions, such as Kurdish, have not been employed. For instance, the *Yaketi Lawani Democrati Rojhalati Kurdistan* (Democratic Youth Union of Kurdistan) has not been transcribed in Kurdish. In addition, if the source of a word has been in the Kurdish language, it has been written in Kurdish accent, for instance, Eran (Iran). However, if the source has been Persian, it has been written in Persian accent, such as Iran (Iran).

Regarding the transliteration of the words to English, in general I have used the most common, already-existing transliterations in English for Kurdish, Persian, Turkish, and other languages. I have followed common sense for transliterating the non-English words to English, through using the general English alphabet, in order to be easily spelled by English readers. The spellings of the names are based on what the authors have preferred. As a result, a name with a single sound may appear in different spellings such as Hussein, Hossein, and Hosein in this book.

Where the letter Ayn (') appears in the beginning of a word such as ('Ali), I have deleted it and used (Ali). But where this letter is located in the middle of a word, I have showed it such as in (Isma'il) or (As'ad). However, when an author has omitted this letter in his or her writings or name, I have followed that author's spellings. For instance, I have used (Said Kaveh) instead of (Sa'id Kaveh).

In short, I am not a translator, but I have had to translate a huge amount of texts from Kurdish, Persian, and Turkish languages to English to be used in this book. While I have not had access to official translators, I hope in future to get the opportunity to consult with some official translators about some words which have been employed here. In addition, regarding the transliteration and transcription, it is possible to use a more advanced and accurate system.

Table of Contents

Preface i
Acknowledgments iii
Dedication vi
Translation and Transliteration... viii
List of Tables xix
List of Figures xx
Acronyms and Abbreviations xxi
    B: Other Political Organizations xxi
    C: Other Countries xxii
Chapter 1: Introduction 1
    1.1. Book Overview 1
        1.1.1. The scope and originality of research. 2
        1.1.2. The central problem of the book. 3
        1.1.3. The original contributions of this research. 3
    1.2. Methodological Aspects 4
        1.2.1. Data collection. 5
        1.2.2. The Interviews. 5
    1.3. Chapter Outline 6
Chapter 2: Theoretical Perspectives 8
    2.1. Introduction 8
    2.2. Perspectives on Nationalism 8
    2.3. National Liberation 19
    2.4. State-Building 21
    2.5. Michels' Iron Law of Oligarchy 22
    2.6. The Analytical Axes 25
Chapter 3: Kurdish Nationalism 29
    3.1. Introduction 29
        3.1.1. Geography 29
        3.1.2. Population. 29

    3.1.3. Language..30

    3.1.4. Cultural diversity..30

    3.1.5. Economy..31

    3.1.6. Political history..31

    3.1.7. The genocide..35

  3.2. Northern Kurdistan (Turkey)..39

  3.3. Southern Kurdistan (Iraq)..43

  3.4. Western Kurdistan (Syria)..48

  3.5. Kurdish Nationalism in Iran, Turkey, Iraq, and Syria.......................................51

  3.6. Analysis and Conclusion..52

Chapter 4: Kurdish Nationalism in Eastern Kurdistan (Iran) 57

  4.1. Introduction..57

  4.2. Constitutional Revolution 57

  4.3. Foreign Influence 59

  4.4. Reza Shah..61

  4.5. Social Movements in This Period...63

    4.5.1. The Jangali Movement..64

    4.5.2. The Revolt of Colonel Pesyan...65

    4.5.3. The Uprising Led by Khiabani..65

  4.6. Kurdish Nationalism in Iran..66

    4.6.1. Kurdish struggles since the beginning of the 20th century...................66

    4.6.2. The movement of Isma'il Agha Shikak (Simko)...................................67

    4.6.3. Other Kurdish movements...90

  4.7. Conclusion and Analysis...93

Chapter 5: The KDP's History (1945-1970) 97

  5.1. Introduction..97

  5.2. *Hizbi Azadi Kurdistan* (Kurdistan Freedom Party)..99

  5.3. The Anglo-Soviet Occupation of Iran and Kurdistan 102

    5.3.1. Struggle in different areas of Kurdistan...103

    5.3.2. Qazi Muhammad visits Baku..104

xi

5.3.3. Sazmani Jawanani Kurd (Kurdish Youth Organization). 105
5.4. *Komalay Jianaway Kurdistan (J.K.)* (Society for the Revival of Kurdistan [J.K.]) 106
    5.4.1. The founding of the J.K. 106
    5.4.2. The goals of the J.K. 109
    5.4.3. The organization of the J.K. 110
    5.4.4. The J.K.'s activities 111
    5.4.5. Qazi Muhammad joined the J.K. 121
5.5. *Hizbi Demokrati Kurdistan* (Kurdistan Democratic Party [KDP]) 124
    5.5.1. The founding of the KDP. 125
    5.5.2. The 1st Congress of the KDP. 128
    5.5.3. The goals of the KDP. 129
    5.5.4. The organization of the KDP. 132
5.6. The Kurdistan Republic 134
    5.6.1. The Cabinet. 136
    5.6.2. The KDP's and the Kurdistan Republic's achievements. 139
        5.6.2.1. Economy. 139
    5.6.3. The Kurdistan Republic and the Iranian government. 149
    5.6.4. The fall of the Kurdistan Republic. 152
5.7. The Soviet Union and the Kurdistan Republic 161
5.8. Continuation of the KDP's Activities 162
    5.8.1. Komitay Komonisti Kurdistan (Communist Committee of Kurdistan [K.K.K.]) or Komitay Boujanaway Hizbi Demokrati Kurdistan (Committee for the Revival of Kurdistan Democratic Party). 163
    5.8.2. The 1st Conference of the KDP. 169
    5.8.3. The Kurdish Revolution in Iraq in September 1961. 173
    5.8.4. Komitay Sakhkaraway Hizbi Demokrati Kurdistan-Eran (Reconstructing Committee of the KDP-Iran). 176
    5.8.5. The 2nd Congress of the KDP-I. 179

5.8.6. Komitay Ingilabii Hizbi Demokrati Kurdistan-Eran (Revolutionary Committee of the KDP-Iran). 185
    5.8.6.1. The reasons for turning to armed struggle of 1967-1968 by the Revolutionary Committee..................186
    5.8.7. The 2nd Conference of the KDP-I. 194
5.9. Examining the Views and Achievements of the J.K. and the KDP 197
    5.9.1. Views on the J.K..................200
    5.9.2. Factors affecting the fall of the Kurdistan Republic. 202
    5.9.3. Views on the KDP and the Kurdistan Republic..................205
    5.9.4. The effects and the defeat of the Kurdish armed struggle of 1967-1968. 207
5.10. Analysis and Conclusion..................209

Chapter 6: The KDP History Since 1971 213
  6.1. The 3rd Conference of the KDP (I)..................213
  6.2. The 3rd Congress of the Kurdistan Democratic Party (Iran) [KDP (I)]. ..216
    6.2.1. The new Program and Constitution of the KDP (I). 218
    6.2.2. The KDP (I) activities..................219
  6.3. The Iranian Revolution of 1979 222
    6.3.1. The KDP (I)'s participation in the 1979 Revolution. 223
  6.4. The KDP (I) and the Islamic Republic of Iran 228
    6.4.1. The Sanandaj War..................229
    6.4.2. Armed conflict after the Revolution. 230
    6.4.3. The Naqadeh War..................231
    6.4.4. The Mangur Tribe..................232
    6.4.5. The Three-Month War. 234
    6.4.6. The Delegation of the Kurdish People..................239
  6.5. The 4th Congress of the PDKI 240
    6.5.1. The Democratic Party of Iranian Kurdistan (Followers of the Fourth Congress) or PDKI (FFC)..................244

6.5.2. The effects of the Iraq-Iran War on the Kurdish armed struggle in Iran. 258

6.5.3. Conflicts between the PDKI and other political organizations. 259

6.6. The 5th Congress of the PDKI 260

6.7. The 6th Congress of the PDKI 263

6.7.1. The PDKI-Komala clash. 267

6.8. The 7th Congress of the PDKI 272

6.9. The 8th Congress of the PDKI 274

6.9.1. The Fixed List. 274

6.9.2. Hizbi Demokrati Kurdistani Eran, Rebarayati Shorishger (Democratic Party of Iranian Kurdistan-Revolutionary Leadership, or PDKI-RL). 275

6.9.3. The 4th Conference of the PDKI-RL. 278

6.9.4. The Assassination of Ghassemlou. 280

6.10. The 9th Congress of the PDKI-RL 283

6.11. The 9th Congress of the PDKI 283

6.11.1. The assassination of Sharafkandi. 283

6.12. The 10th Congress of the PDKI-RL 285

6.12.1. Unification of the PDKI and the PDKI-RL. 286

6.13. The 10th Congress of the PDKI 287

6.14. The 11th Congress of the PDKI 289

6.15. The 12th Congress of the PDKI 289

6.16. The 13th Congress of the PDKI 290

6.16.1. The split of the Kurdistan Democratic Party (KDP) from the PDKI. 291

6.17. The 14th Congress of the KDP 297

6.18. The 14th Congress of the PDKI 298

6.19. The 15th Congress of the KDP 299

6.20. The 15th Congress of the PDKI 301

6.21. The 16th Congress of the KDP 302

6.22. The PDKI and the KDP since 2015 303

6.23. Summary of the PDKI Clashes with Other Kurdish Groups 308
    6.23.1. Reflections on the PDKI-Komala war and the cases above 310
    6.23.2. The PDKI conflict with the PDKI-RL. 315
  6.24. Analysis and Conclusions 316
    6.24.1. Theories of nationalism and the Kurdish question. 319
Chapter 7: Analyses, Conclusions, Suggestions 322
  7.1. The Political Identity and Struggle of the PDKI 323
  7.2. Revisiting Armed Struggle 325
  7.3. Democracy 328
    7.3.1. Ghassemlou's leadership. 330
    7.3.2. Criticism and judgment 332
    7.3.3. Monopolizing the movement. 333
    7.3.4. Roots of anti-democratic ideas and practices 334
  7.4. Women's status 336
  7.5. Education 340
  7.6. General Conclusions and Suggestions for Fundamental Changes 341
Bibliography 347
Appendices 379
  Appendix 1: Timelines 379
  Appendix 2: The Founders of the J.K. 396
  Appendix 3: The J.K.'s Demands 398
  Appendix 4: The J. K.'s Publications 399
  Appendix 5: The List of the Kurdish Board Which Visited Baku in 1941 401
  Appendix 6: The Declaration of the Kurdistan Democratic Party 402
  Appendix 7: The Six-Article Declaration on 22 January 1946 403
  Appendix 8: The list of the Leadership of the KDP from 1945 to 2016 404
    The 1st Congress of the KDP 404
    The 1st Conference of the KDP-I 405
    The *Komitay Sakhkaraway Hizbi Demokrati Kurdistan-Eran*
(Reconstructing Committee of the Kurdistan Democratic Party-Iran) 406

The 2nd Congress of the KDP-I 406
Komitay Inqilabii Hizbi Demokrati Kurdistan-Eran (Revolutionary Committee of the Kurdistan Democratic Party-Iran or Revolutionary Committee). 408
    The 2nd Conference of the KDP-I 409
    Provisional Leadership of the KDP-I 409
    The 3rd Conference of the KDP (I) 410
    The 3rd Congress of the KDP (Iran) 411
    Komitay Siasy-Nizami (Sia-Mi) (Political-Military Committee or the Sia-Mi Committee) of the KDP (I) 412
    The *Komitay Rabar (K-R)* (Leadership Committee) of the KDP (I) 412
    Yemen 413
    The *Komitay Zagros* (Zagros Committee) of the KDP (I) 413
    The 4th Congress of the PDKI 414
    The *Hizbi Demokrati Kurdistani Eran (Perawani Kongray Chowar)* (Democratic Party of Iranian Kurdistan (Followers of the Fourth Congress) or PDKI (Followers of the Fourth Congress) or PDKI (FFC) 416
    The 5th Congress of the PDKI 418
    The 6th Congress of the PDKI 420
    The 7th Congress of the PDKI (The 40 Years Struggle Congress) 422
    The 8th Congress of the PDKI 424
    Hizbi Demokrati Kurdistani Eran-Rebarayati Shorishger (Iranian Democratic Party of Kurdistan-Revolutionary Leadership [PDKI-RL]) 427
    The 4th Conference of the PDKI-RL 428
    The 9th Congress of the PDKI-RL 430
    The 9th Congress of the PDKI 431
    The 10th Congress of the PDKI-RL 433
    The 10th Congress of the PDKI 434
    The 11th Congress of the PDKI 436
    The 12th Congress of the PDKI 438

The 13th Congress of the PDKI 440
The 14th Congress of the KDP 441
The 14th Congress of the PDKI 443
The 15th Congress of the KDP 446
The 15th Congress of the PDKI 448
The 16th Congress of the KDP 450
Appendix 9: The Cabinet of the Kurdistan Republic of 1946......................453
Appendix 10: Supreme Council of the KDP in May 1946 456
Appendix 11: The Friendship Treaty of Azerbaijan and Kurdistan on 23 April 1946..457
Appendix 12: The publications of the KDP..458
Appendix 13: The Court Martial Charges against Qazi Muhammad............460
Appendix 14: List of People Who Were Executed After the Fall of the Kurdistan Republic..461
Appendix 15: List of the members of the Reconstructing Committee who were prevented to attend in the 2nd Congress..462
Appendix 16: The Declaration of Cooperation between the Revolutionary Committee and the Tudeh Party of Iran 463
Appendix 17: The Scope of Wars between the Peshmergas and the Iranian Government..465
Appendix 18: Organizations of the World Objected the Iranian Regime 467
Appendix 19: A Brief Biography of Abdul Rahman Ghassemlou...............468
Appendix 20: Main Points of the Program and Constitution of the KDP (I).469
Appendix 21: Kurdish Political Organizations 471
Appendix 22: The 8-Article Demands of the Kurds in February 1979.........480
Appendix 23: The Main Points of the 26-Article Plan................................481
Appendix 24: The 6-Article Plan of the PDKI...483
Appendix 25: Democratic Visage 484
Appendix 26: The 10-article Declaration of the PDKI-RL.........................485

Appendix 27: The 6-Point Internal Memo of the Political-Military Commission of the PDKI 486

Appendix 28: The Objectives and Internal Regulation of the PDKI in the 13th Congress 487

Appendix 29: The PDKI-RL's Three-Step Plan 489

Appendix 30: The Main Organizations and Publications of the PDKI and the KDP 490

Appendix 31: The Cooperation Agreement between the PDKI and the Komala 492

    Table 1 493

    Table 2 494

    Table 3 496

    Figure 1 498

INDEX 499

List of Tables

Table 1. Population of the Kurds (Estimated)   493

Table 2. The Size of Kurdish Diasporas   494

Table 3. Women in the Leadership of the
PDKI from 1945 to 2016   496

List of Figures

Figure 1. The PDKI Chart from 1945 to 2016   498

Acronyms and Abbreviations

Acronyms and Abbreviations of the Major Political Parties Related to Iranian Kurdistan.

A: PDKI

KDP	Kurdistan Democratic Party
KDP-I	Kurdistan Democratic Party-Iran
KDP (I)	Kurdistan Democratic Party (Iran)
PDKI	Democratic Party of Iranian Kurdistan
PDKI (FFC)	Democratic Party of Iranian Kurdistan (Followers of the Fourth Congress)
PDKI-RL	Democratic Party of Iranian Kurdistan-Revolutionary Leadership
KDP	Kurdistan Democratic Party

B: Other Political Organizations

CPI — Communist Party of Iran

J.K. — *Komalay Jianaway Kurdistan* (*J.K.*) (Society for the Revival of Kurdistan [J.K.])

KEP — *Komalay Yaksaniy Kurdistan* (Kurdistan Equality Party) or Kurdish Equality Association

Khabat — *Sazmani Khabati Kurdistani Eran* (Organization of Iranian Kurdistan Struggle [Khabat])

Khabat — *Sazmani Khabati Natawayati w Islami Kurdistani Eran* (Organization of Iranian Kurdistan Nationalist and Islamic Revolutionary Struggle)

Komala — *Komalay Shorishgeri Zehmetkeshani Kurdistani Eran* (Komala) (Revolutionary Organization of the Toilers of Iranian Kurdistan. [Komala]). Also, in English called Komala Party of Iranian Kurdistan.

Komala	*Komalay Zahmatkeshani Kurdistan* (Organization of the Toilers of Kurdistan)
Komala (CPI)	Komala Kurdistan's Organization of the Communist Party of Iran (Komala [CPI])
PAK	*Parti Azadi Kurdistan* (Kurdistan Freedom Party [PAK])
PJAK	*Partia Jiyana Azadi Kurdistan* (Party for Free Life in Kurdistan [PJAK])
PSK	*Parti Sarbakhoyy Kurdistan* (Independence Party of Kurdistan [PSK])

C: Other Countries

KDP (Iraq)	*Parti Dimokrati Kurdistan* (Kurdistan Democratic Party)
PUK	*Yaketi Nishtimani Kurdistan* (Patriotic Union of Kurdistan (PUK)
PKK	*Partiya Karkerên Kurdistanê* (Kurdistan Workers' Party [PKK])

Chapter 1: Introduction

The Kurds constitute the largest nation in the world without a state. The struggles of the Kurds in Eastern Kurdistan (Iran), Western Kurdistan (Syria), Northern Kurdistan (Turkey), and Southern Kurdistan (Iraq) have a long history. Modern nationalist struggles of the Kurdish nation in Iran began after WWII, especially with the establishment of the *Komalay Jianaway Kurdistan (J.K.)* (Society for the Revival of Kurdistan [J.K.]) in 1942, and its transformation into *Hizbi Demokrati Kurdistan* (Kurdistan Democratic Party [KDP]) in 1945, and finally renamed as *Hizbi Demokrati Kurdistani Eran* (Democratic Party of Iranian Kurdistan [PDKI]) in 1980. While Iranian Kurdish nationalist movement has been mainly led by the PDKI (see Figure 1), other Kurdish political organizations have also significantly participated in this movement.

This book, based on my dissertation, "Identity, Politics, Organization: A Historical Sociology of the Democratic Party of Iranian Kurdistan and the Kurdish Nationalist Movement," focuses on the Democratic Party of Iranian Kurdistan (PDKI) to investigate Kurdish nationalism in Iranian Kurdistan. This chapter offers a summary of the key aspects of the book.

1.1. Book Overview

There are no comprehensive studies of the PDKI's history and politics in any language. Given the significant role the PDKI has played in championing Kurdish identity and keeping Kurdish nationalism in Iran alive, the lack of a comprehensive study of the KDP and PDKI is rather surprising. This book fills this major gap in existing research about the history and politics of Iranian Kurdish nationalism. The existing research has been largely impeded by the lack of original resources, historical documents, and life histories of the major actors involved in this movement, focusing on the longest-standing Kurdish nationalist party of Iran, the Kurdistan Democratic Party (KDP), later renamed the Democratic Party of

Iranian Kurdistan (PDKI), and its many splinter groups. Since 2006, a faction named KDP split from the PDKI, and presently these two parties are equally the leading the nationalist organizations in Iranian Kurdistan.

1.1.1. The scope and originality of research. This book launches the first full-fledged research, in any language, focusing on the PDKI, as the oldest and most influential political organization. Since the PDKI has never been the subject of a serious study, this book offers the only extensive scholarly project on the subject that employs exhaustive archival research, vast literature review, and extensive open-ended, in-depth interviews with the leaders and cadres of the party. The PDKI holds that the party was founded on 16 August 1945 in Mahabad, Iran, and was officially launched on 23 October 1945 as the party to advocate national rights of the Iranian Kurds and a democratic, federative political system for Iran. The PDKI has historically spearheaded the Kurdish movement in Iran. But other, smaller Kurdish parties have also contributed to this struggle. These parties reflect the social, political, and ideological diversity among the Kurds. *Komalay Shorishgeri Zehmetkeshani Kurdistani Eran (Komala)* or the Revolutionary Organization of the Toilers of Iranian Kurdistan (Komala) is the most important party outside the PDKI lineage, and investigating the relationship between the PDKI and the Komala has also been a part of this study. As well, the study will probe the emergence of Kurdish nationalist movement in Iran that began with the revolt led by Isma'il Agha Shikak (Simko) and continued with foundation of the J.K.

This study attends to: the historical conditions of modern, ethnonational movements; the relations between the PDKI and the Iranian state; the activities of the PDKI and other Kurdish parties; and the theoretical, political, and cultural education within the PDKI. It also considers the conceptions of democracy in the PDKI; its organizational structures and power relations; the splits and reunifications within the PDKI; and class and gender relations within the PDKI.

1.1.2. The central problem of the book. In Iranian Kurdistan, we witness the prolonged presence of a grassroots, nationalist social movement that has persevered and survived for more than seven decades in the face of brutal repression, military occupation, and persistent discrimination. This movement, above all, indicates that *the Kurds in Iran have developed, mostly through socialization and self-didactic political education, a collective sense of distinct Kurdish national identity*. While the origins of *modern* Kurdish movement in Iran goes back to the Kurdish cultural renaissance initiated by the J.K., the movement itself has been led by notable Kurdish intellectuals who have articulated the demands of Kurdish people and provided the Kurds with a vision for their common future. As such, the Kurdish movement must be understood in the context of Iranian and Middle Eastern entry into modernity.

While the PDKI has acted in the name of the Kurdish people, it has mainly represented the "national" dimension of Kurdish demands. Issues of patriarchy, gender discrimination, and class differences within Kurdish society have been treated as secondary, at times bypassed, silenced, ignored, or given cursory lip service. Organizationally, *the PDKI leadership has often undermined the very democratic principles that defined it as a national liberation movement*. The book calls this curious phenomenon the party's "constitutive paradox."

1.1.3. The original contributions of this research. There has been no extensive scholarly research on the PDKI. While there has been research on Kurdish nationalism (Entessar, 1992, Jwaideh, 1961; Koohi-Kamali Dehkordi, 1995; Natali, 2005, Qazi, 2012; Sutton, 1997; Vali, 2011; Yassin, 1995), an MA thesis analyzes the PDKI ideology, organizational structure, leadership, and methods (Mawloudi Sabian, 1994, p. 64). This book is the first extensive scholarly project on the PDKI. *By producing new data, formerly unstudied, this book contributes to literature on nationalist movements in general and the Kurdish movements in particular.*

This study relies on extensive literature and archival research in Kurdish, Persian, English, and Turkish, *the equivalent of more than 60,000 pages of literature.* Many sources here have never been used by other researchers. Thousands of pages from various sources were also consulted but not cited. I conducted *in-depth interviews with 29 high-ranking activists and leaders of major parties. In total, I conducted 93.54 hours of recorded interviews.* As a native Kurdish speaker, I based my research on primary sources in Kurdish, the language of the movement, and the non-Kurdish resources were used as supplemental to the original sources. *I studied Kurdish and non-Kurdish sources that go back 74 years. This is the most comprehensive research on Iranian Kurdish nationalism through the PDKI history.* In addition to several months of fieldwork, *it also took me four years to organize the massive data I had gathered and write this book.*

The primary task of this book is the production of new data. Analytically, this book shows how the Kurdish nationalist movement in Iran is an outcome of Iran's entry into political modernity. Bringing together the concepts of national liberation and nationalism, it highlights the democratic aspect of the movement. Lastly, the book shows and argues that an influential and leading democratic political organization that fights for democracy and social justice can paradoxically and in practice undermine the very democratic values for which it fights. The consequences of this tendency are discussed in the Conclusion.

1.2. Methodological Aspects

This book dwells, by and large, in historical sociology. Methodologically, it entails literature review, discourse and content analysis, in-depth, open-ended interviews, and archival studies. I spent June to December 2012 for fieldwork mainly in the Kurdistan Regional Government (KRG) where I visited Erbil, Koya, Sulaymaniyah, and Qandil Mountain—and where I visited headquarters of Iranian Kurdish parties—and subsequently Bonn, Amsterdam, Stockholm, Oslo, and

London. I spent four months in Kurdistan and two months in Europe. In the PDKI and the KDP areas, I observed *Fergay Siasi-Nizami* (Political-Military Academy), the Education Commission, the Publication Commission, the Libraries, the Women's Union, the Youth Union, and the Student Union. I also visited the Protection Council of Political Prisoners of Eastern Kurdistan, the Children's Section, the Propaganda (*tablighat*) Commission, the TV and Radio Section, the Secretariat Office, and more. While the PDKI imposed recording restrictions for me and denied me participation in their 15th Congress, 23-29 May 2012, the KDP gave me the freedom to do so and allowed me as a guest in its 6th Congress of *Yaketi Lawani Democrati Rojhalati Kurdistan* (Democratic Youth Union of Kurdistan), 29 September-3 October 2012.

1.2.1. Data collection. I have heavily relied on the printed and on-line sources in English, Persian, Kurdish, and Turkish, both scholarly and non-scholarly, as well as party literature, group archives, activist memoirs, commentaries, and websites. Extensive research was needed due to absence of serious research on the subject, in particular no research in English. Periodicals and newspapers—including *Nishtman* (Homeland), organ of the J.K., and *Kurdistan*, Organ of the KDP—were extensively used and constituted the second main source of data. Different periodicals including newspapers and magazines in Kurdish were also consulted. Online sources constitute the third source of data. I found major sources in the Kurdology Institute (Bonn), Kurdish Institute (Stockholm), and International Institute of Social History (Amsterdam).

1.2.2. The Interviews. To conduct and analyze different stages of the interviews, including following purposeful sampling; contacting with the potential participants; taking care of the participants' feelings; creating a climate of trust; considering the fieldworker's position; analyzing of the data; and verifying (validating) procedures, I followed the instructions of various academic literatures. These literatures include (Gall, Gall, and Borg, 2003, p. 178; Legard, Keegan, and

Ward, 2003, pp. 143-145; Zinn 1979, p. 209; Shahidian, 2001, p. 61; Spencer, Ritchie, and O'Connor, p. 217; Ritchie, Spencer, and O'Connor, 2003, pp. 220-48; Creswell, 1998, pp. 201-203, p. 217; Lewis and Ritchie, 2003, pp. 275-76; Patton, 1999, p. 1195).

I tried to recruit equal numbers of participants from the two major factions of the PDKI and the KDP, although I could only approximate this goal. Some leaders of the PDKI (Mustafa Hijri, Hassan Sharafi, Kava Bahrami, Nahid Hosseini, and Ilham Chaichi) warmly accepted my invitation but unfortunately did not keep their pledge. It was not easy to find key informants among women, and some women activists did not take part in the interviews despite their promises. No women in the PDKI leadership participated with the exception of a member of Democratic Women's Union of Iranian Kurdistan (Fatime Osmani). In total, *29 people were interviewed—23 men and 6 women*. This is the party affiliation of the interviewees: the PDKI members, former PDKI members, former PDKI-FFC; Communist Party of Iran (CPI); Organization of Iranian Kurdistan (Khabat); Revolutionary Organization of the Toilers of Iranian Kurdistan (Komala); Party for Free Life in Kurdistan (PJAK); and independent people. All interviews were conducted in Kurdish in 46 sessions and 93.54 hours.

1.3. Chapter Outline

Chapter 2 offers a condensed theoretical overview of the theories of nationalism, national liberation, state-building, Robert Michels' concept of the "iron law of oligarchy," and Peyman Vahabzadeh's "constitutive paradox." It will bring these theoretical aspects together in order to extract a workable theory for the book. Chapter 3 provides a brief account of the historical development of the Kurdish nation and the Kurdish nationalism in Turkey, Iraq, and Syria. Chapter 4 attends to Kurdish nationalism in Iran from the twentieth century to World War II.

It attends to the process of state building in Iran and its consequences for social and nationalist movements in the country.

Chapter 5 offers the original research of this book on the Kurdish nationalist movement from World War II to 1973. It discusses the formation of pioneer political organizations of the Kurdistan Freedom Party and the J.K., the predecessor to the PDKI, before discussing the Kurdistan Republic (Mahabad Republic) and the evolution of the PDKI. Chapter 6 also offers original data and investigates the history of the KDP-I (later PDKI) from 1971 to the present time. It discusses in relative detail the party's transformations and activities, the party's many splits, its participation in the 1979 Revolution, and its relations with other Kurdish opposition parties.

Chapter 7 provides the final general analyses and conclusions, bringing together the themes and data discussed in this book. In particular, it will offer an analysis of how to rebuild and democratize the Kurdish organizations and deepen democratic values within the Kurdish movement.

As Chapter 7 indicates, the book offers the most comprehensive account of the subject using scientific methods through the researcher's objective approach. But it is also a work of advocacy for the rights of the Iranian Kurds and the Kurdish people everywhere. It is hoped that this book may contribute, in a small way, to the struggles of the Kurds for liberation, justice, democracy, and dignity.

Chapter 2: Theoretical Perspectives

2.1. Introduction

This chapter will introduce the main theoretical approaches that will enable the analytical framework for this book. The thematic works of literature that, to varying degrees, account for my analysis will hinge on three axes: nationalism, national liberation, and state-building. Having delved deeply into the various schools of nationalism and national liberation theories,[1] my primary concern is to construct a workable theory rather than critically examine the various aspects of the existing literature (unless the latter is necessary).

2.2. Perspectives on Nationalism

It is not possible to offer a satisfactory review of the vast literature on theories of nationalism in just one book. Numerous scholars have analyzed the emergence of modern nationalism and offered various taxonomies of nationalist movements. Similar to many other concepts in the Social Sciences, views on nation and nationalism remain highly contested. According to McCrone (1998), "There

---

[1] Gottfried Herder (Davis, 1978), Ernest Renan (1994; McCrone, 1998), Elie Kedourie (1993), Ernest Gellner (1997; 1983; 2006), Eric Hobsbawm (1993), Tom Narin (1994), Miroslaw Hroch (McCrone, 1998; Kellas, 1991), Charles Tilly (Spencer and Wollman, 2002), Michael Mann, Anthony Giddens, John Breuilly and Paul Brass (Spencer and Wollman, 2002), Anthony D. Smith (Spencer and Wollman, 2002; McCrone, 1998; Smith, 1989; Smith, 2001b), Hug Seton-Watson (1994), John Hutchinson (2001), Montserrat Guibernau (1996), John Stuart Mill and T. H. Green (Kymlicka, 1995; Mill, 1958), Karl Marx and Friedrich Engels (Spencer and Wollman, 2002; Marx and Engels, 1978; Thompson and Fevre, 2001; Davis, 1978; Löwy, 1976), Lenin and Stalin (Lenin and Stalin, 1970), Rosa Luxemburg (Davis, 1978), Ernesto Che Guevara and Régis Debrey (Davis, 1978), Lois A. West (1997), Floya Anthias and Yuval-Davis (Spencer and Wollman, 2002), Cynthia Enloe (West, 1997), Anne McClintock (Spencer and Wollman, 2002), Deniz Kandiyoti (1996), Nira Yuval-Davis (1997), Lynn M. Kwiatkowski and Lois A. West (1997), Kumari Jayawardena (1986), Sylvia Walby (2006), Gisela Kaplan (1997), Jill Benderly (1997), Valentine Moghadam (1997), Zengie A. Mangaliso (1997), Haunani-Kay Trask (1997), Norma Stoltz Chinchilla (1997), Alma M. Garcia (1997), Patrice LeClerk and Lois A. West (1997), Homi Bhabha (Salehi, 2001), Derrida, Deleuze and Guattari, Kristeva, Spivak, and Bhabha (Leonard, 2005).

simply is no agreement about what nationalism is, what nations are, how we are to define nationality" (p. 3). Nationalism is a political ideology as well as a social and political movement (Gellner, 1983, pp. 1, 124; Sheyholislami, 2008, p. 64). It is not confined to a specific territory or social class. It is a social and political movement that shows "itself in rich and poor countries; it has left-wing as well as right-wing variants; it works with, as well as against, movements of class and of gender" (McCrone, 1998, p. vii). One variation of right-wing nationalism is racist nationalism, although the relationship between racism and nationalism is disputable. In the context of nineteenth-century Europe, many nationalist movements, especially the ones with imperialist drive—e.g., Britain, France, Italy, and Germany—developed in the space in which "scientific racism" prevailed. In addition, in the twentieth century, the Nazi version of nationalism mobilized a racial logic. Theorists like Benedict Anderson and Montserrat Guibernau separate nationalism and racism: whereas nationalism inspires love and creativity that comes from an aspiration for a better, collective life, racism is destructive and spreads hatred. While this is true, it seems that Anderson underrates the reality of racist elements within nationalism and their negative cultural and social consequences (Spencer and Wollman, 2002, pp. 40, 64-65).

The above was meant to show how unsettling the understanding of nationalism could be. Therefore, it is useful to agree on certain classifications. Spencer and Wollman (2002) argue that theories of nationalism, by and large, present a sharp and dualistic distinction between two forms of nationalism: progressive and reactionary. Western nationalism is often received as civic, progressive, political, and liberal, while Eastern nationalism is deemed to be cultural, ethnic, and illiberal (p. 94). Of course, one cannot but object to the prejudicial cliché of the above distinction.

A prevailing kind of categorization of nationalist movements is to group them as primordial and modern. The term "primordialist" was used for the first time by Edward Shils (1957) (Hutchinson and Smith, 1996, p. 8). Primordiality focuses on the role of birth facts in social relationships. This paradigm is made up of different cultural and sociobiological perspectives. "The primordial beliefs are beliefs about relational modes of attachment constitutive of lines of descent, both familial and territorial" (Grosby, 2001, p. 252). Based on common factors, including biology and territory, it is argued that people build different groups. Perennialism represents a modern version of primordialism. Anthony D. Smith (1998) explains that the perennialists look at a nation as a long-term historical development and "tend to drive modern nations from fundamental ethnic ties, rather than from the process of modernization" (pp. 223-224). Walker Connor (1994a), who takes a perennialist position, avers that the word "nation" comes from the Latin verb *nasci*, "to be born," and the Latin noun *nascionem*, meaning "*breed*" or "*race*" (p. 38). This etymology clearly expresses the notion of common blood relations. Connor (1994b) refers to some anthropologists who suggest that a five-stage development of society results in the creation of a nation that includes family, band, clan, tribe, and nation. Nevertheless, this is not an iron law. In his view, a "*nation* refers to a group of people who *believe* they are ancestrally related" (p. 212; original italics).

According to the primordial approach, nations have originated with ethnic groups. Connor (1994a) refines Ernest Barkers' distinction between "ethnic group" and "nation," noting that "a nation is a self-aware ethnic group" (p. 45). This statement reveals the continuity between ethnic groups and nations. Such examples as the disintegration of former Yugoslavia and the formation of (ethnic) Balkan states are often used as the "proof" for this approach. Connor maintains that the American people do not constitute a nation if the precise meaning of the word is employed. He articulates that the term "nation-state" suggests that a nation has its own state, but unfortunately, the word "nation" is too generally used to describe all states. Connor reveals that the world is not largely comprised of nation-states. A survey of the 132 countries in 1971 reveals that only 12 states (9.1%) can be labeled as "nation-states" (Connor, 1994a, pp. 38-39). Likewise, Manuel Castells (1997) differentiates between nations and nation-states, arguing that "nations are, historically and analytically, entities independent from the state" (p. 30).

To illustrate how the primordialists observe a nation, one can refer to scholars who confirm that the formation of the English nation occurred centuries before modernism. Adrian Hastings, a perennialist, states that the English nations had formed in the late fourteenth century, while Leah Greenfield believes that England, in the sixteenth century, was the first nation. In addition, Liobera affirms that the concept of nation is older than the modern era, and people have had a sense of national identity since the end of the medieval era in England. However, according to a survey, only approximately five percent of the English people had this sense of national identity (Spencer and Wollman, 2002, pp. 30-33). Here, we can see how theories of nationalism inadvertently invoke contested readings of history.

In contrast to the primordialist approach, modernists maintain that nations and nationalism are modern phenomena. Like the primordialists, though, the modernists also entail different theoretical perspectives. In analyzing the origins of nations, the modernists do not probe the primeval or medieval but only the modern era (Spencer and Wollman, 2002, p. 34). Most modernists date the birth of nations to the end of the eighteenth century or the French Revolution of 1789, while other modernists date it back to the American Revolution of 1776 or the English Revolution (1649-1660) as the first modern revolution. It is noticeable that these classifications may not always be clear-cut because it is possible to see overlaps between them, and some authors may use different perspectives and classifications. For instance, to clarify the connection between ethnic and civic aspects of nations, Smith writes that "modern nations are simultaneously and necessarily civic and ethnic" (Spencer and Wollman, 2002, p. 95). Similarly, George Schöpflin (2001) asserts that all nations possess both civic and ethnic characteristics. Thus, ethnicity is not just found in the "east." For instance, in the French secular state, values that come from French ethnic culture are dominant in the country (p. 60).

Anthony Smith believes in a "midway" between primordialist and modernist paradigms. Smith's "ethno-symbolism" or "historical ethno-symbolism" approach suggests that the rise of nations can be traced to previous ethnic groups. Nations are made around "ethnic cores," which extended from pre-modern *"ethnie"* (Spencer and Wollman, 2002, p. 28). Smith's concept of "ethnie" reveals two fundamental features: the *myth* of common descent and common historical memories (McCrone, 1998, pp. 52-53). Smith (2001b) states that "historical ethno-symbolism" is a method for the investigation of ethnicity and nationalism that places emphasis on the effects of "myths, SYMBOLS, memories, values and traditions in their formation, persistence and change" (p. 84; original emphasis). Ethno-symbolism differs from primordialism, modernism, and instrumentalism, the latter holding that the elites, in order to gain political and economic interests, create and use nationalism as an instrument to incite people to support them. In contrast to the primordialists, the ethno-symbolists see ethnies and *nations as historical phenomena that change through the process of nation-building*. They reject that the nation is a "given" and a natural constituent of society. In contrast to the instrumentalists and modernists, the ethno-symbolists examine the creation of nations from larger historical trends, which take many of their features from the pre-modern ethnic elements (Smith, 2001b, p. 87). According to Spencer and Wollman (2002), Smith takes a reductionist approach to nationalism while underlining the pre-existing cultural loyalties and discounting political factors. They also argue that Smith holds that nation and nationalism provide a real socio-cultural foundation for world order (p. 29).

Turning to the Marxist historical-materialist view of nationalism, V. I. Lenin understands nationalism as historically progressive because it liberates the masses from feudal passivity, fights against national oppression, and asserts popular sovereignty—all of which are on par with the bourgeois-democratic revolutions of the nineteenth century. However, Lenin overemphasizes the role of the bourgeoisie with respect to the roots of nationalism (Lenin and Stalin, 1970, p. 9; Davis, 1978, p. 87). He defends the "right of nations to self-determination, i.e., the right to secede and form independent national states" (Lenin and Stalin, 1970, p. 11). For Lenin, being an internationalist in an oppressive nation means advocating for the freedom and the right of secession of oppressed nations, even if the chance of separation is only one in a thousand (Lenin and Stalin, 1970, p. 46). Stalin presents a more coherent view of nationalism. Giving a specific definition of "nation," Stalin points out, "*A nation is a historically constituted, stable community of people, formed on the basis of a common language, territory, economic life, and psychological make-up manifested in a common culture*" (Lenin and Stalin, 1970, p. 68; original italics). He emphasizes that only when all of these conditions exist simultaneously will there be a nation. For instance, the Jews have lived in different countries, and thus, they do not constitute a nation (Lenin and Stalin, 1970, p. 68). Stalin proposes that modern nations have come into existence in the era of "rising capitalism," and the bourgeoisie has played the leading role in this process (Lenin and Stalin, 1970, pp. 72-73). Similar to Lenin, Stalin advocated the rights of all nations for self-determination (Lenin and Stalin, 1970, p. 75). The content and the essence of national movements are apparent in Stalin's perspective. He claims that the content of these movements in different places varies from agrarian demands, language features, civic equality (e.g., freedom of religion), and having its own officials and parliament. Relating to national struggles, Stalin emphasizes that under the era of rising capitalism, the struggle is among the bourgeois classes and has always been essentially a bourgeois struggle. Nevertheless, the proletariat should fight against national oppression (Lenin and Stalin, 1970, p. 74).

Stalin's approach to nationalism has been the subject of criticism. His rigid definition of "nation" contains serious limitations. Multilingual nations like Switzerland (which contains four nationalities) are excluded from his concept of a nation. He ignores one of the most fundamental features of a nation—which for Ernest Renan is the sufficient feature (McCrone, 1998)—that people in a specific territory who *believe* that they are a nation play a fundamental role in constituting a nation. To examine the criteria of "historically evolved" and "stability," Pakistan and most of the new nations in Africa do not embrace the elements proposed by Stalin. Poland, in pre-WWI, was divided among three counties and did not have unity regarding economic life, but Stalin still accepted it as a nation. Stalin does not explain how nations could be founded under conditions where there are diverse nationalities (Davis, 1978, pp. 71-72). As a result, Michael Löwy (1976) prefers Lenin's view of nationalism. He stresses that Stalin's theory is dogmatic and restrictive when he claims that the four characteristics of a nation should exist together to qualify for a legitimate national claim. This led Stalin to claim that Georgia was not a nation since it was divided into different principalities prior to the second half of the nineteenth century and did not have a "common economic life" (p. 95).

The historical sociological approaches such as those of Eric Hobsbawm (1993) and Ernest Gellner (1983, 1997) explain nationalism in terms of the process of industrialization of nations and the formation of new classes. For Gellner, nationalism provides the masses with a new language through which they can express their dismay at their formative economic disadvantages. According to Gellner (1983), nationalism provides the masses with a new political language that "enables them to conceive and express their resentments and discontents in intelligible terms" (p. 62). To critique Gellner, James G. Kellas (1991)—who opts for an "integrated theory" of political nationalism—points out that Gellner does not explain the reason for the existence of nationalism in pre-industrial societies such as Scotland in the Middle Ages and England in Queen Elizabeth's period. Also, Kellas argues, Gellner does not provide reasons for the emergence of nationalism in the Third World countries or in "post-industrial" societies governed by "post-materialist values" (p. 44).

Benedict Anderson (2006), an influential modernist theorist, defines a nation as "an imagined political community—and imagined as both inherently limited and sovereign" (p. 6). He explains that it is imagined in four following ways: a nation is "imagined" since "the members of even the smallest nation will never know most of their fellow-members"; it is "limited" because even the largest nation is finite; it is imagined as "sovereign"; and a nation is "imagined as a community, because, regardless of the actual inequality and exploitation that may prevail in each, the nation is always conceived as a deep, horizontal comradeship" (Anderson, 2006, pp. 6-7). Print technology (print-capitalism) had a fundamental effect in creating nationalism. The scope of print material connected people to each other. Also, maps have had the function of creating the image of a nation bound together (Anderson, 2006).

Certain components of Anderson's thoughts are questionable. Kellas (1991) points out that Anderson's conditions for the rise of nationalism are vague since print-capitalism could both create and destroy nations. Many languages and ethnic groups have died out or been weakened during the process of struggling against the nations that have access to print media. Moreover, Anderson's analysis of the relationship between religion and nationalism is problematic. Kellas states that nationalism does not always replace religion, and the two sometimes cooperate to achieve the same goals. Some churches or mosques in countries like Ireland, Poland, Armenia, Israel, and Iran have indeed supported nationalism (pp. 47- 48).

According to Afshin Marashi (2014), since the 1980s, a new type of cultural nationalism has emerged that considers "the nation" as a cultural category. The new approach underlines "the distinctively modern processes that work to make, shape, or construct a particular constellation of symbolic associations comprising a national identity" (pp. 9-10). John Hutchinson (2001) is a leading proponent of cultural nationalism. As he indicates, some scholars believe that cultural nationalism is a reactionary phenomenon. Hans Kohn claims that there are two types of Western and Eastern nationalisms. Western nationalism is rational and political, while Eastern nationalism is mystical and cultural. Cultural nationalism first appeared in Eastern Europe and Asia as a reaction to Western European nations. However, Eastern countries were conscious of their social backwardness and refused rationalist forms of citizenship and instead applauded an ideal ancient nation (Hutchinson, 2001, p. 41). The supposed "irrationality" of eastern nationalism results from the weakness of civic institutions (Schöpflin, 2001, p. 61). Hutchinson (2001) criticizes Kohn, pointing out that Kohn disregards the modernizing elements of cultural nationalism and its reformist nature. Kohn also neglects the appearance of cultural nationalism in "advanced" Western societies like England in the late nineteenth century (p. 42). According to Hutchinson (2001), scholars have disdainfully treated cultural nationalism, regarded it as regressive and temporary, and disappearing gradually with full industrialization. However, more "recently, there has been something of a re-evaluation of the moral and symbolic dimension of cultural nationalism, which recognizes its distinctive communitarian ethos and politics, its socially innovative qualities, and its embeddedness in the modern world" (p. 40).

Some theoreticians of nationalism consider the role of the intellectuals in the nationalist movements negatively. Elie Kedourie takes a critical position against nationalism, calling it a disease scattered from the West to the world. Nationalist doctrines were generated by intellectuals who were marginalized from politics due to the effects of rationalism from the Enlightenment. Kedourie blames the intellectuals who created a theory based on the assumption that nations are natural bodies of the human race. These intellectuals turned to Romanticism and created nationalism after a certain image of a nation. Herder and Fichte were among these intellectuals. Likewise, intellectuals from colonial societies who were educated in the West became alienated from their native cultures, and their main aim was to achieve power and privilege. Kedourie's position is criticized because he does not consider the kind of nationalism that is supported by the official intellectuals who already have power and status (Guibernau, 2010, pp. 139-140). However, Kedourie's perspective concerning the detrimental role of intellectuals in nationalism is questionable. Montserrat Guibernau (2010) asserts that although intellectuals may assist sub-state nationalism, they are not after economic privileges or a desire for power. Many intellectuals have a genuine love for their nation and make an effort to see their nations flourish, especially under the states that oppress the nation culturally, economically, or politically. Within these movements, groups, and parties that fight for national rights, the feeling of belonging to a nation is created through the establishment of camaraderie among its members. Yet, it is also true that among intellectuals, there also exists competition. In this case, "[t]hey struggle to become more influential, obtain more recognition or be offered a better job" (p. 146).

Montserrat Guibernau (1996) declares that nations have five dimensions: psychological, which means the consciousness of constituting a group, as well as cultural, territorial, political, and historical dimensions. She defines a nation as "a human group conscious of forming a community, sharing a common culture, attached to a clearly demarcated territory, having a common past and a common project for the future and claiming the right to rule itself" (p. 47). Assessing Guibernau's understanding of the nation, Sheyholislami (2008) writes that this definition rejects the essentialist view of the nation as a natural and perennial object while recognizing the nations that do not have states (p. 48).

Concerning the concept of stateless nations, Guibernau (1999) explains that "nations without states" are "nations which, in spite of having their territories included within the boundaries of one or more states, by and large, do not identify with them" (p. 16). Some nations without states include Catalonia, Quebec, Scotland, the Basque, Flanders, Palestinians, Tibetans, and the Kurds. Nationalisms of these nations are socio-political movements that aim to obtain the right to self-determination (Guibernau, 1999, pp. 16, 18; Guibernau, 1996, p. 101).

Here, I offer general conclusions about nation and nationalism. Regarding the concept of "nation," ethno-symbolism offers an intermediary as well as a more inclusive outlook. Thus, in the ethno-symbolist approach, nations are seen as modern phenomena which have roots in pre-modern cultures. As a result, I argue that *nations are both a real and constructed phenomenon,* and nations have both objective and subjective features. The objectivity of nations is reflected in their language, culture, religion, economy, and territory. The subjective aspect is shown in the will of people who believe in being a nation while trying to create and maintain a national identity. The *final factor in defining a nation is the subjective one* involving the decision and the will of people to call themselves a nation and live together. Finally, *a nation is, or wants to establish, a self-ruling community based on some relatively shared factors such as territory, language, culture, economy, historical memory, and legal rights.* Self-ruling or self-determination may have different forms, such as autonomy, federalism, and, in the radical version, an independent state. Based on this definition, the *Kurds are a nation.*

As for the concept of nationalism, it is settled that nationalism as a political ideology was developed in the nineteenth century in Europe. Nationalism as a reality could have been around earlier, and on this more research and analysis are needed in both Europe and the rest of the world. Nationalism was born as an ideology and a sentiment as well as a social and political movement that aims at preserving and advancing a national identity by achieving and maintaining a nation's social and political self-determination. With respect to the reasons for the advent of nationalism, it can be concluded that there are multi-factored causes for the emergence of national movements. Some of these factors include the advancement of modernity, establishment of modern states, emergence of the capitalist mode of production, progression of education, especially after print-capitalism, the Industrial Revolution, uneven development, the emergence of core and periphery areas, anticolonial liberation movements against imperialism, reactions against official nationalism, the fight against the internal colonialism, and the struggle for identity.

As for the discussion of the essence of nationalism—whether it is progressive or reactionary—there is no agreement among scholars. As both an ideology and a movement, nationalism is a double-edge phenomenon: it can be progressive or reactionary and right- or left-leaning. Where nationalism is on par with the expansion of democracy and social justice, it is regarded as progressive. If it acts as a barrier to these objectives, it is deemed to be reactionary. What is important is to recognize that within every nationalist movement, it is possible to find both reactionary and progressive sides.

2.3. National Liberation

Frantz Fanon (2004) argues that colonialism creates a Manichaean condition in which the world within a colonized country is divided between the imperial colonizer and the oppressed colonized. In this binary context, the language of the colonized people is one of violence since anti-colonial violence is the only method that can deliver the colonized from the colonizer's violence. Anti-colonial violence has an "enlightening" effect on the masses, encouraging them to join the struggle for national liberation (Fanon, 2004, p. 52). Writing in the context of the Algerian war of liberation, Fanon rejects the attempts by French colonizers to help and "develop" Algeria through the expansion of universities, civil services, and, importantly, the labor unions (2004, p. 74-76). Pro-liberation colonized intellectuals often have a tendency to romanticize the past (Fanon, 2004, p. 148).

Because colonialism destroys culture (Fanon, 2004, p. 170), the war of liberation involves a rebuilding of the national culture. The outcome of national liberation is a nationalist consciousness, the emergence of a new people, but Fanon was suspicious of this national consciousness. He observed that many liberated nations in Africa, under corrupt leaders, have actually been coopted by their former colonizers and entered into a partnership with them. So, for Fanon, nationalism in the post-WWII age was a consequence of colonization. This is nationalism without decolonization (Fanon, 1994, p. 132), which Fanon rejects. Instead of nationalism, Fanon advocates a pan-African decolonization (Fanon, 2004, p. 106-7). Fanon regards the rise of postcolonial nations as a consequence of the anti-colonial war of national liberation by the colonized nations. It is important to note that for Fanon, an authentic nation emerges only when a colonized people are *liberated*, not when it is granted the right to a nation's sovereignty by imperial powers. There are certain similarities between Fanon's theory and the advocacy of Lenin and Stalin for oppressed nations' self-assertion, although there are important differences in their theoretical views.

Michael Hechter, a Marxist scholar, proposes an argument about "internal colonialism," which is particularly relevant to this book. Hechter rejects the "modernization theory" or "diffusion theory" like that of Karl Deutsch, based on which modernity causes the homogenization of ethnic groups. Hechter suggests that modernization does not necessarily cause the unity of ethnic groups within a state and instead may produce conflicts between ethnicities. This occurs from the inequalities between territories, resulting in downgrading peripheral regions to disadvantage positions. In this case, the peripheries react in a hostile manner to the core. The reason for the existence of Scottish, Welsh, and Irish nationalisms is the reality of "internal colonialism" by the English core (Kellas, 1991, pp. 39-40).

2.4. State-Building

Since my research probes Kurdish nationalism in Iran, it is important to refer to the aspects of state-building before we attend to the actual historical process of state-building and its effect on the Kurdish movement in Iran. Iran has never been colonized by western powers, although western powers have not relented, from the late eighteenth century to today, on manipulating and pressuring the Iranian state to maximize their economic gains from Iranian resources as well as their geopolitical influence.

According to Hobsbawm (1993), a nation as a political idea and a new consciousness was born with the 1789 French Revolution (p. 101). Nationalism is the principle of believing in accordance with national and political units. As it pertains to the relationship between nations, nationalism, and states, Hobsbawm stresses the element of invention and the social engineering of nations and the priority of nationalism. He also writes: "Nations do not make states and nationalism but the other way round" (Hobsbawm, 1993, pp. 9-10).

The scholars within the politico-ideological theories of modernization argue that the state has played a crucial role in developing nationalism in modernity. Within modernist theories of nationalism, scholars such as Michael Mann, Anthony Giddens, John Breuilly, and Paul Brass emphasize the importance of the state (Spencer and Wollman, 2002, p. 45). Giddens defines nationalism as "the cultural sensibility of sovereignty, the concomitant of the co-ordination of administrative power within the bonded nation-states" (Spencer and Wollman, 2002, p. 46). Mann argues that nationalism developed because states needed to communicate with their citizens. As such, we have different forms of nationalism in Britain, Austria, Prussia, and France because of different kinds of communication. The purposes of communication were different; for instance, in the conflict between the states, the main priority of the states was to mobilize people for war. Giddens claims that early nationalisms were grounded in the state's mobilization of various classes of people against an enemy. Breuilly stresses that nationalism is a modern political phenomenon related to the development of the state. Brass asserts that elites created nationalism in order to obtain political and economic advantages for the groups they represent (pp. 46-47). McCrone (1998) writes that based on the ideas of Breuilly and Mann, nationalism is fundamentally a political movement related to *state formation* in Europe in the nineteenth century. Breuilly underscores the political identity of a nation and gives a secondary role to other interests. Thus, the aim of a nation is to ensure political sovereignty within an autonomous state (p. 95).

The above "political explanation" has been criticized for, firstly, denying the diversity of the state's developmental trends. Secondly, the origins of nationhood in major European states like Britain, France, Germany, and Italy were different from each other. Britain, Italy, and the US may be called "state-nations" rather than "nation-states." In France, the concept of nation came after the establishment of the state, whereas in Germany, it was vice versa. Third, the normative assumption of political approaches about cultural homogeneity is questionable. Nationalism has not been very successful in the creation of cultural homogeneity around the world. Many states are not "nations" because they comprise different ethnic identities, while some nations are not states. Fourth, the political explanation decreases the position of cultural nationalism to the role of a mask for political nationalism (McCrone, 1998, pp. 98-101).

2.5. Michels' Iron Law of Oligarchy

Scholars have investigated the reasons for the emergence of anti-democratic activities within otherwise democratic political organizations. Michels states that some factors that confront the accomplishment of democracy may be categorized as the "tendencies dependent (1) upon the nature of the human individual; (2) upon the nature of the political struggle; and (3) upon the nature of organization"

(Michels, 1968, p. 6). He argues that democracy leads "to oligarchy and necessarily contains an oligarchical nucleus" (Michels, 1968, p. 6). Regarding the role of oligarchy in an organization, Michels concludes that oligarchy in a party's life is inevitable, and the development of this oligarchy imposes problems for the fulfillment of democracy (Michels, 1968, p. 7). Michels uses the principle of the "iron law of oligarchy" to explain the certainty of the growth of oligarchy in an organization. Sigmund Neumann states that Michels' iron law of oligarchical tendencies of social movement dominates the investigation in the sociology of political parties (Michels, 1968, p. 21). Michels stated in 1911 that the fundamental sociological law of political parties might be expressed in these words: "It is organization which gives birth to the dominion of the elected over the electors, of the mandataries over the mandators, of the delegates over the delegators. Who says organization, says oligarchy" (Michels, 1968, pp. 15, 365). Large-scale organizations give their officers a near monopoly of power (Michels, 1968, p.17). Factors contributing to the domination of leaders over the majority of members include economic superiority, historical superiority (traditional and hereditary backgrounds), and intellectual superiority (e.g., education) (Michels, 1968, p. 107). In addition, some resources that give huge advantages to the leaders over the members are superior knowledge, controlling formal means of communication, and skill in the art of politics (Michels, 1968, p. 16). With respect to the reasons for the dictatorial attitude of the leaders, Michels holds that the leaders' despotism does not come "solely from a vulgar lust of power or from uncontrolled egoism, but is often the outcome of a profound and sincere conviction of their own value and of the services which they have rendered to the common cause" (Michels, 1968, p. 222).

As a Marxist, Sidney Hook criticizes Michels for neglecting the social and economic assumptions of oligarchic leadership in the past time. In a socialist society, the monopoly of education for a specific class has been removed. Likewise, the division of labor between manual and intellectual work has been abolished. Therefore, the danger that has been shown by Michels' "iron law of oligarchy" in traditional form has been removed. Maurice Duverger, Sigmund Neumann, and Robert McKenzie argue that Michels' analysis of political parties' behavior has been over-deterministic. The organizational structures of political parties are considerably different (Michels, 1968, pp. 25-28). Some of Michels' ideas are applicable when studying the anti-democratic tendencies of many Kurdish political organizations, including and especially the PDKI.

Another useful concept for the analysis of anti-democratic tendencies of democratic movements is the "constitutive paradox," proposed by Vahabzadeh (2010) in his analyzing the underground Organization of Iranian People's Fedai Guerrillas (OIPFG). The "constitutive paradox" of Fedai Guerrillas' was that "their struggle for freedom from repression and for democratic participation was based on a militant-centrist style of surveillance and disciplinary measures" (p. 242). The OIPFG used disciplinary technologies for its security and survival, which prevented this organization from using its potential to participate in struggles for the development of "democratic and secular socialization and education in Iran" (Vahabzadeh, 2010, p. 243). Similar to the OIPFG, the PDKI has employed similar disciplinary technologies for security and survival, and the PDKI disciplinary style has caused it to ignore democratic principles both internally and externally. Many of its turns and resolutions represent attempts at dealing with this paradox. Now, *if it is an organizational paradox*, then it can be concluded that although the PDKI has struggled for national liberation due to its disciplinary measures and its bureaucratic measures, it has stepped on organizational democratic avenues. However, *if it is a fundamental paradox*, which includes a specific mode of thinking such as ignoring or suppressing rival ideas or participants in Kurdish national liberation, it can be concluded that although the PDKI has struggled for national liberation, its monopolistic ideas and conduct have undermined democratic principles both internally and externally. Therefore, there has existed a constitutive paradox within the PDKI.

2.6. The Analytical Axes

In order to offer an analytical lens on the development of Kurdish nationalism in Iran and the role of the PDKI throughout this book, I will use four theoretical and analytical axes: I will view Kurdish nationalism in Iran in terms of (1) the *rise of nationalism from ethnic solidarity*, (2) and through a *modern and cultural construction of the Kurdish identity*, (3) which has resulted from the process of *state-building* in modern Iran, such that (4) the Kurdish nationalist movement is potentially, though not exclusively, one of *national liberation*. In addition, with respect to the role of the PDKI in the movement, I will refer to Michel's "iron law of oligarchy" and Vahabzadeh's "constitutive paradox."

In the context of Kurdish nationalism, although both primordialist and perennialist have strong currency with a great many Kurdish nationalists, we need to acknowledge that the primoridialist (and related) theories of nationalism cannot provide satisfactory explanatory paradigms. This is because although the Kurds are an ancient people, the Kurdish *nation* is not a given nationhood with fixed cultural characters. Compatible with the modernist approach, Kurdish nationalism has emerged in the modern era while having its roots in the pre-modern Kurdish ethnicity. Therefore, it seems that ethno-symbolism provides a more satisfactory framework for analyzing Kurdish nationalism. Ethno-symbolism can see the Kurdish nation as a historical phenomenon and refutes that the Kurdish nation is a "given." Moreover, ethno-symbolism observes the formation of the Kurdish nations in a historical process, which obtains many of its characteristics from the pre-modern ethnic features. Among the theorists of nationalism, Gellner, an instrumentalist, describes Kurdish society as a pre-industrial society with the sentiments of a nation and calls it a society that is "tribal inside" but "national outside"

(Gellner, 1983, p. 138). Which tribal Kurdish society Gellner refers to remains unclear. Is he referring to the Kurds in the nineteenth and the first decades of twentieth-century Kurdistan under the Ottoman Empire or Iran? Is he referring to the Kurdish territory after WWI and WWII? Kurdistan is not an industrialized region, and a good number of Kurdish cities now have populations between half-a-million to a million. Capitalist relations dominate social, political, and economic relations in Kurdish cities and villages nowadays. In Iran, since the modernizing reforms of Reza Shah (beginning in the 1930s), capitalist relations have developed in Kurdistan. Moreover, since the White Revolution of Mohammad Reza Shah in the 1960s, feudalism in Iran and Kurdistan was fairly abolished and replaced by capitalism. Similar changes have occurred in Kurdish territories under Iraq, Turkey, and Syria. Indeed, the notion of the Kurds as a "tribal nation" is neither realistic nor applicable. Although elements of tribal culture still remain both in rural and urban Kurdistan, these elements no longer define Kurdish nationalism.

The dominant view among the Kurdish scholars and the leaders of the Kurdish political organizations, such as Abdolrahman Ghassemlou, is a modernist perspective. We will see that the PDKI mainly follows Ghassemlou, who advocated Stalin's perspective on nationalism (Ghassemlou, 1965, p. 230). Both Lenin's and Stalin's analyses of nationalism are relevant to the Kurdish nationalist movement. They emphasize the importance of the struggle of oppressed nations for their self-determination. Lenin supports the liberation of colonized people oppressed by imperialism and stresses the importance of these liberations for a world revolution. As with the Iranian case, in which the process of state-building by Reza Shah marginalized the national minorities, Kurds remain the oppressed nation that struggles for liberation against "internal colonialism." While Lenin's and Stalin's theories have currency among Kurdish leaders, the liberatory character of the Kurdish movement, as with Fanon, is clear, although the context is different from that of Fanon's writings. Here, Hechter's concept of "internal colonialism" proves useful for my subsequent analysis. The Kurds have been colonized by the four states of Iran, Iraq, Turkey, and Syria, and Kurdish nationalism is the reflection of the struggle of the "Kurdish periphery" against the "dominant cores" (Arab, Turkish, or Persian) in these countries, to adopt terms from Immanuel Wallerstein (1974). To complicate matters, though, Fanon is insightful since he can account for the postcolonial pan-Kurdish movement in the region today. Kurdistan's being split into four states is *partially* due to the secret Sykes-Picot Agreement (the Asia Minor Agreement) of 1916, in which colonial powers of Britain and France (and Imperial Russia) divided the Middle East more or less into the states that stand today, one might add, at the expense of the Kurds. The 1923 Treaty of Lausanne (see Chapter 3) caused the Ottoman Kurdish regions to be incorporated into different states, including Iraq, Turkey, and Syria (Natali, 2005, p. 25).

Now, with respect to the building of Kurdish national identity as a modern phenomenon, Hutchinson's "cultural nationalism" is partially relevant. The Kurdish intellectuals, poets, writers, musicians, and other artists have had significant roles in producing a nationalist culture for the Kurdish movement. At the present time, in the physical absence of political nationalist organizations, especially in Iranian Kurdistan, Kurdish intellectuals play a fundamental role in developing Kurdish nationalism by focusing on cultural nationalism. However, this cultural nationalism is not totally separate from the political aspect of nationalism but strongly intertwined with it. In Kurdish nationalism, although some intellectuals may participate in the movement due to their own personal interests (and Kedourie addresses this subject correctly), the majority of the Kurdish intellectuals have devotedly taken part in the movement and have played fundamental roles in leading the movement. As such, it is not because of personal gain that the cultural movement led by the intellectuals has such momentum. As a result of the efforts of Kurdish intellectuals to create a national consciousness, one may argue that Anderson's definition of a nation as "an imagined political community" is somehow compatible with our case. However, Anderson's theory cannot account for the oppressive relations to which the Kurds have been subjected as "internally colonized" peoples by the four aforesaid states. Lastly, print-capitalism has certainly had fundamental impacts on the creation and development of Kurdish nationalism.

But we have just begun our journey: we need to turn to Chapter 3, which offers a brief account of Kurdish nationalism in its historical context.

Chapter 3: Kurdish Nationalism

3.1. Introduction

This chapter will offer a general background of Kurdistan's geography, population, cultural diversity, economy, and political history. It continues with the genocide of the Kurds in Kurdistan and traces the historical emergence of Kurdish nationalism in Turkey, Iraq, and Syria before analyzing the effects of these movements on Kurdish nationalism in Iran.

3.1.1. Geography. Kurdistan is located in the Middle East, where the four countries of Iran, Iraq, Turkey, and Syria converge with the majority of the inhabitants being Kurds. There are also Kurdish populations in the Iranian province of Khorasan, in central Anatolia and the Turkish cities of Istanbul, Ankara, and Izmir, and in Armenia, Azerbaijan, and Turkmenistan. Of all Kurds, 43% live in Turkey, 31% in Iran, 18% in Iraq, 6% in Syria, and, 2% in Armenia and Azerbaijan (Gunter, 2009, pp. xxvii-xxviii). The specific geography of Kurdistan's land is a matter of contestation. The whole area of Kurdistan is 581,710 square kilometers (Minahan, 2002, p. 1055; Minahan, 1996, p. 313), although others estimate it at 530,000 (Blau, 2000, p. 1) and 410,311 square kilometers (Madani, 2000, p. 15). Kurdistan is ranked 30 among the world's 194 countries (Madani, 2000, p. 16).

3.1.2. Population. The standard claim is that Kurds constitute the "largest nation" in the world without their own state (Gunter, 2009, p. xxvii). Hassanpour and Mojab (2005) state that the Kurds constitute the fourth largest ethnic group in the Middle East after Arabs, Turks, and Persians (p. 214). As regards the Kurdish population, many researchers estimate it at about 30 million, while Izady (1992) estimates the figure to be closer to 36.2 million in 2000 (p. 119) as opposed to Madani's figure of 29.5 million in 2000 (2000). Hassanpour and Mojab (2005) provide an estimation of the Kurdish population (p. 214) in Table 1. As Gunter (1990) remarks, "a Kurdish diaspora of some 500,000 has formed in western

Europe due to a variety of political, economic, sociological, and educational factors" (p. 103). Hassanpour and Mojab (2005) offer an estimation of the Kurdish diaspora (p. 214) in Table 2.

3.1.3. Language. The Kurdish language is a matter of disputation. It belongs to the Iranian branch of Indo-European languages. Vladimir Minorsky (1877-1966) believes that while there exist differences among the different Kurdish dialects (excluding Zaza and Gurani), there is a significant unity between them since they likely have been derived from Median language. He claims that while the Kurdish language is an Iranian language it is significantly different from Persian. He states that the Kurdish language is related to the Avestan language and the holy book of Zoroastrians since *Avesta* is written in Kurdish. Kurdish language is divided into many dialects (Minorsky, 2007; Minorsky, 2000, p. 43).

Scholars are in disagreement about the classification of the Kurdish language. Izady (1992) suggests that Kurdish vernacular is divided into two main groups. The first is the Kurmanji with the sub-dialects of Bahdinani (northern Kurmanji) and Sorani (Southern Kurmanji); and the second being Pahlawani or Pahlawanic which includes Dimili (or Zaza) and Gurani (p. 167). Hassanpour and Mojab (2005) note that Kurdish language belongs to the Iranian branch of Indo-European languages. The Kurdish language has four dialects including "Kurmanji, Sorani, Zaza/Dimili and Hawrami/Gorani, and Southern dialects. The language has been written for about five centuries, predominantly in Arabic script, but as of the 1930s, also in Cyrillic and Roman alphabets" (p. 215).

3.1.4. Cultural diversity. Kurdistan entails diverse cultures and various religious and ethnic groups. The majority of Kurds are Muslims and mostly Sunnis. Other religions include Judaism, Zoroastrianism, Christianity, Yezidism, Yarsanism (*Ahl-i Haqq*), Alawism, and Sufi Mystic Orders. Ethnic groups include Arabs, Armenians, Assyrians, Persians, Turkmen, and Turks.

3.1.5. Economy. Kurdistan is a rich agricultural and pastoral area and its most important cash crops are tobacco, cotton, wheat, and oat. Oil and water play significant roles in Kurdistan's economy. While oil is the most important underground resource of Kurdistan, the area also contains chrome, copper, iron, coal, lignite, sulphur, lead, gold, silver, salt, zinc, and mercury (Ghassemlou, 1965, pp. 18-19; Yildiz, 2007, p. 9). Due to the repressive policies of the states that govern Kurdistan, the area has been deprived of industrial development. According to McDowall (2004), "No government will willingly surrender control of its oilfields in Kurdistan, be they in Rumaylan (Syria), Batman and Silvan (Turkey), or Kirkuk and Khaniqin (Iraq)" (p. 7).

3.1.6. Political history. Kurds have maintained their cultural identity for millennia and are among one of the ancient civilizations in the world. Yildiz (2007) asserts that the Kurds have evolved from tribes including Guti, Kurti, Mede, Mard, Carduchi, Gordyene, Adianbene, Zila, and Khaldi, which mixed with Indo-European peoples who migrated to the Zagros mountains about 4,000 years ago (p. 7). Bowring (1996) states that the Kurds had developed their homogeneous identity by the fifth century BCE, and Xenophon (431-350 BCE) encountered the people known as "Karduchoi" in 401 BCE. During the following centuries, the Kurds were challenged by competing dynastic ambitions and even during the Mongol onslaught some Kurdish principalities still existed (p. 24). The term "Kurdistan" (koordistan, Kordestan, or Kordestān), used for centuries, means where the Kurds live. Hassanpour (2003) states that the "land of Kurds" was identified in 1076 CE by Ali Kashghari, a Central Asia cartographer. Later the Seljuq Sultan Sanjar (d. 1157) used the word Kurdistan for his Kurdish possessions (p. 114).

The first written description of the Kurdistan's borders appears in *Sharafnāma (Sharaf-Nāme)* by Prince Sharaf al-Dîn Bitlîsiî (Sharaf Khan) in 1596-1597 (Hassanpour and Mojab, 2005, p. 215). Bitlîsiî (2005) divides Kurdish dynasties into three categories. The first category includes the Kurds who "have raised the banner of kingship," whom the historians call "the kings." The second category includes the rulers who did not claim "independent kingship" but sometimes had *Khutba* (preach) recited and coins struck in their names. The third category includes other rulers and emirs of Kurdistan (pp. 18, 20; Bidlici, 2013, pp. 12-13). Five Kurdish dynasties which had royalty status or might be called independent are: "The Marwanids of Diyarbakir and Jazire, the Hasanwayhids of Dinawar and Shahrizur, the Fadluyids of the Great Lur, the princes of Little Lur, and the Ayyubids established by Saladin" (Entessar, 2010, p. 4).

According to Hassanpour (1994), most parts of Kurdistan were independent from the sixteenth to the mid-nineteenth centuries as autonomous Kurdish principalities. The first division of Kurdistan occurred during the Ottoman Empire with the Kasr-i Shirin (Pol-e Zahab) Treaty in 1639 with the Safavid Empire (p. 3). Pirnia and Eghbal Ashtiani (2012) reveal that as a result of the defeat of Shah Ismail I in Chaldiran 1514, Diyarbakir and Kurdistan were appended to the Ottoman Empire (p. 811). A brief explanation regarding the time and reason for the establishment of some Kurdish principalities within the Ottoman Empire is needed. After the battle of Chaldiran in 1514 and the defeat of Shah Ismail I (1487-1524) of Iran, Sultan Selim I, in order to pacify the Kurds, established the Kurdish territory as a buffer zone between the Ottoman Empire and Iran. With the advice of Hakim Idris of Betlis, Sultan Selim I created five hereditary-independent Kurdish Emirates including Bitlis, Hakkari, Bahdinan, Botan, and Hisin-Keif. The Shah of Iran followed the same method to allow the Kurdish Ardelan princes to enjoy extensive governing powers (Bois, 1966, pp. 139-140). The conditions of Kurdish Emirates in Iran were similar to the emirates located in the Ottoman Empire. The Emirates of Bradost, Mukry, and Ardalan were semi-independent and nominally under the Safavid sovereignty. Since the Safavid period, the Kurdish principalities were under the attack of the central government in an attempt to eradicate Kurdish populations. The Ardalan principality was the only one that remained unconquered until the reign of Nasser al-Din Shah (1831-1896), before it was finally conquered in 1865 (Gunter, 2013, p. 33; Mustafa Amin, 2007, p. 605; Entessar, 2010, p. 16). According to Bozarslan (2007), when the Ottoman Empire destroyed the Kurdish principalities in the second half the nineteenth century, it caused wide-ranging insecurity which led to Kurdish revolts against the policy of centralization (p. 39). Kurdish uprisings, according to Bois (1966), included the revolts of Abd el-Rahman Pasha Baban in Sulaymaniyah in 1805; Muhammad Pasha (known as Mir Kor) in Rawanduz (Soran) in 1830; Badr (Badir or Bedir) Khan Beg (Pasha), Emir of Botan in Jezireh in 1842-1846; and Sheikh Ubayd Allah of Nehri, in Iran in 1880 (pp. 140-141). The 1880 revolt of Sheikh Ubayd Allah in Iran was among the most important Kurdish uprisings. Sheikh Ubayd Allah prepared a revolt for the unification of Kurdistan (Borzooyy, 2005, Arfa, 1966, O'Ballance, 1973; Sharafkandi, 1981; Madani, 2000; and Kinnane, 1964). In his letter to the British Consul-General in Tabriz, Sheikh Ubayd Allah stated: "We also are a nation apart. We want our affairs to be in our own hands" (Gunter, 2007, pp. 6-7; 2009, p. 204). British Vice-Consul Clayton believed that Sheikh Ubayd Allah had "a comprehensive plan for uniting all the Kurds in an independent state under himself" (Jwaideh, 2006, p. 80).

At the end of nineteenth century, a new generation of Kurdish nationalist intellectuals—mainly from the aristocratic and privileged families—emerged in the political scene. The *İttihat ve Terakki Cemiyeti* (Committee of Union and Progress [CUP]), also known as the Young Turks was founded in 1889 by young officers and intellectuals with the aim of changing the Ottoman Empire into a constitutional government. In 1907, the Committee held its Congress in Paris with all the opposition parties and organizations including the Kurds who were against the government. In the Congress, the Young Turks agreed that in case they gain power, they would grant political and cultural autonomy to the non-Turkish nationalities (Madani, 2000, 213; Sharafkandi, 1981, p. 32). The Young Turks' 1908 revolution encouraged minorities including the Arabs, Armenians, and Kurds to increase their liberation activities. This resulted in the establishment of Kurdish social, cultural, and political organizations in Istanbul. Emir Badr Khan, General Sharif Pasha, and Sheikh Abdul Qadir of Shamzinan founded the *Kürd Teavün ve Terakki Cemiyeti* (Society for Mutual Aid and Progress of Kurdistan [SMPK]) on 2 October 1908, and they founded *Kurdistan* as their organ (Bois, 1966, p. 142; Özoğlu, 2004, p. 90).

In the last year of WWI, there was a total disarray of the Ottoman Empire. The Fourteen Points declaration by Woodrow Wilson involving the importance of political self-determination for all ethnic minorities was also announced this year. The *Kürdistan Teali Cemiyeti* (Society for the Advancement of Kurdistan [SAK]) was founded on 17 December 1918. Its founders were the same Kurdish notables who were active in previous Kurdish organizations. SAK is regarded as the first Kurdish nationalist organization (Özoğlu, 2004, pp. 81, 83). Özoğlu (2004) explains that a comparison between SAK and SMPK shows an ideological shift regarding Kurdish nationalism. SMPK believed the Kurds should be faithful to the Ottoman Empire, while the SAK emphasized Kurdish distinctness. As Özoğlu (2004) concludes, "*Kurdish nationalism, in the modern sense of the word, emerged after World War I*. The surprising corollary is that Kurdish nationalism is not a cause but a result of the Ottoman Empire's collapse" (p. 125; italics added).

The first division of Kurdistan officially occurred in the Safavid period in 1639. The second division of Kurdistan took place after WWI. After the collapse of the Ottoman Empire, the Kurds had an opportunity to establish a nation-state under the Treaty of Sevres (10 August 1920). General Sharif Pasha was chosen by different Kurdish organizations including the SAK as a Kurdish delegate in the Peace Conference in 1919 and the Treaty of Sevres. The Treaty of Sevres, Section III, Articles 62-64, endorses the creation of a Kurdish State (Bowring, 1996, p. 25). The Turkish War of Independence lasted from 19 May 1919 to 24 July 1923. The

Grand National Assembly of Turkey abolished the Ottoman Sultanate and ended the Ottoman Empire on 1 November 1922. While the Treaty provided hope for the Kurds regarding their own state, the Lausanne Treaty (24 July 1923) rescinded that possibility. The Lausanne Treaty recognized the newly formed Republic of Turkey (proclaimed in October 1923). After the Treaty of Lausanne, the Ottoman Kurdish regions were incorporated into different states including Iraq, Turkey, and Syria (Natali, 2005, p. 25). The Kurdish state was thus never established.

3.1.7. The genocide. The word "genocide" was first coined by the jurist Raphael Lemkin in 1944 concerning the Holocaust. It was accepted by the United Nations General Assembly in 1948 and was approved by the Convention on the Prevention and Punishment of the Crime of Genocide. According to the Article 2 of this convention, genocide has been committed through "(a) Killing members of the group; (b) Causing serious bodily or mental harm to members of the group; (c) Deliberately inflicting on the group conditions of life calculated to bring about its physical destruction in whole or in part; (d) Imposing measures intended to prevent births within the group; (e) Forcibly transferring children of the group to another group" (United Nations, 1948, p. 280). The key factor in the act of genocide is the *intent*, referring to the deliberate destruction of individuals from a specific group. An example would be the 1994 Rwanda genocide of 500,000 to 1,000,000 Tutsis by Hutus (Wilkinson, 1999, p. 252).

The 1994 United Nations Declaration on the Rights of Indigenous Peoples (Article 7) indicates: "Indigenous peoples have the collective and individual right not to be subjected to ethnocide and cultural genocide" (United Nations, 1994, p. 107). But the same UN Declaration in 2007 dropped the concepts of ethnocide and cultural genocide, replacing it with (Article 8): "Indigenous peoples and individuals have the right not to be subjected to forced assimilation or destruction of their culture" (United Nations, 2007, p. 4).

According to Lemkin, genocide is not confined to just the instant destruction of a nation, but intended as a plan aimed to annihilate the foundations of specific national groups' lives. It is also aimed the destroying the specific groups themselves (Rabinbach, 2005, p. 74). Lemkin's emphasizes the cultural genocide and asserts: "Genocide has two phases: one, destruction of the national pattern of the oppressed group; the other, the imposition of the national pattern of the oppressor" (p. 79). Short (2010) concludes that "cultural destruction is '*central* to Lemkin's conception of genocide'" (p. 842).

The Kurds have frequently been the subject of genocide. Bruinessen (1994), argues that in at least two cases, segments of Kurdish populations have been deliberately destroyed. The first is the case of Turkey after the rebellions of the 1920s and 1930s, and the rebellion of Dersim in 1937-1938. The second is the case of Iraq since the mid-1980s. Aside from physical destruction, the Kurds have also been under the policies of *ethnocide*, which involves the annihilation of Kurdish ethnic identity. The assimilation policy has been mostly enforced in Turkey and to some degree in the former Soviet Union. In Iraq, the government's main policy involved the deliberate destruction of Kurdish rural life through total destruction of Kurdish villages and the deportation of the Kurds to strategic villages known as "new towns" (pp. 165-166). Likewise, Beşikçi has analyzed the massacres of Dersim in 1937-1938 and "accused the Turkish government of genocide" (Bruinessen, 1994, p. 168). Bruinessen (1999) emphasizes that the Kurds in Turkey since the late 1920s, and in Iraq during the 1980s have been subjects of various policies of ethnocide. During the genocidal campaign against Dersim (1937-1938), a significant part of population "was deliberately killed and many of the survivors were deported" (pp. 383-384). Chris Kutschera discusses that in repressing the Dersim rebellion the Turkish government committed genocide. Before the rebellion, the government executed mass deportation and planned the "dekurdification" of the territory (Bruinessen, 1994, p. 180). In addition, "cultural genocide" (previously called "ethnocide") was typically accompanied by physical aspects and aimed to eliminate the intellectuals. Cultural genocide has been an integral part of Turkey's policy to eradicate Kurdish and Islamic leaders in 1980s (pp. 325-326).

Iraqi Kurdistan has been the subject of chemical warfare, mass killing, and extensive destruction by the Iraqi government. Bruinessen (1994) highlights an important case regarding the disappearance of the Barzani Kurds who surrendered to Iraq and were relocated to camps near Erbil. In August 1983, eight thousand Barzanis, all men aged between 8 and 70, were gathered in the camps and transferred by army lorries. While some of them were used in experiments with chemical arms, the rest disappeared. The women and children were harshly mistreated and systematically raped. This is "an unambiguous case of genocide by the terms of the 1948 definition in the United Nations Convention on Genocide" (pp.171-172).

The Human Rights Watch (1995) reported that the Iraqi regime had used chemical attacks including mustard and nerve gas against the Kurds during 1987-1988. At least sixty villages and the town of Halabja were targeted by these military operations. Some of these attacks happened before the chemical attack on Halabja with most of them occurring during the Anfal (the spoils) operation (pp. 262-264). Anfal involved a series of military campaigns which consisted of eight separate operations against the Iraqi Kurds lasting from 23 February 1988 to 6 September 1988. In the Anfal operations, more than 1,200 villages were ruined, bringing the total razed villages since 1968 to 4,000 out of 7,000 Kurdish villages (Bruinessen, 1994, p. 175).

According to Max van der Stoel (1992), the special rapporteur of the Commission on Human Rights could not ignore the Kurds' claim that approximately 182,000 persons disappeared through the military operations of the Iraqi regime and "it would seem beyond doubt that these policies, and the "Anfal" operations in particular, bear the marks of a genocide-type design" (p. 29). On the word of the Middle East Watch (1993), since 1975, the Iraqi regime has destroyed some 4,000 Kurdish villages and the number of Kurds who were executed in the eight separate Anfals between February and September 1988, aside from those who were killed in military campaigns, was not less than 50,000 and may even be 100,000. In using the language of the Genocide Convention, the Iraqi regime deliberately destroyed "*the group* [Iraqi Kurds] *in part*" and has committed a complete "crime of genocide" (pp. 20, 32). One of the styles that the Iraqi regime used in annihilation of the Kurds involved using of live mass graves. Yildiz (2007) reveals the existence of 270 mass graves in Iraq containing about 300,000 sets of remains (p. 17).

The international response to the genocide of Kurds in Iraq has been passive: it was ignored by world media. The Halabja massacre caused an international protest but did not result at in any international pressure on Iraq. Instead, the superpowers continued to support Iraq through the Iraq-Iran war (Bruinessen, 1994, p. 172; Conversi, 2006, p. 328). Only after the Iraq-Iran war ended did the international support for the Kurds progressively become evident.

According to the United Nations (1994) "'ethnic cleansing' means rendering an area ethnically homogenous by using force or intimidation to remove persons of given groups from the area" (p. 33). Ethnic cleansing may be done in different ways such as torturing, murdering, arresting, raping, sexual assaulting, forcibly removing civilians, military attacks, the threat of attacks, and malicious property destruction. These actions are recognized as crimes against humanity and could "fall within the meaning of the Genocide Convention' (United Nations, 1994, p. 33). Sinan Esim (1999) claims that since 1923, the Kurds in Turkey have undergone shameful oppression. Recently, the Turkish government launched military repression of the Kurdish national liberation movement involving atrocious instances of ethnic cleaning (p. 20). According to Noam Chomsky (2002), the Turkish "state terrorism" has caused an estimated two million homeless Kurds. By 1994, about 1 million people fled to Diyarbakir after nearly 2,000 villages were destroyed. "Representative Christopher

Smith repeated widely accepted figures when he said in his motion before Congress that 3 million civilians have been displaced from their homes and 2,650 villages destroyed" (1996, Column 673). By 1999, the total number of the Kurds killed by the Turkish military attacks reached over 40,000. Turkey's own Parliament has confirmed that "6,000 Kurdish villages were systematically evacuated of all inhabitants and 3,000,000 Kurds have been displaced" (Fatah, 2006).

In Iran, as Bruinessen (1999) states, Reza Shah emulated many policies of Turkey such as "resettling Kurdish and other tribal groups and suppressing regional cultures, but it stopped, short of destroying Kurdish ethnicity and large massacres" (p. 384). The following sections highlight the history of Kurds in different countries and provide a more detailed examination about genocide and ethnic cleansing.

3.2. Northern Kurdistan (Turkey)

After the collapse of the Ottoman Empire, the Republic of Turkey was established by Mustafa Kemal Pasha (Atatürk) on 29 October 1923. For the purpose of strengthening his position, Atatürk initially talked about the equality of Turks and Kurds in the new state, and on "February 10, 1922, the Grand National Assembly created a draft law for proposed autonomy in Kurdistan" (Natali, 2005, p. 73). However, shortly afterwards, the very existence of the Kurds was denied. Turkey repudiated the Treaty of Sevres and Britain in seeking economic profits developed a new treaty with Turkey. One year after signing the Treaty of Lausanne (24 June 1923) that granted Anatolia to Turkey (Bowring, 1996, p, 25), "Turkish official decree banned all Kurdish schools, organizations and publications, along with religious fraternities and seminars" (Bowring, 1996, p. 26). The policy of assimilating the Kurds in Turkey has been steadfastly pursued since then. After WWI, the Kurdish response to the forcible Turkification of Kurdistan involved several revolts: Kuchgiri rebellion (1920), Sheikh Said uprising (1925), the revolt of Ararat (Agri Dagh or Ağrı Dağı) (1928), and the revolt of Dersim (1937). Nader

Entessar (1992) suggests that in Sheikh Said's uprising in February 1925 was influenced by the Kurdish nationalist organization known as *Ciwata Azadi Kurd* (Kurdish Freedom Society), later called the *Ciwata Kweseria Kurd* (Kurdish Independent Society) or *Azadi* (Freedom or Independence). Sheikh Said's goal was to achieve an independent Kurdish state. A formidable Turkish military deployment put down the uprising by the end of April 1925. Sheikh Said and nine of his compatriots were arrested and hung on June 29, 1925 (pp. 83-84).

Kurdish exiles in Lebanon in 1927 established the organization of *Khoybun* (Independence) under the leadership of Jalalat Badr Khan. According to McDowall (2004), they set up a permanent headquarters in Aleppo and chose Ihsan Nuri as the operational commander. Ihsan Nuri raised the flag of revolt in Ararat in 1928. In Summer 1930, the Turkish army "destroyed over 3,000 non-combatants, men, women and children during their *nettoyage* operations around Arjish and the Zilan plain" (p. 206). Kendal (1980a) states that during the end of summer in 1930 some leaders had fled, and others had been executed (p. 65). During the slaughter, Ihsan Nuri managed to escape to Iran.

The resistance of Dersim was a response to the Turkish policy of repressing Kurdish identity by scattering their population to areas where they would be reduced to no more than five percent of the area's population. Sayyed Reza, the leader of the movement, and his fellow commanders were unable to survive through the winter and surrendered in 1937. The government immediately executed seven leaders, including Sayyed Reza. The Turkish army resumed their aerial bombing and chemical gas attacks in 1938. Estimates hold that 40,000 Kurds were killed (McDowall, 2004, pp. 208-209). Since 1938, the Kurds were defined as the "Mountain Turks," and their Turkification continued for several decades.

In 1965, the Kurdistan Democratic Party of Turkey was formed as a clandestine organization, and a number of Kurdish political organizations were established in the mid-1970s. Gunter (1990) writes that they included the Socialist

Party of Turkish Kurdistan (SPTK, 1974); Revolutionary Democrats; the Kurdish Vanguard Workers Party (PPKK, also known as *Pesheng* or *Vanguard*); the National Liberation of Kurdistan (KUK, 1977); *Rizgari* (Liberation, 1976); *Ala Rirzgari* (Flag of Liberation, 1979); and *Kawa* (1976) (pp. 64-67). These organizations embraced Kurdish nationalism, with the most influential organization being the *Partia Karkaren Kurdistan* (*PKK*, Workers Party of Kurdistan), founded by Abdullah Ocalan on 27 November 1978. In 2002, the PKK reorganized and became the KADEK (Congress for Democracy and Freedom in Kurdistan). Its purpose was to become a legal political party in Turkey. In November 2003, KADEK was renamed *Kongra-Gel* (*KGK*) (People's Congress of Kurdistan), and its platform rejected separatism (Bishku, 2007, p. 95).

The goal of PKK was to achieve an independent, democratic, and unified Kurdistan. In response to the Turkish government's repressive actions, in 1979, Ocalan traveled to the Bekaa Valley in Lebanon and set up a military and political academy to prepare for guerrilla warfare. Since 1984, in the war between the PKK and the Turkish state, "4,500 civilians were killed, around 3,000 settlements evacuated or burned down, and up to three million people internally displaced" (Amnesty International, 2000, p. 241; see also Wahlbeck, 1999, p. 47; Yildiz, 2005, p. 104). The arrest of Ocalan by the Turkish government in 1999 was made possible with the overt collaboration of the United States, Israel, and Kenya. Ocalan was held responsible for "the death of 29,000 people (civilians, soldiers, and PKK militants) who lost their lives in the conflict" (Amnesty International, 2000, p. 241).

The Turkish intellectuals who defend the democratic rights of the Kurdish people also found themselves targets of state repression. A prominent case involves Dr. Ismail Beşikçi (Besikci), a Turkish sociologist who has been imprisoned for many years and tortured for supporting the national rights of Kurdish people. Gunter (1990) states that during the 1970s and 1980s, Beşikçi spent more than a decade in prison because he had affirmed in "his scholarly work that the Kurds constitute a separate, ethnic group" (p. 123). In 1980, Beşikçi stated:

> The official ideology in Turkey continues to maintain in an insistent and obstinate manner that there are no people known as Kurds and no language known as Kurdish…. University circles, political parties, unions, associations, mass media, etc., never touch on the Kurdish question. The aim is to dismiss those who have an interest in the question of Kurdistan… Today, Kurdistan in the center of the Middle East is an international colony that has been divided and served and whose…national and democratic rights have been confiscated. The Kurdish people are a nation partitioned by barbed-wires and fields of mines with on-going efforts to completely cut off the parts from one another. Under these conditions, the political status of the Kurdish people is even lower than that of a colony. Because, for example, in Turkey even their existence is not accepted. The Kurds in Turkey can have rights only to the extent of becoming Turks. The alternative is repression, cruelty, and prison. (Gunter, 1990, p. 48)

Kurdish intellectuals in Turkey, including famous novelist Yaşar (Yashar) Kemal (1923-2015), and even parliament members who defend the rights of Kurdish people are not protected by Turkey's laws (Amnesty International, 1998, p. 337). Although the conflict between PKK and the Turkish government effectively ended in 1999, the limitations on other forms of Kurdish political activism, especially in southern Turkey where representatives of the pro-Kurdish People's Democracy Party (HDP) were put on trial (Amnesty International, 2001, p. 247). In July 1993, the Constitutional Court banned the People's Labour Party

(HEP), which re-emerged as the Democracy Party (DEP). Some of its members were even assassinated (Bowring, 1996, p. 29).

Imperialist powers have supported the Turkish policies of repressing Kurdish people's rights. Esim (1999), a Turkish Marxist activist engaged in Kurdish issues, claims that "Turkey was supported by its NATO allies, above all the United States… in the final analysis, both the United States and the European members of NATO gave their backing, in the policies of successive Turkish governments" (p. 22). Nevertheless, Turkey's treatment of the Kurds has caught the attention of critics in the West, most notably in Europe. Lesser (1999) suggests that the Kurdish question is linked with concerns about human rights in Turkey and as "a factor in negative attitudes toward Ankara's aspiration for full European Union membership" (p. 217).

The history of the Kurdish people's struggle against Ataturkism has proven that assimilation will not resolve Turkey's issues with its Kurdish population. The only way is through a democratic solution that recognizes the self–determination of the Kurds.

3.3. Southern Kurdistan (Iraq)

During WWI, England occupied two Ottoman *vilayets* (provinces) of Baghdad and Basra and later agreed to Sherif Hussein's request for the establishment of an Arab state (Iraq) in 1915. This agreement did not cover the Kurdish province of Mosul, which was occupied by Britain in October 1918. According to Entessar (1992), it was British policy to appoint local Kurdish leaders to administer the Mosul area. One of the influential leaders was Sheikh Mahmoud Barzanji, who was appointed as the Governor of Sulaymaniyah and "revolted against the British and declared independence in May 1919" (p. 50). Sheikh Mahmoud was influenced by United States President Wilson's Fourteen Points (8 January 1918) and by other groups seeking self-determination (Natali, 2005, p. 30;

Vanly, 1980, p. 159). The British suppressed Sheikh Mahmoud's revolt, and he was captured and sent into exile (McDowall, 2004, pp. 157-158).

On 10 August 1920, the Treaty of Sevres was signed between the Allied Powers and the Constantinople Government, including Articles 62, 63, and 64 referring to the establishment of an independent Kurdish state, which included the Mosul *velayat* (Entessar, 1992, p. 51). Several factors contributed to the British defaulting on the Treaty. One factor was the oil resources in Kirkuk, and the British preferred to incorporate the area into their client state of Iraq rather than to establish an independent Kurdish state (Entessar, 1992, p. 52). In August 1921, Emir Faisal (1885-1933), Sharif of Mecca (1854-1931), was appointed as the King of Iraq. Meanwhile, in the face of the growing Turkish threats, Britain pardoned and returned Sheikh Mahmoud in September 1922. In January 1923, Sheikh Mahmoud declared himself "King of Kurdistan." In the following years, until 1931, the revolt continued as the British Royal Air Force (RAF) continuously bombed the insurgents. The last important uprising of Sheikh Mahmoud occurred when the British announced Iraq's independence in 1932. "Denied asylum in Iran, Sheikh Mahmoud made his submission at Panjwin in May 1931, accepting enforced residence in south Iraq" (McDowall, 2004, p. 176). He remained under house arrest until his death in 1956.

In 1943, the movement of Mullah Mustafa Barzani, the leader of the Barzani tribe, began in Barzan and spread quickly. Barzani overran the Iraqi army, forcing them to leave large areas of Erbil and Badinan (Vanly, 1980, p. 163). Some of Barzani's important demands encompassed "the establishment of a Kurdish province (which included oil-rich Kirkuk) under elected Kurdish leaders…. The province would maintain autonomy in cultural, agricultural, and economic affairs" (Entessar, 1992, p. 55). However, the negotiations with the government were fruitless. Finally, in 1945, Iraqi forces and Britain's RAF "managed to force the Kurdish rebels into Iranian Kurdistan, to the above discussed autonomous democratic republic set up in 1946 in Mahabad" (Entessar, 1992, p. 56; Vanly, 1980, p. 163). Barzani supported the Kurdish Republic of 1946 and was appointed head of its military. After Barzani's appointment, the Kurdish Democratic Party (KDP) of Iraq held its first congress in Baghdad on 16 August 1946 with Barzani as its President (in exile) and Hamza Abdullah as its Secretary-General (McDowall, 2004, p. 296). After the Kurdish republic was overthrown by the Iranian military, Barzani escaped to the Soviet Union and stayed there until 1958, when the Hashemite monarchy in Iraq was overthrown by General Abd al-Karim Qasim.

During the Qasim regime (beginning 14 July 1958) and the Ba'ath regime, the relationship between Barzani and the Iraqi state vacillated between negotiations and war. The Iraqi government had never fully recognized the cultural, political, and economic rights of the Kurdish people. A partial step in that direction was the publication of an agreement, known as the Manifesto of 11 March 1970, between the Kurdish movement and the Iraqi regime on "the Autonomy of Kurdistan." The Manifesto provided for the "recognition of the Kurdish language in areas with a Kurdish majority; self-rule; appointment of Kurds to high-level positions in the central government (including a Kurdish vice president); …[and] establishment of a Kurdish academy of letters and a Kurdish university in Sulaymanieh [Sulaymaniyah]" (Entessar, 1992, p. 71). Indeed, President Ahmad Hassan al-Bakr's new plan of 11 March 1974 excluded Kirkuk. Until 1974, this discord had strained the relationship between the Kurds and the Iraqi regime. Another reason why an agreement remained elusive involved the regime's ongoing Arabization of the Kurdish area. The Kurds also rejected Iraqi plans—such as the 1974 Autonomy Law—suggesting "the promise of more aid from the United States, Israel, and the Shah of Iran if Mullah Mostafa Barzani continued to put pressure on the Baghdad government" (Entessar, 1992, p. 76). As a result, the Kurds intensified their fighting, forcing the Iraqi regime to consult with Iran to resolve the issues. On 5 March 1975 Iraq and Iran signed the Algiers Agreement. A few days after the agreement, the Kurdish movement was disbanded, and about 300,000 Kurds fled to Iran (Vanly, 1980, p. 188). After staying in Iran, Barzani traveled to the United States for cancer treatment and died in Washington after the 1979 Revolution in Iran and was buried in the Kurdish city of Oshnavieh in Iran.

The Kurdish resistance split up, and one of its important factions was the Patriotic Union of Kurdistan (PUK), formed on 1 June 1975 under Jalal Talabani. Masoud, son of Barzani, played an important role in establishing the KDP-Provisional Leadership. These two groups played major roles in the Kurdish movement, with smaller organizations, such as the Kurdistan branch of the Iraqi Communist Party (ICP), which actively participated in the ensuing struggles. In May 1987, the Iraqi Kurdistan Front (IKF) was established by major parties and other organizations to orchestrate the struggle against the Iraqi regime. The Front included the KDP, PUK, Kurdish Socialist Party (Iraq) (PASOK), Kurdistan Socialist Party (KSP), Kurdistan Popular Democratic Party (KPDP), Toiler Party, the ICP, and Assyrian Democratic Movement. The relationship between these organizations was marked by atrocities, war, and blood, yet the formation of the Front was a positive step for the Kurdish movement.

The Iraqi Ba'ath state pursued the policy of oppression of the Kurds. It used chemical weapons in Halabja, a town that was briefly occupied by Iran during the Iran-Iraq War and was a center for Kurdish resistance. On 16 and 17 March 1988, Western television crews filmed the horrific scenes on Halabja's streets. Officials from the International Committee of the Red Cross investigated the site and estimated that "some 5,000 Kurds and a much smaller number of Iranian soldiers were killed in the gas attack and the Iraqi shelling of the town. Other estimates exceed 6,000" (Human Rights Watch, 1990, p. 84). The Washington Kurdish Institute (WKI) estimates that between 5,000 and 7,000 people were killed instantly after the attack, and 20,000 to 30,000 were injured. As well, 250,000 people have also been affected, making the Kurdish people "the largest civilian population ever exposed to chemical and biological weapons" (McKiernan, 2006, p. 353).

In 1988, the Iraqi regime commenced the Anfal operations, a series of major attacks against peshmerga (peshmerga or peshmarga; a person who faces death)-controlled areas with chemical and air attacks. At the end of February, Jalal Talabani, the leader of the PUK, "formally accused the regime of genocide, with 1.5 million already deported, and 12 towns and over 3,000 villages razed" (McDowall, 1996, p. 357). In the attacks, lasting six weeks, beginning 19 July 1988, more than 3,000 Kurdish civilians were killed. Red Cross doctors treated hundreds of severely burned children at refugee camps in Turkey, where more than 100,000 Kurds had fled while about 20,000 sought refuge in Iran (Darwish and Alexander, 1991, p. 78). Another policy of the Ba'ath regime involved the forced displacement of the Kurds, beginning in 1985, which displaced about 500,000 Kurds (Human Rights Watch, 1990, pp. 86, 90). Again, the global response to these atrocities was intolerably inadequate.

During the first Gulf War (August 1990-January 1991), when the United States and an international coalition attacked Iraq following Iraq's occupation of Kuwait (August 1990), U.S. President George Bush encouraged Iraqi people to rise up against Saddam Hussain. The city of Basra rose up in March 1991 but was suppressed harshly. Fearing new chemical attacks, thousands of Kurds fled to Turkey, and by April 1991. About two million people were displaced (Abdullah, 2011, pp. 146-148). In mid-April, the U.S.-led Allied Forces established a "safe haven" inside Iraq and prohibited the Iraqi planes from flying north of the 36 parallel (McDowall, 2004, p. 375). "On 20 October 1991, Iraqi forces were withdrawn from the three northern governorates of Erbil, Dohuk, and Sulaymaniyah, and the Kurdish region was placed under economic siege" (Yildiz, 2007, p. 42). This siege was imposed by the Iraqi regime.

The Kurdish Front held an election on 19 May 1992, electing 105 members of the National Assembly with a Presidential election for the post of Leader of the Kurdistan Liberation Movement. In April 2003, the United States-led coalition overthrew Saddam Hussein's Ba'ath regime, creating more political and cultural opportunities for the Kurds. The Kurdish ethnic identity was recognized by the United States officials from the Coalition Provincial Authority and also by the Iraqi Governing Council. They "promised to institutionalize Kurdish autonomy in a federal Iraq" (Natali, 2005, p. 65). At that time, Jalal Talabani had become the president of the pro-American Iraqi government.

3.4. Western Kurdistan (Syria)

Syria is one of the countries created by the British and French imperialists after the Sevres Treaty. But even before that, in May 1916, the Sykes-Picot Agreement carved up the Middle East (Kendal, 1980b, p. 38). After WWI, Syria came under a French Mandate, with parts of Kurdistan annexed to it. In the course of the French mandate (1918-1945), the Kurds in Syria had several cultural and political rights, including establishing political and social organizations, having publications, using the Kurdish language, and participating in the army and administration. The Syrian independence gradually eliminated these rights. Arab nationalism—Ba'athism and Nasserism—and the United Arab Republic (UAR) encompassing Egypt and Syria in 1958 oppressed the Kurds. When Hafez Assad came to power in 1972, improvements in Kurdish conditions were insignificant (Meho, 1997, pp. 15-16).

Three factors helped improve Kurdish national consciousness in Syria: the experience of the French mandate, the impact of the Kurdish uprisings in Turkey and Iraq, and the development of Arab nationalism (Lowe, 2007, p. 289). The first real expression of Kurdish national consciousness in Syria was in "[a] petition to the Constituent Assembly of Syria in June 1928 seeking official use of the Kurdish language… and also the appointment of Kurdish government administrator"

(McDowall, 2004, p. 468; Lowe, 2007, p. 291). Although the Kurds supported the Arab nationalist movement and Syria became independent in 1946, the Kurdish people were subjected to oppression. The Syrian government always had a policy of suppressing the cultural identity of the Kurds while seeking to assimilate minority groups into its dominant culture after 1954 (McDowall, 2004, p. 471). The November 1961 census of the Jezireh region (northern Syria) was intended to identify "illegally infiltrating" Turks intending to "destroy its Arab character." As a result, 120,000 Kurds were excluded as foreigners, and they lost their rights as Syrians. In 1962, the government implemented the Arab Cordon Plan, which envisaged the removal of Kurds along the border of Turkey and the resettlement of the area by Arabs (Nazdar, 1980, p. 216). According to Amnesty International (2002), the Syrian Kurds, including women and children, under the Assad regime have constantly been the subject of mistreatment and torture (p. 237).

Jordi Tejel (2009) asserts that Damascus focused on the establishment of an "Arab belt" by creating a long, well-cultivated strip of land, 280 km in length and between 10 to 15 km wide along the borders of Turkey and Iraq. This plan also included the massive deportation of 140,000 Kurds and their replacement with Arabs (p. 61).

The *Partia Demokrat a Kurdistan—Suriye* (Kurdistan Democratic Party—Syria (KDPS or KDP-S) was formed in July 1957 by Kurdish elites such as Osman Sabri, Nureddin Zaza, and Hamid Haij Darwish. The creation of the KDPS had a great influence on the development of Kurdish nationalism was a response to extreme Arab nationalism. The KDPS demanded "Kurdish political representation, economic development, improved education, and linguistic and cultural freedom" (Lowe, 2007, p. 293). The KDPS was severely repressed in 1960, and most of its leaders, as well as many of its members alongside other Kurds, were arrested (Lowe, 2007, p. 293). Daham Miro, in 1972, formed the Kurdish Democratic Party of Syria, which had a strong relationship with the KDP (Iraq) (p. 297). In 2004, thirteen Kurdish parties were active, while eleven of them had originated with the original (1957) KDPS (Lowe, 2007, pp. 297-298). For many years, Syria has supported the (PKK) in order to undermine the Turkish government. By the estimation of Turkey's intelligence, about 25 percent of PKK guerrillas were Syrian Kurds in the mid-1990s (Lowe, 2007, p. 302).

Although, in recent years, the Syrian regime has been more open to the political and cultural activities of the Kurds, the oppression is still ongoing, with the national rights of the Kurds being denied. This results in the continuing struggles and resistance of the Kurds. A significant example is the revolt of Qamishli on March 12 - 25, 2004. The riot extended to other Kurdish cities and was violently suppressed, leaving many dead, hundreds wounded, and thousands arrested (Tejel, 2009, p. 116).

In the early phase of the Syrian Civil War, when the Syrian military forces left Kurdistan, the Kurdish political organization, including the Democratic Union Party (PYD) as a main force and a branch of PKK, and the Kurdish National Council (KNC), in order to defend the Kurdish area created a Kurdish Supreme Committee (KSC) which founded the People's Protection Units (YPG) as an armed force in 2012. The Kurds established a *de facto* autonomous region known as Rojava (the West, here the Syrian Kurdistan), renamed in 2016 as the Democratic Federal System of Northern Syria, and created three cantons in Afrin, Kobani, and Jazira. Recently, the Syrian Kurds have been engaged in the military campaign against *Da'esh*, the Islamic State of Iraq and Syria (ISIS). The Kurdish women, who were mainly armed by the Democratic Union Party (PYD), established in 2003, have played a fundamental role in this resistance. The Kurdish People's protection (YPG), made of women and men fighters, together with Free Syrian Army forces, attacked Kobani, a Kurdish city in Syria, and drove ISIS from the land it had taken (Bourrie, 2016, p. 17). Another important all-female militia organization that has been established since 4 April 2013 is the Women's Protection

Units or Women's Defense Units (YPJ). It is part of the of the Syrian Democratic Forces (SDF). While the ISIS forces have been defeated in many territories in Syria and Iraq, now (6 March 2017), the Iraqi army and the Kurdish peshmergas of the KRG are fighting to liberate Mosul, which is under ISIS.

3.5. Kurdish Nationalism in Iran, Turkey, Iraq, and Syria

The aim of this section is to discuss some similar and different characteristics of Kurdish nationalism in Iran, Turkey, Iraq, and Syria. One of the similarities between them is that in all of these countries, Kurdish nationalism has been, to various degrees, under the influence of socialist ideas. A difference is that at the present time, the Kurdish nationalism under the PKK is more radical than the others. The second resemblance is regarding the deployment of armed struggle by political organizations in different historical periods in these countries. This form of struggle has been the reflection of the violent response of the governments to the Kurdish demands. Some of the reasons the Kurds to not use armed struggle were the small Kurdish population and the government's use of methods of control and suppression that were not so violent. While in Iraq and Turkey, the Kurds faced extensive physical genocide, Iranian Kurds and especially the Syrian Kurds faced lesser degrees of this type of oppression. In all of these countries, the Kurds were under the cultural genocide; however, the Kurds in Turkey and then in Iran were more under this form of suppression. Whereas in Turkey, for a long period of time, the Kurdish identity has been totally ignored, and the Kurds were called the "mountain Turks," in other countries, the Kurdish identity was acknowledged, and in Iraq, the Kurds were allowed to practice certain cultural rights including studying in the Kurdish language in elementary schools. At the present time, the Kurds in Iraq have a de facto semi-state status; in Syria, an unofficial autonomous territory which is called the Rojava; in Turkey, a strong guerrilla and civil movement under the PKK; and in Iran, a weaker political movement under the Kurdish political parties and a developing cultural and intellectual movement.

3.6. Analysis and Conclusion

Kurdistan has been colonized by the four states of Iran, Iraq, Turkey, and Syria, but the Kurds have never been identified as colonized people. Kurdish nationalism coalesced into a transnational movement in the early twentieth century. The movement has experienced different conditions in each country. Until recently, the Kurds in Iraq have been decimated by decades of atrocity and cultural and sometimes physical genocide, with the worst times under Saddam Hussein's regime. Turkey has tried, in vain, to deny Kurdish identity by calling them "mountain Turks" and has resorted to acts of genocide. Syria has practiced cultural repression and Arabization, as well as imprisonment of Kurdish political leaders. Western powers, protecting their long-term regional interests, have played crucial roles in the oppression of the Kurds. Treaties that made promises to Kurdish nationalists were later rescinded and ignored.

Is there a prospect of an independent Kurdish nation? A national identity has been consistently on the rise among the Kurds. In Iraq, the Kurds have established the Kurdistan Regional Government (KRG) since 1992, a form of autonomy amounting to sub-nationhood. In Syria, the Kurds have established a *de facto* autonomous region known as Rojava since 2012. While the democratic Kurdish political parties pressed for self-determination, they needed to make alliances with Kurdish and non-Kurdish democratic groups. The Kurdish people need broad-based, cross-national organizations to support their struggle for independence. International organizations and Western countries have an obligation to support the building of the Kurdish state.

The nationalist movements of the Kurds in different parts of Kurdistan (Iran, Iraq, Turkey, and Syria) have had profound impacts on each other. These impacts can be categorized as (1) sentimental, sympathetic, moral, and spiritual, (2) cultural, (3) ideological, and (4) political, organizational, and practical. Expectedly, these categories are intertwined. Since this book attends to the struggles of the Iranian Kurds, the following will briefly show the impact of these factors on the Kurds in Iran.

The first aspect of impact is sentimental, sympathetic, moral, and spiritual. The national sentiments of the Kurds transcend the unjust geographical borders that have divided the nation. For instance, in response to the 1999 arrest of Ocalan by the Turkish government, Kurds in many cities around the world—and especially in Iranian Kurdish and non-Kurdish cities—held protests against Turkey. This support showed the connection of Iranian Kurds with the Kurdish movement in Turkey. While the demonstration in the beginning was against Turkey, the United States, and Israel, later, the slogans of people during the demonstrations changed against the Iranian government. These protests elevated the morale and spirit of the Kurds in Iran and encouraged them to pronounce their national feelings against the government.

The second feature of effect is cultural. The cultural products of Kurdish nationalism have affected all the Kurds. For instance, Ahmad (Ahmed) Khani (1650–1706), living in Turkey, wrote *Mem u Zin,* the Kurdish national epic in the late seventeenth century. His poetry has widely affected nationalist feelings in other parts of Kurdistan. In the twentieth century, Hajar translated this work from Kurmaji to Sorani, which is widely used in Iranian and Iraqi Kurdistan. In addition, Haji Qadir Koyi, from Iraqi Kurdistan, produces many revolutionary and nationalist ideas and poems which have extensively affected Iranian Kurds. One of the activities of the J.K. (see Chapter 5) was to print *Gulbjerek la diwani Haji Qadri Koyi blbli nishtmani Kurd* (*Selected Poems of Haji Qadir Koyi, Kurdish Homeland's Nightingale*), in 1943. Moreover, many nationalist songs and poems produced in Iraq Kurdistan have affected the Iranian Kurds. Furthermore, the cultural products of the Iranian Kurds, such as the poems of Hajar (Abdul Rahman Sharafkandi) and Hemin (Sayyed Mohammad Amin Shaikholislami Mukri), have broadly affected the Iraqi Kurds.

The third type of influence is ideological. The Kurdish nationalist ideology of other parts of Kurdistan has affected the emergence and development of Kurdish nationalist ideas in Iranian Kurdistan. Abdul Razzaq Badr Khan was one of the most important Kurdish politicians and intellectuals of his time who lived in Turkey. He and other Kurdish nationalists in Turkey, including other Badr Khanis and Sayyed Taha, played roles in the emergence and development of Kurdish nationalists such as Simko in Iran. Mohammad Rasoul Hawar (1996) states that Isma'il Simko (see Chapter 4) was influenced by the national feelings and intellectualism of Abdul Razzaq Badr Khan, the student of Haji Qadir Koyi (pp. 673-674). In addition, the nationalist ideas of the Iraqi Kurds before and during WWII profoundly affected the Iranian Kurdish intellectuals who later formed the J.K.

The fourth is the political, organizational, and practical impact. The Kurdish nationalist movements in different countries have politically, organizationally, and practically cooperated with each other. For instance, when Sheikh Ubayd Allah conducted a revolt in Iranian Kurdistan in 1880, the Iranian Kurds Hamza Agha Mangur and Feizollah Beg of Begzadeh participated in the uprising (Borzooyy, 2005, Arfa, 1966; O'Ballance, 1973; Sharafkandi, 1981; Madani, 2000; and Kinnane, 1964). In addition, Simko participated in Mullah Salim's revolt in Betlis, Turkey, in the Spring of 1914 (Hawrami, 2006, p. 379). Simko also created a political relationship with Sheikh Mahmoud Barzanji in Iraqi Kurdistan in the Winter of 1922 (Lazarev, 2010, p. 357). Moreover, Mullah Mustafa Barzani and other Iraqi Kurdish nationalists actively participated in organizing the peshmerga forces as well as teaching the Kurdish language during the Kurdistan Republic of 1946 in Iran. Furthermore, Kurdish cadres of the Communist Party of Iraq helped the PDKI to organize its peshmerga section after the Iranian Revolution. Also, as Jalil Gadani (2008a) states, on 25 August 1982, the PDKI released a declaration asking democratic forces of the world to stand against the genocidal treatment by the Iranian government. Jalal Talabani, the leader of the *Yaketi Nishtmani Kurdistan* (Patriotic Union of Kurdistan; PUK), sent a large group of peshmergas known as *Hezi Pishtiwan* (Support Force) to help the PDKI. Talabani himself stayed in Kurdistan for about three months to direct this force. More than 20 of these peshmergas were killed, and tens of them were wounded (Gadani, 2008a, p. 321). Finally, at the present time, for more than 20 years, the Kurdish political organizations such as PDKI have been settled down in Iraqi Kurdistan while the Iraqi Kurds, their political parties, and the Kurdish government comprehensively in all aspects of social life, including politically, socially, and financially have protected the Iranian Kurdish political organizations and their families.

In short, *the Kurdish nationalist movements in different parts of Kurdistan are organic parts of the Kurdish national liberation movement of Greater Kurdistan*. Although these apparently separate movements have different political strategies and tactics, and in some cases, the leading organizations both within a certain county and between different countries in which the Kurds reside have been in violent conflicts with each other, *these movements have extensively cooperated for the liberation of Kurdistan*.

Reasons for these conflicts include ideological clashes, monopolistic ideas and conducts, power-seeking attitudes, personal interests of the leaders, and lack of democratic life experience in Kurdistan. It also includes the interference of the rival states in which the Kurds live, reproducing the violent treatments by the antidemocratic and dictatorial states that dominate Kurdistan and duplicating and normalizing the culture and practice of eliminating others.

It is highly difficult to behave democratically in a society that has never been under a democratic political system: just a small portion of the Iranian Kurds for a very short period (11 months) have lived under the democratic Kurdistan Republic. The political organizations in Kurdistan have been the products of a society in which dictatorial and antidemocratic ideas and practices dominate all of its societal textures, institutions, and organizations. These organizations need comprehensive and constant plans to educate themselves to learn and practice democratic ideas and behaviors. While they emphasize political revolution and reforms to achieve democratic goals, which is undeniable, they underestimate the role of cultural changes in the creation of a democratic society.

To substantiate many of these preliminary conclusions, it is now time to specifically attend to the history of the Kurdish nationalist movement in Iran.

Chapter 4: Kurdish Nationalism in Eastern Kurdistan (Iran)

4.1. Introduction

This chapter attends to the Kurdish nationalist movement in Iran from the beginning of the twentieth century to WWII. Various nationalist movements emerged during this period, and they varied in their importance. After the defeat of Sheikh Ubayd Allah's revolt in 1880 in Iran, one of the most significant movements was the uprising of Isma'il Agha Shikak, known as Simko (1875-1930), the head of the Shikak tribe from the Abdui section, southwest of Urmiya (Urmyeh, Rezaeiyeh). It is somehow a forgotten history that this book revives some important parts of it.

Before entering the discussion on Kurdish nationalism, we need to consider the general political situation of Iran, its neighboring countries, and the foreign powers' influence. The internal and external factors, to different degrees, shaped the emergence, development, or fall of Kurdish movements. The most important external social and political events in the aforementioned period that affected the socio-political movements in Iran include the defeat of Russia by Japan in 1904, the 1905 Russian Revolution, the Young Turk Revolution of 1908, WWI, and the 1917 Russian Revolution. The others comprise the Sevres Treaty of 1920, the Lausanne Treaty of 1923, the dissolution of the Ottoman Empire and Sultanate and the establishment of the Republic of Turkey, the creation of new countries in the Middle East, such as Iraq and Syria, and the formation and continuation of various Kurdish and other social movements in these countries.

4.2. Constitutional Revolution

Some of the most important internal social and political occurrences in Iran that affected Kurdish movements include the Constitutional Revolution of 1905-1911; the manipulative policies of Russian, Britain, and German imperialists; and the military occupation of Iran by Russia, Britain, and Turkey, especially during WWI. Other important occurrences comprise Reza Khan's 1921 coup d'état, the dissolution of the Qajar Dynasty, the establishment of the Pahlavi Dynasty in 1925, and the emergence of new political organizations in the country. Some of the significant movements during this turbulent period were the Jangali movement led by Mirza Kuchek Khan and the establishment of the Soviet Socialist Republic of Iran (Gilan), 1920-1921; the Movement of Azerbaijan led by Sheikh Muhammad Khiabani; and the mutiny of Khorasan officers led by Mohammad Taqi Khan Pesyan.

Scholars have discussed the Iranian Constitutional Revolution of 1905-1911, the effect of the Tobacco Movement of 1891-1892 against the corrupt government of Qajar and foreign domination on this Revolution, the main actors, essence, results, the negative roles Russia, England, America, and Germany, and effects of this Revolution (Daniel, 2001, p. 16; Parsa Benab, 2004, p. 4; Ivanov, 1977, p. 17; Abrahamian, 1982, p. 109; Hatefi, 2001, p. 7; Tabari, 1981, pp. 159-161; Raisnia & Nahid, 1976, pp. 5, 161). As a result of these dynamics, "On December 30, 1906, Muzaffar Al-Din Shah Qajar signed a royal proclamation granting approval for a constitutional monarchy and a national assembly in Iran. The constitution was based on a European model and limited the absolutist powers of the shah" (Price, 2005, p. 135). A new phenomenon in Iran since the Constitutional Revolution was the emergence of social and political parties and organizations. These organizations represented different social classes. The Russian Social Democracy greatly affected the formation of left-wing organizations in Iran. "In 1904, the first Iranian social democratic group (Hemmat) was founded in Transcaucasia" (Nayeri and Nasab, 2006, p. 3). A comprehensive list of the parties and associations (*anjoman*) has been provided by scholars (Agahi,

2006, pp. 9-26; Parsa Benab, 2004, pp. 61-82, 39-45). Similar to the previous Iranian dynasties, women were severely oppressed during the Qajars. They were considered inferior and made to satisfy men's desires. The Royal Qajar harems serve as an example showing the inferior status of women in the society (Azad, 2003, pp. 343, 368, 372). During the Constitutional Revolution, new perspectives regarding the enhancement of women's status rose among male and female intellectuals. Women actively participated in the Revolution. They created many women's organizations engaging in social, cultural, economic, and political activities (Parsa Benab, 2004, pp. 43-46).

In short, the disintegration of feudalism and the struggle of the Iranian people in order to change the political system were some of the fundamental causes of the Constitutional Revolution. It was a bourgeoisie-democratic, anti-despotism, anti-feudalism, and anti-imperialism revolution that was suppressed by the collaboration of the internal reactionary forces with the imperialist forces. Although the Constitutional Revolution gained some important achievements, it remained an unfinished Revolution.

4.3. Foreign Influence

Although Iran technically has never been colonized by a Western power, the policies of foreign countries have greatly affected its social and political situation. During the Qajar era, the colonial countries using different political, economic, and military concessions and agreements changed Iranian society. With the help of Russian military instructors, the Cossack Brigade was established in Iran in 1890, and it was funded through tax incomes of northern Iran. Russia gave two loans to Iran in 1900 and 1901. The total borrowed money was 32,500,000 Manats (60,000,000 Francs). In return, Russia was given control of the tax incomes of northern Iran. Likewise, in 1902, Britain gave a loan to Iran in return for collecting the tax income of southern Iran (Hatefi, 2001, pp. 143-145).

Moreover, Russia occupied Azerbaijan in 1909 and later extended its occupation to other regions, including Tehran, in 1911. Azerbaijan was a battlefield between Russia and the Ottoman Empire. In 1915, the Russian army was stationed in Qazvin. Germans and Ottomans occupied western parts of Azerbaijan and Tabriz in March and May of 1918. In order to support the Anglo-Persian Oil Company, Britain used the area around Ahwaz to attack the Ottomans in Iraq. Britain also formed the South Persia Rifles, a Persian army commanded by Sir Percy Sykes, in 1916 and extended its relationships with different tribes like the Bakhtiaries in Fars and Arabs in Khuzistan under Sheikh Khaz'al. Later, the Cossack Brigade was placed under British control. The British army, under the command of General Lionel Dunsterville, under the pretext of fighting against Germans and Ottomans, mobilized troops in northern Iran and occupied Rasht and Anzali by June 1918. On 12 August 1918, the cabinet of Anglophile Vossugh al-Dowleh was formed (Abrahamian, 2008, pp. 58-60; Ivanov, 1977, pp. 32-33; Daniel, 2001, p. 128; Gheissari and Nasr, 2006, p. 36; Keddie, 2003, p. 74).

Lord Curzon, British Foreign Minister, drafted the 1919 Anglo-Persian Agreement with the help of the Iranian prime minister, Vossugh al-Dowleh. The British gave £160,000 to Vossugh al-Dowleh to push the agreement through Majles. Public reaction to the agreement was extensively against the British and in favor of the Russians. Meanwhile, the Jangalis established the Soviet Socialist Republic of Iran in Gilan (1920-1921) and asked for Bolshevik support. In Azerbaijan, Sheikh Mohammad Khiabani led a revolt against the central government. Shi'i clerics in the Holy City of Karbala issued fatwas against the British. Radical nationalists formed a Punishment Committee in Tehran and announced their decision to avenge the supporters of the Agreement and assassinated four close associates of Premier Vossugh al-Dowleh. Consequently, Vossugh al-Dowleh resigned. By 1920, some provinces were either under the control of the warlords or under the authority of armed rebels. The Red Army dominated Gilan. In reaction, Britain recalled its military forces and began searching for a man to end "anarchy" and "Bolshevik poison" in Iran (Abrahamian, 2008, pp. 60-62). Abbas Milani (2008) claims that Iran was on the threshold of disintegration by 1921 (p. 313). In these critical months, the British, in order to maintain their interests, planned a coup, and they increasingly narrowed their choice down to the capable officer, Brigadier Reza Khan.

4.4. Reza Shah

Reza Khan, later Reza Shah (1878-1944), was the commander of the Cossack Brigade in Qazvin Garrison. He commanded the coup against the Qajar Dynasty on 21 February 1921. The role of the British in supporting the Coup of 1921 is clear. Reza Khan had expressed the British aid to his coming to power but only to serve his country (Makki, 1979, p. 157). Sayyed Zia al-Din Tabatabai, an instrumental figure in the coup, was a known Anglophile politician. Abbas Milani (2008) asserts that Tabatabai supported the 1919 Agreement "and with it, he was irrevocably marked with the infamy of being a British stooge" (p. 313). Tabatabai also had a fundamental role in leading *Komiteh-ye Ahan*, the Iron Committee, a secret Anglophile association whose members took part in the coup (Ghani, 2000, p. 151). Scholars have documented the detailed role of British agents, General William Edmond Ironside, the Commander of Norperforce (North Persia Force), and their Iranian agents in the coup (Axworthy, 2008, p. 217; Makki, 1979, pp. 212-216).

After Reza Khan's coup on 21 February 1921, Ahmad Shah appointed Tabatabai as the Prime Minister on 22 February 1921. Reza Khan became the Commander-in-Chief who proclaimed martial law in Tehran. Many activists and politicians were arrested after the coup. On 30 April 1921, the British military detachment (2,300 British and 9,300 Indians), under the command of Ironside, left Iran. In September 1921, the government disarmed the South Persia Rifles (Makki,

1979, pp. 233-234, 361-362; Ivanov, 1977, p. 53).

In May 1921, Reza Khan became the Minister of War and, in 1923, was appointed the Prime Minister. In 1925, after deposing Ahmad Shah, the last King of the Qajar Dynasty, the Iranian Majles declared Reza Khan as the King of Iran on 12 December 1925. Reza Shah established the Pahlavi Dynasty. When the Anglo-Soviet forces invaded Iran on 25 August 1941, the Iranian army disintegrated within forty-eight hours. The Allies forced Reza Shah to abdicate on 16 September 1941 in favor of his son Mohammad Reza. The Allies exiled Reza Shah first to Mauritius and later to Johannesburg, South Africa, where he died on 26 July 1944 (Ghani, 2000, p. 406). Reza Shah had clear sympathies toward Germany, and the Allies wanted to use Iran as a corridor to help the Soviet Union, protect the oil installations, remove German agents, and prevent the pro-Axis Iranian officers who might remove the unpopular Reza Shah and create a pro-Germany government. When, in 1941, Britain and the Soviet Union asked the Iranian government to expel the Germans, Reza Shah postponed their demand (Abrahamian, 1982, p. 164; Keddie, 2003, pp. 104-105).

During Reza Shah's reign, Iran went through a significant modernization, which resulted in fundamental changes in different areas, including industry, transport, and education. Some steps toward modernization included the formation of a modern army, the foundation of the National Bank of Iran, the opening of the north-south highway, the building of the first cement and tobacco factories and the Trans-Iranian Railway, and the establishment of Tehran University. He formed the "modern Iranian nation-state" and became the "father of modern Iran." The bourgeois and feudal classes were the main social base of Reza Shah. However, his autocratic style resulted in gaining no significant support by the end of his reign (Keddie, 2003, pp. 103-104; Daniel, 2001, p. 135; Safai, 1986, pp. xi-xii; Ghani, 2000, p. 407; Ivanov, 1977, pp. 71-72; Tabari, 1981, p. 188). The military structure of the country as a tool for suppressing opposition was a fundamental feature of the

Reza Shah's autocratic rule. During Reza Shah's reign, military funding made up 30 percent of the country's budget, and the number of army personnel increased from 40,000 to 150,000 (Gheissari and Nasr, 2006, p. 41; Bashiriyeh, 2001, p. 70). Reza Shah, equipped with "troops, tanks, plans, strategic roads, and, of course, Maxim guns," brought tribal chiefs to heel. He killed Simko, the Kurdish leader, and killed or eliminated other Iranian tribal leaders such as Solat al-Dowleh, Sheikh Khaz'al, Quli Khan Mamassani, Doost Muhammad, Sartip Khan, Hussein Khan, and Jafar Quli Khan Sardar As'ad (Abrahamian, 2008, pp. 92-93). Reza Shah seized large amounts of lands and tenements for himself during his reign: by owning about 15 percent of Iran's arable lands, he became the largest landholder in Iran. He also took over some of the most profitable monopolies in the country. Along with state elites and a small number of landed militaries, Reza Shah controlled the largest personal wealth in Iran. More than 300,000 villagers were the peasants of Reza Shah (Paymai, 2002, pp. 173-175; Sharifi, 2008, pp. 90-91; Tabari, 1981, p. 223; Bashiriyeh, 2001, pp. 73-74). Under Reza Shah's autocracy, all political parties were banned, and free elections were prevented (Paymai, 2002, pp. 176-180).

The rise of Reza Shah signifies the *historic process of state-building* in Iran. In creating a modern Iran, *Reza Shah forged a state-sanctioned Persian-centric national identity*, as a result of which not only did he put down tribal revolts, but he also denied the existence of national minorities and suppressed the latter's emerging national consciousness and social movements.

4.5. Social Movements in This Period.

After the first period of the Constitutional Revolution (1905-1911), the struggle of the Iranian people against despotism and imperialism, and for democracy and social justice continued in various forms. The most significant revolutionary movements were the Jangali Movement led by Mirza Kuchek Khan, the mutiny led by Colonel Mohammad Taqi Khan Pesyan, and the revolt led by Sheikh Mohammad Khiabani in Azerbaijan.

4.5.1. The Jangali Movement. Ibrahim Fakhrai (1978) states that in the second year of WWI, the Jangali movement took shape under the leadership of Mirza Kuchek Khan, lasting from 1915 to 1921 (pp. 3-4, 35). The Bolsheviks were involved in Gilan during the Constitutional Revolution of 1905-1911, and their cooperation with Iranian revolutionaries continued in different forms until the 1917 October Revolution. A Bolshevik Revolutionary Committee was established in Anzali in December 1917. In May 1920, the Bolsheviks entered Gilan, and Bolshevik leader Sergo Ordzhonikidze negotiated with Kuchek Khan about the establishment of a revolutionary republic. In June 1920, the Jangalis declared: "Now this national force [the Jangalis] with the help and assistance of all the humanitarians of the world and with the perseverance of the just principles of socialism [...] has entered the stage of the Red Revolution" (Dailami, 1990, pp. 44-46, 55). According to Ivanov (1977), the Jangali movement was Iran's most significant national liberation movement between 1920 and 1922. On 5 June 1920, the Provisional Revolutionary Government and the War Council of the Gilan Republic were established (p. 33).

After Heidar Khan Amuoghly (Tariverdiev) came to Iran, a new *Komiteh-ye Enghelab* (Revolutionary Committee) was established, which included Kuchek Khan and other Gilan leaders. The new government declared the following program: the creation of an Iranian version of the Red Army to attack Tehran, revoking landlords' authorities, abolishing feudalism, and addressing the needs of the city and rural workers (Fakhrai, 1978, pp. 271-273, 302, 327-329). But in September 1921, divisions developed within the Jangali movement, leading to clashes and assassination of Amuoghly (Fakhrai, 1978, 271-273, 368-370, 422; Agahi, 2006, p. 26). In October, Reza Khan, the War Minister, entered Rasht and suppressed the movement. Escaping arrest, Kuchek Khan froze to death shortly after (Bahar, 1978, p. 166). Thus, Iran's only socialist republic disintegrated.

4.5.2. The Revolt of Colonel Pesyan. Colonel Mohammad Taqi Khan Pesyan (1898-1921), born in Tabriz, was a member of the *Hezb-e Demokrat-e Iran* (Democratic Party of Iran), a radical constitutionalist party, which was established in 1910. During WWI, he participated in military activities against the British and Tsarist Russia in Qazvin, Hamedan, and Kermanshah. In 1920, he was chosen as the commander of the Gendarmerie in the Province of Khurasan (Ivanov, 1977, pp. 49-50). Bahar (1978) reveals that after the 1921 coup, Colonel Pesyan, on the orders of Sayyed Zia al-Din Tabatabai, arrested the Qavam-al-Saltaneh, the Governor of Khurasan, and sent him to Tehran. When Qavam-al-Saltaneh became the Prime Minister, Ahmad Shah appointed Najd al-Saltaneh as the Governor of Khurasan on 30 May 1921. Pesyan arrested him and gained control of the region. When the government appointed Samsam al-Saltaneh Bakhtiyari as the Governor of Khurasan, Pesyan organized about 5,000 gendarmes and revolted against the new Governor. His aim was to establish an independent Khurasan Republic. In response, the government provoked the local tribes against him. They united and formed a guerrilla force of about 5,000 armed cavalries and attacked him. Pesyan was killed in this war on 4 October 1921. On 1 December 1921, the government's force entered Mashhad (Bahar, 1978, pp. 140-159).

4.5.3. The Uprising Led by Khiabani. Sheikh Mohammad Khiabani was a radical cleric and a parliamentarian from Tabriz. Khiabani actively participated in the Constitutional Revolution and protested against the humiliating 1919 Treaty. Kiabani's revolt in April 1920 resulted in the gaining control over the provincial government in Tabriz and its surroundings until his death in September 1920 (Parvin, 2011; *Azādīstān*, 1987). During this time, the name of Azerbaijan was changed to Azadistan (Freedom Land). Kiabani had strived to bring cooperation between the revolutionary movements in other parts of Iran, including Jangalis (Fakhrai, 1978, pp. 370-371). However, the course of events did not result in a practical collaboration between these uprisings. The newly appointed Governor of Azerbaijan, Mokhber al-Saltaneh, with the secret support of the revolutionary Gendarmerie Chief and backing of the Cossack Brigade and English Norperforce (North Persia Force) attacked the center of the revolt in September 1920 and killed Khiabani (Raisnia & Nahid, 1976, pp. 257- 258, 261-262; Fakhrai, 1978, 371).

4.6. Kurdish Nationalism in Iran

The nationalist struggles of the Kurds against the central government in Iran from the beginning of the twentieth century to the beginning of WWII are examined in this section and in three parts: (1) the Kurdish struggle for ethnic rights in the aforesaid period, (2) the movement of the Isma'il Agha Shikak (Simko), and (3) other Kurdish protests against the central government.

4.6.1. Kurdish struggles since the beginning of the 20th century. After Sheikh Ubayd Allah's revolt in 1880, the last important Kurdish revolt in Iran during the nineteenth century, the nationalist movements that claimed autonomy or independence in Iranian Kurdistan were rare. Aside from the chiefs' desires to get rid of external interference, there was only one case in Iran that revealed the disposition toward autonomy. This was a short-lived autonomy movement in Sawj Bulaq (Mahabad) in 1886, which was led by the Governor of Mukri. Later, Sheikh Qazi Fattah, the chief mullah of Mahabad, led a movement around 1900, which was supported by some chiefs, especially the Mangur Aghas tribal chiefs. He made two demands: (1) tax increment should be stopped, and (2) the Governorship of Mahabad should be held by a local. In response, the authorities arrested and took him to Tehran (McDowall, 2004, pp. 101-102).

During the Constitutional Revolution of 1906, similar to other parts of Iran, *anjomans* (associations or councils) were established in all Kurdish regions, in the towns of Khoy, Salmas, Urumiya, Mahabad, Saqqiz, Sanandaj (Sinna), Kirmanshah, and some villages. These associations supported the Constitution.

When Qazi Fattah was released at the beginning of the Revolution, he led Mahabad's association (McDowall, 2004, p. 102). The popular *Sedaqat* (Honesty) Association was established by Kurdish intellectuals in 1907 in Sanandaj under Mohammad Mardokh. The Kurdish nationalist movement "was fighting not only for self-rule but also against the tribal chieftains" (Nerwiy, 2012, p. 77). The Constitutional Revolution did not result in recognizing the rights of different nationalities in Iran. Madani (2001) writes that the most important section of the constitution was about *anjomanakari ayalati wa wilayati* (Provincial and District Assemblies) intended to govern the country in a decentralized manner. However, this clause was eliminated due to the opposition of *mashro'eh khahan* (advocates of *Shari'a*) (p. 37).

In July 1918, the leader of the Mukri tribe of Mahabad had "discussed a scheme for an independent Kurdish state under British protection with Lieutenant-Colonel R. L. Kennion, the British consul at Kermanshah, when the later was on tour near Sakiz [Saqqiz]" (Jwaideh, 2006, p. 139). Efforts had been made to organize a pan-tribal movement aimed at Kurdish independence or getting rid of Iranian misgovernment. Some Kurdish chiefs, in July 1918, had seemingly met to examine the possibility of Kurdish independence under British sponsorship, and the suggestion was delivered by a Mukri chief to a British representative in Saqqiz (McDowall, 2004, p. 215).

4.6.2. The movement of Isma'il Agha Shikak (Simko). Simko was the chief of the Shikak tribe in the southwest of Urmiya, Iran. According to Jwaideh (2006), in 1919, two imperative Kurdish leaders, Simko and Sayyed Taha, were closely cooperating "on a plan for the inclusion of the Persian Kurds in an independent Kurdish state" (p. 139). Simko's revolt was the first major Kurdish attempt to establish an independent state by secession from Iran (Entessar, 1992, p. 13). This movement had hardly been studied academically prior to this book. The goal of this section is to introduce and analyze the movement of Simko.

4.6.2.1. A chronology of Simko's movement. The murder of Jafar Agha, the older brother of Simko, by the Iranian government profoundly affected Simko's life. Jafar Agha was the son of Mohammad Agha Shikak. Due to Jafa Agha's influence, Nezam al-Saltaneh, the Governor of Azerbaijan, wanted to eliminate him. An example of Jafar Agha's influence is that formerly, Tsar Nikolas II had invited Jafar Agha, Abdul Razzaq Badr Khan, and Sayyed Taha Shamzinan to Russia (Kutschera, 1994, p. 59). According to Ahmad Kasravi (1970), Mohammad Agha, the Chief of the Shikak tribe, and his son Jafar Agha disobeyed the Iranian government and continued raiding and looting villages for many years. Nezam al-Saltaneh pardoned Jafar Agha and asked him to come to Tabriz in order to control the security of the Armenian region of the city. When in 1905, Mohammad Ali Shah (1872-1925) ascended to the throne, he ordered Nezam al-Saltaneh to kill Jafar Agha. Nezam al-Saltaneh invited Jafar Agha and his followers to his place, where Mohammad Hussein Khan Zargham fatally shot Jafar Agha. The rest of the Kurds fought their way out and escaped, leaving two dead behind. Later, the officials hung the dead bodies of the Kurds upside down at Ali Qapu Palace in Tabriz (Kasravi, 1970, pp. 143-145; Mustafa Amin, 2007, p. 69). When Simko heard about Jafar Agha's death, he vowed vengeance and started a revolt with twelve men around Urmiya and Maragheh (Sajjadi, 2000, p. 214).

While Kasravi and other Iranian writers look down on the resistance of the Kurds and their outstanding figures who fought against the government, calling them raiders and looters, Minorsky (2000) admires the Kurds and writes that Jafar Agha had sometimes looted the rich and divided the loot among the poor. Minorsky personally had met the six men who escaped during Jafar Agha's assassination and was impressed by their bravery (pp. 31, 68). Likewise, Bruinessen claims that Jafar Agha was known as the Robin Hood of the Kurds among Westerners (Hawar, 1996, p. 212-213).

Apparently, one of Isma'il Agha Simko's earliest activities was his conflict with the constitutionalists in Iran. Simko had collaborated with Eghbal al-Saltaneh in confronting the constitutionalists (Malekzadeh, 1992, p. 1113). Concerning Simko's role during the Constitutional Revolution, and his resistance, conflicts, and wars against different groups in the territory, more comprehensive research is needed.

One of the early activities of Simko was his collaboration with Abdul Razzaq Badr Khan, the son of Najib Pasha, the elder son of Badr Khan Pasha. Abdul Razzaq was a student of Haji Qadir Koyi, a prominent Kurdish nationalistic poet and intellectual. Abdul Razzaq was one of the most important Kurdish politicians and intellectuals of his time. He was the Third Secretary of the Ottoman Empire Embassy in Petersburg, Russia, where he learned Russian. He later became the Second Secretary of the Ottoman Empire Embassy in Tehran, Iran. When the Ottoman government became suspicious of him and brought him to Istanbul, he escaped with the help of the Russian Embassy officials in September 1892 and went to Sevastopol and later to Tiflis. Later, he came to Iranian Kurdistan and met with Simko. Abdul Razzaq aimed to strengthen Russian influence in Kurdistan. Jalil emphasizes that Abdul Razzaq was an expert political intellectual, and his analyses were from a tribal perspective. Like Sheikh Ubayd Allah, he believed that it would be easier for the Kurdish revolt to begin in Iranian Kurdistan and then to expand to Kurdistan in Turkey. He believed that because the English had lied to and betrayed the Kurds, the Kurds could ask the Russian Empire to protect an independent Kurdistan (Hawar, 1996, pp. 146-148, 156-159). Abdul Razzaq had an extensive plan for the emancipation of Kurdistan and was organizing various Kurdish activities throughout all of Kurdistan. Hawar (1996) claims Simko was patriotic, a brave revolutionary, and a combatant Kurd whose primary goal was freedom for Kurds and the liberation of Kurdistan. In contrast to most of the tribal chiefs, he was interested in civilization, literacy, intellectualism, and journalism. He was influenced by the national feelings and intellectualism of Abdul Razzaq Badr Khan, the student of Haji Qadir Koyi (pp. 673-674).

One of Simko's cultural activities was his cooperation with Abdul Razzaq for the purpose of establishing a Kurdish school. Abdul Razzaq, with the help of Russians, established the intellectual organization of *Jahandani* in the city of Khoy in 1913. According to Mikhail Semenovich Lazarev, the school was opened on the 24 of December 1913 in Khoy. Due to this event, a huge celebration was organized in the city. The first group of students included 29 people who studied in Kurdish while using the Russian alphabet. They were also studying Russian literature. The school also included a small hospital (Hawar, 1996, pp. 151-153). Jalil mentions the date 27 October 1913 for the official establishment of the school and maintains that Simko, on the 21 of October 1913, brought 29 students, aged from 8-10, from Chehriq (Chehrigh), Somay Bradost, and Khydar to the school. The students were in the uniformed European dress with white Caucasian hats. Forty of Simko's armed men protected them (Hawar, 1996, p. 165).

Simko was actively cooperating with other Kurdish nationalists in Turkey as well. Lazarev (2010) confirms that the most powerful Kurdish revolt took place in Betlis, Turkey, in 1914, under the leadership of Mullah Salim Betlisi. Some people who actively participated in the revolt included Abdul Razzaq, Yousef Kamel, Sheikh Taha, and Simko. They spent three years providing the conditions for the revolt. At the beginning of April 1914, the revolutionaries took over Betlis but were unable to keep it. The Turks brutally suppressed the revolt and hung the revolt's leaders. Zinar Silopi, a pseudonym for the late Qadri Jamil Pasha, maintains that when the October Revolution of 1917 occurred, these Kurdish revolutionaries went back to Turkey. Abdul Razzaq was arrested by the Turks and sent to Mosul, where he was hung without a trial (Lazarov, 2010, p. 289; Hawrami, 2006, pp. 151, 379).

Bruinessen (2006a) states that before 1913, Simko collaborated with pro-Ottoman, anti-Russian Azerbaijanis. However, he turned to the Russians to gain their support in 1913. During WWI, Simko kept himself away from real fighting, while keeping the doors open for all possibilities as well as developing his authority on the borders. At some point, the Russians arrested and sent Simko to prison in Tiflis. Later, they let him live in Khoy if he remained loyal to them. After the Russian Revolution, the Russian army, led by General Baratoff, was called back from Kurdistan to Russia. Simko captured many of their arms, including field guns. In addition, Simko received arms from the Kurdish militia, who had fought for the Turks. At that time, Simko was already widely known as a nationalist leader (pp. 16-17).

When the Ottomans invaded the Kurdish territory in 1908, Simko asked Russia to help him against the Ottomans but the Russians declined. Although the Ottomans promised to appoint Simko as the Governor of Qutur, Salmas, Chehriq, and Soma, he did not accept the offer. Instead, he asked Iran to help him by giving him money and weapons to fight against the Ottomans, but the Iranians refused as well. Finally, Simko launched guerrilla attacks against the Ottomans. In 1911, he asked Russia, once again, for help against the Ottomans, but the Russians, who did not want to destroy their relationships with the Turks, delayed Simko's demand. Simko did not allow the Ottomans to settle in the territory. When the Russians formally invited him to the Caucasus at the end of 1912, the Governor of the Caucasus welcomed Simko as the head of a state, holding a military parade and honoring him with a medal (Hawrami, 2006, pp. 373-375).

The Russian army occupied Urmiya on 11 March 1915 and armed Mar Shimun and the escaped Assyrians and Armenians in the territory. When the Assyrians tried to dominate the region and proclaimed that they wanted to establish their own government, people revolted, and bloody campaigns ensued. Simko, through the Russian Consul, and Mar Shimun tried to solve the problem. However, when the Russians reached the city of Khoy, they arrested Simko on 15 February 1915, accusing him of collaborating with the Ottomans, and sent him to the city of

Tiflis (Hawrami, 2006, p. 379). At the beginning of May 1915, the Russians also arrested Abdul Razzaq, Sayyed Taha, Taymour Khan (Governor of Khoy), and Simko's eight followers and sent them to the city of Jolfa. The Russians also disarmed the Kurdish territory. Finally, they liberated Simko from the prison in April 1916 and negotiated with Iran to recognize Simko's authority because both the Russians and Iranians knew that Simko was the only person who could protect the borders against an Ottoman invasion (Hawrami, 2006, pp. 380-381).

After the October Revolution of 1917, when the Russian army left Iran, they left a lot of weapons that Simko could use (Hawar, 1996, pp. 262,263). During WWI, the Assyrians in Turkey were afraid of experiencing the Armenian fate. Thus, about 25,000 Assyrian Christians, known as Jelus, fled from Turkey to the Urmiya region, doubling the number of their co-religionists in this region. Assyrians also received many armaments from the Russians, leaving Simko worried about their potential power in the region. In an incident, the Assyrian Jelu (Jilu) warriors looted the bazaar of Urmiya on 15 February 1918 and killed 100 Muslims outside the city on 20 February 1918. While the Papal representative, Monseigneur Sontag, tried to stop the disturbance, the American missionary, Dr. Shedd, strongly supported and provoked the Assyrians against Iranians (Hawar, 1996, p. 372; Arfa, 1966, pp. 50-52). The relationship between Simko and the Assyrians and the killing of the Assyrian Patriarch Mar Benyamin Shimun (Mar Shimun) (1887-1918), the religious and political leader of the Assyrians at that time, constitutes an important chapter in Simko's life and his movement. Arfa (1966) indicates that during the second part of WWI, Simko carefully chose a neutral position and avoided joining the Turks as he had done at the start of the war. Mar Shimun was seeking independence, or at least the autonomy, of the Assyrians. He recognized that he should temporarily co-operate with the Kurds (p. 52). While Patriarch Mar Shimun was mostly sympathetic toward the Russians, the British attempted to recruit him by promising him the creation of an independent Assyrian state after the war. Ashor Giwargis (2004) reveals that

> A meeting was held in Uremia [Urmiya] between the Assyrians and the allies, in February 1918, whereby the meeting was limited to the Russian Consul Nikitin, the American Consul Shed, the French officer Cujol, and the English captain Gracy who promised the Assyrian Patriarch in the name of the British Government of an independent State (stretching from the west of Tur-Abdin till the East of Lake Uremia), but in return he asked the Assyrians to abandon the Russians who had already left the war because of the Bolshevik Revolution. Gracy asked the Assyrians to join Britain, which will guarantee them their independent State at the end of the war. The Assyrian leadership had no choice other than joining the English whether they lied or were truthful, but the English were well aware of the fact that the Patriarch sympathized with the Russians.

Regarding the meeting between Simko and Mar Shimun in which Mar Shimun was killed by Simko, Vasily Shumanov writes: on March 3, Mar Shimun, along with some 150 people, arrived at the meeting with Simko (2004). Simko killed Mar Shimun on March 3, 1918, after the negotiations. Kasravi (1977) claims that Mar Shimun wanted to attract Simko toward the Christians and to deceive him. He explains the details of Mar Shimun's assassination by Simko (pp. 726-727). Both the Iranian and British governments were involved in Mar Shimun's assassination (Hawar, 1996, p. 263; Ashor Giwargis, 2004). Mar Shimun's assassination created more disturbances in the area. The Assyrians attacked the innocent Azeries in Urmiya and Salmas, looted and slaughtered many people, including women and children, advanced on Chehriq, Simko's fortress (which Simko had already evacuated, having retreated to the mountains), destroying

Simko's and other people's buildings (Arfa, 1966, pp. 53-54).

When the Ottomans occupied Urmiya at the beginning of summer 1918, the Assyrians moved back to Soldus, now Naqadeh, and Mahabad in order to join the British forces in Sain Qal'eh, Shahindej. On their way, near Miandoab, they were attacked by the Kurds and Iranians, and just a small number of them survived. When WWI ended and the Ottomans left, Simko, using the weakness of the central government in Iran, dominated the north Kurdistan of Iran (Sharafkandi, 1981, p. 65). From 1918, the political relationship between Simko and Sayyed Taha strengthened. By January 1919 a cross-border "pan-Islamic" coalition formed under Simko's leadership among the Kurds near Bashqala. The aim of this cooperation was to impede the returning of the Assyrians and Armenians to the area (McDowall, 2004, p. 116).

Simko's revolt was affected by international and neighboring politics and movements. Since WWI, ideas and activities regarding self-determination and independence have been spreading. President Wilson's 1918 promise of self-determination kindled hope for the non-Turkish people of the Ottoman Empire, encompassing Arabs, Armenians, Kurds, and Assyrians. Such hope materialized in the movements of Sheikh Mahmoud in Iraq and Simko in Iran. After WWI, when the Russians, Turks, and Assyrians left northwestern Iran, Simko filled the vacuum. The Iranian government acknowledged Simko's *de facto* control of the territory and appointed Simko as the Governor of the Kurdish territory west of Lake Urmiya. Simko thought about Kurdish statehood and independence, but his understanding of government was at the tribal command level. Having this type of conception, Simko opposed Tehran's attempts to assign officials to the territory (Eagleton, 1963, pp. 10- 11; Kinnane, 1964, p. 47). Simko revolted in 1919 and occupied Urmiya and Shapur (Salmas) (Hawar, 1996, p. 263).

While the Iranian government gave the title of Sardar Nosrat, Victory Commander, to Simko, they were secretly planning to obliterate him. In May 1919,

Crown Prince Muhammad Ali Mirza sent 45 thousand *tomans* to some Armenians and asked them to kill Simko. They installed a bomb in a candy-like decorated box that was sent as a gift to Simko by Seghatoleslam. However, when Simko received the box, it exploded and killed some of Simko's followers, including two of his brothers, Ali Agha and Khorshid. Consequently, the Shikaks were agitated and burned a few villages in Khoy, which resulted in more enmity between the Iranian government and the Kurds (Mustafa Amin, 2005, p. 423; Hawar, 1996, p. 287-288).

According to Arfa (1966), "In 1920, Simko began to talk openly of Kurdish independence" (p. 58). Arfa (1966) admits that the

> Simko episode may be considered as [*sic*] the first attempt by the Kurds in Iran to create an independent or autonomous region, but the chief actor, Simko, had neither the desire nor the ability to create a state in the modern sense of the word, with an administrative organization. He was chiefly interested in plunder, and as he could not loot his own tribe or the associated tribes, he raided and tried to dominate non-Kurdish regions, like Salmas, Rezaiyeh [Urmiya], and eventually Khoy, reducing the population of these districts to utter ruin and despair. (pp. 63-64)

Arfa statements should be treated with caution. It is not proper to easily conclude that Simko's aim was to create a "personal despotic rule," and it is rather judgmental to claim that Simko did not have the desire or the ability to establish a modern state. Indeed, like such Iranian movements as those of Khiabani, Kuchek khan, and Persian, the severe suppression of Simko's movement did not allow it to develop naturally. Moreover, in the course of the Kurdish uprising, plundering did occur, while in certain cases, even Simko had condemned it. For instance, Simko has claimed that he was very much against the killing and looting of people in Mahabad (Hawar, 1996, pp. 357, 440-442, 446-447; Kavianpur, 1999, pp. 333-

334). In addition, Arfa (1966) maintains that Simko defeated the Iranian army in November 1920 and captured nine soldiers. Simko asked them to describe the mechanism of a machine gun that he had obtained from the army. He awarded gold lira, a Turkish coin, to each of them and made them free (pp. 60). Thus, it is not entirely factual that Simko was chiefly interested in plundering. In contrast, this example shows the generosity, kindness, and humanistic behavior of Simko with the captives.

Simko extended his authority over some other areas of Kurdistan. Arfa (1966) asserts that Simko, due to "his strong personality and reckless bravery, had gained an uncontested authority among the neighbouring tribes, from west of Khoy to north of Saqqez and Baneh" (p. 48). In contrast to Arfa's view, Naqibzadeh (2000) believes that in the course of history, the Kurds were the stooge of other powers, and Simko was basically supported by foreign powers, especially Turkey (pp. 155-156). Although sometimes Simko received help from different powers, which is not necessarily unethical, Simko was an independent leader. According to Minorsky (2007), Simko consciously misled Iranians, Turks, and Russians while choosing a totally independent way (p. 200). In contrast to Naqibzadeh's view, Tabari (1981) writes that the interference and help of the British to Reza Shah made it easy to suppress both Sheikh Khaz'al and Simko (p. 197).

Simko tried to convince Britain and France to help his movement. By the Summer of 1921, Simko had suggested to Britain the attractive view of an independent Kurdistan formed from Iran and Turkey. However, Britain rejected the idea because it was worried about dismantling the border between Turkey and Iran (McDowall, 2004, p. 141). Kutschera (1994) reveals that Simko strived to get help from Britain. In May 1919, he sent Sayyed Taha to Baghdad to negotiate with President Wilson in order to include Iranian Kurdistan in the supposedly forming Kurdish state. In August 1921, Simko also contacted Sir Percy Cox. Simko's negotiations with the British officials, as well as his effort to contact France, produced no results. Finally, rumors had it that Simko tried to gain help from the Soviets. Thus, he sent a delegate to Baku in the spring of 1922. This was the worst time for the Soviets to help because on 26 February 1922, the Soviet Union and Iran had an agreement to normalize their relations, and the Soviets ended up helping the leaders of the Revolutionary Government of Gilan (Kutschera, 1994, pp. 66-68).

The dominant perspective of the Soviet policy about the Kurdish problem during this period is reflected in the letter of 4 June 1924 from Georgy Vasilyevich Chicherin (1872-1936), the Soviet Foreign Minister from 1918-1930 to Petrov, who was in charge of an official of the Comintern. Chicherin claims that the establishment of an independent Kurdistan is against the interests of the Soviet Union, Iran, and Turkey. The Soviets' support of the Kurds would push Turkey and Iran towards Britain. Consequently, the Soviet Union must encourage the Kurds to unite all of their forces to emancipate Kurdistan from Britain and to delay their revolution until a more proper international situation emerges (Hawrami, 2006, pp. 142-143). Mustafa Amin (2007) reveals that when Simko was on the border of Iran and Turkey, *Komali Istighlali Kurdistan* (the Kurdish Independence Association), led by Khalid Baig Jibranli, was preparing itself for a revolt. Khalid Baig asked Simko to contact the Soviets to support Kurdish independence and national rights. Simko sent Ahmad Taqi to visit the Soviet Consul in Urmiya (p. 472), but the effort was fruitless. Simko also had affiliations with the Turks. Simko had an equivocal relation with the Turks. He despised Turkish nationalists and believed they were worse than Iranians in respect to the Kurds. Nevertheless, Simko never cut his relationship with the Turks because he needed their weapons and ammunition (Kutschera, 1994, p. 68).

Simko extended his authority to other areas of Kurdistan in Iran. In 1921, he attacked Sauj Bulaq (Mahabad), killed most of the Iranian gendarmes, around 600, and captured about 300 (Eagleton, 1963, p. 11; Kinnane, 1964, Kavianpur,

1999, p. 47, 334). Kutschera (1994) writes that Simko's advisor, Sayyed Taha, attacked Mahabad on 6 October 1921. The day after, Simko, along with 2,000 cavalries, joined him and severely defeated the government forces. Simko's forces slaughtered the gendarmes. In this battle, one of the great persons of the city, Qazi Latif, was killed, and the homes of some of the great people of the city were looted. Simko later claimed that although he was against looting, it was inevitable (p. 61).

According to Hassan Ghazi (2014) and Susan Meiselas (1997), Miss Augusta Gudhart, one of the missionaries of the American Lutheran Orient Mission in Mahabad, witnessed Simko's forces attack the city. She revealed that the Kurds who searched for money and gold rushed into the various rooms of her home, destroyed her furniture, broke into her already opened cabinets, tore her carpets, and loaded their horses with all the valuable objects that they had acquired. The Kurds also killed a missionary called Mr. George H. Bachimont. Gudhart maintains that in the past, she had met Simko, who spoke French fluently, and he encouraged them to establish a mission in Kurdistan in order to promote civility and literacy. Based on this knowledge of Simko's background, Gudhart and other missionaries decided to approach him. When they complained to him about his men's misbehaviors, Simko responded by expressing his regret about the situation, yet stating that these were wartime conditions. Simko ordered some of his men to take them to their place and aid them. Gudhart asserts that many people were looted (Ghazi, 2014, n.p.; Meiselas, 1997, p. 112).

Mustafa Pasha Yamulki interviewed Simko in Chehriq on 19-20 October 1921. Simko claimed that the goal of his movement was to relieve the Kurds from the Persians' aggression. Regarding the slaughtering of 800 Iranian captives, Simko stated that his forces had already captured them in Urmiya, and they gave these captives clothing and money and released them on condition they would not join Iran. But they did and acted violently and were killed. Concerning the assassination of Mar Shimun, Simko pointed out that he killed Mar Shimun because the Iranian representative asked him to not support the Assyrians and promised to reward Simko. In addition, the Assyrians wanted to conquer Kurdistan. About the future government in Kurdistan, Simko stated that we should wait for the liberation of Kurdistan to see which type of government will be established. It was not important who became the ruler, and he was not looking for it. In regard to pillaging Mahabad's shops and killing people, including Qazi Latif, who was a famous and respected person, and also the looting of Haji Ilkhani, the chief of the Debukri (Dehbukri) tribe, Simko maintained that when Simko's forces wanted to go to Mahabad, they asked all the chiefs to come and support them but they did not come. In this situation, it was impossible to prevent looting, although he was very much against it. He also said that he had sent Sayyed Taha to Baghdad to negotiate with the British, but it was useless (Hawar, 1996, pp. 352-360).

The extent of Simko's relations with non-Kurdish uprisings in Iran needs further investigation. Shamzini claims that Simko had a strong connection with Khiabani's democratic movement in Azerbaijan (Hawar, 1996, p. 196). Swedish Colonel Lundberg, Commander of the Azerbaijan Army, claims that he had obtained some letters revealing relations between Simko and Khiabani's rebels (Hawar, 1996, p. 500). In addition, according to Ali Hasaniani, Amu San, an Azeri Jangali man, claimed that Mirza Kuchek Khan wrote a letter to Simko, which Simko kissed upon receiving and responded to Kuchek Khan. Kuchek Khan's letter stressed unity by forging relations between Gilan and Kurdistan and gaining the cooperation of the Azeries in an uprising for a free and independent Iran. Simko promised cooperation, declaring that in a free Iran, the rights of all Iranian people should be respected. However, before they made an elaborate plan for their cooperation, Reza Shah destroyed them (Hawar, 1996, pp. 204-206).

One of Simko's undertakings was the establishment of an organ for his movement. Simko, under the editorial of secretary of Mullah Mohammad Turjani (Turjanizadeh or Ghizilgi), published the weekly newspaper, *Roji Kurd Shawi Ajam*

(Day of Kurd, Night of Ajam), which later was renamed as the *Roji Kurd* (Day of Kurd), and finally was named the *Kurd*. Unfortunately, only one issue of the *Kurd*, published on 8 June 1922, is available (Hawar, 1996, pp. 298-299). Sajjadi claims that in 1921, three or four issues of the *Kurd* were published in Urmiya. According to Tamaddon, the print house in which the *Roji Kurd Shawi Ajam* was publishing was changed from *Tamaddon* (Civilization), to *Ghairat* (Honour). It was a weekly bilingual newspaper in Kurdish and Farsi (Hawar, 1996, p. 302). As Tamaddon states, "in addition to the paper, custom duty receipts were printed there. Simko ordered a custom duty charge for goods (basically tobacco) being 'exported' out of Urmiyeh to other towns (Maragheh, Khoy, Tabriz, etc.)" (Koohi-Kamali, 2003, pp. 80-81). According to Abbas Vali (2011), the *Roji Kurd* expressed Kurdish nationalist ideas. It used the Sorani dialect and it was the "earliest official use of the Kurdish language in Iran" (p. 13).

Each issue of the *Kurd* has four pages. The second issue has two articles, while the third issue includes two articles and a poem. Simko and Jamal al-Din Al-Hakkari have articles in the second issue of the *Kurd*, which was published between May 27 and 23 July of 1922 (Simko, 1922, pp. 1-3; Al-Hakkari, 1992, pp. 3-4). In the third issue, Mohammad Turjani and Jamal al-Din Al-Hakkari have articles, while Saif al-Qozat has a poem (Turjani, 1922, p. 4; Al-Hakkari, 1922, pp. 2-3; Saif al-Qozat, 1992, p. 3). Overall, the contents of the reviewed issues reveal the unjust and cruel treatment of the Kurds by the government, the resistance and struggle of the Kurds, and the hope that the Kurds would gain control over their own destiny and establish a liberated Kurdistan.

In May 1921, Reza Khan became the War Minister. In the next nine months, he suppressed the revolts of Major Lahuti in Tabriz, Colonel Pesyan in Mashhad, and the Jangalis in Gilan (Abrahamian, 1982, pp. 118-119). At this point, the government seriously focused on suppressing Simko's uprising. On 29 June 1921, Reza Khan asked the Ottoman nationalists to stop supporting Simko. At this time,

Simko's forces were about 3,000 strong, plus an extra 400 escapees from Turkey. On 14 July 1921, the Iranian army severely defeated Simko's force (Makki, 1979, pp. 446-447). Although in 1921 Simko was defeated in one of the major battles, soon after, he became very strong, especially in 1922 when Simko's territory was at its greatest expansion. It had reached Sain Qal'eh (Shahin Dezh) and Saqqiz. Simko was in permanent contact with Southern tribes and had influence in Mariwan and Oraman. Some tribes in Luristan had supported his revolt. He also created friendly relations with many Kurdish chieftains in Turkey and Iraq (Bruinessen, 2006a, pp. 20- 21). To liberate and control Kurdistan, Simko sent two of his respectful representatives, Saif al-Qozat and Sheikh Seraj al-Din, to Baneh, Mariwan, and Sanandaj in order to contact Mahmud Khan Kanisanani, Mahmud Khan Dezli, and Sardar Rashid. Due to the attack of the government on Chehriq, Simko lost the opportunity to liberate southern Kurdistan (Madani, 2001, p. 87).

To suppress Simko's movement, in addition to the Iranian army, Reza Khan also used irregular forces of the Kurds under Khalu Qurban (Khalo Ghorban) and Shahsevan cavalry (Bayat, 2003, p. 229; Eagleton, 1963, p 11). Interestingly, Khalu Qurban's force was with the Jangalis in April 1921, but it "surrendered and enrolled in Reza Khan's forces following Kuchek Khan's defeat in October 1921" (McDowal, 2004, p. 227; Mirza Saleh, 1993, p. 12). According to Makki (1980), when the revolt of Major Abolghasem Lahuti against the government happened in Tabirz on 1 February 1922, the Iranian government sent Khalu Qurban, along with 600 Lors under him, to suppress the revolt (pp. 22, 27). The second issue of the *Kurd* provides a reportage in Persian about the battle between Khalu Qurban and the Kurds on 26 May 1922 (Amin, 2007, pp. 442-443).

To fight against Simko, the government employed its maximum military power. Out of 40,000 Iranian army, approximately 10,000 were deployed to suppress Simko in 1922 (Cronin, 2003, p. 244), although other sources claim the total number to be 15,000, comprised of 8,000 infantry, 1,000 cavalry, 5,000 guerillas, and 1,000 militia under the supervision of the Armenian officers (Kavianpur, 1999, pp. 342). According to Sir Percy Loraine, the British Minister Plenipotentiary in Tehran (1921-26), "If Semitqu [Simko] had scored one more victory, he would have been the chieftain of all western [Kurdish] tribes and would have established a Republic" (Ghani, 2000, pp. 258, 285).

The last battle between Simko and the government occurred in Shakaryazi on 25 July 1922, and the Kurds were decisively defeated. Simko's 10,000 men had been reduced to 1,000. Brigadier-General Amanullah Jahanbani captured the Chehriq Fortress on 12 August 1922. Simko and his remaining men retreated to Turkey. After the defeat of Simko, the Iranian forces destroyed Chehriq Fortress with cannon fire. Malek al-Sho'ara Bahar maintains that in Tehran, Reza Khan, who was the War Minister, held a huge celebration on 20 August 1922 (Kutschera, 1994, pp. 70-71, Bahar, 1978, pp. 265-267; Naqibzadeh, 2000, p. 156).

When Simko entered Turkey, his forces were disarmed by the Turks. They also killed his wife, Jawaher Khan, and arrested his six-year-old son. In October 1922, he went to Irbil, Iraq. On 8 January 1923, he went to Sulaymaniyah to meet with Sheikh Mahmoud Barzanj, who had already proclaimed himself as the King of Kurdistan. Simko was welcomed like a Head of a State (Kutschera, 1994, pp.71-72; Hawar, 1996, p. 557). Simko participated in the Kurdish leaders' meeting headed by Sheikh Mahmoud Barzanji in the Winter of 1922. At the meeting, the leaders decided to cut their relationship with Britain and not cooperate with Turkey (Lazarev, 2010, p. 357).

In 1924, Reza Khan, Prime Minister at the time, pardoned Simko, and in 1925 in Salmas the two met (Naqibzadeh, 2000, p. 156). Reza Khan recognized that the number of his companions was just two cars, and the garrison was empty of soldiers. In contrast, Simko was accompanied by 800 cavalry who were armed and dressed in flamboyant and fearsome Kurdish dress. Thus, Reza Khan was terrified. However, Bahrami, Reza Khan's secretary, observed Simko to be a lovely and noble person. Later, Simko stated that he should have killed Reza Khan, Tahmasebi, and all of their companions at that time (Makki, 1982, pp. 464-465, 470-472; Khajeh-Nouri, 1978, p. 142-144). In 1992, Simko's daughter, Safiyeh Khan, stated that Simko always regretted killing Mar Shimun and not killing Reza Khan who later became Reza Shah. Thus, he could have rescued the Kurds and the Iranians from Reza Shah's dictatorship, and it might have changed the results of many things (Hawar, 1996, p. 625).

After Reza Khan pardoned him in 1924, Simko returned to Iran in 1925 and continued to seek power. He fought against Amer Khan, the Abdui Shikak leader. Defeated again, Simko fled to Iraq and later to Turkey. In 1929, Iran granted him amnesty, even offering him the Governorship of Oshnavieh. But upon arrival, Simko was either ambushed and killed by the Iranian military in Oshnavieh (McDowall, 2004, pp. 220-221; McDowall, 1996, p. 221) or assassinated during negotiations for a settlement of the Kurdish uprising on 21 June 1930 (Entessar, 1992, p. 13). Ali Dehqan (1969) claims that based on the plan of Colonel Sadiq Khan Nowrouzi, the Commander-in-Chief of the Oshnavieh Garrison, Simko was killed on 18 July 1930 in Oshnavieh. His corpse was publicly demonstrated for two or three days in Urmiya (pp. 595-597). Much like other Kurdish leaders throughout the course of history, the Iranian government deceived Simko and killed him, thus ending his revolt.

4.6.2.2. Divergent perspectives on Simko's Uprising. As expected, Simko's revolt has invited conflicting perspectives. For Kasravi (1977), Simko simply aimed at looting, killing, and expanding his territory. His story is reminiscent of the bloodshed committed by Sheikh Ubayd Allah. Simko also wanted Kurdistan to be autonomous and independent. The Europeans had planted the seeds of chaos with the intention of damaging the East in the minds of the Kurds, Armenians, Turkmens, Assyrians, Bakhtiaris, and others (pp. 830, 852). Kasravi's statements insinuate a negative impression of minority movements and the pursuit for independence in the East and in Iran. This bias is especially evident in the case of the Kurdish movements. Thus, Kasravi does not observe the internal reasons for the creation of these movements and strongly emphasizes the external factors. Moreover, he analyzes Simko's revolt in a negative light, reducing it merely to chaos, looting, and bloodshed, thus ignoring the significance of the fight for Kurdish national rights. Finally, his method of researching Simko and his revolt has faults, as he ignores Simko's nationalistic activities in previous periods and his relationship with other Kurdish nationalist activists and movements.

Whether Simko's main concern was becoming a chief for all Kurdish tribes in Iran or struggling for Kurdish identity remains controversial. According to Yassin (1995), "Simko had neither the desire nor the ability to construct a modern Kurdish state. As has been asserted by Koohi-Kamali, recognition by the Iranian central government of Kurdish identity was not a central point in Simko's uprising" (pp. 54-55). Simko was a hero and skillful warrior whom Reza Shah feared. Simko's major shortcoming was his being a tribal chief and not a politician, which made him commit serious errors. His wrong policy about the Assyrians resulted in ethnic conflicts between the two; he aberrantly trusted Ataturk, and as a tribal chief, he was mostly thinking about his own gains, failing to compromise with Sheikh Mahmoud and Sayyed Taha when they did not accept Simko's leadership (Hawar, 1996, pp. 677-678). In contrast, Bruinessen (2006a) emphasizes that Simko "was a clever and opportunist politician who knew with whom to ally himself and when" (p. 16). Mustafa Amin (2007) regards Simko as a Kurdish leader who fought for the establishment of an independent Kurdistan (p. 452).

Some of the weaknesses of Simko's revolt include the lack of a war board, the absence of a political organization or a leadership assembly, and the lack of a clear military-political strategy. Simko's army was composed of tribesmen who were unorganized, untrained, and unskilled in military war. The movement could not advance to the provinces of Kurdistan, Kermanshah, and Ilam. Some of the tribal chiefs in these areas were more affiliated with Sheikh Mahmoud and did not join Simko. Furthermore, Simko did not establish an association of people's representatives and leadership in Kurdistan to provide security and welfare for people. Finally, he could not create relations with other armed uprisings in different parts of Iran. Consequently, the government succeeded in defeating the revolt (Mustafa Amin, 2007, p. 439-440). Bruinessen (2006a) summarizes Simko's revolt shortcomings as follows:

> The most serious weakness of Simko's movement was the absence of any kind of formal organisation. There was just the network of Simko's private relations, no party to organise the followers, [and] no formal government or war council. The major towns, Urmiyeh and Mahabad, were administered by governors appointed by Simko[,] who were both tribal chieftains unrelated to the inhabitants of the towns and simply took over the offices of the previous Tabriz-appointed governors. There was no systematic and equitable taxation; Simko's treasury was filled by indiscriminate looting, although the latter aspect may be severely exaggerated in the sources, most of which are inimical to him. (p. 22)

Simko's revolt was deficient in terms of a distinct nationalist agenda. His movement was primarily motivated by his tribal ambitions, although he was to some degree inspired by his ethnic and nationalist consciousness. His movement did not arise from a dialogue among the Iranian Kurdish intellectuals. It was a reaction to Reza Shah's cultural and linguistic homogenizing policy in order to create a Persian-dominated nation. However, his revolt furnished the basis for the Kurdish nationalist movement in Iran (Ahmadzadeh and Stansfield, 2010, p. 13).

Farideh Koohi-Kamali (2003) analyzes the relations between the economic structural changes in Iranian Kurdistan and its "political demands, namely Kurdish nationalism." From WWI, the three stages of economic development in

Kurdistan have greatly affected how the Kurds requested independence. In Iran, Kurdish nationalism emerged when the dominated traditional tribal economy changed into a society with a market-based economy and social relations. Kurdish nationalism emerged when the Kurdish tribal "face-to-face" society was changed into a society that could "imagine" itself as a nation. The first stage was the tribal consciousness. Simko's revolt during Reza Shah's rule is considered a "face-to-face" phenomenon. The second stage was the phase of national consciousness among the Kurdish leaders, which was demonstrated in the formation of the Kurdistan Republic in Mahabad in 1946. It was the stage of transformation from a "face-to-face" to an "imagined" community. The third stage was the "fully conscious nationalist Kurdish movement" which shows the maximum level of the "imagined" community. This stage started with the Land Reform and the White Revolution of Mohammad Reza Shah in the 1960s and has continued to the present (pp. xi, 11-12).

Simko belonged to a "face to face" tribal society where people were unable to understand abstract concepts like market, nation, state, and a Kurdish nation-state comprised of all Kurds, including tribal, non-tribal, and rival tribes. "In such a society, an abstract concept like nationalism, which presupposes strong, inherent bonds with people one has never seen, is an impossible one to grasp. Simko's movement characterizes that period of Kurdish history" (Koohi-Kamali, 2003, pp. 73, 199). Based on this analysis, Koohi-Kamali (2003) concludes, "Simko was the embodiment of nomadic, tribal society, fighting not in the name of the Kurdish nation but for personal, clan, and tribal grievances" (p. 198).

Concerning the reasons for Simko's revolt, Koohi-Kamali (2003) asserts that the most important motivation for Simko to revolt against the government was the "traditional, almost habitual antagonism" that a lot of many Kurdish tribes felt against the central government. When a tribal chief fights against the central government, it provides prestige and recognition among other tribal leaders. The second reason for Simko to revolt was to take revenge on the Persian government, which killed his brother, Jafar Agha. Thus, when Simko became strong, he fought against the government and, similar to his brother, sustained plundering and looting people in the area (p. 82). According to Koohi-Kamali (2003), although Simko used nationalist rhetoric behavior, he was concerned with strengthening his own power and prestige. An example of this nationalist rhetoric is demonstrated in Simko's letter to Zafar al-Dowleh, the head of one of the Azerbaijan regiments, in which Simko mentioned the Kurdish nation and their right to autonomy. By autonomy, Simko aimed at his and his followers' autonomy. Simko wrote:

> See how the small nations of the world, who [*sic*][which] are not one quarter [*sic*] [one-quarter] of the size of the Kurdish tribes, have received autonomy from great governments such as the Germans. If this great Kurdish nation does not get its rights from Persia, it will consider death far better than life[,] and whether the Persian government grants it or not[,] we will make Kurdistan autonomous, and therefore, not a good thing to be the cause of further loss of life. (in Koohi-Kamali, 2003, pp. 85-86; Kutschera, 1994, p. 65)

Koohi-Kamali (2003) points out that Simko used the nationalist language because, at that period of time, lots of ethnic groups were employing that language, and the Great Powers and the newly formed international institutions understood that language. "What Simko did was to employ a modern means (demand for a Kurdish nation-state as was happening with other ethnic groups at the time) to try to obtain an older, traditional goal" (p. 88). Koohi-Kamali's research regarding Simko's movement contains two major shortcomings that do not allow the author to analyze Simko's movement nature correctly. The first is methodological: her research about Simko's biography and activities is weak and inaccurate. For instance, Koohi-Kamali (2003), referring to Arfa (1966), claims, "Ali Agha from the Avdovi tribe, was the father (or the grandfather) of Jafar Agha and Isma'il Agha (Simko)" (p. 74). However, Arfa correctly states that Mohammad Agha was the father of Simko and Jafar Agha. In addition, as reviewed above, other sources make clear that Ali Agha was the grandfather of Simko. According to the Soviet documents, Ali Agha, Simko's grandfather, participated in Sheikh Ubayd Allah's revolt. Simko and his family have greatly combatted against the Qajars (Hawrami, 2006, p. 373). Koohi-Kamali also makes some claims against Simko without offering any sources. For example, she asserts that Khiabani's movement was basically attacked by conservative tribal forces. "The Shahsavans of Azerbaijan and the Shakak Kurds headed by Isma'il Agha Simko attacked the Democrat forces and brought about their isolation by blocking roads and disturbing the security of the region" (Koohi-Kamali, 2003, p. 87).

The second and more fundamental shortcoming of Koohi-Kamali is epistemological. She offers an economic reductionist perspective in analyzing the relationships between the political views of the movements on the one side and the economic development of societies on the other side. This view believes that the degree of economic development of a society linearly and hugely, almost totally, determines the level of conceptual framework and political thinking and movements of that society. This perspective ignores the dialectical and complex relationship between human minds and the larger environment. The appearance of political thought like nationalism in a specific society, while affected by the economic relations of that society, can also be greatly affected by many other factors. Having this economic reductionist view, Koohi-Kamali mistakenly emphasizes that it is "impossible" for people like Simko, who live in a tribal "face-to-face" society, to understand concepts such as "nation" and "nationalism."

The geopolitics which affected the conceptual formation of Simko and his movement, and the environment influenced by his movement was much larger than a tribal "face-to-face" setting. Indeed, Simko had a strong relationship with other nationalist movements in other parts of Kurdistan. For instance, according to a report by Prince Shakhovski, the Istanbul Committee was under the leadership of Sheikh Abdul Qadir, who was strongly pro-Great Britain. When he was disappointed with the British, he joined the Erzurum Committee, a mostly pro-Soviet organization, which was led by Khalid Baig. The Erzurum Committee, in December 1923, defined the borders of a future Kurdistan. Simko worked under the orders of this Committee. Later, the Erzurum Committee changed its name to *Komitay Nawandi Kurdistan* (Kurdistan's Region Committee) (Hawrami, 2006, p. 436).

According to a report by the Soviet Consul in Erzurum, while the Erzurum Committee aimed for the autonomy of Kurdistan within Turkey, the Kurdistan's Region Committee accepted the slogan of Kurdistan independence. It aimed at organizing a Kurdish leader in the Kurdistan of Turkey to make a mass armed revolt, negotiating with the Soviet Union regarding the assistance of the Kurdish national movement, and later creating a relationship with the Kurdish leaders in Iraqi Kurdistan. Because Simko was famous among the Kurds in Turkey, the Kurdistan Region Committee chose Simko as its symbolic leader in the North. Simko, "in practice," was negotiating with the Soviets his committee goal of establishing an independent Kurdistan. Simko sent a letter to the Consul of the Soviet Union in Urmiya via Kamal Fawzi Baig, a member of the Committee, on 28 November 1923 (Hawrami, 2006, pp. 308-311).

Many authors emphasize the tribal type of leadership of Simko. Hassanpour (2007) maintains that most of the early twentieth-century Kurdish uprisings against the Turkish state (in 1925 and 1937-1938), Sheikh Mahmoud in Iraq (in 1918-1919 and 1922-1924), and Simko in Iran (in 1919-1922 and 1926) were headed by the tribal and feudal nobles (p. 7). Vali (2011) states that there is evidence that reveals the tribal leadership of Simko's revolt, including Simko, "entertained the nationalist idea of a united and independent Kurdistan" (p. 13). Vali (2011) also asserts that although the leadership of Simko's movement advocated for a united and independent Kurdistan, it did not constitute the "strategic objective" of the revolt. The political discourse of *Roji Kurd* mostly ignored the use of the main concepts of "popular democratic politics," which is a feature of modern nationalist language. Simko's movement contained "the paradox of the struggle against national oppression[,] which does not deploy concepts of popular sovereignty, national rights[,] and legitimacy. It is a paradox appropriate to the tribal and autonomist nature of Semko's [Simko's] movement" (Vali, 2011, pp. 13-14).

According to Hawar Khalil Taher Nerwiy (2012), Simko was concerned about his own wealth and power instead of engaging in national or ethnic Kurdish issues. It was essentially a tribal movement. (pp. 79, 81). Ghassemlou (2000) states that Simko proclaimed independence in 1920-1922. A Kurdish program in which the demands of the Kurdish nation movement were formulated was distributed in Urmiya (p. 21). Ghassemlou does not provide more details about this program. Karim Hisami asserts that Simko's revolt was a national uprising, and he struggled for freedom and Kurdish independence (Hawar, 1996, p. 679). Madani (2001) asserts that Simko's national liberating movement dominated all the northern Kurdistan of Iran. He was a great man, an active and brave revolutionary, a pure and spotless Kurd, smart and alert, worldly-wise, dignified, a firm believer, and a political person (pp. 38, 123-124). Finally, Kutschera (1994) regards Simko as one of the fathers of Kurdish nationalism in Iran (p. 62).

4.6.3. Other Kurdish movements. When Reza Khan was gaining more power in the 1920s, he coercively imposed his authority over the Kurdish tribes. He removed the tribal lords to Tehran or other cities in order to end their resistance against the government. The tribal policy of Reza Shah was based on abducting the tribal chiefs, seizing their lands and properties, forcibly settling them, preventing tribes from using their summer pastures, and relocating all the tribes, like the Golbaghi tribe (Nikitin, 1987, p. 432). In the 1920s, the Iranian Kurds protested against the government's policy of Persianization, and a few Kurdish revolts headed by the tribal chiefs appeared. The goal of these chiefs was to keep their independence. In 1923, Sardar Khorshid, the chief of the Kalhur tribe, led a revolt against the government and tried to establish a government in his region and, asking the central government to not interfere with his area. Moreover, the Kurds in Shirvan, in Quchan, Khorasan, revolted under the leadership of Zulfo, a Kurdish peasant. They demanded the abolition of agricultural reform, conscription, and the opium monopoly by the government (Lazarev, 2010, pp. 364-365). By the time Simko was killed in 1930, Reza Shah had already started seizing tribal lands, forcing the nomads to leave their traditional way of life and stay settled in one place. In some cases, Reza Shah relocated entire tribes from their ancient lands. He imposed European dress and outlawed Kurdish schools. The consequence of such behavior towards the Kurdish tribes "was often disease, famine, a loss of purpose, and dignity" (Kinnane, 1964, p. 47). Yassin (1995) lists the chiefs who opposed the government's assimilation policy: Jafar Sultan Jaf, Muhammad (Hama) Rashid Khan, Mahmud Agha Kanisanani, and Amer Khan. These revolts were suppressed, and some leaders were forced into exile until the collapse of Reza Shah's forced abdication in 1941 (p. 58; Ghassemlou, 1965, p. 22; Lazarev, 2010, pp. 283, 291).

    Abbas Khan Sardar Rashid was the son of Ali Khan, who was the son of Mohammad Sadeq Khan, who was the son of Amanullah Khan, the governor of Ardalan Emirate. Sardar Rashid's revolt started at Rawansar in 1917 for the revival of the Ardalan Emirate. Many Tribal chiefs joined him, including Wakil

Jawanrood, Hussein Khan Reza, Jafar San Lahun (Jafar Sultan or Jafer Sultan), Mahmud Khan Kanisanan, Mahmud Khan Dezli, Mohammad Khan Baneh, Sanjar Khan Miawaran, and Hussein Ali Khan Kolyayy. Sardar Rashid also collaborated with Prince Salar al-Dowleh Qajar, brother of the former Mohammad Ali Shah. Sardar Rashid dominated Sanandaj and Kermanshah and ruled the territory. In order to establish the Ardalan Emirate, Sardar Rashid negotiated with the tribes in 1922 and gathered many warriors from Jawanroodis, Rawansaries, and Sanjabies. Reza Khan ordered Amir Ahmadi to attack Sardar Rashid. Amir Ahmadi recruited Jafar Sultan, Mahmud Khan Dezli, and Hussein Khan Reza to collaborate with the government. Sardar Rashid surrounded himself in Hamadan and was sent as a captive to Tehran. Finally, in 1924, he was imprisoned in Tehran until 1941, when people broke into the Qasr Qajar prison. After his freedom, Sardar Rashid continued to live in Tehran (Sajjadi, 2000, pp. 60-65; Arfa, 1966, p. 66; Naqibzadeh, 2000, pp. 156-157).

4.6.3.1. Mullah Khalil's Revolt. One of the undertakings of Reza Shah in the process of nation-building and modernization was forcing men to wear Western-style, uniformed outfits and a so-called "Pahlavi hat" in 1927. Later, in 1936, he also imposed an "unveiling" law for women. When many men protested against this change, on 4 January 1929, the Parliament of Iran ratified a four-article law about the uniformed dress. The first article makes it clear that all people who do not have a certain dress based on their jobs should were a uniformed dress, including the Pahlavi hat and a suit (Makki, 1983, pp. 71-72). Entessar (2010) argues that through such laws, the state imposed cultural uniformity and assimilation, thus ignoring cultural differences and minority rights. It was in reaction to this policy that the national awareness of minorities appeared (p. 8). The most significant movement against the imposition of uniformed dress in Kurdistan was the armed revolt of Mullah Khalil of Goramari (Goromari), the religious leader of the Mangur tribe located between Mahabad and Sardasht. The uprising began around late 1928 and early 1929 and continued for about six months until the mid-spring of 1929 (Nerwiy, 2012, p. 86; Samadi, 1998, pp. 91, Afkhami, 1989, pp. 33-38; Borzooyy. 2005, p. 324). Mullah Khalil's revolt was supported by the Gawork tribe and the residents of Mahabad, which the rebels planned to occupy. The several clashes between the Kurds and the Iranian army left many killed from both sides. The cavalry from the tribes of Mamash and Dehbokri supported the army in pushing the rebels back. In the mid-spring of 1929, Iranian airplanes bombarded the main Mangurs strongholds, including Il Taymour and Khalifan, looted the people, burned many villages, and the villagers, including women and children, had to escape to the mountains searching for shelter. Mullah Khalil, along with the other rebels, had to leave for Iraq by way of the Qalatasian Bridge, and the revolt was suppressed. Later, Mullah Khalil was pardoned, came to Kurdistan in Iran, and settled in the village of Mirawa (Afkhami, 1989, 7-21, 33-38, 60-61; Borzooyy. 2005, pp. 322, 324, 326; Samadi, 1998, p. 92; Madani, 2001, p. 142).

4.7. Conclusion and Analysis.

The Constitutional Revolution represents Iran's entry into political modernity, but it ignored the national rights of minorities in Iran, movements and revolts for national liberation, social justice, and democratic representation. Iranian constitutionalism, the first democratic movement in Asia, eventually decayed into the autocracy of Reza Shah, who rose to power in the chaotic aftermath of the Constitutional Revolution and launched the nation-building project through which, ideologically, modern Iran was identified with the Persians. As such, Reza Shah repressed the national minorities' movements for their meaningful inclusion in the new, modern Iran, as a result of which the revolts of early twentieth-century Iran took the form of autonomy-seeking movements. But constitutionalism also unleashed the revolutionary potential in the country and especially in the regions where regional and national grievances had remained unaddressed. This chapter has highlighted the most important revolt of this period, focusing on the proto-nationalist Kurdish uprisings. The Kurdish revolts were, in some part, a reaction to the new Iran's official nationalism in Iran. Some of these Kurdish uprisings remained territorial, while others extended into much larger areas, including the cities. They were mostly led by the tribal chiefs or local nobles who demanded keeping their local power against the central government. Although trapped in local tribal demands (and some of these movements sometimes were collaborating with the state against the other rebellions), they also sometimes cooperated with each other and with the other nationalist movements in other parts of Kurdistan (e.g., Iraq). The most important of these movements was Simko's revolt, which struggled for the formation of an autonomous Kurdistan.

The assimilative policies of Iran's new, modern state can be clearly seen in the different factors that affected the emergence of Mullah Khalil's uprising, which was against the centralization policy of the government. The tribal chiefs supported the revolt because the government had curtailed their local authority as well as the authority of the Sunni clerics. In addition, people also were against compulsory military service imposed by Reza Shah. Moreover, the cruelty and unjust behavior of the government officials created people's dissatisfaction. The government's denial of the Kurdish cultural identity by imposing the new dress code triggered serious resistance. So, we witness a case that clearly shows a cultural-nationalist uprising against Reza Shah's official, strong-handed, assimilative, and Persianate nationalism.

Simko's movement can be defined within the framework of national-liberation launched against the internal colonialism of rising modern Iranian state-building and attempts at the Persianization of Iranian diversity. Clearly, Simko's revolt cannot be identified with the types of national-liberation movements that emerged post-WWII. As such, we must classify it as a *proto-nationalist and proto-*

national-liberation movement in that due to the absence of the cultural element propagated by Kurdish intellectuals, the nationalist self-consciousness is absent, and Kurdish identity is mainly understood in tribal terms. To qualify my analysis, let us remember that Simko's revolt had a "national" character because it ambitiously aimed at the creation of an independent Kurdish state, including the whole of Kurdistan, and the protection and development of Kurdish identity. In addition, it was "liberatory" because Simko aimed to emancipate an oppressed nation and achieve the right to self-determination. Precisely, because of the tribal structure of the uprising and Simko's chieftain leadership, his revolt had a serious democratic deficit that disqualified his movement as strictly a national-democratic and national liberation movement. That is why I regard it as a proto-nationalist and proto-national-liberation movement.

Therefore, I argue that Simko's rebellion should be observed as part of the other nationalist movements in Iran, Turkey, and Iraq. This is evidenced by his forging strong relations with other movements as well as other Kurdish nationalist groups and personalities During the course of his revolt, Simko strived to create a harmonized struggle among the other Kurdish nationalists, although his efforts were eventually fruitless. The reason was that other Kurdish leaders more or less relied on their own personal perspectives and interests. Indeed, the Kurdish nationalist movement had not grown enough at that period to be capable of establishing a strong political organization to lead the movement. In short, national consciousness and the political-organizational experience were so weak among the Kurds in Iran that they could not launch a harmonized struggle.

An important deficiency of Simko's revolt was the lack of a modern political organization based on democratic principles, as well as the absence of a clear and detailed nationalist program and strategy. The tribal style of leadership gave enormous power to Simko. Although an extensive number of people from different social classes participated in the movement, the Kurdish movement in Iran mainly remained under Simko's control. The concentration of power in the hands of Simko let him make some decisions that were disadvantageous to the movement. In addition, the absence of a well-organized social institution affected the method of "taxing" in rebel-controlled areas, which sometimes took the form of "looting" based on discrimination and intrusion into working people's lives.

While all the aforementioned weaknesses affected the defeat of the movement, other factors also played an important role in his defeat. The most crucial element was a lack of support for his movement by a foreign power(s), which instead supported the Iranian state. Another major factor was the military prowess of the Iranian state as well as the collaboration of Turkey with Iran. While Simko's movement had its weaknesses and was far from the modern Kurdish nationalist movement that later emerged in Iran, it must be recognized as a proto-nationalist movement that affected Kurdish nationalism in years to come.

The undeveloped Kurdish society had not experienced modem economic, social, and political structures and organizations, as it was deeply immersed in feudal and tribal culture, as well as Islamic values and patriarchal worldviews. However, in conjunction with the growing nationalist sentiments in the region, the formation of the modern nation-state in Iran *inadvertently* created elementary conditions for the cultural revival of the Kurds. And with that the seeds of proto-nationalism that were planted by Simko's movement, in a matter of only a few years, began to bear fruits. The next chapter will attend to not only the revival of Kurdish nationalism in Iran but, more importantly, the emergence of modern Kurdish nationalism and national liberation.

Chapter 5: The KDP's History (1945-1970)

This chapter essentially encompasses the Kurdish nationalist movement in Iran from WWII to 1973. The main focus is on the formation and history of the *Hizbi Demokrati Kurdistan* or Kurdistan Democratic Party (KDP), while it discusses the emergence of *Hizbi Azadi Kurdistan* (Kurdistan Freedom Party) and *Komalay Jianaway Kurdistan* (Society for the Revival of Kurdistan [J.K.]). In addition, while addressing the main social and political events that have affected Kurdistan, the focus will primarily be on the emergence of Kurdish political organizations, their goals, structures, and changes. These changes will be discussed with respect to the important meetings, conferences, congresses, and splits of these organizations.

5.1. Introduction

The emergence and development of the Kurdish movement and its political organizations have occurred along with larger social and political contexts of Iran and the world. The most important event was WWII and its consequent Anglo-Soviet occupation of Iran on 25 August 1941. The Soviets occupied the northern and northwestern parts of Iran, including Azerbaijan and northern parts of Kurdistan. The British controlled southern parts of Kurdistan and the south of the country. Reza Shah abdicated on 16 September 1941 in favor of his son Mohammad Reza Shah. Reza Shah was then exiled to South Africa, where he died in 1944. Paradoxically, foreign occupation created relaxed political conditions that resulted in the formation of dozens of political parties and organizations, including the pro-Soviet *Hezb-e Tudeh-ye Iran* or the Tudeh Party of Iran (2 October 1941) (Parsa Bonab, 2004, pp. 235-259). In Azerbaijan, the *Ferqeh-ye Demokrat-e Azerbaijan* or Azerbaijan Democratic Party (3 September 1945). In Kurdistan, *Hizbi Azadi Kurdistan* or Kurdistan Freedom Party (June 1938), *Komalay Jianaway Kurdistan* (J.K.) or Society for the Revival of Kurdistan (J.K.) (16 August 1942), and the

Kurdistan Democratic Party (KDP) (23 October 1945), later *Hizbi Demokrati Kurdistani Eran* (Democratic Party of Iranian Kurdistan [PDKI]), were established.

The establishment of the KDP and the Kurdistan Republic, aside from the internal factors of the development of Kurdish nationalism in the political context of Iran, was also affected by the policies of the Soviet Union, the emergence of the Azerbaijan Democratic Party, and the Azerbaijan National Government. The history of the KDP was also affected by the Tudeh Party, the oil nationalization movement under the leadership of Prime Minister Dr. Mohammad Mosaddiq (Mossaddegh) in the 1950s, and the CIA-MI6 engineered *coup d'état* of 1953 that toppled Mosaddiq. Also, it was shaped by the White Revolution of 1963 and, finally, the Kurdish nationalist movement in Iraq.

Kurdistan was a feudal society. The majority of Kurds were peasants and under severe exploitation by the landlords supported by cruel gendarmes. In addition to class oppression, the Kurds also were under national and religious repression. By 1945, the population of Iranian Kurdistan was 3,000,000, of which only 10 percent lived in the cities, and 95 percent of the Kurdish population was illiterate (Gadani, 2008a, pp. 15-16; Qazi, 2005, p. 41; Hisami, 2011, p.15; Ghassemlou, 2000, pp. 14-15).

Prior to WWII, the intellectual awakening of Kurdistan was partly under the influence of Kurdish intellectuals in Iraqi Kurdistan. For example, issues of the Kurdish magazine *Galawej* were sent from Iraq to Qazi Muhammad in Mahabad. Intellectuals of the Iraqi Kurdistan, such as Mullah Ahmad Fawzi, actively enlightened the Kurds in Iran. The formation of literary groups in 1938 provided an opportunity for discussing Kurdish nationalism in Iranian Kurdistan (Homayoun, 2004, p. 7; Hemin, 1999, p. 11, 14-15; Hisami, 2011, p. 17).

5.2. *Hizbi Azadi Kurdistan* (Kurdistan Freedom Party)

Hizbi Azadi Kurdistan (Kurdistan Freedom Party) has been known by other names, including *Komalay Azadikhowazani Kurd* (Association of Freedom-seekers of Kurd), *Komalay Azadikhowazi Kurdistan* (Association of Freedom-seekers of Kurdistan). It is also known as *Hizbi Azadikhowai Kurdistan* (Freedom-seekers of Kurdistan Party), and *Hizbi Azadikhowazi Kurd* (Freedom-seekers of the Kurd Party). This party, according to the letter from the J.K. to Molotov, was established in June 1938, but the announcement of the establishment was at the beginning of 1939 (Sardashti, 2002b, pp. 101-103). Established under Aziz Zandi (aka Aziz Almani, the German Aziz), the Kurdistan Freedom Party is certainly the first modern Kurdish nationalist party of Iranian Kurdistan. The founders of the party included Aziz Zandi, Hussein Frouhar, Hussein Mikaeili, Karim Yahou, Ghafour Mahmoudian, and Muhammad Amin Ratebi (Gohari, 1999, p. 29).

According to Jamal Nabaz, the Kurdistan Freedom Party was a clandestine party established around June 1938 under Aziz Zandi in Mahabad. The party survived until the entrance of the Soviet Union into Kurdistan in August 1941. At that time, the party distributed an announcement that welcomed the Soviet army to Kurdistan. Zabihi claims that Zandi, by some of his friends, was recognized as a "*napak*" (unclean) person. Nabaz maintains that after disagreement among the members, Zandi and Ghafour Mahmoudian left the party, and the Party collapsed. Later, some other members of the party, along with some other intellectuals, founded the J.K. (Gohari, 1999, pp. 9, 11-12).

The J.K. documents regard the J.K. as the continuation of the Kurdistan Freedom Party. Qasim Ilkhanizadeh, a member of the J.K., has told Hassanov, the Soviet Union Consul in Tabriz, that the J.K. (which here signifies the Kurdistan Freedom Party) had been established before the Soviet Union's entrance to Kurdistan. In addition, in a report of the J.K. CC to Molotov, Soviet Union's Minister of Foreign Affairs, dated 28 December 1944, the history of the Kurdistan

Freedom Party has been addressed as the history of the J.K. According to this report, the J.K. had been formed in June 1938 (Gohari, 1999, pp. 22, 24, 227-228).

Hoshang Tawfiq claims that before the emergence of the Kurdistan Freedom Party, a few communities and political organizations had existed, but they did not have platforms, specific slogans, and strategies (Gadani, 2008b, p. 152). In contrast, the Kurdistan Freedom Party, which had a leftist program established, but it could not succeed (Hemim, 1999, p. 20). According to Hisami (2011), the platform of the Kurdistan Freedom Party included 28 articles: the unity of Kurds, Armenians, Turks, and Assyrians in Kurdistan; development of the Kurdish, Armenian, and Turkish languages and establishment of Kurdish and Armenian schools in all cities and villages. Other articles were providing armaments in Kurdistan to struggle against dictatorship and fascism, teaching the ideology of democracy and freedom based on the principle of the republic system; and obtaining the foreign concessions for the establishment of industrial plants such as tractor factories. Still, some other articles included freeing the culture, literature, and language of all small nations and respecting their nationality; creating laws based on Islam while encouraging other nations to practice based on their own tradition and religious laws; and founding free medical, agricultural, law, and historical schools. Finally, the program included establishing clubs, theatres, and cinemas and publishing various liberal, national, social, agricultural, economic, and business-related newspapers and magazines (Hisami, 2011, pp. 17-18).

One of the activities of the Kurdistan Freedom Party was to send a representative to the border of Iran-Iraq in May 1939 to negotiate with some Iraqi Kurds concerning the cooperation between them for the liberation of Kurdistan (Sardashti, 2002b, p. 105). The party also participated in the revolt of the Kurds in Urmiya. The Kurdish revolt in the territory of Urmiya (1941-1942) was led by Omar Khan Shikak, Rashid Baig Jahangiri, Taha Harki, and Zero Baig Bahadiri.

The reasons for the revolt were to fight against the government's attempts to bring back the army to Kurdistan and fortify the gendarmerie outposts, distribute arms among the Turks, who were the government's supporters, and disarm the Kurds in the area. The Kurdistan Freedom Party had relations with the Kurdish revolt in the territory of Urmiya. When the Kurds surrounded Urmiya, this party distributed a declaration in which they asked the Iranian government officials to leave Urmiya (Sardashti, 2002b, pp. 109-110). Moreover, according to Bolourian (1997), the Kurdistan Freedom Party, in a handwritten declaration, encouraged the Kurdish people to support the youth who were struggling for the independence of Kurdistan. In regard to this activity, the police arrested a young man named Haji Khosraw and tortured him. In addition, the police exiled some others, like Hussein Frouhar and Muhammad Ratebi, to Shiraz and Kerman (Bolourian, 1997, pp. 16-17).

While there are different perspectives regarding the dissolution of the party and the role of its leader, Aziz Zandi, Yasin Sardashti, relying on Kutschera's research, states that the Soviet Union dissolved this party because it attacked gendarmes. In addition, after this event, the conflict between the leadership of the party developed so that Zandi and the minority of the party left the struggle, while Frouhar and others eventually established the J.K. (Sardashti, 2002b, pp. 113-114). According to Gohari (1999), Aziz Zandi was against the Kurdistan Freedom Party's relations with the Soviet Union. Consequently, his friends accused him of being a supporter of Nazi Germany (p. 32). Although the Kurdistan Freedom Party was not as influential and well-organized as the later-established J.K., it immensely contributed to the development of Kurdish nationalism in Iranian Kurdistan. Yasin Sardashti states that the Kurdistan Freedom Party, and especially the J.K., which was a petite-bourgeois organization, had great roles in the revival of the national spirit in the territory (Hawrami, 2007, p. 5).

5.3. The Anglo-Soviet Occupation of Iran and Kurdistan

The Anglo-Soviet forces occupied Iran on 25 August 1941. On 27 August 1941, the Soviet planes bombed Mahabad. About 20 people were killed, and several residences and the city's market were partly destroyed. On 28 August 1941, the Red Army entered the city, and the Iranian army surrendered without resistance (Samadi, 1984, p. 6; Samadi 1998, p. 106; Hemin, 1999, pp. 17-19). The occupation led to the residents' acquiring weapons by entering garrisons or disarming escaping officers and soldiers and securing between 15,000 to 20,000 rifles, machine guns, cannons, and ironclads (Sardashti, 2002b, p. 50). In the fall of 1942, the Soviets unloaded some light weapons and ammunition near *Pirdi Sour* (Red Bridge) in Mahabad and informed Qazi Muhammad. On that night, 400 men registered, each receiving a Brno rifle along with 100 bullets. In addition, two carts of rifles and ammunition were carried to the city to be given to the qualified people (Homayoun, 2004, pp. 34-35). The Soviets also assisted the J.K. before its transformation into the KDP. During the fall of 1945, the Russians covertly gave 1,200 rifles, taken from the Iranian gendarmes, to the J.K. (Kinnane, 1964, p. 50).

Golmorad Moradi (1996) argues that when the Allies entered Iran, Mahabad was not occupied, and according to the agreements of Iran with the Allies, the Iranian army was not permitted to conduct military activities in this area. As a result, Mahabad became the center for the political and cultural activities of the Kurdish people (pp. 28-29). The government appointed Ali Agha Aliar Dehbukri (Amir As'ad) as Mahabad's Governor in March 1942. After a while, because he had a background of family hostility with Qazi Muhammad and people were not cooperating with him, he had to leave the city. In the aftermath, the government appointed Sari'al-Qalam as Mahabad's Governor. However, he was just a formal Governor because he was practically under the control of Qazi Muhammad (Homayoun, 2004, pp. 37-38).

5.3.1. Struggle in different areas of Kurdistan. After the Allies' occupation of Iran, Kurdistan witnessed incidents of armed revolts. In September 1941, Muhammad Rashid Khan attacked Baneh and, in a two-day war, occupied the garrison and took more than 7,000 weapons and equipment. Soon, many Kurdish Baigs and tribal chiefs joined him and occupied the territories of Marivan, Sardasht, Nawsoud, Paveh, and Saqqiz. Hamah Rashid Khan's forces reached 12,000. In October 1941, he contacted the British to support the intendancy of Kurdistan and its liberation from Iran's suppression. The British did not offer support. On 7 October 1941, Hamah Rashid Khan attacked Diwandareh but was defeated. In addition, on December 20, 1941, Iran heavily bombarded Saqqiz, and he had to withdraw and leave the city. On 10 February 1942, in an epic battle in which 300 Iranian officers and soldiers were killed and many were arrested, Muhammad Rashid Khan occupied Saqqiz again. Consequently, the Iranian government, with the support of the British, granted the semi-autonomy of Muhammad Rashid Khan, which lasted until autumn 1944 (Sardashti, 2002b, pp. 55-62). In May 1942, the Iranian army under Colonel Arfa, with the support of the Tileco tribes, defeated Muhammad Rashid Khan in Saqqiz. Then, ironically, Muhammad Rashid Khan was appointed Governor of Baneh (Bana). In the summer of 1942, Baneh was again occupied by the Iranian army under General Houshmand Afshar, who tormented, tortured, executed, plundered, and seized people's property (Khoshhali, 2001, p. 16). When, in 1944, Muhammad Rashid Khan occupied Marivan, the British supported Iran against him. The well-equipped Iranian army, under Brigadier Houshmand Afshar, along with about 10,000 tribal chief's forces of Galbaghi, Tilakoyy, Manmi, and the forces of Mahmoud Khan Kanisanani, attacked Muhammad Rashid Khan and reoccupied Marivan. The latter retreated, forcing the people of Baneh to leave the city. In order to prevent the Iranian forces from having access to the wealth of the city, he burned down Baneh and fled to Iraq (Sardashti, 2002b, pp. 62-64).

The Kurds also revolted in the northern parts of Iranian Kurdistan, in the territory of Urmiya. For instance, Omar Khan Sharifi (Shikak), a Simko ally who was in prison, was released. He gathered a significant force of 20,000 militiamen, attacked gendarmerie stations, controlled the area between Sha Awa and Maku, and declared independence from Tehran. He also allied with the Jalali and Milani tribes and subsequently made a Kurdish flag. They developed their revolt and, at the beginning of 1942, surrounded Urmiya. The tribal chiefs of Harki and Shikah, in a gathering in a Sunni mosque in Urmiya, decided to unite the Kurds and create a government. On 28 April 1942, the Kurds in the city held a demonstration, cut the telegraph wires, and killed several gendarmes. On 30 April 1942, the Kurds and the Soviet Union consul, who came from Tabriz, had a meeting in the village of Askarabad, Khoy. The Kurds offered eight suggestions to the Iranian government (Sardashti, 2002b, pp. 73-74).

5.3.2. Qazi Muhammad visits Baku. Before continuing with the subject, due to the outstanding role of Qazi Muhammad in leading the nationalist movement in Kurdistan, his brief biography seems only appropriate. Born in 1900 in Mahabad, Qazi Muhammad married Mina Khanim in 1930. When his father, Qazi Ali, who was the Qazi (judge) of Mahabad, died in 1931, people chose Qazi Muhammad as the judge of Mahabad, and he resigned from the Education Office to accept the new position (Homayoun, 2004, p. 23). Qazi spoke Kurdish and was familiar with English, French, Russian, Persian, and Turkish languages (Homayoun, 2004, p. 22). Soon after joining the J.K., Qazi Muhammad became its leader.

Many authors regard Qazi Muhammad as a courageous person and administrator. For instance, before the establishment of the Kurdistan Republic when the tribes attacked Mahabad, Qazi acted bravely in standing on the front barricades to defend (Hemin, 1999, p. 28). He took over the responsibility of securing the city and organized the people to protect the city against burgling and invading. He also solved food shortages in Mahabad through the city's employers. As Mahabad's judge, he was known for settling disputes. Due to his popularity, the people gave him the title *Pishwa (Peshawa)* or Leader (Jalaeipour, 1990, pp. 23-24). In short, Qazi was a knowledgeable, organized, brave, popular, and progressive Kurdish nationalist who played a profound role in leading the Kurdish nationalist movement, especially during WWII.

Soon after the occupation, Qazi tried to meet British and American officials in order to attract their support to the Kurdish cause. His first meeting with the representatives of Britain and the United States took place on 25 September 1941 in Mahabad (Gadani, 2008a, p. 23). Qazi also hosted de Crespigny, the British Air Vice-Marshal in Iraq, and Urquhart, the Britain Consul in Tabriz, in mid-October 1942 (Kutschera, 1994, p. 203). However, it seems he did not get the expected support from them. After observing the social condition of Kurdistan and the influence of the tribal chiefs, the Soviet officials invited influential chiefs, religious leaders, and intellectuals to Baku. Qazi Muhammad was the intellectual figure among them. The first visit to Baku—comprising of a 30-delegate Kurdish party—took place, according to Kutschera, between 25 November and 5 December 1941. The aim of the Soviet Union, they surmised, was to preserve a peaceful space in Kurdistan (Kutschera, 1994, pp. 197-198; Gohari, 1999, p. 116; Homayoun, 2004, p. 34; Mustafa Amin, 2007, pp. 48-49). However, Omar Agha Aliar, the son of Ali Agha Aliar, who was one of the delegates, claims that the delegation involved only 20, while Eagleton suggests a list of 19 persons (Samadi, 1998, p. 154; Eagleton, 1963, p. 133; Appendix 5). During the first visit to Baku in 1941, the Kurdish delegation observed the industrial, agricultural, cultural, and artistic advancements of the Soviet Republic of Azerbaijan (Jalaeipour, 1990, pp. 33-34).

5.3.3. Sazmani Jawanani Kurd (Kurdish Youth Organization). After the Red Army entered Kurdistan, under the influence of a Russian officer Jafarov, who was a Kurd from Armenia, Ghani Bolourian learned about Komsomol (Communist Union of Youth), and at the end of *Khakalewa* (21 April) 1942, he established the *Sazmani Jawanani Kurd* (Kurdish Youth Organization) in *Baghi Mikaili* (the Mikail Garden) under the Ashkawti Nouradin (Nouradin Cave) in Mahabad. The participants chose Ali Mawlawi, Ahmad Salehian, Qadir Mahmoudzadeh, and Aziz Farhadi as the organizers and Bolourian as the leader (Bolurian, 1997, pp. 21-22). After Qazi Muhammad became a member and the leader of the J.K. in 1944, J.K. leadership successfully asked *Sazmani Jawanani Kurd* (the Kurdish Youth Organization) to join the J.K. in October-November 1944. So, the organization renamed itself *Rekkhrawi Lawani Komalay J.K.* (J.K. Youth Organization), with Bolourian still being its leader (Bolourian, 1997, pp. 32-33, 44). Before the formation of the J.K. (and during the J.K. period) and after the founding of the Kurdistan Republic, the Kurdistan Youth Organization attracted many young intellectuals. The Kurdistan Republic and especially Qazi Muhammad paid special attention to the youth. The majority of these youth had socialist ideas and were under the influence of the Soviets and the Tudeh Party (Hussein, 2008, p. 106).

5.4. *Komalay Jianaway Kurdistan (J.K.)* (Society for the Revival of Kurdistan [J.K.])

Modern Kurdish nationalism in Iran was born with the foundation of *Komalay Jianaway Kurdistan* (*J.K.*) (Society for the Revival of Kurdistan [J.K]), an organization that precedes subsequent Kurdish nationalist organizations. Of course, the formation of the J.K. as a modern Kurdish nationalist organization in Mahabad in 1942 was strongly affected by the previous Kurdish nationalist organizations in Iraqi and Iranian Kurdistan.

5.4.1. The founding of the J.K. According to Muhammad Amin Siraji, the establishment of the J.K. had been affected by the Kurdish intellectual movement in Iraqi Kurdistan, the Iraqi Kurdish publications, books, and memoirs, and the defeat of Sheikh Mahmoud's movement. Abdul Rahman Zabihi's letters to the Russians reveal that the formation of the J.K. dates back to 1941. After Reza Shah's fall, a situation appeared in Iranian Kurdistan that caused the surge of the Kurdish nationalist movement (Karimi, 1999, pp. 193, 195). Zabihi claims that the Kurdistan Freedom Party, the J.K., and the KDP, in fact, were one party. They emerged under three different conditions: before WWII, after the occupation of Iran by the Allies and the removal of Reza Shah, and after WWII. In addition, the activities of these organizations were a chain of Kurdish nations' struggle against occupation and imperialism (Abdullahi, 2008, p. 142). Therefore, the name, date of foundation, and the founders of the J.K. have been the subject of scholars' contention. The perfect name of the J.K., according to Zabihi and Qasim Ilkhanizadeh, is *Komalay Ziyanaway Kurdistan* (Society for Revival of Kurdistan). The second issue of the J.K. organ *Nishtman* (Homeland) (October-November 1943) holds that it was established on 16 August 1942 (Gohari, 2002, pp. 40-41; Ghassemlou, 1965, p. 76; Ghassemlou, 2000, p. 27; Shapasandi, 2007, p. 25; Karimi, 1999, p. 298; Eagleton, 1963, p. 33; Gohari, 1999, pp. 10-11; Roosevelt, 1980, p. 136; Karimi, 2008, p. 32). The number of founders of the J.K. is also debatable. Qadir Modarresi, one of the founders of the J.K., suggests two different lists—one including 18 and the other 10 names (Samadi, 1998, p. 111; Samadi, 1984, p. 10; Samadi, 1981, p. 15; Shapasandi, 2007, p. 24; see Appendix 2).

Modarresi and Shapasandi, a J.K. member, claim that Frouhar was the leader of the J.K. for two years; Karimi states that Frouhar was the leader of the J.K. until October 1944; and Arfa writes that in April 1943, hundreds of the J.K. members chose a CC and elected Rahman Zabihi as the chairman (Samadi, 1981, p. 15; Shapasandi, 2007, p. 21; Karimi, 2008, p. 21; Arfa, 1966, p. 77). Hashem Shirazi, claiming to be one of the founders of the J.K., asserts that none of the founders of the J.K. had higher education compared to him, having equal to a high school diploma, the highest among them all (p. 111). The J.K. leaders were the elites of their society at that time, and Zabihi was the leader and the most intellectual person in the J.K.

Zabihi claims that he finished the six-year elementary school in four years and, in 1938, he finished his middle school (grade 9 of 12) in Urmiya. When Giw Mukriani opened Photoshop in Mahabad in 1932, he also opened a French class for the youth. Zabihi studied for a few months in this class (Karimi, 1999, p. 446). According to Hashim Shirazi, Zabihi could read and write Kurdish, French, English, and Arabic in addition to speaking Armenian (Karimi, 1999, p. 58). Mustafa Amin states that Zabihi knew Kurdish, Persian, Turkish, and Arabic, as well as the basics of French and English (Karimi, 1999, p. 529).

After the fall of the Kurdistan Republic (see below), Zabihi went to the Iraqi Kurdistan. In the beginning, he tried to revive the J.K. and published the newspaper *Nishtman*, but he did not succeed. In Iraqi Kurdistan, he cooperated with the KDP (Iraq); in Syria, he cooperated with the Kurdish activists in the establishment of the Kurdistan Democratic Party of Syria; he returned to Iraq on 14 July 1958 and continued his cooperation with the KDP (Iraq) and later became a member of the KDP (Iraq) Politburo. Zabihi was an internationalist Kurdish nationalist. He published his works in different magazines in Iran and Iraq. Zabihi also became a prominent Kurdish lexicographer. According to Amir Hassanpour, the most important Kurdish dictionary is Zabihi's *Qamousi Zmani Kurdi* (Kurdish Language Dictionary) (Karimi, 1999, pp. 446, 530-531). The ideological perspectives of Zabihi are controversial. He considered himself a Marxist theorist; however, Jamal Nabaz emphasizes that while Zabihi proudly called himself a Marxist, theoretically and practically, he was far from Marxism. Siraji claims that while Zabihi was called *Mamosta Ulama* (Master of Scientists) because of his knowledge in every area, he was against communists (Karimi, 1999, pp. 220, 223, 253, 408).

Mullah Qadir Modarresi, one of the founders of the J.K., states that after the summer of 1941, some people from the Hiwa Party (Hope Party) of the Kurdistan of Iraq came to establish a branch of this party in Mahabad. On 13 August 1941, Said Hama Qala Bostanchi informed Modarresi and some other people, including Muhammad Nanavazadeh, to go to the Amin al-Islam Garden to meet three foreign guests. While Zabihi and Frouhar were also there, Zabihi introduced them to the guests, including Colonel Mir Haj and Mustafa Khoshnaw, who were from the Hiwa Party. The guests wanted to establish a branch of the Hiwa Party in Mahabad. The negotiation continued the next day in *Baghi Khizi* (the Sand Garden). They convinced the guests that they wanted to establish their own party while using the experiences of the Hiwa Party. After some appraisals, the J.K. was established (Samadai, 1994, pp. 108-110). A clarification about Mir Haj and others is needed: Ibrahim Ahmad claims that Mir Haj was not a member of Hiwa because, at that time, Hiwa was split into two sections. Some people, including Ibrahim Ahmad, Mir Haj, and Khoshnaw, established a group to create a party in the name of Hiwa or another name (Karimi, 1999, p. 179). Modarresi maintains that this group of people, who constituted a committee, after taking an oath and announcing their faithfulness to the party and its constitution, gathered in *Baghi Goweze* (the Walnut Garden) to share the responsibilities. They chose Frouhar as the Head of the Committee and Zabihi as the Secretary (the Head of Publications) (Samadi, 1998, p. 112; Samadi 1984, p. 10; Shirazi, 2000, p. 101).

5.4.2. The goals of the J.K. The ultimate goal of J.K. was the formation of an independent Kurdish state. According to Arfa (1966), the J.K. aimed at, first, obtaining autonomy for the Kurdish region in Iran and later unifying all Kurdish regions in an independent state (p. 73; Sardashti, 2002b, p.116). Khalil Fahimi, the Consultant Minister and the Governor of Western Azerbaijan, visited Mahabad and was respectfully received by Qazi Muhammad (Homayoun, 2004, p.36). When Fahimi traveled to Mahabad, the J.K. prepared a letter to him dated 14 January 1944 (Gohari, 1999, pp. 43-44; Sardashti, 2002b, p. 125; Yassin 19995, p. 114; Gohari,

1999 p. 44). Appendix 3 shows these demands.

The goals and methods of struggle of the J.K. expressed in its organ, *Nishtman*, Issue 1 (June 1943): some obstacles to the advancement of the Kurdish society include internal enmity, divisions, self-ruining, money-worshiping, and xenophilia. The J.K., *Nishtman* declares, strives to take off the chain of captivity from the neck of the Kurdish nation and create an orderly, united Kurdistan where all the Kurds live freely. Many people believe that the Kurdish nation should be liberated through the use of force and weapons. However, they are wrong. The Kurds should understand that today, compared with machine guns, cannons, tanks, planes, and so on, a rifle is like a firecracker. The way of civilization is the only way for the Kurds in order to achieve freedom and independence. In addition, in *Nishtman*, Issue 5 (January 1945), the J.K. explains that according to its constitution, the J.K. had been established based on Islam, Kurdish nationalism, civilization, and peace-seeking. All of its laws and regulations will be compared with Islamic laws and then will be used (Karimi, 2008, pp. 3-4, 110).

5.4.3. The organization of the J.K. After its establishment, the J.K. created rules for membership. Modarresi stresses that each new member, after performing ablution, should seven times take an oath to the Quran, the map of Kurdistan, and the flag of Kurdistan:

1. To not commit treason to the Kurds in any way.

2. To struggle for the independence of Kurdistan.

3. To not reveal any party secret by language, pen, or sign.

4. To remain as a member of the party to the end of life.

5. To know all Kurdish men as his/her brothers and all Kurdish women as his/her sisters.

6. To not join any party or group without J.K.'s permission.

(Samadi, 1998, pp. 110-111)

According to Modarresi, members should be born from a Kurdish father and mother. The non-Muslim Kurds took an oath to their religious books (Samadi, 1998, p. 112). Siraji maintains that the J.K. initially imposed restrictions on the membership of Sheikhs, Mullahs, and Aghas to the party, but later, these were removed (Karimi, 1999, p. 198). According to Modarresi, the J.K. invited many Aghas and Mullahs to join, and they accepted. These included, in Bukan, Haji Rahman Agha Ilkhanizadeh, Qasim Agha Ilkhanizadeh, Kak Abubakr Ilkhanizadeh, Haji Kaka Muhammad Karim Hamzeh-yy, Sheikh Kamil, and many others in other territories of Kurdistan (Samadi, 1998, p. 114; Samadi, 1984, p. 11).

With respect to the organizational structure, disciplines, and development of the J.K., Gohari (1999) provides some useful information. The organization was based in *Katla* (District), *Idaray Mhalli* (Territory Office or the City Committee), *Idaray Nawandi* (Central Office, or the CC), *Konfransi Mhalli* (Territory Conference), and the *Kori Balay Raweji Hayati Nawandi* (Higher Consulting Gathering of the Central Committee). The CC was located in Mahabad. Each of the cities of Mahabad, Bukan, Oshnavieh, Urmiya, Sardasht, Saqqiz, Sanandaj, Tehran, Kermanshah, Erbil, and Sulaymaniyah had a City Committee and five Districts. Each year, the City Committees held conferences and sent their representative to the Congress. The J.K. has held two congresses. The first was held on 16 August 1943 and the second one in January 1945. Since 1945, the J.K. organization was turned into an open organization, which opened the way for joining good and bad people, and that, in turn, prepared the way for J.K.'s collapse. In March 1945, the J.K. sent two members to visit Omar Khan Sharifi, and they established the J.K. organization in Salmas territory. The tribal chiefs were the heads of the organization in this territory (Gohari, 1999, pp. 37-39).

5.4.4. The J.K.'s activities. The J.K. performed different types of organizational, social, and political activities. Some of these activities included holding a congress, creating its branches to Iraqi and Syrian Kurdistan, organizing shows, publishing different cultural and political materials, bringing a press to Mahabad, submitting its demand to the Iranian government, and creating relations with the Soviet Consul. Other activities comprised organizing a demonstration, creating and conducting a protest and attacking the Central Police Station in Mahabad, supporting Kurdish protests in different parts of Iranian Kurdistan against the Iranian government, and establishing a Kurdish school. In the following, some of J.K.'s activities will be addressed only briefly, while the others will be discussed in more detail. According to Qazi (2012), the 1st Congress of the J.K. was held in the Mountain of *Qalay Sarim* (Sarim Fortress) outside Mahabad on 13 May 1943 (p. 126). The CC of the J.K., in the wide meeting in the Mountain of *Qalay Sarim,* decided to overt some of its activities. Gohari summarizes the main accomplishments of the J.K. in 11 points (Gohari, 2002, pp. 43-45).

Madani (2001) maintains that about 25 members of the J.K. gathered in this meeting [Congress]. They compared the programs of the J.K. and the Communist Party of the Soviet Union and, found common grounds and decided to establish friendly relations with the Soviet Union (p. 229). The J.K. selected a CC in April 1943 (Vali, 2011, p. 44) or sometime in Spring 1943 (Sabian, 1944, p. 35). After the Congress, the J.K.'s activities were extended. By the end of 1943, the J.K. had a membership of between 10,000 and 15,000 in Iran (Qazi, 2012, p. 130).

Another activity of the J.K. was supporting Kurdish protests against the government in different parts of Iranian Kurdistan. The J.K. supported the Kurdish movement of the tribal chiefs in Oraman and Marivan against Brigadier Houshmand Afshar (Sardashti, 2002b, pp.126-127). The J.K. tried to gain the support of the great powers by trying to attract Britain and the Soviet Union to the Kurdish movement. In order to attract Britain's support for the Kurds, in *Nishtman*, Issue 3, 4 (November 1943-January 1944), the J.K. admired Britain's two accomplishments of establishing a Kurdish Radio station in Palestine and publishing the journal *Dangi Giti Taza* (Voice of New World) in Baghdad. In this article, J.K. addresses Britain as the protector of freedom and independence and as the supporter of the small nations of the world (Gohari, 1999, p. 75-76) The relations between the J.K. and the Soviets will soon be explained.

The J.K. also staged a protest by its leaders and members, attacking the Mahabad Police Station on 15 February 1945 (Sardashti, 2002b, p. 126). This event has been described and analyzed in different ways. According to Sardashti, a demonstration led by Hussein Frouhar and Aziz Khan Kirmanj ended with the reading of a declaration and the attack and disarming of the police station of Mahabad on 15 February 1945. During the attack, two policemen, three gendarmes, and a Kurd, Awlay [Abdullah] Mina Khalandi, were killed (Hawrami, 2007, p. 21; Khoshhali, 2001, pp. 270-273). Homayoun (2004) writes that a group of angry individuals, in order to expel Governor Sari'al-Qalam from Mahabad, misused the protestors' feelings and unexpectedly attacked Mahabad's Police Station. They killed several policemen and vandalized the Station. The residents of Mahabad, who mostly had secretly been the J.K. members and strived to create a secure and peaceful city, became very angry and withstood them (pp. 35-36). But Gohari (2002) admits that attacking the Police Station was based on the guidance of the J.K. leaders (p. 25). Bolourian states that after the occupation of the Police Station, Major Qubadi, the Head of the Station, and Sari'al-Qalam, Mahabad's Governor, left the city. The government was still paying the employees' salaries of the other offices in Mahabad. Later, the government, with the Russians' permission, appointed Amir As'ad, who created the *Intezamat-e Ashayeri* (the Tribal Regiment), which included 300 armed peasants. Amir As'ad was against the activities of *Sazmani Jawanani Kurd* (the Kurdish Youth Organization), and the *Intezamat-e Ashayeri* (Tribal Regiment) surrounded the office of this organization. But Major Abdullaov, the Russian officer in charge of Mahabad's security, prevented Amir As'ad's forces and made him and his forces leave the city within 24 hours (Bolourian, 1997, pp. 25-26, 29-31; Khoshhali, 2001, pp. 270-273).

Frouhar, who was one of the leaders of the J.K., organized this protest. It should be addressed that the J.K. did not provide any document that proves that the party was behind the attack. It is more probable that Frouhar had done a sectarian and individualistic action. It seems that Frouhar had done these types of wilful actions a few other times, too. Therefore, Blourian claims that the J.K. leader was a terrorist and that the party was a terrorist-producing organization (Shapasandi, 2007, p. 52). For example, Bolourian (1997) claims that Frouhar provoked Hashem Farhadi to kill Rahmat Shafe'i, the wealthiest and a respectful person in Mahabad. Nevertheless, Farhadi did not find him, and when Rahman Shafe'i, brother of Rahmat Shafe'i, attacked Farhadi, Farhadi shot and killed him with a pistol. Later, Farhadi was found and killed by the armed men of Abdullah Bayazid Agha (pp. 44-48). Likewise, Sardashti (2002b) maintains that Frouhar, in the Sayyed Nizam Mosque in Mahabad, threatened with his pistol certain wealthy figures who were the supporters of the government and wanted to create a party against the J.K. (Sardashti, 2002b, pp. 123-124).

5.4.4.1. The J.K. in Iraq and Syria. One of the activities of the J.K. was to extend the organization to other parts of Kurdistan, including Iraq and Syria. Abdul Qadir Dabbaghi went to Sulaymaniyah and established the branch of the J.K. (Abdullahi, 2008, pp. 175-176). According to Eagleton (1963), in March 1944, Muhammad Amin Sharafi was sent by the J.K. to Kirkuk to meet the members of the Hiwa Party. Later, in the summer of 1944, some members of the Sulaymaniyah branch of the Hiwa went to Mahabad for the second time. One-and-a-half years later, activists from Iraq, Syria, and Turkey went to Mahabad to visit the Kurdish leaders (p. 36). Ibrahim Ahmad asserts that the first time the J.K. contacted the Hiwa Party, it contacted the section of Rafigh Hilmi, which was affiliated with Britain (Abdullahi, 2008, p. 213). Ibrahim Ahmad claims that when the J.K.'s Sulaymaniyah branch, including two women, Bahiya Faraj and Nahida Sheikh Salam, was established, they chose him as the Secretary (Karimi, 1999, p. 263). It seems that the J.K. in Iraqi Kurdistan had created a women's organization. *Yaketi Jinani Kurdistan* (Women's Union of Kurdistan) was led under Nahida Sheik Salam, Naima Khan (sister of Ibrahim Ahmad), and Zakiya Baban (Hussein, 2008, pp. 39-40). Mojab (2001) asserts that the J.K. emphasized one of the bases of democracy, which was "independence from foreign rule." The J.K. "paid lip service to the other requirements of democratic life, such as gender equality and did not even consider the abolishing of feudal relations. Women were the property, and the chaste mother, of the nation" (p. 76).

Ibrahim Ahmad states that the name of the organization of the J.K. in Iraqi Kurdistan was the J.K.'s Iraqi Kurdistan branch. The J.K. established branches in Zakho, Shaqlawa, Duhok, and Erbil and an office in Syria (Karimi, 1999, pp. 262-263). It created relations with the Kurdish and non-Kurdish organizations in Iraq, Turkey, and Syria. For instance, in Iraq, the J.K. had friendly relations with *Komalay Hiwa* (Hope Party), the Iraqi Communist Party, *Parti Rizgari Kurdistan* (Kurdistan Liberation Party), and Mullah Mustafa Barzani (Gohari, 1999, p. 132).

An important political activity of the J.K. was creating a pact with the Hiwa Party. A prevalent mistake exists among the scholars regarding the participants of this pact, as they believe that the representatives of the Kurds of Iran, Iraq, and Turkey (some scholars also add Syria) participated in *Paymani Se Snour* (Three-borders Pact) (Abdullahi, 2008, pp. 179-180). According to *Nishtman*, Issue 7, 8, 9 (March-April-May 1945), the representatives of the J.K. and the Hiwa Party held a conference on the borders of Iran, Iraq, and Turkey in the mountain of Dalanpar. After three days of negotiations, they signed an agreement known as the Three-borders Pact. The goal of the agreement was to expand the struggle and establish extensive political relations between these organizations. The Three-borders Pact was approved by the Consulting Board of the CC of the J.K. This approved copy was supposed to be exchanged with the Hiwa Party's copy of the agreement soon (Karimi, 2008, p. 163). Abdul Rahman Sharafkandi (Hajar) (1997), who was one of the participants in this conference, reveals that the conference was held in the month of Jozardan (May-June), and the agreement included 12 points. The representatives of the Hiwa Party at the conference were Sheikh Ubayd Allah Zinwe and Sayyed Aziz Shamzini. The delegates of the J.K. included Qasim Qadiri Qazi, Abdul Rahman Sharafkandi (Hajar), and Abdul Rahman Zabihi. Hajar maintains that while the J.K. quickly published the agreement in *Nishtman*, they were informed that the Hiwa Party had not been satisfied with the agreement and it should not have been published. Therefore, they tore out the page containing the agreement from *Nishtman* (Abdullahi, 2008, pp. 180-181; Hajar, 1997, pp. 64-65).

After publishing *Nishtman*, Issue 7, 8, 9 (March-April-May 1945), Zabihi was arrested by the Iranian army. According to Ubayd Allah Ayyubian, for a short time and for an unknown reason, Zabihi was arrested by the J.K., and a few days after he was released, he, Qasim Qadiri Qazi, and Muhammad (Dilshad) Rasouli went to Urmiya for a party mission but were arrested by Major-General Zanganeh in Balanish, Urmiya on 5 August 1945. According to *Kurdistan*, Issue 14 (13 February 1946), they were released after spending eight months in a Tehran prison (Abdullahi, 2008, pp. 101-102, 107-123; Karimi, 2008, pp. 29, 106; Saleh and Saleh, 2007, pp. 55, 76). But it seems that they had been arrested for about six months. The clarification about these dates is significant because it reveals that when the KDP and the Kurdistan Republic were established, Zabihi, as the most important leader of the J.K., was actually in prison. Indeed, some believe that Zabihi was against Qazi Muhammad's attempt to rename the J.K. to the KDP. However, he could not prevent this process because of his imprisonment.

5.4.4.2. *Cultural works and publications of the J.K.* One of the undertakings of the J.K. was organizing Kurdish shows. During its activity, the J.K. facilitated three plays. The first was *Salah al-Din* (*Saladin*), written by Qazi Muhammad and staged in Mahabad. The second, titled *Dayki Nishtman* (*Mother of Homeland*), is believed to have also been written by Qazi Muhammad, although according to Bolourian Mir Haj brought this play from Iraqi Kurdistan. Ahmad Sharifi states that Ibrahim Ahmad from Kurdistan of Iraq wrote it. This play was performed in Mahabad, Naqadeh, and Oshnaviyeh. Its cast of twelve actors included activists such as Abdullah Nahri, Bolourian (with three roles), and Abdullah Hakimzadeh (with two roles). The third play was *Tabibi Ejbari* (*Compulsory Doctor*), staged in 1946 at Shahpour High School in Saqqiz (Hussein, 2008, pp. 22-24; Bolourian, 2000, p. 35; Kutschera, 1994, p. 218; Shapasandi, 2007, p. 58 of Appendix). Due to its strong Kurdish nationalist theme, *Dayki Nishtman* (*Mother of Homeland*) turned out as the most popular play, staged since the beginning of summer 1945 for 40 days in Mahabad, 4 days in Naqadeh, and also in Qshnavieh (Bolourian, 1997, pp. 38, 40-41). Bolourian (1997) maintains that on the Russians' recommendation, they replaced the original king with a president at the end of the play The *Mother of Homeland* (pp. 43-44; pp. 138-139). In this opera, the Kurdish homeland, figured as the mother, "was represented as abused by three ruffians, 'Iraq', 'Iran', and 'Turkey', finally to be rescued by her stalwart sons" (Roosevelt, 1980, pp. 138-139). According to Manaf Karimi, women and girls who were not allowed in the theatre watched the play from the back of the windows, on the walls, and back of the roofs were not able to hold back their tears (Homayoun, 2004, p. 39). Homayoun's account reveals the low status of Kurdish women at the time. *Mother of Homeland* had a great impact on the people's sentiments and directed them toward patriotic thoughts (Homayoun, 2004, pp. 38-39).

Among other cultural activities of the J.K. was providing an opportunity to teach the Kurdish language in Mahabad. During the last year of the J.K. and establishment of the KDP, two Kurdish schools, *Galavej* and *Azadi*, were established in Mahabad (Gadani, 2008a, pp. 19-20). According to the *Kurdistan*, Issue 10 (4 February 1946), the *Galavej* night school was established on 2 June 1945 in the house of Ahmad Gadani. In this school, Kurdish and Russian language lessons were taught (Saleh and Saleh, 2007, p. 39). Another undertaking of the J.K. was publishing various political and cultural materials in the Kurdish language. The most important of these publications was *Govari Nishtman* (the magazine Homeland). According to Shapasandi, the circulation of *Nishtman* was between 700 and 800 (Shapasandi, 2007, p. 70 of Appendix). The list of publications is provided in Appendix 4.

5.4.4.3. *The J.K. and the Soviet Union.* At the time of the formation of the J.K. in 1942, the Soviet Union was not in favor of an autonomous Iranian Kurdistan. Molotov, the Soviet Minister of Foreign Affairs, in a letter to Smirnov, the Soviet Ambassador to Iran, on 31 August 1942, argued that the struggle of the Iranian Kurds for autonomy and independence, based on its social nature, was a reactionary defense of the separatist Kurdish feudal lords against the policy of centralism in Iran (Gohari, 1999, pp. 85-88). Nerwiy (2012) writes that in Molotov's letter, "polarization intensified between the two ethnic groups, the Kurds and the Azeris. The priority was given to the Azeris, and the Kurds were considered unreliable and in the service of British imperialism" (pp. 234-235). After the Battle of Stalingrad (from 23 August 1942 to 2 February 1943), the policy of the Soviet Union regarding the Kurds changed. Nerwiy (2012) states that the Soviet Union, employing the notions of the right of nations to self-determination, raised the motto of "liberty for the Kurds and the Azeris from the oppression of the Persians" (p. 237). To obtain the trust of the Russians, the J.K. tried to be close to them in Mahabad. Thus, Zabihi created good relations with the Soviet Union Consulate. The Soviets helped him publish the J.K. publications, including *Nishtman*, *Diari Komala* (*J.K.'s Gift*), and other publications in Tabriz (Shapasandi, 2007, p. 23).

According to Hassanov, the Soviet Consul in Urmiya, the J.K. sent a telegraph, signed by 312 famous Kurds, to Iran's Parliament and newspapers. The telegraph demanded the Iranian government grant the Caspian oil concession to the Soviet Union. In addition, for the same purpose, they held demonstrations in the

Kurdish areas. For instance, on 10 February 1944, the J.K. held a demonstration in Mahabad in which 3,000 people participated (Gohari, 1999, p. 124). On 13 September 1944, Zabihi met Hassanov and told him that about two years ago, they had formed the J.K. Zabihi said that they wanted to work in the Soviet's order (Hawrami, 2008, p. 112). According to Gohari (1999), on 27 September 1944, Zabihi wrote a letter to Hassanov in which he made several requests from the Soviets: officially recognize the J.K., help the development of the J.K., prevent the Iranian army from approaching Mahabad, and order the Kurdish tribal chiefs to not interfere in political affairs. The other requests comprised solving the J.K.'s equipment and technical problems and using the Soviet influence in the areas of Sardasht, Bukan, Miandoab, Mahabad, Oshnavieh, Naqadeh, and Urmiya to help end the authority of Iran in these areas; and recognize these areas as the Free Kurdistan. Another J.K.'s demand was to establish a Provisional Kurdish Government with the help of the youth and educated, wise Kurdish people of Iran, Iraq, and Syria in order to control the economy and administrative powers of these areas. The J.K. asked the Soviets to accept the Provisional Kurdish Government as a "brother republic" of the Soviet Union and make it a member of the greater Soviet Union. The J.K. demanded the Soviets make a plan to liberate other areas of Kurdistan and, to accomplish the above points, to send consultants to the J.K. (pp. 91-94). In a letter to the Consul of the Soviet Union in Tabriz dated 5 December 1944, Zabihi reported about the Hiwa Party and asked about opening a Soviet cultural entre in Mahabad, Bukan, Naqadeh, and Oshnaviyeh (Abdullahi, 2008, pp. 206-207). Also, in a letter to Hasanov dated 23 December 1944, Zabihi provided a list of 22 J.K. activists (Gohari, 1999, pp. 50-51, 232; Karimi, 1999, p. 624) As such, the J.K. created strong connections with the Soviets. The following letters of Zabihi to the Soviet Consul show that the J.K. trusted the Soviets to the extent that it revealed its organizational activities and even the names of some of its active members to the Soviets. On 27 September 1944, in a letter to the Consul of the

Soviet Union in Tabriz, Zabihi wrote that the J.K. had recently established a branch of its organization in Sulaymaniyah. He revealed that this branch asked the J.K. to write more about the Soviet Union in its organ. Moreover, he stated that the embassy of Britain was publishing a Kurdish journal *Dangi Giti Taza* (Voice of New World) (Karimi, 1999, pp. 624, 607).

Hashemov and Akbarov, from the Soviet Consulate in Urmiya, wrote that based on Moscow's orders, they had changed their relations with the J.K. since August 1945. They told the Kurds that the slogan "Independence for Kurdistan" was not realistic because it was mostly supported by the enemies of the Kurds (Hawrami, 2008, p. 137). Likewise, Gohari (1999) states that the report of the Soviet Consulate in Urmiya, signed by Hashimov and Akbarov, revealed that since June 1945, their relations with the J.K. had turned for the better. They suggested that the J.K. struggle for the equality rights of the Kurds within the framework of the Iranian laws for the democratic foundations of the country (p. 94).

One of the activities of the J.K. was its demand on the Soviet Union to establish a Soviet Cultural Relations Society in Mahabad. Then, Soviet Consul Matveyev visited Mahabad on 11 and 12 January 1945, where he met members of the J.K. who asked the Soviets to establish an Iranian-Soviet Cultural Relations Society in Mahabad and help them to find a typography. They requested the Soviets to establish a Kurdish Radio Program in Moscow that broadcasts in a Kurdish dialect that the Iraqi Kurds could also understand. In addition, they asked the Soviets to help the liberation of Kurdistan from the exploitation of three countries, Iran, Iraq, and Turkey, as well as the unification of the Kurds into a state (Hawrami, 2008, p. 122-123). Gohari (1999) maintains that the J.K.'s leaders, since 11 January 1945, asked the Soviets several times to establish *Komalay Pewandiyakani Farhangi Soviet* (Soviet Cultural Relations Society) in Mahabad. Finally, under Major Abdullaov, an Azeri Soviet Union officer, the Kurdistan-Soviet Cultural

Relations Society was established in Mahabad on 12 May 1945 (Gohari, 1999, pp. 120-122). Hashemov reports that in a meeting, a group of leaders was chosen to direct *Komalay Pewendiye Kelturiyekan* (Soviet Cultural Relations Society). Qazi was chosen as the head and Muhammad Keywanpur as the assistant (Hawrami, 2007, p. 25). The Kurdistan-Soviet Cultural Relations Society in Mahabad caused the development of the cultural relationship between the Kurds and the Soviet Union. Hemin (1999) was a member of the Kurdistan-Soviet Cultural Relations Society. This institution translated Kurdish writings into Azeri and Russian. One of these translations was Hajar's *Alakok* (Salsify) poem, which was translated by an Azeri Soviet, Master Jafar Khandan, to Azeri (p. 22).

5.4.5. Qazi Muhammad joined the J.K. Before joining the J.K., Qazi Muhammad had created strong connections with the Soviets. Maximov, the Soviet Consul in Urmiya, reported on 7 October 1943 that the representatives of all Kurdish leaders from Shapur to Saqqiz, including Qazi Muhammad, participated in the wedding of the son of Qarani Agha Zarza (Commander or Governor of Oshnavieh). They had a meeting in which they swore to the Quran and agreed:

1. To be faithful to the Soviet government to not act against the Soviet Union and its army in Iran and not make treaties with any country without the permission of the Soviets.

2. To act against the plunderers and punish them in order to end the lootings.

3. To preserve the unity of the Kurdish nation and be faithful to the principle of "all for one and one for all" (Hawrami, 2008, pp. 72-73).

Qazi Muhammad had always supported the J.K. in practice. However, there existed certain concerns among some of J.K.'s leaders about asking him to join the party. Shapasandi (2007) stresses that Zabihi and some of the J.K.'s founders thought that the J.K.'s leadership might face risk in asking Qazi to join the organization. Others like Mir Haj and Mustafa Khoshnaw, including the J.K., believed that Qazi was practically the leader of the Kurdish nation. Shapasandi maintains that after a while, Qazi was selected as the J.K.'s leader: among the supporters of Qazi Muhammad, who constituted the majority, this created harshness toward Zabihi, and its imprint remained even after the fall of the Republic of Kurdistan (pp. 25-26). Hajar (1997) states that they wanted Qazi to cooperate with the J.K., but he looked down upon them. The J.K. felt that without having a great leader, the tribes and other famous people would not be satisfied with the J.K.'s leader, Hussein Frouhar. The J.K. asked its followers to participate in Qazi's speeches, and consequently, he felt that the party was strong. Hajar asserts that J.K. asked Qazi to join, and he accepted. Very soon, it was decided that Qazi Muhammad became J.K.'s leader (p. 69).

Arfa (1966) states that the Soviets realized that a highly authoritative person was needed to lead and attract the tribal chiefs to the movement. For this reason, they advised the J.K. to bring in Qazi Muhammad. Qazi joined the J.K. but never became a CC member. He was rather the spiritual leader of J.K. (p. 77). Eagleton (1963) asserts that Qazi was not a CC member of the J.K.; also, he did not join the KDP (p. 57). According to Kinnane (1964): "In October 1944, Qazi Muhammed was invited to join *Komala* [J.K.] and accepted immediately" (p. 49). Qazi Muhammad became the leader of the J.K. in October-November 1944. His alias in the J.K. was Yazdi at the beginning, but later changed to Binayy (Gohari, 1999, p. 109; Moradi, 1996, p. 41; Shapasandi, 2007, p. 27 of Appendix).

After joining, Qazi strengthened the J.K.'s relations with the Soviets. Hawrami (2007) writes that, after his return from Tehran, Qazi met with the Soviet Vice-Consul, N. K. Qoliyov, in Tabriz on 20 February 1945. In his conversation with Qoliyov, Qazi described his meeting with the Iranian officials, including Prime Minister Sa'ed, the Shah, the Head of General Staff of the Iranian Army, General Haj Ali Razmara, the War Minister Ibrahim Zand, the Consultant Minister, Fahimi, and the new Prime Minister, Bayat. Sa'ed had asked Qazi about the news, which stated that the Kurds wanted to proclaim an independent Kurdistan. Qazi rejected this statement and explained to Sa'ed that the Iranian government ignored problems of health and education in Kurdistan. He explained to the Shah that based on the Kurds' Sunni religion, the people should serve their King, and the Kurds have always been faithful to the King (pp. 13-18).

In a meeting with the Soviet Vice-Consul N. K. Qoliyov on 20 February 1945, Qazi demanded the following from the Soviets:

1. The opening of the Community of the Cultural Relationship of the Soviets with Iran in Mahabad.
2. The opening of a course in learning the Russian language.
3. To allow a direct relationship in order to strengthen commercial relationships with the Soviets for selling the Soviet industry in Mahabad, as well as for buying our commodities by their commercial organizations.
4. A printing apparatus to be given to us. (Hawrami, 2007, pp. 19-20)

One of the activities of the J.K. was raising the Kurdistan flag on the top of the building of the Soviet Cultural Relations Society in Mahabad. This occurred due to celebrating the victory over Fascism in WWII (Gohari, 2002, p. 44). It is noticeable that in his contact with the Soviet Union's official, Qazi expressed his wish for the independence of Kurdistan. Hashemov, the Soviet Consul in Urmiya, in his report on 1 May 1945, stated that during his visit to Qazi Muhammad, the whole time, Qazi was leading the conversation on the subject of the independence of Kurdistan. Qazi stated that he owned a big piece of land; however, he wished to establish a government like the Soviet Union, although he might lose his property (Hawrami, 2007, pp. 20-22). Qazi's statement also revealed his personal, radical perspective regarding the land question in Kurdistan and his inclination toward the socialist system of the Soviet Union. According to Gazi (2012), Qazi Muhammad strongly believed in democracy, freedom, socialism, and the Soviet Union (Qazi, 2012, p. 298). Qazi also created a friendly relationship with the Azerbaijan national movement. According to Parsa Benab (2004), *Ferghe-ye Demokrat-e Azerbaijan* (Azerbaijan Democratic Party) was established on 3 September 1945 under Jafar Pishevari in Tabriz. In its 12-Point Program, this party asked for cultural and political autonomy for the people of Azerbaijan under a national government within a united and independent Iran. At that time, the Tudeh Party had a vacillating position regarding the national question in Iran. Thus, the branch of the Tudeh Party joined the Azerbaijan Democratic Party (pp. 281-282). According to Mianali Alieza (2005a), when the Azerbaijan Democratic Party was established, Qazi went to Tabriz to congratulate the party's founding. Many Kurds in Mahabad and Naqadeh sent congratulatory telegrams as well and named Qazi as their representative (pp. 57-58, 60).

The J.K. continued to develop its activities in the following months.

5.5. *Hizbi Demokrati Kurdistan* (Kurdistan Democratic Party [KDP])

This section discusses the formation of the KDP in 1945 in Mahabad, the establishment and fall of the Kurdistan Republic in 1946 in Iranian Kurdistan, the revival of the KDP's activities after the fall, and the holding of the 1st conference of the KDP in Kurdistan in 1955. It also brings up the formation of *Komitay Sakh Karaway Hizbi Demokrati Kurdistan-Eran* (Reconstructing Committee of the Kurdistan Democratic Party-Iran or Reconstruction Committee) in the Iraqi Kurdistan in 1963 and the 2nd Congress of the KDP in Iraqi Kurdistan in 1964. Moreover, it considers the foundation of *Komitay Inqlabii Hizbi Demokrati Kurdistan-Eran* (Revolutionary Committee of the Kurdistan Democratic Party-Iran or Revolutionary Committee) in the Iraqi Kurdistan in the summer of 1966, which led the armed movement of 1967-1968, and, finally, holding the 2nd Conference of the KDP in the Iraqi Kurdistan in 1969.

Before discussing the above, a brief explanation of the entrance of the Barzani tribe to Iranian Kurdistan is addressed because it greatly affected the Kurdish movement in Iran. On 10 October 1945, about 4,000 armed Barzanis and 1,000 women and children who were under attack by the Iraqi government and the British forces took refuge in Iranian Kurdistan (Qazi, 2012, p. 153; Mustafa Amin, 2007, p. 84; Eagleton, 1963, p. 54). Gadani writes that when the Barzanis' uprising in 1945 was suppressed by Iraq, and most of their villages were burned and ruined, about 10,000 Barzanis, nearly 1,500 of them armed, entered Iran in the autumn of 1945. With the agreement of the KDP and some tribal chiefs, they were settled in the areas of Margawar, Targawar, Oshnavieh, Naqadeh, Piranshahr, Mahabad, and Bukan. Muhammad Amin Manguri states that Qazi Muhammad, on the Soviet Union's recommendations, sent lots of resources to them. Also, the Aghas of these villages provided for the livelihood of these families. In March 1946, Mullah Mustafa Barzani was respectfully received in Mahabad, and later, his forces came to the city and, after arming them, they were sent to the Saqqiz front (Gadani, 2008a, pp. 32-33; Manguri, 2001, pp. 47, 49).

5.5.1. The founding of the KDP. The proliferation of the modern political and social organization in Iran, the formation of the Azerbaijan Democratic Party, and the second visit of Qazi Muhammad to Baku significantly influenced the formation of the KDP.

Two different ideas exist among scholars regarding the date of the KDP's formation. The first group, including Jalil Gadani, Abbas Vali, and Rahim Qazi, believes that the KDP was established before the second visit of Qazi Muhammad to Baku and essentially on 16 August 1945 (Gadani, 2008a, p. 24; Qazi, 2012, p. 148; Vali, 2011, pp. 25, 50, 149). Gadani, Qazi, and Vali have not revealed documents proving their claim. Indeed, none of the outstanding members of the

J.K., who even later joined the KDP, have mentioned that the KDP was established before Qazi's second visit to Baku.

The second group of scholars believe that the KDP was established after the second visit of Qazi Muhammad to Baku. The second visit of Qazi and a group of Kurds, who were invited by Atakishiyev, a Soviet Union Army General, to Baku was, as widely believed, in September 1945. Roosevelt (1980) states that on 12 September 1945, Captain Namazaliov, the Soviet Union Town Commandant in Miandoab, took the Kurdish board to Tabriz, and from there, they went to Baku. After four days of staying in Baku and meeting Mir Jafar Baqirov, the leader of Azerbaijan of Russia, they returned to Kurdistan (Roosevelt, 1980, p. 140; Sardashti, 2002b, p. 139). According to Eagleton (1963), the list of people on the second visit to Baku was Qazi Muhammad, Ali Rayhani, Muhammad Hussein Khan Saifi Qazi, Manaf Karimi, Qasim Ilkhanizadeh, Abdullah Qadiri, Hamza Agha Nalosi, and Nouri Baig Baigzadeh (p. 133; Gohari, pp. 46-47; Gadani, 2008a, p. 32).

Before discussing the negotiation of the Kurdish delegation with Baqirov, it should be noted that the views of the Soviet Union's officials were different from Baqirov's perspectives. Hawrami (2008) asserts that Baqirov and Pishevari were against the autonomy of Kurdistan and asked the Soviet leaders to give cultural autonomy to Kurdistan within the framework of Azerbaijan. However, Moscow wanted to create separation movements in Kurdistan, Azerbaijan, Gilan, Khorasan, and other parts of Iran in order to weaken and subdue the Iranian government (p. 203). The Kurdish representatives had different perspectives from Baqirov. Yassin (1995) states that the Kurds asked for the Soviet Union's military and financial help, and they also wished to establish an independent state (p. 121). Baqirov replies that:

> There was no need for the Kurds to hurry the formation of their own
> state. Kurdish freedom must be based on the triumph of popular

forces not in Iran alone but also in Iraq and Turkey. A separate Kurdish state was a desirable thing to be considered in the future when the entire 'nation' could be united. In the meantime, Kurdish aspirations should be achieved within autonomous Azerbaijan. (Eagleton, 1963, p. 44; Yassin, 1995, p. 155)

The Kurdish representatives rejected the idea of being under Azerbaijan. When Baqirov observed their will to be autonomous, he respected their decision (Yassin, 1995, pp. 155-156). In addition, Baqirov promised the Kurds assistance with military equipment, accepting Kurdish students in the Baku Military College, asking Pishevari to accept 80 Kurdish students in the university, which would be established in Tabriz, a printing house, and financial assistance. Moreover, Baqirov advised transforming the J.K. into the Democratic Party of Kurdistan to help progress the Kurdish movement (Eagleton, 1963, p. 45). According to Manaf Karimi, Baqirov said that the J.K. demands the Greater Kurdistan. This may cause a war with Iran, Iraq, Syria, and Turkey and the so-called Third World War (Abdullahi, 2008, p. 147).

Hajar (1997) claims that when Qazi Muhammad returned to Mahabad from Baku, he was told that Russia was not satisfied with the J.K.'s designation because the J.K. struggled for the liberation of the whole Kurdistan, and this made Great Britain and Turkey angry. Qazi Muhammad said that we should change our name to the KDP and demand autonomy (p. 72; Homayoun, 2004, p. 45; Hisami, 2011, p. 27; Mustafa Amin, 2007, p. 86). According to Balaki, the KDP was not founded on 16 August 1945. He claims that the presence of the Red Army in Kurdistan and the visit of Qazi to Baku had affected the establishment of the KDP. Possibly in Baku, they suggested to him to form a party. However, it was not the Soviets that created the party; Qazi Muhammad established the KDP (Personal communication, September 28, 2012).

According to the organ of the KDP, *Govari Kurdistan* (the magazine Kurdistan), Issue 1 (6 December 1945), *Hizbi Demokrati Kurdistan* (Kurdistan Democratic Party [KDP]) was established and distributed its declaration on 23 October 1945 in Mahabad. In addition, the KDP held its 1st Congress on 24 October 1945 (Hussein, 2008, p. 533). It should be noted that the KDP, to show its continuity with the J.K., officially has accepted 16 August 1945 as its foundation date. According to the *Kurdistan*, Issue 1 (6 December 1945), *Bayannamay Komalay Demokrati Kurdistan* or *Bayannamay Hizbi Demokrati Kurdistan* (Declaration of the Kurdistan Democratic Party) was an announcement about the establishment of the Kurdistan Democratic Party, released on 23 October 1945. Two versions of the declaration are available: the hand-written and the print versions. Both versions are in both Kurdish and Persian languages. The hand-written version contains the names of 39 people. Said Ibrahimzadeh's name appears only in this copy. The print version has the names of 72 people; Qazi Muhammad has signed it but has no name on this version. Two points to be noticed are that, firstly, only the names of three of the J.K. leaders appear in the declaration: Seddiq Haidari, Muhammad Amin Sharafi, and Muhammad Yahou. Secondly, the order of the names appears as follows: the clerics, feudal landlords, merchants, government employees, and businessmen like pharmacy and garage owners. This order somehow reveals the nature of the hierarchy in Kurdish society in that era (Saleh and Saleh, 2007, p. 350-355). The Declaration of the KDP contains eight points (See Appendix 6). The main point of the declaration is that the KDP aims to obtain the freedom and autonomy of Kurdistan within the Iranian state.

5.5.2. The 1st Congress of the KDP. The Kurdistan Democratic Party held its 1st Congress on 24 October 1945 in Mahabad (Hussein, 2008, p. 533). The list of the heads and representatives who participated in the congress included people from nine areas. Except for a few names, the list is basically comprised of the names of the tribal chiefs and Aghas (Hussein, 2008, p. 533). In the Congress, the name and the mottos of the J.K. were changed (Bolourian, 1997, p. 58), all the branches of the KDP and their representatives were approved, and they started their activities (Hussein, 2008, p. 534), and the KDP approved a 22-Point Program (Amin, 2007, pp. 92-95; Hisami, 2011, pp. 28-29). The main aim of the KDP was announced as the autonomy of Kurdistan within Iran. The program ignored the land question. The Congress also selected a CC and Qazi Muhammad as the leader of the party. Appendix 8 shows the list of the CCs.

5.5.3. The goals of the KDP. The goals of the KDP were clearly formulated in its 8-Point Declaration and the 22-Point Program. The central goal of the KDP was the establishment of an autonomous Kurdistan within the framework of Iran. Among other important goals were the use of Kurdish as the official language in education and administration in Kurdistan, the recognition of the rights of the minorities such as Assyrian and Armenians in Kurdistan, and the acknowledgment of the equality of men and women in all political, economic, and social areas. The primary goal and other aims of the KDP, frequently announced by Qazi Muhammad, will be considered in this chapter. For now, a few interviews of Qazi Muhammad, before and after the establishment of the Kurdistan Republic, are observed.

In an interview with Shahandeh, the editor of the newspaper *Ferman (Order)*, on 22 December 1945, Qazi stated that the Kurds wanted to live within the framework of Iran, the rule of the constitution and democracy, and preserve the autonomy they now had. Qazi asserted that for four years, the Kurds in Mahabad and its territory had autonomy while nine people were chosen in a congress to lead the issues of Kurdistan and contact the central government (Hawrami, 2007, p. 35). Wadie Jwaideh (2006) reports that, on 1 June 1946, in response to a French journalist, Qazi, stated that the Kurds would be satisfied if the Iranian government recognized the autonomy of Kurdistan. Regarding the potential conflict between the Kurds and the government and the possibility of the other countries' intervention, Qazi stated:

> The situation in Kurdistan is very different from that of Azerbaijan. Our country has never been occupied by Soviet troops, and since the abdication of Reza Shah, neither the Gendarmerie nor Iranian troops have penetrated Kurdistan. We have[,] therefore[,] practically been living independently since that time. Further, we shall never tolerate foreign intervention wherever it comes from. The question of Kurdistan is a purely internal affair to be settled between Kurds and the Central Government. (Jwaideh, 2006, pp. 253-254)

The newspaper *Kurdistan*, Issue 69 (21 July 1946), contains Qazi Muhammad's interview with the representative of the Persian newspaper *Rahbar* (Leader), which belonged to the Tudeh Party. Qazi Muhammad, regarding the scope of the Kurdish democratic movement, responded that the extent of the Kurdish movement includes Maku, Shapur, Khoy, Rezaiyeh (Urmiya), Oshnavieh, Sulduz (Naqadeh), Saqqiz, and Sardasht with the population of about 700,000 or 800,000 people. He claimed that both Azerbaijan and Kurdistan strive for the real freedom and independence of Iran and emphasized that the Kurdish movement has been inspired by Tehran's freedom-seekers. He said that Hajar, in a poem, wrote that the Kurds struggle by the sword and the freedom-seekers in Tehran by their pen. Qazi emphasized that the pen in Tehran did as much as a hundred swords in our territory [Kurdistan] (Saleh and Saleh, 2007, pp. 273-274, 276). Obviously, Qazi and members of the KDP dreamed of an independent Kurdish state that included all parts of Kurdistan located in different countries. Nonetheless, at that time, the political program of the KDP and the political strategy and tactics of the KDP were most aimed at achieving an autonomous Kurdistan within Iran.

An important activity of the KDP after its formation was the establishment of a printing house in Mahabad. The press was provided by the Soviet Union. Two engineers from Czechoslovakia worked for about two months [or two weeks] to install the press (Shapasandi, 2007, p. 72 of Appendix). The KDP published its first issue of *Govari Kurdistan* (the magazine Kurdistan) on 6 December 1945.

The Azerbaijan National Government was established on 12 December 1945 in Tabriz under the Azerbaijan Democratic Party led by Sayyed Ja'far Pishevari. Its establishment constitutes the most significant nationalist, democratic, and radical political and social movement of an oppressed nation in Iran. It affected the whole democratic movement in Iran, including Kurdistan. The Kurdish nationalist movement, led by the KDP, was encouraged to follow its nationalist dreams. The Kurdish people and the KDP strongly supported the Azerbaijan National Government and celebrated its foundation.

Raising the Kurdish flags in Kurdistan was another step toward strengthening the autonomous demands of the Kurds. According to the *Kurdistan*, Issue 3, and the KDP's magazine *Halala* (Buttercup), Issue 1, the flag of Kurdistan was raised on 17 December 1945 on the roof of the *Hayat-i Raeisay Milli* (National Governing Assembly of Kurdistan) in Mahabad. On the following days, the Kurdistan flags were also raised in Naqadeh (18 December 1945), Bukan (28 December 1945), Oshnavieh, and most large villages (Hussein, 2008, p. 770; Gohari, 1999, p. 150; Homyoun, 2004, pp. 58-60).

After raising Kurdistan's flag, in his interview with the Persian newspaper, *Shahbaz* Qazi claimed that the KDP is not a communist party and that only in a council-based government does real democracy exist. He officially recognized the Iranian Constitution. He added that the Higher Council, which controls Mahabad's area, is in connection with the Iranian government. He emphasized that traitors who want to destroy the Kurds stress that Kurdistan demands independence. To reach its aim, the central government accuses Azerbaijan and Kurdistan of separatists.

Qazi maintained that the Kurds did not want autonomy. He said that since the abdication of Reza Shah in September 1941, Gendarmerie and army troops were not present in Kurdistan, and Kurdistan had been practically living independently. He stressed that the Kurds never bear foreigners' interference. The Kurdistan's matters are internal issues to be resolved between the Kurds and the central government (Moradi, 1996, p. 51-55).

By stating that "the Kurds did not want autonomy" and the Kurds "lived in freedom and independence," Qazi meant that the Kurds had practically been autonomous, and they wanted the Iranian state to acknowledge and recognize Kurdistan's *de facto* autonomy. However, the use of the term "independence" by the leaders of Azerbaijan was similar to its use by the Kurdish leaders. According to Mobley (2008), during the negotiation of the Kurds and Azeris with the Iranian government, Pishevari emphasized that the freedom and independence of the Kurds have the same meaning as the freedom and independence of Azerbaijan. He asserted that the Kurds and the Azeris had similar goals and enemies, both going through the same path (p. 65). Statements such as this, it turned out, did not contribute to the Kurdish cause.

5.5.4. The organization of the KDP. The KDP imitated the structure of the communist party (Mawloudi Sabian, 1994). The Soviet Union agents helped the KDP. According to Eagleton (1963), Kakagha helped Mahabad's Army while Babayov and Asadov organized the KDP. The model of the Communist Party was employed for the organization of the KDP. For instance, a Women's Section was created under Qazi Muhammad's wife [Mina Khanim], and a Youth Section was established under Ali Khosrawi. Despite this limitation, the KDP did not have any doctrinaire political direction (Eagleton, 1963, pp. 102-103). In addition, in May 1946, the KDP created a twelve-man Supreme Council in order to expand participation in the hierarchy of the KDP, as well as to handle people's complaints (Eagleton, 1963, p. 102). Appendix 10 shows the list of the Supreme Council of the

KDP, formed in May 1946. The KDP announced a 22-Point Program, and it had an Internal Regulation (Constitution), though this constitution had not been revealed yet. The evidence for the existence of the constitution can be found in the *Kurdistan*, Issue 66 (9 July 1946) where it addresses the party's regulations (Saleh and Saleh, 2007, p. 264). The KDP also organized two chief organizations: *Yaketi Jawanani Demokrati Kurdistan* (Democratic Youth Union of Kurdistan) and *Hizbi Demokrati Jinani Kurdistan* (Democratic Party of the Women of Kurdistan).

The transformation of the J.K. into the KDP has been differently valued by researchers. Regarding the necessity of changing the J.K. to the KDP, Moradi (1996) maintains that it was necessary to change the name of the J.K. because this party was, for more than three years, a semi-clandestine organization and had not taken serious steps toward its 6-article program. In addition, due to having close relationships with Hiwa Party in Iraq and *Khoyboun* (Independence) in Kurdistan of Turkey and Syria, the J.K. was called a nationalist, separatist, and communist party by enemies and especially Great Britain (Moradi, 1996, p. 43). Some researchers, like Karimi, are against the idea which claims that the KDP was the continuation of the J.K. and emphasizes that none of the leaders of the J.K. was among the KDP's leadership (Karimi, 1999, pp. 116, 125-126). In contrast, according to Eagleton (1963), Zabihi, the leader of the J.K., was a member of the CC of the KDP (p. 134).

Some scholars notice the negative effects of changing the J.K. to the KDP. Hassanpour (2007) emphasizes that the foundation of Komalay J.K. in 1942 in Iranian Kurdistan was a milestone. The J.K. converted Haji Qadir Koy's thoughts into a political platform. Nevertheless, when this organization was restructured into the KDP in 1945, it permitted the landlords and tribal aristocrats an important place in the cabinet of the Kurdistan Republic and other institutions of power. The feudal notables played a "betrayal" role in the fall of the Republic (p. 7; see also Hajar, 1997, pp. 72-73).

5.6. The Kurdistan Republic

On 22 January 1946, *Dawlati Jimhouryy Kurdistan* (Kurdistan Republic Government) was announced in Mahabad. Manaf Karimi states that in the days preceding the establishment of the Kurdistan Republic, many Kurdish people from cities and villages came to participate in the ceremony. Tens of thousands attended the ceremony (Homayoun, 2004, p. 47-48). According to the *Kurdistan*, Issue 8, 28 January 1946, "20,000 people" from the northern Kurdistan of Iran participated in the meeting of 22 January 1946 in Mahabad (Saleh and Saleh, 2007, p. 31).

The conditions for and the factors that led to the foundation of the Kurdistan Republic include the weakness of the central government, the prudent support of the Soviet Union, and, most importantly, the existence of a Kurdish national will (Bakhchi, 2007, p. 9). Another factor that affected the establishment of the Kurdistan Republic was the foundation of the Azerbaijan National Government. Clearly, the Azerbaijan National Government was not in favor of the establishment of an autonomous Kurdistan. In winter (before 22 January 1946), Qoliyov, Consul of the Soviet Union in Tabriz, invited some Kurdish and Azeri leaders, including Qazi Muhammad, Saifi Qazi, Pishevari, and Birya, to have a meeting at the Cultural Centre of Azerbaijan and Soviet at Baghe Golestan, Tabriz. The Azeri leaders wanted Kurdistan to be part of Azerbaijan. When Qazi disagreed, saying that let the Kurds be independent and stay on their own feet, Qoliyov and Azeris became upset (Homayoun, 2004, pp. 43-44). Richard A. Mobley (2008) states that the Azeris did not recognize the Kurdistan Republic until a few weeks passed (p. 57). According to (2012), the foundation of the Azerbaijan government created great political anxiety among the Kurds. They recognized that "not only would the Kurdish region come under the control of the Azerbaijan leaders, but the autonomy they enjoyed from 1941 onwards would also disappear" (p. 257).

In his speech during the ceremony on 22 January 1946, Qazi Muhammad maintained that the Kurds established schools for boys and girls, as well as night schools for adults. In addition, books have been translated into Kurdish. Moreover, with the establishment of a print house, they were able to publish magazines and newspapers in Kurdish. Qazi continued that their victory was due to their reliance on people, democracy, and the support of the progressive world. He emphasized that with their resistance and struggle, they had achieved the independence and freedom of the Kurdish nation. After that, many Kurdish tribal chiefs and the KDP leaders delivered speeches, among them two women, Wilma Sayyadian and Khadijeh Haidari. On the same day, the people chose Qazi Muhammad as the President of Kurdistan (Homayoun, 2004, pp. 49-53). Homayoun (2004) affirms that a 6-Point Declaration was announced at the end of the meeting in which people's representatives asked the CC of the KDP and *Anjoman-e Melli-ye Kurdistan* or *Hayat-i Raeisay Milli Kurdistan* (National Governing Assembly of Kurdistan) for certain demands (see Appendix 7). On this day, Qazi Muhammad took the ceremonial oath:

> I swear to God, God's Great Words [the *Quran*], my homeland, the national dignity of the Kurd, and the holy Kurdistan flag that to not withhold from any attempt until my last breath and the sheding of the last drop of my blood, with soul and heart, to preserve the independence and upholding of the flag of Kurdistan, and to be obedient and faithful to the presidency of the Kurdistan Republic and the unity of Kurd[istan] and Azerbaijan. (Saleh and Saleh, 2007, p. 53)

On the same day, representatives of tribal chiefs and the KDP from various cities and villages congratulated and swore allegiance to Qazi Muhammad in the City Hall building (Homayoun, 2004, p. 55). On 22 January 1946, the masses attending the ceremony gave Qazi the title of *Peshawa* (Leader) (Gohari, 1999, p. 110). The Kurdistan Republic did not cover all Kurdish areas of Iranian Kurdistan.

It is estimated that the Kurdistan Republic comprised only between one-third and one-fourth of the Iranian Kurdish territory. The Kurdistan Republic controlled Mahabad, Bukan (Bokan), Naqadeh, and Oshnavieh, whose total population of these areas was about 150,000. The population of Mahabad was 15,000 (Hawrami, 2007, pp. 153-154).

5.6.1. The Cabinet. A few days later, *Heyat-e Raeiseh-ye Melli-ye Kurdistan* (the National Governing Assembly of Kurdistan) that was, in fact, the Cabinet of the Kurdistan Government was formed. To give assurances to the Iranian Government that the Kurds were not separatists, the Cabinet of the Kurdistan Government was named the "Kurdistan National Governing Assembly," and the Ministers were named the Heads (*ra'is*) of the offices (Homayoun, 2004, p. 55). The list of the Cabinet was published on 11 February 1946. Cabinet members were mostly from the known and upper classes of Mahabad and the landlords around Mahabad (see Appendix 9). The northern Kurdistan cities like Urmiya, Khoy, Salams, Maku, and other cities such as Saqqiz and Sardasht did not have representatives in the government (Sardashti, 2002b, p. 139).

The reason for admitting the name Kurdistan Republic Government or just Kurdistan Republic has been arguable. Some may interpret it as a sign of the existence of an independent Kurdish state. Some scholars disagree with this interpretation. Moradi (1996) asserts that, by addressing phrases like nation and free territory of Kurds, Qazi meant free from the chain of dictatorship (p. 49). The Kurdistan government was a *de facto* government. It had neither a legal status in the Iranian Constitution nor did it create its own constitution. Its authority was higher than that of a central government. The ministries were sometimes called "offices" and the cabinet "*Hayat-i Raeisa*" (Governing Council). In addition, the "War Ministry" was sometimes called *Wazarati Hezi Dimokrati Kurdistan* (Ministry of Kurdistan Democratic Force) (Mustafa Amin, 2007, pp. 147-148).

It can be argued that a few factors affected the Kurds in choosing the designation of the Kurdistan Republic. The Kurds were aware of the democratic Republics of the world, having seen the Republic of Azerbaijan in the Soviet Union, and their dream for the political system of Kurdistan was a republic. In addition, as a dream, the Kurds wanted to establish a Kurdistan Republic to possibly unite the Kurds in the Greater Kurdistan within the Kurdistan Republic in the future. The Kurds wanted to show that they had the potential to create their own state independent both from Iran and the Autonomous Azerbaijan Government.

The main objective of the Kurdistan Republic was preserving the *de facto* Kurdistan autonomy that the Kurds enjoyed since the Allies' occupation of Iran and negotiating with the Iranian government to achieve official autonomy within the framework of Iran. In an interview with *Watan Yolinda* (For the Homeland's Sake), Qazi asserted that the Kurds want autonomy (Sardashti, 2002b, p. 161). According to the *Kurdistan*, Issue 1 (11 January 1946), Qazi Muhammad had an interview with the editors Mr. Tafazzoli, from *Iran-e Ma* (Our Iran), Mr. Abbas Shahandeh, from *Farman* (Order), and Mr. Bozorg Alawi from *Rahbar* (Leader). Qazi claimed that the Kurds wanted the Iranian government to abide by the constitution He asserted that the Kurds wanted autonomy, and they had earned it four years previously (Saleh and Saleh, 2007, pp. 1, 4). The Kurdistan Republic was a reality, a Kurdish national will and symbol, and a model for all the Kurds to establish their own dream state in the future. Qazi (2012) reveals that the semi-official newspaper *Ettelaat* (Information), which disseminated the chauvinistic ideas of the Iranian government, sent a reporter to Kurdistan to find out the reason for the influence of Qazi. On 18 June 1946, the reporter wrote that the reason for all Kurdish revolts had been the poverty and backwardness of Kurdistan. According to *Ettelaat*, the reporter had not found even one person who had not believed in Qazi and had not moved based on his demands (p. 205). The Kurdistan Republic was affected and was supported by the Kurds in other countries as well. Qazi (2012) writes that the Russian *Novaya Frimya*, Issue 25 (1949), stated that Kurdistan had turned into a bright light and a guide to the entire Kurdish nation. Groups of Kurds in Turkey, Syria, and Iraq sent letters to the Kurdistan Republic, offering help (p. 191). In February and March 1946, the chiefs of Jalali tribe in Turkey, such as Sheikh Adil and Amar Agha Jalali, contacted Qazi and claimed they commanded a cavalry and were ready to participate in the Kurdish movement in Iran (Qazi, 2012, p. 200). In September 1946, the representatives of the progressive Kurds of Syria, Qadri Baig, the nephew of Jamil Pasha, and the representatives of the Kurds of Turkey, Qazi Wahab, in order to support the Kurdish movement in Iran, visited Qazi Muhammad and offered signed letters of support to him (Qazi, 2012, p.201). Moreover, Fahd, the General Secretary of the Iraqi Communist Party, sent a letter to Qazi in which he supported the Kurdish national democratic experience (Sardashti, 2002b, p. 158). The Kurdish movement and the Kurdistan Republic were not supported by foreign countries, except for the Soviet Union, from which the Kurdistan Republic obtained significant aid (Gunter, 2009, p. 129).

Worried about the effects of the Iranian Kurdish movement on its Kurdish population, Turkey sent troops to the borders of Turkey and Iran (Sardashti, 2002b, p. 167). The British Ambassador to Tehran, Sir Redder Bullard, in his visit to Moscow on 20 December 1941, asked Molotov about the reasons for the visit of the Kurds to the Soviets. Molotov responded that the visit did not include political negotiations. In addition, Turkey, since 2 September 1941, had submitted its protest to Britain regarding the functions of some occupying forces in Iran, which meant the Soviets, which encouraged the Kurds to establish an independent state (Kutschera, 1994, p. 199). After the establishment of the Kurdistan Republic, Sardashti (2002b) writes that at the end of April 1946, Qazi visited Dooher, the Vice-Consul of the United States, in Tabriz and asked the United States to interfere in the problem of the Kurds with Iran in order to end the suppressing policy of the government. The United States's response was not positive (p. 174), while Britain completely supported the Iranian government (Sardashti, 2002b, p. 175).

5.6.2. The KDP's and the Kurdistan Republic's achievements. The Kurdistan Republic created a secure space for people in Kurdistan. It appears that during the Kurdistan Republic, Ghafour Mahmoudian, allegedly a double agent for Britain and Iran, was the only person who was assassinated (on 2 February 1946 in Mahabad). When Qazi heard about this, he became furious and asserted that he had never agreed with such actions (Samadi, 1998, pp. 188-189).

5.6.2.1. Economy. One of the Kurdistan Republic's undertakings was economic development. While Kurdistan was under the economic pressure of the Iranian government, the Kurdistan Republic tried to create commercial relations with the Soviet Union, Azerbaijan, and other parts of Iran (Gadani, 2008a, p. 56). Tobacco exports stood out as the main economic revenue for Kurdistan. Eagleton (1963) states that the Iranian government was supposed to pay for 10 percent of Mahabad's tobacco crop in early 1946 but discarded this purchase. The Soviets stepped up and bought the total tobacco of 1,875,000 kg for the sum of nearly $800,000. This was the most significant commercial deal at that time (pp. 87-88). *Shirkat-i Taraqi,* or Progress Company, was also established under Muhammad Amin Mo'ini, Qasim Utamishi, and Rahman Walizadeh in order to undertake business activities in Kurdistan (Eagleton, 1963, p. 135; Samadi, 1998, p. 172). Qazi (2005) maintains that Ahmad Ilahi exported tobacco to the Soviet Union, exchanging it for glassware, which he sold in Tabriz or Tehran (p. 71). In sum, during the Kurdistan Republic, tractors were brought to Kurdistan for the first time, and the economy of Kurdistan was revived due to trade with Tabriz and the Soviet Union (Hussein, 2008, p. 31).

5.6.2.2. *The class.* While Kurdish nationalism was the main characteristic of the KDP, in general, this party, the Kurdish movement, and the Kurdistan Republic supported social justice, the lower classes, and socialism. Many articles in the KDP's publications reveal the views defending the lower classes and admiring socialist ideas. According to the *Kurdistan*, Issue 2, M. M. Ishqi, in a poem about the life of a poor female student, writes that the brilliant and magnificent clothes of some girls come from the sucking of the proletarian's blood. In the near future, the feudal landlords and the bourgeoisie will be eliminated, and there will come the day when whoever does not work does not eat (Hussein, 2008, pp. 554-555). Abdullah Hijab, an alternate member of PDKI CC, asserts that the KDP and the Kurdistan Republic were pro-Soviet. In its programs, the KDP approved socialism and condemned imperialism (Girami, 2013, p. 6). While the KDP supported the lower classes, some examples reveal that it did not radically stand against the upper classes (Hussein, 2008, pp.564). In contrast to the Kurdistan Republic, the Autonomous Azerbaijan government took a radical position regarding the rights of the deprived classes. When the Azerbaijan National Government came to power, 437 landlords left Azerbaijan. The Azerbaijan government distributed 257,066 acres of land among 209,096 peasants (Mianali, 2005a, p. 271).

5.6.2.3. The youth. One of the important achievements of the KDP was the foundation of the youth organization called *Yaketi Jawanani Demokrati Kurdistan* (Democratic Youth Union of Kurdistan). It was established based on the Kurdish Youth Organization, which approximately had been created on 20 April 1942 in Mahabad. Ghani Bolourian was in charge of the Kurdish Youth Organization in Mahabad. It was joined the J.K. in November 1943 and renamed the J.K.'s Youth Organization. When the J.K. was replaced by the KDP on 23 October 1945, it was renamed the Democratic Youth Union of Kurdistan. Rahim Kharazi was later put in charge of this organization (Bolourian, 19997, pp. 22, 32-33; Qazi, 2005, pp. 62-63). The date of the foundation of the Democratic Youth Union of Kurdistan is not clear. According to some research, its name as, the Youth Union of Kurdistan first time appeared in the newspaper Kurdistan on 2 February 1946. It is claimed that the Democratic Youth Union of Kurdistan was established between 13 and 23 July 1946. However, it can be argued that because the first issue of *Govari Hawari*

Nishtman (Magazine Shout of Homeland), the magazine of the Democratic Youth Union of Kurdistan, was published on 21 March 1946, therefore, the organization had been established before this date ("Komitay Barewabari", 2015; Saleh and Saleh, 2007, p. 32; Hussein, 2008, pp. 106-107; Abdullahzadeh, 2011, pp. 12-15). It is concluded that since the transformation of the J.K. to the KDK, the Democratic Youth Union of Kurdistan has been a part of the KDP though it has been called by different names. The Democratic Youth Union of Kurdistan, under Seddiq Anjiri, published *Govari Hawari Nishtman* (Magazine Shout of Homeland) and the newspaper *rojnamay Hawari Nishtman* (newspaper Shout of Homeland). Also, this organization established three types of night classes in the Galawej School (Hussein, 2008, pp. 106-107, 713-755; Saleh and Saleh, 2007, pp. 313, 337).

5.6.2.4. The women's status. Compared to the J.K., the KDP and the Kurdistan Republic provided much more opportunities for the participation of women in the Kurdish nationalist movement. Shahrzad Mojab (2001) asserts that in the Kurdistan Republic, the educational and political situation of women was drastically different from the previous pre-modern types of Kurdish statehood. However, in both types, the state power was exercised based on a male-favoring gendered model. The Kurdish government provided the conditions for the participation of women in social life. Nevertheless, women entered the public area "in support of the national case rather than the activists in the women's movement or leaders or active cadres of the ruling party" (pp. 71-72). There is no indication to prove that the women who supported the Kurdistan Republic had (liberal) feminist inclinations (Mojab, 2001, pp. 84-85).

According to the *Kurdistan*, Issue 24 (13 March 1946), on 8 March 1946, women held a conference at the Kurdish-Soviet Cultural Society (Kurdistan-Soviet Cultural Relations Society) in Mahabad. Many of the participants, including women, delivered speeches. Mina Khanim, Qazi's wife, emphasized the importance of education for women and girls and the advancement of women in the

Soviet Union (Saleh and Saleh, 2007, p. 99). Mojab asserts that the conference did not address March 8, International Women's Day (Mojab, 2001, p. 81). According to the *Kurdistan*, Issue 25 (17 March 1946), *Hizbi Demokrati Jinani Kurdistan* (Democratic Party of the Women of Kurdistan) was established under Mina Khanim on 15 March 1946 (Saleh and Saleh, 2007, p. 103). Two versions of the organization's name have been reported in the pages of the *Kurdistan*: *Yeketi Jinani Demokrati Kurdistan* (Union of Democratic Women of Kurdistan) and the *Hizbi Yayan* (Ladies' Party) (Mojab, 2001, p. 81).

Ten women worked under Mina Khanim. The *Kurdistan*, Issue 77 (15 August 1946) reports the revenues and expenditures of the Democratic Party of the Women of Kurdistan (21 March 21 to 19 June 1946). The report reveals that the party had assigned ten women as the heads of ten districts of Mahabad (Saleh and Saleh, 2007, p. 308; Mojab, 2001, p. 81). For the first time, a Women's Committee was established in Mahabad, and many women undertook social activities like teaching, journalism, health services, speaking in ceremonies and celebrations, singing, and artistic works. Some of the active women who were associated with the *Kurdistan* or delivered speeches at ceremonies and celebrations were Mina Qazi, Amaneh Dawoudi, Ziba Ayyoubian Markazi, Shah Sultan Khanoum Fattahi Qazi, Rana Frouhar, Kolthum Sultanian, Nazakat Haj Rashidi, Khadijeh Haidari, Wilma Sayyadian, Kobra Azimi, Halab Ismail Faraji, Saltanat Dawoudzadeh, Eshrat Azimi, Iran Bolouri, Farideh Zand, Rouqya Qadiri, and Mazar (Mawzar) Bilazada (Homayoun, 2004, pp. 61-62; Hussein, 2008, p. 250).

Among other activities of women was the celebration of the International Workers' Day. According to the *Kurdistan*, Issue 46 (11 May 1946), the Democratic Party of the Women of Kurdistan celebrated May Day on 1 May 1946 (Saleh and Saleh, 2007, p. 188). The primary goal of the Women's Party was to organize adult women in order to attract their support for the Republic. The party's activities included establishing literacy classes for women, holding gatherings, fundraising for the Kurdish national army, taking part in demonstrations, writing in newspapers, and weaving clothes and socks for peshmergas (Mojab, 2001, p. 82). Besides, women also participated in Kurdish publications in other parts of the country (Hussein, 2008, pp. 173, 192-193). Women in other parts of Kurdistan, such as Iraqi Kurdistan, also financially assisted the Kurdistan Republic (Sardashti, 2002b, p. 158).

Although the Women's Party showed women's participation in political life, it "justified their exclusion from the decision-making ranks of the KDP…. [The Women's Party] also formalized the segregation of the rank-and-file along gender lines, each having its own organization. Clearly, the two were not on the same footing" (Mojab, 2001, p. 86). While Mojab's points are valuable, it should be addressed that it is unfair to the women activists in Kurdistan 70 years ago to be judged by the standards of the present time. Indeed, the women's achievements during the Kurdistan Republic were progressive for its time.

5.6.2.5. The minorities. The Kurdistan government valued minority rights. It made it compulsory for Jewish children, girls and boys, to register in a Kurdish-Hebrew school in Mahabad (Khoshhali, 2001, pp. 53-54). Nerwiy (2012) asserts that the Kurdistan Republic was popular amongst the Kurdish people since it protected the rights of other ethnic groups, including Jews, Azeris, and Armenians (p. 257). The Jews supported the Kurdistan Republic. *Kurdistan*, Issue 20 (27 February 1946) reports that Khizir Dawoudzadeh, the representative of the Jews in Mahabad, sent a congratulatory message to *Kurdistan* and wished that freedom would expand to all Kurdish territories. In addition, the *Kurdistan*, Issue 22 (4 March 1946), revealed that the Jewish community in Mahabad held a two-day celebration for independence and introduced Qazi on 13 February 1946 (Saleh and Saleh, 2007, pp. 78, 85). In 1945, about 60 Jewish families were living in Mahabad. When the Kurdish schools were established in Mahabad, a school headed by Dawoudzadeh was founded for Jewish children in order to teach them their mother tongue (Homayoun, 2004, pp. 62-63). Dawoudzadeh encouraged the parents to register both their girls and boys (Mustafa Amin, 2007, p. 157).

5.6.2.6. The army. The Kurdistan Republic established *Wazarati Hezi Dimokrati Kurdistan* (Kurdistan Democrat Force Ministry), also known as the War Ministry (Mustafa Amin, 2007, p. 148, 181; Sardashti, 2002b, p. 144). The Ministry established a Kurdish army called *Hezi Dimokrati Kurdistan* (Kurdistan Democratic Force), comprised of soldiers called peshmerga from the peshmergas of Mullah Mustafa Barzani, Kurdish citizens, and Kurdish tribal forces. Barzani's army was a milestone for the foundation of the Kurdish army. In October 1945, Barzani and 9,000 followers reached Mahabad's outskirts, and in early March of 1946, Barzani's armed forces in Mahabad were more than 3,000 (O'Ballance, 1973, pp. 49, 52). It must be noted that some tribal chiefs conducted military activities against the Kurdistan Republic. According to Ezat (1995), on 1 May 1946, Aziz Moradi, the Commander of the Kurdistan Democratic Force in Bukan, reported that the Dehbukri Aghas had prepared themselves to attack, having gathered tribesmen in villages like Hamamiyan and Mirava (p. 455).

According to Kinnane (1964), in February 1946, the Soviets gave 5,000 Bren and Colt machine guns and rifles, tank destroyers, and Molotov Cocktails to the Kurdish Republic. Later, the Kurds also received ten Russian trucks, as well as ten old American trucks and ten jeeps. In addition, the Soviets sent a military officer to Kurdistan for military training of the Kurds. Most of this training was conducted by the four Kurdish-Iraqi officers who had come with Barzani to Mahabad (p. 52). The total Soviet military help to the Republic reached 10,000 rifles, pistols, and machine guns and about 20 trucks. In addition, in March 1946, the Soviets sent Major Salah al-Din Kazimov (aka Kak Agha or Kakagha), along with some Kurdish officers who had come to Iran with Barzani, for the military training of the Kurds (Kutschera, 1994, p. 213).

The exact number of the Kurdish peshmergas is disputed. The War Minister claimed it to be 45,000. Shamzini claimed 10,000-11,000, Arfa 12,000, Eagleton 12,750. According to Gadani, during the Kurdistan Republic, about 2,000 men received military training. In addition, the tribal forces provided more than 12,000 armed men (Sardashti, 2002b, p. 146; Hussein, 2008, p. 32; Eagleton, 1963, pp. 91-92; Gadani, 2008a, p. 53). Mahmod Mola Ezat (1995) reveals a comprehensive list of the Kurdistan Republic's military ranks with their salaries (pp. 388-389).

5.6.2.7. Cultural and educational works of the KDP and the Kurdistan Republic. Since its foundation and during the Kurdistan Republic, the KDP published several journals and newspapers. The proliferation, volume, extent, and quality of these Kurdish publications were much higher than those of the previous nationalist publications in Iranian Kurdistan. The KDP publications, before and during the Kurdistan Republic, included six magazines and newspapers (Hussein, 2008, pp. 74-78, 82-84, 97, 105, 106-107, 117, 120, 713-775, 759; Gadani, 2008a, p. 51; Saleh and Saleh, 2007, p. 337). Coinciding with the Kurdistan Republic events, Kurdish journalists in Tehran, Sanandaj, Kermanshah, and other parts of Iran were following the events of Kurdistan, Azerbaijan, and Iran (Hussein, 2008, pp. 12, 123-124, 128; Karimi, 1999, p. 628; see Appendix 12).

The KDP established the Kurdistan printing house launched on 10 January 1946 in Mahabad (Gadani, 2008a, p. 49), and a printing house was also founded in Bukan (Hussein, 2008, pp. 33-36), in addition to a radio station, named *Radio Dangi Kurdistan* (Voice of Kurdistan Radio), launched on 30 April 1946 in Mahabad (Gadani, 2008a, p. 51). The next undertaking of the Kurdistan Republic was the establishment of a cinema in Mahabad, which was announced in *Kurdistan*, Issue 62 (27 June 1946) (Saleh and Saleh, 2007, p. 250). The cinema showed movies from the Soviet Union (Gadani, 2008a, p. 51).

Among other educational activities of the Kurdistan Republic was the establishment of different schools in Kurdistan. One of the articles of the KDP Program emphasizes compulsory education of children in primary and secondary schools (Hussein, 2007, p. 33). According to Balaki, the Kurdistan Republic established a mixed school (Personal communication, September 28, 2012). In Mahabad, eight new schools for girls and boys were opened, and the number of students reached 1,600. In addition, in Bukan, Oshnavieh, and Naqadeh, new schools were also established. In Oshnavieh, for the first time a girls' school was opened (Sardashti, 2002b, p. 140). On 21 March 1946, an adult women's school was established in Mahabad. The teacher was Kobra Azimi (Saleh and Saleh, 2007, p. 131). Manaf Karimi reports that Kurdish books and some of the teachers to teach the Kurdish language in schools actually came from Kurdistan of Iraq. After a cultural board made the necessary changes to the books, they were published in the Mahabad print house and were distributed in the schools and public libraries (Homayoun, 2004, p. 120). As well as Kurdish, the Russian language was also taught in Kurdistan. According to the *Kurdistan*, Issue 71 (28, July 1346), Muhammad (Dilshad) Rasouli, the vice-president of the Culture (Education) Office of Mahabad, announced that the Office had opened two evening Russian classes for the public in the Galawej School (Saleh and Saleh, 2007, p. 284).

One of the social programs of the Kurdistan Republic was assisting poor children to continue their education. Gadani (2008a) claims that hundreds of poor children were divided between the rich, who provided the possibility of life and studying for these children (p. 57). Eagleton (1963) states that as the President, Qazi Muhammad's salary was $700 per month, while cabinet members' salaries stood at $65 per month. But Qazi would not accept money for his work (p. 83) and donated his salary to the Kurdish schools (Qazi, 2005, p. 70).

The founding Kurdish National Library was another cultural achievement of the Kurdistan Republic. The *Kurdistan*, Issue 25 (17 March 1946), announced that Qazi ordered the foundation of the national library in Mahabad, and according to *Kurdistan*, Issue 64 (2 July 1946), *Kitebkhanay Farhang* (Culture Library) was founded next to Galawej School in Mahabad (Saleh and Saleh, 2007, pp. 103, 255).

Another educational task of the Kurdistan Republic was to provide educational opportunities for the youth by sending them to Baku and Tabriz. In April-May 1946, about 80 young men were sent to study in the Soviet Union in Baku. Some youths were also sent to Tabriz for military training (Gadani, 2008a, p. 51). According to Abdullah Qazi, 33 young men were sent to Tabriz for six months for military training (Qazi, 2005, p. 75).

The next significant cultural activity was the extension of the Kurdish literary relations with the Azerbaijanis as well as the Soviet Azeris. A collection of Hajar's poems titled *Alakok* (Falsify), Hajar's other poems, and his biography were translated to Azari by Jafar Khandan, a knowledgeable Soviet officer. They were published by *Soviet Madaniyat Evi* (Soviet Cultural House; Soviet Cultural Society in Azerbaijan) in Tabriz. These publications were the newspaper *Watan Yolinda* (For Homeland's Sake), the magazine *Shafaq* (Aurora), and a book titled *Shaeirlar Majlisi* (Poets' Sessions). In addition, Khandan published them in the magazine *Azerbaijan,* which was published in Baku (Hussein, 2008, pp. 846-847).

5.6.2.8. *Kurdistan-Azerbaijan relations.* Since the beginning of the Azerbaijan movement, the Kurds had tried to create friendly relations with the Azeris: the KDP congratulated the establishment of the Azerbaijan National Government. Eagleton (1963) states that the Soviet Union's officials advised the Kurds to send five representatives to participate in the Provincial National Assembly in Tabriz. The Kurds sent Saifi Qazi, Haji Mustafa Dawoudi, Manaf Karimi, Karim Ahmadain, and Wahab Bolourian to that Assembly. The delegates realized that they had been considered not as separate delegates of Kurdistan but as specific constituencies like other cities of Azerbaijan. After three sessions, they returned to Kurdistan (p. 60). This policy of the Azeris created tensions between the Kurds and Azeris so that when the Kurdistan Republic was founded, the Azeris did not initially recognize it. According to Nerwiy (2012), from the establishment of the Republic of Kurdistan until April 1946, the "newspaper *Azerbaijan*, organ of the Azerbaijan Democratic Party, mentioned no issue about the Kurds and the Kurdish government" (p. 209). The Azeris planned to subordinate the Kurdish Republic to Azerbaijan (Mobley, 2008, p. 42). Another factor that created tension between the Kurds and the Azeris was the condition of the borders between them (Mobley, 2008, p. 55). Some cities, such as Miandoab, Naqadeh, Urmiya, Khoy, Shapur, and Maku, in the Province of Western Azerbaijan, comprise mixed Kurdish-Azeri populations. When the Azerbaijan government attempted to control these territories, it faced the opposition of the Kurds. In addition, the radical land reform initiated by the Azerbaijan government created conflicts in Kurdistan.

Mobley (2008) reports that in 1946, the land reform in Azerbaijan irritated the Kurdish khans (tribal chiefs). When the land conflict with Kurdistan was not resolved through diplomatic efforts, the Azeris threatened the Kurds with military force. However, the Azeris' small army was unable to face the Kurdish tribes. Tabriz relied on the non-military tactics of the Soviets to solve the problem. Mobley shows the scope of these conflicts ranging from June to September 27, 1946. On August 9, Qazi and Pishevari met in Urmiya to solve the disagreements (Mobley, 2008, pp. 45-46, 91-92). Eagleton (1963) states that in mid-April 1946, the Soviet Union officials encouraged the two governments to negotiate and solve their problems (p. 82). On 23 April 1946, the Friendship Treaty of Azerbaijan and Kurdistan was signed in Tabriz (Mianali, 2005a, p. 430; Homayoun, 2004, p. 69; Saleh and Saleh, 2007, p. 183; see Appendix 11).

In order to divide the Kurds and Azeris and destroy their friendship, Prime Minister Qavam al-Saltaneh secretly sent a telegraph to Qazi Muhammad. In response, Qazi exposed Qavam al-Saltaneh's deceptive policies, stating that he could not destroy the friendship between Azeri and Kurdish peoples (Mianali, 2005b, pp. 432-433). After the Treaty, the cooperation between Azerbaijan and

Kurdistan expanded to include military cooperation (Abdul Karim Hawezi, 2001, pp. 95, 99, 103).

5.6.3. The Kurdistan Republic and the Iranian government. During its tenure, the Kurdistan Republic negotiated with the Iranian government regarding the demands of the Kurds. Based on the Treaty with Azerbaijan and a profound trust in them, the Kurds also gave authority to Pishevari to negotiate with the government for both the Kurds and Azeris.

Sardashti maintains that the joined Kurdish and Azeri representatives went to Tehran on 28 April 1946. Their main demand was autonomy. They returned home on 13 May 1946 empty-handed (Hawrami, 2007, p. 129). However, in the negotiation with Tehran and while having a Friendship Agreement with the Kurds, the Azeris treated Kurdistan as a part of Azerbaijan and not an equal partner (Homayoun, 2004, p. 70).

While the government was negotiating with the Azeris and the Kurds, it conducted a war against the Kurds. The First Mamasha War between the Kurds and the government occurred on 29 April 1946 when 700 Iranian troops, supported by artillery, tanks, armor-clad, and two planes, attacked the Kurdish trenches near Baneh. Under Colonel Mustafa Khoshnaw, the peshmerga withstood the attack around the village of Mamasha. The army retreated with 100 casualties, leaving behind 30 captured soldiers and a tank. The Kurdistan government asked the tribal forces to move from Mahabad toward Saqqiz. These forces were also ready to move toward southern Kurdistan and occupy the garrisons in Sardasht, Baneh, Saqqiz, and Sanandaj. But Qazi Muhammad and the Kurdish government authorities did not wish to earn autonomy through war. Arfa claims that the Iranian army included 600 men. The army "sustained heavy losses and had to retreat to Saqqez" (Homayoun, 2004, pp. 63-64; Abdul Karim Hawezi, 2001, p. 56; Sardashti, 2002b, p. 197; Arfa, 1966, p. 90). Haji Baba Sheikh Siadat, Muhammad Rashid Khan, Mullah Mustafa, most of the tribal chiefs, and the KDP's members believed

Kurdish forces should liberate Saqqiz, Sanandaj, and Kermanshah. But Qazi was searching for a peaceful solution (Sardashti, 2002b, p. 195). A ceasefire agreement was made between Major-General Razmara and Qazi Muhammad in the village of Sara. According to Sardashti, the ceasefire came into effect on 26 May 1946 between the Kurdish representatives under Ezat Abdul Aziz and Major-General Razmara (Homayoun, 2004, p. 68; Hawrami, 2007, p. 138; Arfa, 1966, p. 91).

The negotiations continued between the Kurds and the Azeris with the government. It was supposed that Peshevari would represent the Kurds, too. Sardashti claims that Mozaffar Firouz and Azeri leaders signed a 15-article Agreement in Tabriz on 13 June 1946. In this agreement, the only thing mentioned about the Kurds was that they could study the Kurdish language until the fifth grade (Hawrami, 2007, pp. 129, 157). The Pishevari-Firouz treaty stayed silent concerning the Kurdish request for an autonomous Kurdistan. Article 13 of the Agreement recognized the Kurds as people who live in Azerbaijan but *not* as citizens of the Kurdistan Republic (Vali, 2011, p. 60). The Kurds were unsatisfied with the Azeri leaders because they prioritized Azerbaijan's interests and disregarded the Kurds' demands in the negotiations.

After the Firouz-Pishevari Agreement, Qazi Muhammad went to Tabriz to meet with the Azerbaijani leaders about their agreement with Iran. However, the Iranian government took the opportunity and, with command of Qavam al-Saltaneh and Razmara, the army, in order to open the Saqqiz-Baneh road, attacked the Kurds again in Mamasha on 15 June 1946 (Homayoun, 2004, pp. 66-67). On 15 June 1946, Mir Haj, the commander of Branch 2 of Barzanis, reported that the Iranian regime bombed the Kurds using airplanes and cannons (Ezat, 1995, p. 629). This was when the Iranian army attacked the Kurds in Mamasha for the second time. According to the *Kurdistan*, Issue 66 (9 July 1946), the Mamasha War occurred on 15 June 1946 when Major-General Razmara ordered the 4th Army under Brigadier Homayouni to move from Saqqiz and attack the Mamasha Hill on the Mountain

Malqarni. The Iranian army included 3,000 soldiers, 8 cannons, two airplanes, and two tanks (Saleh and Saleh, 2007, p. 262; Abdul Karim Hawezi, 2001, pp. 64-65). The government asked Qazi Muhammad and Dr. Salamullah Jawid, Minister of Interior of Azerbaijan, to negotiate the evacuation of the Iranian forces from Saqqiz, Sardasht, and Baneh. The negotiations occurred on 28 June 1946. Qazi Muhammad requested the extension of all rights of the Agreement of 13 June 1946 to Kurdistan (Khoshhali, 2001, p. 78). The negotiations were useless.

Some evidence shows that Qazi trusted Qavam al-Saltaneh's policies regarding Kurdistan. According to *Kurdistan*, Issue 65 (5 July 1946), in an interview with the *Iran-e Ma* (Our Iran), Qazi asserted that the Kurdish nation had faith in the pure intentions of Qavam al-Saltaneh and was sure that the Kurdish problem would be solved in the interest of democracy and freedom for all and the Kurdish nation's rights (Saleh and Saleh, 2007, p. 260). In July 1946, a delegation under Colonel Firouz went to Mahabad and told Qazi that, at that time, the central government was not ready to grant autonomy to the Kurds unless they put their weapons down. Qazi responded that he could not ask this from the Kurds (Khoshhali, 2001, p. 79).

On 16 October 1946, the governments of Kurdistan and Azerbaijan established a Common Defense Commission and agreed on the eight points (Khoshhali, 2001, p. 82; Sardashti, 2002b, pp. 207-208). Although the Kurds did not have strong relations with the democratic Iranian political organizations, they attempted to cooperate with them. According to the *Ettelaat*, on 5 September 1946, Qazi sent a telegraph to Qavam al-Saltaneh, the leader of the Democratic Party of Iran, the Tudeh Party, and the Democratic Party of Azerbaijan, and agreed to participate in a front (Hawrami, 2007, p. 47). In a telegraph on 25 November 1946 to the *Kouhestan* (Mountain), the KDP congratulated the cooperation of six freedom-seeking political parties, including the KDP, the Azerbaijan Democratic Party, the Socialist Party, and the *Jangal Party* (*Ejtema'iyoun*) (Hawrami, 2007, p.

47; Madani, 2001, pp. 303-304). In November 1946, Pishevari made another secret agreement with the Iranian government. One of the points of agreement was that Azerbaijan was supposed to give up the control of Zanjan; instead, the government gave control of the two Kurdish cities of Sardasht and Tikan Tapah (Tekab) to the Azerbaijan government (Mobley, 2008, pp. 82, 106).

While Qazi Muhammad was striving to strengthen the position of Kurdistan by cooperating with the democratic Iranian parties, the unity among the Kurds was collapsing. Some tribes developed secret relationships with the Iranian government. Mobley (2008) reveals that at the end of September 1946, some Kurdish tribal chiefs announced their allegiance to the government in return for the government's treating them in the future. The representative of Omar Khan Shikak met with Dooher, the Vice-Consul of the United States in Tabriz, a few times. Dooher acted as the mediator between the chiefs and the central government and exchanged their letters (pp. 75-76).

The negotiations of the Kurds and Azeris with the Iranian government were fruitless. The government was deceiving them and preparing itself for a major attack on Azerbaijan and Kurdistan.

5.6.4. The fall of the Kurdistan Republic. After a series of negotiations, Iran and the Soviet Union made a concession over the Caspian oil on 4 April 1946. It was also agreed that the Soviet Union not interfere in Azerbaijan's affairs as it was considered an internal Iranian issue. Besides, the Soviet Union pledged to withdraw the Red Army from Iran, and it evacuated Iran by 9 May 1946. Later, on 22 October 1947, Iran's parliament rejected the Iran-Soviet pact (Khoshhal, 2001, pp. 69-70; Nerwiy, 2012, p. 252; Hawrami, 2008, p. 315). The withdrawal of the Red Army allowed the Iranian government to suppress Azerbaijan and Kurdistan's democratic movements without any hindrance. The Iranian government, on the pretext of providing security for the parliament election, but in reality, for the purpose of suppressing Azerbaijan and Kurdistan, deployed a military force of

25,700 soldiers to the borders of Kurdistan and Azerbaijan, 18,700 of which on the Kurdistan borders. In addition, the Gendarmerie and tribal forces that supported the government were already in the territory. The Iranian army was equipped with 3200 machine guns, 70 mortars, 104 cannons, 55 tanks and armored vehicles, and 50 airplanes (Qazi, 2012, pp. 275-276). George Allen, the United States Ambassador, approved the Iranian government's decision to send security forces all over the country to establish order (Madani, 2001, p. 305).

On 5 December 1946, the Kurdish leaders formed a War Council, including 10 officials, in Mahabad. The Council decided to defend the liberated Kurdish territory. It was approved to hold a meeting in Abbas Agha Mosque the next day to consult with people regarding this subject (Sardashti, 2002b, p.210). On 6 December 1946, in the meeting in Abbas Agha Mosque in Mahabad, Qazi Muhammad and Sadr Qazi supported the idea of not letting the army enter Mahabad. Others, such as Sayyed Muhammad Ishaqi, Mullah Abdullah Modarresi, and Mullah Hussein Majdi, thought that the defense was useless and that Kurdistan did not have a chance against the army, and therefore, the Kurds should allow the army to enter Mahabad (Sardashti, 2002b, p. 210). In the yard of Abbas Agha Mosque, the majority of people decided to not resist the Iranian army (Homayoun, 2004, p. 89; Hemin, 1999, pp. 24-25).

On 8 December 1946, while in Zanjan, the Shah ordered the army to attack Azerbaijan and Kurdistan. On 10 December 1946, the army defeated the Azerbaijan Fadai force, entered Mianeh, and then occupied Maragheh. The discord within the leadership of Azerbaijan caused Pishevari to flee to the Soviet Union, while Dr. Jawid and Ali Shabestari, who had already established contacts with the Iranian government, wrote a telegraph to the government on 12 December 1946 in which they surrendered themselves. On 13 December 1946, the army, without any resistance, entered Tabriz (Sardashti, 2002b, pp. 211-212).

On the night of 11 December 1946, Qazi Muhammad announced his surrender to Iran. He asked Mullah Mustafa Barzani to withdraw his forces from the fronts. The documents of the party, printing house, and Qazi's office were burned by the orders of Qazi and Kurdistan Republic leaders. In the morning, along with the Iranian officials, he went to *Mizgawti Sour* (Red Mosque) in Mahabad. In his speech, he mentioned two reasons for this decision: first, the United States and Britain supported the Iranian government. Second, Azerbaijan was unfaithful to the Kurds because without seeking the Kurdish opinion, it had surrendered to the Iranian government (Manguri, 2001, p. 101).

After the collapse of the Azerbaijan government on 13 December 1946, members of the KDP's CC and Mullah Mustafa Barzani asked Qazi Muhammad to leave Iran for Iraq or the Soviet Union. As well, the British Consul in Tabriz asked him to go to England via Iraq, just as the Americans asked him to leave Iran. However, he rejected all of these suggestions. Qazi Muhammad announced a unilateral cease-fire and issued the following announcement:

> The Iranian army reached Tabriz, and without having the ability to defend itself, Pishevari's government collapsed. After much negotiation, we decided to leave our trenches and welcome the Iranian army. Now, I ask the Iraqi Kurds to return to Iraq and ask the Iranian Kurds to surrender to the nearest Iranian post. Your brother, Qazi Muhammad. (Khoshhali, 2001, pp. 251-252)

On 16 December 1946, Mullah Mustafa Barzani returned to Mahabad and asked Qazi to leave the city (Sardashti, 2002b, p. 214), which he rejected. Qazi talked to Brigadier Homayouni on 16 December 1946 and, along with Saifi Qazi, Haji Baba Sheikh Siadat, and several others, he surrendered to Homayouni in the village of Hamamian in Bukan (Hussein, 2008, p. 43). After negotiation with

Homayouni, Qazi Muhammad and others were allowed to return to Mahabad and prepare the conditions for the peaceful return of the Iranian army to Mahabad

The last visit of Mullah Mustafa Barzani and Qazi Muhamad took place on 17 December 1945 in Mahabad. Once again, Barzani asked Qazi to leave Iran, but Qazi replied that he knew that he would be executed, but he stayed so that the Kurdish people would not be hurt. Qazi Muhammad took the flag of Kurdistan on his desk, kissed it, and gave it to Barzani, saying: "Keep Kurdistan's flag with you. I hope you do not let this flag fall" (Homayoun, 2004, p. 92-93). On 16 or 17 December 1946, Qazi handed over 3,000 rifles, 120 machine guns, two cannons, and grenades to the Barzanis (Eagleton, 1963, p. 115; Homayoun, 2004, p. 121). On 17 December 1946, Qazi and other leaders of the Kurdistan Republic went to the village of Gok Tapa to welcome the Iranian army under Colonel Ghafari (Gohari, 1999, p. 151). The Iranian army entered Mahabad, and thus, the Kurdistan Republic came to an end (Eagleton, 1963, p. 115). On 21 December 1946, Sadr Qazi was arrested in Tehran, brought to Mahabad, and imprisoned with the other Qazis in the Mahabad Garrison (Qazi, 2012, p. 300). Finally, on 22 December 1946, Qazi Muhammad, Muhammad Hussein Saifi Qazi, and Haj Baba Sheikh Siadat were arrested in Mahabad (Homayoun, 2004, p. 8; Samadi, 1984, p. 14).

5.6.4.1. *Trial and execution of the Qazis*. A court-martial was held under Colonel Parsi Tabar, Military Commander of Mahabad, and the public prosecutor, Colonel Fiuzi, the Force Chief of Staff. Captain Sharif was the court-appointed attorney for Qazi Muhammad. Because he faithfully defended Qazi and believed that charges against him were unfair, Brigadier Homayouni (who, after the occupation of Mahabad, became Major-General Homayouni) became angry with him. In 1947, Captain Sharif had been promoted to Major, but because of his defending Qazi he was demoted (Homayoun, 2004, pp. 95-96).

When Qazi Muhammad was asked to explain why he surrendered himself, he exclaimed that Sadr Qazi had deceived him; otherwise, he knew that the Iranian government did not have a trace of honor (Manguri, 2001, pp. 105-106). Captain Kiumarth Saleh, the reporter for the Iranian army magazine who attended the Qazis' trial, states that on 26 January 1947, the Iranian delegation, under Colonel Gholam Hussein Azimi, entered Mahabad and held a trial for the Qazis. The charges against the Qazis were vague, and they expressly rejected the charges (Saleh, 2003, p. 9). But because it was a formality (*farmayeshi*) court and the sentences had already been issued in Tehran, the officials did not provide any evidence. In a few hours, the Qazis' death sentences were handed down (Saleh, 2003, pp. 6-7; see Appendix 13).

On 22 January 1947, the Qazis were sentenced to death (Qazi, 2012, p. 307). However, the government postponed the carrying out of the sentences. During the trial of Qazis, the United States Ambassador, George Allen, its Consul in Tabriz, Lester Sutton, its former Vice-Consul Gerald F. P. Dooher in Tabriz, the American Church representative in Tabriz, Livingston Bentley, and the British Consul in Tabriz, Kars, had traveled to Kurdistan and even met the Qazis in prison (Qazi, 2012, p. 310; Khoshhali, 2001, p. 290).

While General Homayouni wanted to execute the Qazis on 23 January 1947, he received a telegraph from Tehran ordering him to pause. Before their execution, the government transferred them to hidden locations in Tehran where, on 5 February 1947, the Kurds from Ardalan, Sanandaj, Ilkhanizadeh, and Fahimi met them. They asked the Qazis to recant, issue a declaration asking the Kurdish tribes to disarm, issue announcements against the Tudeh Party and the Soviet Union to announce that they had provoked the Qazis, and ask forgiveness in letters to the Shah and the Prime Minister. In this case, they would be freed. George Allen and General Herbert Norman Schwarzkopf told Qazis that if they followed the United States' policy regarding the Kurds, they would be set free. Qazi Muhammad rejected the offers while claiming that he would not betray his nation (Qazi, 2012, pp. 311-313). During his imprisonment, Qazi Muhammad contacted the Soviet

Consulate in Tabriz on 27 February 1947, asking them to liberate the Qazis (Qazi, 2012, p. 315).

During the trials of the Qazis, the government provided a petition demanding the execution of Qazi Muhammad (Samadi, 1998, pp. 191-192). It turned out that government agents, including Officer Muhammad Attari and Sheikh Abdul Rahman, took the petition to the peoples' homes for signing. Even Mullah Hussein Majdi, the Minister of Justice, and Mullah Seddiq Sedqi had signed the petition (Qazi, 2005, p. 100; Karimi, 1999, p. 397).

Kiumarth Saleh maintains that, after three months, another Iranian delegation went to Mahabad to hold an appeal court for the Qazis. The delegation comprised Colonel Reza Nikoozadeh (Public Prosecutor), Colonel Rajab Atayy (Head of the Court), Captain Hussein Solh Jou, and Captain Nabavi (state-appointed Attorney for the Qazis). The Qazis' defenses included 114 pages, but nobody had read it in the previous three months. On 29 March 1947, the Court held its second session and ended at 12 PM. The Court sentenced all of them to death (Saleh, 2003, pp. 19-20, 36). On 31 March 1947, between 3 and 6 AM, first Qazi Muhammad, and then Muhammad Hussein Saifi Qazi and Abulqasim Sadr Qazi were executed at *Maidani Chowar Chira* (Four Light Square) in Mahabad (Samadi, 1998, pp. 179-183). Under the gallows, Muhammad Hussein Saifi Qazi shouted, "Long Live the Peshaway [Leader; i.e., Qazi Muhammad] of the Kurdish Nation," "Long Live Liberation," and "Long Live Stalin." At the time of his execution, the rope broke, and he fell. When the officers tried to hang him for the second time, he shouted at them that they, their feeble shah, and their way of governing were worn out like this execution rope (Qazi, 2012, pp. 328-329). Many experts believe that Razmara and the United States Ambassador George Allen attended the hanging and did not leave until they were sure that the Qazis were executed (Shirazi, 2000, p. 130; Qazi, 2012, pp. 325-326). According to Badr al-Din Saleh (2003), Captain Kiumarth Saleh revealed Qazi Muhammad's testament in which he addressed the

Kurdish nation (pp. 46-48).

The Qazis faithfully and radically defended the Kurdish nation and finally gave their lives to obtain the right of self-determination for the Kurdish nation and establish a just, democratic system in Iran.

After the death of Qazis (31 March 1947), the government also hung four other Kurds in Mahabad on 7 April 1947. In addition, 11 people were already had been executed in Saqqiz and Bukan on 14 February 1947. In total, 18 people were executed in Kurdistan (Homayoun, 2004, pp. 109-110; Khoshhali, 2001, p. 269; see Appendix 14). Samadi (1998) reveals the names of 27 Mahabad residents who were imprisoned and seven who escaped to Iraq (pp. 173-174; Homayoun, 2004, p. 94; Manguri, 2001, p. 159). According to Roosevelt (1980), the Iranian regime resorted to repression in order to reverse the accomplishments of the Kurdistan Republic. "The Kurdish printing press was closed, the teaching of Kurdish was prohibited, and all books in Kurdish were publicly burned" (p. 149).

5.6.4.2. The Kurdish Liberation Movement. After the fall of the Kurdistan Republic, some Kurds continued their resistance. The Kurdish liberation movement lasted until June 1947, when the Kurdistan peshmergas resisted the Iranian government (Qazi, 2012, p. 289). On the same night when Qazi Muhammad was arrested, 1,150 armed peshmergas in Mahabad, under the officer Muhammad Mawloudian, joined Mullah Mustafa Barzani's peshmergas who were in the territories of Naqadeh and Oshnavieh (Qazi, 2012, p. 293). At the beginning of January 1947, a meeting of 27 heads of *Hezi Peshmergay Kurdistan* (Kurdistan Peshmerga Forces) under Sheikh Ahmad Barzani was held. They called themselves the *Najatdari Kurdistan* (Liberator of Kurdistan). They posed four demands to the Iranian government: First, all of the peshmergas of Iran and Iraq who had fought for the independence of Kurdistan, including the participants in the Barzani's movement, should be pardoned. Second, the Iranian and Iraqi governments should compensate for all the causalities they caused the Barzanis. Third, they should grant

Kurdistan its independence, and all political parties should be free. Fourth, the government should not disarm the Kurds. In addition, in the meeting, it was decided that in order to strengthen all sides, they should contact the Tudeh Party and the KDP (Iraq) (Qazi, 2012, pp. 294-295). In order to revive the Kurdistan Republic, Mullah Mustafa visited and asked Sayyed Abdullah Afandi [Gailani], the grandson of Sheikh Ubayd Allah of Nehri and the CC member of the KDP] to be the President of the Kurdistan Republic. He said that he was too old and unable to accept such a responsibility (Abdul Karim Hawezi, 2001, p. 127).

Another resisting territory was around Maku and Urmiya, under Zero Baig Bahadiri (Harki). Even Haidar Baig, a tribal chief of Kurdistan in Turkey, along with its cavalry, joined them. They killed 700 soldiers, captured 320, obtained 500 rifles, and after the death of Qazi Muhammad, they executed 19 officers. Also, in Saqqiz and Bukan, resistance continued under Ahmad Khan Farouqi and Ali Khan Sherzad (Qazi, 2012, pp. 293-294, 317, 330-331). Six months after the fall of the Kurdistan Republic, when they were pardoned by the government, the Shikaks were disarmed (Mamadi, 1999, p. 11).

5.6.4.3. The Barzanis' fight. According to Bakir Abdul Karim Hawezi, the commander of the front of Sardasht and Baneh, the KDP (Iraq) was established in February 1946. Qazi Muhammad, for two reasons, asked to dissolve the party: first, to prevent damages to the Kurdistan Republic that might have been caused by Turkey and Iraq, supported by the Allies, and second, the KDP in Iran was a party for all Kurdistan. The Kurdish Republic provided all kinds of support to the Kurds in Iraq. Mullah Mustafa agreed to the dissolution of the KDP (Iraq) (Abdul Karim Hawezi, 2001, pp. 16, 37, 39-40). On 21 December 1946, Barzani went to Tehran and visited the Shah, the Prime Minister, and other Iranian authorities. The government gave him three suggestions (Manguri, 2001, p. 58; Sardashti, 2002b, p. 222). It was supposed that the Barzanis would leave Iran on 4 February 1947. On 21 February 1947, the Iranian army, accompanied by the tribal forces of

Shahsewan, Dehbukri, Mamash, Mangur, Piran, and Zarza, under Major-General Homayouni, using planes, tanks, and armored vehicles, savagely attacked Barzanis. For two months, while retreating toward the Iraqi border, the Barzanis were attacked by the Iranian forces and fought against them in winter conditions. Four officers of the Tudeh Party had escaped and joined the Barzanis; they were Captain Rais Dana, Lieutenant Kamali, Lieutenant Fatemi, and Lieutenant Yaqoubi (Manguri, 2001, pp. 59-60; Abdul Karim Hawezi, 2001, pp. 13, 136).

On 11 March 1947, the Iranian army attacked the Barzanis (Sardashti, 2002b, p. 223). On 20 March 1947, Major-General Homayouni met the Commander of Police in Iraq, Sayyed Ali Hijazi, in Haji Omran. They planned to suppress the Barzanis. Turkey established three bases on the borders of Turkey and Iran in order to persecute the Barzanis (Manguri, 2001, p. 72). On 13 April 1947, the Barzanis passed the Gadar River and entered Iraq (Sardashti, 2002b, p. 224). On 16 April 1947, through the Gadar Bridge, the Barzanis surrendered themselves to the Iraqi government. However, 500 of them who were able to carry weapons stayed with Mullah Mustafa Barzani. They entered Iraq on 20 April 1947. From then, until 25 May 1947, they moved from the borderland of Iraq and Turkey while facing clashes with the military forces of these countries. They entered Iran on 26 May 1947 (Zarbakht, 1998, pp. 33, 46; Abdul Karim Hawezi, 2001, p. 136). Manguri (2001) states that on 28 May 1947, based on trust between Barzani and the Soviet Union, Mullah Mustafa moved toward the Soviet Union (p. 86).

According to Eagleton (1963), the Barzanis marched about 350 kilometers in 14 days (p. 129). The Iranian military deployed a force of about 8,000 soldiers, five artilleries, twelve tanks, five groups of mortars, and six airplanes to repress the Barzanis (Manguri, 2001, p. 88; Homayoun, 2004, pp. 121-122). According to Kazim Shandri, on 16 and 17 June 1947 (based on the report of Mir Haj Ahmad Aqrawi, on 17 and 18 June 1947), all Barzanis passed the Aras River to the Soviet Republic of Azerbaijan (Zarbakht, 1998, pp. 34, 62). An investigation commission regarding the function of the Iranian commander officers of the Fourth Army during the operations against Barzani, from 28 May to June 11, 1947, under Lieutenant General Shahbakhti, addressed that in the Showt event, 31 Iranian army men were killed and 35 were wounded. Zarbkhat claims that the number of Iranian armies was twentyfold, about 10,000 forces, compared to that of the Barzanis (Zarbakht, 1998, pp. iv, 93, 116-119). In short, the Barzanis, under Mullah Mustafa Barzani, actively participated in the Kurdish nationalist movement and the Kurdistan Republic, strived to revive the Kurdistan Republic after its fall, and heroically resisted and fought against the Iranian army. They sought refuge in the Soviet Union and returned to Iraq after Abd al-Karim Qasim seized power on 14 July 1958 through a coup that ousted the monarchy.

5.7. The Soviet Union and the Kurdistan Republic

While the existence of a Kurdish national will was important and necessary, the occupation of Iranian Kurdistan by the Soviet Union was a major factor in the development of Kurdish nationalism, the emergence of nationalist organizations, and the establishment of the Kurdistan Republic of 1946. The Soviet Union also played a major role in creating the Azerbaijan National Government, which in turn affected the foundation of the Kurdistan Republic. Also, the Soviet Union provided much larger support to Azerbaijan, and it furnished assistance to the Kurdish movement as well. This support included political, economic, military, educational, and cultural.

As the Soviet Union was the greatest supporter of the Azerbaijan National Government and the Kurdistan Republic, the inevitable withdrawal of the Soviet Union from Iran was the most important factor in allowing the Iranian government to suppress the movements of Azerbaijan and Kurdistan. While some may see an opportunistic move of the Soviet Union in making a concession over the Caspian oil and withdrawal of its forces from Iran, it appears that the Soviet Union had to remove its forces from Iran. Even after the fall of the Kurdistan Republic, the Soviet Union provided various assistance to the Kurdish movement, including giving refuge to the Barzanis. However, it is true that the support of the Soviet Union of the Kurdistan Republic gave a huge hope to the Kurdish people, so they interpreted this help as everlasting and unlimited support for the future of the Republic. Whether the Soviet Union promised unconditional and unlimited help to the Kurdish leaders needs more investigation. To date, such promises have not been revealed.

5.8. Continuation of the KDP's Activities

Some KDP members continued with limited activities after the fall of the Kurdistan Republic. Since 1946, tracts known as *shabnameh* (literally, "nocturnal letters") against the Shah were clandestinely distributed in Mahabad and other Kurdish cities, especially in schools. A radio station called *Radio Serri* (Secret Radio), established in Soviet Azerbaijan, broadcasts the news about Mahabad and other cities of Kurdistan. This radio positively brought new hopes to the Kurdish people. Gradually, some KDP cells (including "family cells") were formed (Gadani, 2008a, pp. 74-75). In a meeting on Bolourian's invitation on 2 March 1948, Bolourian, Qadir Mahmoudzadeh, Aziz Farhadi, and Muhammad Shapasandi decided to revive the KDP. In order to get help printing the declaration of the foundation of this group, they contacted Ehsan Tabari, a CC member of the Tudeh Party in Tehran. Tabari advised them that it was early to publish a declaration and told them to secretly revive the party's cells. They disagreed with Tabari; therefore, Bolourian and Shapasandi traveled to Iraqi Kurdistan to get help from the KDP (Iraq) around 20 March 1948. They met with Sheikh Latif, son of the great Sheikh Mahmoud Barzanji, who sent them to his village, Sitak, where they met with Qizilji and Zabihi. Sheikh Latif helped them acquire a printing device. They published the magazine *Rega* (Way), the organ of *Komalay Jiani Kurd* (Party of Life of Kurd), in October-November 1948. The reason for choosing this name was to prevent the suppression of the members of the KDP in Iran by the Iranian government. With the help of Hamza Abdullah, the General Secretary of the KDP (Iraq), Bolourian delivered the magazine to Mahabad. Only one issue of *Rega* (Way) was published, according to which the goal of the Kurds was to establish a democratic autonomous government within a central, democratic government in Iran under the Iranian Constitution (Bolourian, 1997, pp. 78-82, 85, 90, 93-95; Hisami, 2011, p. 40; Karimi, 1999, p. 628).

It must be pointed out that the KDP members in the Soviet Union also continued their activities. Rahim Saif Qazi and Ali Galawej, who were living in Soviet Azerbaijan, published the *Kurdistan* as the organ of the KDP as a part of the newspaper *Azerbaijan* from 1947 to 1962. Finally, the Tudeh Party closed *Kurdistan* (Hisami, 1988, p. 10).

5.8.1. Komitay Komonisti Kurdistan (Communist Committee of Kurdistan [K.K.K.]) or Komitay Boujanaway Hizbi Demokrati Kurdistan (Committee for the Revival of Kurdistan Democratic Party). Bolourian was a prominent member of the KDP who participated in the establishment of *Komitay Boujanaway Hizbi Demokrati Kurdistan* (Committee for the Revival of the Kurdistan Democratic Party; henceforth, the Committee, which is also called the *Komitay Komonisti Kurdistan* (Communist Committee of Kurdistan [K.K.K.]) at approximately the end of December of 1950. The members of this Committee were Bolourian, Rahim Sultanian, Karim Weysi, Rahim Kharazi, Aziz Hisami, and Abdullah Ishaqi [later Ahmad Tawfiq]. In addition, Aziz Yousefi and Seddiq Khatami were in prison at that time. Later, Yousefi joined the leadership of the KDP. This committee contacted some of the KDP committees in Sardasht, Saqqis, Naqadeh, and some villages. The Mahabad committee led all of these committees (Bolourian, 1997, p. 107; Gohari, 2002, pp. 65-66; Gadani, 2008a, p. 75; Hisami, 1997, p. 117). In addition, in the last month of the Summer of 1948, a group including Karim Hisami gathered in Muhammad Yar market and established *Komalay Lawani Lade* (Association of Village Youth). Their purpose was the revival of political struggle, and they focused on creating cells in different villages and urging peasants to revolt against the oppression of the feudal (landlords) (Hisami, 2011, pp. 36, 40).

5.8.1.1. *Cooperating with the Tudeh Party of Iran.* In 1949, the Association of Village Youth joined the K.K.K. After the establishment of the K.K.K., Rahim Sultanian and another member went to the Soviet Union embassy in Tehran for consultation, guidance, and financial and intellectual help. It was suggested that they join the Tudeh Party. Consequently, they contacted the Tudeh Party, which suggested they, under the name of the KDP, work for the Tudeh Party. The Tudeh Party appointed one of its cadres, Sarm al-Din Sadiq Waziri, as the contact person between the party and the Mahabad Committee. As a result, the K.K.K. dissolved itself and joined the Tudeh Party but continued its activity using the designation KDP. The KDP members sold the Tudeh Party publications, including *Be Soy-e Ayandeh* (Toward Future) and *Shahbaz* (Royal Falcon) in Mahabad. At this time, the KDP did not publish a magazine in Kurdish and did not print propaganda about Kurdish rights and culture. Functioning as a Tudeh Party branch, the KDP only existed in the name (Hisami, 2011, pp. 41-42; Hisami, 1997, pp. 119-120).

In 1950, the KDP leadership—Bolourian, Rahim Sultanian, and Rahim Kharazi—traveled to Tabriz to ask the Azerbaijan Democratic Party to help them theoretically. Abdul Rahman Ghassemlou was the representative of the Tudeh Party and participated in the KDP's committee in Mahabad. Later, the Tudeh Party sent Ihsannollah (for seven months) and then Jawhari (for a month) to help the KDP. Besides, Sadiq Waziri and Anjiri were also cooperating with the KDP. Gadani claims that in 1952 (elsewhere, he said in 1953), *Komitay Hawkari Azerbaijan wa Kurdistan* (Committee of Azerbaijan and Kurdistan Cooperation, or

KAK) with the Tudeh Party was founded. Kurdistan's representative in the KAK at first was Sadiq Waziri and then Abdul Rahman Ghassemlou. In the Spring of 1953, the Tudeh Party sent two cadres, Abdul Rahman Ghassemlou and Behnam, to Kurdistan, where the first training course for the KDP cadres was formed. These two parties were so close that the KDP members could join the cells of the Tudeh Party in Tehran and other cities and vice versa. The KDP developed its activities in Sanandaj, Saqqiz, Baneh, Bukan, Sardasht, Naqadeh, Urmiya and its surroundings. The KDP leaders were Rahim Sultanian, Ghani Bolourian, Aziz Yousefi, Abdullah Ishaqi, and Karim Weysi (Bolourian, 1997, p. 112-114; Gadani, 2001, p. 122; Gadani, 2008a, pp. 77-78, 94-95, 110-111; Qazi, 2010, p. 24).

5.8.1.2. The elections of the 17th parliament in 1951. The elections of the 17th Parliament took place in 1951. Sarm al-Din Sadiq Waziri was the candidate from the Tudeh Party in the Mahabad riding and was supported by the KDP. Hashem Shirazi states that another candidate in Mahabad was Sayyed Hassan Emami—Friday prayer leader of Tehran, who was living in Tehran. Based on the Shah's recommendation and through a huge fraud, Emami "won" the election and was selected as Madabad's representative for the parliament. Ghassemlou claims that Waziri received 1535 votes out of 1850 total ballots cast (82.97%), Gadani claims 85% and Hisami 99% (Shirazi, 2000, pp. 189, 191, 202; Ghassemlou, 2000, pp. 222-223; Gadani, 2008a, pp. 91-92; Hisami, 2011, p. 47).

In the Autumn of 1950, the National Front of Iran brought to light the nationalization of the oil industry, and its leader, Dr. Mohammad Mosaddiq, was seriously struggling with this issue. The parliamentary bill of oil nationalization was ratified on 15 March 1951 in the parliament and on 20 March 1951 in the Senate. Mosaddiq became the Prime Minister on 29 April 1951. On 21 July 1952, demonstrators in Tehran held a massive rally in support of Mosaddiq's premiership (after he had resigned due to his conflict with the Shah), in which several were killed. The KDP participated in the protests in this period, in particular those supporting oil nationalization (Gadani, 2008a, pp. 83, 85-87, 90).

Besides, the Committee of the KDP in Mahabad extended its activities among different groups of people. Various party committees were established in Mahabad, including the Saddlers Committee, Bakery Committee, and Shoe Makers Committee. Moreover, to attract the peasants, the party tried to recruit tribal chiefs into the party (Bolourian, 1997, pp. 114-115).

5.8.1.3. *The Peasants' Movement in 1952-1953.* Under the premiership of Dr. Mosaddiq, a Bill known as "Bill 20 Percent" was ratified in 1952, according to which the landlords, after obtaining their interests from the peasants, were required to return 20 percent of their income to the village councils (Gadani, 2008a, p. 90). In Mahabad, *Komiteh-ye Dehqanan-e Sarasari-ye Kurdistan* (The Peasant Committee of throughout Kurdistan) was formed under Karim Hisami. The committee led the peasants' struggle in Kurdistan for radical land reforms and prevention of the expelling of the peasants in villages by the landlords. In some villages, the peasants took control of their villages. Some newspapers in Tehran in 1952 claimed that Kurdistan had become a communist land (Hisami, 2011, p. 50).

The ratification of the "Bill 20 percent" pushed the feudal landlords, in collaboration with the government, to act against the peasants. On the other hand, the Kurdish peasants in Mukrian territory secretly united when, in January-February 1952 (Hisami and Amir Qazi date it as 1953), many villages revolted against the landlords. The KDP supported the peasants by propagandizing their interests and helping them financially. The Commander of Mahabad's Brigade, Colonel Mozaffar Zanganeh, with the collaboration of the landlords, severely suppressed the revolt. The peasants were killed and looted, while men, women, and children were thrown into the water. Some of the activists, including Haji Qasim Khayat, were imprisoned or fled. The majority of these people struggled for the KDP to their last breath. It was revealed that when the army and the landlords were suppressing and persecuting the rebels, some landlords assisted the peasants. In 1953, during the conflict between the villagers and the Aghas in Chomi Majid Khan, in the village of Saroqamish, Salar Qazi gave refuge to the villagers. Hemin claims that from 1950 to 1953, the KDP was under the influence of the Tudeh Party, emphasizing the class struggle, the overthrow of the fogeyism, and the establishment of democracy in Iran. The KDP therefore gave insufficient attention to the nationalistic struggle (Gadani, 2008a, p. 93-94; Hisami, 2011, pp. 50-51; Qazi, 2010, pp. 29-33; Bolourian, 1997, pp. 119-124; Hemin, 1999, pp. 36, 38).

5.8.1.4. The 4th World Festival of Youth and Students in Romania in 1953.
In late Spring 1953 (5 June, according to Gadani), the Youth Organization in Mahabad held a meeting in Baghi Mikaili (Mikail Garden), which included youth from all over Kurdistan, in order to choose representatives to send through the Tudeh Party to the 4th World Festival of Youth and Students in Bucharest, Romania. The army under Brigadier Mozaffari attacked the meeting and killed Hassan Ramazani. 70 were arrested in the subsequent demonstration. Some women attacked gendarmes, soldiers, and military policemen, disarming some of them. People took sanctuary in Mahabad's Telegraph Office. After three days, the arrested demonstrators were released (Hisami, 2011, p. 55; Gadani, 2008a, pp. 95-97). According to Hisami, from Kurdistan, the youth chose nine people, including Amineh Mawlawi, daughter of Muhammad Mawlawi. Under Karim Hisami, they went to Tehran, where 90 youths, including Hisami, were chosen to participate in the Festival (Hisami, 2011, pp. 56-57; Gadani, 2008a, pp. 95-97; Bolourian, 1997, p. 137).

5.8.1.5. The Coup d'état of 1953. On 16 August 1953, the Shah left Iran for Baghdad and thereafter to Italy. In Mahabad, people celebrated his departure. On 17 August 1953, the greatest rally since 22 February 1946 was held in Mahabad's Abbas Agha Mosque, where Hassan Dawoudi, Dr. Hussein Ayyoubi, Sayyed Aziz Ayyoubian, Seddiq Haidari, and two women delivered speeches. Hemin read the poem "*da bro ay shahi khaein, Baghda niway reyat be*" ("Go Away the Traitor Shah, Baghdad Be Your Halfway"), which elevated the people's excitement. Two days later, on 19 August 1953, the Shah returned to power after a coup that overthrew the democratically elected Prime Minister Dr. Mosaddiq. Many of the KDP members escaped to the Mangur villages, where the Mangurs, both peasants and Aghas, gave asylum to them (Hemin, 1999, pp. 40-42; Gadani, 2008a, pp. 100-101).

After the coup, Abdullah Ishaqi, Hussein Frouhar, and the brave Kurdish woman, Gula Rehan, were arrested. The rest of the KDP leaders left Mahabad and covertly sought refuge in the villages of the Mangur area while other cadres hid in the areas of Gawirk, Swesnayati, Baneh, Naqadeh, and Sharweran. In practice, the leadership of the KDP was in the hands of Ghani Bolourian, Aziz Yousefi, Seddiq Khatami, Hashim Aqal al-Tolab (Qadir Sharif), and Muhammad Amin Ratebi (Gohari, 2002, p. 67). After the fall of Dr. Mosaddiq, Ghassemlou for a while hid in Qazi Muhammad's home where, with the help of Mina Khanim, he organized hidden political activities in Tabriz, Urmiya, and Tehran (Ali Mahmood Shekhani, 2007, p. 109).

After the 1953 coup, for security purposes the KAK was dissolved. However, some KDP cadres stayed in Tabriz. In the Winter of 1954, in a meeting in Tabriz—which included Hisami, Bolourian, Aziz Yousefi, Qadir Yousefi, and Sulayman Mo'ini—the publishing of *Kurdistan,* under Ghassemlou, was discussed. After the fifth issue of *Kurdistan*, its printing house, which belonged to the Azerbaijan Democratic Party, was discovered by the government. Six or eight issues of *Kurdistan* were published in this period. Bolourian states that the circulation of the *Kurdistan* was 2,000, of which 100 were sent to Iraq and Turkey (Hisami, 2011, pp. 66, 70; Gohari, 2002, p. 68; Bolourian, 1997, pp. 152-153; Gadani, 2008a, pp. 110-111).

Some women who participated in the KDP before and after the coup included Mina Khanim (Qazi Muhammad's wife), Khanma Khanim (Rahim Saifi Qazi's wife), Ismat Khanim Qazi (Qazi Muhammad's daughter), Sa'adat Hisami, Habiba, Zenab, Zerin, Khat Zenab, Ayshe Rash Gadani, and Eran Khanim Husseinzadeh. Jalil Gadani, who was also a KDP member at that time, states that these women delivered most of the party's publications, letters, and messages. They also performed great roles in protecting the cadres (Gadani, 2001, pp. 16-17; Hisami, 1986, p. 247). Unfortunately, the extent of women's participation in Kurdish nationalism in this period has not been the focus of the Kurdish authors.

5.8.2. The 1st Conference of the KDP. The 1st Conference of the KDP, which Sayyed Rasoul Dehqan called a "meeting," was initiated in the Summer of 1955 with the help of Sayyed Rasoul Dehghan on the Kevi Qalata Rash (the Black Fortress Mountain) at the village of Sayyed Away Babi Gawra in Piranshahr. Among the 15 cadres who took part in the Conference were Abdul Rahman Ghassemlou, As'ad Khodayari, Abdullah Ishaqi, and Aziz Yousefi. The most important decisions of the conference included the following: (1) the new proposal for the KDP's platform was approved, and the party was renamed as *Hizbi Demokrati Kurdistan-Eran* (Kurdistan Democratic Party-Iran); (2) leadership members were chosen from the attendees and absentees; and (3) the Conference decided to end its direct relations with the Tudeh Party effective immediately. One of the reasons for severing relations with the Tudeh Party was that the Tudeh Party did not take the necessary action against the Coup d'état, which was against Mosaddiq. The Conference chose a leadership under Ghassemlou as the Director General of the KDP (Gadani, 2008a, pp. 112-116; Bolourian, 1997, pp. 155-156; Gohari, 2002, p. 98; Hassanzadeh, n.d., p. 111; Ali Mahmood Shekhani, 2007, pp. 110-113; see Appendix 8). Although the Party's official name was the Kurdistan Democratic Party-Iran or KDP-I), the party still called itself the KDP in its official documents.

In the Spring of 1955, the KDP-I assigned Ghassemlou to deliver two letters to the Soviet Communist Party and the leadership of the Tudeh Party in Europe (Bolourian, 1997, pp. 155-156). After returning to Iran, Ghassemlou contacted Arsalan Pouya, a member of the Provincial Committee of the Tudeh Party, in 1957 (according to Hisami, in 1956), not knowing that Pouyan was secretly working for the Iranian intelligence or SAVAK. Ghassemlou and his cousin Isma'il Ghassemlou were subsequently arrested. They promised to cooperate with the Iranian government and were released after 48 hours (Gohari, 2002, p. 71). Ghassemlou's brief arrest and having been freed so quickly created suspicions about him among the KDP leaders. In addition, regarding the discord between Ahmad Tawfiq and Ghassemlou, Mawloudi Sabian (1994) states that in 1956, Bijan Khan, one of the chiefs of Dehbukri, caused the police to arrest Ghassemlou and Tawfiq, but Tawfiq escaped to Iraq. He was suspicious about how Ghassemlou was freed (pp. 115-116, 118). Later, the KDP-I appointed Ghassemlou to attend the World Festival of Youth and Students in Moscow in 1957. But while in Czechoslovakia, he contacted the Tudeh Party again. Therefore, the KDP-I decided to send Tawfiq to the Festival. While in Czechoslovakia, Ghassemlou created problems for Tawfiq, and he could not go to Moscow. Upon return, Tawfiq expressed his anger toward Ghassemlou (Gadani, 2001, p. 23).

On 14 July 1958, Abdul Karim Qasim grabbed power in Iraq through a coup, and soon afterward, Mullah Mustafa Barzani returned to Iraq from the Soviet Union. His return brought hope to the Kurdish people, and the supporters of the KDP-I multiplied. However, the backlash was that many of the KDP-I cadres were spending too much time in Iraqi Kurdistan instead of focusing on Iranian Kurdistan's events. After the imprisonment of Aziz Yousefi in 1958, the only remaining leadership member of the KDP-I was Tawfiq. He and Qadir Sharif rarely contacted the KDP-I cadres inside Iranian Kurdistan (Gadani, 2008a, pp. 123-124).

5.8.2.1. The raids on the KDP-I in 1959. In 1959, SAVAK struck the heaviest blow to the KDP-I and the Kurdish nationalist movement. Isma'il Ghassemlou, one of the cadres whom the KDP-I had promised to send to Europe so he would continue his education, was arrested in the Winter of 1959 in Baneh and collaborated with the government. In prison, he told Gadani that he wanted to take revenge on Abdul Rahman Ghassemlou and Tawfiq for not having sent him abroad. Later, in mid-Autumn 1959, the government arrested about 250 (according to Dehghan, 120, according to Gadani, 150) members of the KDP-I (Hemin, 1999, p. 42; Hassanzadeh, n.d., p. 113; Hisami 2011, p. 95; Qazi, 2010, p. 441; Gadani, 2008a, pp. 124-130). After the raids in 1959, about 270 cadres and members of the party sought refuge in Sulaymaniyah in Iraqi Kurdistan. They established *Komoni Sulaymaniyah* (Sulaymaniyah's Commune) under the leadership of Tawfiq, Qadir Sharif, Hashim Husseinzadeh, Qasim Sultani, and Mullah Baqir. The Commune lasted until 1961. Due to the lack of a democratic process, the Commune witnessed endless conflicts. Tawfiq, supported by Mullah Mustafa Barzani, dominated the Commune. Due to the Tawfiq's unfriendly leadership, the majority of the Commune either were expelled from or left Sulaymaniyah or alternatively surrendered to the Iranian officials (Kaveh, 2005, 32; Khizri, 2003, p. 13).

Disagreements had already existed within the KDP-I, but the period between 1958 and 1971 can be characterized as one of crisis and fragmentation of the KDP-I. Aside from the existence of different ideological perspectives within the party and the lack of strong leadership, a crucial factor in creating the crisis was the effect of the Iraqi Kurdish movement on the party, especially after the Kurdish Revolution in September 1961. When the KDP-I leadership was established in Iraq, it did not have a united leadership either in Iran or Iraq. The KDP-I consisted of two different streams of thought. The first, led by Ghassemlou, was leftist, democratic, and progressive, while the second, under Ahmad Tawfiq, had strict nationalistic views. Qazi claims that the first tendency was that of the traditional left and pro-Tudeh, while the second insisted on having an independent organization and getting rid of the influence of the Tudeh Party (led by Tawfiq and Sulayman Mo'ini). Peshnimaz, a CC member of the KDP-I, asserts that Tawfiq was known to have disliked leftists (Hassanzadeh, n.d., pp. 114-115; Qazi, 2010, pp. 404-406, Peshnimaz, 2012, p. 105).

A certain root of the conflict was the significant disagreement between Tawfiq and Ghassemlou, who were now in the Iraqi Kurdistan. Basically, Tawfiq had serious doubts about Ghassemlou and claimed that he had promised General Taymour Bakhtiar, the Head of SAVAK, to cooperate in addition to being with the Tudeh Party. Tawfiq believed the KDP-I should liberate Kurdistan with the assistance of the United States (Gadani, 2008a, p. 131). Consequently, in 1960, Tawfiq tried to assassinate Qasim Sultani and Ghassemlou. However, Jalal Talabani saved Sultani, while two members of the Iraqi Communist Party saved Ghassemlou's life in Sulaymaniyah (Hisami, 1998, pp. 87-89; Sardashti, 2002a, pp. 8-9). Ghassemlou was teaching at the university in Baghdad. Tawfiq claimed that Ghassemlou was a spy, and when Barzani reported this to the Minister of Interior of Iraq, Ghassemlou was expelled from Iraq. On 1 March 1960, he left Iraq for Prague (Hisami, 1998, pp. 89-90; Hisami, 2011, p. 97; Hassanzadeh, 2012, p. 59). Madani asserts that Tawfiq killed As'ad Khodayari on the pretext that he was cooperating with the SAVAK. Indeed, Khodayari, on the orders of the KDP-I, was in contact with Mr. Kanzi, a retired Captain and the first chief of SAVAK in Mahabad. Tawfiq also ordered the execution of Ghassemlou. However, Rasha Ghachaghchi helped Ghassemlou to escape and saved him (Personal communication, October 13, 2012). Tawfiq treated his rivals with cruelty and even assassinated them, as was the case with killing As'ad Khodayari (Bolourian, 1997, p. 188; Hisami, 1998, p. 87; Hassanzadeh, n.d., p.116).

Tawfiq grew powerful in the party for two reasons. First, he was very active, devoted, popular, disciplined, and brave in decision-making and in armed operations. Second and more importantly, he was supported by Mullah Mustafa Barzani. When some party members met Barzani and claimed that Tawfiq was a dictator, he responded that he would not exchange Tawfiq for all of them put together (Hassanzadeh, 2012, pp. 60-61). Thus, Ghassemlou, accompanied by his family and later Hisami, returned to Europe in 1960. Many PDK-I members returned to Iran, and some of them were arrested and convicted (Gadani, 2008a, p. 137-139).

5.8.3. The Kurdish Revolution in Iraq in September 1961. In September 1961, a Kurdish revolt started in Iraq (Gadani, 2008a, p. 138). The revolt against the Iraqi government was mainly led by the KDP (Iraq) and its leader, Mullah Mustafa Barzani. The Iranian government, due to its hostility toward the Iraqi government, decided to support the Kurdish struggle. Iran also expected, through the KDP (Iraq), to nullify KDP-I activities in Iran and destroy the organization. The KDP-I strongly and practically supported the Kurdish Revolution. However, some of the members of the KDP-I tried to keep their organizational and political independence and continue their struggle inside Iranian Kurdistan. These members were in opposition to Tawfiq, who faithfully obeyed Mullah Mustafa. Tawfiq suppressed the opposition inside the KDP-I. On the other hand, the KDP (Iraq), to protect their revolution and also under the influence of Iran, followed a wrong policy based on suppressing those opposing Tawfiq. This policy resulted in handing over to Iran, as well as murdering some leaders and members of the KDP-I. The activities of the KDP-I in Iraq must be considered under the said political conditions in Iraqi Kurdistan.

The KDP-I members established *Komitay Barewabaryy Hizbi Dimokrati Kurdistan-Iran* (Directing Committee of the Kurdistan Democratic Party-Iran) in Koya. The members included Ahmad Tawfiq, Said Kaveh (Kowestani), Sulayman Mo'ini, Salah al-Din Mohtadi, and Muhammad Ilkhanizadeh. The Committee mainly focused on deploying assistance from Iranian Kurdistan to the Kurdish movement in Iraq and established some bases in the villages of Sone, Zinwe Shekh, and Sangasar. Besides, instead of publishing *Kurdistan*, Tawfiq began publishing a weekly newsletter titled *Disan Barzani* (Again Barzani) (Sardashti, 2002a, pp. 9-10, 45).

Masoud Barzani (2004b) emphasizes that after the beginning of the September War, the leaders and the peshmerga of the KDP-I participated in the revolution (p. 190). Qazi (2010) maintains that at the beginning of Spring 1965, the KDP-I had a group of 30 peshmergas, under Tawfiq, in front of Qaladiza and Sangasar that cooperated with the KDP (Iraq) against the Iraqi regime (pp. 126-127; Gadani, 2008a; p. 140). Regarding the activities of Tawfiq, Barzani (2004a) states that when John F. Kennedy was assassinated in 1963, Mullah Mustafa provided a condolence letter and, through Tawfiq, sent it to the United States Embassy in Tehran (p. 154).

The KDP-I also conducted activities in other parts of Iran. In 1961, after the beginning of the Kurdish Revolution in Iraqi Kurdistan, a secret committee named *Komitay Barewabari Katii Hizbi Demokrati Kurdistan-Eran* (Temporary Directing Committee of the Kurdistan Democratic Party-Iran) was established in Tehran to help the Kurdish movement in Iraq. The founders were Salah al-Din Mohtadi, Aziz Jian, Muhammad Amin Siraji, Fatih Sheikh al-Islami, Mustafa Ishaqi, Sulayman Shafe'i, and Amir Qazi. The Committee tried to contact the KDP (Iraq), help the peshmergas of the KDP-I in Iraq, and connect to the Kurdish Student Association in Europe. After a year, Sulayman Mo'ini met Amir Qazi in the village of Shekhlar in Bukan and delivered a bunch of the KDP-I's newsletter, *Disan Barzani,* to him (Qazi, 2010, pp. 46-48).

The discord among them, especially with Tawfiq, was continuing. Mullah Awara [a popular and active cadre of the party], while not claiming to be a leader of the KDP-I, created a new line of organization in the territory of Sardasht and advocated for the KDP-I. Likewise, in 1962 and 1963, Muhammad Ilkhanizadeh and Salah al-Din Mohtadi, under the influence of a party called the KAJIK, which was similar to the J.K., founded the *Komalay Rizgari* (*Kurdistan*) (Kurdistan Liberation Committee). They conducted some organizing activities in the areas of Sardasht and Bukan. Later, this Committee sent a letter to the Iraqi Ba'ath Party on 5 July 1971. The letter contained the 15-article program of the Committee (Hassanzadeh, n.d., p. 116; Khizri, 2003, p. 27; Gadani, 2008a, pp. 142-143; Hisami, 1990, pp. 59-63).

In 1963, some young Kurdish intellectuals—including Rastgar, Madani, Sharifzadeh, Siraji, Haidari, and Hamza Bayazidi—traveled to the Iraqi Kurdistan (Sardashti, 2002a, p. 10; Gadani, 2008a, p. 139; Qazi, 2010, p. 80). In 1963, a party base was established in Sone. The members of the Sone base, including Sulayman Mo'ini, established a few committees for conducting political activities in Iran, including collecting financial and material help for the Kurdish Revolution in Iraq (Peshnimaz, 2012, pp. 113-114, 128).

As mentioned, the KDP-I published the magazine *Disan Barzani* (Again Barzani). The magazine mainly aimed at defending Barzani against his opponents (Hassanzadeh, n.d., p. 115). The KDP-I also cooperated with the Kurdish movement in Iraq in diplomatic ways. When Iran, Turkey, and Syria sent their armies to the borders to support the Iraqi government and attack the Kurds, Mullah Mustafa Barzani wrote a letter to the Soviet Union. Similarly, Tawfiq sent a letter (through Khidir Marasana) to Seddiq Anjiri in Tehran, and he delivered it to the Soviet Embassy. After a few days, Radio Moscow threatened these governments, stating that if they interfered in the Kurdish affairs, the Soviets would not remain silent. Consequently, these countries recalled their forces (Gadani, 2008a, p. 140).

Tawfiq was practically the leader of the KDP-I and did not answer to anyone. He had a cynical mind: in 1960, without any investigation, he ordered the killing of As'ad Khodayari, who was one of the best friends of the KDP-I, on his way from Qaladiza to Sone. Such conduct, especially in 1963 and 1964, caused many cadres and members in Iraq to turn their backs on Tawfiq. Hassan Rastgar, Hossein Madani, Said Kowestani, and others met Mullah Mustafa a few times and explained the situation to him, but he was furious at them (Gadani, 2008a, pp. 140-141). Regarding the characteristics of Tawfiq, Peshnimaz (2012) states that Tawfiq was very brave, fearless, active, honest, strongly against Kurdistan's enemies, and patriotic. However, most KDP-I members were against the dictatorship of Tawfiq (Peshnimaz, 2012, pp. 105, 133).

Some members of the PDK-I in Europe cooperated with the Tudeh Party in order to defend Kurdish nationalism. The KDP-I members, such as Hisami, produced and broadcast programs about the Kurdish nationalist movement through the Tudeh Party's *Radio Peyk-e Iran* (Iran Courier). According to the State Department in Washington, D.C. (1982), *Peyk-e Iran was* broadcasting its programs first from East Germany and later from Bulgaria and was active from 1957 to 1976. As early as 1961, the radio had a Kurdish program under Ali Galawej and Hassan Qizilji, and since 1964, under Karim Hisami (Hisami, 2011, pp. 106-108).

The Tudeh Party tried to unify the KDP-I and the Tudeh Party. Hisami opposed the suggestion regarding the unification of these parties, claiming that they do not have the authority to talk for the KDP-I. Thus, the proposal was rejected. Finally, it was decided to publish the *Kurdistan* in the Kurdish language, with Ghassemlou being its nominal editor. After writing and typing them, the articles were sent to Prague, where Ghassemlou published and distributed the paper. The Tudeh Party paid the expenses for the Kurdish paper. In all, 26 issues of the *Kurdistan* were published from 21 January 1965 to Spring 1970 (Hisami, 2011, pp. 108-109).

5.8.4. Komitay Sakhkaraway Hizbi Demokrati Kurdistan-Eran (Reconstructing Committee of the KDP-Iran). The discord between Tawfiq and other cadres of the KDP-I was not improving. In the Summer of 1963, some party members established *Komitay Sakhkaraway Hizbi Demokrati Kurdistan-Eran* (Reconstructing Committee of the Kurdistan Democratic Party-Iran or Reconstructing Committee). It should be noted that although the name of the party was officially KDP-I, almost all writers of the KDP-I alternatively use the name KDP. Therefore, they use *Komitay Sakhkaraway Hizbi Demokrati Kurdistan* (Reconstructing Committee of the Kurdistan Democratic Party).

Disagreement exists about the date and founders of the Reconstructing Committee (Sardashti, 2002a, p. 12; Hisami, 1997, p. 55; Peshnimaz, 2012, p. 152; Gadani, 2008a, pp. 169-170). Hassanzadeh states that according to Hossein Madani, the Reconstructing Committee was established in the Autumn of 1963 by Qadir Sharif, Hossein Madani, Hassan Rastgar, and Said Kowestani. The Committee added two other members, Mullah Awara and Mullah Abubakr Falsafi, as well as Rasoul Peshnimaz and Qadir Qazi (Mamand), as alternate members of the Committee. The Committee announced its constitution in a declaration criticizing Tawfiq. Moreover, in June-July 1964, the Committee created three organizational teams and sent them for political activities in Iranian Kurdistan. Gadani states that Rasoul Peshnimaz, Mamand Qazi, and Hassan Naghadehei were chosen as the alternates of the Committee (Hassanzadeh, n.d., pp. 116-117; Gadani, 2001, p. 130).

In a declaration dated 17 June 1964, the Reconstructing Committee called Tawfiq a traitor. It listed his "anti-party" activities and asserted that he had deviated from the party's way, creating discord between political organizations and treating Ghassemlou with hostility. Thus, the CC summoned him for investigation in the Summer of 1958. The CC, in September 1959, wrote him a letter and took away his responsibilities, but Tawfiq had already stolen the printing devices of the party and continued distributing his ideas in the name of the party and revealing the party's secrets and Isma'il Ghassemlou's confessions. When the Provisional Committee of the party was established after 3 November 1959, it investigated Tawfiq, and he resigned on 1 May 1961. He contacted William Eagleton, the top United States intelligence officer in the Middle East. At the beginning of the Kurdish movement in Iraq (1961), on the orders of the United States, Tawfiq traveled to Lebanon for training and contacted SAVAK agents there. On his return, he brought Dana Adams Schmidt, a correspondent for *The New York Times* in the Middle East, to observe the Kurdish movement in Iraq. Moreover, from 1958 to 1959, he stole most of the financial help of the Kurdish people. Finally, the Reconstruction Committee declaration suggests people to not trust the declarations and newspapers, which were published by Tawfiq and his follower Sulayman Mo'ini (Sardashti, 2002a, pp. 52-62).

The Reconstruction Committee declaration was harsh. The activities of Tawfiq need to be analyzed fairly. For instance, regarding the subject of Dana Adams Schmidt, an alternative analysis observes Tawfiq's action positively. For example, according to Barzani (2004b), an outstanding activity of Tawfiq was that he brought Dana Adams Schmidt from Beirut to observe the Kurdish movement in Iraq in 1963. His articles were published in *The New York Times* and *Christian Science Monitor*, and he also wrote a book, *Journey Among Brave Men* (1964). These publications primed the world opinion for recognition of the Kurdish revolt in Iraq (p. 190).

At that time, the KDP (Iraq) also went through a split. The splinters were called *Bali Maktabi Siasi* (Political Bureau Wing) or the KDP (Iraq) Political Bureau, and led by Ibrahim Ahmad and Jalal Talabani. The Reconstructing Committee relied on the Political Bureau Wing. However, Mullah Mustafa Barzanis' wing of the KDP (Iraq) attacked the Political Bureau Wing and pushed it to retreat to Iran (Gadani, 2008a, p.142). The conflicts between these two wings affected the KDP-I, too.

The discord among the KDP-I leaders created different factions within the party led by Tawfiq, Mohtadi, and the Reconstruction Committee. Tawfiq created fear among the members and also disarmed some of the peshmergas (Qazi, 2010, p. 72; Peshnimaz, 2012, pp. 135-136, 149; Qazi, 2010, pp. 87-91). Hassan Rastgar, a political activist, a long-time member of the KDP, and a former General Secretary of the Democratic Party of Iranian Kurdistan (PDKI-RL), claims that when he and other Reconstruction Committee members were in Zinwe Shekhan, Tawfiq, and Barzanis disarmed them (Personal communication, October 15, 2012). Anjiri and Mo'ini, who were friends of Tawfiq, realized that the people had left them. Besides, Tawfiq needed to legitimize himself. Thus, the party needed to hold a congress (Gadani, 2008a, p.143).

5.8.5. The 2nd Congress of the KDP-I. The 2nd Congress of the KDP-I was held between the villages of Sheni in Sardasht and Sone in Qaladiza in December 1964. The 2nd Congress elected 15 cadres as the CC (Khizri, 2003, p. 48) and Tawfiq as the leader of the party (Gadani, 2008a, p. 145; see Appendix 8). The 2nd Congress chose several cadres to the CC in absentia. For instance, when Hajar, who had never been a member of the party, heard that he was elected to the CC, he made fun of the news. In addition, the congress chose Barzani as the head of the party. In the Congress, *Hayati Sikertariyay Hizibi Demokrati Kurdistan* (Secretariat Board of the Kurdistan Democratic Party) was founded, but in practice, Tawfiq was the party and the party was Tawfiq. The Secretariat Board was only rubber-stamping Tawfiq's wishes. In the Congress, for the first time in KDP-I's history, *Komitay Chawaderi Barz* (Higher Inspection Committee) was established (Hassanzadeh, 2012, p. 61; Hassanzadeh, n.d., pp. 120, 121; Gadani, 2008a, pp. 145-146).

Mohammad Khizri, a former, long-time member of the KDP, claims that 54 people participated in the 2nd Congress, of which all except five or six people were from the most undeveloped sectors of society (Personal communication, November 22, 2012). In Peshnimaz's report, 200 and in Gadani's, 300 members participated in the 2nd Congress. None of the delegates were chosen based on the constitution by the KDP-I cells. Instead, they were mostly invited by Tawfiq and

Mo'ini, and thus, the majority of the participants were under the authority of Tawfiq (Peshnimaz, 2012, p. 167; Gadani, 2008a, pp. 143-144). According to Peshnimaz, 13 members of the KDP-I, who were also members of the Reconstructing Committee, were not allowed to attend the 2nd Congress. Peshnimaz states that when they reached the congress venue, Tawfiq's gunmen did not let them enter, except for Mirza Khidir Marasana (Gadani, 2008b, pp. 155, 157). Peshnimaz (2012) reveals the list of 14 people, including Peshnimaz, who were not allowed to participate in the Congress (p. 167; see Appendix 15).

According to Kkizri (2003), the party approved a program that emphasized independence, a federative system, and a constitution based on which each Kurdish person could become a member of the party. Tawfiq's report to Congress attacked the leadership of the Kurdistan Republic because they were submissive and inefficient individuals, and he called many cadres and members of the party, such as Ghassemlou, spies and traitors, to the party. When Sulayman Mo'ini became a member of the CC, he read his written speech in which he called Tawfiq an incompatible pessimistic dictator (pp. 41-43, 47, 51).

According to Anjiri, the Congress did not approve the expelling of the Reconstructing Committee members or Tawfiq's criticism of the Kurdistan Republic leaders. Nonetheless, Tawfiq published his report as the resolution of the Congress. This resulted in a new season of disharmony among the leadership of the party. For instance, Tawfiq typed a letter of resignation to the party, an act Anjiri called childish (Khizri, 2003, pp. 63-66).

The resolution of the 2nd Congress of the KDP was published in November 1964. According to this document, the Congress started with the anthem *Ay Raqib* (Lo the Enemy), and then a combatant clergy recited the Surah Al-Fath (The Victory) from *The Quran*. The declaration criticized the leadership of the party during the Kurdistan Republic, stating that they submitted themselves to their fate. They did not use the opportunity to strengthen the Kurdish government, Kurdish army, and peshmergas. Before the enemy prepared and became able to break the Kurdish nation, the party and the Kurdistan Republic's leaders had, in fact, prepared the conditions for the enemy to invade the Kurdish nation, the government, and the party. The leaders were hopelessly looking forward to the Iranian government's movement in order to put the Kurds in catastrophe. The declaration criticized the Soviet Union, which, under the influence of their ignorant consultants and the Azerbaijan leaders, thought that the Kurdish Republic was strong enough to protect itself, and as such, they did not support the Kurdish movement when the latter needed it. Besides, the resolution emphasized that the parliamentary struggle in Iran was a treachery and the method of the real struggle for national liberation was armed, revolutionary revolt against colonialism, the Shah, and the government, and abolishing the foundation of the Iranian state—that is, capitalism and feudalism. The experiences of Cuba, Algeria, and many other places had shown that the victory of the revolution depended on organizing the peasants for armed struggle in the mountains and deserts and creating relationships with the exploited national toilers. The declaration names some members of the party as *rou rash* (denigrated), those who wanted to destroy the party, namely Ghassemlou. It asserts that when these members were arrested, they surrendered themselves to SAVAK and worked as spies (Sardashti, 2002a, pp. 64-66, 68, 73).

The 2nd Congress has been criticized from different angles. Amir Qazi criticized the 2nd Congress resolution for disrespectfully attacking the Kurdistan Republic and its leaders; attacking the KDP (Iraq) Political Bureau; unjustly accusing Dr. Ghassemlou; and finally, accusing some of the cadres and members of the KDP-I (Qazi, 2010, pp. 124-125; Hassanzadeh, n.d., p. 119).

After the Congress, discord persisted within the party. Dehqan asserts that after the 2nd Congress, a real party did not exist. Each of the leaders had relations with a group of their friends. Sometimes these groups were returning to Iranian Kurdistan and were accusing other groups (Qazi, 2010, p. 445; Bakhchi, p. 10).

When the CC did not accept Tawfiq's resignation, he demanded that he needed some relaxation and wanted to go to Qandil Mountain for three months. It was accepted. He went to Qandil in May 1965. After three months, he went to the village of Shekhan, where he trained the cadres, but in fact, he was plotting against the CC (Khizri, 2003, pp. 70-73, 103; Gadani, 2008a, p. 148). Only four members in the CC were vigorously directing the party's activities in Iraqi and Iranian Kurdistan: Anjiri, Mo'ini, Naho Pashayy (Bapir Shikak), and Mullah Rahim Wirdi. These members organized other cadres and members to establish party cells and committees in Kurdistan of Iran (Khizri, 2003, pp. 76-78). Khizri claims that after the Congress, while he was armed, he traveled to the territory between Mahabad and Miandoab for organizational activities and stayed there for nine months (Personal communication, November 22, 2012). In the Spring of 1966, Bapir Shikak and his five friends were killed in a clash with the gendarmes in Somay Bradost (Qazi, 2010, p. 131; Khizri, 2003, p. 150).

For a while, Tawfiq was far from the Pishdar region. During this period, gradually a strong relationship between the Reconstructing Committee and some leaders of the KDP-I was created. Rastgar states that when Tawfiq was in Sheikhan territory, Anjiri, Sulayman Mo'inio, and Abdullah Mo'ini (Gadani adds Amir Qazi) in Qaladiza met them. They made an agreement with Rastgar and other members of the Reconstructing Committee to join them as substitute members of the CC, allowing them the authority of CC members. Therefore, they joined the party (Personal communication, October 16, 2012; Gadani, 2008a, pp. 146-147). The KDP-I members, including Mo'ini and Rastgar, had returned to Iranian Kurdistan, where in the village of Pana Sar, they clashed with the gendarmes. As a result, a gendarme was wounded, and the rest of them surrendered. After treating the wounded, the peshmergas returned their weapons and released all of them. At that time, the KDP (Iraq) removed some of the KDP-I's bases at the border (Gadani, 2008a, p. 147).

The Iranian government was pushing the KDP (Iraq) to arrest and submit the members of the KDP-I to Iran. In the Spring of 1966, when SAVAK asked the KDP (Iraq) to submit Tawfiq to Iran, Barzani sent him to the village of Kani Masi along with six or seven cadres, ordering them to stay out of sight (Khizri, 2003, pp. 103-104; Gadani, 2008a, pp. 151-152; Peshnimaz, 2012, p. 180). Not all of the CC members and cadres were in favor of the political and especially armed activities of the KDP-I in Iranian Kurdistan. According to Qazi (2010), Anjiri's view was changing. He believed that in that condition, the party should not use arms, hold meetings, or direct political struggle. He suggested that the members hide themselves. He was also strongly against Tawfiq (p. 132; Khizri, 2003, p. 97).

Later, Tawfiq escaped to Baghdad. Sanar Mamadi claims that Tawfiq explained that he escaped from the exiled place to Baghdad because one of his friends in the politburo of the KDP (Iraq) told him that the Parastin, the security forces of the KDP (Iraq), and SAVAK planned to assassinate him. Qazi states that Tawfiq complained that Barzani and KDP-I members were unfaithful and disrespectful to him. Later, Tawfiq was arrested and killed by the Iraqi government. The KDP had tried through 64 for Tawfiq's freedom. The Iraqi officials told him that Tawfiq was a double spy who worked for both the Iraqi government and Mullah Mustafa Barzani (Mamadi, 1999, p. 49; Qazi, 2010, p. 207; Hassanzadeh, 2012, p. 66). Hassanzadeh (2012) states that when Tawfiq was sent away, the KDP-I was, in fact, comprised of individuals, not an organization (Hassanzadeh, 2012, p. 65). But even these individuals did not work in harmony; in fact, they were in discord.

One of the outcomes of the conflict within the KDP's leadership was the assassination of Anjiri. Anjiri and Said Kaveh were living together in the village of Darband in the territory of Balakayati. At the end of April 1966, they visited the village of Lewja and then went to the village of Marout to visit Khalid Hisami, the poet. Anjiri sent Said Kaveh to the village of Darband. Ajiri wanted to see Mullah

Mustafa; thus, he stayed in Hisami's home, whence he disappeared, possibly at the beginning of May 1966 (Sardashti, 2015, p. 52).

Sardashti states that the majority of the people, including Said Kaveh, Rasoul Peshnimaz, Hassan Rastgar, Mullah Muhammad Khizri, and Muhammad Amin Siraji, believe that the chief reason for killing Anjiri was the conflicts within the KDP-I. They claimed that Tawfiq had planned this assassination through his nephew, Hassan Ishaqi, along with three peshmergas, Mirad Rasoul Ali Laylan, Mirad Hasil, and Muhammadi Mirza Awla (Abdullah) (Sardashti, 2015, pp. 99-100). Tawfiq had confessed to Mullah Sayyed Rashid that he had ordered his nephew, Hassan Ishaqi, to kill Anjiri on the road between the villages of Lewja and Souraban on the slope of the village of Wasan (these villages are in the area of Nawdasht and Doli Balayan) (Hassanzadeh, n.d., p. 121). Hisami claims that after the 1979 Revolution, SAVAK investigated Hassan Ishaqi because he had confessed to SAVAK that he had killed Anjiri (Khizri, 2003, p. 122).

It is revealed that Mo'ini while cooperating with Tawfiq, had his own specific thoughts and plans regarding conducting political and even military activities in Iranian Kurdistan. For instance, according to Hisami (1988), on 23 September 1965, Mo'ini sent a letter through the Iraqi Communist Party to Karim Hisami in Europe. He stressed that he and his friends in the KDP wanted to open the way for the struggle of others. They calculated that they could confront the Iranian forces and could make the biggest strike on the Iranian government. This strike would affect the whole country (Hisami, 1988, p. 25). On 2 January 1966, Hisami (1988) responded to Mo'ini's letter, suggesting that at that stage, Mo'ini and his friends had better take their next steps in consultation with Barzani (pp. 26, 32).

Mo'ini had also tried to forge relations with the Soviet Union. Hisami (1988) maintains that on 12 February 1966, Reza Radmanesh [the General (First) Secretary of the Tudeh Party of Iran (1948-1969)] sent a letter to Hisami, which indicated that Sulayman Mo'ini had sent, via Radmanesh, a letter to the Communist Party of the Soviet Union (p. 37).

5.8.6. Komitay Inqilabii Hizbi Demokrati Kurdistan-Eran (Revolutionary Committee of the KDP-Iran). In this section, the establishment and activities of the Revolutionary Committee of the KDP will be addressed through a relatively chronological history of the KDP. The relationship of this Committee with the Kurdish movement in Iraq under the KDP (Iraq) and cooperation with the Tudeh Party will also be reviewed. Once again, it should be noted that although the name of the party was officially KDP-I, almost all writers of the KDP-I alternatively use the name KDP. Therefore, they use the name *Komitay Inqilabii Hizbi Demokrati Kurdistan* (Revolutionary Committee of the Kurdistan Democratic Party, or Revolutionary Committee). The alternative name is the *Komitay Inqilabii Hizbi Demokrati Kurdistan-Eran* (Revolutionary Committee of the Kurdistan Democratic Party-Iran or Revolutionary Committee). It is also known as *Komitay Shorishger* (Revolutionary Committee).

According to Said Kaveh (Kowestani), the Revolutionary Committee was established in the Summer of 1966 in the village of Alana in the territory of Balakayati. The Committee members were (1) Muhammad Amin Siraji, (2) Isma'il Sharifzadeh (Mullah Aziz), (3) Salar Haidari, (4) Mullah Ahmad Shalmashi (Mullah Awara), (5) Said Kaveh, (6) Sanar Mamadi, and (7) Mullah Abdullah Abdullahi (Mullah Sarbaz) (Kaveh, 2005, p. 73). On 3 September 1946, Kowestani wrote a letter to Hisami in which he informed the latter about the establishment of the Revolutionary Committee (Hisami, 1988, p. 43). Hisami adds that despite Kutscher's writing, the original founders of the Committee were not eleven men: they were originally seven and then grew to 21 cadres (Mamadi, 1999, pp. 45, 55-56; Sardashti, 2002a, p. 25; Peshnimaz, 2012, p. 166; Khizri, 2003, p. 135; Hassanzadeh, n.d., p. 122; Hisami, 1988, p. 79).

5.8.6.1. The reasons for turning to armed struggle of 1967-1968 by the Revolutionary Committee. The reasons for the establishment of the Revolutionary Committee included elevating Kurdish nationalistic sentiments of the members, the rise of armed struggle and liberation movements in the world, the presence of disagreements within the KDP-I, and the belief in initiating struggle inside Kurdistan and mobilizing people. It also consisted of the cooperation between the Iranian government and the Kurdish leaders in Iraq against the KDP-I, the Iranian regime's demobilizing of the Kurds (especially in the villages), and the return of activists such as Dr. Kourosh Lashai—a Maoist from the Revolutionary Organization of the Tudeh Party—from China to Kurdistan (Gadani, 2001, p. 127). Regarding the goals of the Revolutionary Committee, Gadani (2008a) claims that the Revolutionary Committee decided to return to Iran in the Spring of 1967 in order to unite the members and launch an armed struggle against the Iranian government. The Committee also decided to contact the Iraqi Communist Party and the Tudeh Party to receive financial support from them. The number of members who participated in this campaign was not more than one hundred. They tried as much as possible not to engage in armed clashes until they had created a strong popular base (Gadani, 2008a, pp. 152-153).

Certain dubious documents hold that Isma'il Sharifzadeh had relations with the leftist intellectuals of Azerbaijan, Alireza Nabdel and Behrouz Dehqani, who both later became the original members of the Organization of Iranian People's Fedai Guerrillas (OIPFG). Vahabzadeh (2010) states that the OIPFG was established when two founding groups, under Bijan Jazani and Massoud Ahmadzadeh, respectively, merged after meetings between 6 and 11 April 1971 (pp. 16, 31). Sharifzadeh and Siraji were members of the Tehran Committee of the KDP in the early 1960s. This Committee was a group comprised of Kurdish university students in Tehran (Vahabzadeh, 2010, p. 12). According to Hamid Momeni (1979), when Sharifzadeh was a university student in Tehran, he took part in Marxist activities. In 1964, due to the Iranian government's persecution, about 2,000 Kurdish activists escaped to Iraq. They included Sharifzadeh, an engineering student, Muhammad Amin Siraji, a law student, and Abdullah Mo'ini, a student in Mahabad. In Winter 1967, Sharifzadeh wrote letters to Iranian intellectuals in different cities, his student friends, and Kurdish students in Tehran. He asked them for help and encouraged them to join the struggle instead of gathering in teashops and talking idly about action. It is said that he contacted Alireza Nabdel, who did not accept the Sharifzadeh's group policy and asked for more time for his response until his investigations were complete. As the armed struggle gained momentum, their relationship broke off. Yet, others claim that Sharifzadeh had never contacted Nabdel, and Nabdel and Dehqani were only indirectly related to Sharifzadeh, but they did not accept Sharifzadeh's views and did not help him (Momeni, 1979, pp. 48-49, 53-54).

It can be concluded that certain leaders of the Revolutionary Committee theoretically believed in an armed struggle in that situation. When Sharifzadeh was in the Iraqi Kurdistan, he sent a letter to Hisami. He stated that Mullah Mustafa Barzani, on the orders of Iran, persecuted and surrendered their friends, while Jalal Talabani supported them. Sharifzadeh emphasized that a revolutionary storm had enveloped Iran, and the masses had reached the conclusion that the only way to freedom was to pick up weapons and go to the mountains. He stressed that not only for Iran but for all oppressed and exploited nations, the armed uprising of the working masses is "guerrilla warfare," which should start in the countryside and prepare masses of peasants for armed struggles (Hisami, 2011, pp. 120-121). Some researchers believe that the reason for some members of the KDP-I to initiate armed struggle was to protect their lives. Khizri emphasizes that Mo'ini and other peshmergas did not wish to make a revolt but they had to, because they were fearful of being handed over to Iran. Consequently, armed struggle of the 1967-1968 was imposed on the Branch 3 of the KDP-I. They did not have any plan for their revolt.

The next factor that affected turning to armed struggle was the effect of liberation movements around the world. At this time, liberation movements in Asia, Africa, and Latin America were in their heights under the leadership of leftist groups (Khizri, 2003, pp. 128, 155-156).

Some cadres of the party did not join the Revolutionary Committee. Dehqan states that the Committee members wanted to use Mo'ini and later take over the leadership. Dehqan asserts that he and Amir Qazi disagreed with this movement and remained neutral. They believed that first the discord among the leadership should be resolved, a clear policy should be determined, organizational activities should be set up, and later armed struggle should be started (Qazi, 2010, pp. 446-447). An alternative perspective belongs to Amir Qazi, claiming that the emergence of the 1967-1968 movement was ignited by Mo'ini (Qazi, 2010, pp. 195-196, 198).

5.8.6.2. Activities of the Revolutionary Committee. One of the activities of the Revolutionary Committee was publishing three issues of the newspaper *Tishk* (Ray). While in Iran, Mo'ini also published the newspaper *Roj* (Sun), the organ of the Branch 3 of the KDP-I, in Autumn 1966 (Hisami, 2011, pp. 110-111; Hassanzadeh, n.d., p. 122; Khizri, 2003, pp. 142; Hisami, 1988, p. 205). In Autumn 1966, Mo'ini also sent a letter and an issue of *Roj* (*Sun*) to Hisami through the Iraqi communists. Hisami, at the request of Radmanesh, translated the contents of *Roj* (Sun) into Persian and gave it to Radmanesh for broadcasting in *Radio Peyk-e Iran* (Iran Courier). In addition, Mo'ini sent a letter, via Radmanesh, to the Communist Party of the Soviet Union (Hisami, 2011, p. 111).

Due to the intrigues of Tawfiq, members of the Revolutionary Committee were persecuted, arrested, and turned over to Iran by the KDP (Iraq). To protect their lives, some members inevitably returned to Iran but were ambushed by the Iranian gendarmes (Hisami, 2011, pp. 110-111). Three members of the Revolutionary Committee contacted the Tudeh Party (Hisami, 2011, p. 111). Siraji and Sulayman Mo'ini wrote a letter to Hisami and asked him to return to Kurdistan.

Hisami wrote a letter on 2 January 1966 to Radmanesh, asking to help him go to the Iraqi Kurdistan. Radmanesh accepted. Hisami returned to Iraq in April 1967 and had a meeting with the leaders of the Revolutionary Committee including Sharifzadeh. They discussed the movement and their relations with the Tudeh Party. On 19 May 1967, Hisami left Baghdad for Syria and Germany. In Berlin, he met Iraj Iskandari [later, the General (First)) Secretary of the Tudeh Party of Iran (1969-1979) who agreed to help the Revolutionary Committee. On 18 July 1967, Siraji, in a letter to Hisami, wrote that they had joined Mo'ini. When they returned to Iran, they chose a 21-cadre (including Hisami) Revolutionary Committee leadership (Hisami, 2011, pp. 111, 113-115).

The peshmergas of the Revolutionary Committee carried out activities within Iranian Kurdistan. During 1967-1968, Sulayman Mo'ini and other peshmergas had stayed for three nights in the house of Abdullah Qazi in the village of Konade (Kohneh deh) (Qazi, 2005, pp. 176-177, 180). Although they tried not to engage with the Iranian armed forces, the attacks of the army forced them to defend themselves. For instance, in July 1967, the first group of peshmergas who fell under gendarmerie attack, using helicopters, was the group under Naho Pashayy and his friends in Salmas. In a heroic battle, Naho Pashayy and his four friends were killed. Besides, five peshmergas were attacked by the Iranian forces in the village of Sarawan in Piranshahr. They killed nine soldiers before seeking refuge in the village of Alana, which was controlled by the Iraqi Kurdish movement. But the Kurdish forces attacked them and, while they killed one of them and wounded another, they inevitably surrendered to Iran and were later executed (Gadani, 2008a, pp. 154-155). Also, Sulayman Mo'ini's peshmergas engaged in a conflict in the territory of Mangurayati in which five gendarmes, and Silaman (Sulayman), son of Bapir Agha, were killed by the peshmergas (Qazi, 2005, p. 182). In Summer 1967, Sulayman Mo'ini and his comrades were attacked by the Iranian forces who used a helicopter, in the village of Spisang, and Mo'ini's peshmergas killed a few gendarmes. Abdullah Mo'ini was wounded in this battle (Gadani, 2008a, p. 155). Finally, on 13 October 1967, Mullah Mahmoud Zangana was killed in a shootout with the gendarmes in Bairam, Mahabad. His corpse was put on public display for three days in Mahabad, Piranshahr, and Naqadeh (Hisami, 1988, pp. 47-48).

The cooperation between the Revolutionary Committee and the Tudeh Party became more serious. On 9 February 1968, a meeting was held in Baghdad between Radmanesh and Ghassemlou from the Tudeh Party, and Siraji, Mo'ini, and Hisami from the Revolutionary Committee. They signed a joint declaration that regarded armed revolt positively and as inevitable. The declaration announced their goal to gradually expand armed struggle in Iran (Hisami, 2011, pp. 116-119; Kaveh, 2005, pp. 82-83). Appendix 16 shows this declaration.

The activities of the peshmergas elevated the Kurdish people's spirit, and many supported the movement. However, the Iranian government used some Kurds who collaborated and participated in military activities against the Kurdish movement. The Kurds used the word *jash* (traitor; originally, "little donkey") to refer derisively to a Kurd who supported an anti-Kurd government. In 1968, the government allocated 30-40 million tomans for suppressing the Kurdish movement while it chose Lieutenant General Oveissi as the Commander of the Iranian forces. He later became the Commander-in-Chief of Iranian Gendarmerie (Gadani, 2008a, p. 155). Between 10,000 and 12,000 gendarmes under General Oveissi were deployed from Tehran to the Jaldian Garrison, a village in Piranshahr, West Azerbaijan. In addition, they hired 1200 jash, most from Kermanshah and Lorestan (Sardashti, 2002a, p. 34).

The role of Barzanis in pushing some of the leaders of the KDP-I to create the Revolutionary Committee, and in suppressing the Revolutionary Committee had been addressed by researches. Hossein Madani, a member and political consultant of the KDP, and a previous member of the Politburo of the PDKI-RL, claims that it was said that the Revolutionary Committee, without informing Mullah

Mustafa Barzani, had contacted Gamal Abdul Nasser, the President of Egypt, and received funds and weapons from him. For this reason, Barzani was angry with the Committee (Personal communication, October 13, 2012). Qadir Wirya, a member of the Politburo of the KDP, states that the Revolutionary Committee did not aim to create a wide movement in Iranian Kurdistan; it was imposed on them. They felt that their lives were endangered by the leaders of the Kurdish movement in Iraq. One of the weaknesses of the Iraqi Kurdish movement under Barzani was that they killed or turned in members of the armed uprising of 1967-1968 to Iran (Personal communication, October 22, 2012).

In addition to the attacks of the Iranian army, the Revolutionary Committee members were also under attacks by the KDP (Iraq). Many sources reveal that the prominent leader of the uprising, Sulayman Mo'ini, was killed by the KDP (Iraq). In mid-spring 1968, it was heard that Mo'ini and Khalil Shawbash were arrested through Qala Tagarani (an Iranian secret agent) by Seddiq Afandi. Amir Qazi asked Barzani not to kill or turn in Mo'ini to Iran. After they both were killed, Mo'ini's body was submitted to Iran. His body was displayed in public in Sardasht, Piranshahr, Naqadeh, and then given to his father in Mahabad (Qazi, 2010, p 187, 190; Hisami, 2011, p. 119-120; Gadani, 2001, p. 29). Regarding the death of Sulayman Mo'ini, Idris Barzani, son of Mullah Mustafa Barzani, had reportedly said that for the interests of the revolution, one sometimes must drink his brother's blood (Qazi, 2010, p. 192).

The second big loss for the Revolutionary Committee was the death of Sharifzadeh and his three friends after a six-hour heroic battle against about 400 Iranian forces in the village of Darena in Baneh on 2 May 1968. Siraji who had already returned to Iraq, was secretly living under the Iraqi Communist Party and Jalal Talabani (Gadani, 2008a, p. 156; Khizri, 2003, pp. 21-22). The third misfortune of the peshmergas was the arrest of the Mullah Awara through some traitor Kurds in the village of Diwalan in Sardasht in mid-spring 1968 and his execution on 2 September 1968 (Hassanzadeh, n.d., p. 124). In June 1968, Abdullah Mo'ini and Mina Sham were killed in a heroic battle. After that, a group of 25-30 peshmergas went to Bakrajo where the headquarters of the KDP (Iraq) Political Bureau was located. Later the peshmergas along with the KDP (Iraq) Political Bureau and the Iraqi government attacked the KDP (Iraq) and occupied Qaladiza. Another group of 25 peshmergas were under the KDP (Iraq) in Erbil. However, the KDP (Iraq) surrendered Salih Lajani and Sulayuman Karqashan to Iran where they were executed in Jaldian (Qazi, 2010, pp. 193-194). Gadani and Sardashti have provided some detailed information about the scope of the clashes between the peshmergas and the Iranian government (Gadani, 2008a, pp. 156-159; Sardashti, 2002a, pp. 77-79, 82; see Appendix 17). Mostafa Shalmashi, a member of the Politburo of the KDP, states that after the leaders of armed struggle were killed, some of the peshmergas continued to fight for five to seven months before returning to the Iraqi Kurdistan (Personal communication, November 14, 2012).

After the deaths of Mo'ini and Sharifzadeh, and the capture of Mullah Awara, a meeting was held on 14 September 1968 in Germany, in which the following from the KDP-I and the Tudeh Party participated: Reza Radmanesh, Abdul Samad Kambakhsh, Iraj Iskandari, Abdul Rahman Ghassemlou, Hassan Qizilji, and Karim Hisami. In the meeting, the letter of Siraji was read. The meeting came to the conclusion that it was unpractical and useless to continue armed struggle in Kurdistan under present conditions (Hisami, 2011, pp. 120-121). The Tudeh Party, in a declaration in October 1968, announced that the Iranian government had sent more than 12,000 army and gendarmes to suppress the Kurds. During the last two months, dozens of Kurdish freedom-fighters had been executed without trials (Hisami, 2011, p. 122). The Tudeh Party, in November 1968, wrote a letter to all democratic parties and organizations in the world and asked them to oppose the Iranian government's crimes against the Kurds. The KDP-I distributed a declaration to many freedom-seeking parties and forces of the world. After the distribution of the Tudeh Party's declaration, many dissident parties and organizations in the world condemned the Iranian government (Hisami, 1988, pp. 165-177; Hisami, 2011, p. 123; Gadani, 2008a, pp. 163-164; Sardashti, 2002a, pp. 43-44; see Appendix 18). The Iranian government brutally suppressed the Kurdish movement. Under Lieutenant General Oveissi hundreds from different parts of Kurdistan were arrested, sent to Jaldian garrison, and tortured. Some were executed or were imprisoned in Urmiya, and more than 100 Kurds were sent to Falak ol-Aflak Prison (Castle) in Luristan (Gadani, 2008a, p. 160).

Aside from some productive cooperation between the KDP (Iraq) and the KDP-I, the wrongheaded policy of the KDP (Iraq) regarding the KDP-I, before, during, and after the establishment of the Revolutionary Committee, is well documented. Some of the party's members, alive or dead, were turned over to the Iranian government. In addition, some of the peshmergas of the KDP (Iraq) were cooperating with the Iranian forces in persecuting the Kurds in Iran. In Spring 1967, for example, Abdul Wahab Otroushi, a chief of the KDP (Iraq), arrested five party peshmergas, including Mam Askandar, and turned them over to Iran in Nawsoud. They were sentenced to two to five years prison terms. Otroushi, in Summer 1967, imprisoned Mullah Rahim Wirdi in the Biyara Prison and, after a month, ordered his killing. The KDP (Iraq) submitted these peshmergas to Iran where they were executed: Salih Lajani, Sulayman Karqashan, Ali Gowe Rash, Qadir Chil Koch, Qadir Panira, Muhammad Amin Shirej, Abdullah Bayza Qinja, and so on (Hassanzadeh, n.d., pp. 123-124; Khizri, 2003, pp. 83, 166-167, 11 of Appendix; Gadani, 2008a, 159-160).

Many years later, Masoud Barzani addressed the policy of the KDP (Iraq) regarding the Kurdish movement in 1967-1968. Masoud Barzani (2004b) writes that the revolution in 1967 had to take unfortunate actions that were inevitable. It arrested Sulayman Mo'ini, the opponent of Ahmad Tawfiq, killed him, and delivered his corpse to Iran. According to Masoud Barzani, Sulayman Mo'ini had relied on the "*Jashakani 66*" (the 1966 traitors, meaning the KDP [Iraq] Politburo lead by Ibrahim Ahmad and Jalal Talabani), and cooperated with the Iraqi regime against the Kurdish Revolution (p. 191). Amir Qazi (2010) claims that Masoud Barzani's view regarding the killing of Sulayman Mo'ini is unjust because he had not had any relations with the Iraqi government or with the group of Ahmad and Talabani (p. 409). If the KDP (Iraq) openly addressed its political mistake regarding the KDP at that time, it would have helped the creation of a more productive and trustful relationship between the Kurds.

5.8.7. The 2nd Conference of the KDP-I. The 2nd Conference of the KDP-I was held on 17 August 1969 in one of the villages of the Qandil Mountains in the Sangasar region. The Conference aimed to rebuild the CC in order to gather the scattered members of the party. The Conference asked Ghassemlou and Hisami to return to Kurdistan and continue their cooperation with the KDP-I. The Conference also asked Tawfiq to clarify his position in regards to his relations with the KDP-I, because the party wanted to be independent and rid itself of the influences of others. At the end of Winter 1970 (after 11 March 1970), Ghassemlou returned to Iraq (Gadani, 2008a, pp. 174-175; Ali Mahmood Shekhani, 2007, p. 121). Tawfiq did not participate in the 2nd Conference and sent letters to the CC and the Conference in which he announced his resignation from the CC. The leadership, through Mullah Sayyed Rashid, asked Tawfiq to retract his resignation, but he declined. Finally, after the declaration of 11 March 1970, the party accepted his resignation (Hassanzadeh, n.d., p. 125-126).

The 2nd Conference amended the CC. After choosing three new members, the new CC included Ahmad Tawfiq, Ghani Bolourian, Aziz Yousefi, Amir Qazi, Mullah Sayyed Rashid Saqqizi, Mamosta Abdullah Hassanzadeh, Hassan Rastgar, and Mamosta Hemin. As it was mentioned, Tawfiq did not participate in the Conference, and Bolourian and Yousefi were in prison. The leadership, elected in the 2nd Conference, was against the armed struggle of 1967-1968 (Hassanzadeh, n.d., p. 125).

On 11 March 1970, the declaration of the Iraqi government about the autonomy of the Kurds was announced (Gadani, 2008a, p. 175). Amir Qazi, Hemin, and Hassanzadeh visited Mullah Mustafa Barzani and asked him to remove restrictions on the KDP-I's activates. They were disappointed when Barzani told them that he could not help them. However, Barzani stated that because the situation had changed and the KDP (Iraq) now had ministers in the Iraqi government, the KDP-I could negotiate with the Iraqi government about its political activities in Iraq (Hassanzadeh, n.d., p. 127). After the declaration, Ghassemlou returned to Iraq. He contacted the KDP-I leaders in order to unite and reconstruct the KDP-I. In the Spring of 1970, Ghassemlou called Amir Qazi to join him and renew the KDP-I. Qazi claims that while he and other leaders of the KDP-I did not have a problem working with Ghassemlou, they did not agree about working with Ghassemlou's friends, such as Hisami, Rizwani and Siraji, who were supporters of the Tudeh Party. They especially emphasized Siraji, whom they thought was responsible for the calamity of the 1967-1968 movement. The negotiations took a few months (Qazi, 2010, p. 211) and resulted in the formation of *Komitay Sarkirdayati Katii Hzibi Dimokrati Kurdistan* (Provisional Leadership Committee of the Kurdistan Democratic Party), also called Provisional CC or Provisional Leadership. In June 1970, the KDP-I bases merged in Hiran and Nazanin. When the parties of Ghassemlou and the KDP-I gathered again, it was revealed that the party members had two different views, which caused discord among them. Siraji previously had Maoist ideas and had later become a supporter of the Tudeh Party. Amir Qazi, Mamosta Abdullah Hassanzadeh, and others had nationalist perspectives. Nevertheless, these two outlooks gradually converged. However, both Tawfiq and Ghassemlou announced that they would not work with each other. Finally, a Provisional CC was selected. Hassanzadeh states that, in a meeting in a teahouse on the street of Abunawas in Baghdad, six people, including Ghassemlou, chose a CC of eight members. This was against the party's principles and made the party membership furious. The Provisional CC was supposed to prepare the conditions for a conference. Thus, a committee for writing the party constitution was chosen. On 30 September 1970, Ghassemlou returned to Bulgaria, where he, Hisami, and Qizilji wrote the KDP-I program. They choose the following slogan: "Overthrowing the Dictatorial Regime of Shah and Establishing an Iranian Federative Republic." At the beginning of October 1970, Ghassemlou had a consultation with Iraj Iskandari, the new General Secretary of the Tudeh Party, in Prague. Iskandri suggested this slogan: "Democracy for Iran, Autonomy for Kurdistan." When Ghassemlou returned to Kurdistan, the latter slogan was accepted by the KDP-I. On 1 May 1971, the commission distributed the platform and constitution among the members in order to read and be prepared to discuss them at the next conference (Gadani, 2008a, pp. 176-177; Ali Mahmood Shekhani, 2007, p. 122; Hassanzadeh, n.d., p. 129; Hisami, 2011, pp. 126-127; Hisami, 1990, p. 20; see Appendix 8).

Regarding the impact of Ghassemlou on the party, Hassanzadeh claims that from 1960 to 1970, Tawfiq's line dominated the party. His views had moved away from the party's directions from the original principles of the party. The leaders were not aware of the principles of a political party. Everything changed when Ghassemlou returned to the party. He had the experience of working with political parties, both his party and the Tudeh Party, as well as knowledge about the modern parties. Also, the role of Ghassemlou in creating a relationship with the Iraqi government was crucial. After the declaration of 11 March 1970, on Barzani's recommendation, the KDP-I, for the first time (through Sami Abdul Rahman), created relations with the Iraqi government and received financial help (Hassanzadeh, nd., p. 129; Hassanzadeh, 2012, pp. 71-72, 162-163). At this time, the KDP-I resumed the publication of the *Kurdistan*, starting in Winter 1971 (Gadani, 2008a, p. 179).

The declaration of 11 March 1970 made some members of the KDP-I see that they should, as soon as possible, return to Iranian Kurdistan and launch an armed struggle against the Iranian government. Other members rejected the idea until a formidable organization was in place. On 13 May 1971, the Provisional CC published a declaration that pointed out that the CC believed that the main method of struggle for the liberation of Kurdistan from the Shah's regime and imperialism was armed struggle. However, key conditions like the alliance between the Iranian democratic forces and an appropriate external situation for launching armed struggle did not yet exist. The declaration held that the CC should prepare the party's organization and educate political and military cadres to participate in the broader Iranian revolution and use its connections with the forces outside of Kurdistan in participation in armed struggle (Gadani, 2008a, pp. 178-179; Hisami, 1990, pp. 20-21).

The history and struggles of the KDP-I since 1971 will be discussed in the next chapter.

5.9. Examining the Views and Achievements of the J.K. and the KDP

The J.K.'s and the KDP's ideological, political, and social views are reflected in their publications *Nishtman* and *Kurdistan* (both journal and newspaper). A comparison between the perspectives of the J.K. and the KDP clearly reveals the existence of similarities between them. In fact, we find the continuity of the outlooks of the J.K. within the KDP. For one thing, such similarity can be attributed to the authors of the J.K. also writing for KDP publications. The J.K. and the KDP had a democratic and just nationalist perspective mixed with traditional, religious, non-scientific, patriarchal, and sometimes even racist outlooks. This is why we need to focus on the views of the J.K. and the KDP regarding class, religion, gender, and race.

(a) Class. Many articles in the J.K. and the KDP publications reveal that these parties defended the oppressed classes, often by criticizing mullahs, sheikhs, and landlords. Hassanpour states that the majority of people in Kurdistan, during the beginning period of Zabihi's life, lived in the villages dominated by feudalistic and tribal relations (Karimi, 1999, p. 22). In *Nishtman*, Issue 1 (June 1943), the J.K. stressed that one of the main reasons for the backwardness of the Kurds was the greediness of the Kurdish tribal chiefs who received funds from the government. The J.K. advised them to throw out this greediness because it delays Kurdistan's independence (Karimi, 2008, pp. 5-6). This article indicates that the J.K. did not have a profound understanding of the social classes, and its critique of the higher classes was based on ethics. In *Nishtman*, Issue 5 (January 1945), Hemin criticized Aghas in a poem and said they were idlers, thieves, thoughtless, and unclean. The Kurdish homeland had been in ruins due to their cruelty, and they are a thousand times worse than the foreigners (Karimi, 2008, p. 32). In *Nishtman*, Issue 2 (October 1943), M. Farrokh wrote an article about the great October Revolution in Russia (Karimi, 2008, p. 56). The ideas of supporting the rights of the lower classes and socialism are frequently observed in the KDP's publications. The *Kurdistan*, Issue 3 (March 1946) contains a translated article about socialism (Hussein, 2008, p. 571), while the *Kurdistan*, Issue 4 (May 1946) covers an article about Scientific Socialism. In their poems, Hajar and Hemin admire Lenin, Stalin, and the Red Army. In the same issue, Muhammad Majdi, in a poem, praises the Russian hammer and sickle (Hussein, 2008, pp. 613, 628-629, 644).

(b) Islam. The Islamic beliefs strongly constituted the ideas of the J.K. followers. The J.K. used Islamic ideas to fortify nationalist struggle and constituted a criterion for membership. Appeal to Islam was present in J.K. publications (Karmi, 2008, p. 10). The Islamic outlook repeatedly appears in the KDP's publications, too. For instance, in the *Kurdistan*, Issue 6-7 (June-July 1946), M. S. Qizilji, in a poem, asks the prophet Muhammad to help the Kurdish nation to get

its freedom (Hussein, 2008, p. 656). According to the *Kurdistan*, Issue 14 (13 February 1946), the CC of the KDP gave gifts, including a *Quran* and two *barmals* (a cloth cover for the praying of the Muslims), to Qazi Muhammad. He accepted *The Quran* and said that there is nothing as dear and great as *The Quran*, and returned the *barmals* as gifts to the KDP (Saleh and Saleh, 2007, p. 55).

(c) Patriarchy. According to Hassanpour (2001), "Patriarchal domination is ubiquitous in the Kurdish language in everyday acts of writing and speaking, poetry and prose, music, lexicography, and other contexts" (p. 257). This patriarchal language has been frequently observed in Kurdish publications before the J.K., the J.K. era, and thereafter. While some articles in the J.K. publications advocated the improvement of women's status, many others looked down upon women. For example, in a poem in *Hawar* (*Shout*), Hajar wrote that a wise of the earth prefers a mannishly dying to a womanly living (Karimi, 2008, p. 336). Such a gendered outlook repeatedly shows itself in the KDP's publications (Hussein, 2008, pp. 536, 671).

(d) Racism. Some articles in the J.K. publications reveal racist views. In *Nishtman,* Issue 2 (October 1943), addressing the Kurdish people, Hemin wrote that they are from a pure nation and a pure race. Their grandfathers in Kurdistan lived free and independent (Karimi, 2008, p. 41). Even six decades after the establishment of the J.K., Shirazi (2000), an influential member of the J.K. asserted that Mahabad's people are from the pure and untouched Aryan race (Shirazi, 2000, p. 31). The KDP publications contain racist ideas. In *Kurdistan*, Issue 4 (May 1946), Saif al-Qozat, in a poem, praises the Kurds for being the only pure-blooded people in Iran because they had not mixed with Turks and Arabs (Hussein, 2008, p. 611). Humiliating accounts of other peoples were often invoked to make the "natural beauty" of the Kurds stand out (Hussein, 2008, pp. 697-700). In short, while the goals and the programs of the J.K. and the KDP were clearly anti-racist, racist expressions existed in their publications. It should be mentioned that the

racial views expressed in the J.K. and the KDP publications were mainly related to admiring the Kurdish nation instead of looking down on other nations. None of these authors claimed that, for instance, the Kurdish nation is superior to other nations. In addition, racist views were not based on a theoretical perspective but mainly a reflection of the humiliation of the dominant, aggressive nationalism of the governments that ruled over Kurdistan.

5.9.1. Views on the J.K. Some scholars maintain that the J.K. had major weaknesses. Hawrami (2007) asserts that the J.K. lacked a proper constitution, doctrine, and program, and its critique of the Kurdish structure was just a moral critique. In addition, the J.K. did not have faith in the power of society. So, the J.K. did not provide a clear strategy for the independence and liberation of Kurdistan (p. 125). Omar Balaki, a member of the Politburo of the KDP, claims that the goal of the J.K. was to create an independent Kurdistan, but it was a very closed organization and hardly developing (Personal communication, September 28, 2012).

The ideology and political perspectives of the J.K. have also been discussed by scholars. The ideology of the J.K. was based on nationalism and religion. Religion has fortified Kurdish nationalism (Mawloudi Sabian, 1994, pp. 65-66, 162). Nabaz claims that the J.K. had a Kurdish nationalist ideology that belonged to petit-bourgeois intellectuals (Gohari, 1999, p. 99). Hemin (1999) emphasizes that the members of the J.K. were from different classes and had different political and philosophical perspectives. Nevertheless, they all fought for the liberation of Kurdistan (Hemin, 1999, p. 21). Hawrami (2008) asserts that the J.K. was neither on the right nor the left of the political spectrum, and it did not tie itself to any of the great powers. It was a classic progressive Kurdish nationalist party that demanded the freedom of the Kurds. It was a democracy-seeking, anti-fascist, anti-reactionary, and political representative of an exploited nation. The J.K. was like a front comprised of all the classes and beliefs, such as the supporters of the Soviets,

England, America, and Iran, as well as independence and autonomy (p. 109). Finally, Hassanpour asserts that the idea of bourgeois democracy in Kurdistan appeared first in the poems of Haji Qadir Koyi (1817-1897). About forty years later, his ideas were materialized in the political organization called the J.K. The majority of the founders and members of the J.K. came from petit-bourgeoisies. Nevertheless, the J.K. did not surpass Haji Qadir's ideas. Out of the key democratic struggles in Kurdistan—namely, the liberation of peasants from the exploitation of the landlords, the liberation of women from patriarchal relations, and the emancipation of the Kurds from Iranian national oppression—the J.K.'s agendas and activities were focused on the national oppression of the Kurds (Karimi, 1999, pp. 23-24).

In short, the J.K. was the first well-organized modern Kurdish progressive nationalist political organization in Iranian Kurdistan that fought for the Kurds' right to self-determination. The J.K. defended the oppressed classes, was anti-reactionary, praised socialism, and was anti-fascist. It supported the advancement of women. Altogether, it was a leftist organization, while its main perspective remained Islamic.

The J.K. had some major shortcomings. Its dominant worldview was influenced by patriarchal, traditional, and Islamic cultures. One of the effects of this outlook was to look down on the abilities of women in their social and national struggles. Therefore, the J.K. mainly ignored the mobilization of women in Iranian Kurdistan. The next shortfall of the J.K. was that it lacked a profound class analysis of society. Its critique of the upper classes, such as the landlords, was mainly a moral critique. It also did not have a deep analysis of race. These caused some of its members to use racial expressions in J.K. publications. Another weakness of the J.K. was that it fell short in terms of having an inclusive political ideology, program, and constitution. It did not have a clear strategy to achieve the independence of Kurdistan. Finally, the J.K. leaders' ideological, political, educational, and organizational understanding was lower than that of other Iranian political parties at that time. Despite all of these weaknesses, the J.K. significantly affected the development of the Kurdish nationalist movement in Iran.

5.9.2. Factors affecting the fall of the Kurdistan Republic. Scholars, historians, politicians, and commentators have variously analyzed the reasons for the fall of the Kurdistan Republic. While both external and internal factors contributed to the defeat of the movement, the most fundamental reasons were external rather than internal. The most crucial reason was the armed interference of the United States and Britain in the Iranian issues. The government of Qavam al-Saltaneh made a military pact with the United States; the Americans controlled the Iranian army, gendarmerie, and police. The military invasions of Azerbaijan and Kurdistan were under the leadership of General Herbert Norman Schwarzkopf. At the same time, the majority of Kurdistan, including Sanandaj, Kermanshah, Marivan, Oraman, Shah Abad, and Qasr-e Shirin, were under British control. Therefore, any type of Kurdish armed movement would be confronted by the British. Another external factor was that the Soviet Union did not support the Kurdish movement to the extent it assisted the Azerbaijan movement. Under the influence of the Azerbaijan leaders, the Soviet Union observed the Kurdish movement as part of a democratic movement within Azerbaijan, not as an independent movement. The Soviet Union's military assistance to Kurdistan was limited. It did not provide the Kurds with cannons, tanks, planes, and anti-plane artillery, as it did with Azerbaijan. The next external factor was the treachery of some of the Azerbaijan leaders, who surrendered themselves to the Iranian government and opened the way for the returning army to Azerbaijan. Finally, another external factor was Qavam-al-Saltaneh's crafty diplomacy: he made an oil agreement with the Soviet Union. Qavam al-Saltaneh promised to fight for democracy and deceived the Soviet Union (Qazi, 2012, pp. 360-364, 366, 368).

One of the internal factors contributing to the defeat of the movement was that the Kurdish government could not attract the peasants to the movement. It did not provide the opportunity for them to properly participate in the government's and the party's organizations. The next internal reason was the lack of cooperation of the Iranian democratic forces, except between the Tudeh Party and the Azerbaijan Democratic Party. The cooperation between the Kurdish movement and the democratic forces in Iran remained only on paper. The further internal element was that the Kurdish government and the party leaders had weak social and revolutionary knowledge. Without mastering Marxism-Leninism, leading a democratic and social movement could not be correctly guided. In addition, the leadership of the movement, especially Qazi Muhammad, was deceived by the promises of the Iranian officials after the defeat of Azerbaijan. Finally, another internal factor was that Qazi Muhammad did not radically punish the traitors such as Omar Khan Shikak, Sheikh Abdullah Afandi Gailani, Abdullah Agha Ilkhanizadeh, and Rahmat Shafe'i. Instead, he provided the opportunity to Omar Khan Shikak and Abdullah Agha Ilkhanizadeh to work in the Party and the government (Qazi, 2012, pp. 369-372, 374-376).

According to Ghassemlou (2000), "The main reasons for the failure of the Kurdistan Republic were the internal weakness of the movement, the inner weakness of the party, and for the most part, the weakness of the leadership of the Kurdistan Democratic Party." He asserts that the external factors included the fall of the Azerbaijan government, the United States and Great Britain's support for the Iranian government, and the lack of the expected support of the Kurdistan Republic by the Soviet Union (pp. 138, 145, 151-152). Others enumerate the following reasons for the fall of the Kurdistan Republic: the Iranian government's imposed economic sanctions against Kurdistan; the treacheries of certain Kurdish tribal leaders; the economic weakness and backwardness of Kurdish society, intellectual weakness of Kurdistan; and the retreat of the Russians (Moradi, 1996, pp. 62-64,

83; Sardashti, 2002b, pp. 216-220; Shapasandi, 2007, p. 62; Saleh, 2003, pp. 3-5). Parsa Benab (2004) states that two important factors caused the fall of the Kurdistan Republic. The first factor was the cooperation of the United States and Great Britain against the Soviet Union at the beginning of the Cold War, which caused Qavam al-Saltaneh to become the Prime Minister. Their ultimatum in 1946 caused the Red Army to evacuate the Kurdish territories. As Mullah Mustafa Barzani had brilliantly claimed, this was not the defeat of the Kurds by the Iranian army; it was the defeat of the Soviet Union by the United States and Great Britain. The second and main factor was that the Kurdish leaders had inadequate knowledge and experience (pp. 314-315).

Some scholars have emphasized the external factors. Jwaideh (2006) asserts that "[p]robably the single most direct cause of the collapse of both Azerbaijan and Mahabad Republic was the Soviet Union's decision, made under intense pressure from the Western powers, to withdraw its military forces from Iran in May 1946" (p. 260). Madani claims that the main reason for the fall of the Kurdistan Republic was the lack of support from an international superpower. He believes that the lack of tribal support was not an important factor because the tribes always supported the dominant power (Personal communication, October 13, 2012). Said Shams, a Kurdish academician, claims that external factors had a fundamental role in the fall of the Kurdistan Republic. The international balance had changed against the Republic. The United States and Britain pushed the Soviet Union, and the Soviet Union could not support the Republic. Shams adds that the Soviet Union was the only country that condemned Qazi Muhammad's execution (Personal communication, October 18, 2012). The strength of the United States' influence over the Soviet Union and the former's ultimatum. According to the Shah of Iran, Mohammad Reza Pahlavi (1980), when the Russians did not withdraw their army on 2 March 1946, "Truman sent a polite note to the Russians on March 6. It was ignored. A stiffer letter followed, and on March 24, Moscow announced the Soviet troops would pull out. By May, the Red Army had officially departed" (p. 75).

Some scholars have addressed the possibility of the resistance of the Kurdistan Republic against the suppression of the Iranian army (Sardashti, 2002b, p. 220; Hawrami, 2008, p. 239; Qazi, 2005, pp. 94-95). Although it was possible to resist the government, and it might have brought up some positive effects on the Kurdish and Iranian democratic movement, nonetheless, in the long term, the lack of a strong Iranian movement and their support of Kurdistan was very unlikely for the Kurdish movement to succeed.

5.9.3. Views on the KDP and the Kurdistan Republic. Controversial perspectives exist about the nature, achievements, and outcomes of the Kurdish movement and the Kurdistan Republic. For various reasons, some question the Kurdish movement and the Kurdistan Republic as an authentic nationalist movement. Strangely, Naqibzadeh (2000) claims that in WWII, the Mahabad Republic was established not by the Kurdish people but by a thousand rebels who were related to the foreigners. The geographical area of this Republic was smaller than a village. However, paradoxically, he claims that the total population of Mahabad was 30,000. He asserts that at the present time, the government's task is to give correct historical knowledge [to the Kurds] to prevent the disturbance of national security and the territorial integrity of the country (p. 179). Naqibzadeh is an Iranian scholar whose views regarding Kurdish nationalism are incorrect, biased, and discriminative. For instance, he totally ignores the existence of a Kurdish nationalist movement, which led to the establishment of the Kurdistan Republic. He also humiliates the Kurdish nation and discards the Kurdish people's knowledge about their own identity, history, and dreams. He ignores the national rights of the Kurdish people.

Nerwiy (2012) applies the theoretical views of Gellner and Smith to the Kurdish national movement in 1945-1946. He states that for Gellner transition to an industrial society is necessary for the development of a nationalist movement. However, Kurdistan was mainly an agricultural society during the period, with more than 90 percent of the Kurdish population being illiterate. Nerwiy concludes that the Kurdish movement in 1946 was not a proper nationalist movement (p. 256). According to Nerwiy (2012), a crucial reason for the creation of the Republic of Kurdistan was a "reaction of the self" in response to the "action of the other." The establishment of the Autonomous Government of Azerbaijan inspired the Iranian Kurds both politically and psychologically to rapidly announce the Republic of Kurdistan (p. 257). It seems that Nerwiy ignores the realities of the Kurdish nationalist movement in favor of upholding Gellner's theory. In contrast, Amir Hassanpour (2007) states that, in the Kurdistan Republic of 1946, which was a modern state, the landed, tribal, and religious notables compromised with the urban middle classes (p. 7). According to Kutschera, the Kurdistan Republic was the first Kurdish movement led by the intellectuals (Gadani, 2008a, p. 69). Ghassemlou states that the most important achievement of the Kurdistan Republic was that the Kurdish people, after a long period, obtained their national freedom. The Kurdish movement of 1945-1946 was a part of the peoples' struggle against imperialism and fascism, as well as the democratic struggles of the Iranian and international proletariat (Gadani, 2008a, p. 68). In Ezat's view, the Kurdistan Republic was the greatest political change and national incident in contemporary Kurdish history; it encouraged the revival of Kurdish history, literature, language, art, and culture; it revived the economy of the region; and it established a political and national structure of the Kurdish nation. The Republic provoked the class consciousness of the Kurdish nation; it helped the Kurdish nationalist movement in the Greater Kurdistan to flourish; and it revealed the Kurdish nation's ability to create the Republic's institutions and initiated the popular movements of youth and women (Gadani, 2008a, pp. 69-70).

Concerning the characteristics of the Kurdish movement during 1941-1947, Qazi (2012) states that the most unique characteristic of the Kurdish movement was that it was nationalist, patriotic, and democratic. It was nationalist because the movement incorporated all classes within Kurdish society. At the same time, it had an internationalist feature because it accepted the national minority rights in Kurdistan. It was a democratic movement because it favored the toiling classes, struggled against the Iranian reactionary and feudalist forces, and was an inseparable part of the common international struggle against fascism and colonialism. Another feature of the movement was that the KDP, which was comprised of the most progressive members of the Kurdish society, led the movement. One of the important ideas of the KDP was that it did not separate the struggle of the Kurdish people from those of other Iranian peoples, just as it did not separate itself from the struggles of the Kurds in other countries. Finally, the most significant political feature of the movement was the establishment of the Kurdish national government that led the Kurdish people for eleven months (Qazi, 2012, pp. 353-355, 357, 358).

5.9.4. The effects and the defeat of the Kurdish armed struggle of 1967-1968. According to Gadani (2008a), the 1967-1968 Kurdish armed uprising produced several important results in retrospect. There should have been much more focus on the political and organizational issues and, as much as possible, non-engagement in armed struggle. The loss of the Revolutionary Committee members greatly damaged the struggle of Iranian and especially Kurdistan's people during the Iranian Revolution of 1979. However, the uprising ruined the Iranian state's plans for the assimilation of the Kurdish culture and diminished the effects of the White Revolution in weakening Kurdish nationalism. The uprising strengthened Kurdish national sentiments, weakened the morale of the opponents of the Kurds, and revealed that despite the Shah's claim, Iran was not an "island of stability." The movement created a revolutionary spirit among Kurdish and Iranian youth who believed in launching armed struggle against the Shah, as did the People's Mojahedin Organization of Iran (PMOI) and the Organization of the Iranian People's Fedai Guerrillas (OIPFG). In sum, the uprising provided significant momentum for the members of the KDP-I to move toward unification (pp. 168-169).

Regarding the reasons for the defeat of the movement of 1967-1968, Qazi (2010) writes that, firstly, it was an untimely movement that did not rely on a proper analysis of the condition. The 1967-1968 uprising showed that its leaders were rather irresponsible with regard to the KDP-I and the Kurdish people. The movement resulted in the deaths of many Kurdish activists and caused the imprisonment and exile of thousands of Iranian Kurds. Secondly, at that time, the KDP-I members had major disagreements amongst themselves. Thirdly, the leaders of the movement did not realize the real power of the Iranian regime in suppressing the movement. Fourthly, the Kurdish Revolution in Iraq, supported by Iran, positioned itself against armed struggle by the Iranian Kurds. The Kurdish movement in Iraq did not rely on a Kurdish strategy. Many members of this Kurdish movement in Iraq, especially Sami Abdul Rahman, had relations with the Iranian government and acted against the Iranian Kurdish activists; thus, they greatly damaged the Kurdish movement of 1967-1968 (pp. 196-199).

Salah al-Din Mohtadi writes that the armed uprising of 1967-1968 was a turning point in the political, social, and cultural history of the Kurdish nation in Iran. It was the beginning of growing leftist and revolutionary movements in Iran, and it was part of the liberating revolution of the New Left in the world, which spanned from Beijing to Paris and Latin America to the Persian Gulf and Dhofar (Khizri, 2003, n.p.). Dr. Miro Aliyar, member of the PDKI Politburo, states that the main reason for the defeat of the 1967-1968 armed uprising was the lack of a solid social base in Kurdistan. Besides, discord existed among the leadership, and the Kurdish movement in Iraq negatively affected the Iranian Kurdish movement

(Personal communication, October 22, 2012). Dr. Hossein Khalighi, a previous professor of philosophy at Tabriz and Sanandaj Universities and a previous member of the CC of the PDKI, claims that the armed struggle was imposed on the Revolutionary Committee as they faced the dilemma of having to stay in the Iraqi Kurdistan and be killed, or return to Iranian Kurdistan and be killed as the heroes of the struggle (Personal communication, December 1, 2012).

In conclusion, among the reasons that led some of the leaders, cadres, and members of the KDP-I to initiate an armed uprising in Iranian Kurdistan that lasted for about 18 months in 1967-1968 was the belief of some members of the KDP-I, in keeping the independence of the organization. In addition, it was the existence of discord among the KDP-I leadership and members, the actuality of limiting the organizational work of the KDP-I in Kurdistan of Iran by the KDP (Iraq), and the fear of submitting and being terrorized by members by the KDP (Iraq). Moreover, there were the effects of the discourse of armed struggle in Iraqi Kurdistan and around the world and the unrealistic analysis of the Kurdish and Iranian revolutionary power in confronting the Iranian regime.

While many members and supporters of the movement lost their lives or were tortured or imprisoned by the Iranian government, the heroic struggle of the 1967-1978 movement became a model for many revolutionaries in Kurdistan and Iran, revived Kurdish nationalism, especially in Iranian Kurdistan, and left its revolutionary impression on the Kurdish culture and literature, especially Kurdish poetry.

5.10. Analysis and Conclusion

The analysis of the foregoing shows us how the formation of the KDP, the Kurdistan Republic, and the Kurdish armed uprising of 1967-1968 can be understood on the axes of nationalism, national liberation, and state-building in Iran. The Kurdish nationalist movement in Iran during WWII led to the establishment of the KDP and the formation of the Kurdistan Republic, creating the first modern Kurdish democratic nationalist phenomenon in Iran. For the first time, the popular Kurdish nationalist movement in Iran was led by Kurdish intellectuals. We can clearly see that this struggle was connected to the struggles of the Iranian intellectuals and the Iranian leftist and national forces for democratic self-assertion, best expressed on the national level through the democratically-elected government of Dr. Mosaddiq and the oil nationalization movement. In the context of post-WWII and the Soviet occupation of Kurdish territories, Kurdish nationalism was epitomized by the Kurdistan Republic, which tried to negotiate with the Iranian government for its semi-independence. But in the context of the failed experience of the Kurdistan Republic, the 1953 coup in Iran, and the return of dictatorship, and in the context of the rebellious 1960s, the Kurdish nationalist movement gradually acquired national liberation dimensions, as evidenced by the Kurdish uprising of 1967-1968. Iran's Kurdish nationalist movement was greatly incited, affected, or assisted by the complex political conditions of its time, including the Kurdish nationalist movement in other parts of Kurdistan, especially Iraq, policies of the Soviet Union, democratic movement in Iran, and especially in Azerbaijan. Without the cultural and educational campaigns of the J.K., the Kurdistan Republic is unimaginable. The Kurdistan Republic was the first Republican Kurdish state in Iranian history. The Kurdistan Republic acquired great democratic achievements and, for the most part, showed the ability and the eligibility of the Kurdish nation to create its own state and conduct its destiny. It positively changed the political, social, and cultural situations in Kurdistan. The Kurdistan Republic profoundly affected the development of the Kurdish nationalist movement in the whole of Greater Kurdistan, as well as democratic movements and ideas in Iran. Of course, the Kurdistan Republic, led by the KDP, had many shortcomings. The fall of the Kurdistan Republic was the result of many internal and external dynamics. Considering the total achievements and possible potentials of the Kurdistan

Republic at that time, the main factor for its fall was external. The collaboration of the United States, Great Britain, and the Iranian government that resulted in the withdrawal of the Soviet Union's army from Iran was the foremost factor in the fall of both the Azerbaijan National Government and the Kurdistan Republic. The fall of Azerbaijan and the lack of strong support of Kurdistan by democratic forces in Iran were another important external reason. An often-missed factor was the Iranian state's increasing attempts at becoming a repressive state—that it conclusively achieved after the 1953 coup—allied with the imperialist forces and on its way to complete the process of a modern, authoritarian state-building that had started during the reign of Reza Shah. The rise of Kurdish nationalism should, therefore, be understood in relation to the consolidation of a Persianate, homogenizing, and centralist Iranian state that did not recognize the cultural rights of the national minorities, let alone their right to self-determination or a federative political system that would accommodate national and cultural differences within the country.

While the peak of the Kurdish nationalist movement in Iran was during the Kurdistan Republic of 1946, after its fall, the KDP was still the only leading organization that spearheaded the Kurdish movement. Compared with the previous Kurdish movements, such as Simko's revolt, the KDP introduced democratic and just ideas to the organization and the Kurdish struggle. However, the organization still suffered from the deeply-rooted tendency of patriarchal-tribal lordship (in the manner of Simko's leadership), endemic to the traditional Kurdish society, to lead the struggle. From Simko's movement to the J.K. and to the KDP, we witness the transformation of the traditional lordship into Michel's "iron law of oligarchy": the movement now acquired a modern, democratic organization, but it was still ruled by authoritarian figures such as Ahmad Tawfiq, supported by patriarch Mullah Mustafa Barzani, who regularly ignored or sidetracked the party constitution in order to advance his personal agendas. Likewise, even a leader from a younger generation, such as Ghassemlou, often ignored the party's principles due to his unique knowledge and position in the party. Here, we are confronted with an interesting organization that captures what Vahabzadeh (2010) has called a "constitutive paradox": a social movement-based organization that leads people's struggles for democratic rights functions and thrives through non-democratic ways.

Chapter 6: The KDP History Since 1971

This chapter discusses the history of the KDP-I from 1971 to the present time. The establishment of the 3rd Conference and the 3rd Congress of the party launched its modernization. Since the 3rd Conference, the KDP-I changed its name to the KDP (I), and in the 4th Congress, it changed to the Democratic Party of Iranian Kurdistan (PDKI). During this period, *three major formal splits* in the PDKI occurred: (1) after the 4th Congress, the PDKI (Follower of the Fourth Congress) or PDKI (FFC); (2) after the 8th Congress, the PDKI-Revolutionary Leadership or PDKI-RL; and (3) after the 13th Congress, the Kurdistan Democratic Party (KDP). In addition, this chapter reviews the role of the PDKI in the Iranian Revolution of 1979, its relations with the Iranian government, other Kurdish political organizations, and major Iranian political organizations that were active in Kurdistan. Due to the fundamental role played by Ghassemlou within the party, a brief excerpt of his biography is also presented in Appendix 19.

6.1. The 3rd Conference of the KDP (I)

The 3rd Conference of the KDP-I was held on 21 June 1971 in Koya, Iraq, in which 32 people participated (Hisami, 2011, p. 129). In the Conference, the name of the party changed to the *Hizbi Democrati Kurdistan (Eran)*, Kurdistan Democratic Party (Iran), or KDP (I) (Hassanzadeh, n.d., p. 131). At the Conference there was a disagreement regarding the naming of the Conference. Ghassemlou emphasized that the 2nd Conference of the KDP-I was not lawful. Thus this 3rd Conference of the KDP (I) should be actually called the 2nd Conference. Ghassemlou also pushed for the candidacy of Muhammad Amin Siraji. These issues created disharmony within the party. The Conference chose a CC, a Politburo, and Abdul Rahman Ghassemlou as the General Secretary (Gadani, 2008a, pp. 182-183; see Appendix 8). Tawfiq did not participate in the Conference and resigned from the CC. The CC and the Politburo contacted Tawfiq three times, asking him to accept the party's discipline. On 25 June 1970, it was decided to ask Tawfiq, Abdul Rahman Zabihi, and Mullah Rashid to join the party, but they rejected. In response, without revealing any names, Tawfiq claimed that there were spies within the party, asking the party to hand them over to him so he would interrogate, torture, extract confessions, and execute them. This was his condition for returning to the party! Tawfiq occasionally distributed declarations against the party, in which he presented himself as the party and the CC. As a result, in the *Kurdistan*, Issue 12 (2 January 1972), the party announced that Tawfiq, due to his anti-party activities, had been expelled from the party (Hassanzadeh, 2012, p. 68; Hassanzadeh, n.d. p. 132; Gadani, 2008a, pp. 183-184; Peshnimaz, 2012, p. 249). In the Summer of 1972, the Politburo was informed that Tawfiq had gone missing while in Baghdad. The party appointed Siraji to contact Iraqi officials who denied any knowledge about Tawfiq's disappearance. Later, though, it was revealed that after being tortured, Tawfiq had been executed by the Iraqi authorities (Gadani, 2008a, p. 184; Hassanzadeh, n.d., 132).

The 3rd Conference of the KDP (I) was the beginning of a great change in the party because it made the party independent. The Conference also adopted a progressive program and a constitution. The KDP (I) made principled relations (*ravabet-e osuli*) with the Kurdish and Iranian political organizations, as well as with the Iraqi government. The new issues of the *Kurdistan* were now better typeset and contained higher quality material. In order to educate the members, the party published and distributed an internal organ named the *Tekoshar* (Struggler) (Gadani, 2008a, pp. 184-185). The next significant impact of the Conference was that the CC initiated a Commission—under Hisami and including Rastgar, Rasoul Peshnimaz, Karim Hadad, and Qadir Werdi—to re-establish KDP (I) branches inside Iranian Kurdistan. These succeeded, especially in the territories of Mahabad, Sardasht, and Baneh. But while on an assignment on 22 March 1973, Qadir Werdi, a CC member, was ambushed and killed in Baneh (Gadani, 2008a, pp. 198-190;

Hassanzadeh, n.d., pp. 133-134).

An achievement of the party in this period was holding three-month courses at the end of 1972 to train its cadres. Twenty-one members participated in these courses in which Ghassemlou, Siraji, and Hisami were the instructors (Hisami, 2011, p. 135 Gadani, 2008a, p. 189). Another activity of the KDP (I) before and after the 3rd Conference was cooperation with General Dr. Mahmoud Panahian. Siraji reveals that after the assassination of the former Head of Iranian intelligence (SAVAK), Taymour Bakhtiar, in exile in Iraq by SAVAK agents in 1970, Panahian established a Front. The Front had a radio station in Baghdad run by Zabihi. Panahian and Captain Morad [Aziz] Razmavar [previous member of the Tudeh Party of Iran] were trying to establish a political Front of leftist parties that included the KDP (I) (joined the Front on 15 July 1971), the Azerbaijan Democratic Party, some Balouches, Arabs from Ahwaz and Abadan, Tawfiq, Zabihi, Shapasandi and his friends as independents. The Front had a radio station named *Radioy Shoreshgerani Eran* (Iranian Revolutionaries' Radio), run by Zabihi. The Front also published a newspaper in Persian, Azeri, and Kurdish titled *Rah-e Ettehad* (Path to Unity), or in Kurdish, *Regay Yaketi* that ran from April 1971 to October 1973—31 issues in total. The Kurdish part was organized under Zabihi and Siraji (Shapasandi, 2007, pp. 70-74; Karimi, 1999, pp. 200-207; Gadani, 2008a, pp. 187-188).

In Baghdad, the Iranian Nation's United Front was formed, and Mamadi was part of this organization. He introduced 25 cadres to be trained for guerrilla operations in Iranian Kurdistan. Mamadi also contacted Tawfiq in Baghdad, who joined the leadership of the Iranian Nation's United Front. It was decided that Tawfiq and his group of 25, after finishing military training, would join Mamadi's forces in Iranian Kurdistan. When Mamadi and his six friends were delivering arms to Iran, they were attacked by Barzanis. Mamadi was injured and, captured and handed over to Iranian authorities after 16 days. Soon, Mamadi managed to escape from prison but was arrested again in Tabriz on 21 March 1972 and was released on 25 October 1978 (Mamadi, 1999, p. 67-68, 74-84). Gadani (2008a) states that when the Iranian Revolutionaries Radio was established under General Panahian in 1971 in Iraq, the Politburo, on 15 July 1971, approved to cooperate with the Radio if it broadcast the KDP (I) policy. Siraji was appointed as the party's representative on the Radio. When Mamadi was turned in to Iran, General Panahian prepared a declaration in which he severely condemned Barzani, but the KDP (I) opposed this declaration, and consequently, the cooperation between the party and General Panahian was terminated (pp. 187-188).

The next activity of the KDP (I) since September 1971 was creating diplomatic relations with the Lebanese Communist Party, the Progressive Socialist Party of Lebanon, and the Bulgarian Communist Party—all through Hisami (Gadani, 2008a, p. 188; Hisami, 2011, p.131). The party also cooperated with the Tudeh Party. Stationed in East Germany at that time, the Tudeh invited the KDP (I) representative to a meeting. Hisami had a discussion with Iskanari and Noureddin Kianouri [the General (First) Secretary of the Tudeh Party of Iran (1979-1984)] about the KDP (I). Iskandari accepted that the KDP (I)'s Program was progressive and anti-imperialist. Kianouri announced that the Program was a Marxist program and the KDP (I), a Marxist party. However, he argued that based on Lenin's theory, a country should have just one Communist party, thus encouraging the KDP (I) to join the Tudeh Party. Kianouri emphasized that the KDP (I) should be a branch of the Tudeh Party. In contrast, Hisami emphasized creating a political front. So, the meeting did not reach any agreements (Gadani, 2008a, pp. 188-189; Hisami, 2011, p. 132).

6.2. The 3rd Congress of the Kurdistan Democratic Party (Iran) [KDP (I)]

The 3rd Congress of the KDP (I), in which 49 members participated, was held in Baghdad on 22 September 1973. The party retained its name: KDP (I) (Ali Mahmood Shekhani, 2007, p. 125, 127; Hassanzadeh, n.d., p. 136). Ghassemlou was elected as the General Secretary of the KDP (I). For the list of the CCs, see Appendix 8. It should be addressed that although in the 1st Conference of the KDP in 1955, the name of the party changed to the KDP-I, in the official documents and the literature of the party, it had been addressed as the KDP. In addition, in the Program and Constitution of the Party in the 3rd Congress, the name of the party appeared as the KDP. Between the 3rd and 4th Congresses, the KDP (I) was the party's official name. The CC makeup after the 3rd Congress was disharmonious. Some members did not believe in the party's program and constitution, others favored socialist countries, while some regarded the Soviet Union to be imperialist. The Program and Constitution were approved thanks to the influence of Ghassemlou and due to his impressive knowledge, theory, and reasoning (Hassanzadeh, 2012, pp. 165-166).

Some of the main conflicts in the 3rd Congress were over the following. Firstly, Ghassemlou questioned the legality of the 2nd Congress, but the 3rd Congress approved it as legal. Nonetheless, except for some political analyses, the 3rd Congress rejected most of the decisions made by the 2nd Congress, especially the ones that erroneously attacked the Kurdistan Republic. Secondly, members such as Hisami and Siraji emphasized that "socialism" was the final goal of the KDP (I), while others drew on a *sosializmi adilana* (just socialism) (Qazi, 2010, pp. 229-231; Gadani, 2008a, pp. 194-195). According to Shalmashi, three tendencies existed in the 3rd Congress regarding socialism: (1) one that focused on Kurdish nationalism and disregarded socialism; (2) one that was against the socialist countries, calling them revisionists; and lastly, (3) one that believed in the "actually existing socialism." In this context, Ghassemlou introduced the idea of democratic socialism. Lastly, Congress approved a "compatible socialism" ["just socialism"] (Personal communication, November 14, 2012). Hisami asserts that the party was not a class party and did not believe in class struggle. The KDP (I) accepted "just socialism" in order to attract people to the party since socialism was prevalent in the world at the time (Hisami, 1997b, pp. 299, 307).

One of the disputes within the Congress was about the armed struggle of 1967-1968. Amir Qazi and others called the 1967-1968 revolt treacherous, while Ghassemlou, Hisami, and Siraji praised it. Others, such as Hassanzadeh, Rastgar, and Hemin, were in-between (Hassanzadeh, 2012, pp. 97-98). While the Congress admitted that the armed struggle of 1967-1968 was a golden point in the history of the party, Amir Qazi believed that because the revolt was not based on the CC's decision, it was a non-party movement, and its remaining leaders should be punished (Hassanzadeh, n.d., p. 137). Hisami (1997b) confirms that choosing armed struggle was due to the influence of "quasi-revolutionary" and Maoist ideas, without calculating the concrete territorial and international conditions, as well as the forces of the party and the enemy (Hisami, 1997b, pp. 308-310). With regard to the ideological changes in the party, Mawloudi Sabian (1994) asserts that, in 1953, the dominant ideology of the KDP was that of the Tudeh Party. Since 1960, when Ahmad Tawfiq dominated the party, the party has inclined toward the right. In the 3rd Congress of the party, the KDP (I) turned to the Left (pp. 70, 72, 74). Congress accepted armed struggle as the main method of struggle against the regime (Hassanzadeh, n.d., p. 137).

According to Aliyar, the 3rd Congress launched the party's political independence, which was initiated by Ghassemlou (Personal communication, October 22, 2012), and Amir Hassani holds that since the 3rd Congress, Ghassemlou revived and changed the KDP (I) into a modern political party (Personal communication, October 19, 2012).

6.2.1. The new Program and Constitution of the KDP (I). The most important organizational change in the party was the improvement of the new

Program and Constitution, which was, with some changes, the same as the Program and Constitution ratified in the 3rd Conference (see Appendix 20).

6.2.2. The KDP (I) activities. The party asked the Iraqi government for a half-hour program through Radio Baghdad. Permission was granted, and for a while, the party was broadcasting its program through *Radioy Dangi Kurdistani Eran* (Iranian Kurdistan Voice Radio). After 11 March 1974, armed conflict between the Iraqi government and Kurds in Iraq started again. In a statement in mid-Summer 1974, the KDP (I) called this conflict "brother-killing" and asked them to start negotiations. Soon after, the Iraqi government imposed limitations on the KDP (I) activities under the pretext that the KDP (I) had not condemned Mullah Mustafa Barzani in its statement. On 15 January 1975, the Iraqi government asked the KDP (I) to stop publishing *Kurdistan* unless the party condemned Barzani as an American agent. So, the KDP (I) stopped publishing the *Kurdistan*. Later, when the relations between Iran and Iraq became normalized, Iraq asked the KDP (I) not to attack Iran in its radio program. But the party refused, and its radio program was shut down (Hisami, 2011, pp. 141-143; Gadani, 2008a, pp. 197-198; Hassanzadeh, n.d., p. 139).

The KDP (I) attempted to cooperate with the opposition to the Iranian regime. Ghassemlou sent a representative to visit Khomeini in Najaf in 1973-1974, but the Ayatollah refused to see him (Ali Mahmood Shekhani, 2007, p. 138). The KDP (I) established training courses for cadres starting on 3 March 1974 and lasting 25 days. Two women—Rounak, Siraji's wife, and Khadija, Karim Hadad's wife—also attended the course that was taught by Ghassemlou (philosophy, economy, politics, Kurdish problems, and international relations) and Hassanzadeh (Kurdish language). Rounak shone as the best student in this course (Peshnimaz, 2012, p. 265). The KDP (I) made new efforts to cooperate with the Tudeh Party. On 31 July 1974, a meeting was held in Leipzig, East Germany, with the Tudeh representatives Iraj Iskandari, Kianouri, and Ali Galawej, and the KDP (I) representatives

Ghassemlou, Siraji, Hisami, and Qizilji. Ghassemlou suggested that they call this an official meeting between the representatives of the KDP (I) and the Tudeh Party Politburo. Iskandari accepted this suggestion, but Kianouri disagreed, citing that the Tudeh had not "recognized" the KDP (I). Kianouri suggested that it was a meeting of the Tudeh Party with "some Iranian Kurds." When Iskandari and Galawej accepted Ghassemlou's suggestion, Kianouri left the meeting (Hisami, 2011, pp. 138-139), which turned out to be fruitless.

After their work in Europe was done, in a meeting in Sofia, Bulgaria, on 2 August 1974, Ghassemlou decided to stay in Europe despite Hisami and Siraji's disagreement. He wrote a letter to the KDP (I) and asked to choose Hisami as the Alternate General Secretary. While there was not such position in the constitution of the KDP (I) at the time, the CC in Kurdistan of Iraq selected Hisami for this position (Hisami, 2011, p.140).

On 6 March 1975, the Algiers Agreement between Iraq and Iran was signed. On 8 March 1975, the Iraqi government asked Siraji to inform the KDP (I) to end its activities and not travel to Iran without the government's permission (Hisami, 2011, p. 143). One of the outcomes of the Algiers Agreement was the ceasing of activities of armed Iraqi Kurdish groups against the Iraqi government. Soon, the leaders and the masses of the Iraqi Kurdish movement, based on an agreement with the Iranian government, left the Kurdistan of Iraq for Iran. The KDP (I) tried to give a message to Barzani through Hassanzadeh. Before he reached the leaders of the KDP (Iraq), they had passed the border to Iran. The message asserted that Barzani should transfer his forces to Iran and struggle against the Iranian government. In this case, the KDP (I) would join the struggle and, under the KDP (Iraq)'s leadership, would take part in the war (Hassanzadeh, n.d., p. 143; Hisami, 2011, p. 143).

According to Gadani (2008a), some members of the CC held a Plenum in Varna, Bulgaria, on 13 May 1976. Based on Ghassemlou's proposal, the Plenum approved the creation of *Komitay Siasy-Nizami (Sia-Mi)* (Political-Military Committee or the Sia-Mi Committee). It aimed at transferring the party's leadership and members to Iran, finding weapons, and establishing the three-member committees in Kernamshah, Sanandaj, Urmiya, Tabriz, Tehran, and Mahabad. The CC selected some cadres to the Sia-Mi Committee, but the committee could not do anything. When Ghassemlou and Amir Qazi returned to Iraq, the CC held a meeting on 21 November 1976. The Sia-Mi Committee was set up. Despite the opposition of the CC, Ghassemlou went back to Europe on 27 November 1976. A few days later, Sadoun Shakir, who was in charge of the Iraqi Intelligence Service, asked the party to leave Iraq (Gadani, 2008a, pp. 203-205; Hisami, 2011, p. 148; Qazi, 2010, p. 244; see Appendix 8).

The Iraqi government, in April 1977, arrested several members of the party's leadership and transferred their families to Ramadi. Consequently, the CC and some other cadres, in a meeting in May 1977, decided that certain CC members should go into hiding. A *Komitay Rabar (K-R)* or Leadership Committee was established in order to prepare for dangerous times ahead (Gadani, 2008a, p. 206; see Appendix 8). As the result of Ghassemlou's diplomacy, on 8 January 1977, Ghassemlou and Hisami went to the Democratic Republic of Yemen and visited the leaders of South Yemen, Abdul Fattah Ismail and Salim Rubai Ali, who warmly received them (Gadani, 2008a, p. 205; Hisami, 2011, p. 150). Later, in a meeting in Paris, the CC followed up on the subject of the Sia-Mi. On 26 July 1977, the CC of the KDP (I) held a meeting in Paris in the house of Chris Kutschera and chose five cadres as the Politburo. Later, the party sent 10 people to Yemen for military training under Hashim Karimi and underwent political and military training for four months (Hisami, 2011, p.152; Gadani, 2008a, p. 207; Ali Mahmood Shekhani, 2007, p. 311; see Appendix 8).

On 15 February 1978, Hisami went to Beirut and visited George Habash, the leader of the Popular Front for the Liberation of Palestine, the Lebanese

Communist Party, and the Lebanese Communist Labor Organization. He also visited Kamal Junbalat, the leader of the Progressive Socialist Party of Lebanon, and Abu Ayad, the Deputy Chief and Head of intelligence for the Palestine Liberation Organization. They all expressed support for the KDP (I) (Hisami, 2011, p. 153). At this time, the party was under pressure from the Iraqi government to leave the country (Hisami, 2011, p. 152). On 25 October 1977, the KDP (I) sent Rasoul Peshnimaz to Iranian Kurdistan to assess the possibility of political activities (Gadani, 2008a, p. 209). By 1978, the party increased its activities by sending groups to Kurdistan.

6.3. The Iranian Revolution of 1979

The revolutionary struggle of the Iranian people against Shah's authoritarian regime and his imperialist supporters and for democracy profoundly developed in 1978. The revolution resulted in the overthrow of the Shah on 11 February 1979. While millions of people—political organizations from the most radical to the conservatives, Left to Right, and communist to Islamic—participated in the revolution, the leadership was mainly under the Shi'i forces led by Ayatollah Khomeini, which led to the establishment of the Islamic Republic of Iran.

The Kurdish people widely participated in the revolution. Nevertheless, the political and ideological tendency in Kurdistan was in favor of democratic, nationalist, and leftist groups, although Islamic tendencies were also present. Among the Kurdish organizations, the KDP (I) was the best-known party to participate in the revolution. An influential Maoist group of Kurdish intellectuals also emerged soon after the Revolution, calling itself the Komala. As well, Iranian political organizations such as the OIPFG and the Tudeh Party were also active in Kurdistan and absorbed many Kurdish intellectuals. Other Iranian groups, though not influential, and new Kurdish organizations also were active in Kurdistan (see Appendix 21).

6.3.1. The KDP (I)'s participation in the 1979 Revolution. In 1978, with the Iranian people's rising protest against the regime, the KDP (I) increased its activities by sending party cells to Iranian Kurdistan. Two teams under Sayyed Rasoul Dehqan (June 1978) and Hashim Karimi were deployed to Iran. They returned to Iraq after carrying out their duties (Gadani, 2008a, p. 209). One of the party's activities related to the death of Aziz Yousefi, who was released in the Summer of 1977 after spending 25 years in prison and died on 4 June 1978 in Tehran. When his body was brought to Mahabad, thousands of people participated in his funeral. Jalil Gadani eulogized Yousefi at his tomb. On the third day after the funeral, 8 June 1978, more than 20,000 people walked to Yousefi's grave. Jalil Gadani, Hawsat Dabbaghi, Fowziyeh Jawanmard, and Sulayman Tikan Tapa delivered speeches. On their way back, the protesters shouted slogans against the regime, turning the event into a demonstration. Forty protesters were arrested, and 16 of them were imprisoned in Urmiya. In most of the demonstrations in the Kurdish cities, the KDP (I) members were the main organizers since, at this time, no other political organization except the KDP (I) was known among the people (Gadani, 2008a, p. 220; Gadani 2001, pp. 45-46). Elsewhere, Jalil Gadani, the oldest and most veteran cadre of the KDP and the previous General Secretary of the PDKI-RL, maintains that on the third day of Yousefi's death, about 30,000 marched between Azadi Fourway and Mawlawi Fourway (Personal communication, October 21, 2012).

However, Gadani's statements regarding the organizers of these events are questionable. As a matter of fact, many of the main organizers in this event and many other protests during the revolution were intellectuals who were not members and supporters of the KDP (I). In fact, some organizers belonged to the OIPFG, the Tudeh Party, and the organization that later became the Komala. Gohari (2002) reveals the names of some of the organizers of the demonstrations relating to Yousefi's death, revealing that some organizers were Tudeh supporters. Later, the majority of the organizers that Gohari mentioned above separated from the PDKI and joined the Tudeh Party, the PDKI (FFC), and the Organization of Iranian People's Fadaian (Majority) (pp. 13-14). In November 1978, the political prisoners were released in groups. When Ghani Bolourian was freed and returned to Mahabad, 60,000 people welcomed him at Tabriz Boulevard (Gadani, 2008a, pp. 223-224; Gadani, 2001, p. 189). The aforementioned number of protestors is rather questionable since the population of Mahabad was about 50,000 at the time (Hassanzadeh, n.d., pp. 148-149).

The Kurds in Tehran also actively participated in the revolution. In creating the Kurdish Community in Tehran, Gadani played a significant role. In late Autumn of 1978, the Kurdish Community in Tehran organized a demonstration in which the Kurdish anthem, *Ay Raqib* (Lo the Enemy), was sung, and they were joined by tens of thousands of people (Gadani, 2008a, p. 223).

In the Spring of 1978, Sayyed Rasoul Dehqan visited Mahabad, Naqadeh, and Piranshahr for more than two months for political purposes. When Ghassemlou returned to Iraq, around the first week of November 1978, *Komitay Zagros* (Zagros Committee) was established. Its members were: (1) Abdul Rahman Ghassemlou, (2) Amir Qazi, (3) Hashim Karimi, (4) Sayyed Rasoul Dehqan, (5) Mullah Hassan Shiwasali, (6) Abdullah Hassanzadeh, (7) Muhammad Amin Siraji. They returned to Iran on the last week of November 1978 (Hassanzadeh, n.d., pp. 146-148; Gadani, 2008a, p. 224; see Appendix 8). The Zagros Committee practically could not work as an organization until the fall of the regime. Two members, Amir Qazi and Hashim Karimi, were not able to go to the assigned territories. The contacts between the Committee members were basically by phone and between two members. Thus, the decisions were not made collectively. The center of the decision-making was in Mahabad, where Ghani Bolourian and Abdullah Hassanzadeh were in regular contact with each other. Ghassemlou returned to Mahabad two or three times to visit the other two (Hassanzadeh, n.d., p. 148).

In Mahabad, the KDP (I) did not have headquarters. Thus, they had to ask Kurdish spiritual and political leader Sheikh Izz al-Din Husseini to provide them with a place (Qazi, 2010, p. 248). The KDP (I) members who returned to Kurdistan during the revolution numbered around 40 and had disagreements among themselves. The Party did not have any organization in Iranian Kurdistan (Gadani, 2008a, pp. 321). The Committee in each city was allowed to recruit only one per one-thousand of the population as the party's members per year. For instance, in Mahabad, with an estimated population of 50,000, the Committee could recruit only 50 members. The committee members were allowed to be in direct contact with only three members. These regulations were not properly functional in those conditions. With the support of some young women and men, the party founded *Yaketi Lawani Mahabad* (Mahabad Youth Union) and *Yaketi Jinani Mahabad* (Mahabad Women's Union). Later, these organizations branched out to other cities of Kurdistan (Hassanzadeh, n.d., pp. 148-149).

On the 11 February 1979 uprising that ended the regime, Bolourian (1997) states the people attacked Mahabad Police Station and disarmed it on 12 February 1979. On the same day, people attacked and disarmed Mahabad Gendarmerie Headquarters. Several died during the attack (Bolourian, 1997, pp. 290-291). On 17 February 1979, the Provisional Government emissaries to Kurdistan—Ayatollah Nouri, Dariush Forouhar, Ismail Ardalan, and Dr. Muhammad Mukri—arrived in Mahabad and were stationed in the hotel at the Mahabad Dam. On 18-19 February 1979, they met with the Kurdish leaders like Ghassemlou, Bolourian, and Sheikh Izz al-Din Husseini, the Komala and the OIPFG cadres, in Mirza Rahim Kharazi's house (Bolourian, 1997, pp. 292-293; Gohari, 2002, p. 23). According to Ahmad Askandari (2015), the Kurdish representatives provided an 8-Article Demand that included Kurdistan's right to self-determination within a federative Iran (see Appendix 22).

Before continuing this discussion, a brief explanation about Qiaday Mowaqati Parti (Provisional Leadership of the KDP [Iraq]) looks useful. After the Algiers Agreement of 1975 between Iran and Iraq and the defeat of the Kurdish movement in Iraq, Barzani and thousands of peshmergas and their families fled to Iran. Barzani died on March 1, 1979. In the 9th Congress of the KDP (Iraq), which was held in Zewa, Maragawar, Urmiya (December 4-13, 1979), Masoud Barzani was elected as the leader of the party. The Congress chose a temporary leadership named Qiaday Mowaqati Parti (Provisional Leadership of the KDP [Iraq]). After the Iranian Revolution of 1979, the Provisional Leadership of the KDP (Iraq) had a cooperative relationship with the government. The historical hostility between this organization and the PDKI was intensified. The PDKI and some other political organizations in Iran and Kurdistan were calling Barzani and the Provisional Leadership of the KDP (Iraq) as traitors, agents of imperialism, CIA, Mossad, MIT, and Iran. Article 8 asked the Iranian government to cut all contacts with this group and to expel its leaders. Later, the Provisional Leadership of the KDP (Iraq) cooperated with Iran and fought against the PDKI.

The Kurdish delegation can be criticized for inserting Article 8 regarding Provisional Leadership as a demand (see Appendix 22). Not only are the claims of Article 8 questionable, but it largely destroyed the relationship between the KDP (Iraq) and the Iranian Kurdish organizations, especially the KDP (I). Gadani (2008a) stresses that it was not clear why Ghassemlou accepted Article 8 demanding that *Qiaday Mowaqati Parti* (Provisional Leadership of the KDP [Iraq]) should leave Iran (Gadani, 2008a, p. 228).

The role of the KDP (I) in controlling the Mahabad Garrison was crucial. The party historians have shed light on this subject. On 23 January 1979, the people attacked the Mahabad Garrison. They did not succeed, and 29 people were killed or wounded. On 11 February 1979, though, many police and gendarmerie stations in Kurdistan were disarmed by the people. On the night of 11 February 1979, representatives of the leftist organizations in Mahabad discussed the idea of attacking the Mahabad Garrison again with Ghani Bolourian. The party rejected it and claimed that many people might be killed. Beginning the next day, for three days, people attacked the Garrison. Fifty-six civilians were killed or wounded. The KDP (I) contacted some patriotic officers inside the garrison and Major Abbasi, who was in town. On 19 February 1979, through a smart plan made by the patriotic officers and non-commissioned officers, the Garrison was taken. During the attack, Brigadier Pezeshkpour was slightly injured. The prominent role in controlling the Mahabad Garrison was played by Colonel Iraj Qadiri, Ahmad Jawidfar, Karim Pourqobad, and Hamid Gohari. The civilians who had attacked the garrison walked away with light weapons. The party obtained about 50 to 60 assault rifles, but later, it obtained 500 rifles by breaking into the garrison depot. Some light weapons were distributed among the people, and 100 rifles were given to the Mahabad Council, which functioned as the city's popular militia. After the occupation of the Mahabad Garrison, the KDP (I) distributed the weapons to different cities. There was a protest around the garrison against the party's control over weapons. The people also acquired weapons by attacking other military stations. Later, the party gained even more weapons from the garrisons of Sardasht and Nawsoud. The occupation of the garrison negatively affected the Provisional Government's view of the KDP (I) (Hassanzadeh, 2012, pp. 197-199; Hassanzadeh, n.d., pp. 153-154; Gadani, 2008a, p. 229; Peshnimaz, 2012, pp. 431-434; Gohari, 2002, p. 79).

On 2 March 1979, the KDP (I) held a mass demonstration at Mahabad [*Abiari*, now *Azadi*] Stadium. Hassanzadeh asserts that between 100,000 and 150,000 people participated, but Bolourian (1997) rightly holds that only a few thousand attended the demonstration (p. 301). Ghassemlou delivered a speech announcing that the KDP (I) was no longer an underground party. Thereafter, the party opened offices in Kurdish cities, and thousands signed up for membership (Gadani, 2008a, p. 230; Gadani, 2001, p. 160; Hassanzadeh, n.d., p. 153).

The role and the extent of the KDP (I)'s participation in the Iranian Revolution have been discussed by other leaders who later established the PDKI and the KDP. Aliyar maintains that the party's leaders came back to Kurdistan before the Iranian Revolution and started organizing, but they were practically late in participating in the Revolution (Personal communication, October 22, 2012). Khalighi believes that the KDP (I) did not organize Kurdish people before the revolution, and when the party returned to Kurdistan, its activities were limited to Mahabad, Bukan, Saqqiz, and some other areas, but they did not pay attention to Southern Kurdistan including Sanandaj, Kermanshah, and Ilam (Personal communication, December 1, 2012). Rastgar also asserts that the KDP (I) organization in Iran before the revolution was very weak. After the revolution, the party did not have great influence over the people, only over very small numbers of the youth. The meeting of the party in Mahabad Stadium on 2 March 1979 revived the party to a small extent (Personal communication, October 16, 2012).

Other active parties in Kurdistan included the Komala, *Rekkhrawi Ganj u Lawani Kurdistan* (Kurdistan Youth Organization), supporters of Sheikh Izz al-Din, the Fedai Guerrillas (later to split into factions), the Tudeh Party [of Iran], and some small leftist groups (Qazi, 2010, p. 257).

6.4. The KDP (I) and the Islamic Republic of Iran

Iranian Kurds, including the KDP (I), regarded the Provisional Government as a revolutionary government. They negotiated with the government's delegates. The main thrust within the post-revolutionary state was to reject the Kurdish demands and use military force against the Kurds. While the Kurdish forces, in general, did not wish to engage in a war with the central government, the conditions provided the opportunity for them to resist the Iranian military. As such, several armed clashes occurred between the two sides. The Kurdish political organizations were not totally unfaultable in triggering military campaigns against the Kurds, but the Iranian regime was, in fact, the main culprit in creating civil war in Kurdistan. The Kurds defended freedom, democracy, and their national rights, while the Iranian regime aimed to suppress them. This conflict has continued to this date. The most important conflicts in 1979—the Sanandaj war, the Naqadeh war, and the Three-Month War—will be discussed below.

6.4.1. The Sanandaj War. The 8-Article Demands of the Kurds were ignored by the central government. Instead, on 18 March 1979, three days before the Iranian New Year or Nowruz celebrations, the government imposed a war on the Kurds in Sanandaj (Bolourian, 1997, p. 296; Gadani, 2008a, p. 230). The clash occurred when Khomeini ordered the invasion of Kurdistan (Hassanzadeh, 2012, p. 484). The war known as the Bloody Nowruz in Sanandaj was instigated when the commanders of the garrison, under the pretext of people attacking the gendarmerie and police stations, invaded the city. The garrison used cannons, mortals, DshK [in Kurdish, *Doshka*] (Soviet-made heavy machine gun), and helicopters against the people. At least 450 civilians were killed, and the city was heavily damaged. Later, a government delegation traveled to Sanandaj and negotiated with some of the representatives of political organizations in Kurdistan, as well as Sheikh Izz al-Din Husseini and Ahmad Mofizadeh, and the war ended. According to Hassanzadeh, some small, inexperienced armed groups in Sanandaj played a role in causing this war (n.d., pp. 155-156; also, Saedi, 2012, pp. 508, 514, 519).

The Sanandaj war had great implications for the KDP (I) policy regarding the state-building process in post-revolutionary Iran. The government held a referendum on 30-31 March 1979 to establish the Islamic Republic. The results were announced on 1 April 1979. Among the KDP (I) leaders, different views existed regarding the referendum. A KDP (I) delegation traveled to Qom to visit Ayatollah Khomeini on 28 March 1979. The Ayatollah told them to negotiate with Prime Minister Mehdi Bazargan, which they did (Bolourian, 1997, p. 300). Hisami

(2011) states that on 28 March 1979, when the KDP (I)'s delegates visited Ayatollah Khomeini, Sheikh Izz al-Din Husseini, under the influence of the Komala, boycotted the upcoming referendum in a statement. Hisami maintains that, although the KDP (I) had already decided to participate in the referendum, after visiting Khomeini and under the influence of Sheikh Izz al-Din, three members of the Politburo, without returning to Mahabad to consult with the CC, decided to boycott the referendum (p. 159; see also Hassanzadeh, n.d., p. 158; Gadani, 2008, p. 231).

On 3 August 1979, the government held elections for the Assembly of Experts for the constitution. According to Gadani (2008a), Ghassemlou was elected by the voters in Western Azerbaijan Province with 113,773 votes, but he did not participate in the meeting of newly-elected Assembly of Experts members with Ayatollah Khomeini (Gadani, 2008a, p. 231; Hassanzadeh, n.d., p. 163).

6.4.2. Armed conflict after the Revolution. While during a revolution, the people's and political organizations' decisions, actions, and their effects are not easily predictable, and even the experienced leaders can be confused about their own plans, the political parties have more responsibility for what they decide and act during the revolution. Here, there are some questions that can be posed for deeper investigation in the future. Was it necessary for the Kurdish groups in Kurdistan, in particular the PDKI, to attack and disarm the Iranian garrisons and stations in Kurdistan after the victory of the Iranian Revolution? What would occur if, instead of planning to disarm the garrisons, the PDKI had planned to encourage people to a peaceful way of political struggle for the Kurdish cause? What were the results of obtaining a great number of arms in the hands of the Kurdish people and political groups? It can be argued that political parties could choose more peaceful tactics and strategies in their struggle for the Kurdish cause. The very condition that there existed armed people in Kurdistan had many impacts on the Kurds and the Iranian government. Firstly, it encouraged and pushed the Kurds to choose an armed struggle. Secondly, it caused the Iranian government, at the time feeling threatened by the United States, to be more suspicious about the Kurdish people and its political organizations and treat them more violently. That is to say, while Kurdish nationalism had just demands, the armed struggle did not make the struggle for the Kurdish cause easier, and it created enormous causality for the Kurds.

6.4.3. The Naqadeh War. Naqadeh is a city located in West Azerbaijan province, and its inhabitants are a combination of the Kurds and the Turks (Azeris). In Spring 1979, a war occurred between the Kurds and the Turks that lasted four days. The conflict first happened in the city and was extended to some villages. During this war, which was basically planned by some factions and characters of the Iranian state, thousands of people were engaged, and hundreds of them, mostly the Kurds, were killed. In addition, thousands of Kurds had to escape from Naqadeh to the other Kurdish cities and villages.

The Naqadeh war occurred when, on 20 April 1979, the KDP (I) held a large demonstration in the Sports Field [now Takhti Stadium] located in the Turkish part of the town (Bolourian, 1997, p. 303; Hassanzadeh, 2012, p. 202). Gadani (2008a) blames agents of the central government for instigating the war (p. 230). According to McDowall (2004), "As the rally commenced, shots were fired, which rapidly led to heavy fighting. As Azeri bands moved on to loot Kurdish villages, at least 200 died, and some 12,000 Kurds were made homeless" (p. 270). Many KDP (I) leaders, while accepting that the war was imposed by the government agents on the Kurds, criticize the KDP (I) for having held that demonstration in Naqadeh in the first place. It is not clear why the party held this rally in the Turkish part of Naqadeh (Qazi, 2010, p. 278).

When Ghassemlou decided to hold a rally in Naqadeh that included the party's armed peshmergas, members such as Siraji questioned Ghassemlou's decision. The Azeri Committee of Naqadeh sent an official letter to the KDP (I), asking the party not to hold the rally in the Turkish part of the town. Members of the KDP (I)'s Naqadeh committee were also against it. But Ghassemlou insisted (Hisami, 2011, p. 162; Peshnimaz, 2012, p. 440). Peshnimaz later criticized himself for having taken armed peshmergas to Naqadeh while having known about the murky relations between the Kurdish and Turkish Committees of Naqadeh. Brigadier Zahir Nejad and Mullah Hassani, the Friday Prayer Imam in Urmiya, were planning against the Kurds (Peshnimaz, 2012, p. 441). Hissam (2011) states that on 25 April 1979, Tabrizi, the Governor of Tabriz, Derakhshan, the Assistant to the Interior Ministry, Seifi, the Governor of Maragheh, and Major Jawad Moazen, Ayatollah Taleqani's representative, entered Naqadeh and ended the conflict. During the Naqadeh war, hundreds of families sought refuge in Mahabad and were housed in the Youth House (Hisami, 2011, pp. 163-166). In the Naqadeh war, more than 500 Kurds and Turks were killed (Kaveh, 2005, pp. 90-92).

Hassanzadeh states that thousands of Kurds and Azeris participated in this conflict. The war lasted four days, and with the support of the army, it ended with the victory of the Azeris. While the war was planned by the agents of the government, Hasanzadeh argues, the KDP (I) was also culpable. The party's leaders in Naqadeh did not have a realistic view of the potential dangers of holding a large, armed Kurdish rally in this town (n.d., p. 159). For the second time, the KDP (I) representatives under Ghassemlou visited Ayatollah Khomeini in the late Spring of 1979 to discuss the Naqadeh war. The third meeting with the Ayatollah involved Jalil Gadani, accompanied by the peasants of the region. Gadani holds that these meetings did not change Khomeini's views about Kurdistan (Gadani, 2008a, p. 231).

6.4.4. The Mangur Tribe. One of the strategies of the Iranian government to confront the Kurdish political parties was arming chiefs of the Mangur tribe in Mahabad. The Mangur armed forces and the KDP (I) engaged in armed clashes after the Iranian Revolution in 1979. Ibrahim Nawzari, the chief of the Mangur tribe, accompanied by some other Mangur chiefs, visited Ghassemlou and informed him that the government had told them to go to Urmiya and receive money and arms. Ghassemlou argued that the Mangurs, in the past, had assisted the party. The Mangurs did not take any weapons when the Mahabad Garrison was looted, and some of them had been killed by the party's peshmergas. To compensate, Ghassemlou decided to let them go and get weapons from the government. He also stated that the party could take the weapons from them. Thus, after the Naqadeh War, the officials gave 220 rifles to the Mangur tribe and 120 rifles to the Zarza tribe. When the Mangurs got weapons and the party asked for their weapons, they refused to give up their weapons, arguing that they were poor and needed the weapons. These tribal chiefs were receiving the weapons against the KDP (I) and also forcing the peasants to pay them the 10-year tribute after the land reform in Iran. The party held three meetings with the Mangurs and advised them to stop looting and harassing people, but it was useless. On 16 July 1979, the KDP (I) attacked them: one of the Mangurs was killed, and the others escaped to the Jaldian Garrison in Piranshahr. In a week, the Aghas were disarmed, and most of their weapons were confiscated. As Sayyed Rasoul Dehqan claims, the party made a grave mistake in attacking them. Later, to calm down the Mangurs, Bolourian visited them and gave them Kalashnikovs as gifts. Nevertheless, later when the military forces entered and controlled Mahabad, the Iranian military recruited some Mangurs and used them against the KDP (I) (Bolourian, 1997, pp. 306-308; Hisami, 2011, p. 172; Peshnimaz, 2012, pp. 466, 469, 475-476; Hassanzadeh, n.d., pp. 161-162).

Further clashes between the Mangurs and the KDP (I) were still to occur. According to Peshnimaz (2012), after the Three-Month War and the 4th Congress of the PDKI, the party committed many wrongdoings against the Mangurs (p. 525), thus pushing the Mangurs toward the government. The PDKI and its remaining leaders owe an apology to the Mangurs.

6.4.5. The Three-Month War. In July 1979, the KDP (I) sent weapons to Paveh and Marivan. A few days later, the government attacked Paveh. On 14 and 15 July 1979, the party sent forces to Paveh (Peshnimaz, 2012, p. 454.). The Paveh War started on 15 August 1979 when the KDP (I) held a rally to celebrate the anniversary of the party's establishment. Gadani emphasized in his speech that the reactionary rulers in Tehran were preparing to attack the Kurds. He asserted that to defend democracy, the KDP (I) should arm people and let them defend themselves (Gadani, 2001, pp. 56-57). The government imposed a war on the people of Paveh that lasted for a week. While people took sanctuary in the village of Qori Qala, Dr. Mostafa Chamran, the Deputy Prime Minister of Iran for Revolutionary Affairs at the time who, due to fighting against the Kurds, soon became the Defense Minister of Iran, wildly attacked people. The government also used the commando and air forces. In this war, a jet and a helicopter were shot down by the Kurds (Gadani, 2008a, p. 234). On 18 August 1979, Ayatollah Khomeini ordered the Chief of the Army General Staff, the Commander-in-Chief of Gendarmerie, and the Commander-in-Chief of the Revolutionary Guard Corps to command the Iranian forces in Kurdistan to prosecute the wicked invaders, arrest and deliver them to the officials, and close the borders to prevent the wicked from fleeing abroad (Khomeini, 1979a, p. 3).

On 19 August 1979, the Islamic Revolutionary Council, which directed the policies of post-revolutionary Iran, outlawed the KDP (I). According to the Revolutionary Council, the KDP (I) was supported by foreign and counter-revolutionary agents that intended to break Kurdistan away from Iran through a revolt, provoking people into looting, murdering, and causing the bloody events of Sanandaj, Naqadeh, Marivan, and Paveh, as well as attacks on the garrisons in Mahabad and Sanandaj. Collaborating with the KDP (I) would now constitute a counter-revolutionary act against the state, punishable by law (Islamic Revolutionary Council, 1979, p. 1). In his 20 August 1979 statement, in a declaration addressing the Kurdish people of Iran, Ayatollah Khomeini announced that after the revolution, some groups affiliated with the foreigners conducted activities against the Islamic movement and even boycotted the referendum. The KDP (I) was directly affiliated with the United States and Israel and was an evil party. Khomeini announced that the KDP (I) was an illegal party. The party's criminal leaders had created brother-killing wars, and they wanted to push the country toward blasphemy. Therefore, the respectful Kurdish people should prevent their children from joining this party. Khomeini asked the Kurds to cooperate with the police, reveal the KDP (I) leaders' hideouts, and turn them into officials (Khomeini, 1979b, p. 3). The Ayatollah statement has been widely interpreted as a declaration of war against the Kurds.

While the government was already attacking the Kurds (in the town of Paveh), the Iranian military widely invaded Kurdistan after the declaration. The Kurds, mainly under the political parties, resisted the invasion. The war lasted for about three months and was known as the Three-Month War. Gohari (2002) writes that the Three-Month War started with Khomeini's declaring Jihad against the Kurds that lasted from 19 August to 17 November 1979 (p. 80). Although it was not a jihad, the military invasion of Kurdistan resulted in many innocent and defenseless people's deaths, imprisonment, execution, persecution, and displacement. Many areas were destroyed by the Iranian forces. The scale of this invasion reached much more than the Kurdish opposition groups. The aim was to suppress Kurdish nationalism.

On the morning of 3 September 1979, Iranian fighter jets flew over Mahabad, and by noon, the army had entered the city while they waited at the Governing Building Square (Hisami, 2011, p. 179). Before the army entered, the KDP (I) leaders and thousands of people left the cities. The party was not prepared for the war (Gadani, 2008a, p. 243-245). When the party was established in the villages of Bnokhalaf and Kani Zard in Sardasht, Ghassemlou asked Talabani and

Abu Jamil (who was in charge of the Iraqi Communist Party's peshmergas) for assistance. They responded that they could send some commanders to the KDP (I). When Ghassemlou asserted that the Iraqi government wanted to help the party, Talabani emphasized that the party should not put itself in the arms of the Iraqi government. Likewise, Abu Jamil emphasized that the KDP (I) had better not to make war than to throw itself into the arms of the Iraqi regime. When Ghassemlou insisted that the party should fight, Talabani and Abu Jamil recommended that the KDP (I) make a one-time request to the Iraqi government to give the party comprehensive help, including weapons, money, gas, and cars. Later, Iraq provided 25,000 dinars, old Chinese Kalashnikovs, and a few RPGs (Bolourian, 1997, pp. 317-318). Seeking the Iraqi government's assistance during the Three-Month War caused certain members of the KDP (I) who supported the Tudeh Party to question the party (Bakhchi, 2007, p. 16).

The party quickly organized peshmergas in different units called *Hez* (Force). These Forces included Martyr Mo'ini Force, Martyr Awara Force, Martyr Peshawa Force, Arbaba Force, Aziz Yousefi Force, Shaho Force, Sharifzadeh Force, Kelashin Force, and Bayan Force (Gadani, 2008a, p. 246). Another Force was the *Hezi Gharaman* (Hero Force) (Mamadi, 1999, pp. 97-99). In a resolution, the CC ordered the establishment of village councils comprised of five persons to collect aid for the peshmergas, help the party's peshmergas and members, and solve the problems of people in the village. The party announced that people should not sell their weapons and those who could afford it should buy weapons; nobody in the villages should contact the army or the officials; those collaborating with the government or do not obey the village council in supporting the peshmergas would be punished (Hisami, 2011, p. 181).

When the government took control of Kurdish towns, the government's agents and military forces created an atmosphere of horror among the people: many Kurds were arrested, and the notorious "hanging-judge" Sadeq Khalkhali sentenced many to death in different towns (Gadani, 2008a, p. 247). In Saqqiz, Khalkhali executed four innocent persons, including a wounded 12-year-old boy. In Mahabad, he executed a Baha'i who had not engaged in any type of political activity (Hisami, 2011, p. 182). Forces under Defense Minister Chamran attacked and killed many in Paveh, Nawsoud, Marivan, Saqqiz, and Baneh (Gadani, 2008a, p. 234). Besides, on 2 September 1979, the Revolutionary Guards and Mullah Hassani massacred 46 (or 68 according to Hassanzadeh) defenseless people in the village of Qarne (Hisami, 2011, p. 178; Hassanzadeh, n.d., pp. 164-165).

The Kurds resisted the state's repression. Gadani claims that one of the most important operations against the government was totally destroying the *Sotun-e Gard-e Jawidan* (Immortal Guard Column) near Baneh. In this operation, tens of army trucks were burned, hundreds of army forces were killed and captured, and a large amount of military equipment, weapons, and ammunition were gained by the Kurdish peshmergas (Gadani, 2008a, p. 247).

In an open letter dated 12 October 1979, the KDP (I) asked for a truce and negotiation with the government (Bolourian 1997, pp. 323-324). A central government delegation, including Forouhar, Sabaghian, Sahabi, and Shakiba, came to Mahabad on 3 November 1979 (Hisami, 2011, p. 183). This delegation held negotiations with the KDP (I) representatives—Bolourian, Hassanzadeh, Hisami, and Aziz Mamle—in the hotel at the Mahabad Dam. Forouhar claimed that Khomeini was ready to grant many significant demands of the Kurds' demands, but he did not like the word *khodmokhtari* (self-determination). Forouhar suggested the word *khodgardani* (self-governing) (Bolourian 1997, p. 324) instead. According to Hassanzadeh, after the negotiations, a Tudeh Party delegation—including Mohammad Ali Amouyy and Mohammad Reza Shaltouki—met Bolourian in Mahabad and gave him a plan named *Tarh-e Khodgardani* (Self-Governing Plan) (Hassanzadeh, n.d., p. 174). Later, Forouhar used the term *khodgardani*. However, on 20 December 1979, the Persian daily *Ettelaat* published a document titled "Right and Duties of the Self-Governing Regions" (Hassanzadeh, n.d., pp. 174-176).

After about three months, certain factors caused the Iranian authorities to temporarily stop the war in Kurdistan and negotiate with the Kurds. Firstly, the Iranian army and the inexperienced Revolutionary Guards Corps had sustained huge human and military casualties. Secondly, Sadeq Zibakalam, the delegate of the premiership of Iran, visited Kurdistan, and his report about the realities of Kurdistan had positively affected some Iranian authorities. Thirdly, some authorities wanted to solve the conflict peacefully. Finally, the Iranian state needed to comprehensively prepare itself and make effective plans and strategies for defeating the Kurds and controlling Kurdistan once and for all.

Ayatollah Khomeini sent an important, reconciliatory message to the people of Kurdistan on 17 November 1979. He saluted the Kurdish people for being faithful to the Islamic Republic and preventing the plot of the enemies. He stated that the reports of the special delegation showed that the Kurdish people did not want to secede from Iran. He asked the Kurdish people to unite with all Iranians against the plunderers led by the United States. He revealed that he was aware of the oppression of the Kurds. However, other Iranians such as Turks, Lurs, Arabs, Balouchis, Persians, and Turkmens had also been deprived. He asked the special delegation to continue negotiating with religious and political leaders and other classes of Kurdish people in order to provide for their demands. He emphasized that Islam had condemned all types of discrimination. Under Islam and the Islamic Republic, the right to govern internal and territorial issues and to remove all types of cultural, economic, and political discrimination belonged to all Iranians, including the Kurds (Khomeini, 1979c, p. 3). The Ayatollah's message created hope among the Kurds who celebrated on the streets of the Kurdish cities. In short, the 17 November 1979 message by Ayatollah Khomeini led to a ceasefire and promised to grant rights to the Kurds (Gadani, 2008a, p. 247; Hassanzadeh, n.d., p. 168).

The KDP (I) held a rally in Mahabad on 20 November 1979, and Ghassemlou optimistically gave a positive response to Ayatollah Khomeini's message (Gadani, 2008a, p. 247; Hisami, 2011, p. 185). Kutschera states that in this rally, in which about 100,000 participated, Ghassemlou spoke positively of Khomeini. Gadani estimates that at most 50,000-60,000 rallied (Gadani, 2001, pp. 164-165), but this figure is also exaggerated since the total population of Mahabad at that time was about 50,000 (see above).

6.4.6. The Delegation of the Kurdish People. The *Lejnay Nowenarayati Gali Kurd*, or the Delegation of the Kurdish People, was established in Mahabad on 22 November 1979 (Bolourian, 1997, p. 324). It included the KDP (I), the Komala, the OIPFG, and Sheikh Izz al-Din Husseini (Saedi, 2010, p. 163). Sheikh Izz al-Din was the head, and Ghassemlou was the speaker of the Delegation (Gadani, 2008a, p. 249). After a few meetings, the Delegation offered a 26-Article Plan (*Galalay 26 Madayy*) on 25 December 1979. It was written by Sarm al-Din Sadiq Waziri [Jurist, solicitor general] with the collaboration of Aziz Mamle [Jurist, Lawyer]. The 26-Article Plan was taken to Tehran. Similar to the previous 8-Article Demands, the central government did not pay attention to it, and it did not have any positive outcome (Gadani, 2008a, p. 249; Gohari, 2002, pp. 16-17). The main point of the 26-Article Plan was asking for the autonomy of Kurdistan within Iran (see Appendix 23).

On 6 December 1979, the Delegation of the Kurdish Nation announced that despite the acceptance of the ceasefire by the Kurds, the government had bombed the villages of Mamkan, Mingol, and Somanabad (between Urmiya and Salmas) on 28 November 1979 using six helicopters. In addition, in the cities of Sanandaj, Saqqiz, and Paveh, the government had fortified its military forces. Likewise, Sanandaj had been surrounded by the green beret detachment (Hisami, 2011, p. 187). The Delegation of the Kurdish Nation and the government representatives held a meeting in Mahabad on 11 December 1979 (Hisami, 2011, pp. 192-193).

The central government was represented by Hashem Sabaghian, Ezzatollah Sahabi, and Forouhar (Gadani, 2008a, p. 249). Bolourian states that Sabaghian had already announced that the government did not recognize the Komala and the OIPFG as the representatives of the Kurdish people. Therefore, the Kurdish delegation asked Sheikh Izz al-Din not to introduce the political affiliations of the representatives. However, in the first and only meeting of the Kurdish delegation and the government representatives on 11 December 1979, Sheikh Izz al-Din introduced the political affiliations of all Kurdish representatives. In the meeting, the 26-Article demand was submitted to the government representatives. Nevertheless, Sabaghian stated that they did not want to have a meeting with the Komala and the OIPFG. Therefore, the negotiation was ended (Bolourian, 1999, pp. 326-327). This was the first and only negotiation between the Kurds and the government. Later, the PDKI provided a shorter version of the 26-Article Plan on 1 March 1980; it was known as the 6-Article Plan (see Appendix 24). Gadani and Hassanzadeh reveal that soon after the 4th Congress, the PDKI sent a delegation including Bolourian, Abdullah Hassanzadeh, Fawziyeh Qazi, Nawid Mo'ini, and Ahmad Qazi (a friend of the PDKI) to meet President Bani Sadr on 27 February 1980. The delegation prepared a 6-Article Plan named *Reous-e Kolli-ye Tarh-e Khod Mokhtari* (General Outline for Autonomy) and gave it to the government representatives—Forouhar, Sabaghian, and Sahabi—on 1 March 1980 to deliver it to President Bani Sadr. The plan was rejected by the Council of Guardians (Gadani, 2008a, pp. 263-264; Hassanzadeh, n.d., p. 185, 187).

6.5. The 4th Congress of the PDKI

After the selection of the representatives by the city conferences, the 4th Congress of the PDKI was held in Mahabad's Cinema Omid from 19 to 24 February 1980 (Gadani, 2008a, p. 258). Three hundred ten delegates, each representing 200 members, participated in the Congress. At this time, the party reportedly had about

60,000 members (Hassanzadeh, n.d., p. 180). Ghassemlou was elected the General Secretary (see Appendix 8). In this Congress, the name of the party changed to *Hizbi Demokrati Kurdistani Eran* or the Democratic Party of Iranian Kurdistan (PDKI). The number of party members is disputable. Shalmashi claims that, during the Iranian Revolution, 200 cadres and peshmergas of the party returned from Iraq to Iran. However, in the 4th Congress, representatives of 30,000 members participated (Personal communication, November 15, 2012). A huge discrepancy exists regarding the number of the party's members in the above statements. It can be concluded that according to Gadani, each of the 310 delegated represented 100 members, but according to Hassanzadeh, each represented 200 members. Therefore, the total members were between 31,000 and 62,000.

According to the Program of the party, the Kurdish people participated in the 1979 revolution to deepen the anti-imperialism struggle, establish a democratic political system in Iran, remove the suppression of Iranian nations, and achieve autonomy for Iranian Kurdistan. The 4th Congress supported the Iranian Revolution and Ayatollah Khomeini's leadership (Hisami, 2011, pp. 216-217). The 4th Congress led to increased discord among the leaders. Gadani (2008a) states that some people who did not succeed in the leadership provoked Ghani Bolourian, who obtained more votes than Ghassemlou. Also, believing that the PDKI should be a branch of the Tudeh Party and in order to weaken the PDKI, the Tudeh Party prompted Bolourian, who was confused about what he wanted, against the party. To prevent discord, after the Congress and contrary to the Party's Constitution, Bolourian was asked to become the leader of the party, but he rejected it. Also, in the First Plenum [perhaps 28 February 1980], he was offered to become the General Secretary, but he did not accept (Gadani, 2008a, p. 262).

Hosein Bakhchi (2007) explains that in the 4th Congress, the main conflict was between Ghassemlou, who wanted to impose his program on the Congress, and Siraji, who was trying to advance the goals of the Tudeh Party. Bakhchi provides detailed information about the subjects that were discussed in the Congress, including socialism, *Simay Demokrat* (Democratic Visage), and the *Listay Fix* (Fixed List) of the CC (Bakhchi, 2007, pp. 18-23).

The shortcomings of the 4th Congress have been addressed by many party leaders. Bakhchi (2007) states that the Congress chose *Komitay Bazrasi* (Inspection Committee) under the watch of Ghassemlou. The Inspection Committee began investigating the members who were known to be pro-Tudeh Party. The activities of this Committee created more discord within the party (p. 19). The Congress resulted in the establishment of more individual wilfulness and authoritarianism within the party (Bakhchi, 2007, p. 22). Between the 4th and the 5th Congresses, the party was conducted by a weak centralism and moved toward concentrating the power in the hands of two persons in the Politburo (Qazi, 2010, p. 334).

The 4th Congress was full of dishonesty, deception, cheating, and faction-making. It opened the way for the culture of disharmony among the party youth (Kaveh, 2005, p. 95). Kowestani (Kaveh) claims that the Inspection Committee, after the 4th Congress, was the Politburo's tool for scrutinizing the ideas of the members (Hisami, 1997a, p. 60). Some evidence shows that Ghassemlou had done some manipulation in the Congress. For instance, according to Gadani, Mustafa Hijri was not a member of the PDKI but was invited by Ghassemlou as a guest to the 4th Congress on 19 February 1980. Ghassemlou suggested that Hijri put his name on the list, and he was selected as a CC member (Gadani, 2015). Khizri states that the party brought several guests to the 4th Congress, such as Colonel Chia and Captain Afshin, who did not know the meanings of politics, party, and congress (Personal communication, November 22, 2012).

As discussed, after the 4th Congress, the PDKI offered a 6-Article Plan to the government, but it was rejected (Gadani, 2008a, pp. 263-264; Hassanzadeh, n.d., p. 185, 187). In the first parliamentary elections after the 1979 revolution (held on 14 March 1980), the PDKI candidates obtained between 57 and 97 percent of the popular vote within the Kurdish regions. But, the government, upon Ayatollah Khomeini's instructions, nullified the election results in Kurdistan. Clearly, in most parts of Kurdistan, the PDKI candidates for the parliamentary election won the majority of the votes. In Mahabad, the PDKI candidate, Ghani Bolourian, received 97.4 percent of the popular vote (Hassanzadeh, n.d., p. 188; Gadani, 2008a, pp. 273-274; Bolourian, 1997, p. 331).

All previous negotiations between the Kurds and the government were fruitless. Instead, the government planned to suppress the Kurds. In early Spring 1980, the government attacked the town of Kamiaran and other cities and territories of Kurdistan (Gadani, 2008a, pp. 274-275). Before the Iranian New Year, the government deployed forces to northern and southern Kurdistan. In the second war in Sanandaj, before the New Year (21 March 1980), about 2,400 defenseless civilians were killed. Colonel Sadri, the Commander of the Sanandaj Garrison, asserted that they were firing 400 mortar-shells on the city each hour. After 26 days, the peshmergas left the city in order to prevent the destruction of the city and the death of civilians (Hassanzadeh, n.d., p. 194; Gadani, 2008a, p. 275). In this new war against the Kurds, the government also imposed economic sanctions against Kurdistan (Hassanzadeh, n.d., p. 195).

Within the chaotic conditions in Kurdistan, the PDKI moved towards the preparation for armed struggle. Hosein Bakhchi, a political activist and a previous member of the CC of the PDKI (FFC), argues that, after the 4th Congress, Ghassemlou acted against the policies approved by Congress. This happened for multiple reasons: the government was wasting time to resolve the Kurdish question; the radical factions of the regime were creating problems in Kurdistan; and Iraq was ready to help the Kurds for its own interests. Therefore, a few weeks after the Congress, it was said that the party wanted to move outside the cities to conduct armed activities (Personal communication, November 5, 2012).

One of the changes within the PDKI was pressuring certain members. The CC, through the Inspection Committee, put members of the Youth Organization of PDKI and members of Mahabad's City Committee on trial. In addition, they also dismissed the leadership of the Youth Organization of PDKI because of their stance against the Ba'ath regime and in favor of the Tudeh Party. The Youth Organization changed its name to *Yaketi Lawani Hizbi Demokrat* (Youth Union of the Democratic Party) (Bakhchi, 2007, p. 23). After the 4th Congress, the PDKI hostility toward the Tudeh Party increased. The PDKI attacked the Tudeh Party's offices and set the Tudeh Mahabad office on fire, and it also persecuted, arrested, assaulted, and disrespectfully treated Tudeh members (Bakhchi, 2007, p.23).

The discord within the PDKI developed quickly, leading to a split in the party.

6.5.1. The Democratic Party of Iranian Kurdistan (Followers of the Fourth Congress) or PDKI (FFC). The discord among the PDKI leaders caused the split of *Hizbi Demokrati Kurdistani Eran* (*Perawani Kongray Chowar*), Democratic Party of Iranian Kurdistan (Followers of the Fourth Congress) or PDKI (FFC), from the PDKI on 15 June 1980. Unlike the other splits before and after the 4th Congress, this was a clearly political split.

Bolourian claims that before the parliamentary elections (14 March 1980), Ghassemlou had told him that the Iraqi government had asked Ghassemlou to go to Baghdad and visit the Iraqi officials. Although Bolourian disagreed, the Politburo sent Abdullah Hassanzadeh to Haj Omran to visit the Iraqi officials (Bolourian, 1997, p. 333). Hassanzadeh traveled to Haj Omran and Kirkuk and returned in about a week. In the Politburo meeting, Hassanzadeh revealed the 7-Point Plan of the Iraqi government, which was supposed to be approved by the PDKI. Bolourian maintains that although he had not seen the actual Iraqi proposal, it contained these seven points: (1) two Iraqi officers should stay with the PDKI to assist and supply funds and military equipment to the PDKI; (2) two members of the Politburo should stay in Iraq for consultation; (3) the PDKI should provide its intelligence to Iraq regarding the movement of the Iranian military forces near the Iraqi border and about the Iranian garrisons close to the border including the types and numbers of their weapons; (4) the PDKI should inform Iraq concerning the types of planes and helicopters used by Iran; (5) the PDKI should promote the idea of overthrowing of the Iranian regime; (6) the PDKI should prevent the Iraqi Kurds in Iran to move toward to the Iraqi border in order to fight against the Iraqi government; (7) the PDKI should inform Iraq about Iran's relations with other countries and report the weapons Iran had bought from them (Bolourian, 1997, pp. 338-339).

Bolourian maintains that, in the meeting, he announced that it was treason to accept the Iraqi proposal. Nevertheless, the meeting approved it. He adds that he boycotted the party and did not participate in the Politburo meetings. He decided to leave Iran and go to Iraq and join the Kurdish political parties who were struggling against Saddam. However, Ghassemlou sent several letters to Bolourian (through Hassanzadeh) in order to find a solution. In his last letter, Ghassemlou asked him to attend the CC meeting to discuss his views. Bolourian attended the CC meeting of 7 May 1980 in the village of Brayma. He stated that the Politburo had undermined the resolutions of the 4th Congress. He maintained that the politburo should be dissolved and the CC should select a new Politburo and General Secretary. He also stated that he and Ghassemlou should not be selected as members of the Politburo. According to Bolourian, when there was a break in the meeting, Ghassemlou told members that the Tudeh Party under Kianouri [the General Secretary since 1979] was trying to dissolve the PDKI. Upon resumption, the meeting chose the same Politburo and reappointed Ghassemlou as General Secretary (Bolourian, 1997, pp. 340-343).

Gadani (2001) rejects the existence of the 7-Point Plan of the Iraqi proposal of the Iraqi government altogether (pp. 108-109, 201-202). According to Hisami (1992), the Iraqi government pushed the party representative, Siraji, to send a party delegation to Baghdad for negotiations with the Iraqi government. The CC chose delegates under Hisami, including Siraji, Fatah Kawian, and someone named Fatah. They went to Haj Omran and later to Erbil. Five delegates, under Abu Ahmad, the Head of Iraqi Intelligence Service (*Mukhabrat*), represented the Iraqi government. Abu Ahmad stated that they did not support the Kurds' negotiations with the Iranian government regarding autonomy. He said that Iraq was ready to provide everything for the PDKI if it accepted five conditions. Hisami maintains that he rejected these conditions, which included:

1. To end negotiations with Khomeini's regime.

2. A representative of the Iraqi government is to permanently participate in the meetings of the Central Committee of the party.

3. A representative of the Iraqi government is to participate in the party's Peshmerga Commission.

4. A representative of the party is to permanently stay in Baghdad as a contact with the Iraqi government.

5. A representative of the party is to be in contact with the Iraqi embassy in Europe in order to exchange news. (pp. 250-253)

According to Hisami (1995), without consulting with the CC, Ghassemlou later sent Hassanzadeh to Iraq to accept the 7-Point Plan suggestions of Iraq and imposed them on the CC. Bolourian was against affiliation with the Ba'ath regime (p. 35).

Two basic views prevailed among the PDKI members. The first view, coming from the followers of the Tudeh Party, held that the PDKI should defend the Iranian revolution under Ayatollah Khomeini against imperialism and the creation of a national democratic government. Only then will autonomy for the Kurds would be granted. The second view, which was advanced by Ghassemlou, tied the party's support of the revolution to the granting of autonomy to the Kurds.

Gradually, Ghassemlou's wing ignored the contents of the 4th Congress, and while the government did not accept autonomy, the PDKI announced that in order to force the government to continue with the negotiations, it was necessary to initiate long-term guerrilla warfare. Bakhchi believes that the party should have made such a crucial decision in a congress, conference, or at least in a plenum (Bakhchi, 2007, pp. 26-28).

After the Plenum, discord within the party grew. Hisami (2007) argues that Bolourian and Ismail Haji visited the Organization of Iranian People's Fedai Guerrillas (Majority) base, asking them for support, but they advised that they would not support a split (p. 168).

6.5.1.1. The split of the PDKI (FFC). The PDKI (FFC) split from the PDKI through a published declaration on 15 June 1980. Siraji maintains that the first declaration of the PDKI (FFC) was written by Ali Galawej, the CC member of the Tudeh Party (Gadani, 2001, p. 109). Siraji and Farouq Keikhosrawi encouraged Bolourian to part ways with Ghassemlou. They provided him with a declaration that he read and to which he made some changes. This became the declaration of the PDKI (FFC). Bolourian states that Galawej told him later that if he were, at that time, in Kurdistan, he would not have allowed the split. Bolourian claimed that only later he found out that the split was not a good idea, and he should have stayed in the party to disseminate his ideas among the party members (Bolourian, 1997, pp. 344-346).

The splinters included seven members of the CC plus some cadres and peshmergas. However, the splinters left some friends within the PDKI to inform them about developments within the party (Gadani, 2008a, pp. 281-282; see Appendix 8). Some of the key views of the PDKI (FFC) were as follows. Autonomy was the right of the Kurdish people, and its essence was embodied in Khomeini's message of 17 November 1979. However, the Iranian government had attacked Kurdistan, shed blood, destroyed cities, and displaced thousands of families.

Therefore, a brother-killing war had been continuing in Kurdistan. Within both sides of the conflict, both revolutionary and counter-revolutionary elements existed. Certain tendencies within the Iranian government agreed with ending the oppression of the Kurds. The government suggested the *Tarh-e Khodgardani* (Self-Governing Plan), but Ghassemlou, in Chowar Chira Square in Mahabad, called it *Tarh-e Sargardani* (Displacement Plan) (Gohari, 2002, p. 32).

6.5.1.2. The PDKI and the PDKI (FFC). The PDKI made a statement about the split dated 18 June 1980 in which it called the splinters "*Taqmi Hawt Kasi*" (Group of Seven People), traitors, and jash. Hissami claims that while he condemned the split, he was against name-calling (Hissamio, 2011, pp. 218-219; Hisami, 1997a, p. 61). The splinters were charged with surrendering Piranshahr and Sargirda to the government and participating in the enemy's attacks against the Kurdish people (Gadani, 2008a, pp. 281-282). In return, the splinters called the PDKI "*Bandi Ghassemlou*" (Ghassemlou's Gang). The Tudeh Party supported the splinters (Bakhchi, 2007, p. 31). All in all, the position of the PDKI regarding the PDKI (FFC) was even harsher. Two CC members, Mamosta Hemin and Farouq Keikhosrawi, and many rank-and-file members who had affinities with the splinters were arrested and imprisoned by the PDKI. The party also assassinated Jafar Karroubi, a peshmerga of the PDKI (FFC), and his brother, Ali Karroubi, an ordinary person (Bakhchi, 2007, p. 32; Peshnimaz, 2012, p. 545).

Shalmashi states that the PDKI asked Hemin to come to the Politburo Office in Dolatou for negotiations. The party provided quarters for him, and after three or four months, he returned home. Shalmashi claims that some of the party's leaders had not agreed with bringing Hemin there (Personal communication, November 15, 2012). Kamal Karimi, a member of the Politburo of the KDP, states that the way in which the PDKI approached the PDKI (FFC) was illogical (Personal communication, September 4, 2012). Khalighi asserts that the PDKI hastily and wrongly labeled Bolourian a traitor and jash (Personal communication, December

1, 2012). In Wirya's view, although the PDKI (FFC) did not serve the interests of the Kurdish struggle, the PDKI's treatment of the splinters was wrong. He maintains that the PDKI's position regarding the KDP (Iraq), which was in Iran at the time, was also mistaken because it pushed the KDP (Iraq) to become closer to the Iranian government (Personal communication, October 22, 2012).

Madani asserts that he is completely against the PDKI's culture of calling its critics traitors. The PDKI called Bolourian a jash, but people never accepted this label. He adds that when, during the Iranian revolution, Bolourian was released from prison and returned to Mahabad, he was welcomed by 30,000 to 40,000 people (Personal communication, October 14, 2012). Rastgar discloses that in a plenum, the majority voted that the word jash should not be used by the party, especially against Hemin, who was an honorary member of the CC when he split, and Hassanzadeh left the Plenum in protest. Ghassemlou told the members that the party had lost Hemin, and now he would not allow losing Hassanzadeh as well (Personal communication, October 17, 2012).

It should be addressed that after the split, the relations between the PDKI and the Tudeh Party deteriorated rapidly. Hisami (1997a) claims that, after the declaration, the PDKI began arresting the followers or members of the party's Youth Union who were supporters of the Tudeh (p. 173). On the other side, the Tudeh Party propagandized against the PDKI, calling it counter-revolutionary (Hisami, 2011, p. 220). Moreover, Gadani (2008a) asserts that on 9 July 1980, the daily *Ettelaat* published a false report that was taken from the organ of the Tudeh Party, the *Mardom*. According to the so-called "report," "Dr. Ghassemlou has received $9 million from NATO." On 11 July 1980, Ghassemlou sent a harsh letter to *Ettelaat*, in which he reaffirmed the struggle of the PDKI against American imperialism and rejected such shameless accusations. Amusingly, Ghassemlou insisted that the readers of *Mardom* in Kurdistan were less than the numbers of one's fingers (Gadani, 2008a, pp. 280-281).

6.5.1.3. The PDKI (FFC)'s activities and fate. When, in early Spring 1980, the government attacked the Kurds, the PDKI was preparing itself for a long-term war. The government destroyed Kurdish cities and villages and killed many innocent people. The PDKI had to evacuate the cities and relocate to the mountains. During this period, the PDKI (FFC) chose a semi-open presence based on the policy of "critique and unity" with the regime. And yet, some of its members were arrested and sent to Urmiya prison (Bakhchi, 2007, p. 37). The PDKI (FFC) set up a CC, including the previous but also new members, including Muhammad Amin Siraji, Qadir Khalidi, Nasser Khoshkalam, and Hosein Bakhchi. Three Kurdish cadres of the Tudeh Party were delegated to attend the party, with two of them attending the CC meetings. Bolourian, Siraji, and Dr. Rahim Saifi Qazi were in Tehran. The party lost its independence in decision-making: it was now the Tudeh policies that were carried out through the PDKI (FFC) in Kurdistan (Bakhchi, 2007, pp. 38-39). The PDKI (FFC) published *Kurdistan* as its organ and published about 30 issues between the Spring of 1980 and the Winter of 1983 (Bakhchi, 2007, p. 37).

Sanar Mamadi was the Chief of the Mamadi tribe and a CC member of the PDKI. He did not obey the PDKI orders. The government, apparently to solve the Kurdish problem, contacted Mamadi. Mamadi believed that the government's intention was to reach a compromise by negotiating through Mamadi. Therefore, he asked Ghassemlou to send a representative of the Politburo to Mamadi to assist him regarding negotiation with the government (Bakhchi, 2007, pp. 41-42). It seems that Ghassemlou did not help Sanar and was unsatisfied with his actions. The PDKI, in its Plenum on 5-9 April 1981, called Mamadi and Rahman Karimi traitors and expelled them from the party. Their dismissal was not due to their political perspectives. Mamadi and Isma'ilzadeh had a conflict with the PDKI because their authority in their territories was in danger (Bakhchi, 2007, pp.42-43). On 17 April 1981, with the cooperation of the Tudeh Party and the PDKI (FFC), Rahman Karim,

Mamadi, and Jahangir Isma'ilzadeh issued a statement and joined the PDKI (FFC) (Bakhchi, 2007, p. 43).

As follows, about the end of Summer 1981, a disastrous war occurred between the government and the PDKI in northern and western parts of Urmiya, including the city of Oshnavieh. In this war, the government, with the cooperation of the PDKI (FFC) and especially the KDP (Iraq), fought against the PDKI.

Ahmad Safa states that Karimi, the commander of the Awara Force, and Rahman Piroti, the commander of the PDKI in Oshnavieh, also split from the PDKI and joined the PDKI (FFC). The party started a base in the village of Shinawe, close to the base of the KDP (Iraq), and created an armed column. Moreover, *Komitay Shoumal* (North Committee) was established: it included Safa as the organizational head, Mamadi as its military head, and Karimi as the head of the political bureau (Personal communication, December 8, 2012).

The pressure of the PDKI was a major factor in pushing the PDKI (FFC) to go to northern Kurdistan in Iran and towards the government. Safa maintains that they sought refuge in the territories controlled by the government. The party did not intend to fight against the PDKI. Safa was in charge of the party's base in Rajan. At this time, Bolourian was negotiating with the representatives of Ayatollah Khomeini and President Muhammad Ali Rajai. They maintained that if the PDKI cooperated with the KDP (Iraq) and withdrew the anti-revolutionaries from northern Kurdistan, the KDP (Iraq), which was settled in Iranian Kurdistan as refugees after the Algiers Agreement in 1975, could replace them, and the government would meet the demands of the PDKI (FFC). Later, the PDKI (FFC) received 200 guns from the government, distributing most of them to Mamadi and some 20-30 rifles to Mullah Rahman Piroti and Mullah Qadir Khalidi. During the battles that forced the PDKI to leave the territory, 20 to 30 armed PDKI (FFC) peshmergas participated. Then, the government asked the PDKI (FFC) to return the weapons and began exposing the previous activities of Mamadi that had led to the death of civilians. Since Mamadi did not want to return the weapons, he contacted the PDKI and stated that it was Karimi's idea to cooperate with the government. When the PDKI asked him to compensate for his previous errors, Mamadi arrested and killed Karimi (Safa, Personal communication, December 8, 2012). According to Bakhchi (2007), Karim, Mamadi, and Isma'ilzadeh negotiated with the government not as the CC members of the PDKI (FFC) but as individuals. He added that Mamadi's murder of Karimi won him a seat as a consultant member of the PDKI CC (pp. 45-47; Mamadi, 1999, pp. 175-177).

It should be noted that the KDP (Iraq) played a negative role during the suppression of the Iranian Kurdish nationalist movement. This party actively cooperated with the Iranian government in attacking the PDKI peshmergas. Hassanzadeh (2012) claims that, after the revolution, the KDP (Iraq) opened fire at the demonstrators in Oshnavieh, killing and injuring several. This is when the hostilities between the PDKI and KDP (I) began (p. 132). One of the factors that created conflict between these two parties was that the 8-Article demand was against the KDP (Iraq). Besides, the KDP (Iraq) accused the PDKI of pulling the corpse of Mullah Mustafa Barzani from his grave. Also, in the northern and western parts of Urmiya, in cooperation with the government, the KDP (Iraq) attacked the peshmergas of the PDKI (Gadani, 2008a, pp. 302-303). Qazi (2010) states that the KDP (Iraq) also attacked the PDKI in the liberated areas of northern and southern Kurdistan, killing about 200 PDKI peshmergas (p. 332). The war in the northern and western parts of Urmiya, which started at the end of the Summer of 1981 and lasted a few months, resulted in the domination of the government forces in this area.

The Tudeh Party helped the PDKI (FFC) organizationally and financially, as did the Fadaian (Majority). Moreover, in Tehran, the Tudeh Party held training courses for the CC members of the PDKI (FFC) in philosophy, history, economy, and politics. The *Kurdistan* continued its publication in the Spring of 1981 in the printshop of the Tudeh Party. To negotiate a political merger, the Tudeh Party, the Fadaian (Majority), and the PDKI (FFC) held meetings in Tehran (Bakhchi, 2007, p. 50), most likely during 1981-1982.

During the same period, the PDKI, the Komala, and the government were pressuring the opposition groups in Kurdistan. Bakhchi (2007) writes that in Mahabad, the Komala killed Mustafa Sharwerani, a Tudeh Party supporter, and arrested Khalid Badrnia, a supporter of the Fadaian (Majority) but he was later released. Reports hold that at this time, the PDKI probably took some members of the PDKI (FFC) outside of the city and shot them. The Komala also assassinated Mullah Karim Shahrikandi, a Kurdish patriotic clergy, on 22 March 1982 in Mahabad (pp. 51-52). It is also likely that it was the Komala who assassinated Taha Parsa and Karim Khayati, members of the Fadaian (Majority), and Qadir Abdullah Pour, who supported the Iranian government in Mahabad. The Komala imprisoned Ahmad Moqtaderi and Khalid Badrnia, members of the Fadaian (Majority) from Bukan and Mahabad, respectively. Ebrahim Jahangiri maintains that the Komala also assassinated Mullah Karim Shahrikandi on 22 March 1982 and Mullah Omar Shahin in Mahabad. The PDKI assassinated Omar Ahmad Mihali in the village of Talaw on 13 July 1985. Kamal Isma'ilzadeh, a military commander of the PDKI, was also reportedly executed, along with his pregnant wife, by the PDKI when he rejoined the PDKI after having surrendered himself to the Iranian government. Their execution created great uproar within the party ranks. It is also said that Mullah Khalid Azizi was assassinated by either the PDKI or the Komala. These individuals were assassinated only because their political views were different from the abovementioned political organizations (Jahangiri, 2012).

Likewise, the Iranian government persecuted, arrested, and killed members of the PDKI (FFC). In one instance, the supporters of the PDKI (FFC) were caught by a group of regime's armed force (pasdars or the police) while writing slogans on the walls in Mahabad. Although they introduced themselves to the police, they were shot at, and two of them lost their legs. Many members of the PDKI (FFC) were also imprisoned. In Baneh, the government arrested Nasser Khoshkalam, a CC member of the PDKI (FFC), and tortured and executed him on 24 April 1983 (Bakhchi, 2007, pp. 52-53). The government also arrested Rahim Nadir Ahmadi and tortured and imprisoned Hassan Hatami. Both were from Mahabad, and both were members of the PDKI (FFC) (Bolourian, 1997, pp. 348, 360).

On 6 February 1983, the government arrested Kianouri, the Tudeh General Secretary, and other leaders of the party. These arrests were followed by a wholesale prosecution of the Tudeh members in mid-spring 1983. These raids also included members of the PDKI (FFC) and the Fadaian (Majority). So, followers of these parties in Kurdistan escaped to the mountains of Iraqi Kurdistan and were sheltered by the Iraqi Communist Party for the next five years (Bakhchi, 2007, pp. 53-54).

The Plenum of the PDKI (FFC), held in the mountains of Lolan in mid-summer 1983, decided that Bolourian, Siraji, and Nawid Mo'ini should travel abroad in order to consult with the Tudeh Party. Muhammad Amin Chira from the Tudeh Party accompanied them (Bakhchi, 2007, pp. 58). In the Spring of 1984, the followers of the PDKI (FFC) in the mountains sent letters to their leadership, asking them to return. Later, they received a telegram from Siraji informing them that they would continue their struggle under the name of the Tudeh Party. It was later revealed that Bolourian was chosen as a member of the Politburo and Siraj as a CC member of the Tudeh Party. In a meeting of the CC, the cadres criticized the leaders who, without informing them, had joined the Tudeh Party and had, in effect, terminated the PDKI (FFC). Nevertheless, the majority supported the unification of the two parties (Bakhchi, 2007, pp. 66-69). Bolourian claims that when he was in Prague, Hamid Safari, a Tudeh Party leader, informed him that Ghassemlou announced that if the PDKI (FFC) were dissolved into the Tudeh Party, the PDKI would accept collaborating with the Tudeh. Bolourian had responded that he would not stand in the way, thus agreeing with the dissolution (Bakhchi, 2007, p. 69). Gradually, based on their personal plans, the mountain group left for Syria, Iraq, Turkey, Soviet Azerbaijan, and Afghanistan. They eventually settled in Europe, Canada, and other Western countries (Bakhchi, 2007, p. 69).

Bolourian frequently had asked the Tudeh Party leaders and the Soviet Union authorities to pay attention to the Kurdish problem and, at the very least, allow Kurdish programs to be broadcast from radios *Solh wa Taraqi* (Peace and Progress) and *Zahmatkeshan* (Toilers). But his requests were ignored (Bakhchi, 2007, p. 73). After a few years, almost all Kurdish members of the Tudeh Party and the Fadaian (Majority), including Bolourian and Siraji, left these groups due to changes in their political views and continued their activities in the Kurdish areas (Bakhchi, 2007, pp. 70-71). On 30 March 1990, the majority of the Kurdish cadres and members of the Tudeh Party in Europe announced their leaving the party. Bolourian and Siraji, on 30 March 1990, declared that they had joined the Tudeh Party without being fully aware of the essence of the Tudeh leadership and its non-democratic structure, and they now had decided to leave the Tudeh Party (Bakhchi, 2007, pp. 80, 90-91).

6.5.1.4. The PDKI's activities since Spring 1980. In the Autumn of 1979, the party started its temporary radio broadcasting until 14 or 15 June 1980, when the party launched its own radio station and a program called *Radioy Dangi Kurdistani Eran* (Iranian Kurdistan Voice Radio). Besides, after the split of the PDKI (FFC), in a rally in Mahabad, Ghassemlou stated that the main issue was whether or not to put the party's arms down. Eighty thousand demonstrators reportedly shouted against it (Hassanzadeh, 2012, p. 273). Clearly, this report is flatly exaggerated since the population of Mahabad at the time was about 50,000 (see above).

The Iraq-Iran War started on 22 September 1980 when Iraq attacked Iran. The PDKI announced its position in a statement that asserted that Ayatollah

Khomeini or the President should accept and officially announce the 6-Article Demand regarding Kurdistan's autonomy, end the military occupation of Kurdish cities, and withdraw the Revolutionary Guards and the hired jash troops from Kurdistan. Once these conditions are met, the PDKI would fight the enemy alongside Iranian troops (Gadani, 2008a, pp. 283-284).

The Iranian regime was not only fighting the peshmergas. It attacked and murdered the ordinary people, continued economic sanctions against Kurdistan, and closed down schools in the region (Hassanzadeh, 2012, p. 290). For more than two weeks, Mahabad was under cannon and mortar fire, and more than 150 defenseless civilians were killed (Gadani, 2008a, p. 285; Hisami, 1997a, p. 94). The Iranian military forces also raided the rural communities. Hussein Rasouli Azar, in his interview with Herish Nasseri regarding the slaughtering of people in the village of Indirqash (Agrigash), states that on 4 November 1980, the Iranian regime's force of Qarapapaqs (Black Hats), the *Basij* [Mobilization. The Organization for Mobilization of the Oppressed] militias and the Revolutionary Guards, under Mullah Hassani, attacked the village of Indirqash (Agrigash) near Mahabad without any pretext. They burned down houses and murdered 31 innocent people, including women. Rasouli Azar states that he knew some witnesses who saw the invaders raping women and girls, who remained silent about the incident to protect their honor (Nasseri, 2012). The massacres of the Kurdish civilians in the villages of Qalatan, Kulij, and Sofian in Oshnavieh, Indirqash (Agrigash) in Mahabad, and Sarokani in Piranshahr were reminders of the massacre of Qarne in 1979 (Gadani, 2008a, p. 287).

In its Plenum, 5-9 April 1981, the PDKI leadership called Rahman Karimi and Sanar Mamadi traitors, expelled them, and claimed that they would be punished by a revolutionary tribunal. Karimi was accused of being a government spy, having contacts with the Revolutionary Guards and the army, carrying out the operation of Piranshahr in favor of the government, slandering the PDKI leaders, and collaborating with Mamadi. Likewise, Mamadi was charged with having relations with General Oveissi and other Royalists, receiving money from them, exploiting and expelling the toilers in the villages under his authority, and having a feudalistic manner in party's activities (Gadani, 2008a, pp. 291-292). A year earlier, in the Brayma Plenum, Ghassemlou had stated that Mamadi had split from the PDKI along with Jahangir Isma'ilzadeh. Mamadi had contacted the United States Embassy in Ankara and received funds. He was charged with smuggling heroin. Mamadi strongly rejects these charges (Mamadi, 1999, pp. 180, 185). Despite these accusations, interestingly, after the 6th Congress of the PDKI and in a Plenum held in mid-Winter 1983, Mamadi was elected consultant member of the CC (Gohari, 2002, p. 81).

On 7 May 1981, four Iraqi helicopters and two fighter jets attacked the village of Dolatou in the territory of Sardasht, using Napalm bombs on the prisons of the PDKI, in which 42 people were killed and 50 were wounded. These included six peshmergas killed and several wounded. The PDKI, in a declaration, severely condemned this attack (Gadani, 2008a, p. 295).

The People's Mojahedin Organization of Iran (PMOI), on 20 June 1981, held a demonstration in Tehran in which tens of thousands participated. Their slogan was "Down with the reactionaries, long live freedom." In clashes with the Iranian security forces, tens of the demonstrators were killed and hundreds wounded. As PMOI became an underground group due to its armed uprising against the regime, in the following months, many PMOI cadres and members moved to Kurdistan and stayed as guests of the PDKI. For a while, they used the PDKI's radio station, and the two began expanding their cooperation (Gadani, 2008a, p. 298).

During 1980-1981, the diplomatic relations between the PDKI and foreign countries developed. French doctors came to Kurdistan with the PDKI arrangements to treat the wounded and the sick of the party. The PDKI sent a message to the French President, François Mitterrand, expressing their gratitude for his support of the Kurdish struggle (Gadani, 2008a, p. 295-296).

Before the 5th Congress, the PDKI joined the PMOI-led National Council of Resistance of Iran (NCRI). The decision was made by Sharafkandi and Ghassemlou, not by the CC. According to Qazi (2010), that way of decision-making was a coup-like method (p. 327). Gadani (2008a) asserts that Massoud Rajavi, the head of the NCRI and leader of the PMOI, sent a letter to Ghassemlou, dated 25 October 1981, that contained the program of the Democratic Islamic Republic of Iran. The program asserted the approval of the autonomy of Kurdistan in the framework of the Iranian territory. After many rounds of negotiations, a declaration signed by the PDKI Politburo was published on 17 November 1981. It announced the official joining of the PDKI with the NCRI. But Gadani insists that the decision to join the NCRI had never been discussed in the plenums of the PDKI. After six months of negotiations, in the Spring of 1985, due to the ongoing negotiations between the PDKI and the Iranian regime, the NCRI expelled the PDKI, and the PDKI, in a declaration on 2 April 1985, accepted this decision (Gadani, 2008a, pp. 305-307, 357).

An important change in the PDKI policy at this time was adopting the slogan "down with the Iranian government." Hassanzadeh (2012b) states that before the 5th Congress, he wrote an article for the PDKI's radio program. The article, approved by Sharafkandi, included the slogan, "Down with the Islamic Republic of Iran" (p. 177).

6.5.2. The effects of the Iraq-Iran War on the Kurdish armed struggle in Iran. The Iraq-Iran War started on 22 September 1980 when Iraq attacked Iran. It was discussed that an important reason for the split of the PDKI (FFC) from the PDKI was its opposition to the PDKI's relationship with the Iraqi regime. The Iraq-Iran War had different effects on the armed struggle in Iranian Kurdistan. Some of them include the following. Firstly, the Iraqi regime, even before the Iraq-Iran War, had encouraged the Kurdish groups to oppose the Iranian government. This war caused the Iraqi government to support the Kurdish groups even more and practically. While the Kurdish groups received political, social, financial and military support from the Iraqi government, they also used the Iraqi territory as a rear for the Kurdish armed struggle against the Iranian government. Secondly, the war created hopes among the Kurds that this war would weaken the Iranian government, from which the Kurds would benefit. Thirdly, this war produced great hope among the Kurds in Iran, and one result of such hope was to extensively participate in the armed struggle led by the political organization in Kurdistan. Fourthly, the cooperation of the Kurds with the Iraqi government caused the Iranian government to accuse the Kurdish movement of being affiliated with foreign countries that, as part of the imperialist power's plan against the Iranian revolution, tried to destabilize the Iranian state. Using this logic, the Iranian state successfully provoked non-Kurdish people, mobilized large groups of non-Kurdish militiamen, and deployed them to suppress the Kurdish nationalist movement.

6.5.3. Conflicts between the PDKI and other political organizations. While fighting against the Iranian government, the PDKI engaged in many clashes with various Kurdish and non-Kurdish political organizations. It has also cooperated, to varying degrees, with other groups. These include the PDKI cooperating with the Organization of Revolutionary Workers of Iran (Rah-e Kargar) and the Iranian People's Fedai Guerrillas (Liberation Army of the Iranian Peoples [LAIP]) in 1985 in Baneh (Gadani, 2008a, p. 369).

The PDKI was in conflict with the Tudeh Party of Iran, the PDKI (FFC), the Komala, *Komalay Yaksaniy Kurdistan* (Kurdistan Equality Party) (KEP), *Sazmani Khabati Kurdistani Eran* (Organization of Iranian Kurdistan Struggle) or the Khabat, the Organization of Revolutionary Workers of Iran or the Rah-e Kargar, the Organization of Struggle for the Emancipation of the Working Class or the

Peykar, the Iranian People's Fedai Guerrillas, the Organization of Iranian People's Fadaian (Majority), *Sazman-e Kar-e Iran* (Labour Party of Iran) or the Toufan, *Hizbi Demokrati Kurdistani Eran-Rebarayati Shorishger* (Iranian Democratic Party of Kurdistan- Revolutionary Leadership) or the PDKI-RL, and *Hizbi Demokrati Kurdistan-Eran* (Kurdistan Democratic Party-Iran) or the KDP-I, which in the 14th Congress changed its name to *Hizbi Demokrati Kurdistan* (Kurdistan Democratic Party) or the KDP. We will review the major conflicts soon.

6.6. The 5th Congress of the PDKI

The 5th Congress of the PDKI, known as *Kongray Shahidan* (Martyrs' Congress), was held in the village of Shiwajo in the region of Rabat, Iran, 6-9 December 1981 (Gadani, 2008a, p. 311). The Congress elected Ghassemlou as the General Secretary and Sadiq Sharafkandi as the alternate General Secretary, a position that had only existed since the 5th Congress, in which the PDKI approved the slogan, "down with the Islamic Republic of Iran" (see Appendix 8). This, however, did not mean that the PDKI was actually able to overthrow the regime. It meant that it was impossible to solve the Kurdish problem within the existing regime (Hassanzadeh, 2012, p. 297). Hoshmand Ali Mahmood Shekhani, an Iraqi Kurd academician, states that this slogan was a mistake because it was not the duty of the Kurdish movement, however, theoretically, to challenge the power of Tehran and also because Ghassemlou believed in peaceful solutions. Therefore, the party should have opted for negotiations (Ali Mahmood Shekhani, 2007, pp. 160-151). In this Congress, Ghassemlou also introduced the idea of *Simay Demokrat* (Democratic Visage). Ghassemlou argued that democratic personality was essential for the democratization of a country or a political party. Thus, he outlined a code of conduct for the PDKI cadres (Monazzami, 2011, p. 34; see Appendix 25).

The organizational set up of the PDKI had been based on the principle of democratic centralism, approved by the 3rd Congress. The leading organs in the

PDKI include the Congress, Conference, CC, and Politburo. The executive organs are comprised of the Commissions and the local executive units. The cadres had 5 ranks in the PDKI (Mawloudi Sabian, 1994, pp. 96, 98). The military section was under the Political-Military Commission, and the latter under a Politburo member. The PDKI's peshmergas had been organized in *Hezes* (Forces). Each *Hez* (Force) included four *Liqs* (Branches), each Branch had four *Pals* (Twig), each *Pal* contained four *Dasta* (Groups), and each Group comprised 12 peshmergas. Therefore, each Force included 768 people (Mawloudi Sabian, 1994, p. 128). The PDKI peshmergas were organized in 11 Forces, including Zagros, Douy Rebandan, Bistoun, Qandil, Peshawa, Bayan, Gia Rang, Zimziran, Arbaba, Kela Shin, and Spi Sang. The International Institute for Strategic Studies in London estimated the number of the peshmergas to be 10,000-12,000 strong, which seems higher than the real number of the total Forces, about 8,448 (Mawloudi Sabian, 1994, pp. 129-130). And yet, Shalmashi believes that the PDKI had 12,000-15,000 peshmergas (Personal communication, November 15, 2012).

While fighting against Iranian forces, the PDKI provided education in some rural areas, trained teachers, medical cadres, and judges, and divided lands among the landless peasants (Hassanzadeh, n.d., pp. 202-203; Gadani, 2008a, pp. 299-300, 312-313).

On 25 August 1982, the PDKI released a declaration asking democratic forces of the world to stand against the genocidal treatment by the Iranian government. Jalal Talabani, the leader of the *Yaketi Nishtmani Kurdistan* (Patriotic Union of Kurdistan) or PUK, sent a large group of peshmergas known as *Hezi Pishtiwan* (Support Force) to help the PDKI. Talabani himself stayed in Kurdistan for about three months to command this force. More than 20 of these peshmergas were killed, and tens of them were wounded (Gadani, 2008a, p. 321). The Support Force, comprised of 1,500 (or 1,700) PUK peshmergas, took part in the PDKI heavy clash with the Iranian army on the Piranshahr-Sardasht highway (in late August or early September 1982). At least 15 PUK peshmergas were killed and dozens wounded (Hassanzadeh, 1996, pp. 24-29; 2012, pp. 340-343). On 26 January 1983, the government attacked the villages of Qaragol, Sawzi, and Sarchinar, killing women and children and burning down houses and even animals. In Qaragol 18 and in Sawzi, 9 people were killed, and many disappeared (Gadani, 2008a, p. 323).

When the government raided the Tudeh Party and arrested its leadership in the Spring of 1983, the PDKI issued a statement (dated 8 May 1983) in which it asserted that although the Tudeh Party supported the reactionary Iranian regime and spied on the PDKI, the party still condemned the arrest and torture of the Tudeh members and supporters. The statement maintained that the PDKI would protect the security of the members and followers of the Tudeh Party if they came to Kurdistan (Gadani, 2008a, pp. 326-328; see also Gohari, 2002, p. 20).

One of the cruel actions of the government was the execution of 59 mostly young civilians from Mahabad. In a joint statement dated 5 June 1983, the Politburos of the PDKI declared that on 2 June 1983, the Iranian government had executed 59 civilians in Mahabad. They announced 7 June 1983 as a public mourning day and asked the Kurdish people in Kurdistan's cities to close their offices, schools, shops, corporations, and factories ("Shared Declaration", 1983, p. 1). From 20 February 1983 to 6 August 1983, according to Gadani (2008a), the PDKI peshmergas conducted 179 operations and captured four military bases. In these operations, the PDKI forces reportedly killed 6,339, wounded 2,127, captured 328 soldiers, and lost 249 peshmergas (p. 333).

Meanwhile, discord within the PDKI continued between the 5th and 6th Congresses. Hisami (2011) reports that before the 6th Congress, dozens of experienced cadres accused of criticizing party leadership were expelled arbitrarily (p. 252). Amir Qazi was one of those who criticized the party's leadership and policies and opposed dictatorship. Later, this group established a new organization called *Parti Sarbakhoyy Kurdistan* (Independence Party of Kurdistan) (Qazi, 2010, pp. 362-364).

By the end of Summer 1983, the party, due to the occupation of the territories by the Iranian army and pushing back the Kurdish peshmergas toward the border of Iran-Iraq, had to move the Politburo office to the Iraqi Kurdistan, in the territory of Mawat (Shinkayati). There, they informed the Iraqi government of this transfer to Iraqi soil. Likewise, the bases of OIPM and the Komala were moved to Shinkayati. By 1985, the government had recaptured and controlled almost all of Kurdistan, pushing the Kurdish resistance to the border of Iran and Iraq (Hassanzadeh, 1996, pp. 40-43; Ali Mahmood Shekhani, 2007, p. 166).

6.7. The 6th Congress of the PDKI

The 6th Congress of the PDKI, involving 230 representatives, was held in the village of Galala in the territory of Shinkawe on 22-26 January 1984 (Gadani, 2008a, pp. 334-335). Again, Ghassemlou was elected the General Secretary and Sadiq Sharafkandi the alternate General Secretary (see Appendix 8). The key disagreement in the Congress was on the "democratic socialism" proposed by Ghassemlou, who had proposed this concept in his book *Kurta Basek La Sar Sosialism* (*A Brief Discussion on Socialism*). The Congress approved democratic socialism as the final goal of the party (PDKI's Program and Constitution, 1984, p. 16). Ghassemlou's *Brief Discussion* has a longer history. The party has been regarding socialism as its goal for a long time. Aside from the 1960s-1970s, the party always considered itself a leftist party and a friend of communist parties and socialist countries. Ghassemlou, having lived in Prague and through the Prague Spring, had condemned the Soviet invasion of Czechoslovakia in 1968. In the 3rd Conference (1971), Ghassemlou had tried to insert the term "democratic socialism" into the PDKI platform, but the Conference had approved the party's goal to be a "just socialist society." In the 4th Congress (1980), the aim of the party changed to the creation of a "socialist society." In the 5th Congress in 1981, the goal of the party was changed to "a socialist society compatible with the special conditions of our country [Kurdistan]." In the party's Plenum of 1983, Ghassemlou brought up his *A Brief Discussion on Socialism* that argued for a democratic socialism. The pro-Soviet members of the party were against it, but the book influenced other members. Therefore, in the 6th Congress (1984), *A Brief Discussion* was approved, and the objective of the party changed to "democratic socialism." For Ghassemlou, democratic socialism was different from social democracy, as the latter was a reformist approach that defended capitalism in the name of socialism (Hassanzadeh, 1996, pp. 42-48).

In *A Brief Discussion on Socialism*, Ghassemlou states that democracy includes three components: social democracy, economic democracy, and political democracy. In socialist countries, social democracy and economic democracy exist, but these countries lack political democracy. In Western countries, political democracy and social democracy exist, but they lack economic democracy. Ghassemlou prioritizes political democracy. In contrast to social democracy, democratic socialism aims to overthrow capitalism and establish a socialist society that develops democracy (Ghassemlou, 2003, pp. 40-41; Monazzami, 2011, p. 43).

During the discussions over *Brief Discussion*, the Congress had an agitated atmosphere (Hassanzadeh, 1996, p. 56). The idea of democratic socialism was not approved by the Congress, and Ghassemlou left the Congress in protest. Only when Sharafkandi asked him to return to Congress his concept of a Democratic Society was approved in a close vote of 108 in favor, 100 against, and 22 abstained (Khalighi, 2005, pp. 164-165; Hassanzadeh, 1996, p. 56; Qazi, 2010, pp. 369-370; Shalmashi, Personal communication, November 15, 2012; Wirya, Personal communication, October 22, 2012). Clearly, Ghassemlou's leaving Congress and returning to it on the implicit condition that his proposal should be approved was against democratic principles. Ghassemlou succeeded due to backroom threats, incentives, concessions, and his personal charisma. When Ghassemlou observed this situation, he also brought up the subject of *Listay Fix* (Fixed List), a method of choosing the leadership based on voting to one or some fixed list of the members, not to the individuals (see section 6.9.1), but because it was put to the vote through secret ballot, his proposal received only one vote in favor (probably Ghassemlou's own!). This process caused significant numbers of cadres and members to leave (or be expelled from) the PDKI. The Congress' yielding to Ghassemlou's demands encouraged him to try and obtain even greater personal power (Gadani, 2008a, p. 335). Hassani views Ghassemlou as a matchless dictator who did not tolerate any views against his own, and his aforesaid behavior shows he bullied the 6th Congress representatives into approving his views (Personal communication, October 19, 2012).

After the 6th Congress, Ghassemlou translated and distributed a pamphlet written by Michael Rocard, the General Secretary of the French Socialist Party. In a meeting, Ghassemlou defended this pamphlet. But he raged when Hassanzadeh explained that this pamphlet was advocating for social democracy and was different from the democratic socialism approved by the party (Hassanzadeh, 2012, p. 177). The subject of democratic socialism remained a contentious issue. In the end, the party expelled four vocal critics, and another dozen members left the party (Hassanzadeh, 1996, pp.63-64). Aliyar suggests that *A Brief Discussion* and the concept of democratic socialism aimed at making a clear distinction between the PDKI and the Tudeh Party. Although the party's goal is declared to be democratic socialism, in practice, the party has moved toward social democracy (Personal communication, October 22, 2012).

Khalighi reveals that after the 6th Congress, Ghassemlou announced that no one had the right to speak against the democratic socialism within the party. When Mitran, Gohari, Rahimi, and others continued to speak against it, Ghassemlou asked them to sign repentance letters. They refused and left the party (Personal communication, December 1, 2012). For Madani, Ghassemlou did not really believe in democratic socialism, and he moved toward social democracy (Personal communication, October 14, 2012). Rastgar claims that Ghassemlou brought up the subject of democratic socialism not only to mark a distinction between the PDKI and the pro-Soviet Tudeh Party but also to get the West's attention (Personal communication, October 17, 2012). Lotf Pouri confirms this view: Ghassemlou wanted not to be identified with the "actually existing socialism" (Personal communication, October 21, 2012).

The Plenum of the PDKI on 6-15 August 1984 contained two important discussions regarding, first, negotiating with the government, and second, expelling of certain cadres and peshmergas. Negotiating with the Iranian government was against the principles of the NCRI. As a result of the negotiations that took place in Paris and reported by *Kurdistan*, Issue 99, the PDKI was expelled from the NCRI (Gadani, 2008a, pp. 348-349). As regards the second issue, Aziz Mamle, in a letter to Hisami, claimed that the PDKI had expelled Rahim Amiri, Pola Nanavazadeh, Faraydoun Mitran, and Hamed Gohary. Hisami maintains that hundreds of cadres and activists had left the party before being expelled (Hisami, 2011, p.269). Gohari writes that after the 6th Congress, more than 1,000 members surrendered themselves to the Iranian government or left for Iraq. He claims that the PDKI had asked the dissenting members to sign letters pledging to support the party's policy. Gohari asserts that the party's newspaper and radio called them traitors, thieves, and cowards (Hisami, 2011, p. 273). The party believed that since democratic socialism had become the party's political objective, the members could keep their own ideas but did not have the right to speak out against democratic socialism (Hassanzadeh, 2012, p. 389). It was not until the 10th Congress that the members were allowed to disagree and speak against the party's views within the organization (Hassanzadeh, 2012, pp. 389-390).

One of the achievements of the PDKI since 1979 has been educating its members through courses. For instance, in the Spring of 1983, a permanent course called *Zankoy Siasi-Nizami* (Political-Military College) was set up in the territory of Alan, Sardasht. After the 6th Congress, its name changed to *Fergay Siasi-Nizami Hizbi Demokrati Kurdistani Eran* (Political-Military Academy of the Democratic Party of Iranian Kurdistan) (Hassanzadeh, 1996, pp. 65-67).

6.7.1. The PDKI-Komala clash. The *most significant conflict*—in duration, intensity, violence, number of causalities, and negative effects on the Kurdish nationalist movement in Iran—*has been the armed conflict between the PDKI and the Komala*. To date, neither party has offered a comprehensive analysis regarding this subject. Although the PDKI and the Komala have had many smaller conflicts since the Revolution, the main conflict, known as the war between the PDKI and the Komala, lasted for six years, from 1984 to 1990. In considering the reasons for and effects of this bloody clash, the PDKI's leaders and followers and then the Komala's leaders' perspectives will be discussed.

The first clash between the PDKI and the Komala peshmergas occurred on 2 May 1980 in Sardasht. The columns of the two groups' peshmergas ran into each other, and although the Komala peshmergas knew the others were PDKI peshmergas, they nevertheless opened fire on PDKI peshmergas, killing Rasoul Abdullahi (aka Faqe Al Rasouy Alli). Between 1980 and 1984, a few more armed clashes took place. The Komala, especially after it created the Communist Party of Iran [CPI], regarded the war between the Komala and the PDKI as a revolutionary duty. According to the Komala, Kurdistan was divided into capitalist and proletarian classes, represented by the PDKI and the Komala, respectively. In the Komala's view, fighting the PDKI had a higher priority than fighting the government. On 5 September 1982, Komala asserted that there was no fundamental difference between the domination of the PDKI and the Islamic Republic over Kurdistan because both protect the capitalist system and exploit the majority of the society. The Komala emphasized that it would be a fair price to pay if the Komala relinquished territory to the government's control but punished the PDKI by doing that. This is so the analysis went because, in the future, the Komala would be able to confront the government's forces as the ultimate Kurdish fighting force against the Iranian government (Hassanzadeh, 1996, pp. 72-75; Hassanzadeh, 2012, pp. 247-248).

In the views of many of the PDKI researchers, the Komala's antagonism toward the PDKI was based on the Komala's view of the PDKI as a bourgeoisie party. Hassanzadeh (2012) claims that it was the Komala that paved the way to the war (p. 226). Monazzami points out Komala's "triangle theory," formulated by Abdullah Mohtadi, according to which three different groups with different ideologies existed in Kurdistan:

> Komeleh [the Komala] is a group that represents the communists and workers; [the] PDKI is a nationalist party that represents the bourgeoisie in Kurdistan, and the Islamic Republic of Iran represents the bourgeoisie throughout Iran. Then, in order to create a communist society in Kurdistan, according to Muhtadi [Mohtadi], Komeleh [the Komala] had to crush [the] PDKI before it could fight against the Iranian forces. (Monazzami, 2011, p. 48)

The clash between the PDKI and the Komala in Hawraman (Oraman) in 1984 marked the beginning of a major war between these two organizations. Hassanzadeh (1996) asserts that on 16 November 1984, a heavy clash occurred between these two organizations in Oraman in which many, especially from the Komala's side, were killed, and the Komala had to leave the area. A joint commission, including the PDKI, the Komala, and the PUK, investigated the incident (p.78). The commission's effort did not lead to peace. Mohtadi states that the PDKI was not ready to accept its responsibility for killing 13 peshmergas (Saedi, 2010, p. 117). Therefore, the Komala attacked the PDKI in retaliation.

In 1984, the PDKI announced that if the Komala started a war against the party in a territory, the PDKI would fight against the Komala everywhere (Hassanzadeh, 1996, pp. 77-78). Some of the leaders of the PDKI admit that the first attack was the PDKI's doing. Khalighi (2002) reveals that in the first clash in Oraman, the PDKI started the attack. Later, the PDKI apologized to the Komala. The second time, though, the Komala continued the attack in Oraman, and eventually, the PDKI declared an all-out war against the Komala in Kurdistan (pp. 271-272).

After the failure of the joint commission's efforts, the Komala reacted by attacking the PDKI. Hassanzadeh maintains that on 26 January 1985, at midnight, the Komala attacked the PDKI bases in Oraman and killed 19 people, including a wounded person and a woman who had given sanctuary to the wounded person in her home. Soon, the PDKI peshmergas regrouped, attacked, and killed 14 Komala peshmergas. In the aftermath, the Komala asked the PDKI to meet for negotiations, but the party declined, claiming that the Komala had other plans. After this incident, clashes between the two continued until 1988, when the clashes stopped due to the Komala's not having armed units in Kurdistan. On 7 May 1990, the PDKI unilaterally stopped the war, and the Komala accepted it (Hassanzadeh, 1996, pp. 79-80).

In early Autumn 1985, the PDKI Plenum announced that if the Komala accepted that the PDKI was a revolutionary party, the way to a ceasefire and even cooperation would be opened. Thus, both the continuation and end of the war were now in the hands of the Communist Party of Iran (Komala [CPI]) (Gadani, 2008a, p. 359; Ali Mahmood Shekhani, 2007, p. 259; Hassanzadeh, 2012, p. 233). Ebrahim Alizadeh, the General Secretary of the Komala Kurdistan's Organization of the Communist Party of Iran (Komala [CPI]) and the executive member of the Communist Party of Iran (CPI), however, asserts that the PDKI had two conditions for ending the war: (1) the Komala should recognize the PDKI as a revolutionary party, and (2) the Komala should accept the leadership of the PDKI in Kurdistan, according to the PDKI, since the PDKI regarded it as a small group (Saedi, 2012, p.110).

In 1987, a Hexalateral Commission was established to mediate between the PDKI and the Komala. It included Sheikh Izz al-Din, the Rah-e Kargar, and the Kurdistan Equality Party-Iran, as well as three factions of the Fedai Guerrillas in Kurdistan (IPFG, LAIP, and OIPFG). The Commission issued a Three-Point Resolution for stopping the war immediately (Hassanzadeh, 1996, p. 82-83). On 15 July 1987, the IPFG, representing the Appointed Committee of the Hexalateral Commission, asked the PDKI in a letter for a meeting on 19 July 1987. The PDKI, on the same day, replied that the party was too busy to be able to meet on that day, but it would keep the Commission posted. Later, the PDKI sent a proposal to the Komala. The main points were: (1) Both the PDKI and the Komala were participants in the Kurdish movement. (2) Based on the number of casualties, peshmergas, the previous elections in Kurdistan, and the territory under control, the sovereignty in Kurdistan would be under the PDKI. (3) The Komala could have a share in ruling, receiving customs, taxes, and other things based on its weight in the movement. (4) Agreements were to be made about the ceasefire, through negotiations, so that military cooperation between the PDKI and the Komala against the government would be determined. Hassanzadeh maintains that the Hexalateral Commission, in a letter to the PDKI dated 25 July 1987, claimed that the Hexalateral Commission would not pursue the mediations because the PDKI's proposal was against the Commission's efforts to end the conflict (Hassanzadeh, 1996, pp. 84-87). Later, when on 23 April 1988, in a humiliating letter, the Komala declared a ceasefire with the PDKI, but the party did not respond positively to the ceasefire (Hassanzadeh, 1996, p. 81). In fact, the PDKI continued the war for two more years.

The practical reasons for ending the conflict between the Komala and the PDKI were that the leadership of both sides had moved outside of Kurdistan, peshmergas' presence in Iranian Kurdistan had diminished, the exercising of authority was ended in the region, and the political parties lost their power in the area. When the forces moved to Iraqi Kurdistan, the people and political parties there did not accept the war between the Komala and the PDKI (Hassanzadeh, 2012, pp. 238-239).

Gadani maintains that on 26 May 1987, the Hexalateral Commission wrote a resolution that included three points to stop the conflict: (1) to resolve issues in a political way, (2) to guarantee freedom of publicizing and circulating ideas, and (3) to guarantee the right of political-military activities. This resolution was useless because it was a one-sided decision. In late Summer of 1987, the PDKI distributed a 46-page article regarding this subject. The conflict continued until 1988, when the PDKI-RL, on 20 April 1988, announced a unilateral ceasefire, and the Komala accepted (Gadani, 2008a, pp. 351-353). *The war between the Komala and the PDKI is one of the darkest points in the history of the Kurdish nationalist struggle.* As regards the responsibility of these groups in the war, Hassanzadeh (2012) states that the Komala bore greater responsibility than the PDKI. However, the leadership of the PDKI was also at fault (p. 240). Hassanzadeh (1996) also maintains that while creating the war with the PDKI was guilty, it was the Komala leaders' views regarding the PDKI that started the conflict. Long before the war, the Komala had announced its main duty to challenge the PDKI's influence and smash the Kurdish bourgeoisie. In its meetings and rallies, the people were provoked against the PDKI. The party had continuously asked the Komala not to propagandize against other organizations because most activists were armed and did not have political education or democratic tolerance (pp. 69-71).

With respect to the causalities of the war between the PDKI and the Komala, none of these organizations has offered a comprehensive review. The six-year war (1984-1990) between the PDKI and the Komala caused great losses for both parties, as well as the nationalist movement in Iranian Kurdistan (Hassanzadeh, 1996, pp.

69, 87). Hassanzadeh (2012) estimates the casualties of these conflicts to be over 100 for each side (p. 236). According to Mohtadi, who confirms hundreds were killed during this war, the conflict benefited the enemies of the Kurds, as the Kurdish people lost their hope in the movement (Personal communication, September 17, 2012; Saedi, 2010, pp. 7, 109). The Communist Party of Iran CPA) registers 222 Komala peshmergas who were killed by the PDKI in the clashes between the Komala and the PDKI from 1981 to 1989 (Albom-e Janbakhtegan, 2016, n.p.). Mautasam Noorani, a previous alternate CC member of the PDKI, claims that in the war between the PDKI and Komala, more than 500 peshmergas were killed and many wounded from both sides. People lost faith in these parties, and the government occupied the region (Personal communication, September 22, 2012).

6.8. The 7th Congress of the PDKI

The 7th Congress of the PDKI (so-called "40 Years of Struggle Congress") was held in the village of Kani Mew in the Kurdistan of Iraq, 17-20 December 1985 (Gadani, 2008a, p. 361; Hassanzadeh, 1996, p. 133). Ghassemlou was elected the General Secretary, and Sharafkandi the alternate General Secretary of the PDKI (see Appendix 8). In the 7th Congress, when Salam Azizi, a CC member, asked about the financial aid the PDKI had received from the foreign states, Ghassemlou became angry. He asserted, in responding to Ahmad Nastani, that as long as he was the General Secretary, nobody except him should know about the party's finances and assets (Gadani, 2008a, p. 363). Aside from this, for the first time in a resolution, the Conference tasked the leadership with planning to promote women's status in the Kurdish movement (Gadani, 2008a, p. 365). After the Congress, the PDKI contacted the Socialist International. Ghassemlou participated in the 17th Congress of the Socialist International in Lima, Peru (20-23 June 1986) as an observer and for the first time. This experience influenced him and the PDKI to turn to rather "conservative" views (Gadani, 2008a, p. 371). The PDKI became a consultant member of the Socialist International on 11 September 1996 (Hassanzadeh, 1996, p. 142).

According to Gadani (2008a), prior to the 7th Congress and especially since 1985, the PDKI had carried out military, social, diplomatic, and educational activities. Until 1987, the PDKI had published various newspapers and magazines, mostly in Kurdish but also in Persian and French, in addition to about 10 volumes of Kurdish textbooks for elementary schools (pp. 368-390). During this period, the PDKI made several errors. It had hasty joined the NCRI (without CC and Politburo approval) and had been expelled from the NCRI. The party had overlooked the great harm of civil war by attacking two other Kurdish forces in the region, disarming, killing, and looting them. The PDKI-Komala conflict was disastrous and caused great damage to the Kurdish movement. Ghassemlou's *A Brief Discussion* had brought disharmony to the 6th Congress and had damaged the party, the Kurds, and the movement. The party still immensely suffered from authoritarianism, factionalism, ignoring its wrong policies, and personal favors replacing party rules and principles (Gadani, 2008a, pp. 389-390). Although after the previous Congress, many within the party had left or were expelled from the party, discord within the party still continued. The discord remained unresolved in the 7th Congress as some followers of the Tudeh Party still stayed with the party. It was in the 8th Congress (18 January 1988) when they split (21 March 1988) (Hassanzadeh, 1996, p. 136). A significant conflict within the party was concerning *Listay Fix* (Fixed List) (see below).

Later, it was revealed that Ghassemlou had manipulated some conferences that were held to select delegates for the 8th Congress to influence the outcome. For instance, the regional conferences in Germany and England were dissolved, and they could not send delegates to the Congress. In Austria, Sayyed Ahmad Husseini, who was legally elected as a delegate, was replaced by Khosraw Bahrami (Gadani,

2008b, p. 7).

6.9. The 8th Congress of the PDKI

The 8th Congress of the PDKI was held in Sulaymaniyah, Iraq, on 18 January 1988 (Gadani, 2008b, p. 9). Ghassemlou was elected the General Secretary and Sharafkandi the alternate General Secretary. For the list of the CCs, see Appendix 8. After approving some changes to the platform and constitution of the party, the party was criticized for 72 cited cases of corruption revealed by the Review Committee (Gadani, 2008b, p. 9).

6.9.1. The Fixed List. The major conflict in the 8th Congress was over Ghassemlou's proposal that the party leadership be selected out of the Fixed List—an issue that later caused a split within the PDKI. There were two ways of electing the leadership in Congress: individual candidates and the Fixed List. The fundamental disagreement was not over these two methods. The main purpose of the followers of both methods was to prevent the election of individuals from the opposite side of the CC. The philosophy of the Fixed List style was that some people could not effectively work together in the leadership, and this had damaged the party and the movement. Therefore, the Fixed List consisted of those who could smoothly work together in the leadership. Thus, a few different fixed lists could be created and compete with each other. After long debates, those opposing the Fixed List suggested that they would agree to it on the condition that Ghassemlou promised he would cooperate with any Fixed List that won the election. But Ghassemlou rejected this suggestion (Hassanzadeh, 1996, pp. 160-161). Hassan Rastgar was among those Ghassemlou wanted to remove from leadership, and in the 8th Congress, Ghassemlou did not want to work with Rastgar (Hassanzadeh, 2012, p. 416). Likewise, Mustafa Hijri (2015) asserts that Rastgar was careless about the party's duties and mostly spent his time socializing with friends. So, Rastgar was not put on a Fixed List (pp. 73-74). After two days of discussions, between half and two-thirds of the Congress delegates voted in favor of the Fixed List method, about one-third opposed it, and a few delegates cast blank ballots. The elections committee, therefore, suggested a Fixed List of 25 members for the CC. Six individuals on the List declined, so the CC now had 19 members, who joined 7 alternate CC members (Hassanzadeh, 1996, p. 162-165; Hassanzadeh, 2012, p. 418).

According to Khalighi (2002), when in the first round, the Fixed list method was rejected by Congress, Ghassemlou announced that he would not nominate himself for the CC. This was practically an ultimatum, and it resulted in putting the Fixed List to a second vote, in which by adding just one more vote, this method was approved (p. 322). After adding this one vote, 58 members voted for the method of the Fixed List. In the Fixed List, after six members of the CC withdrew, 19 members of the CC remained. The Congress voted on this list as follows: 75 in favor, 4 abstained, and 65 opposed (Khalighi, 2005, pp. 176-177). Gadani (2008b) claims that Ghassemlou held grudges against certain members of Congress and propounded the subject of the Fixed List again. A vote by showing hands was imposed on Congress by deploying threats and incentives. Indeed, 49 percent of the Congress delegates did not have representatives in the CC. After a month, a few thousand members, whose numbers were more than what the constitution required, asked for an extraordinary conference or congress to solve the problems. Ghassemlou rejected their request, although he admitted that the voting manner was a mistake (Gadani, 2008b, pp. 9-13; Gadani, 2015; Khalighi, 2005, p. 177).

6.9.2. Hizbi Demokrati Kurdistani Eran, Rebarayati Shorishger (Democratic Party of Iranian Kurdistan-Revolutionary Leadership, or PDKI-RL). After the 8th Congress, the minority within the PDKI gradually regrouped, visited the party's committees, and argued that the Congress was non-democratic and illegal, and its outcome was nothing short of a coup. They moved their residences from the party's bases. In this schism, about 20 percent of the members split from the PDKI (Hassanzadeh, 1996, pp. 165-166) and formed *Hizbi Demokrati Kurdistani Eran, Rebarayati Shorishger* (Democratic Party of Iranian Kurdistan-Revolutionary Leadership) or PDKI-RL on 21 March 1988. The Splinters issued a 10-article Declaration that accused Ghassemlou of making compromises with the imperialists and distancing himself from the revolution in Kurdistan by ignoring the goals of the PDKI under the influenced Sharafkandi's conservative perspectives. This resulted in dismay among the members, as well as the intensification of the anti-democratic tendencies of the "Sharafkandi-Ghassemlou Faction." Meaningless expulsions within the party had rendered many members passive while many others were expelled. The PDKI's policy, according to the PDKI-RL, had resulted in negotiating with the reactionary Islamic government. This conservative faction had undermined the party's democratic procedures by manipulating members through threats and incentives and imposing the Fixed List. The Declaration emphasized that what happened in the Congress was the consequence of Ghassemlou and his policies and actions in the previous years. These problems threatened to dissolve the party (Gadani, Personal communication, October 21, 2012; Gadani, 2008b, pp. 23-26; see Appendix 26 and Appendix 8).

The first order of business for the PDKI-RL was to declare a ceasefire on 21 April 1988 with the Komala in a statement (dated 19 April 1988), which lamented the great losses to the national democratic movement of the Kurdish nation caused by this protracted conflict (Gadani, 2008b, pp. 42-43). The Komala warmly accepted the PDKI-RL ceasefire, but the PDKI did not accept it and instead issued threats against the Komala. Consequently, the war between the PDKI and the Komala continued for two or three more years. The PDKI accused the PDKI-RL of "selling out the martyrs' blood to the Komala cheaply" (Gadani, 2008b, p. 43). The PDKI Political-Military Commission distributed a 6-Point Internal Memo to the city and territorial committees calling the PDKI-RL *Ladar* (Deviant) and traitors (Gadani, 2008b, p. 41-42; see Appendix 27).

In an article published in *Kurdistan*, Issue 136 (1988), the PDKI accused members of the "deviant group" of having lost faith in the struggle. These individuals, the *Kurdistan* article said, had joined the party having thought of the struggle as expedient and hoped to return home like heroes, but now that they had realized the struggle was long-term, they had lost motivation (Kaveh, 2005, p. 150). In their literature, the two sides called each other *fraksion* (faction, wing: PDKI) and *Ladar* (deviant: PDKI-RL) (Gadani, 2008b, p. 28). Clearly, the PDKI's statements regarding the split are totally biased: if the PDKI-RL members wanted to quit politics, they would have just left the party. However, the conditions under which the PDKI-RL continued its struggle were even harder than those of the PDKI. Also, many leadership and rank-and-file members of the PDKI-RL had fought for Kurdistan for a long time, just as they continued to fight in the next nine years before reuniting with the PDKI on December 28, 1996.

The PDKI-RL received support from many, including previous prominent cadres now residing in Europe. In an open letter to the PDKI leadership dated 30 May 1988, (Sayyed) Hassan Hashimi, Rasoul Peshnimaz, Said Kowestani, Muhammad Khizri, and Khalid Azizi stated that the PDKI had become a hub for political, ideological, and personal conflicts, which had existed for nine years previous. The Kurdish people have been demanding national liberation, democracy, and class struggle, but the PDKI's leadership had not faithfully represented these causes (Kaveh, 2005, pp. 154-159).

The PDKI-RL called the PDKI "Rafsanjani's jash" (Rafsanjani being the President of Iran at the time), while the PDKI called the PDKI-RL "*jash Mujaheds*" [jash means traitor. Hassanzadeh, here, interprets jash as *Zira,* which means imperfect. It can be translated as imperfect Mujaheds or, as I preferred, "Quasi Mujeheds"]. These insulting name-callings hugely damaged the Kurdish movement (Hassanzadeh, 2012, p. 420).

Hassanzadeh (2012) states that although he was against the use of the word *Ladar* (Deviant) or jash for the PDKI-RL, he used these words because it was the party's decision, and he was obligated to do this. He claims that one of the historical mistakes of the party was that the Politburo declared war against the PDKI-RL. Before the declaration was broadcast on the radio, Hassanzadeh and Atiqi asked Ghassemlou to discard this declaration, but he declined. If Ghassemlou had accepted his suggestion, the Politburo would have accepted it, too (Hassanzadeh, 2012, pp. 422, 426). Hassanzadeh's statement reveals the dominant and unique role of Ghassemlou's authority in decision-making in the party. Hassanzadeh (1996) also states that by choosing the name PDKI-RL, the splinters severely damaged the party and the movement. This caused years of clashes between the PDKI and the PDKI-RL, in which many peshmergas were killed and wounded (pp. 174-175).

According to Gadani (2008b), the PDKI called the PDKI-RL traitors and began imprisoning, suppressing, and killing at least 20 members of the PDKI-RL (p.19). Hassanzadeh (2012) holds that the PDKI-RL did not want to fight against the PDKI, and on many occasions, its members fled from the PDKI peshmergas because they did not want to fight. On one occasion, the PDKI-RL peshmergas even surrendered their weapons to the PDKI peshmergas (p. 427).

6.9.3. The 4th Conference of the PDKI-RL. The 4th Conference of the PDKI-RL was held in the town of Ranya, Iraq, 28 June-4 July 1988, in which 113 representatives took part. Jalil Gadani was elected the General Secretary, and Hassan Rastgar was the alternate General Secretary (see Appendix 8). The Conference approved a 13-Point Platform. The Conference held that the party had handed the training of the party's women and youth peshmergas poorly, and it condemned war against the PDKI-RL waged by the Sharafkandi-Ghassemlou Faction. The Conference underscored democratic centralism in directing the party (Gadani, 2008b, pp. 46-50).

While the peshmergas of the PDKI-RL carried out operations against the Iranian military, the PDKI peshmergas attacked the PDKI-RL peshmergas or cadres (on 26 August 1988, 15 September 1988, and 21 September 1988), killing the PDKI-RL cadres Hassan Islami, Khidir Zare', Babakir Khizri, Qadir Khosh Nama, and Motalleb Nabizadeh. On another occasion, the PDKI disarmed some PDKI-RL peshmergas and shot a wounded PDKI-RL peshmerga named Kamram Jamiani (Gadani, 2008b, pp. 54-55, 58, 64). In total, 22 PDKI-RL peshmergas have been killed by the PDKI (Gadani, 2015; Ali Mahmood Shekhani, 2007, p. 181), and perhaps 2 PDKI peshmergas were killed by the PDKI-RL. It is important to note that the PDKI-RL has never attacked the PDKI.

The PDKI-RL published their organ, *Kurdistan*, and a seasonal political-literary magazine, *26 Sarmawaz* (17 December-the anniversary of raising the Kurdistan flag over Mahabad in 1945), and it established *Radio Dangi Kurdistani Eran* (Iranian Kurdistan Voice Radio) on 1 May 1988. In all, the PDKI-RL published 80 issues of *Kurdistan*, 20 issues of *26 Sarmawaz*, and 10 issues of the magazine *Rowangay Lawan* (Youth View). It also established many political and literacy classes for women and the elderly. Among the plays that PDKI-RL members staged was *Hawar* (Shout), which was about the struggle of Kurdish women against exploitation (Gadani, 2008b, pp. 44, 143-144, 146).

After the 8th Congress of the PDKI, two important events occurred in Iran, which affected the PDKI's policies. Firstly, on 18 July 1988, the Iran government accepted the United Nations Security Council Resolution 598 that ended the war with Iraq (Gadani, 2008b, p. 55). Secondly, Ayatollah Khomeini's death was officially announced on 4 June 1989. In 1989, Ghassemlou focused on the creation of an Iran-wide front, which was supposed to include democratic organizations and personalities. His analysis went like this: after the ceasefire between Iran and Iraq and Khomeini's death, the Iranian regime would move toward its collapse. He predicted that in a more open space, the creation of a wide front would gain momentum. Although he did not succeed in creating the front, he kept working on it until he was assassinated in July 1989. Clearly, his estimation was wrong (Ali Mahmood Shekhani, 2007, pp. 297-298). On 3 August 1988, in his letter to Javier Pérez de Cuéllar, the Secretary-General of the United Nations, Ghassemlou claimed that since 1979, more than 40,000 people in Kurdistan had been killed and hundreds of thousand misplaced. The central government, to suppress the Kurdish people, sent 200,000 military forces to Kurdistan and established 3,000 military bases in the villages and mountains of the Kurdish territory (Hassanzadeh, 1996, pp. 188-189).

6.9.4. The Assassination of Ghassemlou. After the end of the Iran-Iraq war in August 1988, the Iranian government had fortified its forces in Kurdistan, and Ghassemlou had been convinced that the liberation movement in Kurdistan could not attain victory through armed struggle. Besides, nine years of armed conflict with the Iranian state, as well as clashes against the Komala and the PDKI-RL, had weakened the PDKI. These conditions had exhausted the people, and they needed a break from conflict (Ali Mahmood Shekhani, 2007, pp. 182-187). Thus, under Ghassemlou, the PDKI started negotiating with the Iranian government during 1988-1989.

In Autumn 1988, Ghassemlou met with the Iranian agents in Vienna. This meeting was arranged by Dr. Fazil Rasoul. Later, Ahmad Ben Bella (former President of Algeria) and Jalal Talabani (from PUK) joined the negotiations. The Politburo, the CC, and even the members in charge of the party's organization in Vienna were not aware of the negotiations. Only Abdullah Qadiri Azar, a member of the CC who was in charge of the party's foreign relations, knew about it. Ghassemlou had also informed his wife, Helena Kreulich, in a letter from France. Only after his return to Kurdistan (possibly between mid-January and the end of February 1989) did Ghassemlou inform the Politburo about these meetings. Expectedly, the Politburo and the CC criticized him for keeping them in the dark

(Hijri, 2015, pp. 9-10). The negotiations were supposed to continue in the Spring of 1989 (Hijri, 2015, p. 10). The Politburo decided that in the next round of negotiations, instead of Ghassemlou, a PDKI delegation under a leading member should participate, and Ghassemlou accepted. In its 28 February-5 March 1989 meeting, the CC also approved the Politburo's decision (Hijri, 2015, pp. 12-13). However, Ghassemlou ignored the party's decision and personally continuation the negotiations. Hijri (2015) states that the Politburo did not hear about the continuation of negotiations until it heard about the assassination of Ghassemlou on 13 July 1989 (p. 13).

The Islamic Republic representatives wanted the negotiations to be conducted in secret and only with Ghassemlou. While the CC clearly rejected the government's suggestion, unfortunately, the Politburo and Ghassemlou accepted it. The first round of negotiations was held in early January 1989 in Vienna, with the presence of Jalal Talabani and Ahmad Ben Bella and the PUK providing the security for the gathering. The Iranian government, based on a plan, spread the news about the secret negotiations, but it accused the PUK of doing so. In the mid-spring of 1989, while Sharafkandi was in Europe, the Politburo proposed that the Iranian government continue the negotiations with Sharafkandi. The Iranian negotiators rejected this proposal and asked that the PUK be excluded from the negotiations (Hassanzadeh, 1996, pp. 197-199, 205).

At the end of December 1988 and the beginning of 1989, two or three meetings were held in Vienna in which Talabani, Ben Bella, and in some meetings, Nawshirwan Mustafa Amin participated (Hassanzadeh, 2012, p. 354). Previously, through Talabani, negotiations between the government and the PDKI were held in Vienna on 1 July 1987. Later, the first round of new negotiations was held in Vienna on 28 December 1988 and lasted for two days. In addition, in the negotiations on 20 January 1988, the Iran representatives apparently accepted the demand for autonomy for Kurdistan but announced that they had to return to Iran to discuss with the Iranian authorities. The second round of new negotiations started on 12 July 1989 in Vienna. The negotiations continued on 13 July 1989, during which the Iran representatives assassinated Ghassemlou, Abdullah Qadiri Azar, and Dr. Fazil Mullah Mahmoud Rasoul. In the shootout, one of the Iranian representatives, Muhammad Rahimi, was also wounded (Ali Mahmood Shekhani, 2007, pp. 189-201). The cassettes of the negotiations reveal that the Iranian government's representatives were actually assassins (Hassanzadeh, 1996, p. 202). Ghassemlou and Ghadiri were buried at the Père Lachaise Cemetery in Paris (Hassanzadeh, 1996, p. 206). Carol Prunhuber (2009) has investigated the role of the Iranians who allegedly participated in the assassination of Ghassemlou and the position of the Austrian government regarding this subject (pp. 209, 304-305). More information about the assassination of Ghassemlou is available in Khalighi, 2005, p. 286; Ali Mahmood Shekhani, 2007, p. 208; and Gadani, 2008b, p. 65).

In a declaration dated 18 July 1989, the PDKI-RL condemned the Iranian government for assassinating Ghassemlou. The declaration announced that Ghassemlou

> had even betrayed his own past by declaring that there was no military solution to the Kurdish problem in Iran. Unfortunately, Dr. Ghassemlou became a tragic victim of his own political mistake and comprising stance toward the reactionary terrorists who govern the Islamic Republic. (Entessar, 1992, p. 43)

Likewise, Rastgar, one of the PDKI-RL's leaders, condemned the assassination of Ghassemlou, but he also stated that Ghassemlou had led the brother-killing war and was a jash of the Iranian regime (Rastgar, 2011).

6.10. The 9th Congress of the PDKI-RL

The 9th Congress of the PDKI-RL was held in the village of Qala Sayda in Doli Shawre in Ranya, Iraq, 12-19 August 1990 (Gadani, 2008b, p. 67). Gadani was elected the General Secretary and Rastgar the alternate General Secretary (see Appendix 8). The party used the derogatory title "Jama'ati Sharafkandi" (the Sharafkandi's Band) instead of the previously denigrating "Sharafkandi-Ghassemlou Faction" for the PDKI (Gadani, 2008b, p. 73). In its Plenum in Spring 1991, the PDKI-RL announced that the party was ready to unconditionally negotiate with the PDKI while suggesting a Three-Step Plan to solve their problems Gadani, 2008b, pp. 79-83; see Appendix 29). When Sharafkandi and his friends were assassinated in Berlin on 17 September 1992, the PDKI-RL sent a high-ranking delegation led by Hossein Madani to participate in their funeral. Nonetheless, the PDKI, until their 10th Congress, remained hostile to the PDKI-RL (Gadani, 2008b, p. 89).

6.11. The 9th Congress of the PDKI

The 9th Congress of the PDKI was held on 22 December 1991 in Gali Badran, near the village of Zargali in the area of Nawchia, in Iraqi Kurdistan. The Congress was titled the "Ghassemlou Congress" because he was born on *Shabe Yalda* (winter solstice) (Hassanzadeh, 1996, p. 226). Sharafkandi was elected the General Secretary and Hijri alternate General Secretary (see Appendix 8).

6.11.1. The assassination of Sharafkandi. After the assassination of Ghassemlou, the assassination of Sharafkandi on 17 September 1992 by the Iranian government was the most important attack on the PDKI. Much evidence reveals that the party, especially Sharafkandi, committed grave mistakes by ignoring security issues.

Sadiq Sharafkandi, along with Fatah Abdoli, Homayoun Ardalan, and Nouri Dehkurdi, participated in the 19th Congress of the Socialist International, 15-17

September 1992, in Berlin, Germany. After the Congress, Sharafkandi and his friends gathered for dinner in Mykonos Restaurant for informal discussions with some Iranian opposition groups and personalities, including the Fadaian (Majority), *Jomhourikhahan-e Melli*-ye Iran (National Republicans of Iran), and *Hezb-e Demokratik-e Mardom-e Iran* (People's Democratic Party of Iran). At 11 PM, two armed men entered the restaurant and opened fire, killing Sharafkandi, Abdoli, Ardalan, and Dehkurdi (Hassanzadeh, 1996, pp. 233-235; Hassanzadeh, 2012, p. 453). Prior to the Congress, Sharafkandi had stated that he would cancel the gathering with Iranian opposition in Germany because he had heard that the regime's agents had been searching for him. Nevertheless, he somehow ended up agreeing to that fateful meeting (Hijri, 2015, p. 39). On 10 April 1997, a German court issued its verdict about the Mykonos attack. This was the first time that a European court expressly indicted the highest ranks of the Iranian state, including the "Supreme Leader Ayatollah Ali Khamenei and the President Ali Akbar Hashemi Rafsanjani, in ordering the killings of the KDPI's [PDKI's] leader and the other incidents" (Entessar, 2010, p. 49).

After the assassination of Sharafkandi, the alternate General Secretary, Hijri, became the General Secretary of the PDKI. On 13 March 1993, six Iranian fighter jets bombed the bases of the Politburo, peshmergas, the hospital, and the fields of the peasants using cluster bombs, killing four and injuring dozens (Hassanzadeh, 1996, p. 247). The Kurdistan Regional Government (KRG; est. 1992) had provided bases for the PDKI and the Kurdish refugees. The Iraqi Kurds, using trucks of the KRG and their own, significantly helped in transporting the PDKI's camps (Hassanzadeh, 1996, pp. 264-265). In addition, on 9 November 1994, six Islamic Republic war planes bombed a PDKI base in the city of Koya in Iraqi Kurdistan in which three PDKI activists and an Iraqi Kurdish woman were killed, and the PDKI and people in the vicinities sustained destruction (Hassanzadeh, 1996, p. 269). Moreover, since 1991, Iranian forces have infiltrated

Iraqi Kurdistan and assassinated dozens of cadres of the PDKI and other Kurdish opposition groups (Hassanzadeh, 1996, p. 266). Furthermore, the Iranian government continued to suppress the Kurds and political organizations in Kurdistan. According to Gadani (2008b), until 1990, the number of followers of the PDKI and the PDKI-RL who had been executed by the Iranian government in Iran was 742, while 130 villages were destroyed, and 68 people from the different Kurdish parties were assassinated [in Iraq] by Iran (p. 130).

After the 9th Congress, two factions were created within the PDKI regarding the unification with the PDKI-LR. The first faction, which included Hijri, disagreed with the unification. They thought that due to the changes in lifestyles and struggles of the PDKI-RL—namely, improving their personal lives, seeking asylum in European countries, and sending family members to Europe—the unification was not in favor of the PDKI, and it even prevented the party's activities and progress. The second faction supported the unification for different reasons. This included some leaders, cadres, and peshmergas. Most of the cadres and peshmergas did not properly know the leaders of the PDKI-RL. Hassanzadeh was the leader of this faction and claimed that he wanted to "melt" (*Towandnawa, zowb kardan*; read: dissolve) the PDKI-LR into the party. The dispute between these factions continued, and before the 10th Congress, it took undemocratic forms. At the 10th Congress, the second faction won, and Hassanzadeh became the General Secretary, tasked with preparing for the unification (Hijri, 2015, pp. 102-104).

6.12. The 10th Congress of the PDKI-RL

The 10th Congress of the PDKI-RL was held on 1-5 May 1994 in Ranya, Iraq. The Congress changed the long-lasting slogan of the party, "democracy for Iran and autonomy for Kurdistan," into "democracy for Iran and the right of self-determination for Kurdistan." Perhaps the creation of new republics after the collapse of the Soviet Union had affected the change in the PDKI-RL's slogan. In addition, the Congress confirmed the party's existing policy regarding the "faction" (PDKI), but it also proposed resolving the discord between the two parties. The Congress mandated the PDKI-RL leadership to seriously encourage women to take part in the Kurdish movement (Gadani, 2008b, pp. 101-102, 110-111). Gadani was selected as the General Secretary and Rastgar the alternate General Secretary (see Appendix 8).

The Iranian government, using its influence through the PUK, succeeded in closing the radio stations of the PDKI-RL and the PDKI in 1996. However, the PDKI opened another radio station far from the authority of both the Kurdish government established by the KDP (Iraq) and the PUK in Kurdistan. The PUK promised the PDKI-RL that if it shut down its radio station, the Iranian regime would stop attacking the PDKI-RL. Despite this agreement, many cadres and peshmergas were still assassinated by the Iranian agents. In addition, the PUK was responsible for killing four PDKI peshmergas in Koya in December 1997 when the 11th Congress was held (Gadani, 2008b, pp. 113-114; Hassanzadeh, 2012, pp. 364-366).

6.12.1. Unification of the PDKI and the PDKI-RL. Strong demand for the unification of the two factions came from the Kurdish people in Iran and the Iraqi Kurds. On 2 April 1994, 42 writers, literary personalities, and poets of the Iraqi Kurdistan published an open letter asking the two parties to reunite (Gadani, 2008b, p. 122). Nevertheless, certain figures in each party were still against unification. These include a significant number of PDKI members (Gadani, 2008b, p. 122), but they had different reasons to oppose the unification. For instance, Hijri (2015) distrusts the PDKI-RL, asserting that the real reason behind the PDKI-RL's push for unification was its inability to provide stipends for its cadres and peshmergas, and the unification would solve the PDKI-RL financial crisis so that they would regroup and split away again (p. 86). Yet, on 21 February 1994 and after its 9th Congress, the PDKI declared a unilateral ceasefire with the PDKI-RL, which the latter accepted. Then, after the 10th Congress of the PDKI (12-19 April 1995), the PDKI ended its boycott against the PDKI-RL, which again the latter accepted and started visiting the Politburo of the PDKI (Hassanzadeh, 1996, pp. 177-178).

Gadani (2008b) offers a detailed account of the negotiations between the two parties in May-July 1995 (pp. 119-120, 123). In its unification plan document, the PDKI wrote the "PDKI-RL" (with quotation marks), and the unification was postponed for a long time until the quotation marks were removed. The 6th Plenum of the PDKI-RL (19 September 1996) selected Rastgar as the General Secretary and Gadani as the alternate General Secretary. After dozens of rounds of negotiations, Rastgar and Hassanzadeh signed a plan for unification, which was far from the spirit of democracy and "brotherhood." Nevertheless, the PDKI-RL accepted the plan in the interest of the Kurdish nation (Gadani, 2008b, pp. 124, 135).

The 7th Plenum of the PDKI-RL was held on 27-29 December 1996 in Erbil. During the Plenum on 27 December, the Politburo paid a visit to the PDKI in Koya. On 28 December, after the removal of the quotation marks, Hassanzadeh (PDKI) and Rastgar (PDKI-RL) signed the 20-Article Unification Agreement. On 30 December 1996, the PDKI announced that its Plenum had approved the unification. The content of the agreement has never been publicly released (Gadani, 2008b, pp. 136-137; Hassanzadeh, 2012, pp. 471-472). On 8 January 1997, a magnificent celebration in which both parties participated was held (Gadani, 2008b, pp. 138, 218). After the unification, the two parties continued their activities under the PDKI.

6.13. The 10th Congress of the PDKI

The 10th Congress of the PDKI was held in Erbil, Iraq, on 12 April 1995, in a venue provided by the Iraqi Communist Party (Hassanzadeh, 2012, p. 494).

Hassanzadeh was elected the General Secretary, and Hijri the alternate General Secretary (see Appendix 8). As mentioned, the Congress ended the boycott of the PDKI-RL, but more importantly, the Congress recognized the right of minority members within the party to express their views. Before the 10th Congress, members could only express their position against the party's decisions in their own units, but now they were able to express their views publicly (and even publish them) six months prior to the next Congress. This is very significant, as the PDKI was the first of all Kurdish parties to recognize its internal minorities to express their opinions (Hassanzadeh, 1996, pp. 282-283).

Although the scale of the armed conflict between the Iranian government and the Kurdish groups had dramatically diminished, the Iranian agents started assassinating the Iranian Kurdish activists in Iraq in 1994. The assassinations of the PDKI members by Iran caused the death and injury of about 300. Between 110 and 115 were killed. The Iraqi Kurdistan government can be criticized because it did not protect the security of Iranian Kurdish groups (Hassanzadeh, 2012, p.473). Alizadeh lists the names of 207 Iranian Kurdistan activists who were assassinated or wounded in Iraqi Kurdistan between 1991-1997 (Saedi, 2012, pp. 680-692). Later, in 1996, however, the Iranian army, in cooperation with the PUK, initiated an extensive attack, using Katyusha rockets, on the bases of the PDKI in Koya. The attack damaged almost all the houses in the base, but it left no casualties (Hassanzadeh, 2012, pp. 367-372).

The PDKI had agreed to the PUK's condition to cease its military operations in Iran. In fact, both the KDP (Iraq) and the PUK had barred the PDKI from carrying out operations in Iran. But in fact, the PDKI was unable to carry out operations. Except for *Yaketi Shorishgerani Kurdistan* (Kurdistan Revolutionaries Unity), the PDKI was the only remaining party to fight against the Iranian army, but the latter had lost logistical support for its campaigns, and its military potential had diminished. In the past, the party had 12,000 peshmergas and 30,000 to 40,000

Popular Supporting forces, but at this point, its forces were reduced to a few thousand (Hassanzadeh, 2012, p. 372). On 24 July 1996, the PDKI declared that it would not carry out attacks against the Iranian forces (Hassanzadeh, 2012, p. 376). The PDKI officially stopped armed operations within Iran by July 1996.

6.14. The 11th Congress of the PDKI

The 11th Congress of the PDKI was held in Kirkuk, Iraq, on 22 December 1997. Hassanzadeh was selected as the General Secretary, and Hijri was the alternate General Secretary (see Appendix 8). Recall that the 10th Congress had approved of the minorities within the party to have a right to reveal and publish their ideas internally, even if these ideas were against the party's views, within six months before the next Congress. The 11th Congress removed the six-month limit, making it free for everyone to express their ideas without any time limit (Hassanzadeh, 2012, p. 469). This was clearly a step forward in democratizing the internal regulations of the party.

Disagreements within the PDKI were intensified during the next congresses. After the unification, the PDKI members who were against the PDKI-RL frequently and secretly continued to refer to the former PDKI-RL members using derogatory terms and created factions against them. Some PDKI members, including Mustafa Hijri, had accepted the Congress' decision for unification, but now they thought it was the wrong decision (Hassanzadeh, 2012, p. 479).

6.15. The 12th Congress of the PDKI

The 12th Congress of the PDKI was held in Kirkuk, Iraq, on 24 November 2000. Hassanzadeh was elected the General Secretary, and Hijri the alternate General Secretary (see Appendix 8). According to the 12th Congress, Internal Regulations of the PDKI, Article X: Central Committee: "3. No one can be elected to the office of Secretary-General for more than two consecutive terms"

(Democratic Party of Iranian Kurdistan, 2000). This was another step in democratizing the party. Around the 12th Congress, the previous members of the PDKI-LR suggested replacing the party's slogan, "autonomy for Kurdistan," with "federalism." Those opposing the idea argued that this change was treasonous to Ghassemlou's way (Hassanzadeh, 2012, pp. 480, 491). The discord between the opponents and the proponents of the unification was deepened in the 12th Congress. Hassanzadeh (2012) writes that many people within the PDKI who were against the unification had voted for it but later tried their best to break this unity (p. 481). While the majority of the 12th Congress was in the Rastgar's wing, the other wing opposed it, and the conflict became intensified. Both wings approached Hassanzadeh to find a solution. He proposed a CC list containing 12 cadres from the majority wing and 10 from the minority wing, plus himself. This list was approved by the Congress (Hassanzadeh, 2012, pp. 496-500).

In the 12th Congress the clashes between the minority wing led by Hijri and the majority led by Rastgar were intensified (Hassanzadeh, 2012, p. 496). But the 12th Congress approved that forming secret factions would constitute treachery. Hijri's wing was a minority in the 12th Congress, but by creating a hidden faction, it grew into a majority in the 13th Congress (Hassanzadeh, 2012, pp. 480, 500).

6.16. The 13th Congress of the PDKI

The 13th Congress of the PDKI was held in Koya, Iraq, on 3 July 2004. Mustafa Hijri was elected the General Secretary, and Hassan Sharafi the alternate General Secretary (see Appendix 8). The 12th Congress had approved of "3. The strategic slogan of the PDKI is 'Democracy for Iran and Autonomy for Iranian Kurdistan'" (Democratic Party of Iranian Kurdistan, 2000). The 13th Congress changed it to: "3. The strategic slogan of PDKI is the establishment of a democratic federal Iran and the attainment of Kurdish national rights in Iranian Kurdistan" (Democratic Party of Iranian Kurdistan, 2004). The term "democratic centralism," which existed in previous internal regulations, was omitted, but the principles of democratic centralism were kept (Democratic Party of Iranian Kurdistan, 2004). Appendix 28 shows the general objectives and partial internal regulations approved by the 13th Congress. The PDKI has adhered to these internal regulations without major changes to this day.

6.16.1. The split of the Kurdistan Democratic Party (KDP) from the PDKI. After the 13th Congress, a group of dissenters split from the PDKI by publishing a declaration on 6 December 2006. They called themselves *Hizbi Demokrati Kurdistan,* or Kurdistan Democratic Party (KDP), in the party's 14th Congress on 6 March 2008. The process leading to the split, a contested account indeed, is as follows. Representing the point of view of the PDKI, Hijri (2015) claims that when, in the 13th Congress, the supporters of unity did not get the majority in the leadership, they started a non-democratic confrontation against the new leadership. On 18 June 2005, the minority boycotted the plenum (pp. 105, 158). Hijri (2015) maintains that the main figure of this minority after the 13th Congress was Hassanzadeh, who was supported by the previous members of the PDKI-RL (p. 167). Hijri (2015) asserts that the PDKI-RL reunited with the PDKI to prevent the former's dissolution. In actuality, the PDKI-RL was not really united with the PDKI and waited for an opportunity to split again. When this faction could not gain the majority in the 13th Congress, they split on 6 December 2006 (p. 100). They could have remained within the party and, through a democratic process, absorbed the majority of the members and peshmergas (Hijri, 2015, p. 94). This reveals that they did not consider the interests of the Kurdish people again (Hijri, 2015, p. 92). Hijri (2015) repeats criticisms against Hassanzadeh: that he was a weak leader, held all power in his own hands, and was more interested in party infighting rather than fighting against the Iranian government (pp. 183, 190-191, 192-193).

In regards to sharing responsibilities with the minority, Hijri (2015) writes that after the Congress, the important posts of the party remained with the minority faction: Mustafa Mawloudi was in charge of the Financial Commission, Kamal Karimi in charge of the party's Relations in Erbil, Omar Balaki in charge of the radio, and Baba Ali Mehrparwar in charge of the party's Publication. Moreover, Hassan Rastgar and Baba Ali Mehrparwar remained members of the Politburo (p. 123). The leaders of the minority faction tried to attract party cadres by promising to send them abroad, provide them with better stipends, and choose them as CC members (Hijri, 2015, p. 128).

On 29 July 2006, the minority faction submitted a 20-Point Declaration to the leaders of the PDKI (Hassanzadeh, 2015, p. 76). On 27 November 2006, the PDKI leaders responded with a 17-point Proposal, agreeing to most of their minority's demands, but the minority faction ignored it, having already decided to leave the PDKI (Hijri, 2015, pp. 131-132). Two and a half years after the 13th Congress, they surprisingly split so that their followers, including two of their CC members, were faced with a *fait accompli* (Hijri, 2015, p. 129). Two or three of their leaders were holding meetings, deciding about their programs and resolutions, and dictating their decisions to the others (Hijri, 2015, p. 197). The splits imposed heavy setbacks on the Kurdish movement, having forced the parties to be occupied with their internal affairs for several years and caused them to forget the struggle, which in turn gave opportunities to their enemy and planted the seeds of hopelessness among the Kurdish people (Hijri, 2015, p. 5).

Naturally, the views of the minority faction are different. The 12th Congress had approved the freedom to criticize the party (Hassanzadeh, 2015, p. 23). Hijri had created a hidden faction before the 13th Congress. Gadani emphasizes that Hijri, after the 12th Congress, undermined the party's regulations and created a faction in the party. Hijri, in a letter to some members such as Rahim Qadiri, stated that the party had been destroyed and the only way to change was to change the leadership. In a Plenum, he confessed to the creation of a hidden faction, but the party ignored his punishment. Hassanzadeh did not ask for his punishment because he thought that it would not be accepted. It was also found out that five members who belonged to Hijri's faction were attempting to create a faction. Some of them were suspended for six months, while some others were demoted (Gadani, 2015; Hassanzadeh, 2012, pp. 501-503; Hassanzadeh, 2015, p. 24).

Although everyone could stand as a candidate and no Fixed List existed for two weeks before the Congress, the names of the 13 persons belonging to the Hijri's wing were made known to all as the next CC members (Hassanzadeh, 2012, p. 513). In the 13th Congress, they decided to choose 21 members for the CC, 13 from Hijri's side and 8 from the others (Hassanzadeh, 2012, p. 511). Hassanzadeh (2012) claims that after the 13th Congress, Mustafa Hijri did not properly incorporate the minority wing into the leadership and the key positions in the party because Hijri thought he had the majority (p. 505). Taymour Mostafayy, a Politburo member of the PDKI, has asserted that the General Secretary should solely serve the interests of the majority (his friends), neglecting the minority (Hassanzadeh, 2012, p. 526). Based on this view, Hijri's wing removed two out of four people in the *Shahidan* (Martyrs) organization of the party, claiming that this section of the organization did not need four people. Soon after, they replaced them with two people who were from Hijri's wing (Hassanzadeh, 2012, p. 509).

It seems that the PDKI, after the 13th Congress, had limited the activities of the minority members. Hassanzadeh emphasizes that when Ehsan Houshmand [a Kurdish sociologist, reformist, and national reformist activist] wrote an article against the PDKI, Hassanzadeh made a taped interview responding to Houshmand. However, the tape was never distributed abroad. In addition, after the 13th Congress, Hijri extensively "cleansed" the party. For instance, they changed the composition of the organization of *Hezi Parezgari* (Protective Force) so that out of 31 cadres, just one cadre from the minority wing remained, and he was never called to the meetings. Hassanzadeh provides more examples regarding the limitations that the party created for him and the misbehaviors of the Hijri's wing (Hassanzadeh, 2012, pp. 522-525). Likewise, Khalighi (2005) maintains that it was supposed that he would participate in seminars in Finland and Canada, but the party prevented him (p.16).

By harassing members of the opposition, the party intended to push them to leave. For instance, in one particular case, to make a member either be submissive to the party decisions or leave the party, the PDKI leadership changed his organizational position and residence and punished him eight times within two months. They used this phrase: *"Daparyawa biparewa, napariyawa awa halita"* (if you pass to our side, so do it; otherwise, this is your condition) (Hassanzadeh, 2012, p. 525).

After the 13th Congress, with the development of the discord within the party, a committee known as the *Opozisioni Newkhoy Hizbi Demokrati Kurdistani Eran* (Internal Opposition of the Democratic Party of Iranian Kurdistan) was established. It contained 25 members, including eight CC and Politburo members. The committee and executive committee of five members included Abdullah Hassanzadeh, Hassan Rastgar, Mustafa Mawloudi, Qadir Wirya, and Osman Rahimi. The Opposition group announced its demands in a 20-Point Declaration to the party on 29 July 2006 (Hassanzadeh, 2012, pp. 527, 562-562). The key demands of the 20-point Declaration included: (1) The party is to recognize the Opposition and have dialogue with it. (2) The party must fulfill the resolutions approved by the 12th and 13th Congresses regarding the freedom of expression in the internal organizations of the party. (3) In the past two years, hundreds of members have been either punished, displaced, and their positions taken, or were rewarded and given positions. A committee, including the representative of the Opposition, is to be established to review all of the cases and nullify the unhealthy decisions. (4) The party should support the Women and Youth organizations. (5) In contrast to the previous congresses, there is no balance between the representatives of the different wings in the CC. To compensate for this shortcoming, three suggestions were offered: the vacant seat of Khalid Azizi in the CC must be given to the Opposition, the vacant seats of the alternates of the CC must be given to the Opposition, and within each organ whose head is from the majority, its substitute must be from the minority. (6) Members of the two wings should be allowed to express their ideas within the party's radio, newspaper, and television without investigating them. If the Opposition's view is against that of the party, it should be distributed in the internal publication of the party, *Tekoshar* (Struggler), as has been approved in the 12th and 13th Congresses (Hassanzadeh, 2012, pp. 561-562).

The PDKI responded to the demands of the minority with a 17-point Proposal on 27 November 2006, to which the Opposition responded on 1 December 2006. Four of the PDKI points were not related to the Oppositions' demands, and interestingly, the PDKI rejected 12 points out of 13 demands of the Opposition and accepted just half of the last point (Hassanzadeh, 2012, pp. 540, 565-570; Hassanzadeh, 2015, pp. 82-85). The minority members claim that they tried they were left with not choice but to leave the PDKI. Gadani begged Hassanzadeh that, if still there was the slightest chance of staying, they should try not to leave (Hassanzadeh, 2012, p. 544). Hassanzadeh (2012) concludes that, in the 13th Congress, the majority led by Hijri wanted to eliminate the minority. The minority was left with two options: "be slave or split" (p. 501).

When the problems between the majority and minority wings in the PDKI were not resolved, the Opposition wrote a Declaration about its separation from the PDKI. Before publicizing it, though, the Opposition took the Declaration to the PDKI leaders, but they received it with indifference. Therefore, the Opposition split from the PDKI by publicizing the Declaration under the long designation of "A Group of the Members of the Politburo and the CC, and Alternates and Consultants of the CC of the Democratic Party of Iranian Kurdistan" on 6 December 2006. This group distributed a declaration titled *Hela Gishtiyakani Rebazi Ema* ("General

Principles of Our Way"; aka "General Principles") in which they chose the name the Kurdistan Democratic Party-Iran or KDP-I on 9 December 2006, and shortly after, changed it to the Kurdistan Democratic Party or the KDP, in the party's 14th Congress, held on 6 March 2008 (Hassanzadeh, 2012, pp. 529, 544; Kurdistan Democratic Party-Iran, 2006). At the beginning of 2006, the KDP comprised 15 percent of the PDKI membership, but by 2012, the KDP had attracted more than 50 percent of the PDKI membership (Hassanzadeh, 2012, p. 549).

The PDKI did not call the splinters the KDP but *Taqmi Hassani Rastgar* (Hassan Rastgar's Group) (Hassanzadeh, 2012, p. 543). In recent years, the PDKI has called them "our old friends." In fact, the PDKI has always been very sensitive and possessive about the previous splinters who had used names for their parties that resembled that of the PDKI. Referring to the previous split from the PDKI, Hijri (2015) emphasizes that according to the constitution of the party, the leaders of the majority of the party who have been chosen in a lawful congress have the right to use the name of the party, not the minority. In countries where the law prevails, the court decides about the parties' claims over designations. Therefore, the PDKI was right in defending its right to the party's name (Hijri, 2015, p. 95).

Hijri's statements can be criticized on different grounds. The constitution of the party does not address "the right to use the name of the party." He ignores that the name of the splinters was not the PDKI but the PDKI-RL—a different designation. Moreover, he does not explain why the PDKI did not choose civilized and peaceful ways to protect its presumably lawful right to the party's name and why it conducted violent, military attacks on the PDKI-RL in which 22 peshmergas of the latter party were killed. Hijri (2015) believes that the parties that choose the same name as the mother party exploit the history of the mother party for their own present interests. These types of parties will gradually become weak and leave no effect on society (p. 96). If Hijri's claim is correct, then why did the PDKI not let the PDKI-RL die out on its own but instead attacked the PDKI-RL using military force? Was it so crucial to destroy that PDKI-RL so fast? In contrast to Hijri's view, even though the PDKI attacked the PDKI-RL, the latter party was not destroyed and survived for nine years. Instead, finally, despite its presumed principle in its constitution, the PDKI had to accept the designation PDKI-RL in order to officiate its unification with the latter.

After the separation of the KDP, the PDKI continued to launch uncivilized and violent activities against the splinters (KDP) that included a communication boycott and beating some KDP members. Hassanzadeh claims that after the split, the PDKI members physically attacked the KDP members. These include stabbing the KDP member Arash Zamani (25 times) in his home (he survived) and the beating of the KDP members in Jejnikan Camp, which led the KDP members to the hospital and the PDKI members to the prison of the KRG! Hassanzadeh emphasizes that the command to beat the members came from the leadership of the PDKI. He claims that Hijri, in a letter to his friends in Romadi, encouraged them to attack the KDP members but not severely. Consequently, the KDP asked the KRG to protect their safety (Hassanzadeh, 2012, p. 550). It was highly probable that if the split occurred in a territory outside of the KRG authority, the conflict between these organizations could have resulted in yet another armed, bloody clash.

6.17. The 14th Congress of the KDP

The 14th Congress of the KDP was held in Koya, Iraq, on 6 March 2006. According to Rahman Naqshi (2015), Khalid Azizi was elected the General Secretary and Mustafa Mawloudi the alternate General Secretary of the KDP (see Appendix 8). As mentioned, the PDKI was against the designation of the KDP, and the former imposed the removal of the latter designation as a precondition for negotiations, but the KDP rejected it (Hassanzadeh, 2012, pp. 577-578).

The KDP's Program and Internal Regulation were not significantly different from the previous ones. The party regarded itself as "democratic Left," but terms such as "scientific worldview" and "democratic centralism" have been taken out of the party's Program, although the latter was still operational within the party (Hassanzadeh, 2012, p. 164). The KDP divisions were parallel to those of the PDKI. A comparison between these two parties reveals the similarity of their organizations as well as the extent of their activities (see Appendix 30).

6.18. The 14th Congress of the PDKI

The 14th Congress of the PDKI was held in Koya, Iraq, 10-14 September 2008. Hijri was elected the General Secretary, and Sharafi the alternate General Secretary (see Appendix 8). The party removed Article 10 from its Internal Regulation that had previously restricted the General Secretary to two successive terms ("Democratic Party" 2008, pp. 87-88). In addition, according to Tahir Mahmoudi, Head of the Social Commission of the PDKI, and Mohayadin Palani, a previous consultant member of the PDKI CC, the 14th Congress decided to choose the heads of the Democratic Women's Union of Iranian Kurdistan and the Democratic Youth Union of Iranian Kurdistan as the alternate members of the CC (Mahmoudi, Personal communication, January 9, 2016; Palani, Personal communication, December 11, 2016).

Two important decisions were made before the 15th Congress. The first related to the party relations with the KDP, and the second with the Komala. Regarding the first, the Plenum of the party on 1 August 2012 approved that the CC can negotiate with the "previous friends" (KDP) in order to solve their problems and bring them back to the PDKI. The 15th Congress approved this decision ("Komiteh Markari-ye," 2012, p. 254). The second achievement of the PDKI was signing a cooperation agreement with the Komala. For about a year prior to the 15th Congress, the PDKI and the Komala were holding negotiations. These resulted in the signing of a cooperation agreement between them on 21 August 2012 ("Komiteh Markari-ye," 2012, p. 254; "Hezb-e Demokrat-e Kurdistan-e," 2012;

see Appendix 31).

6.19. The 15th Congress of the KDP

The 15th Congress of the KDP was held in Koya, Iraq, 23-29 May 2011. In this Congress, Khalid Azizi was elected the General Secretary and Mustafa Mawloudi the alternate General Secretary of the KDP (Naqshi, 2015; see Appendix 8). According to Hassan Hatami, an alternative member of the CC of the KDP, with the approval of the CC, the Politburo selected five members as consultant members of the Politburo (Hatami, Personal Communication, May 6, 2017; "Kurdistan Democratic," 2015; see Appendix 8). Since the Congress, the KDP has established and strengthened its organizations and presence within the Kurdish movement. With respect to the main differences between the two parties, Hassanzadeh argues that the KDP has concentrated on the democratization of the party, whereas the PDKI has focused on centralization. The KDP members express their ideas freely internally and externally, and regardless of the opinions expressed, the party members are regarded as valued members. In contrast, the PDKI has punished members who were in favor of the unification of the two parties (some had signed a petition) and had communicated with the KDP members (Hassanzadeh, 2012, p. 547). While Hassanzadeh's statements are *partially* correct, a closer look at the internal relations within the KDP shows that in terms of democratizing party life, the KDP faces major shortcomings.

In 2012, the PDKI announced that some cadres, peshmergas, and members (of the KDP) who had separated a few years back, in 2006, in protest to the KDP leaders, had created a group named *Goroupi Halwest* (Position Group). The Position Group, in a declaration dated 21 June 2012, announced their separation from the KDP and joining the PDKI ("Democratic Party", 2012). This is the strange story of this faction: Lotf Pouri, the main character of this group, explains that since the 10th Congress of the PDKI (1994), regional factions emerged in the party. These regions included the North, Middle, and South of Iranian Kurdistan. Regionalism was used to get power. In and after the 13th Congress (2004), the discord between the two factions—Hijri and the splinters (KDP)—erupted. The minority—that is, the splinters (KDP)—emphasized the necessity for reforms, freedom of expression, decentralization of the leadership, utilizing the experiential wisdom of elderly members and the youth, and strengthening the nationalist aspect of the party. Lotf Pouri maintains that one year (2003) before the 13th Congress (2004), he and some other members created a group named the *Rawti Reform* (Reform Trend) within the PDKI. The aim of this group was to reform the party. The Reform Trend joined the minority oppositions and split from the PDKI (2006), and it continued its activity within the KDP. The space for activity and criticism was satisfactory within the KDP until after the 14th Congress of the KDP, when the party officially, without announcing, dissolved the Reform Trend. Gradually, by threatening or promising posts to the members of the Reform Trend, the KDP ended its activities (Personal communication, October 21, 2012). Lotf Pouri maintains that the KDP gradually abandoned democratic principles. When the Reform Trend members lost hope in making reforms within the KDP, Lotf Pouri and some other members created another group named the *Goroupi Halwest* (Position Group). The group's aim was to struggle for the unification of the KDP and the PDKI. However, the KDP started reproaching, suspending, and expelling some members of the Position Group (Lotf Pouri, Personal communication, October 21, 2012). Lotf Pouri states that about 70 members, cadres, and peshmergas of the Position Group in Kurdistan and Europe split from the KDP (Personal communication, October 21, 2012).

Aside from some tactical changes, the KDP upheld political activity (instead of armed operations) and support for the civil rights movement within Iranian Kurdistan and the rest of Iran as its policy. Although the KDP peshmergas have occasionally attended political activities in Iranian Kurdistan, they have not engaged in military clashes with the Iranian forces. However, they have been attacked by the Iranian military when present on the Iranian side of the border and have sustained causalities.

The PDKI has consistently boycotted all presidential and parliamentary elections in Iran, but the KDP's approach has been different. In the Presidential elections of 2009, the KDP announced on 14 May 2009 that it supported the reformist candidate Mehdi Karroubi, for he had defended the rights of minority groups (Politburo of the Kurdistan Democratic Party, 2009a, p. 5). Later, on 19 June 2009, the KDP Politburo supported the nationwide protest movement against the rigged elections known as the Green Movement (Politburo of the Kurdistan Democratic Party, 2009b, pp. 1-2).

6.20. The 15th Congress of the PDKI

The 15th Congress of the PDK was held in Koya, Iraq, 29 September-3 October 2012. Hijri was voted in as the General Secretary, and Sharafi, the alternate General Secretary (see Appendix 8). The Congress decided the heads of the Democratic Women's Union of Iranian Kurdistan, the Democratic Youth Union of Iranian Kurdistan, and the Democratic Student Union of Iranian Kurdistan automatically become the alternate members of the CC (Kurdistan Media, 2012). The 15th Congress of the PDKI approved and emphasized the fulfillment of the two previous decisions of the party—that is, to continue negotiating with the KDP and to reach an agreement with the Komala ("Komiteh Markari-ye," 2012, pp. 254-255). In total, aside from some critiques about these undertakings, both of these subjects have had positive political and moral effects on the Kurdish people. The continuation of the PDKI's activities after the 15th Congress, including its new political plans and its relations with the KDP, will be discussed in the rest of this chapter.

6.21. The 16th Congress of the KDP

The 16th Congress of the KDP was held in Koya, Iraq, 6-11 February 2016. The Congress voted Khalid Azizi as the General Secretary and Mustafa Mawloudi as the alternate General Secretary (Hatami, Personal Communication, May 6, 2017; see Appendix 8). The 16th Congress removed the Internal Regulation, Article 18, that limited the position of the Secretary-General to two successive terms ("Kurdistan Democratic Party," 2016a, p. 35) so that the KDP could choose Khalid Azizi for a third successive term. It seems that the Congress, due to disagreements among the members, agreed to choose Azizi as the General Secretary, and Azizi accepted this position on the condition that the composition of the leadership remains exactly the same, to which the Congress consented (Hatami, Personal Communication, May 6, 2017). Concerning the nature and the magnitude of discord within the KDP more research is needed.

Regarding the forms of struggle, the 16th Congress of the KDP emphasized that the party believed in multi-directional forms of struggle in Iran. The party criticized the Kurdish political organizations that treated civic activities and creative engagements of the Kurdish elite in Iranian Kurdistan with suspicion. Although since the 14th Congress the KDP had tried for a long time to revive its peshmergas' presence in Iranian Kurdistan, it was only in the past two years, since 2014, when its presence increased. The Congress maintained that the Kurdish people have warmly welcomed the peshmerga presence. The KDP has always actively supported the civil society struggles of the Kurdish people. The peshmerga presence in Iranian Kurdistan meant to develop political and organizational aspects and make connections with the people. The peshmergas' activities should be viewed as just one type of multi-directional struggle and not a substitute for civil society activism ("Kurdistan Democratic," 2016b, pp. 30, 32-33).

The 16th Congress maintained that while the Iranian government's treatment of the Kurds has been persistently one-dimensional and suppressive, the dominant, subversive discourse of the opposition, including the Kurds, has also been one-dimensional. While it is logical to overthrow and boycott this regime, Congress declared it is not correct to ignore other methods of challenging the regime. The Congress, therefore, invited people to engage in cultural politics, attending the fields of struggle and creating cultural and human rights organizations. According to the KDP, after the 15th Congress, the Supreme National Security Council (SNSC) of Iran called the KDP for negotiations. The KDP representatives met with the Iranian delegates a few times to discuss solving the Kurds' issues. Expectedly, the negotiations turned out fruitless because the government was not serious. The Congress believed that the party should not reject the negotiations but should be conscious of the government's plots ("Kurdistan Democratic," 2016b, pp. 34-35).

As for its relations with the PDKI, the KDP Congress supported the PDKI decision in their 15th Congress, which approved of negotiating with the KDP. The KDP provided a plan and submitted it to the PDKI. As the PDKI had had problems with the name of the KDP, the KDP suggested using the designation "*doo layani Demokrat*" (two parts of Democrat) or "*demokratakan*" (Democrats). The PDKI never provided a written plan. After the last negotiations among the Politburos of the two parties, probably in 2015, it was revealed that the PDKI's aim was not the unification of the two parties; rather, the PDKI expected the KDP to join the former. The KDP rejected the position that one of the parties (PDKI) was the original Democratic Party and the other only secondary ("Kurdistan Democratic," 2016b, pp. 40-41).

6.22. The PDKI and the KDP since 2015

While both parties have been cooperating to find a way for unification, Hijri wrote a book in 2015 in which he severely attacked Hassanzadeh and the KDP. Hijri's book proved to be detrimental to the inter-party relations. In his book, Hijri claims that Hassanzadeh has brought shame to himself by leading the split and breaking the hearts of patriotic Kurds. It is a type of disgrace that has no political and organizational justifications: a black blot on Hassanzadeh's reputation after so many years of Party activity and an unhappy end of his life (Hijri, 2015, pp. 136, 161). Hijri (2015) states that the separatists faced a meaningful defeat when some of their members, including *Goroupi Halwest* (Position Group), split from them (p. 13). The split of the Position Group proves the KDP's failure to fulfill the promises of *Hela Gishtiyakan* (General Principles) and the subject of unity with the PDKI (Hijri, 2015, p. 136). Hijri claims that according to a member of the Position Group, the KDP leadership planned to harness greater and get arbitrary power for itself, which caused the pacification of a significant number of the CCs (Hijri, 2015, p. 140).

In response, Gadani criticizes Hijri and states that it seems like Hijri was specifically asked to write his meaningless book, which is full of accusations, to postpone the process of unification and create an obstacle in the process of negotiation between the two parties (Gadani, 2015). Gadani, likewise, accuses Hijri of having allegedly ordered a bomb to be detonated among members of the PDKI-RL in 1996. Fortunately, claims Gadani, the PDKI cadres found out about the bombing attempt and neutralized it (Gadani, 2015). Gadani mentions Hijri as having a king-like mentality: no matter who splits from his party and why, Hijri views that person as a traitor and jash (Gadani, 2015).

Hassanzadeh (2015) claims that until recently, Hijri, under the pretext of defending Ghassemlou, was confronting the splinters, calling them enemies because they were critical of Ghassemlou (p. 7). Hijri and others ordered the invasion, clubbing, and stabbing of the members, cadres, and peshmergas of the KDP during the few weeks after the split (Hassanzadeh, 2015, p. 19). After the 13th Congress, the members of the Opposition were humiliated by expulsion, punishment, and displacement (Hassanzadeh, 2015, p. 32). Hijri, to attract people to the PDKI, promised them positions and salaries, as well as sending the prospective members to Europe (Hassanzadeh, 2015, p. 44). In regards to the Position Group, Hassanzadeh (2015) admits that his party has not fulfilled the promises in the General Principles. However, unlike the Position Group, he claims that the KDP has not retreated from these principles (p. 50). In short, the abovementioned disputes have created a negative climate and damaged the process of negotiation between the two parties.

Since the early Spring 2016, the PDKI has chosen a new policy regarding its activities in Iranian Kurdistan. On 18 March 2016, Mustafa Hijri sent the PDKI's message to the Kurdish people for the new Kurdish year (20 March 2016). He stated that the PDKI intends to organize its abilities in both the mountains and cities and create a strong force to create a new life far from submissiveness and injustice for the Kurdish people. He promised the Kurdish youth in Eastern Kurdistan that the PDKI, in the new year of 2016, would provide the opportunity for them to join the lines of the PDKI peshmergas so that they start an honorable life and leave humiliation behind. After televising his message and in an interview with Rudaw TV, Hijri also stated that the party is sending its peshmergas to Iranian Kurdistan to mix with the Kurdish people. When he was pressed to explain why many PDKI supporters and peshmergas had left the party for Europe, Hijri replied that the members' leaving for Europe was a plot of the Islamic Republic meant to weaken the struggle (Hijri, 2016).

This new PDKI plan has been the subject of criticism. Although the PDKI officially announced its plan in 2016, it had already begun sending its peshmergas to Iranian Kurdistan in 2015 when both the KDP and the PDKI each sent a group of about 15 to 20 peshmergas to the Qandil Mountains on the border town of Oshnavieh in Iran. Muhammad Reza Eskandari criticizes these parties for lacking a clear vision about what they intend to achieve by sending peshmergas inside Iranian Kurdistan. Eskandari believes that if the intent is to stage armed struggle, the conditions are not ripe, nor do the Kurdish parties have a clear strategy or formidable military force and extensive support line. Eskandari estimates that, at best, the total combined qualified military personnel of these two parties is about 400 peshmergas who are equipped with old weapons. They stand no chance against the Iranian state (Eskandari, 2015).

More to the point, the Politburo of the PDKI announced that a team of the PDKI peshmergas deployed to the village of Qara saqal, Oshnavieh, was attacked by the Iranian military on 15 June 2016. Seven peshmergas were killed, and many homes in the village were destroyed by shelling ("Politburo of the Democratic," 2016a). According to the Roji Kurd, a Kurdish independent website, five armed clashes occurred between the PDKI and the Iranian forces between 9 November 2015 and 26 June 2016. In total, 56 Iranian soldiers have been killed and 98 wounded, while 9 peshmergas from the PDKI have been killed (Roji Kurd, 2016, June 26). No other reliable sources were found to confirm these figures.

In reaction to the peshmergas' presence in the region, the Iranian government has shelled the bases of the Iranian Kurdish forces located on the Iraqi side of the border. The bombings have caused casualties and the displacement of many, in addition to the destruction of agricultural land. On 17 July 2016, the PDKI declared that Mohsen Rezaee, former Commander-in-Chief of the Revolutionary Guards, had criticized some countries for supporting the Iranian Kurdish political organizations. Rezaee threatened Masoud Barzani and stated that if Barzani could not solve this problem, Iran would launch a destructive operation against these organizations ("Politburo of the Democratic," 2016b).

Enayat Fani, BBC Persian anchor, interviewed Hijri on 20 September 2016 regarding the PDKI's latest strategy called *Rasan* (Rising or Re-rising of the PDKI). According to Hijri, *Rasan*, which was announced in Hijri's New Year 2016 address, included armed struggle as well as awakening, encouraging, and giving hope to the Kurdish people. Hijri stated that the PDKI wanted to be present in the region but not attack the Iranian forces. The Iranian forces, however, have attacked the peshmergas. When asked about the real effects of this strategy, Hijri responded that the PDKI's presence in the region has positively affected the morale of the Kurdish people and boosted the PDKI's popularity. Hijri admitted that it was, in fact, the Kurdish youth who pushed the PDKI to choose this form of struggle (Fani, 2016).

Fani flagged two problems with this strategy: the first is the PDKI's inability to confront the regime, and the second is that the Kurdish civil activists have objected to the PDKI's plan that has militarized Kurdistan and negatively affected political development in Kurdistan. In response, Hijri pointed out that Iran has only intensified security in Kurdistan in the past 20 years (Fani, 2016). He also mentioned that the PDKI rejected the KRG's ultimatum that Iranian Kurdish groups should stop armed operations against the Iranian state, thus insisting on the party's existing programs and plans. But he also confirmed the PDKI's decision to reduce the numbers of the PDKI's peshmergas inside Iranian Kurdistan. Hijri adds that the PDKI's plan is to reduce the number of peshmergas who move from Iraqi Kurdistan to Iran on a daily basis and organize the forces inside Iranian Kurdistan (Fani 2016).

The party calls its new strategy *Rasan,* referring to its "rising" (resurgence). But *Rasan* has no clear theoretical basis, and aside from a few armed clashes between the PDKI peshmergas and the government forces, it has not produced any measurable outcome either. Clearly, the present conditions in Iranian Kurdistan do not invite armed struggle. Here is where the KDP differs from the PDKI. Although the KDP's peshmergas are present in Iranian Kurdistan, it seems it has managed to avoid clashes with the Iranian military. Instead, the KDP pays greater attention to political and cultural struggles, and has more hope for a Kurdish civil rights movement compared to the PDKI.

Khalid Azizi, the General Secretary of the KDP, states that the Iranian opposition outside the country has distanced itself from the Iranian people in the past 38 years. Only a small portion of the Iranian people engage in political activities. The opposition has not successfully incorporated the daily problems

Iranians face into its politics, and thus, the opposition has not succeeded in motivating the Iranians into political activism. In contrast, the ongoing conflicts between the conservatives, moderates, and reformists within the Iranian ruling class have indeed affected the people and mobilized them toward various movements (Roji Kurd TV, 2016, March 27). Azizi argues that the Kurds alone cannot overthrow the Islamic Republic, and the Kurdish movement should be regarded as a part of a wide-ranging Iranian movement. The KDP tries to end the Islamic regime and establish a democratic state in which the Kurds can obtain their national rights (Roji Kurd TV, 2016, March 27).

6.23. Summary of the PDKI Clashes with Other Kurdish Groups

The history of the PDKI is riveted by unending armed clashes with other Kurdish parties. These include disarming, detaining, killing, and executing the members of these parties. These conflicts, as is expected, have produced significant negative effects on the Kurdish society. Although the PDKI clashes with other Kurdish organizations have already been discussed, there are a number of cases that deserve a closer look because these cases have allowed the leaders and cadres of the party to also critically reflect on the nature of the PDKI's continued crises. Ironically, the PDKI equally and "democratically" suppressed political organizations in Iranian Kurdistan. The conclusion will argue that these attacks reveal the pathology of the PDKI's life and politics. A general inference about the nature of these conflicts is that they occurred over authority, especially because of the PDKI's attitude to eradicate other organizations and monopolize the leadership of the Kurdish movement in Iran.

(a) As early as the Fall of 1979, the PDKI peshmergas attacked the Kurdistan Equality Party (or Kurdistan Equality Association) peshmergas in the village of Mawlanawa, Saqqiz, killing one and arresting four, just because the

Kurdistan Equality Party peshmergas were speaking to the people in the mosque. The PDKI peshmergas threw a grenade into the mosque to kill the rest of the Kurdistan Equality Party peshmergas, but nobody was hurt. The next day, in protest against the PDKI, the Education Office and all schools of Saqqiz were closed. The people and the majority of the political organizations present in Saqqiz supported the rally organized by the Kurdistan Equality Party against the PDKI. As a result, the PDKI released the four peshmergas it had captured (Kurdistan Equality Party, 2015).

(b) One of the cruelest actions of the PDKI was attacking the office of the Peykar [Organization of Struggle for the Emancipation of the Working Class] in Bukan on 26 February 1981 and carried out by Karim Khaldar, a PDKI commander (Khalighi, 2002, p. 273), without any reason. Three activists were killed in this attack (Hassanzadeh, 2012, p. 238), and the *Peykar*, Issue 97, contains the statements from the Komala, the Rah-e Kargar [Organization of Revolutionary Workers of Iran], and the People's Fedai Guerillas (Minority), condemning this attack (Ayoubzadeh, 2002).

(c) The PDKI and the Khabat [Organization of Iranian Kurdistan Struggle] engaged in several armed clashes between 1980 and 1984, in which several Khabat peshmergas were wounded. The PDKI attacked Khabat bases in Shqoif in Saqqiz, Singan in Oshnaiye, Rabat territory, and in Bukan territory. In these attacks, the PDKI confiscated the weapons, arrested the peshmergas, and beat them. The PDKI regularly arrested Khabat couriers and destroyed their newspapers, not to mention the party had beaten Khabat peshmergas who were in *jawla* (moving around a territory for military practice) many times. Nuranifard reports that in a meeting, the PDKI leaders wanted to eliminate it and monopolize the leadership of the Kurdish resistance (Nuranifard, Personal communication, September 8, 2012).

(d) The PDKI arrested and imprisoned members of the Tudeh Party, the Fadaian (Majority), and the PDKI (FFC) (Gohari, 2002, pp. 20-21). On one occasion, the PDKI attacked the peshmergas of Fadaian (Majority), killing Reza Pirani from Mahabad. Mautasam Noorani confirms these attacks and points out that in these conflicts, the party was in error (Personal communication, September 22, 2012).

Many Kurdish activists, the PDKI, and the KDP cadres (former or present) have been critical of the PDKI's violence against other Kurdish groups. Dr. Miro Aliyar, a member of the Politburo of the PDKI, blames the non-democratic political culture among the Kurdish organizations for these attacks (Personal communication, October 22, 2012). Jalil Gadani, the most veteran cadre of the KDP and the previous General Secretary of the PDKI-RL, condemns all of the PDKI's armed activities against other political parties in Kurdistan. In regard to the aforementioned attack on Peykar's office in Bukan, Gadani insists that this attack was not the PDKI's policy, and the Politburo was not even aware of it until after the incident (Personal communication, October 21, 2012). Dr. Hossein Khalighi, the previous member of the PDKI CC, confirms that the attack against Peykar was inexcusable, but he also mentions that the PDKI did not put the wayward members responsible for the attack on trial (Personal communication, December 1, 2012). Abdollah Hejab, a political activist, cadre of the PDKI, and its previous consultant member of the CC, calls these attacks unlawful and believes that the PDKI must answer these actions (Personal communication, December 6, 2012). Mohammad Khizri, the veteran member of the KDP, also confirms the PDKI's unlawful imprisonment of followers of the Tudeh Party, the Fadaian (Majority), and the Komala in the village of Qom Qal'eh. But the worst thing the PDKI did, Khizri argues, was the assassination of Jafar Karroubi (Khizri's best friend), a peshmerga of the PDKI (FFC) (Personal communication, November 22, 2012).

6.23.1. Reflections on the PDKI-Komala war and the cases above. Madani states that in its literature, the PDKI deems itself as the sole agent capable of resolving the "Kurdish Question." The party was authoritarian and thought that deciding about war and peace in Kurdistan was its exclusive prerogative, and thus, it never had any respect for the rights of minority groups (Personal communication, October 14, 2012). Hossein Madani, member and a political consultant of the Politburo of the KDP and previous member of the Politburo of the PDKI-RL, who was in charge of the PDKI's office in Bukan when the party's peshmergas attacked the Peykar, confirms that this attack was the act of wayward individuals, although, he claims, he had offered the Peykar members an apology afterward (Personal communication, October 14, 2012).

Mostafa Shalmashi, a member of the Politburo of the KDP, also blames the lack of democratic culture within the PDKI for attacking the smaller groups. Shalmashi also confirms the previous accounts of the Bukan incident, although he mentions that in the party's Plenum, the Bukan incident was investigated, and some members' party responsibilities and assignments were taken away from them (Personal communication, November 15, 2012).

Shams emphasizes that the nature of these conflicts was power. These conflicts had roots in sectarianism, a disease of the Left. Although the PDKI was the most monopolistic organization in Kurdistan, the Komala was equally monopolizing in its territories (Personal communication, October 18, 2012). The PDKI's war with the Komala has been discussed above. The ultimate reason for this war was power and authority over the Kurdish resistance (Ali Mahmood Shekhani, 2007, p. 256). Hassani emphasizes that the war was simply over authority, just as the splits within the PDKI and the Komala were over power and authority (Personal communication, October 19, 2012).

Interestingly, Khalighi interprets the want of power as the desire to rule the people due to the authoritarian policies and outlooks of these two parties the Komala claimed to represent the toiling masses, while the PDKI asserted itself as the "owner" of the Kurdish movement (Khalighi, 2002, pp. 269-270). The casualties of the PDKI-Komala war were victims of the power-hungry and ultra-leftist policies combined with chauvinistic ideas (Khalighi, 2005, p. 19).

Amir Qazi, leader of the Independence Party of Kurdistan (PSK) and the previous member of the Politburo of the KDP, goes further by calling these clashes meaningless (Qazi, 2010, p. 376). Khadija Mazour, a woman and a member of the CC of the KDP, likewise condemns these clashes because they all damaged the Kurdish society. She claims that while the PDKI was not the only guilty party in creating conflicts, it was the main guilty party because the PDKI considered itself the supreme champion of the field (Personal communication, October 11, 2012). Kwestan Ftoohi, a woman and a CC of the KDP, too, stresses that the party has been arrogant and monopolist (contrary to the party's Program). Although both the PDKI and the Komala were culprits, the party was guiltier because it was the greater organization. The party should have resolved the issues with the Komala peacefully, even if it took a hundred dialogues with them (Personal communication, October 9, 2012). Sohaila Qadri, a woman and an alternate member of the CC of the KDP, states that the main two reasons for the war between the PDKI and the Komala were, firstly, the lack of understanding of democracy and the recognition of the minorities' rights, and secondly, the Komala's provocations. She emphasizes that both of these parties should officially apologize to the Kurdish people (Personal communication, October 21, 2012), a sentiment also expressed by Rambod Lotf Pouri, member of the CC of the PDKI (Personal communication, October 21, 2012).

Shahla Dabaghi (2012), a writer, human rights activist, and previous supporter of the PDKI (FFC), states that the war between the PDKI and the Komala was overpowering. The Komala's gravest mistake was to consider itself a progressive, leftist group and the PDKI a backward, nationalist, and tribal party (Personal communication, November 25, 2012). Aliyar wishes for an unbiased commission's analysis regarding the war between the two parties (Personal communication, October 22, 2012).

But there are leaders and cadres that still blame the war largely on the Komala. Stating that the PDKI-Komala war has claimed 700-900 lives from both sides, Hejab largely blames Komala's ideology for this conflict. That said, neither the PDKI nor the Komala has been brave enough to critically analyze the conflict (Personal communication, December 6, 2012). Khalighi also claims that while the PDKI regarded itself as the "owner" of the Kurdish movement, the Komala regarded itself to be a Marxist-Leninist organization and the PDKI a bourgeois party. Because these organizations were undemocratic, their ideological conflict led to their conflictual interests and, thus, to war against each other. But Khalighi still largely blames the Komala for the war (Personal communication, December 1, 2012). Madani emphasizes that the Komala was creating disturbances and did not allow the PDKI members to spread their ideas in Kurdistan (Personal communication, October 14, 2012). Similarly, Shalmashi holds both of these organizations guilty but believes that the Komala provided the pretext for the war by identifying the "bourgeois" PDKI and the Iranian regime. That said, in the continuation of the war, the PDKI is to blame (Personal communication, November 15, 2012). Qadir Wirya, a member of the Politburo of the KDP, also blames the war on a lack of democratic experience in leadership, which has led to authoritarian overviews and conduct. The Komala, in certain aspects, was guiltier: it called the PDKI a bourgeois party and aimed to replace the PDKI as the leading organization in the Kurdish movement. On the other hand, the PDKI did not allow other organizations to confront it (Personal communication, October 22, 2012).

Contrary to the above, some PDKI cadres differ: Khizri found the PDKI culpable for starting the war when the party killed 15 Komala peshmergas (Personal communication, November 22, 2012). Hassan Rastgar, a veteran member of the KDP and a previous General Secretary of the PDKI-RL, indicates that the nature of the war between the PDKI and the Komala was ideological and over authority. The

PDKI could not launch ideological propaganda due to its shortage of theoretical knowledge, while the Komala was ideologically formidable. So, the PDKI did not want to lose its authority in Kurdistan (Personal communication, October 17, 2012).

Now, the reflections of the Komala leaders are equally interesting. They agree that the Komala has made serious mistakes in the past, but they still regard the PDKI as the main culprit. According to Abdullah Mohtadi, the General Secretary of the Komala, Ghassemlou is to blame for the war (Saedi, 2010, p. 7) when the PDKI attacked and killed 13 Komala peshmergas on 16 November 1984. The PDKI had an authoritative mentality and thought that others should either be slaves to the PDKI or cease activity (Saedi, 2010, pp. 107-108). Said Kowestani, a previous prominent cadre of the PDKI, reveals that the PDKI had planned to attack the Komala (Saedi, 2012, pp. 562-566). Ebrahim Alizadeh is the General Secretary of the Komala Kurdistan Organization of the Communist Party of Iran (Komala [CPI]) and the executive member of the Communist Party of Iran (CPI). Alizadeh, regarding the attack of the PDKI on other groups as well as on the Komala in Barda Sour, which was the first conflict between the PDKI and the Komala, maintains that the PDKI has attacked different, smaller groups in Kurdistan. The PDKI wanted to cleanse Kurdistan of these alleged obtrusive organizations. The party did not worry about Peykar's power but its waspish language. In regards to the Komala, the situation was different because the Komala was a powerful force (Personal communication, September 13, 2012). According to Alizadeh, the PDKI even dissolved the village councils that were created by the Komala (Saedi, 2012, p. 562). Thus, Alizadeh largely blames the war on the PDKI (Saedi, 2012, p. 106), but he also makes an interesting observation: the conflict between the PDKI and the Komala was neither overpowering nor classic class warfare between the bourgeoisie and the proletariat. Rather, it was over democracy and unconditional freedom for communist activity in Kurdistan. His evidence is the fact that almost all of the leftist organizations in Kurdistan experienced armed invasions by the PDKI (Saedi, 2012, pp. 109-110).

6.23.2. The PDKI conflict with the PDKI-RL. Although at the time of the split (2006), Ftoohi stayed with the PDKI, she nonetheless stresses that the conflict was due to the lack of tolerance within the party, and that is why the PDKI under Ghassemlou imposed a war on the PDKI-RL (Personal communication, October 9, 2012). Sohaila Qadri, a female alternate member of the CC of the KDP, largely blames the PDKI for the conflict (Personal communication, October 21, 2012). Karimi echoes this verdict, pointing out that as a result of this split, hundreds of the cadres and peshmergas of the PDKI and PDKI-RL left these parties by either surrendering themselves to Iranian authorities, staying in the Iraqi Kurdistan or leaving for the West (Personal communication, September 4, 2012). Khalighi points out that the PDKI mistreated the PDKI-RL members through smear campaigns and physical assault (Personal communication, December 1, 2012). Madani reveals that at the time of the split, Ghassemlou had stated that he would have the PDKI-RL kicked out of Kurdistan by the Ba'ath Party and Saddam (Personal communication, October 14, 2012). Wirya points out that while the PDKI mistreated the PDKI-RL members and even disarmed them, the PDKI-RL chose not to clash with the PDKI (Personal communication, October 22, 2012), a point verified by Shalmashi (Personal communication, November 15, 2012). Finally, Lotf Pouri states that the PDKI should not have conducted war against the PDKI-RL (Personal communication, October 21, 2012).

The PDKI and the Komala, while leading a war against the Iranian government, engaged in a long-term war against each other. This war has had many negative effects on the Kurdish people, the Kurdish nationalist movement, and on them both. Although both sides correctly admit that they had roles in the creation of the war and made mistakes, they each believe that the other side carried greater responsibility. Based on the aforementioned explanations and the general policy of the PDKI in creating many conflicts with many other organizations in order to strengthen its grip and keep its dominant role in Kurdistan, the PDKI was more responsible for the creation and continuation of the war between these two parties.

The conflict between the PDKI and the PDKI-RL reveals that the PDKI, especially under Ghassemlou, had treated the PDKI-RL with greater cruelty compared to other organizations, so much so that the PDKI campaign against the PDKI-RL has been criticized even by many present leaders and cadres of the PDKI.

6.24. Analysis and Conclusions

Decades of conflict between Kurdish nationalist organizations and, above all, the branches that have stemmed from the original Kurdistan Democratic Party (KDP) that was established in 1945, on the one hand, and two different regimes in Iran have proven the following. While the Kurdish movement has been opting for certain policy flexibilities in regard to finding a solution for the "Kurdish Question," the Iranian state (both monarchical and Islamic) has been unwaveringly suppressive toward the Kurdish movement. Being a part of the national struggle of the Kurds in the Greater Kurdistan, since 1971, the PDKI has created strong connections with the other Kurdish movements in the region and especially with that of Southern Kurdistan (Iraq). Above all, since the retreat of the PDKI and other Kurdish organizations, along with thousands of their followers, to Iraqi Kurdistan, where they have been housed for 25 years, it is important to remember the crucial, daily assistance of the KRG and the Kurdish people and organizations that have sustained the Iranian Kurds.

This chapter shows the agonizing, bloody, and conflictual history of the PDKI since its modernization in 1971. We have seen that since 1971, and especially after the Iranian Revolution of 1979, major discord has existed within the leadership of the PDKI. While, in some cases, ideological and political disagreements have caused these discords and splits, the main root of them all has been the struggle over power in the party and in society. The conflicts within the party have resulted in three major splits. The last major discord exploded in the 13th Congress and resulted in the split of the KDP. Clearly, the PDKI is responsible for violent and anti-democratic actions against the KDP after the split. The conflict within the PDKI was not about the political tactics, strategy, and ideological beliefs of the organization. The essence of the discord within the PDKI, which resulted in a split, was the conflict over power, position, and democracy in the party. However, the process of getting power from the majority was through undermining the democratic principles—the very principles approved by the party. For instance, during the 13th Congress and later, the majority led by Hijri, through limiting, punishing, and eliminating many of the minority members, especially from the key positions, intensified the already existing discord within the party. Under those conditions, the struggle of the minority gradually shifted more toward the struggle for democracy. From these statements, it is not concluded that the minority, when they were in power, had created a totally democratic party: they did not. Nevertheless, ignoring the minority's rights and discarding democratic conduct by the majority was so deep it was unacceptable for the minority members.

In general, the many splits in the PDKI have negatively affected the political and social relationships among the former and present comrades, the Kurdish political organizations, and the Kurdish society. These are symptoms of deep crises within the Kurdish national movement in Iran. The history of the PDKI since 1971 reveals that the PDKI has sustained its struggle for Kurdish national liberation to the present time. The history of the PDKI since 1971 reveals that the PDKI has sustained its struggle for Kurdish national liberation to the present time. The objectives of the PDKI and its offshoots have been national liberation as the final wish (independence and creation of a Kurdish state) and a limited extent of national liberation as the primary goal (autonomy or self-governance within the state of

Iran). These parties, at present, are increasingly encountering a nationalist movement that faces adverse conditions imposed on them, as well as the endless discord and conflict the party has brought upon them due to its undemocratic organizational life.

Clearly, the PDKI and its offshoots are part of the pan-Kurdish struggle in the region. But, the possible favorable outcomes for the Iranian Kurdish movement are diminishing. Referring to Fanon's perspectives, it can be argued that the violent armed struggle of the PDKI and other Kurdish political organizations has been a reflection of the violent language of the Iranian internal colonizing state. In the process of state-building under Reza Shah, in the process of "repressive development" (Vahabzadeh, 2010) under Mohammad Reza Shah, and in the age of the Islamic Republic's discourse of emancipation of the Iranian nation against the forces of "international arrogance" (estekbar-e jahani) through the creation of a strong state, the Kurds have been excluded from these political processes. The "Kurdish Question," therefore, is symptomatic of Iranian Kurdistan's political underdevelopment imposed by the Iranian state. Kurdistan's economic development, in other words, has come at the cost of its political underdevelopment. Nevertheless, the Kurdish struggle for autonomy and dignity has had an "enlightening" effect on the Kurdish people and encouraged many to participate in the movement, but this does not mean that the forms of struggles launched by the Kurdish opposition in Iran have been the right from the start or flawless.

Now, we have come full circle. In order for the Kurdish rights to autonomy and national recognition to become a part of the public discourse, and in order for these rights to be recognized by the Iranian state at some point—*if* that is at all possible—the Kurdish political groups must bring themselves fully to this age. They must abandon their tribal, authoritarian, and sectarian policies and inner/organizational life. Michel's "iron law of oligarchy" fully applies to the

Kurdish opposition groups, as we clearly witness a ruling elite—all men—reigning over these parties, trying to exclude their rivals and monopolize power in their own hands. These aging parties have no place for women or youth. *Whether the existing parties can accommodate the requirements for liberation movements in our age remains the key question at this time.*

Here, we can see how Vahabzadeh's term, "constitutive paradox," applies to the PDKI and its offshoots: *the very party that has been unwaveringly struggling for the democratic rights of the Kurds has done so only through deeply undemocratic means and policies*. The democratic future of a liberated nation, in other words, is fought for by undemocratic organizations. It can be concluded that the PDKI's relations with other political organizations in Iranian Kurdistan and its own splinter groups have been steadily undemocratic. Of course, these authoritarian ideas and practices, to a great degree, have been the reflection of the Kurdish and Iranian societies, which have been under dictatorial states and undemocratic cultures for so long. While other political organizations were not faultless, the PDKI's antidemocratic practices greatly damaged the process of development of democratic relationships between political organizations and among the Kurdish people in Kurdistan. In recent years, the party has accepted democratic principles but has repeatedly undermined them.

6.24.1. Theories of nationalism and the Kurdish question. Although linking theories of nationalism to the Kurdish nationalist movement is highly significant and needs separate research, some will be briefly applied by focusing on Kurdish nationalism in Iran.

Writers such as Hechter, Lenin, Stalin, and Fanon related certain nationalist movements to the struggle of people against colonialism or internal colonialism. These perspectives attribute a national liberation and progressive character to these movements. Kurdish nationalism within the Greater Kurdistan is the national struggle of the Kurds against the internal colonialism of four states: Iran, Iraq, Turkey, and Syria. The emergence of modern Kurdish nationalism by the early 20th century can be traced as follows. It was against the Ottoman Empire and later the Turkish Republic under Ataturk, the campaigns of Sheikh Mahmoud Barzanji against the British and the Iraqi government since 1919, the movement of Simko against Reza Shah, and the Kurdish nationalist movement in Syria. These nationalist movements have been, in some part, the reflection against the emergence of the dominant nationalisms and colonizer states in these countries. The Kurdish national liberation movements have been led in different forms by different political organizations in these countries.

Some scholars, such as Anderson and Guibernau, distinguish between nationalism and racism. Kurdish nationalism can be categorized as anti-racist nationalism. For instance, the Kurdish Republic of 1946 and today's KRG in Iraq have recognized the rights of minorities in their territories. Moreover, the Kurdish political parties in Iran, Iraq, and Syria, such as the PDKI, the Komala, and the PKK, have emphasized the fulfillment of the minorities' rights in Kurdistan and created a just and democratic society.

For Gellner, nationalism provides the masses with a new language through which they can express their dismay at their formative economic disadvantages. Kurdish nationalism contains comprehensive political, social, cultural, and economic demands. It has opened the way for people to struggle for different aspects of justice and democracy. These demands have been reflected in the programs and constitutions of the Kurdish political organizations. Gellner describes Kurdish society as a pre-industrial society with the sentiments of a nation; however, evidently, Kurdish nationalism is much stronger than qualifying it just as "sentiments."

Some scholars such as Hobsbawm, Mann, Giddens, Breuilly, and Brass emphasize the importance of the state in creating nationalism. While the states have played fundamental roles in creating nationalism, Kurdish nationalist movements have been mainly developed for the establishment of a Kurdish state. However, the Kurdistan Republic and especially the KRG have greatly affected the development of nationalism.

Kedourie claims that nationalist doctrines were generated by intellectuals who were marginalized from politics due to the effects of rationalism from the Enlightenment. Related to Kurdish nationalism, although some intellectuals may participate in the movement due to their own personal interests, the majority of the Kurdish intellectuals have devotedly taken part in the movement and have played fundamental roles in leading the movement. Indeed, many intellectuals, including the leaders of Kurdish nationalism, such as Ghassemlou and Sharafkandi, have devoted their lives to the Kurdish cause.

Finally, ethno-symbolists like Smith examine the creation of nations from larger historical trends, which take many of their features from the pre-modern ethnic elements. Modern Kurdish nationalism has created a massive body of literature that emphasizes the existing Kurdish nation is deeply rooted in the emergence and changes of the ancient Kurds who had originally lived in tribes, then developed into an ethnic group, and later became a nation. These historical forms of social identities have also been reflected in the Kurdish poems and verses.

Chapter 7: Analyses, Conclusions, Suggestions

It is hoped that this book has succeeded in providing valuable data on the history and politics of the Democratic Party of Iranian Kurdistan (PDKI)—as well as its predecessors and offshoots—within the vast and multiple contexts of nationalism and national liberation movements, history of the Middle East, history of Iran, and history of the Kurdish peoples. *This book provides arguably the most comprehensive account of the subject to this day and in any language:* it has not only relied on enormous research of archival sources, but it has also brought the views, opinions, analyses, and recollections of the leading figures of Iranian Kurdish groups, as well as Kurdish activists and analysts. *This book, however, does not pretend to be a detached and dispassionate scholarly work. While unwaveringly objective in its approach, this book recognizes the fundamental and inalienable rights of the Kurdish people—the largest nation without a state—and, in particular, the right of the Iranian Kurds to self-determination.*

In the final chapter, the acronym PDKI or the party will also be used as a common historical name to refer to the various organizations that were formed from the original KDP in 1945. When it is necessary, each branch of the PDKI will be specifically addressed. This chapter offers analyses, conclusions, and suggestions regarding the Kurdish nationalist movement in Iran as spearheaded by the PDKI. It considers such themes as identity, politics, and organization of the party and attends to the political identity and struggle of the PDKI in Kurdish nationalism, the evaluation of the quality of the PDKI and the KDP regarding democracy, women, education, and proposing some suggestions for initiating fundamental changes in these parties.

But before I proceed, it is important to acknowledge that the Iranian Kurdish nationalist movement, and thereby the PDKI and its offshoots, stand at a historic threshold. As mentioned, the PDKI is the product of very specific historical circumstances, and even more so is the renewed modernization party since 1971 and, in particular, after the 1979 revolution. The Iranian state has proven itself, time and again, unwilling to yield to nationalist movements, let alone grant autonomy to the national minorities within a federal system. The Kurdish society in Iran has also changed dramatically, and with the recent surge in civil society activism, while showing respect for the Kurdish nationalist organizations (in exile across the mountainous borders), the new generations of Kurdish activists have deeply engaged in civil society activism. The key question, therefore, is this: *is there not a mismatch between these nationalist parties (above all, the PDKI) and the current realities and the new generation's views and aspirations within Iranian Kurdistan?* There is no point denying that today's Kurdistan is *not* the Kurdistan of the 1980s in which militant activism of the PDKI and the Komala style seemed practical and useful. If we agree with these two points, then I argue *the only path for the PDKI's survival as a meaningful political organization is its total renewal as a modern nationalist party, well-tuned to the realities, aspirations, and worldviews of the people of Iranian Kurdistan.* This means that today, Iranian Kurdish nationalism must find paths other than the one form which it has arisen—that is, the post-WWII national liberation route.

In light of these observations, let us have a final analytical encounter with the PDKI.

7.1. The Political Identity and Struggle of the PDKI

The previous chapters have shown that the original KDP spearheaded the Kurdish nationalist movement (a) in the context of the Iranian state-building in the early twentieth century—through which the national identity and culture were associated largely with the Persians—thus alienating, to varying degrees, Iran's national minorities, and (b) in the context of post-WWII national liberation movements in Asia and Africa, and in this particular historic junction, with the short-lived support of the Soviet Union. Thus, as regards its identity, the PDKI has unwaveringly been a Kurdish nationalist organization. In its main direction, this party has been a democratic Kurdish nationalist organization and the most influential in leading the Kurdish national movement in Iran. The nationalist essence of the party, since its establishment, has been influenced by socialist ideas. The establishment of a socialist society has been clearly addressed in its program as the final goal of the party. Due to its foundation in the post-WWII era, even the party's organizational structure is modeled after the communist parties and based on the Leninist principle of democratic centralism. Although later the party removed democratic centralism from its constitution, it has still kept its principles. Under the influence of socialist ideas, the party has accepted many values of social justice and democracy, including advocacy for women's rights. And yet, the party recognizes itself as a democratic nationalist and leftist organization, not a socialist one. The long-term goal of the party is to establish a democratic socialist society. The party is a member of the Socialist International, and its goals and policies, in practice, have become closer to social democracy.

This book has shown that the PDKI originates with the state-building process in Iran through which the national minorities were alienated from the centralized government and homogenized national discourse. As such, the party has emerged against the internal colonization of minorities by the (Persianized) Iranian state, thus attaining the quality of a national liberation movement. And yet, except for the brief period of the Kurdistan Republic, the party has never been in a position to launch such a movement. As such, the liberatory aspect of the party has been more or less a subtext of its discourse, while the element of nationalism and fighting for autonomy within the Iranian state has been dictated upon the party by the political realities of undemocratic states in Iran and in the region. Thus, the strategic goal of the party, for a long time, has been obtaining democracy for Iran and autonomy for Iranian Kurdistan. This demand is more complex than meets the eye:

it requires a fundamental shift in the Iranian political structure—that is, a shift toward a democratic-federative Iran.

7.2. Revisiting Armed Struggle

While the PDKI has used different methods of struggle in the past, it has, especially after the Iranian Revolution of 1979, engaged in long-term armed struggle against the Iranian regime. The party leaders and cadres have extensively reflected on the reason for armed struggle (Aliyar, Personal communication, October 22, 2012; Madani, Personal communication, October 14, 2012; Lotf Pouri, Personal communication, October 21, 2012; Rastgar, Personal communication, October 16, 2012; Hassani, Personal communication, October 19, 2012; Wirya, Personal communication, October 22, 2012; Gadani, Personal communication, October 21, 2012; Hassanzadeh, 2012, pp. 273, 301, 485, 489-490). They agree that after 1979, the already-armed Kurdish people and parties rightly defended their democratic rights in the face of a government that only ignored their demands and suppressed them. But their being armed provided the government with a pretext to attack them. If the armed Kurdish groups had not opted for an armed standoff against the government, the Kurds' conflicts with the state would not have resulted in a devastating civil war that has detrimentally affected the relations between the Kurds and the Iranian state to this day. That said, the Iranian regime has been the main factor in the creation, extension, and continuation of civil war in Kurdistan. To date, the Iranian state has not shown the slightest interest in considering, let alone accepting, some of the Kurdish demands. The present government of President Hassan Rouhani does not have the capacity to solve the Kurdish problem either. Only a wise, strong, and stable Iranian government can provide a peaceful and civilized way for initiating reforms that will result in the establishment of a democratic political system in Iran and fulfill the demands of the Kurds.

The Kurdish nationalist struggle in the form of armed struggle in Iran, under the political parties and especially the PDKI, politically and militaristically has failed. Not only did armed struggle not overthrow the government, it has not even pushed the government to negotiate with the Kurds. So, it is important here to enumerate the reasons for the failure of the Kurdish armed movement in Iran. These include (1) The huge difference between the strong financial, social, and military resources of the government and the fragile resources of the Kurdish movement. (2) The lack of strong support throughout Iran for the Kurdish movement, to the extent that even some key Kurdish territories did not actively participate in the movement, and the government was able to mobilize the masses for the suppression of the Kurds. (3) The lack of permanent strong foreign political, financial, and military support for the Kurdish movement. (4) The failure of the Kurdish organizations struggling for Kurdish rights to create a united front. (5) From the former, there arose perpetual internal conflicts, splits, and discords within the Kurdish parties and movement. These clashes diminished the morale and hopes of the Kurdish people in supporting the armed struggle. (6) The regime's severe suppression of the ordinary people, as well as supporters of the Kurdish political parties, has caused fear among the people. In sum, *the subjective and objective conditions for the victory of the Kurdish movement in Iran did not exist*. Seriously misunderstanding these conditions, the Kurdish political organizations proposed and practiced unrealistic, often flatly faulty, strategies and tactics, which mainly concentrated on the armed struggle against the Iranian state. Armed struggle has caused the death of thousands of people in Kurdistan, including members of the Kurdish and non-Kurdish political organizations. Likewise, thousands of the government forces lost their lives in the civil war, and although the exact number of these casualties remains unknown, one estimate holds that since the establishment of the Islamic Republic of Iran, 50,000 Kurds, have been killed (Khalighi, Personal communication, December 1, 2012), of which an estimated 5,000 (Lotf Pouri, Personal communication, October 21, 2012) or 6,000 casualties

(Noorani, 2012, Personal communication) belong to the PDKI and some 3,000 (Saedi, 2010, p. 392) (or in another figure, 2,300 including 102 women [Saedi, 2012, pp. 91, 693-696]) belong to the Komala. Further research is needed to find out the casualties of other groups in Kurdistan.

To these figures, there must be added thousands of Kurds who have been affected by displacement, great psychological trauma, and living in a region with a perpetual and disproportionately heavy military presence. Armed struggle has also left behind a culture of violence in Kurdish society. This book has shown many instances in which violent suppression of one another—resulting in hundreds of casualties—had become the moral syntax of the Kurdish opposition. As this culture of violence and intolerance grew, it also repressed the culture of tolerance, dialogue, and negotiation.

However, a one-sided view of the Kurdish armed struggle is not faithful to the reality of the Kurds in Iran: armed struggle has elevated the nationalist sentiment and morale of the Kurds, having shown that it was possible to resist the government's oppression. It has indeed attracted several generations of youth and women to the nationalist struggle and has brought the Kurdish nationalist movement to the attention of all Iranians and the international scene. Indeed, armed struggle has been a method for a just struggle. However, armed struggle has left the Kurdish nationalist movement between a rock and a hard place. It has transformed the Kurdish movement for autonomy into a zero-sum game with objectives so ambitious the Kurds neither strategically nor practically could have won. In hindsight, the proper struggle of the Kurds after the Iranian Revolution of 1979 should have been political, cultural, and educational. The Kurds should have aimed at creating comprehensive, deep, and widespread democratic, nationalist ideas among the Kurdish people—ideas that would have organized the Kurds and attracted non-Kurdish Iranians to support the Kurdish cause. Such an approach, however, does not mean that the government would have accepted the Kurdish demands or would not have suppressed the movement. But at the very least, this alternative approach would have dramatically diminished the tremendous human and economic damages sustained by the Kurds and other Iranians. In addition, it would have allowed the new generations of Iranian Kurds to come up with new, innovative forms of struggle for the recognition of Kurdish rights in conjunction with the country's long struggles for democratic citizenship.

Since Spring 2016, obviously, in response to the demands of the Kurdish civil society, the PDKI has announced the *Rasan* (Rising or Re-rising) of the party, which strongly emphasizes the Peshmergas' presence within Iranian Kurdistan. However, this new policy is still devoid of a clear theoretical view and strategy. The KDP also seems to follow a similar policy, but its goal is to avoid armed standoff with the Iranian forces as much as possible. Whether this new policy, to be present in Iranian Kurdistan, indicates the party's uncertain move toward self-repatriation in Iranian Kurdistan remains to be seen. If it does, though, this policy is insufficient, unsure, and miles away from the expectations of the Kurdish civil society activists and the potential Kurdish civil society has to offer for an internal push for change.

7.3. Democracy

Offering a pathology of the undemocratic organizational life of the PDKI requires us to look at the symptoms carefully. As a nationalist party, the PDKI has struggled for the democratic rights of the Iranian Kurds. During its long history, the party has made some important democratic achievements best exemplified by the unique experience of the Kurdistan Republic. The party's structure represents, at least in theory, a democratic, modern party. Nevertheless, the party has consistently ignored democratic values, both internally and externally. I have used the concept of "constitutive paradox" to refer to this curious aspect of the party, an aspect that has increasingly embodied Michels' "iron law of oligarchy": the party's oligarchy has been holding fast to power, unyielding to change, unable to transform and update the party, and belligerent towards criticism (ironically, by the party's very own inner circle). These leaders have utilized their unique, superior knowledge of the party's inner workings, their contacts with the regional powers, controlling financial resources of the party, monitoring formal means of communications, and their skillful manipulative politics. The arch example of such an oligarchical leader is Ghassemlou. Compared to other elites within the party, he was highly knowledgeable and exceptionally skillful in manipulating party procedures to achieve his desired outcomes. As previously discussed, after the 3rd Congress (1973), Ghassemlou managed to have the party's program and constitution approved while the CC was in total disarray and the CC members had diverging, even conflicting, ideas (Hassanzadeh, 2012, pp. 165-166). Therefore, as per Michels' theory, the role of the leadership in the PDKI has been crucial not only to the party's achievements but, more importantly, to the party's failures. Yet, there has been a lack of fair criticism toward the party's leaders, and thus, it has been impossible for the party to learn from and correct its mistakes, move forward, and succeed in effectively mobilizing the masses. Anderson (2007) asserts that while the main Kurdish nationalist political organization of the KDP, the PUK, the KDPI [PDKI], and the PKK have made huge sacrifices to maintain the foundations of Kurdish nationalism, they are also somehow responsible for the failure of the effective mobilization of the movement. This is, to some degree, the deficiency of these organizations' leadership. The states in the region have exploited the rivalries among these organizations and have divided and conquered the Kurds (p. 124).

  To maintain authority, to achieve greater power, or to weaken other cadres' powers within a political party requires unlawful activities. The PDKI history shows how these illegitimate and unethical methods of power-grab have been continuously engineered. Some examples include the elimination (even physical) of dissenting members, expelling them from the party, pushing them to leave the party, suspending them for unnecessary periods of time, punishing them severely, changing their geographical positions, and altering their organizational responsibilities. More examples are preventing or limiting them from disseminating their ideas, restricting their intellectual or practical potential, promising them to provide higher positions or opportunities, subjecting them to character assassination, and boycotting and humiliating them. The history of the party is full of evidence of the employment of all of these methods. Certainly, such an atmosphere impedes democracy and robs the members of an opportunity to cultivate democratic, humanist, and revolutionary characters within the party. In contrast, this environment prevents the growth of love, friendship, democratic culture, and the intellectual and practical potential of the members. Contrary to the aforementioned requirements for a democratic movement, a significant portion of the politics in the party has been about acquiring greater power within the party. One of the reasons for the existing long-term stability of the conflict over gaining and maintaining the power positions in the party is the support of the party's body for this phenomenon. Indeed, conflict over power among the general members is as prevalent as it is at the highest levels of the party. *Unfortunately, this is the culture of the party.*

7.3.1. Ghassemlou's leadership. Like any other charismatic and strong leader, Ghassemlou has been praised and criticized by many leaders of the PDKI. Some claim that he did not impose his will on the party and always tried to convince his opponents (Peshnimaz, 2012, p. 267), while others assert that he was against the cult of personality in the party (Hejab, Personal communication, December 6, 2012). Still, others believe that Ghassemlou was not a dictator, and in fact, in many congresses, he accepted defeat (Wirya, Personal communication, October 22, 2012). Others, however, depict a different picture: Ghassemlou wanted everything under his authority (Rastgar, Personal communication, October 16, 2012) and micromanaged the party to the minute detail (Gadani, Personal communication,

October 21, 2012). It is said that Ghassemlou had once reportedly said, "The Politburo utters its words, and the General Secretary does his job"—a statement that reflects his view of the party leadership (Karimi, Personal communication, September 4, 2012). It is said that Ghassemlou was charismatic but failed to deploy his charisma properly; thus, he fell into partisanship and factionalism (Khalighi, Personal communication, December 1, 2012). To these views, one could add his reported lack of tolerance and expulsion of his opponents (Shams, Personal communication, October 18, 2012), which at the time resulted in the physical elimination of his opponents (Hassani, Personal communication, October 19, 2012).

There are lessons to be learned here: (1) Compared to other leaders of the PDKI, Ghassemlou has had the most fundamental role in the modernization of the party and the establishment of theoretical principles of democratic ideas in the party and in Kurdish society. However, in practice, Ghassemlou, more than any other leader of the PDKI, has undermined the democratic principles within and outside the party. (2) Ghassemlou theoretically and powerfully believed in making a strong, unified organization and the most comprehensive front within the Kurdish and Iranian political organizations. Nonetheless, in practice, more than any other leader of the PDKI, Ghassemlou created disunity, conflicts, and wars within his party and with other political organizations. (3) Ghassemlou was, therefore, the leading person in the establishment of democratic principles as well as in ignoring and undermining them. (4) Ghassemlou's mistakes not only negatively affected the party and the movement in his time but their negative legacy has stayed with the party to this day. As a result, sadly, some of the leaders of the party have continued methods of eliminating the opposition within the party as a tradition.

The malignant growth of unresponsive leadership, an unfortunate legacy of Ghassemlou (and before him, Tawfiq), has unfortunately branched out within the party. There are numerous examples of authoritarian conduct by Sharafkandi after he succeeded Ghassemlou (1991) (Khalighi, 2002, pp. 178-179), or Hijri after them (Hassanzadeh, 2012, p. 480) or Khalid Aziz, the leader of the KDP (Ahangari, 2016, June 6).

Clearly, here, Ghassemlou is no longer the name of a man but the designation for a critical, even terminal, condition: we are dealing with the paradoxical situation in which to create a modern, democratic organization to advance the democratic rights of the Iranian Kurds has gone through the creation of an undemocratic, unresponsive, and oligarchic leadership that moves the movement one step forward while simultaneously causing it to fall back two steps.

7.3.2. Criticism and judgment. In offering a pathology of the undemocratic aspects of the Kurdish nationalist parties, it is important to discuss the lack of a culture of criticism, self-reflection, and judgment. In the party, fair and analytical criticisms of the parties' policies and members' activities are rarely found. In the previous chapters, we have seen how the leaders typically responded to the criticism: by apparently quitting their responsibilities (huffing; Kurdish, *ziz boon*; Persian, *qahr kardan*) or by threatening, pressuring, and boycotting their critics. In other words, criticizing the leadership has caused punishment to the extent of suspending or expelling the critics. Sometimes, it has resulted in the split of the party (Kaveh, 2005, p. 236). Smear campaigns against critics have been very common, at times even brutal. Examples of brutality or threats of violence abound (Khizri, 2003, p. 46). According to Khalighi, many criticisms have their roots in bigotry and the culture of tribalism of the backward communities of the Kurdish nation (Khalighi, 2005, pp. 11, 18, 24). More often, though, the purpose of criticizing others has been to ruin their personalities. The non-scientific and unethical method of the writers and members of the party has destroyed and humiliated the personalities of individuals and political organizations and has damaged the prestige of the party.

7.3.3. Monopolizing the movement. An important aspect of undermining democratic principles of the PDKI was its serious attempts to forcibly and violently render subordinate, or even eliminate, other political organizations in Kurdistan. The range of PDKI's anti-democratic actions against other organizations has varied from threats, attacks, beatings, and detaining to assassinating members of other parties, attacking their offices, and disarming and waging war against them. The record of the PDKI's relations with other Kurdish and non-Kurdish organizations is clearly anti-democratic.

Among these conflicts, the most extensive and long-lasting conflict was the war between the PDKI and the Komala, during which hundreds of peshmergas from both sides lost their lives in vain. While both of these organizations were guilty of making this war, the share of the PDKI was greater. We have already seen the details of this bloody conflict, but here it is important to remember that the war was a dark legacy of Ghassemlou, who had insisted that the Komala should have accepted the PDKI as a revolutionary party, which the Komala refused to do due to its Maoist analysis of the Kurdish classes and forces. Only after the death of Ghassemlou and Sharafkandi did the PDKI agree to a ceasefire with the Komala (Hassanzadeh, 2012, p. 404). As some PDKI leaders have already pointed out (Khalighi, 2005, p. 180), these incidents indicated a power grab and the acquisition of authority when the leadership of a *party,* in fact, deemed itself as the leader of the *movement*. Here, we are dealing with a party that does not recognize the *irreducible diversity* of the Kurdish society in Iran, and as such, *it is under the illusion that one party can represent the entire Kurdish society*. The monopolistic policies of the PDKI have not only imposed a setback on the fight for the rights of the Kurds in Iran, but they have also greatly damaged the struggles of the Kurdish people for democracy.

Another reason for the maintenance of such conflict in the party is the unfortunate support of the masses in Kurdish society. Firstly, the lack of democratic political organizations in Iranian Kurdistan leaves no choice for many people but to support the existing parties. Secondly, to the extent that these parties undermine democratic principles internally and externally, in the final judgment of the majority of the Iranian Kurds, they are still much better than the central government that does not even pretend to recognize the rights of the people, a state that has been widely and profoundly suppressing fundamental democratic elements. Thirdly, the culture of rivalry and power-seeking in Kurdish society is dominant not just as a legacy of tribalism but also due to the dominant culture of capitalism, which emphasizes individualism and personal interests in society. The party has not seriously educated its members, supporters, and the Kurdish society about democratic principles and practices.

It seems that due to the historical anti-democratic experiences and especially the experiences of the 4th, 8th, and 13th Congresses, the minds of some of the PDKI leaders and members have been vaccinated against the invasion of democratic viruses!

7.3.4. Roots of anti-democratic ideas and practices. Anti-democratic ideas and practices of the Kurdish political parties have social roots. The factors that have affected the creation and continuation of these anti-democratic tendencies in theory and practice are summarized in this manner. (1) The predominance of Islamic traditions, which contain anti-democratic teachings and behaviors, among Iranian Kurdistan, as well as in Iran and the Middle East. (2) The influence and, since 1979, the domination of Islamic doctrines in the structure of the Iranian state. (3) The domination of patriarchal relations and structures in society that have significantly been fortified by religious teachings. (4) The domination of patriarchal ideas and practices in the Iranian state. (5) The diffusion of patriarchal and anti-democratic ideas and practices through the official education system in Iran, as well as unofficial institutions (e.g., the mosques). The Iranian education system has been anti-democratic, anti-egalitarian, pro-exploitation, racist, patriarchal, sexist, homophobic, and discriminatory. (6) The existence of despotic and dictatorial political systems in Iran. The Kurdish society has never been under democratic rule, except and to a limited degree, during the Kurdistan Republic in 1945-1946. (7) The Iranian government has severely suppressed political opposition for a long time. Due to the lack of democracy and freedom of expression in Iran and Kurdistan, democratic culture has only developed weakly. (8) The capitalist system dominates Iran and Kurdistan. This system encourages a culture of individualism and competition for personal profit. The capitalist ethos has been aided by the traditional, tribal, religious, patriarchal, and anti-democratic culture, especially in Kurdistan. (9) The violent suppression of people by the governments has left very limited space for peaceful political struggle and dialogue between the people and the governments. Therefore, many political organizations in Iran and Kurdistan have chosen violent forms of struggle against the governments. (10) The Kurds in other countries, especially in Iraq and Turkey, have been under violent suppression by their respective governments. Thus, they had chosen armed struggle against these regimes. This form of activity has caused these parties to significantly ignore the democratic principles within their organizations and in their relations with other organizations. In addition, these parties have repeatedly waged wars against each other. For a long period, resolving disagreements by force and violence had become a culture within the Kurdish society. The Iranian political organizations, especially the PDKI, have been affected by the Kurdish parties in Iraq, imitating the latter's violent political culture. (11) Armed struggle has, on the one hand, prevented the appropriate conditions for democratic practice within the Kurdish parties and, on the other hand, reduced women's participation in organized struggle. (12) Another factor in preventing the development of democratic culture within the Kurdish political organization has been the lack of deep understanding of democracy in theory and practice by the Kurdish political organizations and especially by their leaders. The PDKI has never had a systematic and comprehensive plan to educate and train its members regarding the theories and practices of democracy. Instead of focusing on political and social training, the preference of the party has been military education. (13) Although the Kurdish political parties, including the PDKI in general, have had some positive effects on the improvement of democratic ideas and behaviors in Kurdistan, they have also disseminated and practiced religious ideas. A sad example of this is the PDKI's exploiting the religious sentiments of the Kurds in its propaganda against communism and the "immoral" relationships between the men and women in the Komala during its conflict with the latter. Interestingly, the PDKI, for a long time and to this day, has been starting its daily radio programs by reciting verses from the *Quran*.

Unfortunately, it seems that the internalization of anti-democratic values by the party's leading cadres is so deep that although some of them have lived parts of their lives in Western societies and have been familiar with democratic ideas, in practice, they were significantly under the influence of their anti-democratic culture. How can the party resolve this paradoxical situation that keeps an oligarchy in power and deprives the party of proper social, cultural, and political development?

7.4. Women's status

The status of women within the party has become the *measure* for the extent of the party's intended but shaky renewal. Since the establishment of the party in 1945, women have vastly participated and bravely fought for democratic Kurdish nationalist goals and have also been encouraged and trained by the party to partake in a struggle for women's rights and gender equality. Despite these facts, women's status in the party and in the Kurdish movement has not radically improved, and women have only occupied minor positions in leadership. Since the establishment of the J.K., the culture of humiliation of women has been reflected in the organization's publications and has continued in the J.K.'s transformation into the party. Qazi Muhammad has certainly played a crucial role in attracting women to fight for democratic nationalism and women's rights, but he has also made patriarchal remarks like "[I]t is worse for a man to flee his nation than to wear women's trousers" (Qazi, 2012, pp. 281-282).

Compared to the women's participation at all levels in the PKK or the Rojava experience, the lack of women's participation in the Iranian Kurdish movement is visible. According to Fatime Osmani, a member of the PDKI's Democratic Women's Union of Iranian Kurdistan, in the course of the party's history, the women fighters in the party's ranks have been significantly absent. After the Revolution, when the less educated women joined the PDKI, the party helped these women but it has never regarded women as a practical and intellectual force. Therefore, the party has never had specific training/education plans for them, and women have been marginalized. Osmani believes that most men in the party do not believe in women's rights, and the majority of the PDKI women are financially dependent, which impedes women's initiatives and autonomy. Comparing the situation of women in the PDKI to that of the Komala, Osmani claims that the Komala gives women more opportunities in their activities because it is more open-minded. The PDKI women are more conservative and think that they should do the types of activities that men deem fit for them. To solve women's problems, Osmani maintains, there should be plans for challenging women's internalized patriarchal values (Personal communication, October 15, 2012).

Yet there is another challenge: the male leaders of the party take the initiative for the so-called empowerment of PDKI women, thus robbing women of their subjectivity and agency. *But here, I would like this book to echo the (long-silenced) voices of women.* Khadija Mazur, member of the KDP CC, reminisces that at the 8th Congress of the PDKI, Ghassemlou asked her to stand as a CC candidate, and he would teach her everything she needs to know. Mazur turned down this offer as well as the offer to stand as a candidate for an alternate CC member in the 10th Congress. Then, in the 11th Congress, she was chosen alternate CC member, and since the 14th Congress of the KDP, she has been a member of the CC. Mazur's story shows that women do not have enough self-confidence to take greater responsibilities in the party. Mazur states that based on the mechanism of "positive discrimination" in favor of women, 25 percent of the participants in the 14th Congress of the KDP were women, which was a record number in the party's history. In addition, based on the said mechanism, five women were chosen for the leadership. However, Mazur is against this form of "affirmative action" as she believes that women should be educated, prepared, and deserve to accept important responsibilities. Mazur is critical of the women's organization in the KDP, claiming that instead of assigning serious tasks to women, this organization has wasted their time by giving women the responsibility to make tea for others (Personal communication, October 11, 2012).

Kwestan Ftoohi, a CC member of the KDP, emphasizes that the "women's question" is a national issue, and it is not of secondary nature. Echoing the challenges already mentioned by other woman activists of the party, she points out that women are deterred from greater participation due to child rearing and that child care has never been a priority for the party. Furthermore, many girls who have joined the party have been returned to their homes and encouraged to get married. Therefore, Ftoohi states that the party has never believed in women because of the domination of the patriarchal mentality over the leadership that has not left behind deeply religious doctrines. She claims that the institutions of education of the party including the *Ferga* (School or College) of Political and Military, and the Education Commission, should concentrate on teaching equality. The Democratic Women's Union of Kurdistan, Ftoohi argues, is a tool in the hands of the party. This organization has not dared to break the taboos involving reactionary traditions in the community (Personal communication, October 9, 2012).

Sohaila Qadri, an alternate CC member of the KDP, blames the subaltern position of women in the party on the lack of a systematic program for training women. Women, on the other hand, have not tried to educate themselves either. Qadri argues that if men have patriarchal tendencies, they cannot show them because they will feel ashamed (Personal communication, October 21, 2012). Golaleh Sharafkandi, a CC member of the KDP, makes a rather interesting observation: she asserts that the party has not allowed for the recognition of women's values. The party has generally supported women *but has not considered them as activists*. Due to long residence in Iraqi Kurdistan and the growth of political Islam, the views that encourage women's participation have declined. Sharafkandi states that she has fought in order to stabilize the mechanism of "positive discrimination" in favor of women in the KDP. Sharafkandi concludes that the crucial mechanism to educate women is to give posts to them so that they can reveal their potential, find self-confidence, and even compete with men for the post of General Secretary (Personal communication, November 26, 2012). The extent of patriarchy within the Kurdish parties can hardly be exaggerated, according to the writer, human rights political activist, and previous supporter of the PDKI (FFC), Shahla Dabaghi. She points out that after the 1979 Revolution, the PDKI established the Women's Union, but its goal was to serve nationalism, not women (Personal communication, November 25, 2012).

These women activists talk about their lived experiences in the ranks of the party, and they allow us to see clearly the many challenges the women of Kurdistan face. In short, since the establishment of the PDKI, and especially after the Iranian Revolution, the women in the PDKI have increasingly participated in the nationalist struggle led by the party. In general, the party has positively affected the development of women's potential in the party and society. However, some obstacles that have prevented the worthy progress of women in the party include the domination of patriarchal ideas and practices in the organizations and the lack of comprehensive, systematic, and qualitative programs for educating women within the organizations and in society. Other hindrances are the historical weakness of women's educational levels and the lack of collective self-confidence of women in their own practical and intellectual capacities. Consequently, *the women in the party have not flourished intellectually and practically to any significant level commensurate with today's progressive and militant women's world*. For the longest part of the party's history, women have not attended the leadership, and in the present time, their participation in the higher levels of leadership remains rather rare. While the progressive ideas among the party's women are developing and they are increasingly fighting for women's rights even within their organization, the party needs to conduct a fundamental reform to improve the women's status in the party as well as in society. This is a vital part of struggles for justice and democracy. *Tokenistic efforts and "positive discrimination" tend to solidify the oligarchical rules of the old-time party leaders. The "women's question" in Kurdistan, therefore, can only be resolved by the Kurdish women's agency.*

7.5. Education

The idea of Kurdish rights and Kurdish autonomy within a federative Iran, advanced by the PDKI, has begotten democratic values involving the notion of the inalienable rights of a nation. Although the party has been holding many training and educational courses for its members and for the Kurdish people within its territories, its efforts have fallen short in many areas. The party has not been very serious about educating its members, and thus, it has not had a stable, continuous, and specific educational system based on its strategic goals. Training of the cadres in the party has disproportionately focused on military training, and education has not appropriately concentrated on women's education to empower them and end patriarchal ideas and practices within the party. Its existing training programs are not scientific, progressive, and research-based. The PDKI has not cultivated a culture of learning, seeking knowledge, and keeping up-to-date with the world of activism, not even among the party elite. As such, the party has completely neglected creating and promoting intellectual pursuits such as producing theoreticians, party archivists to preserve its historical documents, and critical thinkers and creative and independently minded members. The ruling oligarchy within the party, time and again, has created only obedient subjects through internal politics based on carrots and sticks.

The very fact that the party has not been able to metamorphose into a party in sync with our age—a transformation that the PKK and the Rojava experience have proven to be possible—is very telling: we can observe that the lack of proper progress within the party is due to its lack of attention to education. The party will not succeed without fundamentally revisiting this crucial issue. In the end, it should be emphasized that deep critical research is needed about the PKK and the Rojava, and this comparison between these parties is not an approval of all policies of the PKK or Rojava.

7.6. General Conclusions and Suggestions for Fundamental Changes

Kurdish nationalism in Iran, since 1945, was led by the KDP, later the PDKI, and its many offshoots (through splits and reunifications), among which the most important has been the KDP that emerged through the 2006 split.

The key conclusion of this book is that while the PDKI has, for many years, been the main party in keeping the idea of Kurdish rights within the public discourse and leading the Kurdish democratic and nationalist movement in Iranian Kurdistan, it has also been the (leading) party that has, time and again, undermined democratic principles and values both inside and outside itself. As a result, both the PDKI and the KDP need to introduce fundamental reforms in order to democratize their ideas, practices, and organizations. Without such fundamental changes, I argue, the party will soon lose its relevance, as the younger generation within Kurdish society in Iran has now engaged in the forms of struggles—above all civil society activism—other than those of the party, which is rooted in the post-WWII age of national liberation.

In the case of the PDKI, we have seen the curious emergence of a simultaneously suppressive and democratic political organization and social movements. Based on this observation, we are dealing with an influential and leading national-liberation political organization, one that has been fighting to assert and institutionalize the inalienable rights of the Kurdish nation in Iran to self-determination, democracy, and social justice. But this organization has, in practice, widely undermined the democratic values and aspirations at the heart of its struggle, and as such, it has damaged the wider democratic social movement to which it belongs. The concepts of "constitutive paradox" and the "iron law of oligarchy" have paved the way for theorizing this "suppressive and democratic" aspect of Kurdish nationalism in Iran.

Due to the complexities of the Middle East region, where the Kurdish nation has been split between four undemocratic states, Kurdish liberation in Greater Kurdistan has taken multiple routes. The Kurdish movements in each of the four countries (Iran, Iraq, Turkey, and Syria) have historically tried to enter into some kind of arrangement with their states. In Iran, this is found in the PDKI's strategic slogan of an autonomous Kurdistan within a federative Iran. That said, this book recognizes the rights of the Kurds to have their own state. As such, while struggling for autonomy within a federative system, the Kurdish movements need to concentrate on the creation of a Kurdish state. This will have to be the PDKI's strategic goal—an objective to be pursued along with the pulse of the Kurdish movement in the region and the geopolitical developments in the four states where the Kurds live.

Therefore, the formation of a comprehensive front comprised of all Kurdish political parties, organizations, and intellectuals seems like a strategic plan. But in the meantime, it is important for the Kurds in Iran to create an alliance with the progressive Iranian political forces. These two orientations are not mutually exclusive. That said, realistically, the proper intellectual conditions for the formation of such fronts in Iran or in the region do not exist. This rather somber statement, alas, is supported by the conflicted history of the PDKI, which was at the heart of this book. At the present time, the PDKI and the KDP have not resolved the major disagreements (since their split), and even if they reunite, the united party will most likely confront a huge discord within the organization. Consequently, the very likely possibility of future splits remains. Thus, the most logical move would be the respectful cooperation of these parties for the creation of a democratic front including other Kurdish organizations.

A general comparison between the PDKI and the KDP shows that, in regard to their programs, constitutions, final goals, and political strategies, these parties are similar. With respect to political tactics, while still their major political strategies and tactics focus on peaceful and civil forms of struggle, the PDKI, especially since the spring of 2016, has shown inclinations toward using armed operations in Iranian Kurdistan. Although it does not reject armed action in principle, the KDP has primarily focused on peaceful political struggle and civil movement activities. In the organizational field, the PDKI and the KDP are also similar (see Appendix 30). The KDP is more open than the PDKI to moving toward, accepting, and practicing democratic reforms within their organization; its leadership is more educated and consists of greater numbers of women (see Table 3).

In regard to the relationship of the PDKI with other Kurdish organizations, the party should critically analyze its previously damaging conflicts with them, including the Komala. The party and the Komala should provide and make public a profound analysis of the roots, continuation, and results of the armed conflicts and officially apologize to the Kurdish people. Besides, while the PDKI in the past has extensively suppressed other political parties, the party needs to officially criticize its anti-democratic practices and apologize to these parties.

Looking to the future, the most appropriate and realistic form of struggle for the Kurdish political activists and organizations is peaceful, oppositional political struggle along with other democratic forces in Iran. Thus, the perception of the style of struggle should be transferred from military to peaceful and civic. Armed struggle and militant activities need to be discarded, while the military training of the peshmergas within the party should be reduced to the level of protecting the security of the party members housed within Iraqi Kurdistan. Since ancient times, the Kurds have proved that they are courageous in defending their existence. *Today, more than ever, the Kurds need peshmergas and guerrillas of wisdom, knowledge, and science.*

This turn requires organizational changes. The necessity for extensive reforms in these parties is so dire that there are projections that if these parties do not seriously consider a grave overhaul, they will have no admirable future. Any party that thinks it can save itself through charismatic leadership has signed its death warrant (Ahangari, 2016, March 29). Each of the PDKI and the KDP needs to create a Reform Committee. This can be a significant step in democratizing the Kurdish militant organizations. The Committee's task is to gather, analyze, and propose to the CC the ideas about the reforms that need to be done in the party. The key areas of reform include the following. (1) The total reconstruction of the leadership of the Kurdish political parties is an urgent duty. An entirely new leadership consisting of highly educated and modern-minded members of the party with extensive knowledge of the social sciences, especially on political and sociological subjects, is needed. The leadership should create a strong and extensive core of highly educated people as consultants in various areas of knowledge required for the thriving of the party. (2) The PDKI and the KDP should strongly focus on the improvement of women's status within the party and provide greater opportunities, compared to the general education in the party, for women's education. These parties should open the way for bringing younger generations, including women, to all levels of leadership. A quota system can be used based on which about 50 percent of the CC and about 50 percent of the Politburo need to be under the age of 40, and 50 percent or more women need to be in the Politburo and the CC of the party. Also, the general secretary's position must be limited to two terms, and when the general secretary is a man, his alternate should be a woman, and vice versa. The most important step for these parties is to provide extensive, continuous courses of the highest quality to improve the education of women at all levels of the organization in order to cultivate the intellectual and practical potential of women. The parties need to encourage women to take responsibility and attract to the leadership the educated women who affiliate with or are close to these parties and live in Europe or other Western countries. Lastly, the parties' women also need to bravely step forward, educate themselves, and take responsibility. (3) These parties need to found the Council of the Previous Leaders of the party whose members are still the members of the party. This Council chooses two representatives to attend the CC's meetings in which they are eligible to cast two votes. In addition, in any case, one of the representatives should be a woman. (4) The educational system of these parties should be built on a democratic education system based on critical, dialogical, and revolutionary methods. This system relies on comprehensive necessary teachings for all members, uses scientific methods for research in the social sciences, cooperates with and engages in dialogue with the public, including experts outside the party and aims to make fundamental reforms to democratize the party. While the PDKI and the KDP's final goals remain the creation of a democratic socialist society, they have the potential to move toward the employment of revolutionary critical pedagogy. This pedagogy presents an alternative education system for these parties "by creating a democratic, multicultural curriculum in order to bring social justice into educational environments" (Jahani Asl, 2007, p. 115). This system emphasizes the "philosophy of the education system, ethnicity, culture, gender, sexuality, class, and content and methods of teaching" (Jahani Asl, 2007, p. 117). The final goal of the revolutionary critical pedagogy is to create a socialist society based on equality and justice and end all types of oppression, discrimination, and exploitation. (5) The political and social analyses proposed by these parties should be based on scientific methods of research. Besides, education needs resources. Each of the PDKI and the KDP needs to create a modern system to store a publicly accessible party archive. While the culture of studying and researching in these parties is very weak, they need plans to resolve this problem.

The key question is this: *do these parties have the potential to create such radical reforms?* The will for this kind of fundamental change is rather frail, but the potential and the will in the body of these parties, especially among the youth, women, and the more educated members, are stronger. This potential can be enhanced in the following ways. These parties can cooperate with the pro-reform members of the party in Kurdistan and in Western countries. It can also cooperate with non-party educated people, including the academics and intellectuals of the Iraqi Kurdistan. In addition, these parties can approach highly educated volunteers or paid professionals to teach all, especially the CC members of the party, in different areas. Moreover, these parties can create productive relations with the Western states, their political parties, community organizations, and intellectuals in order to theoretically and practically learn the principles of democracy. The age and the conditions for making the PDKI and the KDP relevant to the present realities of the Kurdistan of Iran are present. The question is, are these parties ready? Only time can tell.

Bibliography

Abdul Karim Hawezi, B. (2001). *Gashtek ba Komari Mahabad da: Birawariyakanim la Rojhalati Kurdistan (1944-1947)* [*A journey over the Mahabad Republic: my memoirs about the Easter Kurdistan (1944-1947)* (2nd ed.).]. Erbil: Aras Publishers.

Abdullah, T. A. J. (2011). *A short history of Iraq* (2nd ed.). Harlow, England: Pearson.

Abdullahi, K. (2008). *Sebari Azadi: Hawraz u Nshewakani Mejoy Khabati Komalay Je. Kaf (J.K.) 1321-1324* [*Shadow of freedom: Ups and downs of history of J.K.'s social struggle 1942-1945*]. Sulaymaniyah: Shvan Press.

Abdullahzadeh, L. (2011). *Awir Denawayak la Mejooy Yaketi Lawani Demokrati Kurdistani Eran* [*Looking Back at the History of the Democratic Youth Union of Iranian Kurdistan*]. n.p.: *Democratic Youth Union of Iranian Kurdistan* Publication.

Abrahamian, E. (1982). *Iran between two revolutions*. Princeton: Princeton University Press.

Abrahamian, E. (2008). *A history of modern Iran*. Cambridge: Cambridge University Press.

Afkhami, I. (1989). *Qiam-e Mulla Khalil w radde farman-e Reza Shah* [*The Revolt of Mullah Khali and resuming of Reza Shah's order*]. Tabriz: Hadi Press.

Agahi, A. H. (2006). Tarikh-e ahzab-e Iran [History of parties of Iran]. Retrieved January 27, 2006, from http://www.rahetudeh.com

Ahangari. K. (2016, March 29). Kawe Ahangari: Har chashna khabateki tak rahandi la Rojhalati Kurdistan Shkist ahenet [Kawe Ahangari: Any one-dimension struggle in the Eastern Kurdistan will fail]. Retrieved from http://www.dengiamerika.com/content/iran-kurdish-party/3221194.html

Ahangari. K. (2016, June 6). Ragayandin sabarat ba dastpekrdni tekoshanm la Hizbi Demokrati Kurdistani Eran da [Announcement regarding starting my activity in the Democratic Party of Iranian Kurdistan]. Retrieved from http://peshmergekan.com/kurdish/index.php?option=com_content&view=article&id=6996:2016-06-06-21-08-14&catid=34:babetekan&Itemid=34

Ahmadzadeh, H., and Stansfield, G. (2010). The political, cultural, and military re-awakening of the Kurdish nationalist movement in Iran, *Middle East Journal*, 64(1), 11-27. Doi: 10.3751.64.1.11

Albom-e Janbakhtegan [Album of Devotees]. (2016, March 31). Retrieved from http://www.yadihawrean.com/index.php

Al-Hakkari, J. (1922, July 23). *Kurd*, pp. 2-3. Retrieved from http://ruwange.blogspot.ca/2014_05_01_archive.html

Al-Hakari, J. (1922, between June 8 and July 23). *Kurd*, pp. 3-4. Courtesy of Hassan Ghazi.

Ali Mahmood Shekhani, H. (2007). *Abdul Rahman Ghassemlou: Jian u roli siasi la bizoutnavay rizgarikhowazi Kurd da (1930-1989): Towejinawayaki mejouyy siasiya* [*Abdul Rahman Ghassemlou: His life and political role in the Kurdish liberation movement (1930-1989): A political historical Study*]. Erbil: Shahab Press.

Aliyar, M. (2012, October 22). Personal communication.

Alizadeh E. (2012, September 13). Personal communication.

Amnesty International. (1998). Amnesty International Report. United Kingdom: Amnesty International Publication.

Amnesty International. (2000). Amnesty International Report. United Kingdom: Amnesty International Publication.

Amnesty International. (2001). Amnesty International Report. United Kingdom: Amnesty International Publication.

Amnesty International. (2002). Amnesty International Report. United Kingdom: Amnesty International Publication.

Anderson, B. (2006). *Imagined communities: Reflections on the origin and spread of nationalism*. London: UK Verso.

Anderson, L. (2007). The role of political parties in developing Kurdish nationalism. In M. M. A. Ahmed, and M. M. Gunter (Eds.), *The evolution of Kurdish Nationalism* (pp. 123-148). Costa Mesa: California: Mazda Publications, Inc.

Arfa, H. (1966). The Kurds: An historical and political study. London: Oxford University Press.

Askandari, A. (2015, March 3). Qatgnameh-ye 8 Madehey-ye Mahabad, Qiadeh-ye Mowaqat, wa Kurdistan-e Iran: 30 Bahman 1357(Madabad's 8-Article Demand, Provisional Leadership, and Iranian Kurdistan: 19 February 1979). Retrieved from http://asre-nou.net/php/view.php?objnr=33905

Awraz, A. (2012, September 20). Personal communication.

Axworthy, M. (2008). *A history of Iran: Empire of the mind*. New York: Basic books.

Ayoubzadeh, A. (2002). Chap la Rojhalati Kurdistan: Komala w dozi nasionali kurd [Left in Eastern Kurdistan: Komala and the Issue of Kurdish nationalism (Vol. 1).]. n.p.: Nima Verlang.

Azad, H. (2003). *Posht-e pardeh- haye haramsara* [*Behind the harems' curtains*] (9th ed.). Oromiyeh: Anzali.

Bahar, M. (1978). *Tarikh-e mokhtasar-e ahzab-e siasi-ye Iran* [*Brief history of political parties in Iran*] (Vol. 1) (2nd ed.). Tehran: Sepehr Publication.

Bakhchi. H. (2007). *Lekdabiran: Pedachonawayak ba sar choneti pek hatini Perawani Kongray Chowari Hizbi Demokrati Kurdistani Eran* [*Split: A review of the manner of establishment of the Followers of the Fourth Congress of the Democratic Party of Iranian Kurdistan*].

Balaki, O. (2012, September 28). Personal communication.

Barzani, M. (2004a). *Masoud Barzani w bzoutnaway rzgarikhowazi Kurd* [*Masoud Barzani and the Kurdish liberation movement* (Part III, Vol. 1).]. Erbil: Education Ministry's Print house.

Barzani, M. (2004b). *Masoud Barzani w bzoutnaway rzgarikhowazi Kurd* [*Masoud Barzani and the Kurdish liberation movement* (Part III, Vol. 2).]. Erbil: Education Ministry's Print House.

Bashiriyeh, H. (2001). *Mavane'e Tosa'ehye siasi dar Iran* [*Obstacles to political development in Iran*] (2nd ed.). Tehran: Gam-e No.

Bayat, K. (2003). Reza Shah and the tribes: An overview. In S. Cronin (ed.), *The making of modern Iran: State and society under Reza Shah, 1921-1941*. London: Routledge.

Benderly, J. (1997). Rape, feminism, and nationalism in the war in Yugoslav successor states. In L. A. West (Ed.), *Feminist nationalism* (pp.201-219). New York: Routledge.

Bidlici, M. S. (2013). *Sharaf-Nāme: Mezhooy mala mirani Kurdistan* [*Sharaf-nāme: The history of Kurdish dynasties*] (6th ed.). (Hajhar, Trans). Tehran: Payyz Publication.

Bishku, M. B. (2007). The resurgence of Kurdish nationalism in northern-Kurdistan-Turkey from the 1970s to the present. In M. M. A. Ahmed, and M. M. Gunter (Eds.), *The evolution of Kurdish Nationalism* (pp. 78-97). Costa Mesa: California: Mazda Publications, Inc.

Bitlîsiî, P. S. (2005). *The sharafnāma, or, The history of the Kurdish nation* (Vol. 1). (M. R. Izady, Trans.). Costa Mesa, California: Mazda Publishers, Inc.

Blau, J. (2000). Masaleh-ye Kord: Barresi-ye tarikhi wa jame'eh shenasi [Le problème Kurde: Essai sociologique et historique]. (P. Amin, Trans.). Sanandaj: Kurdistan University Publication. (Original work published 1963)

Bois, T. (1966). *The Kurds* (M. W. M. Welland, Trans.). Beirut, Lebanon: Khayats.

Bolourian, G. (1997). *Alehkok: Basarhatakani siasi jianim* [*Salsify: My political adventures*]. Stockholm: Författares Bokmaskin.

Borzooyy, M. (2005). *Bar wa dokhi siasi Kurdistan (1880-1946)* [*The political situation of Kurdistan (1880-1946)*] (N. M. Abdulghadir, Y. K. Choopan, and S. Alipour, Trans.). Hawler, Kurdistan: Ministry of Education Publications.

Bourrie, M. (2016). *The killing game: Martyrdom, murder and the lure of ISIS*. Patrick Crean Editions.

Bowring, B. (1996). The Kurds of Turkey: Defending the Rights of Minority. In K. E. Schulze, M.
Stokes and C. Campbell (Eds.), Nationalism, minorities and diasporas identities and rights in the
Middle East (pp. 23-35). New York: Tauris Academic Studies.

Bozarslan, H. (2007). Kurdish nationalism under the Kemalist Republic: Some hypotheses. In M. M. A. Ahmed, and M. M. Gunter (Eds.), *The evolution of Kurdish Nationalism* (pp. 36-51). Costa Mesa: California: Mazda Publications, Inc.

Bruinessen, M. V. (1994). Genocide of Kurds. In I. W. Charny (Ed.), *The widening circle of Genocide: Genocide: A critical bibliographic review* (Vol. 3, pp. 165-191). New Brunswick, NY: Transaction Publishers.

Bruinessen, M. V. (1999). Kurds, genocide of. In I. W. Charny (Ed.), *Encyclopaedia of Genocide* (Vol. 2, pp. 383-385). Santa Barbara, California: ABC.CLIO, Inc.

Bruinessen, M. V. (2006a). A Kurdish warlord on the Turkish-Persian frontier in the early twentieth century: Isma'il Agha Simko. Retrieved from http://www.hum.uu.nl/medewerkers/m.vanbruinessen/publications/Bruinessen_Simko.pdf

Chinchilla, N. S. (1997). Nationalism, feminism, and revolution in Central America. In L. A. West (Ed.), *Feminist nationalism* (pp.201-219). New York: Routledge.

Chomsky, N. (2002). *Alpaslan Işıklı - Noam Chomsky e-mail discussions*. Retrieved from http://www.universite-toplum.org/text.php3?id=61

Connor, W. (1994a). A nation is a nation, is a state, is an ethnic group, is a.... In J. Hutchinson, and A. D. Smith (Eds.), *Nationalism* (pp. 36-46). Oxford: Oxford University Press.

Connor, W. (1994b). *Ethnonationalism: The quest for understanding*. Princeton, New Jersey: Princeton University Press.

Conversi, D. (2006). Genocide, ethnic cleansing and nationalism. In G. Delanty, and K. Krishna (Eds.), *The SAGE handbook of nations and nationalism* (pp. 320-333). London: SAGE.

Congress of Nationalities for a Federal Iran (CNFI). (n.d.). Asasnameh-ye Kongreh-ye Melliyatha-ye Iran-e Federal [Constitution of the Congress of Nationalities for a Federal Iran]. Retrieved from http://iran-federal.org/1274-2/

Cronin, S. (2003). Reza Shah and the disintegration of Bakhtiyari power in Iran, 1921-1934. In S. Cronin (Ed.), *The making of modern Iran: State and society under Reza Shah, 1921-1941*. London: Routledge.

Creswell, J. W. (1998). *Qualitative inquiry and research design: Choosing among five traditions*. Thousand Oaks: SAGE Publication.

Dabaghi, S. (2012, November 25). Personal communication.

Dailami, P. (1920). The Bolsheviks and the Jangali revolutionary movement, 1915-1920. *Cahiers du monde russe etsoviétique*, 31(1), 43-59. doi: 10.3406/cmr.1990.2201

Daniel, E. L. (2001). *The History of Iran*. Westport: Greenwood Press.

Darwish, A., and Alexander, G. (1991). *Unholy Babylon: The secret history of Saddam's war*. London: Victor Gollancz LTD.

Davis, H. B. (1978). *Toward a Marxist theory of nationalism*. New York: Monthly Review Press.

Dehqan, Ali (1969). *Sarzamin-e Zardosht: Owza'-e Tabi'I, siasi, eqtesadi, farhangi, ejtema'i, tarikhi-ye Rezaeiyeh* [*Zoroaster's land: Political, economic, cultural, social, and historical conditions Rezaeiyeh*]. Rezaeiyeh: Ibn-e Sina Publications.

Democratic Party of Iranian Kurdistan. (2000). Democratic Party of Iranian Kurdistan: Program and Internal Regulations Adopted in the XIIth Congress (24-26 November 2000). Retrieved from http://www.pdk-iran.org/english/doc/program_html.htm

Democratic Party of Iranian Kurdistan. (2004). Democratic Party of Iranian Kurdistan: Program and Internal Regulations adopted in the XIIIth Congress (3-7 July 2004). Retrieved from http://www.pdk-iran.org/english/doc/Program%20and%20Internal%20Regulations%2013th%20congress.htm

Democratic Party of Iranian Kurdistan. (2008). Balganamakani Kongray Chowardahami Hizbi Demokrati Kurdistani Eran: Kongray gasha kirdin u ba jamawaritir kirdni khabat (20 ta 24y Kharmanani 1387 hatawi, 10 ta 14 y Septambri 2008y zayyni) [The documents of the 14th Congress of the Democratic Party of Iranian Kurdistan: The congress of flourishing and more popularizing of struggle (10-12 September 2008]. n.p.: Democratic Party of Iranian Kurdistan's Publication Commission.

Democratic Party of Iranian Kurdistan (2012). Etelaiyeh-ye daftar-e siasi-ye Hezb-e Demokrat-e Kurdistan-e Iran [Declaration of the Politburo of the Democratic Party of Iranian Kurdistan]. Retrieved from http://www.kurdistanmedia.com/farsi/idame/1479

Eagleton, W. (1963). *The Republic of Kurdistan of 1946*. London: Oxford University Press.

Entessar, N. (1992). *Kurdish ethnonationalism*. Boulder and London: Lynne Rienner Publishers.

Entessar, N. (2010). Kurdish politics in the Middle East. Lanham, Md: Lexington Books.

Esim, S. (1999). NATO's ethnic cleansing: The Kurdish question in Turkey. *Monthly Review: An Independent Socialist Magazine*. 51 (2), 20-28. doi: http://dx.doi.org/10.14452/MR-051-02-1999-06_4

Eskandari, M. R. (2015, May 31). Mobarehzeh-ye ahzab-e Sharq-e Kurdistan ba che manteq wa poshtewaneh-ey? [The struggle of the Eastern Kurdistan' parties by which logic and support?]. *Giareng*. Retrieved from http://www.giareng.com/giarengs-map/farsi/1461.html

Ezat, M. M. (1995). *Dawlati Jimhuri Kurdistan: Nama w dokument* [*The Republic of Kurdistan: Correspondence and documents* (Vol. 2).]. Stockholm: APEC.

Fakhrai, I. (1978). *Sardar-e jangal: Mirza Kuchek Khan* [The forest commander: Mirza Kuchek Khan] (8th ed.). Tehran: Javidan Printing Institution and Publication.

Fanon, F. (1994). *Toward the African Revolution* (H. Chevalier, Trans). New York: Grove Press.

Fanon, F. (2004). *The Wretched of the Earth* (R. Philcox, Trans). New York: Grove Press.

Fatah, R. (2006). The accepted genocide of Kurds in Turkey. Retrieved from http://www.kurdmedia.com/article.aspx?id=13491

Ftoohi, K. (2012, October 9). Personal communication.

Gadani, J. (2001). *Ba nabeta droy pash mirdou* [*Lets to not become the lie of after the dead* (2nd ed.).]. Paris: n.p.

Gadani, J. (2008a). *50 Sal khabat: Korta mejouyaki Hizbi Demokrati Kordistani Eran [50 Years Struggle: A brief history of the Democratic Party of Iranian Kurdistan* (2nd ed., Vol. 1).]. Duhok: Khani Press.

Gadani, J. (2008b). *50 Sal khabat: Korta mejouyaki Hizbi Demokrati Kordistani Eran [50 Years Struggle: A brief history of the Democratic Party of Iranian Kurdistan* (3rd ed., Vol. 2).] Duhok: Khani Press.

Gadani, J. (2012, October 21). Personal communication.

Gadani, J. (2015 April 30). Wilamek ba "Nsko w Dabran" (A respond to "*Decline and Division*"). Retrieved from https://goo.gl/Di0tSF

Gall, M. D., Gall, J. P., and Borg, W. R. (2003). *Educational Research: An introduction* (7th ed.). Boston: Allyn and Bacon.

Garcia, A. M. (1997). The development of Chicana feminist discourse. In L. A. West (Ed.), *Feminist nationalism* (pp. 247-268). New York: Routledge.

Gellner, E. (1983). *Nations and nationalism*. Ithaca, NY: Cornell University Press.

Gellner, E. (1997). *Nationalism*. London: Weidenfeld and Nicolson.

Ghani, C. (2000). *Iran and the rise of Reza Shah: From Qajar collapse to Pahlavi rule*. London: I.B. Taurts Publishers.

Ghassemlou, A. R. (1965). *Kurdistan and the Kurds*. Prague: Publishing House of the Czechoslovak Academy of Sciences.

Ghassemlou, A. R. (2000). *Chil sal khabat la penavi azadi: Kortayak la mezhooy Hezbi Demokrati Kordstani Eran [Forty years combat for liberty: A brief history of the Democratic Party of Iranian Kurdistan]*. np: Democratic Party of Iranian Kurdistan Publication.

Ghassemlou, A. R. (2003). *Kurta Bas [Brief discussion]*. Sweden: Ketab-I Arzan Press.

Ghazi, H. (2014). Kew u shakh u dashti khoshin bo dilim: Augusta Gudhart, dosti gawray gali Kurd [Its mountain and desert make my heart happy: Augusta Gudhart, Kurdish nation's great friend]. Retrieved from http://ruwange.blogspot.be/2009/03/blog-post_14.html

Gheissari, A., and Nasr, V (2006). Democracy in Iran: History and the quest for liberty. Oxford: Oxford University Press.

Giwargis, A. (2004). The Patriarch Mar Binyamin Shimmun A Martyr of the Assyrian Nation and the Church of the East. *Zinda Magazine*, 10(3). Retrieved from http://www.zindamagazine.com/html/archives/2004/3.15.04/

Girami, A. (2013). Komari Kurdistan u khowendnaway amro [Kurdistan Republic and today's reading.]. *Govari Wilat* (*Magazine Wilat*), 1, 4-7. Retrieved from https://issuu.com/welat/docs/wilat_1

Gohari, H. (1999). *Komalay Ziznaway Kurdistan* (*The Society for the Revival of Kurdistan*). Stockholm: Rabun.

Gohari, H. (2002). *Rastiyakan bokhoyan dadwen* [*The truths talk themselves*]. Stockholm: Sverge.

Grosby, S. (2001). Primordiality. In A. S. Leoussi (Ed.), *Encyclopedia of nationalism* (pp. 252-255). New Brunswick (USA): Transaction Publishers.

Guibernau, M. (1996). *Nationalism: The nation-state and nationalism in the twentieth Century*. Cambridge: Polity Press.

Guibernau, M. (1999). *Nations without states: Political communities in a global age*. Cambridge, UK: Polity Press.

Guibernau, M. (2010). Catalonia: Nationalism and intellectuals in nations without states. In M. Guibernau and J. Rex. (Eds.), *The ethnicity reader: Nationalism, Multiculturalism and migration* (2nd ed.) (pp. 138- 154). Polity Press.

Gunter, M. M. (1990). *The Kurds in Turkey: A political dilemma*. Boulder: Westview Press.

Gunter, M. M. (1999). *The Kurdish predicament in Iraq: A political analysis*. New York: St. Martin's Press.

Gunter, M. M. (2009). *The A to Z of the Kurds*. Lanham, Toronto, and Plymouth, UK: The Scarecrow Press, Inc.

Gunter, M. M. (2013). The contemporary roots of Kurdish nationalism in Iraq. Kufa Review, 2 (1), 29-48. Retrieved from http://www.uokufa.edu.iq/journals/index.php/Kufa_Review/article/viewFile/26/pdf_19

Hassani, A. (2012, October 19). Personal communication.

Hassanpour, A. (1994). The Kurdish experience. *Middle East Report*. No.189 (189), 2-23.

Hassanpour. A. (2001). The (Re) production of patriarchy in the Kurdish language. In S. Mojab (Ed.), In S. Mojab (Ed.), *Women of a non-state nation: The Kurds* (pp. 227-263). California: Mazda Publishers, Inc.

Hassanpour, A. (2003). The making of Kurdish identity: Pre-20th century historical and literary sources. In A. Vali (Ed.), Essays on the origins of Kurdish nationalism (pp. 106-162). California, Costa Mesa: Mazda Publishers, Inc.

Hassanpour, A. (2007). Ferment and Fetters in the Study of Kurdish Nationalism [Review of the book *Kurdish notables and the Ottoman state: Evolving identities, competing loyalties, and shifting boundaries*, by H. Ozoglu]. *H-Turk, H-Net Reviews*. Retrieved from http://www.h-net.org/reviews/shorew.php?id=13540

Hassanpour, A., and Mojab, S. (2005). Kurdish Diaspora. In M. Ember, C. R. Ember, and I. Skoggard (Eds.) Encyclopaedia of Diasporas Immigrant and Refugee Cultures Around the World (pp. 214-224). Retrieved from http://download.springer.com.proxy.lib.sfu.ca/static/pdf/38/chp%253A10.1007%252F978-0-387-29904-4_21.pdf?auth66=1414704613_896d543a05ef8d11f27f275726446e84&ext=.pdf

Hassanzadeh, A. (1996). *Niw sada tekoshan: Awrek la rabirdouy khabat u tekoshani Hizbi Demokrati Kudistani Eran [Half a century struggle: A look at the struggle and activity of the Democratic Party of Iranian Kurdistan* (Vol. 2).]. n.p.: Democratic Party of Iranian Kurdistan Publication.

Hassanzadeh, A. (2012). *Azmouni khabat: Awrek la jian u khabati Abdullah Hassanzadeh (Vitouweji Hayas Kardo)* [*Strugle's experience: A look at the life and struggle of Abdullah Hassanzadeh (Hayas Kardo's interview)* (2nd ed.).]. Sweden: Ketab-I Arzan Press.

Hassanzadeh, A. (2012, August, 6). Personal communication.

Hassanzadeh, A. (2015) *Roun krdnawa, yan halbastni mejou?!: Khowendnawayak bo ktebi "Nsko w Dabran"* [*Clarification, or making history?!: A reading of the book Decline and Division*]. Retrieved from http://peshmergekan.com/kurdish/index.php?option=com_content&view=article&id=5814:2015-04-29-19-44-29&catid=28:jwebunawe&Itemid=59

Hassanzadeh, A. (n.d.). *Niw sada tekoshan: Awrek la rabirdouy khabat u tekoshani Hizbi Demokrati Kudistani Eran* [*Half a century struggle: A look at the struggle and activity of the Democratic Party of Iranian Kurdistan* (Vol. 1).]. Retrieved from http://www.kurdistanukurd.com/?page_id=60&paged=3

Hatami, H. (2017, May 6). Personal communication.

Hatefi, R. (2001). *Enghelab-e natamam: Zamineh-hay-e siasi va eghtesadiy-e Enghelab-e Mashrooteh-ye Iran* [*The unfinished revolution: The political and economic backgrounds of the Constitutional Revolution of Iran*]. np: Publication of Tudeh Party of Iran.

Hawar, M. R. (1996). *Simko (Esma'il Axayi Shukak) u Bizutnewey Netewayetiy Kurd* [*Simko and Kurdish national movement*]. Stockholm: APEC Publishing.

Hawrami, A. (2006). *Kurd la arshivi Rusia w Soviet da* [*Kurd in the archive of Russia and Soviet*]. Hawler: Mukiryani Establishment for Research and Publication.

Hawrami, A. (2007). *Roodawakani Rojhalati Kurdistan labalga namay Sovieti da 1945-1947* [*The Eastern Kurdistan's events in the Soviet document[s] 1945 1947*]. Sulaymaniyah: Shvan Press.

Hawrami, A. (2008). *Rojhalati Kurdistan la sardami Dowam Jangi Jahani da: (Ba pey labalga namakani arshivi Yaketi Soviet* [*Eastern Kurdistan during the Second World War: (According to the documents of Soviet Union archives)*]. Sulaymaniyah: Shvan Press.

Hejab, A. (2012, December 6). Personal communication.

Hezb-e Demokrat-e Kurdistan-e Iran [wa] Hezb-e Komaleh-ye, Kurdistan-e Iran [Democratic Party of Iranian Kurdistan, and Komala Party of Iran.]. (2012). *Tawafoqnameh-ye Moshtarak-e Hezb-e Demokrat-e Kurdistan-e Iran wa Hezb-e Komaleh-ye Kurdistan-e Iran* [The Shared Agreement between the Democratic

Party of Iranian Kurdistan and the Komala Party of Iran]. Retrieved from http://www.kurdistanmedia.com/farsi/idame/2462

Hijri, M. (2015). *Nisko w Dabran [Decline and Split]*. Sulaumaniyah, Kurdistan: Sardam Press.

Hijri, M. (2016, March 18). Mustafa Hijri bo Rudaw: Awsal peshmergakanman danerinawa bo Rojhalati Kurdistan [Mustafa Hijri for Rudaw: This year, we will send our peshmergas to the Eastern Kurdistan]. Retrieved from http://peshmergekan.com/kurdish/index.php?option=com_content&view=article&id=6797:2016-03-18-18-43-58&catid=32:chalaki&Itemid=57

Hemin (Sayyed Mohammad Amin Shaikholislami Mukri). (1999). *Tarik u Roun: Golbzherek la she'arakani Hemim (Dark and bright: A collection of Hemin's poems)*. Kurdistan, Iraq: Binkay Adabi Peshawa Publication.

Hisami, K. (1986). *La birawariyakanim: La mindaliyawa ta Sali 1957(Bargi Yakam) [From my memoirs* (Vol. 1).]. Uppsala, Sweden: (n.p.).

Hisami, K. (1988). *La birawariyakanim: 1965-1970 (Bargi Seyam) [From my memoirs* (Vol. 3).]. Stockholm: Ketab-I Arzan Press.

Hisami, K. (1990). *La birawariyakanim: 1970-1975 (Bargi ChowahamSeyam) [From my memoirs* (Vol. 4).]. Stockholm: Shilan Tryckeri.

Hisami, K. (1992). *La birawariyakanim: 1970-1975 (Bargi Shasham) [From my memoirs* (Vol. 6).]. Stockholm: n.p.

Hisami, K. (1995). *Hikayat Kirdin ya nousini mejou: Halwstek la sar "Niw sada tekoshan" nousini "Abdullah Hassanzadeh" (Story telling or writing history: A view on "Half a century struggle" written by Abdullah Hassanzadeh]*. Stockholm: n.p.

Hisami, K. (1997a). *Gashtek ba new birawariyakanda [A review of the memoires]*. Stockholm: Roj Press.

Hisami, K. (1997b). *Pedachoonawa: Bzoutnavway nishtimaniy Kurd la Kurdistani Eran (1947-19978) [Re-examining: Kurdish patriotic movement in Iranian Kurdistan (1947-1978)* (Vol. 2).]. Sweden: Ketab-I Arzan Press.

Hisami, K. (2011). *Khaterat-e Karim Hisami [Karim Hisami's memoirs]*. Sweden: Ketab-I Arzan Press.

Hobsbawm, E. J. (1993). *Nations and nationalism since 1780: Program, myth, reality* (2nd ed.). Cambridge: Cambridge University Press.

Homayoun, S. (2004). *Peshwa-ye bidari: Khaterat-e Said Homayoun* [*Leader of wakefulness: Memoirs of Said Homayoun*]. Erbil: Aras Press and Publisher.

Human Rights Watch. (1990). Human rights in Iraq. New Haven: Yale University Press.

Human Rights Watch. (1995). *Iraq's crime of Genocide: The Anfal campaign against the Kurds*. New Haven and London: Yale University Press.

Hussein, H. (2008). *Rojnamavani Kurdi: Sardemi Komari Dimokrati Kurdistan 1943-1947* (*Kurdish journalism: During the Democratic Republic of Kurdistan 1943-47*). Lebanon: Green Gallery.

Hutchinson, J., and Smith, A. D. (Eds.). (1996). *Ethnicity*. Oxford: Oxford University Press.

Hutchinson, J. (2001). Cultural nationalism. In A. S. Leoussi (Ed.), *Encyclopedia of nationalism* (pp. 40-43). New Brunswick (USA): Transaction Publishers.

Islamic Revolutionary Council. (1979 August 19). *Ba tasvibe Shoray-e Enqelab-e Eslami Hezbe Demokrat-e Kurdistan ghair-e qanouni e'alam shod* [With the approval of the Islamic Revolutionary Council the Kurdistan Democratic Party (Democratic Party of Iranian Kurdistan) was made illegal]. *Kayhan (Extraordinary)*. p. 1.

Ivanov, M. S. (1977). *Tarikh-e novin-e Iran* [*History of modern Iran*] (H. Tizabi and H. Ghaem Panah, Trans.). Tehran: Tudeh Party of Iran Publication.

Izady, M. R. (1992). *The Kurds: A concise handbook*. Washington: Tylor and Francis

Jahangiri, E. (2012, December 30). E'dami shorishgerana ya tirori jiabiran [Revolutionary execution or assassination of the opponents]. Retrieved from http://ebrahim-jahangiri.blogspot.ca/search?updated-min=2012-01-01T00:00:00-08:00&updated-max=2013-01-01T00:00:00-08:00&max-results=50

Jahani Asl, M. N. (2007). *A democratic alternative education system for Iran: An historical and critical study* (Master's thesis). Burnaby Campus, Simon Fraser University. Vancouver, Canada.

Jalaeipour, H. (1990). *Qazi Muhammad: Kurdistan dar salhaye 1320-1324* [*Qazi Muhammad: Kurdistan in the years of 1941-1946*]. Tehran: Amir Kabir Publications.

Jalil, J. (2002). *Kordhay-e Empratoory-e Osmani* [*The Kurds of the Ottoman Empire*] (S. Ashti, Trans). Tehran: Paniz Publications.

Jayawardena, K. (1986). *Feminism and nationalism in the Third World*. New Delhi: Kali for Women.

Jwaideh, W. (2006). *The Kurdish national movement: Its Origin and Development*. Syracuse, New York: Syracuse University Press.

Kandiyoti, D. (1996). Women, ethnicity, and nationalism. In J. Hutchinson, and A. D. Smith (Eds.), *Ethnicity* (pp. 311-316). Oxford: Oxford University Press.

Kaplan, G. (1997). Feminism and nationalism: The European case. In L. A. West (Ed.), *Feminist nationalism* (pp.3-40). New York: Routledge.

Karimi, A. (Ed.). (1999). *Jian u basarhati Abdul Rahman Zabihi (Mamosta Ulama)* [*The Life and fortunes of Abdul Rahman Zabihi (Master Scientists)*]. Gothenburg, Sweden: Zagros Media Press.

Karimi, A. (Ed.). (2008). *Nishtman: Blaw karaway biri Komalay J.K.* [*Nishtman: The distributer of the J.K.'s thought*]. Sulaymaniyah: Shvan Press.

Karimi, A. (2012, November 29). Personal communication.

Karimi, K. (2012, September 4). Personal communication.

Kaveh. S. (2005). *Wardanawa: Roudaw, rowanga, rakhna, terownini gishti* [*Re-examining: Event, view, criticism, public opinion*]. n.p.: n.p.

KDP (I)'s Program and Constitution. (1973). Barnama wa Asasnameh-ye Hezbe Demokrat-e Kurdistan (Iran): Mosawab-e Kongereh-ye sewom-e Hezb (mehr mah-e 1352-September 1973) [The Kurdistan Democratic Party of (Iran)'s Program and Constitution: Ratified in the Third Congress of the party (September 1973)]. n.p.: n.p.

Kasravi, A. (1970). *Tarikh-e Mashruteh-ye Iran* [*History of the Iranian Constitution*] (8th ed.). Tehran: Amir Kabir Publication.

Kasravi, A. (1977). *Tarikh-e Hejdah saleh-ye Azarbaijan ya sarnewesht-e gordan wa daliran* [*Eighteen-year history of Azerbaijan or the destiny of heroes and braves*] (8th ed.). Tehran: Amir Kabir Publication.

Kavianpur, A. (1999). *Tarikh-e Urmiya* [*History of Urmiya*]. Tehran: Azer Kohan Publications.

Keddie, N. R. (2003). *Modern Iran: Roots and results of Revolution*. New Haven Yale University Press.

Kedourie, E. (1993). *Nationalism* (4th ed.). Oxford UK: Blackwell.

Kellas, J. G. (1991). *The politics of nationalism and ethnicity*. New York: St. Martin's Press.

Kendal, N. (1980a). Kurdistan in Turkey. In G. Chaliand (Ed.), *People without a country: The Kurds and Kurdistan* (pp. 47-106). London: Zed Press.

Kendal, N. (1980b). The Kurds under the Ottoman Empire. In G. Chaliand (Ed.), *People without a country: The Kurds and Kurdistan* (pp. 19-46). London: Zed Press.

Khajeh-Nouri, I. (1978). *Bazigarn-e asr-e talayy* [*The politicians of the golden age*] (2nd ed.). Tehran: Sepehr Press.

Khalighi, H. (2002). *Jan u jian* [*Suffering and life* (Vol. 3).]. Sweden: Author

Khalighi, H. (2005). *Jan u jian wa vilami rakhnagiran* [*Suffering and life and responding the critics* (Vol. 4).]. Sweden: Author

Khalighi, H. (2012, December 1). Personal communication.

Khizri, M. (2003). *Laparayak la tekoshan u joulanaway salakani1342-1347(1963-1968) i Hizbi Demokrati Kurdistan* [*A page from the struggle and the movement of the Kurdistan Democratic Party during the years of 1963-1968*]. Sweden, Stockholm: n.p.

Khizri, M. (2012, November 22). Personal communication.

Khomeini, R. A. (1979a, August 19). Imam: Nagozarid Ashrar Bogrizand [Imam: Do not let the wicked to escape]. *Kayhan*. p. 3.

Khomeini, R. A. (1979b, August 20). Imam: Sarkerdagan-e Hezb-e democrat ra dastgir konid. [Imam: Arrest the leaders of the Democratic Party]. *Kayhan* (3rd ed.). p. 1.

Khomeini, R. A. (1979c, November 18). Haqe edarah-ye Omour-e dakheli wa mahalli wa raf'e har gouneh tanb'iz mota'alleq be tamam-e mellat ast [The right to administer internal and territorial Issues and remover all types of discriminations belong to the whole nation]. *Kayhan*. p. 3.

Khoshhali, B. (2001). *Qazi Muhammad wa Jomhuri dar ayeneh-ye asnad [Qazi Muhammad and the Republic on the mirror of documents]*. Hamadan: Ferdowsi Press.

Kinnane, D. (1964). *The Kurds and Kurdistan*. London: Oxford University Press.

Komitay Barewabari Gishti Yaketi Lawani Demokrati Rojhalati Kurdistan. (2015). Bayannama ba bonay diari kirdini salyadi damazrani Yaketi Lawani Demokrati Rojhalati Kurdistan [Declaration on determining the anniversary of the establishment of the Democratic Youth Union of Kurdistan]. Retrieved from http://www.kurdistanukurd.com/?page_id=66

Komiteh Markari-ye Hezb-e Democrat-e Kurdistan-e Iran [Central Committee of the Democratic Party of Iranian Kurdistan]. (2012). Gozaresh-e komiteh markari be panzdahhomin congreh-ye Hezb-e Democrat-e Kurdistan-e Iran [The report of the Central Committee to the 15th Congress of the Democratic Party of Iranian Kurdistan]. Retrieved from http://www.kurdistanmedia.com/farsi/idame/6537/asnad

Koohi-Kamali, F. (2003). *The political development of the Kurds in Iran: Pastoral nationalism*. New York: Palgrave Macmillan.

Kurdistan Democratic Party. (2015). Barnama w Perawi Newkhoy Hizbi Demokrati Kurdistan, pasand krawi Kongray Chowardayam [Program and Internal Regulations of the Kurdistan Democratic Party adopted in the Fourteenth Congress]. Retrieved from http://www.kurdistanukurd.com/?page_id=17

Kurdistan Democratic Party. (2016a). Barnama w Perawi Newkhoy Hizbi Demokrati Kurdistan, pasand krawi Kongray 16 (17 ta 21y Rebandani 1394, 6 ta 11 Fewriyay 2016) (Program and Internal Regulations of the Kurdistan Democratic Party adopted in 16th Congress (6-11 February 2016). Retrieved from http://www.kurdistanukurd.com/?page_id=17

Kurdistan Democratic Party. (2016b). Raporti komitay nawandi bo Kongray Shazdayami Hizbi Demokrati Kurdistan, 16 ta 24y Rashamay 1386 (6 ta 14y Marsi 2008)

[Central Committee's report to the Sixteenth Congress of the Kurdistan Democratic Party (6-14 March 2008)]. Retrieved from http://www.kurdistanukurd.com/?page_id=17

Kurdistan Democratic Party-Iran (2006). Hela Gishtiyakani Rebazi Ema [General Principles of Our Way]. Retrieved from http://www.kurdistanukurd.com/?page_id=17

Kurdistan Equality Party. (2013, August 28). Barz u barez be salyadi shahid booni peshmerga w rabari yaksanikhowaz. Mamosta Qandil (Be high and respectful on the anniversary of martyring the equality-seeking peshmerga and leader, Mamosta Qandil). Retrieved from http://yeksani.simplesite.com/419852183

Kurdistan Equality Party. (2015, November 25). Chonyati shahid krani hawre Hassan Eqbali la layan "H.D.K.I" wa (The way of martyring friend Hassan Eqbali by the PDKI). Retrieved from http://yeksani.info/article/82

Kurdistan Freedom Manifesto. (2006). Manifisti Azadiy Kurdistan: Programi "*Parti Azadiy Kurdistan*" (Kurdistan Freedom Manifesto: The program of the Kurdistan Freedom Party [PAK]). Retrieved from http://pazadik.org/Zanyary.aspx?Jimare=3

Kurdistan Media (2012, October 10): Sikerteri Gisti Hizbi Demokrat, halbjerdra [The General Secretary of the Democratic Party [PDKI], was selected]. Retrieved from http://www.peshmergekan.com

Kutschera, C. (1994). *Jonbesh-e melli-ye Kord* [*The Kurdish National Movement*]. (I, Younesi, Trans.). Tehran: Negah Publications.

Kwiatkowski, L. M. and West, L. A. (1997). Feminist struggles for feminist nationalism in the Philippines. In L. A. West (Ed.), *Feminist nationalism* (pp.147-168). New York: Routledge.

Kymlicka, W. (1995). *Multicultural citizenship: A liberal theory of minority rights*. Oxford: Clarendon Press.

Lazarev. S. M. (2010). *Mezhooy Kurdistan* [*Kurdistan History*] (2nd ed.). (H. A. Sargawi, Trans.) Hawler: Rojhelat Publication.

LeClerk, P. and West, L. A. (1997). Feminist nationalist movements in Quebec: Resolving contradictions? In L. A. West (Ed.), *Feminist nationalism* (pp. 220-246). New York: Routledge.

Legard, R., Keegan, J., and Ward, K. (2003). In-depth interviews. In J. Ritchie and J. Lewis (Eds.), *Qualitative research practice: A guide for social science students and researchers* (pp. 138-169). London: SAGE Publications.

Lemkin, R. (1944). *Axis rule in occupied Europe: Laws of occupation, analysis of government, proposals for redress*. Retrieved from http://www.heinonline.org.ezproxy.library.uvic.ca/HOL/Page?handle=hein.cow /axisrul0001&id=137&collection=beal&index=

Lenin, V. I., and Stalin, J. (1970). *Selections from V.I. Lenin and J.V. Stalin on national colonial question*. Calcutta: Calcutta Book House.

Leonard, P. (2005). *Nationality Between Poststructuralism and Postcolonial Theory*. Palgrave Macmillan.

Lesser, I. O. (1999). Ethnic and religious strains in Turkey. In L. Brinder (Ed.), Ethnic conflict and international politics in the Middle East (pp. 209-222). Ganinesville: University Press of Florida.

Lewis, J., and Ritchie, J. (2003). Generating from qualitative research. In J. Ritchie and J. Lewis (Eds.), *Qualitative research practice: A guide for social science students and researchers* (pp. 138-169). London: SAGE Publications.

Lotf Pouri, R. (2012, October 21). Personal communication.

Lowe, R. (2007). Kurdish nationalism in Syria. In M. M. A. Ahmed, and M. M. Gunter (Eds.), *The evolution of Kurdish Nationalism* (pp. 287-308). Costa Mesa: California: Mazda Publications, Inc.

Löwy, M. (1976). Marxists and the national question. *New Left Review*, 96, 81-100. *New Left Review I/96, March-April 1976*.

Madani, H. (2000). *Kurdistan u estrateji dawlatan* [*Kurdistan and the strategy of states*] (Vol. 1). Stockholm: Spartyck Tensta.

Madani, H. (2001). *Kurdistan u strateji dawlatan* [*Kurdistan and the strategy of the states* (Vol. 2).]. Stockholm: Spartyck Tensta.

Madani, H. (2012, October 13). Personal communication.

Madani, H. (2012, October 14). Personal communication.

Mahmoudi, T. (2016, January 9). Personal communication.

Makki, H. (1979). *Tarikh-e bist saleh-ye Iran: Kudeta-ye 1299* [*Twenty-year history of Iran: The 1921 Coup d'état*] (Vol. 1) (2nd ed.). Tehran: Amir Kabir Publications.

Makki, H. (1980). *Tarikh-e bist saleh-ye Iran: Moghadamat-e taghyyr-e saltanat* [*Ttwenty-year history of Iran: Preludes tochanging the monarchy*] (Vol. 2) (4nd ed.). Tehran: Bongah-e Tarjomeh va Nashr-e Ketab.

Makki, H. (1982). *Tarikh-e bist saleh-ye Iran: Aghaz-e saltanat-e diktatory-ye Pahlavi* [*The twenty-year history of Iran: The beginning of Pahlavi's dictatorial monarchy*] (Vol. 4). Tehran: Nashr-e Nasher.

Makki, H. (1983). *Tarikh-e bist saleh-ye Iran: Estehkam-e dictatori-ye Pahlavi* [*Twenty-year history of Iran: Consolidation of the Pahlavi dictatorship*] (Vol. 5). Tehran: Nasher Publications.

Malekzadeh, M. (1992). *Tarikh-e Enghelab-e Mashruteh-ye Iran* [*The history of the Constitutional Revolution of Iran*] (Vols. 4-5) (3rd ed.). Tehran: Elmi Publications.

Mamadi, S. (1999). *Hamleh, e'dam, youresh, wa yaweh sarayy-ha-ye Bolourian wa fehresti az khaterat-e siasi-ye man* [*Attack, execution, invasion, and trifles of Bolurian and a list of my political memoirs*]. Sweden. Baran Press.

Mangaliso, Z. A. (1997). Gender and nation building in South Africa. In L. A. West (Ed.), *Feminist nationalism* (pp.130-144). New York: Routledge.

Manguri, M. A. (2001). *Basarhati Siasi Kurd (1914-1958): Yadashtakani Mira Muhammad Amin Manguri.* [*Political adventures of the Kurds (1914-1958): Momories of Mirza Muhammad Amin Manguri* (Vol. 2).]. Sulaymaniyah: Raz Press.

Marashi, A. (2014). Paradigms of Iranian National History: History, Theory, and Historiography. In K.S. Aghaien, & A. Marashi (Eds.), *Rethinking Iranian Nationalism and Modernity* (pp. 3-24). Austin: University of Texas Press.

Marx, K, and Engels, F. (1978). *Manifesto of the Communist Party*. In R. C. Tucker (Ed.), *The Marx-Engels reader* (2nd ed.). (pp. 469-500). New York: W.W. Norton & Company.

Mawloudi Sabian, A. A. (1994). *Tahlil-e Jame'eh Shenakhti Siasi-ye Hezb-e Demokrat-e Kordestan-e Iran* [*Political Sociology analysis of the Democratic Party of Iranian Kurdistan* (Master's thesis)]. Tarbiat Modares University [Professor Training University], Tehran, Iran.

Mazur, K. (2012, October 1). Personal communication.

McCrone, D. (1998). *The sociology of nationalism: Tomorrow's ancestors*. London: Routledge.

McDowall, D. (1996). *A modern history of the Kurds*. London, New York: I-B. TAURIS.

McDowall, D. (2004). *A modern history of the Kurds* (Rev. 3rd.ed.). London, New York: I.B. Tauris.

McKiernan, K. (2006). *The Kurds: A people in search of their homeland*. New York: St. Martin's Press.

Meho, L. I. (1997). *The Kurds and Kurdistan: A selective and Annotated Bibliography*. Weatport, Connecticut: Greenwood Press.

Meiselas, S. (1997). *Kurdistan: In the shadow of history*. New York: Random House.

Mianali, A. (2005a). *Silahla olcholin torpaq!: 1324-1325 ji illarda Azerbaijanda mili-demokratic harakat* [*By-weapon-measured soil!: The Azerbaijan national-democratic movements of the years of 1945-1946* (Vol. 1.).]. Vancouver: Print Depot.

Mianali, A. (2005b). *Silahla olcholin torpaq!: 1324-1325 ji illarda Azerbaijanda mili-demokratic harakat* [*By-weapon-measured soil!: The Azerbaijan national-democratic movements of the years of 1945-1946* (Vol. 2.).]. Vancouver: Print Depot.

Michels, R. (1968). *Political Parties: A sociological study of the oligarchical tendencies of modern democracy* (E. & C. Paul, Trans.). New York: The Free Press.

Middle East Watch. (1993). *Genocide in Iraq: The Anfal campaign against the Kurds*. New York: Human Rights Watch.

Milani, A. (2008). *Eminent Persians: The men and women who made modern Iran, 1941-1979*. (Vol. 1). New York: Syracuse University Press.

Mill, J. S. (1958). *Considerations on representative government*. Indianapolis: The Bobbs-Merrill Company, Inc.

Minahan, J. (1996). Nations without states: A historical dictionary of contemporary national movements (Vol. 2). Westport: Greenwood Press.

Minahan, J. (2002). Encyclopedia of the stateless nations: Ethnic and national groups around the world. (Vol. 2). Westport: Greenwood Press.

Minorsky, V. (2000). *Kord* [*Kurd*] (H. Tabani, Trans.). Tehran: Gostareh Publications.

Minorsky, V. (2007). *Binchinakani Kord wa chand wtareki Kordnasi* [*The origins of the Kurds and some Kurdology articles*] (Vol. 1). (N. Abdullah, Trans.). Sulaymaniyah: Maktabi Bir wa Hoshyari (Y-N-K).

Mirza Saleh, G. (1993). *Reza Shah: Khaterat-e Solayman Behboodi, Shams Pahlavi, Ali Izadi* [*Reza Shah: Memories of Solayman Behboodi, Shams Pahlavi, Ali Izadi*]. Tehran: Sahba Print.

Mobley, R. (2008). *Rawabet-e Jomhouri-ye Kurdistan u Azerebaijan (1945-1946)* [*Study of relations between the Mahabad Republic and Azerbaijan Democrat Republic: the turbulent alliance and its impact upon the Mahabad Republic of 1946*]. (E. Baxtiyari, Trans.). Sulaymaniyah: Shvan Press. (Original work published 1979)

Mohtadi, A. (2012, September 17). Personal communication.

Moghadam, V. (1997). Nationalist Agenda and Women's rightsConflicts in Afghanistan in the twentieth century. In L. A. West (Ed.), *Feminist nationalism* (pp.75-100). New York: Routledge.

Mojab. S. (2001). Women and nationalism in the Kurdish Republic of 1946. In S. Mojab (Ed.), *Women of a non-state nation: The Kurds*. California: Mazda Publishers, Inc.

Momeni, H. (1979). *Dar bareh-ye mobarezat-e Kurdistan* [*On Kurdistan's struggles* (2nd ed.).]. Retrieved from http://www.iran-archive.com/node/5756

Monazzami, A. (2011). *Ghassemlou's ideas of Democracy and Iranian-Kurdish relations in contemporary Iran* (Master's thesis). Available from Master's theses in peace and conflict transformation.

Moradi, G. (1996). *Tajrobeh-ye Yeksal Hokoumat-e Khodmokhtar-e Kurdistan-e Iran marouf be Jomhouri-ye Mahabad 1946-1947* [*The experience of one-year Autonomous Government of Kurdistan in Iran known as Mahabad Republic 1946-1947*]. Sweden: Kitab-I Arzan.

Mustafa Amin, N. (2007). *Hokoumati Kurdistan, Rebandani 1324-Sarmawazi 1325: Kurd la Gamay Soviet da* [*The government of Kurdistan, 22 January-17 December 1946: The Kurds in the Soviet game*]. (3rd ed.). Sulaymaniyah: Tishk Publications.

Mustafa Amin, N. (2007). *Kurd wa ajam: Mezhooy siasi Kordakani Eran* [*Kurd and ajam: Political history of Iranian Kurds*] (3rd ed.). Sulaymaniyah: Roon Publications.

Mustafa Sultani, M, and Watan Doost, S. (2015). *Mabahese "Kongereh-ye Awwal-e Komala": Payyz 1357* [*Discussions of "the First Congress of the Komala": Autumn 1978*]. Retrieved from http://www.komele.nu/archives/635

Narin, T. (1994). The maladies of development. In J. Hutchinson, and A. D. Smith (Eds.), *Nationalism* (pp. 70-76). Oxford: Oxford University Press.

Naqibzadeh, A. (2000). *Dowlat-e Reza Shah wa nezam-e ili: Tasir-e sakhtar-e dowlat-e ghodrat garay-e Reza Shah bar nefooz-e ghabeyel wa 'ashayer* [*Reza Shah's government and tribal system: The impact of the structure of Reza Shahs powers-oriented government on the tribes' influence*]. Tehran: Center for Islamic Revolution Documents Publications.

Naqshi, R. (Ed.). (2015, April 16). Listay andamani rebari Hizbi Demokrati Kurdistan la 66 Sali rabirdou (1945-2011) la 15 Kongray am Hizba da [The list of the leadership of the Kurdistan Democratic Party within its 15 Congresses for 66 years ago (1945-2011).]. Retrieved from http://www.kurdistanukurd.com/?page_id=60&paged=3

Natali, D. (2005). *The Kurds and the state: Evolving national identity in Iraq, Turkey, and Iran*. Syracuse: Syracuse University Press.

Nayeri, K., and Nasab, A. (2006). The rise and fall of the 1979 Iranian Revolution: Its lessons for today. Retrieved August 7, 2006, from https://www.google.ca/?gfe_rd=cr&ei=LTYZVNruBbDP8gfcmYBA&gws_rd=ssl#q=The+rise+and+fall+of+the+1979+Iranian+Revolution:+Its+lessons+for+today

Nazdar, M. (1980). The Kurds in Syria. In G. Chaliand (Ed.), *People without a country: The Kurds and Kurdistan* (pp. 211-219). London: Zed Press.

Nerwiy, H. K. T. (2012). *The Republic of Kurdistan, 1946*. (Doctoral dissertation). Leiden University, Leiden, the Netherlands. Retrieved from https://openaccess.leidenuniv.nl/handle/1887/18583

Nikitin, B. (1987). *Kord va Kordestan* [*Kurd and Kurdistan*]. (M. Qazi, Trans.). Tehran: Nilofar Publications.

Noorani, M. (2012, September 22). Personal communication.

Nuranifard, K. (2012, September 5). Personal communication.

O'Ballance, E. (1973). *The Kurdish revolt: 1961-1970*. London: Faber and Faber Limited.

Osmani, F. (2012, October 15). Personal communication.

Özoğlu, H. (2004). *Kurdish Notables and the Ottoman State: Evolving Identities, Competing Loyalties, and Shifting Boundaries*. Albany: State University of New York Press.

Pahlavi, M. R. (1980). *Answer to History*. Toronto: Clark, Irwin & Company Limited.

Palani, M. (2016, December 11). Personal communication.

Parsa Benab. Y. (2004). *Tarikh-e sad saleh-ye ahzab va sazmanhaye siyasi-ye Iran (1904-2004)* [*A one hundred year history of the Iranian political parties and organizations (1904-2004)*] (Vol. 1.). Washington. D. C.: Rawandi Publications.

PDKI's Program and Constitution. (1984). Barnama wa Asasnameh-ye Hezbe Demokrat-e Kurdistan-e Iran: Mosawab-e Kngereh-ye sheshom-e Hezb [The Democratic Party of Iranian Kurdistan's Program and Constitution: Ratified in the Sixth Congress]. n.p.: The Central Committee of the PDKI's Publication and Propaganda Commission.

Parvin, N. (2011). Azāadīstān. *Encyclopaedia Iranica*. Retrieved from http://www.iranicaonline.org/articles/azadistan

Paymai, N. (2002). *Reza Shah Pahlavi: Az Alasht ta Johannesburg* [*Reza Shah Pahlavi: From Alasht to Johannesburg*]. Washington. D. C.

Patton, M. Q. (1999). Enhancing the Quality and credibility of qualitative analysis. HSR: *Health Service Research* 34(5), 1189-1208.

Peshnimaz, M. R. (2012). *Sarbirday jianim* [*My life adventure* (Vol. 1).]. Sulaymaniyah: Shvan Press.

Pirnia, H., and Eghbal Ashtiani, A. (2012). *Tarikh-e Iran: Az aghaz ta engheraz-e sasanian (jeld-e awal), as sadre eslam ta engheraz-e ghajariyeh (jeld-e dowam)* [*The history of Iran: From the beginning until the overthrow of Sassanians (Vol. 1), and from the beginning of Islam until the overthrow of Qajar (Vol. 2)*] (8th ed.). Tehran: Behzad Publication.

Politburo of the Kurdistan Democratic Party. (2009a) Bayannama: La pewandi lagal newaroki bayannamay "mafi qawmakan u kayatiya ayynakiyanda" [Declaration: Relating to the declaration about the "rights of ethnicities and religious minorities"]. Retrieved from http://www.kurdistanukurd.com/?page_id=26

Politburo of the Kurdistan Democratic Party. (2009b). Bayannama: Pishtiwani la barangar bounaway komalani khalki Eran arkeki hanoukayy ya [Declaration: Supporting the protest of the Iranian people is an urgent duty]. Retrieved from http://www.kurdistanukurd.com/?page_id=26

Politburo of the Democratic Party of Iranian Kurdistan. (2016a). Daftar-e Siasi-ye Hezbi Demokrat-e Kurdistan-e Iran bayniyeh-ey dar rabeteh ba dargiri-ye akhir dar Oshnavieh montasher kard [The Politburo of the Democratic Party of Iranian Kurdistan published a declaration regarding the recent conflict in Oshnavieh]. Retrieved from http://www.kurdistanmedia.com/farsi/idame/24061

Politburo of the Democratic Party of Iranian Kurdistan. (2016b). Hezbi Demokrat be ettehamat wa doroghparakaniha-ye Mohsen-e Rezaee pasokh dad [Democrati Party of Iranian Kurdistan responded to the accusations of Mohsen Rezaee]. Retrieved from http://www.kurdistanmedia.com/farsi/idame/24677

Price, M. (2005). *Iran's diverse peoples: A reference source book*. Santa Barbara: ABC-CLIO.

Prunhuber, C. (2009). *The passion and death of Rahman the Kurd: Dreaming Kurdistan*. New York: iUniverse, Inc.

Qadri, S. (2012, October 21). Personal communication.

Qazi, A. (2005). *Wilati min: Birawariyakani Haji Abdullay Qazi* [*My country: Haji Abdullah Qazi's memories*]. Q. Qazi. (Ed.). Stockholm: n.p.

Qazi, A. (2010). *La birawariya siasiyakanim* [*From my political memories*]. Stockholm: Apec Press.

Qazi, R. (2012). *Bizoutnaway rizgari natawayati gali Kurd u Qazi Muhammad 1941-1947* [*Kurdish nation's liberation movement and Qazi Muhammad 1941-1947*]. Erbil: Aras Publishers. (Original work published as a dissertation in History Science in Baku, 1971)

Rabinbach, A. (2005, Spring). Raphael Lemkin's concept of genocide: Fifty years later, the first conviction was handed down. *IP-Transatlantic Edition*. Retrieved from https://www.google.ca/?gfe_rd=cr&ei=LTYZVNruBbDP8gfcmYBA&gws_rd=ssl#q=Raphael+Lemkin%E2%80%99s+concept+of+genocide:+Fifty+years+later%2C+the+first+conviction+was+handed+down

Ragayandini fraksion la *Komalay Zahmatkeshani Kurdistan* [The announcement of a faction in the Organization of the Toilers of Kurdistan]. (2014). Retrieved from http://parsinews.ir/news/source/a671ffaa85cc7570bb65f3dc98466a23

Rahimi, M. (2016, January 4). Payami mediayy: Yakgirtini Party Sarbakhoyy Kurdistan u Party Sarbasti Rojhalati Kurdistani Eran (Media message: Unity of the Independence Party of Kurdistan and the Eastern Kurdistan Independence Party). Retrieved from https://goo.gl/ZdAnua

Raisnia, R., and Nahid, A. (1976). *Do mobarez-e jonbesh-e Mashruteh: Sattar Khan, Saheikh Muhammad Khiabani* [*Two combatants of Constitution movement: Sattar Khan, Sheikh Muhammad Khiabani*]. Tehran: Agah Publications.

Rastgar, H. (2011). Hassan Rastgar: Pem khosh bou ductour Ghassemlou mabaya ta la maidani siasat shkistim daba w khianatakanm ba chawi khoy nishan daba

[Hassan Rastgar: I wish Dr. Ghassemlou was alive so that I would defeat him in the political field and would show his treasons to him]. Retrieved from http://www.peshmergekan.com/index_a.php?id=6842

Rastgar, H. (2012, October 15). Personal communication.

Rastgar, H. (2012, October 16). Personal communication.

Rastgar, H. (2012, October 17). Personal communication.

Rastgar, H. (2012, October 22). Personal communication.

Rawti Chaksazi w Gashay Komala [Path of Reform and Flourish of the Komala]. (2007). Ragayandini dast bakar bouni Rawti Chaksazi w Gashay Komala [Announcement of the Establishment of the Path of Reform and Flourish of Komala].

Rebarayati Komalay Shorishgeri Zahmatkeshani Kurdistani Eran-Rawti Chaksazi w Gasha [Leadership of the Revolutionary Organization of the Toilers of Iranian Kurdistan-Path of Reform and Flourish]. (2007, September). Retrieved from https://handeran.wordpress.com/2011/06/06/manshet-news-agencys-archive-09-007-9/

Renan, E. (1994). Qu'est-ce qu'une nation? In J. Hutchinson, and A. D. Smith (Eds.), *Nationalism* (pp. 17-18). Oxford: Oxford University Press.

Ritchie, J., Spencer, L., and O'Connor, W. (2003). Carrying out qualitative analysis. In J. Ritchie and J. Lewis (Eds.), *Qualitative research practice: A guide for social science students and researchers* (pp. 138-169). London: SAGE Publications.

Roji Kurd. (2016, June 26). Koy gishti koujraw u brindarakani rejim ta esta ziatir la 154 jash u pasdara [The total number of the regime's killed and wounded to date is more than 154 jash and pasdars]. Retrieved from http://www.rojikurd.net/kujraw-u-brindarekani-rejim-ta-esta-154-kese/

Roji Kurd TV. (2016, March 27). Khalid Azizi: Kurd natowane Komari Islami broukhene [Khalid Azizi: The Kurds cannot overthrow the Islamic Republic] [Video file]. Retrieved from https://www.youtube.com/watch?v=X4-vZmqLhoI

Roosevelt, A., Jr. (1980). The Kurdish Republic of Mahabad. In G. Chaliand (Ed.), *People without a country: The Kurds and Kurdistan* (pp. 135-152). London: Zed Press.

Safa, A. (2012, December 8). Personal communication.

Safai, I. (1986). *Reza Shah-e Kabir dar ayyneh-ye khaterat: Be enzemam-e zendegirameh* [*Reza Shahs in the mirror of memories: Including biography*] (2nd ed.). Los Angeles.

Saif al-Qozat. (1922, July 23). *Kurd*, p. 3. Retrieved from http://ruwange.blogspot.ca/2014_05_01_archive.html

Sajjadi, A. (2000). Tarikh-e jonbeshhay-e Kordesetan [The History of the Kurdish revolts] (2nd ed.). (R. Karimi, Trans). Sanandaj: Kurdistan Publications.

Saedi, B. (2010). *5 sal lagal Abdullay Mohtadi skerteri Komalay Shorishgeri Zahmatkeshani Kurdistani Eran* [*5 years with Abdullah Mohtadi the General Secretary of the (Revolutionary Organization of the Toilers of Iranian Kurdistan)*]. n.p.: Poya Press.

Saedi, B. (2012). *Khabat baraw sarkawtin* [Struggle toward victory (3rd ed.).]. Kurdistan: Intisharati Nawandi Komala [Komala's Central Publications].

Saleh, B. (2003). *Matn-e kamel-e asrar-e mohakemeh-ye Qazi Muhammad wa Sadr wa Saifi Qazi* [*The complete text of the trial of Qazi Muhammad, Sadr and Saifi Qazi*]. (Hiwa, Trans.). Duhok: Tishk.

Saleh, R., and Saleh, S. (Eds.). (2007). *Rojnameyi Kurdistan: Mahabad 1324-1325 Hetawi (1946)* [Magazine *Kurdistan: Mahabad 1324-1325 Solar Hijri Calendar (1946)*]. Erbil: Aras Publishers.

Salehi, F. (2001). A postmodern conception of the nation-state. In A. S. Leoussi (Ed.). *Encyclopedia of nationalism* (pp. 247-252). New Brunswick (USA): Transaction Publishers.

Samadi, S. M. (1981). *Je. Kaf: Chbou? Chi dawist? Wa chi ba sar hat? (J.K.: What was? What wanted? And what happened to it?)*. Mahabad. n.p.

Samadi, S. M. (1984). *Neghahi digar be J.K.: Yaddashtha-ye shakhsi-ye yeki az bonyangozaran-e Jameiyat (Another look at J.K.: Personal notes of one of the founders of the Association)*. Mahabad: n.p.

Samadi, S. M. (1998). *Neghahi beh tarikh-e Mahabad* [*Glimpses of Mahabad history*]. Mahabad: Rahrow Publications.

Sardashti, Y. (2002a). *Khwendnawayaki mejouyy roudawa new khoyyakani Hizbi Dimokrati Kurdistan (HDKA) w joulanaway chakdaranay salani 1967-1968 la Kurdistani Eran* [*A historical reading of the internal events of the Democratic Party of Iranian Kurdistan (PDKI) and the armed movement of the years of 1967-1968 in Iranian Kurdistan*]. Retrieved from http://www.pertwk.com/ktebxane/taxonomy/term/1424

Sardashti, Y. (2002b). *Komari Milli Dimokrati Kurdistan: Lekolinawayaki mejouyy la joulanaway natawayy gali Kurd la Rojhalati Kurdistan* [*Kurdistan National Democratic Republic: A historical research on the nationalist movement of the Kurdish nation in Eastern Kurdistan*]. Retrieved from http://www.pertwk.com/ktebxane/node/1164

Sardashti, Y. (2015). *Geranaway basarhati be besarushowen kiraweki be gilko w mazar (Sadiqi Anjiri Azar)* [*The narration of the destiny of a person who was made to be disappeared and has no tomb (Seddiq Anjiri Azar)*]. Sulaymaniyah: Author.

Schöpflin, G. (2001). Ethnic and civic nationalism (Hans Kohn's typology). In A. S. Leoussi (Ed.). *Encyclopedia of nationalism* (pp. 60-61). New Brunswick (USA): Transaction Publishers.

Seton-Watson. H. (1994). Old and new nations. In J. Hutchinson, and A. D. Smith (Eds.), *Nationalism* (pp. 134-137). Oxford: Oxford University Press.
Sepah-e Pasdaran bayad taqviat shawad [The Army of the Guardians of the Islamic Revolution should be strengthened]. (1980, May 25). *Nameh-ye Mardom* (People's Letter), pp. 1-2.

Serdemî Niwê. (1986). Retrieved from
http://www.kerimhisami.com/web_information.php?item=4

Serdemî Niwê. (1990). Retrieved from
http://www.kerimhisami.com/web_information.php?item=4

Shahidian, H. (2001). "To be recorded in History": Researching Iranian underground political activists in exile. *Qualitative Sociology*, 24(1), 55-81.

Shalmashi, M. (2012, November 14). Personal communication.

Shalmashi, M. (2012, November 15). Personal communication.

Shams, S. (2012, October 18). Personal communication.

Shapasandi, M. (2007). *Birwariyakani Muhammad Shapasandi* [Muhammad Shapasandi's memoirs]. Sulamaniyah: Shvan Press.

Sharafkandi, A. R. (Hajar) (1997). *Cheshti mijewr* [The mosque janitor's food]. Paris.

Sharafkandi, G. (2012, November 26). Personal communication.

Sharafkandi, S (Said Badal). (1981). *Tarikhcheh-ye jonbeshhay-e melly-e Kord: Az gharn-e noozdehom ta payan-e jang-e dowwom-e jahani* [The brief history of Kurdish nationalist movements: From the nineteenth century to the end of the Second World War]. Shiwa Jo: Democratic Party of Iranian Kurdistan Publications.

Shared Declaration of the PDKI and the Komala. (1983, June 5). *Etela'iyeh-ye Moshtarak: Be monasebat-e e'dam-e 59 tan az farzandan-e fadakar-e Kurdistan dar shahr-e Mahabad* [Shared declaration: for the executions of 59 devoted sons of Kurdistan in the city of Mahabad]. The political bureau of the PDKI and the political bureau of the Komala: Reprinting by the PDKI- Europe Organization.

Sharifi, M. (2008). *Imagining Iran: Contending political discourses in modern Iran* (Doctoral dissertation). Universit of Florida. Retrieved from http://ufdcimages.uflib.ufl.edu/UF/E0/02/24/87/00001/sharifi_m.pdf

Sheyholislami, J. (2008). *Identity, discourse, and the media: The case of the Kurds* (Doctoral dissertation). Ottawa: Carleton University.

Shirazi, H. (2000). *Khaterat-e doctor Hashem Shirazi: Az fa'alan-e siasi-ye Kordestan (1298-1377)* [*Memories of Dr. Hashem Shirazi: From the political activists of Kurdistan (1919-1998)*]. Tehran: Tavakoli Publications.

Short, D. (2010). Cultural genocide and indigenous peoples: A sociological approach. *The International Journal of Human Rights*, 14(6), 831–846. Retrieved from https://www.academia.edu/3834426/Cultural_genocide_and_indigenous_peoples_a_sociological_approach

Shumanov, V. (2004). Mar Binyamin Shimmun. *Zinda Magazine*, 10(3). Retrieved from http://www.zindamagazine.com/html/archives/2004/3.15.04/

Simko. (1922, between June 8 and July 23). *Kurd*, pp. 1-3. Courtesy of Hassan Ghazi.

Smith, A. D. (1989). The origins of nations. *Ethnic and Racial Studies*, 12(3), 340- 367. doi: 10. 1080/01419870.1989.9993639

Smith, A. D. (1996). Chosen peoples. In J. Hutchinson, and A. D. Smith (Eds.), *Ethnicity* (pp. 189-197). Oxford: Oxford University Press.

Smith, A. D. (1998). *Nationalism and modernism: A critical survey of recent theories of nations and nationalism*. London: Routledge.

Smith, A. D. (2001b). Ethno-Symbolism. In A. S. Leoussi (Ed.), *Encyclopedia of nationalism* (pp. 84-87). New Brunswick (USA): Transaction Publishers.

Spencer, L., Ritchie, J., and O'Connor, W. (2003). Analysis: Practices, principles and processes. In J. Ritchie and J. Lewis (Eds.), *Qualitative research practice: A guide for social science students and researchers* (pp. 138-169). London: SAGE Publications.

Spencer, P., and Wollman, H. (2002). *Nationalism: A critical introduction*. London: Sage Publications.

Stoel, Max van der (1992). Report on the Situation of Human Rights in Iraq, Prepared by Mr. Max van der Stoel, Special Rapporteur of the Commission on Human Rights, in Accordance with Commission Resolution 1991/74. (E/CN.4/1992/31, 18 February 1992). United Nations Economic and Social Council, Commission on Human Rights. 86 pp. Retrieved from http://www.un.org/en/ga/search/view_doc.asp?symbol=E/CN.4/1992/31

Sutton, P. D. (1997). *The marginalization of Kurdistan: A core-periphery study* (MA thesis). University of Oregon.

Tabari, E. (1981). *Iran dar do sadeh-ye vapasin [Iran at the last two centuries]*. Tehran: Private Company Tudeh Publication.

Tejel, J. (2009). *Syria's Kurds*. London: Routledge.

Thompson, A., and Fevre, R. (2001). The national question: Sociological reflections on nation and nationalism. *Nations and Nationalism*. 7(3), 297-315.

Trask, H. (1997). Feminism and indigenous Hawaiian nationalism. In L. A. West (Ed.), *Feminist nationalism* (pp.187-198). New York: Routledge.

Turjani, M. (1922, July 23). Bayan-e maram [Explanation of aim]. *Kurd*, p. 4. Retrieved from http://ruwange.blogspot.ca/2014_05_01_archive.html

United Nations (1948). Convention on the Prevention and Punishment of the Crime of Genocide. Retrieved from https://treaties.un.org/doc/Publication/UNTS/Volume%2078/volume-78-I-1021-English.pdf

United Nations (1994). Final Report of the Commission of Experts Established Pursuant to United Nations Security Council Resolution 780 (1992). Retrieved from http://www.un.org/en/ga/search/view_doc.asp?symbol=S/1994/674

United Nations. (2007). United Nations Declaration on the Rights of Indigenous Peoples. Retrieved from http://www.un.org/en/ga/search/view_doc.asp?symbol=A%20/61/L.67

Vahabzadeh, P. (2010). *A guerrilla odyssey: Modernization, secularism, democracy, and the Fadai period of national liberation in Iran, 1971-1979*. Syracuse, N.Y.: Syracuse University Press.

Vali, A. (2011). *Kurds and the state in Iran: The making of Kurdish identity*. London I. B. Tauris.

Vanly, I. S. (1980). Kurdistan in Iraq. In G. Chaliand (Ed.), *People without a country: The Kurds and Kurdistan* (pp. 153-210). London: Zed Press.

Wahlbeck, O. (1999). *Kurdish Diasporas: A comparative study of Kurdish refugee communities*. Great Britain: Macmillan Press Ltd.

Walby, S. (2006). Gender approaches to nation s and nationalism. In G. Delanty, and K. Krishna (Eds.), *The SAGE handbook of nations and Nationalism* (pp.118-128). London: SAGE.

Wallerstein, I. (1974). The rise and future demise of the world capitalist system: Concepts for comparative analysis. *Comparative Studies in Society History*, 16(4), 384-415. Retrieved from http://links.jstor.org/sici?sici=0010-4175%28197409%2916%3A4%3C387%3ATRAFDO%3E2.0.CO%3B2-P

West, L. A. (Ed.). (1997). Introduction: Feminism constructs nationalism. In L. A. West (Ed.), *Feminist nationalism* (pp. xi-xxxvi). New York: Routledge.

Wilkinson, R. (1999). Genocide. In Poole, H. (Ed.), *Human Rights: The essential reference* (pp. 252-253). Phoenix, Arizona: Oryx Press.

Wirya, Q. (2012, October 22). Personal communication.

Yassin, B. A. (1995). *Vision or reality? The Kurds in the policy of the great powers, 1941-1947*. Sweden: Land University Press.

Yildiz, K. (2005). *The Kurds in Turkey: EU accession and Human rights*. London: Pluto Press.

Yildiz, K. (2007). *The Kurds in Iraq: Past, present and future*. London: Pluto Press.

Yuval-Davis, N. (1997). *Gender and nation*. London: Sage Publications.

Zarbakht, M. (1998). *Az Kurdistan Eraq ta an souye Roude Aras: Rah peymayy-ye Mullah Mustafa Barzani, 1326* [*From Iraqi Kurdistan to other side of Aras River: Historical walking of Mullah Mustafa Barzani, 1947* (2nd ed.).]. Tehran: Shirazeh Publications and Research.

Zinn, M. B. (1979). Field research in minority communities: Ethical, Methodological and political observations by insider. *Social Problems* 27(2): 209-219.

Appendices

Appendix 1: Timelines

BCE:	
401 BCE	According to Xenophon in *Anabasis*, the Kardouchoi attacked the retreating Greeks.
CE:	
637	The Arab invasion of Iran
Mid-7th century CE	Kurds were Islamized. Saladin fought the Crusaders and founded Ayyubid Dynasty in Egypt and Syria.
1514	Battle of Chaldiran resulted in the foundations of Ottoman-Persian Empire frontier in Kurdistan.
1596	The first written description of the Kurdistan's borders appears in *Sharafnāma* (*Sharaf-Nāme*) by Prince Sharaf al-Dîn Bitlîsiî (Sharaf Khan) in 1596-1597.
Late 17th century	Ahmad (Ahmed) Khani (1650–1706) wrote *Mem u Zin*, the Kurdish national epic.
1781–1925	The Qajar Dynasty
1847	Badr Khan Beg, ruler of last semi-independent Kurdish emirate, submitted to Ottomans.

1880	The Sheikh Ubayd Allah's revolt was defeated in 1880.
1904	The first Iranian social democratic group, Hemmat, was founded in Transcaucasia.
1905-1911	The Constitutional Revolution of Iran
1916	Sykes-Picot Agreement divided Middle East and consequently Kurdistan.
1920	The Iranian Communist Party was founded in which later Heidar Amou Oghly, one of the important leaders of Constitutional Revolution, was chosen to its general secretary.
1925–1979	Pahlavi Dynasty in Iran.
1927 October	Some Kurdish exiles, under the leadership of Jalalat Badr Khan, founded the organization of *Khoybun* (Independence), a pan-Kurdish party, in Lebanon, Syria, in 1927.
1941, August 25	On 25 August 1941 the Red Army entered Azerbaijan and Kurdistan.
1941, September 29	Tudeh Party of Iran, as Iranian Communist Party was established in Iran
1942, December	The first visit of Qazi Muhammad and other Kurdish tribal chiefs to Baku was in December 1941.
1942, August 16	The foundation of the *Komalay Ziyanaway Kurdistan* (J.K.) (Society for Revival of Kurdistan [J.K.]) in Mahabad.

1943, May 13	The 1st Congress of the J.K. was held in the Mountain of *Qalay Sarim* (Sarim Fortress) in Mahabad on 13 May 1943.
1943, July 22	The publication of the first issue of the J.K.'s Magazine *Nishman* (Homeland) on 22 July 1943.
1944, March 7	The establishment of the J.K.'s printing house on 7 March 1944
1944, October 16	Qazi Muhammad went to negotiates with Tehran on 16 October 1944.
1944, end of October-beginning of November	Qazi Muhammad became the member of the J.K. at end of October or beginnings of November 1944.
1945, February 15	Frouhar and Aziz Khan Kirmanj as the J.K. representatives gathered and lectured to people in Abbas Agha Mosque and they attacked and disarmed the Police Station in Mahabad. Five policemen and a Kurd named Abdullah Mina Khaland were killed.
1945, August 16	According to the KDP's historiography, the Kurdistan Democratic Party (KDP) was founded in Mahabad, Iran. It seems that they chose this day to show that the KDP is the continuation of the J.K., which was established on 16 August 1942. Officially, the KDP was established and distributed its declaration in Mahabad on 23 October 1945.

1945, September 12	Qazi Muhammad, on top of a Kurdish board, visited Baqirov in Baku on 12 September 1945.
1945, September 3	Azerbaijan Democratic Party was founded in Tabriz, Iran.
1945, September 12	The second visit of Qazi Muhammad and Kurdish representatives to Baku on 12 September 1945.
1945, October 23	On 23 October 1945, the Kurdistan Democratic Party (KDP) was established and distributed its declaration in Mahabad. According to the KDP's historiography, KDP was founded 16 August 1945 in Mahabad.
1945, October 24	The Kurdistan Democratic Party held its 1st Congress on 24 October 1945 in Mahabad.
1945, November	Qazi Muhammad invited about sixty city and tribal leaders to meet at the Iranian-Soviet Cultural Relations Society in Mahabad.
1945, December 6	The first issue of the magazine *Kurdistan*, the first organ of the KDP, was published on 6 December 1945.
1945, December 12	The Azerbaijan National Government was established on 12 December 1945 in Tabriz under Azerbaijan Democratic Party led by Pishevari.
1946, January 10	The Kurdistan print house was began working on 10 January 1946 in Mahabad.

1946, January 26	The first Issue of the newspaper *Kurdistan*, the organ of the KDP as well as the Kurdistan Republic, was published on 26 January 1946.
1945, December 17	The Flag of Kurdistan was raised on 17 December 1945 on the top of the building of the *Heyat-e Raeiseh-ye Melli-ye Kurdistan* (National Governing Assembly of Kurdistan) in Mahabad.
1946, January 22	The Kurdistan Republic (also known as the Mahabad Republic) was founded under the Kurdistan Democratic Party led by Qazi Muhammad.
1946, February 23	The Women's Union of Kurdistan was established on 23 February 1946 under Mina Khanim, Qazi Muhammad's wife, in Mahabad.
1946, March 15	According to the newspaper *Kurdistan*, Issue 25, 17 March 1946, the *Hizbi Demokrati Jinani Kurdistan* (Democratic Party of the Women of Kurdistan) was established under Lady Mina on 15 March 1946.
1946, April 30	*Radio Dangi Kurdistan* (Voice of Kurdistan Radio) station was established.
1946, July 9	On 9 July 1946, for the second time Qazi, flying by a Soviet plane from Tabriz to Tehran, to negotiate with Tehran.
1946, December 12	The Iranian army entered Tabriz on 12 December 1946.

1946, December 16	Qazi Muhammad on 16 December 1946 talked by phone with the Brigadier Homayouni and along with Saifi Qazi, Haji Baba Sheikh Siadat, and some others went and submitted themselves to Homayouni in the village of Hamamian in Bukan.
1946, December 17	On 17 December 1946, Qazi Muhammad and other leaders of the Kurdistan. Republic went to the village of Gok Tapa to welcome the Iranian army under Colonel Ghafari. The Iranian army smoothly entered Mahabad, which was the announcement of the end of the Kurdistan Republic
1947, March 31	Qazi Muhammad, Saifi Qazi, and Sadr Qazi were hanged by the Iranian government at *Maidani Chowar Chira* (Four Lights Square) in Mahabad on 31 March 1947.
1947–58	According to Kazim Shandri, on 16 and 17 June 1947, and based on the report of Mir Haj Ahmad Aqrawi, on 17 and 18 June 1947, all Barzanis under Mullah Mustafa Barzani passed the Aras River to the Azerbaijan of the Soviet Union.
1951, March 15	The parliamentary bill of nationalization of oil industry was ratified on 15 March 1351 in National Assembly of Iran and on 20 March 1351 in the Senates Assembly.
1955, Summer	The 1st Conference of the KDP, which Sayyed Rasoul Dehqan calls it a meeting, was initiated in summer 1955 on the Kevi Qalata Rash (Black Fortress Mountain) at the back of the village of Sayyed Away Babi Gawra in Piranshahr. The word Iran was

	added to the name of the party and became *Hizbi Demokrati Kurdistan-Eran* (Kurdistan Democratic Party-Iran).
1961, September	The war stated between Barzani-led Iraqi Kurds and Iraqi government.
1957	The Organization for Intelligence and National Security (SAVAK) was the domestic security and intelligence service of Iran from 1957–1979.
1958, July 14	Abd al-Karim Qasim got power on 14 July 1958 through a coup d'état and eliminated the monarchy.
1958, October	Mullah Mustafa Barzani returned from the Soviet Union to Iraq.
1961	The KDP-I also conducted activities in other parts of Iran. In 1961, after the beginning of the Kurdish Revolution in Iraqi Kurdistan, a secret committee named the *Komitay Barewabari Katii Hizbi Demokrati Kurdistan-Eran* (Temporary Directing Committee of the Kurdistan Democratic Party-Iran) was established in Tehran to help the Kurdish movement in Iraq.
1960s	Salah al-Din Mohtadi and Muhammad Ilkhanizadeh created the Party *Rizgari Kurdistan* (Liberation of Kurdistan) [Kurdistan Liberation Committee]. The Kurdistan Liberation Committee sent a letter containing the program of the Committee to the Iraqi Ba'ath Party on 5 July 1971.

1963, Autumn	The *Komitay Sakhkaraway Hizbi Demokrati Kurdistan-Eran* (Reconstructing Committee of the Kurdistan Democratic Party-Iran) was established in Autumn 1963 by: 1. Qadir Sharif. 2. Hossein Madani. 3. Hassan Rastgar. 4. Said Kowestani. Later, on 17 June 1964, in a declaration, announced its existence.
1964, December	The 2nd Congress of the KDP-I was held between the villages of Sheni in Sardasht and Sone in Qaladiza in December 1964. The Congress chose Ahmad Tawfiq as the leader of the KDP-I.
1966, Summer	According to Said Kaveh (Kowestani) the *Komitay Inqlabii Hizbi Demokrati Kurdistan* (Revolutionary Committee of the Kurdistan Democratic Party) was established in summer 1966 in the back of the village of Alana in the territory of Balakayati, whose members were: 1. Muhammad Amin Siraji. 2. Isma'il Sharifzadeh (Mullah Aziz). 3. Salar Haidari. 4. Mullah Ahmad Shalmashi (Mullah Awara). 5. Said Kowestani. 6. Sanar Mamadi. 7. Mullah Abdullah Abdullahi (Mullah Sarbaz).
1969	Foad Mustafa Sultani, Muhammad Hussein Karimi, Mosleh Sheikh al-Islami, and Abdullah Mohtadi founded an organization in autumn 1969 which later named as the Komala.
1969, August 17	The 2nd Conference of the KDP-I was held on 17 August 1969 in one of the villages of the Qandil Mountain in Sangasar area. The aim of the conference was to rebuild the central committee.
1970	The March Manifesto in Iraq guaranteed Kurdish autonomy.

1970, probably June	The *Komitay Sarkirdayati Katii Hzibi Dimokrati Kurdistan* (Provisional Leadership Committee of the Kurdistan Democratic Party) [also called Provisional Central Committee or Provisional Leadership] was formed more likely in June 1970.
1971, June 21	The 3rd Conference of the KDP-I was held with the 32 participants in the city of Koya in Iraq, on 21 June 1971. Abdul Rahman Ghassemlou was selected as the General Secretary
1973, September 22	The 3rd Congress of the KDP (I) was held in Baghdad on 22 September 1973 in which 49 people participated.
1974	The war started between Iraqi Kurds and Iraqi government.
1971, February 8	The Organization of Iranian People's Fedai Guerrillas (OIPFG) also known as 'Cherikhaye Fadai Khalgh', and 'Fadaian-e Khalgh', and 'Fadaiyan' was established in Iran.
1975, March 15	In 5 March 1975 Iraq and Iran signed the Algiers Agreement based on which Iran ended to support the Iraqi Kurds.
1975, June 1	Jalal Talabani established the Patriotic Union of Kurdistan (PUK).
1976, May 12	On 12 May 1976, in Varna, Bulgaria, the Central Committee of the KDP (I) held a meeting in which Ghassemlou proposed the *Siasi-Nizami* (*Sia-Mi*) (Political-Military Committee) Plan.

1977, May	In May 1977 the *Komitay Rabar (K-R)* (Leadership Committee) of the KDP (I) was established in order to prepare itself for crucial time.
1977, July 27	The Central Committee of the KDP (I) held a session in Paris in the house of Chris Kutschera on 27 July 1977. It was decided to continue the plan of Si-Mi. They chose and sent 10 people to go to Yeman to have a military training.
1978, November, First week	When Ghassemlou returned to Iraq, after a while, about the first week of November 1978, the *Komitay Zagros* (Zagros Committee) was established.
1978, November 27	The *Partiya Karkerên Kurdistanê* (Kurdistan Workers' Party [PKK]), a left-wing Kurdish organization in Turkey Kurdistan, was founded by Abdullah Ocalan on 27 November 1978.
1979, February 11	The Iranian revolution against Mohammad Reza Shah was victorious.
1979, February 16	*Komalay Shorishgeri Zehmetkeshani Kurdistani Eran (Komala)* (Revolutionary Organization of the Toilers of Iranian Kurdistan [Komala]) was revealed itself on 16 February 1979, five days after the victory of the Iranian Revolution of 11 February 1979.
1979, February 17, 18	On 17 February 1979, Ayatollah Nouri, Dariush Forouhar, Dr. Ismail Ardalan, and Dr. Muhammad Mukri, went to Mahabad and on 18 February 1979, they met some Kurdish figures like Qassemlou, Bolurian, and Sheikh Izz al-Din Husseini.

1979, March 21	*Komalay Yaksaniy Kurdistan* (Kurdistan Equality Party) (KEP) or Kurdish Equality Association was established under the general Secretary Mamosta Sayyed Rashid Husseini and some of his friends including Mamosta Abdullah Zaki (Mamosta Qandil) in Saqqiz on 21 March 1979.
1979, April 1	On 12 Farvardin 1358 (1 April 1979), the Iranians voted for the Islamic Republic.
1979, April 20	The Naqadeh war occurred when the KDP (I) hold a large meeting, including many peashmargas, in the Turkish territory of Naqadeh, on 20 April 1979.
1979, February 19	On 19 February 1979, Mahabad's garrison was captured by people.
1979, August 18	On 18 August 1979, Ayatollah Khomeini in a declaration ordered the Chief of the Army General Staff, the Commander-in-Chief of Gendarmerie, and the Commander-in-Chief of the Army of the Guardians of the Islamic Revolution, to command the Iranian forces in Kurdistan to persecute the wicked and invaders, arrest and surrender them to the officials, and close the borders to prevent the wicked from fleeing abroad.
1979, August 19	On 19 August 1979, the Islamic Revolutionary Council in a declaration announced the PDKI an illegal party.
1979, August 19	"The Three-Month War" between the Kurds and the Iranian government lasted from 19 August 1979 to 17 November 1979.

1979, November 17	On 17 November 1979, Khomeini declared a cease-fire and promised granting the rights of the Kurds.
1979, November 22	The *Lejnay Nowenarayati Gali Kurd* (Board of the Representatives of the Kurdish People) was established in Mahabad on 22 November 1979.
1979, December 25	A Kurdish Board was formed to negotiate to the government. The members of the board comprised of the KDP-I, the Komala, the Organization of Iranian People's Fedai Guerrillas (OIPFG), and Sheikh Izz al-Din Husseini. In the board, Sheikh Izz al-Din Husseini was the chief and Ghassemlou was the speaker. On 25 December 1979 the Kurdish Board provided a 26-Article Declaration which was taken to the Iranian Board to Tehran. Similar to the previous 8-Article Demands the government did not pay attention to it and it did not have any positive outcome.
1980, February 19-24	The 4th Congress of the PDKI was held in the Cinema Omid in Mahabad from 19 to 24 February 1980.
1980, March 1	On 1 March 1980, the KDP-I provided a shorter version of the 26-Article Declaration which known as the 6-Article Declaration. It was sent through a board to Tehran to the Iranian President, Abolhassan Banisadr.
1980, March 13	The first parliamentary election after the Iranian Revolution of 1979 was held in Iran.

1980, March Before 21	In the second war in Sanandaj, before the New Year in 21 March 1980, about 2,400 defenseless people of the city were killed by the government.
1980, June 15	The *Hizbi Demokrati Kurdistani Eran (Perawani Kongray Chowar)* (Democratic Party of Iranian Kurdistan (Followers of the Fourth Congress) or PDKI (Followers of the Fourth Congress) or PDKI (FFC) separated from the PDKI on 15 June 1980.
1980, August 28	The *Sazmani Khabati Natawayati w Islami Kurdistani Eran* (Organization of Iranian Kurdistan Nationalist and Islamic Struggle) (Khabat) was established under Sheikh Jalal al-Din Husseini, brother of Sheikh Izz al-Din Husseini, in Baneh on 27 August 1980. In the 3rd Congress of the *Khabat* in 2005, the name of the organization changed to the Organization of Iranian Kurdistan Struggle (Khabat).
1980–88	The Iran–Iraq War occurred from 1980 to 1988.
1981, December 6-9	The 5th Congress of the PDKI known as the *Kongray Shahidan* (Martyrs Congress) was held in the village of Shiwajo in the territory of Rabat, Iran, from 6-9 December 1981.
1983, June 2	On 2 June 1983 the Iranian government executed 59 people from Mahabad in Urmiya.
1984, August 15	The PKK insurgency in Turkey began.

1984, January 22-26	The 6th Congress of the PDKI was held in the village of Galala in the territory of Shinkawe from 22-26 January 1984 in which 230 representatives of the party participated.
1985, December 17-20	The 7th Congress of the PDKI (the 40 Years Struggle Congress) was held in the village of Kani Mew in Kurdistan of Iraq from 17-20 December 1985.
1987–88	Saddam Hussein conducted genocidal *Anfal* campaigns against Iraqi Kurds.
1988, January 18	The 8th Congress of the PDKI was held in Sulaymaniyah, Iraq, on 18 January 1988.
1988, March 21	The *Hizbi Demokrati Kurdistani Eran, Rebarayati Shorishger* (Democratic Party of Iranian Kurdistan-Revolutionary Leadership [PDKI-RL]) split from the PDKI on 21 March 1988.
1988, June 28- July 4	The 4th Conference of the PDKI-RL was held in the city of Ranya, Iraq 28 June-4 July 1988, in which 113 representatives were taken part. Jalil Gadani was selected as the General Secretary and Hassan Rastgar as the alternate General Secretary of the party.
1989, July 13	On 13 July 1989, Dr. Abdul Rahman Ghassemlou, Abdullah Qadiri, and Fazil Rasoul were assassinated while negotiating with the Iranian government, by the Iranian diplomat terrorists including Sahraroudi, Haji Mostafawi, and Bozorgian in Vienna, Austria.

1990, August 12-19	The 9th Congress of the PDKI-RL was held in the village of Qala Sayda in Doli Shawre in Ranya, Iraq, from 12-19 August 1990.
1990	The *Parti Sarbakhoyy Kurdistan* (Independence Party of Kurdistan [PSK]) was established under Amir Qazi in the first month of summer 1990.
1991	The *Yaketi Shorishgerani Kurdistan* (Kurdistan Revolutionaries Unity) was established in 1991 under Said Yazdanpanah. Later its named changed to the *Parti Azadi Kurdistan* (Kurdistan Freedom Party [PAK]) which was founded in its first Congress on 10-12 October 2006.
1991, December 22	The 9th Congress of the PDKI was held in a place called Gali Badran, near the village of Zargali in the area of Nawchia, in Kurdistan of Iraq on 22 December 1991.
1991, August 2	The Iraqi occupation of Kuwait in 2 August 1990 and the subsequent military intervention by the U.S.-led Allied Forces in January 1991 had crucial consequences for the Kurdish movement. The Gulf War ended in February 1991 with the defeat of Iraq. This new situation opened a great opportunity for the Kurdish rebellion.
1992, May 19	Elections was held in Iraqi Kurdistan.
1992, July 4	The Kurdistan Regional Government (KRG) was created in Iraqi Kurdistan.

1992, September 17	Dr. Sadegh Sharafkandi, the leader of the PDKI, Fatah Abdoli, and Homayoun Ardalan were assassinated by the agents of the Islamic Republic at Mykonos Restaurant in Berlin on 17 September 1992.
1992, October 4	The KRG parliament declared Iraqi Kurdistan a constituent state in a federal Iraq.
1993, June	The Peoples Labor Party (HEP) was banned in Turkey and the Democracy Party (DEP) succeeded it.
1994–98	A civil war between the KDP (I) and the PUK happened in Iraqi Kurdistan from 1994 to 1998.
1994, May 1-5	The 10th Congress of the PDKI-RL was held in Ranya, Iraq, from 1-5 May 1994.
1995, April 12	The 10th Congress of the PDKI was held on in Erbil, Iraq, on 12 April 1995.
1996, December 28	On 8 Bafranbar 1375 (28 December 1996), an Agreement, including 20 Articles, between the PDKI and PDKI-RL was signed, based on which the PDKI-RL joined the PDKI and these parties continued their struggle under the name of PDKI
1997, December 22	The 11th Congress of the PDKI was held in Kirkuk, Iraq, on 22 December 1997.
1999, July	As a replacement for the MED-TV, the MEDYA-TV started to broadcast.

1999, February 16	Abdullah Ocalan was captured in Kenya by Turkey and returned to Turkey.
2000, November 24	The 12th Congress of the PDKI was held in Kirkuk, Iraq, on 24 November 2000.
2004, April 25	The *Partia Jiyana Azadi Kurdistan* (Party for Free Life in Kurdistan [PJAK]) was formed on 25 April 2004 in Kurdistan.
2004, July 3	The 13th Congress of the PDKI was held in Koya, Iraq, on 3 July 2004.
2006, October 10-12	The *Parti Azadi Kurdistan* (Kurdistan Freedom Party [PAK]) was founded in its first Congress on 10-12 October 2006. Originally the name of the party was *Yaketi Shorishgerani Kurdistan* (Kurdistan Revolutionaries Unity) which was established in 1991 under Said Yazdanpanah.
2006, December 6	The *Hizbi Demokrati Kurdistan-Iran* (Kurdistan Democratic Party-Iran [KDP-I]) separated from the KDP on 6 December 2006. In the 14th Congress on 6 March 2008, its name changed to the *Hizbi Demokrati Kurdistan* (Kurdistan Democratic Party [KDP]).
2008, March 6-14	The 14th Congress of the KDP was held in Koya, Iraq, from 6-14 March 2008.
2008, September 10-14	The 14th Congress of the PDKI was held in Koya, Iraq, on 10-14 September 2008.

2011, May 23-29	The 15th Congress of the KDP was held in Koya, Iraq, from 23-29 May 2011.
2012, September 29-October 3	The 15th Congress of the PDK was held in Koya, Iraq, from 29 September-3 October 2012.
2016, February 6-11	The 16th Congress of the KDP was held in Koya, Iraq, from 6-11 February 2016.

Aside from other sources, Gunter (2009) has been used throughout this Timeline.

Appendix 2: The Founders of the J.K.

The founders of the J.K. according to Ali Karimi:

1. Rahman Zabihi. 2. Hussein Frouhar. 3. Abdul Rahman Emami. 4. Qadir Modarresi. 5. Najmadin Tohidi. 6. Muhammad Nanavazadeh. 7. Ali Mahmoudi. 8. Muhammad Ashabi.
9. Abdul Rahman Kiani. 10. Seddiq Haidari. 11. Qasim Qadiri (Karimi, 1999, p. 63).

The founders of the J.K. according to Hashem Shirazi:

1. Hussein Frouhar. 2. Rahman Zabihi. 3. Najmadin Tohidi. 4. Muhammad Nanavazadeh. 5. Muhammad Yahou. 6. Abdul Rahman Emani. 7. Mullah Qadir Modarrasi. 8. Muhammad Shapasandi. 9. Abdullah Dawoudi. 10. Qasim Qadiri. 11. Hashem Shirazi. Shirazi maintains that there were some others who he is not sure about them (Shirazi, 2000, p. 101)

The founders of the J.K. according to Qadir Modarresi (claimed in 1981):
It is interesting that Modarresi provides two different lists for the founders of the J.K. in his writings. In 1981 he provides this list: 1. Muhammad Nanavazadeh 2. Abdul Rahman

Zabihi. 3. Hussein Frouhar (Zeringaran). 4. Abdul Rahman Emami 5. Qasim Qadiri. 6. Mullah Abdullah Dawoudi. 7. Muhammad Yahou. 8. Qadir Modarresi. 9. Seddiq Haidari Farouqi 10. Abdul Rahman Kiani (Samadi, 1981, p. 15).

The founders of the J.K. according to Qadir Modarresi (claimed in 1984):
1. Abdul Rahman Zabihi. 2. Muhammad Nanavazadeh. 3. Hussein Frouhar. 4. Abdul Rahman Emami. 5. Qasim Qadiri. 6. Mullah Abdullah Dawoudi (Malay Hajoke). 7. Muhammad Yahou. 8. Qadir Modarresi. 9. Seddiq Haidari Farouqi. 10. Abdul Rahman Kiani. 11. Muhammad Shapasardi. 12. Muhammad Ashabi. 13. Najmadin Tohidi. 14. Hamed Mazouji. 15. Ali Mahmoudi. 16. Muhammad Salimi. In addition, two people participated from the Kurdistan of Iraq: 17. Mir Haj. 18. Mustafa Khoshnaw (Samadi, 1998, p. 111; Samadi, 1984, p. 10).

The founders of the J.K. according to William Eagleton:
1. Rahman Halavi. 2. Muhammad Amin Sharafi. 3. Muhammad Nanavazadeh. 4. Rahman Zabihi. 5. Hussein Frouhar (Zargari) 6. Abdul Rahman Emami. 7. Qasim Qadiri. 8. Mullah Abdullah Dawoudi. 9. Qadir Modarresi. 10. Ahmad Ilmi. 11. Aziz Zandi. 12. Muhammad Yahou. 13. Mir Haj from Iraq (Eagleton, 1963, p. 133).

Appendix 3: The J.K.'s Demands

The J.K.'s demands to the Iranian government were:

> 1- The Iranian government should acknowledge the Kurdish language as the official tongue in all Kurdish territories with a population of over 3 million.
>
> 2- Kurdish should be the official language in education, administration, and justice.
>
> 3- The state officials in Kurdistan should be Kurds.
>
> 4- All financial resources gathered in Kurdistan should be expended in Kurdistan in the construction of schools and hospitals.
>
> 5- These demands should be brought out in parliament and given legal status.
>
> 6- These are our demands in the present circumstances. Yet the future goal shall be self-determination, based on the legitimate right of all peoples to self-determination. Negotiation to this end should be conducted after the war, and there may be no doubt that the Kurds will determine their own future.
>
> 7- If the Kurdish people are enabled to determining their future, then Iran should be dealt with as a neighbour. (Yassin, 1995, p. 114)

In addition, according to Gohari (1999), the Soviet agents in Iran provided a report on 12 October 1945 regarding the minimum program of the J.K., which included:

> -The land reform: To divide all government, endowed, and feudal lords' lands among the toilers, peasants, and herders.
>
> -To return the lands which have been grasped unlawfully by the government and feudal lords to the peasants.
>
> -To try for the development of commerce and industry in Kurdish areas.
>
> -To grant the rights of toilers, peasants, herders, and craftspersons.
>
> -To struggle against the authority of feudalism and the central government.
>
> -To strive for the improvement of public services like health and education.
>
> -To ceaselessly try for radically democratizing of the social life of the Kurds. (p. 44)

Appendix 4: The J. K.'s Publications

Komalay Jianaway Kurdistan (J. K.) (Society for the Revival of Kurdistan [J. K])'s Publications:

1. Govari *Nishtman* (the magazine Homeland). According to Shapasandi, the circulation of *Nishtman* was between 700 and 800 (Shapasandi, 2007, p. 70 of Appendix). The *Nishtman* was often written by Zabihi who was indeed a skilful writer. His articles were also publishing in Turkish magazine *Watan Yolinda* (For Homeland's Sake). Zabihi was very talented. While he knew different Kurdish dialects, he was familiar with English and French (Samadi, 1984, p. 13). Most issues of the *Nishtman* were published in Tabriz. Zabihi provided a small press from Tabriz and brought it to Mahabad on 7 March 1945. It was supposed to print *Nishtman* with this device thereafter (Karimi, 2008, p. 318; Shapasandi, 2007, pp. 28). Shapasandi writes that after the publication of 5th Issue of *Nishtman*, the relationship between Zabihi and the Soviet Consulate became cold. Perhaps the Soviets asked the Khalifehgari print house to create some problem for J.K. publications. Before, Shapasandi and Zabihi rented a house in Tabriz where they were typesetting and then taking it to the Khalifehgari Print Houses for printing. From number 6 to 9 of *Nishtman* were published in this way (Shapasandi, 2007, p.34). Shapasani does not offer any source to support his guess about the relationship between the Soviets and the Khalifehgari's limitation policy of the Kurdish publications. The dates of the publication of the Issues of this magazine are: Issue 1, June 1943; Issue 2, October 1943; Issue 3, 4, November 1943-January 1944; Issue 5, January 1945; Issue 6, February 1945; Issue 7, 8, 9, March-April-May 1945. In addition, after the fall of the Kurdistan Republic, Zabihi in Iraqi Kurdistan, Sitak, published *Nishtman,* Issue 10, October 1948. According to Shapasandi (2007), the circulation of Issue 10 of *Nishtman* was 500 of which Bolourian took 100 and brought to Iran in 21 October 1948 (Shapasandi, 2007, pp. 48-50). There is no document to prove that Bolourian had participated in that process. Regarding *Nishtman*, Issue 10, according to Karimi (1999), Zabihi has told that in that Issue, instead of choosing the name of the J.K., he chose the name of *Nehzati Mqawmat* (Resistance Movement) for the organization. Karimi maintains that that Issue contained some subjects which were against the KDP (Iraq) and Hamza Abdullah (Karimi, 1999, p. 236). Logically, Zabihi should have

continued the publications of *Kurdistan*. Instead, he continued to publish the *Nishtman*. Therefore, he published the *Nishtman* Issue 10 in Kurdistan of Iraq. This was the last Issue of *Nishtman*. The publication of *Nishtman* reveals that although Zabihi actively participated in construction of the Kurdistan Republic, he was more committed to and interested in the J.K.'s ideals, as well as its revival.

2. *Diari Komalay J.K. Bo Lawakani Kurd* (*The Society of J.K.'s Gift for the Kurdish Youth*), published in 1943.

3. *Gulbjerek la diwani Haji Qadri Koyi blbli nishtmani Kurd* (*A selected poems of Haji Qadir Koyi the Kurdistan homeland's nightingale*), published in 1943.

4. *Dasta guleki jowan u bon khosh la baghi nishtman parwari* (*A beautiful and fragrant bouquet from the garden of patriotism*), published in 1943.

5. Govari *Hawari Kurd* (the magazine Shout of Kurd), Issue 1, in September 1945. It was published in September 1945 around the changing of the J.K. to the KDP. It was one of the J.K.'s publications under Sayyed Muhammad Hamidi (Hussein, 2008, p. 71).

6. *Rojjimeri taybati Komala bo Sali 1322* (The J.K.'s calendar for the year (1943-1944).

7. *Rojjimeri taybati Komala bo Sali 1323* (The J.K.'s calendar for the year (1944-1945).

8. *Govari Awat*, (the magazine Wish), Issue 1, 23 October 1945. Shapasandi reveals that after the arrestment of Zabihi, he decided by himself and published the magazine *Awat* (Wish) on 23 October 1945. It was the only Issue of the *Awat*. The J.K.'s CC, through Muhammad Yahou, admonished him for publishing this magazine without their permission. In addition, they informed him that a printing device to Mahabad and he should provide some cadres to work on the press. The press reached to Mahabad in October 1945. Two Russian engineers worked two weeks and established the press. Mullah Qadir Modarresi was the responsible for the printing house while Mullah Sayyed Muhammad Hamidi was the editor of the newspaper *Kurdistan* (Shapasandi, 2007, pp. 28-29).

9. According to Gohari (1999), the J.K. also had an internal publication for the J.K.'s members, under Zabihi, called *Rojnamay Mirow* (*Newspaper Human*) (p. 34).

Appendix 5: The List of the Kurdish Board Which Visited Baku in 1941

The Kurdish board which for the first time visited Baku under Qazi Muhammad, according to Omar Agha Aliar (son of Ali Agha Aliar) included 20 people:

1. Ghazi Muhammad, 2. Ali Agha Aliar (Amir As'ad), the chief of the Dehbukri Tribe. 3. Qarani Agha Amir Ashayer, the Chief of Mamash Tribe. 4. Haji Baba Sheikh Siadat. 5. Majid Khan Mir Mukri. 6. Ali Khan Nozari Mangur. 7. Bayazid Agha Azizi Gawirk. 8. Muhammad Hussein Saifi Qazi. 9. Rashid Baig Harki. 10. Zero Baig Harki 11. Sartip Shikak. 12. Hassan Tilo Shikak. 13. Kak Hamza Qadiri Mamash. 14. Ahmad Khan Farouqi Faizollah Baigi. 15. Hassan Omary Shikak. 16. Muhammad Agha Vosough Ghassemlou. 17. Muhammad Amin Faizollah Baigi. 18. Tro the son of Sayyed Taha. 19. Qoytas Mamadi Shikak. 20. Omar Aliar (the son of Amir As'ad) (Samadi, 1998, p. 154).

Egleton suggests a list of 19 people. A comparison between the list of Eagleton and Aliar shows that Eagleton drops from the Aliar's list these names: Ali Khan Nozari Mangur, Sartip Shikak, Tro the son of Sayyed Taha, Qoytas Mamadi Shikak, Muhammad Agha Vosough Ghassemlou, and Muhammad Amin Faizollah Baigi. Nevertheless, he adds the followings: Taha Harki, Sayyed Muhammad Seddiq (Sheikh Pusho), Muhammad Amin Shikak, Hurko Baigzadeh, and Nouri Baig Baigzadeh (Eagleton, 1963, p. 133; Samadi, 1998, p. 154).

Appendix 6: The Declaration of the Kurdistan Democratic Party

The Declaration of the Kurdistan Democratic Party contains the following eight points:

> 1. The Kurdish people in Iran should have freedom and self-government in the administration of their local affairs, and obtain autonomy within the limits of the Iranian state.
>
> 2. The Kurdish language should be used in education and be the official language in administrative affairs.
>
> 3. The Provincial Council of Kurdistan should immediately be elected according to constitutional law and should supervise and inspect all state and social matters.
>
> 4. All state officials must be of local origin.
>
> 5. A single law for both peasants and notables should be adopted and the future of both secured.
>
> 6. The Kurdish [Kurdistan] Democratic Party will make a special effort to establish unity and complete fraternity with the Azerbaijani people and the other peoples that live in Azerbaijan (Assyrians, Armenians, etc.) in their struggle.
>
> 7. The Kurdish [Kurdistan] Democratic Party will strive for the improvement of the moral and economic state of the Kurdish people through the exploration of Kurdistan's many natural resources, the progress of agriculture and commerce, and development of hygiene and education.
>
> 8. We desire that the people living in Iran be able to strive freely for the happiness and progress of their country. (Roosevelt, 1980, pp. 140-141; Ghassemlou, 2000, pp. 37-38; Saleh and Saleh, 2007, pp. 354-355; Yassin, 1995. p. 152)

Appendix 7: The Six-Article Declaration on 22 January 1946

Homayoun (2004) affirms that a Six-article Declaration was announced at the end of the meeting on 22 January 1946 in which people's representatives asked the CC of the KDP and the "*Anjoman-e Melli-ye Kurdistan*" or *Hayat-i Raeisay Milli Kurdistan* (National Governing Assembly of Kurdistan) for the following demands:

1. To establish a relative freedom in the areas in which the Kurds are living.
2. To hold the National Parliament election.
3. To form the National Government of Kurdistan and the Council of Ministers.
4. To found the Kurdish armed force in the Kurdish areas.
5. To set up commercial and economic relations with the neighbouring country [the Soviet Union].
6. To form friendly relationships with the Azeri brothers. (pp. 53-54)

Appendix 8: The list of the Leadership of the KDP from 1945 to 2016

The 1ˢᵗ Congress of the KDP

The 1ˢᵗ Congress of the KDP was held on 24 October 1945 in Mahabad.

Eagleton maintains that the Congress selected Qazi Muhammad as its leaders, and the following Central Committee:

1. Haji Baba Sheikh Siadat
2. Muhammad Hussein Khan Saifi Qazi
3. Manaf Karimi
4. Sayyed Muhammad Ayyoubian
5. Abdul Rahman Ilkhanizadeh
6. Ismail Ilkhanizadeh
7. Ahmad Ilahi
8. Khalil Khosrawi
9. Karim Ahmadain
10. Haji Mustafa Dawoudi
11. Muhammad Amin Mo'ini
12. Mahmoud Walizadeh
13. Muhammad (Dilshad) Rasouli
14. Muhammad Amin Sharafi
15. Abdul Rahman Zabihi (Eagleon, 1963, p. 134).

The list of the Central Committee of the 1ˢᵗ Congress of the KDP according to Gadani:

1. Peshawa Qazi Muhammad (Leader of the KDP)
2. Muhammad Hussein Saifi Qazi.
3. Haji Baba Sheikh Siadat.
4. Manaf Karimi.
5. Sayyed Muhammad Ayyoubian.
6. Abdul Rahman Ilkhanizadeh.
7. Khalil Khosrawi.

8. Karim Ahmadin.

9. Haji Mustafa Dawoudi

10. Muhammad Amin Mo'ini.

11. Mahmoud Walizadeh.

12. Muhammad (Dilshad) Rasouli.

13. Sayyed Abdullah Gailani.

14. Omar Khan Sharifi (Shikak).

15. Zero Baig Bahadiri (Harki).

16. Rashid Baig Jahangiri.

17. Ismail Ilkhanizadeh.

18. Ahmad Ilahi.

19. Muhammad Amin Sharafi.

20. Abdul Rahman Zabihi (Gadani, 2008a, p. 31).

Rahman Naqshi adds the following to the list:

21. Seddiq Haidari.

22. Mustafa Sultanian.

23. Wahab Bolourian (Naqshi, 2015, April 16).

***

The 1st Conference of the KDP-I

The 1st Conference of the KDP, which Sayyed Rasoul Dehqan calls it a meeting, was initiated on the Kevi Qalata Rash (the Black Fortress Mountain) at the back of the village of Sayyed Away Babi Gawra in Piranshahr in summer 1955. Hassanzadeh claims that the 1st Conference was held in the Spring 1955.

According to Hassanzadeh, the 1st Conference chose the following leadership:

1. Abdul Rahman Ghassemlou (the director general, and internal and outside relations),

2. Ghani Bolourian (the southern area especially Sanandaj),

3. Aziz Yousefi (Urmiya, the northern area, and printing),

4. Rahmat Allah Shariati (the southern area especially Sanandaj),

5. Abdullah Ishaqi (Mahabad and its area),

6. Dr. Ali Mawlawi (consultant member) (Hassanzadeh, n.d., p. 111).

***

The *Komitay Sakhkaraway Hizbi Demokrati Kurdistan-Eran* (Reconstructing Committee of the Kurdistan Democratic Party-Iran)

The *Komitay Sakhkaraway Hizbi Demokrati Kurdistan-Eran* (Reconstructing Committee of the Kurdistan Democratic Party-Iran) was established in Autumn 1963 by: 1. Qadir Sharif. 2. Hossein Madani. 3. Hassan Rastgar. 4. Said Kowestani. Later, on 17 June 1964, in a declaration, announced its existence.

The founders of the Reconstructing Committee were:

1. Hassan Rastgar

2. Hossein Madani

3. Said Kowestani

4. Qadir Sharif

5. Mullah Awara

6. Mullah Abubakir Falsafi.

In addition, three people were selected as the alternate members:

1. Hassan Naghadehei,

2. Mullah Rasoul Peshnimaz,

3. Qadir Qazi (Mamand) (Gadani, 2008a, p. 170; Hassanzadeh, n.d., pp. 116-117; Sardashti, 2002a, p. 12).

***

The 2nd Congress of the KDP-I

The 2nd Congress of the KDP-I was held between the villages of Sheni in Sardasht and Sone in Qaladiza in December 1964. The congress chose Ahmad Tawfiq as the leader of the KDP-I.

According to Khizri, the list of the Central Committee members included:

1. Seddiq Anjiri.

2. Ahmad Tawfiq.

3. Sulayman Mo'ini (Fayq).

4. Mullah Sayyed Rashid Husseini (Saqqizi).

5. Mullah Rahim Wirdi.

6. Amir Qazi.

7. Naho Pashayy (Bapir Shikak).

8. Sayyed Kamil Imami (Hashimi).

9. Habib Qaragowezi (Warzer).

10. Sarm Al-Din Sadiq Waziri.

11. Rahim Jawanmard Qazi.

12. Abdul Rahman Sharafkandi (Mamosta Hajar).

13. Dr. Ali Mawlawi.

14. Aziz Yousefi.

15. Ghani Bolourian.

Gadani and Hasanzadeh omit Sarm Al-Din Sadiq Waziri and Sanar Mamadi. In addition, Hassanzadeh replaces Rahim Jawanmard Qazi with Dr. Rahim Qazi

The *Komitay Chawaderi Barz* (the Higher Inspection Committee) included:

1. Abdullah Mo'ini.

2. Mullah Qadir Lachini.

3. Raouf Mullah Hassan (Wasta Raouf Khayat).

4. Sayyed Haji Kalawe.

5. Sayyed Tahir Imami (Hashimi) (son of Sayyed Kamil Hashimi).

6. Mullah Karim Sardakosani (Azizi).

7. Mullah Najmadin Kawkabi.

8. Sayyed Rasoul Dehqan.

9. Mustafa Ishaqi (Qoula).

10. Abdullah Mawlawi.

11. Rashid Falahi (Rashay Qachaqchi) (Gadani, 2008a, p. 145; Hassanzadeh, n.d., pp. 120-121; Khizri, 2003, pp. 48-49).

***

***Komitay Inqilabii Hizbi Demokrati Kurdistan-Eran* (Revolutionary Committee of the Kurdistan Democratic Party-Iran or Revolutionary Committee).**

The *Komitay Inqilabii Hizbi Demokrati Kurdistan-Eran* (Revolutionary Committee of the Kurdistan Democratic Party-Iran or Revolutionary Committee) was established
was established in the back of the village of Alana in the territory of Balakayati, in Summer 1966, whose members were:

Isma'il Sharifzadeh (Mullah Aziz),

Muhammad Amin Siraji,

Mullah Ahmad Shalmashi (Mullah Awara),

Said Kaveh (Kowestani),

Sanar Mamadi,

Mullah Abdullah Abdullahi (Mullah Sarbaz)

Salar Haidari (Kaveh, 2005, p. 154).

The list according to Gadani included:

Sulayman Mo'ini (Fayq),

Isma'il Sharifzadeh (Mullah Aziz),

Muhammad Amin Siraji,

Mullah Ahmad Shalmashi (Mullah Awara),

Bapir Shikak (Naho Pashayy),

Abdullah Mo'ini,

Sanar Mamadi

Mullah Abdullah Abdullahi (Mullah Sarbaz) (Gadani, 2008a, pp. 152-153).

***

The 2nd Conference of the KDP-I

The 2nd Conference of the KDP-I was held in one of the villages of the Qandil Mountain in Sangasar area on 17 August 1969. The aim of the conference was to rebuild the Central Committee.

The new Central Committee included:

1. Ahmad Tawfiq.
2. Ghani Bolourian.
3. Aziz Yousefi.
4. Amir Qazi.
5. Mullah Sayyed Rashid [Husseini] Saqqizi.
6. Momosta Abdullah Hassanzadeh
7. Hassan Rastgar
8. Mamosta Hemin (Gadani, 2008a, pp. 173-174).

***

Provisional Leadership of the KDP-I

The *Komitay Sarkirdayati Katii Hzibi Dimokrati Kurdistan* (Provisional Leadership Committee of the Kurdistan Democratic Party) [also called Provisional Central Committee or Provisional Leadership] was more likely established in June 1970.

The members of the Provisional Leadership ware:

1. Abdul Rahman Ghassemlou.
2. Amir Qazi.
3. Mamosta Hemin.
4. Muhammad Amin Siraji.
5. Hassan Rastgar.
6. Mamosta Abdullah Hassanzadeh.
7. Yousef Rizwani.
8. Karim Hisami.

A commission for writing the platform and constitution of the party was chosen whose members were:

1. Abdul Rahman Ghassemlou.
2. Karim Hisami.
3. Muhammad Amin Siraji.
4. Mamosta Abdullah Hassanzadeh.

***

The 3rd Conference of the KDP (I)

The 3rd Conference of the KDP (I) was held with the 32 participants in the city of Koya in Iraq, on 21 June 1971. Abdul Rahman Ghassemlou was selected as the General Secretary. The followings were chosen as the member of the Central Committee:

1. Abdul Rahman Ghassemlou.
2. Karim Hisami.
3. Muhammad Amin Siraji.
4. Mamosta Hemin.
5. Mamosta Abdullah Hassanzadeh.
6. Hassan Rastgar.
7. Rasoul Peshnimaz
8. Qadir Werdi
9. Sayyed Rasoul Dehqan
10. Amir Qazi.
11. Karim Haddad

The Politburo was comprised of:
1. Abdul Rahman Ghassemlou (Geneal Secretary).
2. Karim Hisami.
3. Muhammad Amin Siraji.
4. Mamosta Hemin.

5. Mamosta Abdullah Hassanzadeh. (Gadani, 2008a, pp. 182-183; Hassanzadeh, nd., pp. 130-131).

***

The 3rd Congress of the KDP (Iran)

The 3rd Congress of the KDP (Iran) was held in Baghdad on 22 September 1973. Abdul Rahman Ghassemlou was selected as the General Secretary.

The chosen Central Committee member of the party included:

1. Abdul Rahman Ghassemlou.
2. Karim Hisami.
3. Muhammad Amin Siraji.
4. Mamosta Abdullah Hassanzadeh
5. Mamosta Hemin.
6. Muhammad Mohtadi
7. Amir Qazi.
8. Dr. Hassan Shitwi
9. Dr. Sultan Watamishi
10. Hashim Karimi
11. Rasoul Peshnimaz
12. Ghani Bolourian
13. Aziz Yousefi

Note: Hassanzadeh omits Bolourian and Yousefi from the list.

The Politburo members were:
1. Abdul Rahman Ghassemlou.
2. Mamosta Abdullah Hassanzadeh
3. Karim Hisami.
4. Dr. Sultan Watamishi
5. Muhammad Amin Siraji

The alternate members of the Central Committee were:

1. Karim Hadad

2. Mullah Ismail Haji.

3. Muhammad Rasoul Hassanpour

4. Mullah Salam Nijnayy [Shafi'i] (Gadani, 2008a, p. 196; Hassanzadeh, nd., pp. 137-138).

***

Komitay Siasy-Nizami (Sia-Mi) (Political-Military Committee or the Sia-Mi Committee) of the KDP (I)

On 12 May 1976, in Varna, Bulgaria, the Central Committee of the KDP (I) held a meeting in which Ghassemlou proposed the *Siasi-Nizami* (*Sia-Mi*) (Political-Military Committee) Plan. When Ghassemlou and Amir Qazi returned to Iraq, the Central Committee held a meeting on 21 November 1976. The Sia-Mi Committee was established. Its members were:

1. Abdul Rahman Ghassemlou.

2. Amir Qazi.

3. Muhammad Amin Siraji.

4. Mamosta Abdullah Hassanzadeh.

After two days Mamosta Abdullah Hassanzadeh withdrew and

4. Mullah Ismail Haji was replaced (Gadani, 2008a, p. 203-205; Hisami, 2011, p. 148).

***

The *Komitay Rabar (K-R)* (Leadership Committee) of the KDP (I)

In May 1977 the *Komitay Rabar (K-R)* (Leader Committee) of the KDP (I) was established in order to prepare itself for crucial time. This Committee included:

1. Muhammad Amin Siraji.

2. Sayyed Rasoul Dehqan.

3. Rasoul Peshnimaz.

4. Hashim Karimi.

5. Karim Hadad.

6. Hassan Shiwasali.

7. Mullah Ismail Haji.

The day after, Muhammad Amin Siraji disagreed with and being in the Committee. Thus, Karim Hisami was replaced him as the leader of the Committee (Gadani, 2008a, p. 206).

***

Yemen

The Central Committee of the KDP (I) held a session in Paris in the house of Chris Kutschera on 27 July 1977. It was decided to continue the plan of Si-Mi. They chose and sent 10 people to go to Yemen to have a military training. These people who were under Hashim Karimi included:

1. Hassan Rastgar.
2. Hashim Karimi.
3. Sayyed Rasoul Dehqan.
4. Faqe Abdullah Qalarashi.
5. Mullah Seddiq.
6. Mullah Hassan Shiwasali.
7. Mirza Ali.
8. Muhammad Bukani.
9. Mullah Osman (Jalal Mirawayy).
10. Mullah Mahmoud Qazani (Gadani, 2008a, 2007).

***

The *Komitay Zagros* (Zagros Committee) of the KDP (I)

When Ghassemlou returned to Iraq, after a while, about the first week of November 1978, the *Komitay Zagros* (Zagros Committee) was established. The leaders who returned included

1. Abdul Rahman Ghassemlou.
2. Mamosta Abdullah Hassanzadeh.
3. Amir Qazi.
4. Hashim Karimi.

5. Salim Babanzadeh.

6. Sayyed Rasoul Dehqan.

7. Mullah Hassan Shiwasali.

8. Muhammad Amin Siraji (Hassanzadeh, n.d., p. 147; Gadani, 2008a, p. 224).

***

The 4th Congress of the PDKI

The 4th Congress of the PDKI was held in the Cinema Omid in Mahabad from 19 to 24 February 1980. Abdul Rahman Ghassemlou was chosen as the General Secretary.

The Central Committee included:

1. Ghani Bolurian.

2. Abdul Rahman Ghassemlou.

3. Jalil Gadani

4. Hassan Shiwasali.

5. Fawzieh Qazi.

6. Amir Qazi.

7. Mustafa Shalmashi.

8. Dr. Sadiq Sharafkandi.

9. Rahman Karimi.

10. Mamosta Abdullah Hassanzadeh

11. Jahangir Ismailzadeh.

12. Farouq Keikhosrawi.

13. Sargord (Major) Abbasi.

14. Nawid Mo'ini.

15. Sanar Mamadi.

16. Hassan Rastgar.

17. Ahmad Azizi.

18. Kamal Dabbaghi.

19. Qadir Abdi.

20. Hashim Karimi.

21. Rahim Saif Qazi.
22. Mustafa Hijri.
23. Abubakir Hidayati.
24. Sayyed Rasoul Dehqan.
25. Hossein Madani.
26. Mamosta Hemin.

Mamosta Hemin was chosen as the honorary member of the Central Committee.

The Politburo included:
1. Abdul Rahman Ghassemlou.
2. Ghani Bolourian.
3. Jalil Gadani.
4. Dr. Sadiq Sharafkandi. [Mustafa Hijri].
5. Amir Qazi.
6. Mamosta Abdullah Hassanzadeh.
7. Mustafa Shalmashi.

Moreover, the first plenum of the party selected the followings as the alternate members:
1. Sayyed Hassan Hashimi.
2. Osman Asrary.
3. Faraydoun Mitran.
4. Rasoul Peshnimaz.
5. Sayyed Ali Rahmani.
6. [Abdul] Rahman Haji Ahmadi.
7. Hussein Ibrahimi.
8. Salim Babanzadeh.
9. Aziz Mamle.
10. Shapour Firouzi.
11. Hassan Sharafi.

12. Rahman Kajehyy.

13. Taha Haq Talab.

14. Taha Atiqi.

15. Hakim Razayy.

16. Zobaideh Talebpour.

Furthermore, the congress selected and inspection Committee which included

1. Fatah Kawian.

2. Iraj (Sarhang, Colonel) Qadiri.

3. Qadir Shahabi.

4. Seddiq Qawi Panjeh.

5. Dr. Khosrawi.

6. Said Sultanian.

7. Sarhang (Colonel) Rabiei.

8. Sarwan (Lieutenant) Afshin.

9. Rahman Aria (Mohandes, Engineer).

10. Ali Hassaniani.

11. Muhammad Pour Azar.

While Gadani adds Mustafa Hijri instead of Dr. Sadiq Sharafkandi to this list of the Politburo, Hassanzadeh omits Hijri from the list. Hassanzadeh omits Salim Babanzadeh from the list of the alternate members of the CC (Gadani, 2008a, p. 259; Hassanzadeh, n.d., pp. 180-183).

***

The *Hizbi Demokrati Kurdistani Eran* (*Perawani Kongray Chowar*) (Democratic Party of Iranian Kurdistan (Followers of the Fourth Congress) or PDKI (Followers of the Fourth Congress) or PDKI (FFC)

On 15 June 1980 six members of the Central Committee of the PDKI along with Mamosta Hemin who was chosen as the honorary member of the Central Committee by issuing a declaration announced their separation from the party. They established the *Hizbi Demokrati Kurdistani Eran* (*Perawani Kongray Chowar*) (Democratic Party of Iranian Kurdistan (Followers of the Fourth Congress [FFC]) or PDKI (FFC). Ghani Bolourian was the leader of the PDKI (FFC).

These people were:

1. Ghani Bolurian.
2. Fawzieh Qazi.
3. Farouq Keikhosrawi.
4. Nawid Mo'ini.
5. Ahmad Azizi.
6. Rahim Saif Qazi.
7. Mamosta Hemin.

Later, the following Central Committee members of the PDKI also joined the party:

1. Rahman Karimi
2. Sanar Mamadi.
3. Jahangir Isma'ilzadeh

Finally, the complete number of the members of the Central Committee who were chosen or joined the PDKI (FFC) included:

1. Ghani Bolurian.
2. Fawzieh Qazi.
3. Farouq Keikhosrawi.
4. Nawid Mo'ini.
5. Ahmad Azizi.
6. Rahim Saif Qazi.
7. Mamosta Hemin.
8. Muhammad Amin Siraji.
9. Qadir Khalidi.
10. Nasser Khoshkalam.

11. Hussein Bakhchi.

12. Rahman Karimi

13. Sanar Mamadi.

14. Jahangir Isma'ilzadeh

The Politburo included:

1. Ghani Bolurian.

2. Rahim Saif Qazi.

3. Muhammad Amin Siraji.

The consultant members of the Central Committee were:

1. Ahmad Safa.

2. Rahman Piroti.

3. Abdullah Qoreshi.

4. Rahmat Atri (Bakhchi, 2007, pp. 38-39, 45; Bakhchi, Personal communication, November 5, 2012; Gadani, 2001, p. 109; Gadani, 2008a, pp. 281-282; Safa, Personal communication, December 8, 2012).

***

The 5th Congress of the PDKI

The 5th Congress of the PDKI known as the *Kongray Shahidan* (Martyrs Congress) was held in the village of Shiwajo in the territory of Rabat, Iran, from 6-9 December 1981. Abdul Rahman Ghassemlou was selected as the PDKI's General Secretary and Sadiq Sharafkandi as the alternate of the General Secretary.

The Central Committee included:

1. Aziz Mamle.

2. Abdul Rahman Ghassemlou.

3. Jalil Gadani.

4. Taifour Bathayy.

5. Ahmad Jawidfar (Hajar).

6. Mamosta Abdullah Hassanzadeh.

7. Hashim Karimi.

8. Hassan Sharafi.

9. Mustafa Shalmashi.

10. Hossein Madani.

11. Dr. Sadiq Sharafkandi.

12. Hassan Rastgar.

13. Fatah Kawian.

14. Ali Kashifpour.

15. Baba Ali Mehrparwar.

16. Kamal Dabbaghi.

17. Mustafa Hijri.

18. Rahim Muhammadzadeh.

19. Said Kowestani.

20. Hakim Razayy.

21. Rahman Aria (Mohandes, Engineer).

22. Amir Qazi.

23. Sayyed Rasoul Dehqan.

24. Abdullah Bahrami.

25. Nabi Qadiri.

The Politburo members were:

1. Abdul Rahman Ghassemlou.

2. Dr. Sadiq Sharafkandi

3. Mamosta Abdullah Hassanzadeh

4. Mustafa Shalmashi.

5. Jalil Gadani.

6. Fatah Kawian.

7. Mustafa Hijri

The alternate members of the Central Committee were:

1. Sayyed Hassan Hashimi

2. Tahir Aliar.

3. Rahim Baghdadi.

4. Shapour Firouzi.

5. Ali Kitabi.

6. Abdullah Ibrahimi.

7. Ghani Ghanipour.

8. Behrouz Kurd Ahmadi.

The consultant members of the Central Committee were:

1. Rahman Kajehyy.

2. Azim Afsar.

3. Jafar Hamidi.

4. Hassan Shiwasali.

5. Ghafour Hamzayy.

6. Homayoun Ardalan.

7. Aziz Lahimi.

Hassanzadeh adds Abdullah Ezatpour to the list. Also, after Ahmad Jawidfar killed, the Central Committee chose Behrouz Kurd Ahmadi as the Central Committee member (Hassanzadeh, 1996, pp. 10-11).

***

The 6th Congress of the PDKI

The 6th Congress of the PDKI was held in the village of Galala in the territory of Shinkawe from 22-26 January 1984. Abdul Rahman Ghassemlou was selected as the General Secretary and Sadiq Sharafkandi as the alternate of the General Secretary of the PDKI.

The chosen Central Committee based on their higher votes included:

1. Hassan Rastgar.

2. Abdul Rahman Ghassemlou.

3. Jalil Gadani.

4. Tahir Aliar.
5. Hashim Karimi.
6. Dr. Sadiq Sharafkandi.
7. Mustafa Hijri.
8. Mamosta Abdullah Hassanzadeh.
9. Hassan Sharafi.
10. Mustafa Shalmashi.
11. Homayoun Ardalan.
12. Hossein Madani.
13. Fatah Kawian.
14. Hassan Shiwasali.
15. Ali Kashifpour.
16. Dr. Hussein Khalighi.
17. Sargord (Major) Aliar.
18. Rahim Muhammadzadeh.
19. Shapour Firouzi.
20. Baba Ali Mehrparwar.
21. Ghafour Hamzayy.
22. Nabi Qadiri.
23. Hakim Razayy.
24. Jahangir Ismailzadeh.
25. Abdullah Bahrami.

In the first plenum after the congress, the following were chosen as the Politburo:

1. Abdul Rahman Ghassemlou.
2. Dr. Sadiq Sharafkandi.
3. Mamosta Abdullah Hassanzadeh.
4. Hashim Karimi.
5. Jalil Gadani.
6. Hassan Sharafi.

7. Hassan Rastgar.

The alternate members of the Central Committee were:
1. Abubakir Rad.
2. Muhammad Amin Majidian.
3. Morad Qadiri.
4. Rahman Rahimi (Chako).
5. Jafar Hamidi.
6. Seddiq Farokhian.
7. Fatah Abdoli.

In addition, the following were chosen as the consultant members of the Central Committee:
1. Sanar Mamadi (Hassanzadeh, 1996, p. 60).
2. Hassan Ayoubzadeh (Mamosta Goran).
3. Seddiq Babayy.
4. Abdullah Ezatpour.

Hassanzadeh omits Morad Qadiri from the list of the alternate members. Hassanzadeh omits Mamadi and Ayoubzadeh and adds Morad Qadiri, and Rahim Baghdadi to the list of the consultants (Gadani, 2008a, p. 342; Hassanzadeh, 1996, pp. 58-60).

***

The 7th Congress of the PDKI (The 40 Years Struggle Congress)

The 7th Congress of the PDKI (the 40 Years Struggle Congress) was held in the village of Kani Mew in Kurdistan of Iraq from 17-20 December 1985. Abdul Rahman Ghassemlou was selected as the General Secretary and Sadiq Sharafkandi as the alternate of the General Secretary of the PDKI.

The congress chose the followings as the Central Committee members:
1. Abdul Rahman Ghassemlou.

2. Hashim Karimi.

3. Dr. Sadiq Sharafkandi.

4. Mustafa Hijri.

5. Hossein Madani.

6. Jalil Gadani.

7. Fatah Kawian.

8. Seddiq Babayy.

9. Ali Kashifpour.

10. Hassan Rastgar.

11. Mamosta Abdullah Hassanzadeh.

12. Muhammad Amin Majidian.

13. Hassan Shiwasali.

14. Hakim Razayy.

15. Nabi Qadiri.

16. Hassan Sharafi.

17. Osman Rahimi.

18. Abdullah Qadiri.

19. Jafar Hamidi.

20. Abubakir Rad.

21. Abdullah Ezatpour.

22. Salam Azizi.

23. Dr. Hussein Khalighi.

24. Fatah Abdoli.

25. Baba Ali Mehrparwar.

The following were selected as the Politburo members:

1. Abdul Rahman Ghassemlou.

2. Dr. Sadiq Sharafkandi.

3. Hassan Sharafi.

4. Hashim Karimi.

5. Hassan Rastgar.

The alternate members of the Central Committee were:
1. Rahman Rahimi (Chako).
2. Sadoun Abbasi.
3. Ibrahim Lajani.
4. Kamal Karimi.
5. Hassan Ayoubzadeh.
6. Ismat Abdi.
7. Colonel Iraj Qadiri.
8. Mahmoud Dashti.
9. Shapour Firouzi.
10. Muhammad Nazif Qadiri.

On 11 December 1986, the third plenum of the PDKI selected these people as the consultant members of the Central Committee:
1. Ghafour Hamzayy.
2. Rahim Muhammadzadeh.
3. Abdullah Sharifi.

Hassazadeh adds Shapour Shojai Fard and Omar Sharifzadeh to the list (Hassanzadeh, 1996, pp. 137-140).

***

The 8th Congress of the PDKI

The 8th Congress of the PDKI was held in Sulaymaniyah on 18 January 1988. Abdul Rahman Ghassemlou was selected as the General Secretary and Sadiq Sharafkandi as the alternate of the General Secretary of the PDKI.

The election Committee suggested the Fixed List of the 25 people for the Central Committee as follows:

1. Abdul Rahman Ghassemlou.
2. Dr. Sadiq Sharafkandi.
3. Dr. Hussein Khalighi.
4. Mustafa Hijri.
5. Hassan Sharafi.
6. Baba Ali Mehrparwar.
7. Salam Azizi.
8. Fatah Abdoli.
9. Hassan Shiwasali.
10. Ibrahim Lajani.
11. Mansour Fatahi.
12. Muhammad Nazif Qadiri.
13. Jafar Hamidi.
14. Taimour Mostafayy.
15. Ghafour Hamzayy.
16. Abdullah Sharifi.
17. Mahmoud Dashti.
18. Sayyed Reza Diroudgar.
19. Abdullah Qadiri.
20. Jalil Gadani.
21. Fatah Kawian.
22. Hossein Madani.
23. Seddiq Babayy.
24. Kamal Karimi.
25. Abubakir Rad (Hassanzadeh, 1996, pp. 163-164).

Before voting to the Fixed List of 25 people, six members of the Central Committee in the list including the followings withdrew themselves from the list.
1. Jalil Gadani.
2. Hossein Madani.

3. Fatah Kawian.

4. Seddiq Babayy.

5. Kamal Karimi.

6. Abubakir Rad.

The Central Committee of the PDKI were:

1. Abdul Rahman Ghassemlou.

2. Dr. Sadiq Sharafkandi.

3. Mustafa Hijri.

4. Hassan Sharafi.

5. Baba Ali Mehrparwar.

6. Dr. Hussein Khalighi.

7. Salam Azizi.

8. Fatah Abdoli.

9. Hassan Shiwasali.

10. Ibrahim Lajani.

11. Mansour Fatahi.

12. Muhammad Nazif Qadiri.

13. Jafar Hamidi.

14. Taimour Mostafayy.

15. Ghafour Hamzayy.

16. Abdullah Sharifi.

17. Mahmoud Dashti.

18. Sayyed Reza Diroudgar.

19. Abdullah Qadiri.

The Politburo of the PDKI included:

1. Abdul Rahman Ghassemlou.

2. Dr. Sadiq Sharafkandi.

3. Mustafa Hijri.

4. Hassan Sharafi.

5. Baba Ali Mehrparwar.

The alternate members of the PDKI were:

1. Seddiq Firouzi.

2. Muhammad Ali Anayati.

3. Sayyed Ahmad Husseini.

4. Mustafa Mawloudi.

5. Omar Hamidi.

6. Abdullah Ibrahimi.

7. Rahman Rahimi (Chako).

The consultant members of the PDKI were:

1. Abdullah Ezatpout.

2. Ahmad Nastani.

3. Sayyed Rasoul Sayyed Ahmadi.

4. Shaho Husseini.

5. Kawa Bahrami (Hassanzadeh, 1996, pp. 163-164, 167).

***

Hizbi Demokrati Kurdistani Eran-Rebarayati Shorishger (Iranian Democratic Party of Kurdistan-Revolutionary Leadership [PDKI-RL])

On 21 March 1988, the PDKI-RL split from the PDKI and announced a 10-Article Declaration.

The Declaration of the PDKI-RL, published on 21 March 1988, was signed by the followings:

1. Jalil Gadani.

2. Hassan Rastgar.

3. Fatah Kawian.

4. Hossein Madani.

5. Nabi Qadiri.

6. Seddiq Babayy.

7. Abubakir Rad.

8. Osman Rahimi.

9. Ali Kashifpour.

10. Sarhang (Colonel) Iraj Qadiri.

11. Kamal Karimi.

12. Ismat Abdi.

13. Shapour Firouzi.

14. Rahim Muhammadzadeh.

15. Shapour Shojai Fard (Gadani, 2008b, pp. 39-40).

***

The 4th Conference of the PDKI-RL

The 4th Conference of the PDKI-RL was held in the city of Ranya, Iraq from 28 June-4 July 1988, in which 113 representatives were taken part. Jalil Gadani was chosen as the General Secretary and Hassan Rastgar as the alternate General Secretary.

The 4th Conference of the PDKI-RL chose the following Central Committee:

1. Jalil Gadani.

2. Hassan Rastgar.

3. Hashim Karimi.

4. Fatah Kawian.

5. Sayyed Ibrahim Karimi.

6. Hossein Madani.

7. Ali Kashifpour.

8. Osman Rahimi.

9. Kamal Karimi.

10. Shapour Firouzi.

11. Seddiq Babayy.

12. Nabi Qadiri.

13. Omar Sharifzadeh.

14. Abubakir Rad.

15. Sarhang (Colonel) Iraj Qadiri.

16. Mozafar Mitran.

17. Shapour Shojai Fard.

The Politburo of the PDKI-RL included:

1. Jalil Gadani.

2. Hassan Rastgar.

3. Fatah Kawian.

4. Hossein Madani.

5. Nabi Qadiri.

In addition, the alternate members of the Central Committee included:

1. Faysal Irandoust.

2. Rahim Salihzadeh

3. Muhammad Mirwati.

4. Mullah Khidir Omarzadeh.

5. Morad Mehraban.

6. Amir Qadiri.

The consultant members included:

1. Osman Fatahi.

2. Rashad Husseini.

3. Najmadin Zor Asna.

4. Badir Shikak (Gadani, 2008b, pp. 51-52).

***

The 9th Congress of the PDKI-RL

The 9th Congress of the PDKI-RL was held in the village of Qala Sayda in Doli Shawre in Ranya, Iraq, from 12-19 August 1990. Jalil Gadani was chosen as the General Secretary and Hassan Rastgar as the alternate General Secretary of the party.

The 9th Congress of the PDKI-RL chose the following Central Committee:

1. Jalil Gadani.
2. Hashim Karimi.
3. Faysal Irandoust.
4. Hassan Rastgar.
5. Shapour Firouzi.
6. Kamal Karimi.
7. Nabi Qadiri.
8. Sarhang (Colonel) Iraj Qadiri.
9. Abubakir Rad.
10. Fatah Kawian.
11. Osman Rahimi.
12. Hossein Madani.
13. Khalid Hassanpour.
14. Mozafar Mitran.
15. Said Baigzadeh.

In addition, the first plenum of the party chose Jalil Gadani as the General Secretary and Hassan Rastgar as the alternate General Secretary of the party on 25 August 1990. The Politburo of the PDKI-RL included:

1. Jalil Gadani.
2. Hassan Rastgar.
3. Hashim Karimi.
4. Fatah Kawian.
5. Nabi Qadiri

Moreover, the alternate members of the Central Committee included:

1. Mullah Khidir Omarzadeh.
2. Muhammad Mirwati.
3. Fatah Rihani.
4. Hashim Rostami.

The second plenum chose these consultant members of the Central Committee of the party:

1. Amir Qazi.
2. Haji Golawi.
3. Sirwan Hafidi.
4. Morad Hafidi.
5. Sayyed Ibrahim Karimi (Gadani, 2008b, pp. 74-75).

***

The 9th Congress of the PDKI

The 9th Congress of the PDKI was held in a place called Gali Badran, near the village of Zargali in the area of Nawchia, in Kurdistan of Iraq, on 22 December 1991. It was called the Ghassemlous' Congress because he was born on *Shabe Yalda* (the night of the winter solstice) (Hassanzadeh, 1996, p. 226). Sadiq Sharafkandi was chosen as the General Secretary and Mustafa Hijri as the alternate General Secretary.

The members of the Central Committee of the PDKI were:

1. Dr. Sadiq Sharafkandi.
2. Hassan Shiwasali.
3. Dr. Hussein Khalighi.
4. Baba Ali Mehrparwar.
5. Hassan Sharafi.
6. Rahman Rahimi (Chako).
7. Mustafa Mawloudi.
8. Ghafour Hamzayy.
9. Mahmoud Dashti.

10. Muhammad Ali Anayati.
11. Fatah Abdoli.
12. Mustafa Hijri.
13. Muhammad Nazif Qadiri.
14. Abdullah Sharifi.
15. Salam Azizi.
16. Mansour Fatahi.
17. Abdullah Ibrahimi.
18. Shaho Husseini.
19. Mamosta Abdullah Hassanzadeh.

The first plenum chose the followings as the Politburo members:
1. Dr. Sadiq Sharafkandi.
2. Mustafa Hijri.
3. Hassan Sharafi.
4. Baba Ali Mehrparwar.
5. Mamosta Abdullah Hassanzadeh.

The alternate members of the Central Committee were:
1. Ibrahim Salih Rad (Ibraim Lajani).
2. Hassan Qadirzadeh.
3. Muhammad Shahrawan.
4. Loqman Mehfar.
5. Sayyed Rasoul Sayyed Ahmadi.
6. Kawa Bahrami.
7. Sayyed Ahmad Husseini.
8. Omar Hamidi.

The consultant members of the PDKI were:
1. Sayyed Ibrahim Hashimi.

2. Omar Balaki.

3. Sayyed Reza Diroudgar.

4. Ahmad Badkani.

5. Taimour Mostafayy (Hassanzadeh, 1996, pp. 227-229).

***

The 10th Congress of the PDKI-RL

The 10th Congress of the PDKI-RL was held f in Ranya, Iraq, from 1-5 May 1994. Jalil Gadani was chosen as the General Secretary and Hassan Rastgar as the alternate General Secretary.

The Congress chose the following Central Committee:

1. Faysal Irandoust.

2. Fatah Kawian.

3. Hashim Karimi.

4. Hassan Rastgar.

5. Hossein Madani.

6. Jalil Gadani.

7. Nabi Qadiri.

8. Osman Rahimi.

9. Kamal Karimi.

10. Said Baigzadeh.

11. Abubakir Rad.

12. Mullah Khidir Dolagrami.

13. Khalid Hassanpour.

14. Sarhang (Colonel) Iraj Qadiri.

15. Hashim Rostami.

The Politburo of the PDKI-RL included:

1. Jalil Gadani.

2. Hassan Rastgar.

3. Hashim Karimi.

4. Fatah Kawian.

5. Nabi Qadiri

In addition, the alternate members of the Central Committee included:

1. Sayyed Ibrahim Karimi.

2. Sirwan Hafidi.

3. Mamosta Bebash.

4. Muhammad Amin Rashidi.

Moreover, the second plenum of the party in January-February 1995 selected the first three people, and the third plenum on 23 May 1995, the last four people in the following list, as the consultant members of the Central Committee of the party:

1. Sayyed Abdullah Husseini.

2. Khalid Wanawsha.

3. Khidir Muhammadpour.

4. Qasim Qazi.

4. Saleh Khizirpour (Rabati).

5. Nasir Pirani.

4. Jafar Manguri (Gadani, 2008b, pp. 112, 116).

***

The 10th Congress of the PDKI

The 10th Congress of the PDKI was held in Erbil, Iraq on 12 April 1995. Hassanzadeh was chosen as the General Secretary and Mustafa Hijri as the alternate General Secretary.

The congress chose the followings as the Central Committee of the PDKI:

1. Hassan Sharafi.

2. Mustafa Hijri.

3. Sulayman Kalashi.

4. Muhammad Ali Anayati.

5. Salam Azizi.

6. Omar Balaki.

7. Muhammad Nazif Qadiri.

8. Qadir Wirya.

9. Taimour Mostafayy.

10. Isma'il Bazyar.

11. Mustafa Mawloudi.

12. Hassan Qadirzadeh.

13. Omar Hamidi.

14. Sayyed Ahmad Husseini.

15. Muhammad Shahrawan.

16. Baba Ali Mehrparwar.

17. Hussein Nazdar.

18. Loqman Mehfar.

19. Mamosta Abdullah Hassanzadeh.

The members of the Politburo were:

1. Mamosta Abdullah Hassanzadeh.

2. Mustafa Hijri.

3. Hassan Sharafi.

4. Baba Ali Mehrparwar.

5. Salam Azizi.

The alternate members of the Central Committee included:

1. Rostam Jahangiri.

2. Sayyed Rasoul Sayyed Ahmadi.

3. As'ad Ahmadi.

4. Sayyed Mansour Nasiri.

5. Sayyed Ibrahin Hashimi.

6. Ahmad Nastani.

7. Mautasam Noorani.

8. Karim Mahdawi (Saqqizi)

The consultant members of the Central Committee included:

1. Rahman Rahimi (Chako).

2. Kawa Bahrami.

3. Sayyed Reza Diroudgar (Hassanzadeh, 1996, p. 277-281).

***

The 11th Congress of the PDKI

The 11th Congress of the PDKI was held in Kirkuk, Iraq, on 22 December 1997. Hassanzadeh was selected as the General Secretary and Hijri as the alternate General Secretary.

The congress chose these people as the Central Committee:

1. Abdullah Hassanzadeh.

2. Mustafa Hijri.

3. Hassan Rastgar.

4. Hassan Sharafi.

5. Baba Ali Mehrparwar.

6. Jalil Gadani.

7. Hossein Madani.

8. Fatah Kawian.

9. Salam Azizi.

10. Osman Rahimi.

11. Kamal Karimi.

12. Sulayman Kalashi.

13. Muhammad Nazif Qadiri.

14. Qadir Wirya.

15. Taimour Mostafayy.

16. Isma'il Bazyar.

17. Hassan Qadirzadeh.

18. Muhammad Shahrawan.

19. Shaho Husseini.

20. Mustafa Mawloudi.

21. Rahman Rahimi (Chako).

The members of the Politburo included:

1. Mamosta Abdullah Hassanzadeh.

2. Mustafa Hijri.

3. Hassan Rastgar.

4. Hassan Sharafi.

5. Baba Ali Mehrparwar.

The alternate members of the Central Committee included:

1. Muhammad Ali Anayati.

2. Loqman Mehfar.

3. Rostam Jahangiri.

4. Sayyed Rasoul Sayyed Ahmad.

5. Sayyed Mansour Nasiri.

6. Sayyed Ibrahin Hashimi.

7. Karim Mahdawi (Saqqizi).

8. Sayyed Ahmad Husseini.

9. Sayyed Ibrahim Karimi.

10. Khadija Mazur.

The consultant members of the Central Committee were:

1. Muhammad Hassanpour.

2. Sayyed Reza Diroudgar.

3. Miro Aliyar.

4. Khosraw Bahrami (Naqshi, 2015, April 16).

***

The 12th Congress of the PDKI

The 12th Congress of the PDKI was held in Kirkuk, Iraq, on 24 November 2000. Abdullah Hassanzadeh was selected as the General Secretary and Mustafa Hijri as the alternate General Secretary.

The congress chose these people as the Central Committee:

1. Mamosta Abdullah Hassanzadeh.
2. Mustafa Hijri.
3. Hassan Rastgar.
4. Osman Rahimi.
5. Kamal Karimi.
6. Sulayman Kalashi.
7. Loqman Mehfar.
8. Mustafa Mawloudi.
9. Rahman Rahimi (Chako).
10. Hassan Sharafi.
11. Baba Ali Mehrparwar.
12. Jalil Gadani.
13. Hossein Madani.
14. Fatah Kawian.
15. Omar Balaki.
16. Muhammad Nazif Qadiri.
17. Qadir Wirya.
18. Taimour Mostafayy.
19. Isma'il Bazyar.
20. Hassan Qadirzadeh.
21. Muhammad Shahrwan.
22. Sayyed Ibrahim Hashimi.
23. Mullah Ahmad Rahimi.
24. Sayyed Reza Diroudgar.
25. Kawa Bahrami.

The members of the Politburo were:

1. Mamosta Abdullah Hassanzadeh.
2. Mustafa Hijri.
3. Hassan Rastgar.
4. Hassan Sharafi.
5. Baba Ali Mehrparwar.

The alternate members of the Central Committee were:

1. Ali Kasnazani.
2. Muhammad Ali Anayati.
3. Karim Mahdawi (Saqqizi).
4. Muhammad Hassanpour.
5. Hussein Nazdar.
6. Sayyed Ibrahim Karimi.
7. Khadija Mazur.
8. Mautasam Noorani.
9. Muhammad Salih Qadiri.
10. Muhammad Kasrayy.
11. Khalid Azizi.

The consultant members of the Central Committee were:

1. Omar Shadab.
2. Khalid Wanawsha.
3. Tahir Kasili.
4. Miro Aliyar.
5. Khosraw Abdullahi.
6. Said Baigzadeh (Naqshi, 2015, April 16).

***

The 13th Congress of the PDKI

The 13th Congress of the PDKI was held in Koya, Iraq, on 3 July 2004. Mustafa Hijri was selected as the General Secretary and Hassan Sharafi as the alternate General Secretary. The congress chose these people as the Central Committee:

1. Mustafa Hijri.
2. Hassan Sharafi.
3. Hasan Rastgar.
4. Muhammad Nazif Qadiri.
5. Baba Ali Mehrparwar.
6. Rostam Jahangiri.
7. Hassan Qadirzadeh.
8. Muhammad Salih Qadiri.
9. Shaho Husseini.
10. Omar Balaki.
11. Rahman Rahimi (Chako).
12. Sayyed Ibrahim Hashimi.
13. Mullah Ahmad Rahimi.
14. Mustafa Mawloudi.
15. As'ad Ahmadi.
16. Kamal Karimi.
17. Hussein Nazdar.
18. Khalid Azizi.
19. Taimour Mostafayy.
20. Isma'il Bazyar.
21. Kawa Bahrami.
22. Loqman Mehfar.
23. Sayyed Reza Diroudgar.

The members of the Politburo included:
1. Mustafa Hijri.

2. Hassan Sharafi.

3. Hassan Rastgar.

4. Muhammad Nazif Qadiri.

5. Baba Ali Mehrparwar.

The alternate members of the Central Committee included:

1. Khadija Mazur.

2. Muhammad Kasrayy.

3. Tahir Kasili.

4. Siamak Wakili.

5. Rahim Manguri.

6. Muhammad Hassanpour.

7. Miro Aliyar.

8. Said Baigzadeh.

9. Khosraw Bahrami.

10. Khosraw Abdullahi.

11. Omar Gholamali.

The consultant members of the Central Committee were:

1. Ali Sorani.

2. Erfan Rahnimoun.

3. Shaho Farazmand.

4. Hemin Sayyedi.

5. Abdullah Bahrami (Naqshi, 2015, April 16).

***

The 14th Congress of the KDP

The 14th Congress of the KDP was held in Koya, Iraq, from 6-14 March 2008. Khalid Azizi was selected as the General Secretary and Mustafa Mawloudi as the alternate General Secretary.

The Congress chose these people as the Central Committee:

1. Khalid Azizi.
2. Mustafa Mawloudi.
3. Hasan Rastgar.
4. Mustafa Shalmashi.
5. Qadir Wirya.
6. Kamal Karimi.
7. Hassan Qadirzadeh.
8. Khadija Mazur.
9. Kwestan Ftoohi.
10. Kowestan Gadani.
11. Sayyed Ibrahim Karimi.
12. Omar Balaki.
13. Siamak Wakili.
14. Ibrahim Ibrahimi (Zewayy).
15. Karim Mahdawi (Saqqizi).
16. Abdullah Bahrami.
17. Eqbal Safari.
18. Aso Hassanzadeh.
19. Mustafa Ma'roufi.
20. Rambod Lotf Pouri.
21. Hemin Sayyedi.

The members of the Politburo were:

1. Khalid Azizi.
2. Mustafa Mawloudi.
3. Hasan Rastgar.
4. Mustafa Shalmashi.
5. Qadir Wirya.
6. Kamal Karimi.

7. Hassan Qadirzadeh.

The alternate members of the Central Committee were:
1. Rahim Muhammadzadeh.
2. Kawe Ahangari.
3. Mawloud Sowara.
4. Muhammad Kasrayy.
5. Soheyla Qadri.
6. Ibrahim Choukali.
7. Khalid Wanawsha.

The consultant members of the Central Committee were:
1. Golaleh Sharafkandi.
2. Muhamad Shahrawan.
3. Massoud Rawandoust.
4. Said Baigzadeh.
5. Sayyed Abdullah Husseini.
6. Muhammad Hassanpour
8. Siamak Qawi Panjeh (Naqshi, 2015, April 16).

***

The 14th Congress of the PDKI

The 14th Congress of the PDKI was held in Koya, Iraq, on 10-14 September 2008. Mustafa Hijri was selected as the General Secretary and Hassan Sharafi as the alternate General Secretary.

The Congress chose these people as the Central Committee:
1. Mustafa Hijri.
2. Hassan Sharafi.
3. Muhammad Nazif Qadiri.
4. Taimour Mostafayy

5. Rahman Rahimi (Chako).

6. Hussein Nazdar.

7. Karim Parwizi.

8. Erfan Rahnimoun.

9. Loqman Mehfar.

10. Tahir Mahmoudi.

11. Shaho Farazmand.

12. Kawa Bahrami.

13. Rostam Jahangiri.

14. Tahir Kasili.

15. Nahid Hosseini.

16. Sadiq Darweshi.

17. As'ad Ahmadi.

18. (Mullah) Ahmad Rahimi.

19. Omar Gholamali.

20. Sayyed Ibrahim Hashimi.

21. Muhammad Sahebi.

22. Shaho Husseini.

23. Miro Aliyar.

24. Khosraw Bahrami.

25. Hassan Shiwasali (as honorary member).

The members of the Politburo included:

1. Mustafa Hijri.

2. Hassan Sharafi.

3. Muhammad Nazif Qadiri.

4. Taimour Mostafayy.

5. Kawa Bahrami.

6. Rostam Jahangiri.

7. Karim Parwizi.

The alternate members of the Central Committee were:

1. Sayyed Reza Diroudgar
2. Sayyed Ezat Husseini.
3. Rahim Manguri.
4. Hawre Isma'ili.
5. Farhad Arshadi.
6. Omid Mandomi.
7. Khosraw Abdullahi.
8. Aso Sayyad.
9. Sadiq Zarza.
10. Sharif Behrouz.

The consultant members of the Central Committee were:

1. Parwana Haidari.
2. Abdollah Hejab.
3. Mohayadin Palani.
4. Mahir Naqshbandi.
5. Luqman Ahmadi.
6. Salam Isma'ilpour.
7. Abdullah Rahimi.
8. Rasoul Muhammadzadeh.
9. Dara Natiq.
10. Nasir Miradi.
11. Khalid Darwija.
12. Ilham Chaichi.
13. Foad Khaki Baigi (Mahmoudi, personal communication, January 9, 2016).

***

The 15th Congress of the KDP

The 15th Congress of the KDP was held in Koya, Iraq on 23-29 May 2011. Khalid Azizi was selected as the General Secretary and Mustafa Mawloudi as the alternate General Secretary.

The Congress chose these people as the Central Committee:

1. Khalid Azizi.
2. Mustafa Mawloudi.
3. Mustafa Shalmashi.
4. Qadir Wirya.
5. Kamal Karimi.
6. Hassan Qadirzadeh.
7. Omar Balaki.
8. Eqbal Safari.
9. Aso Hassanzadeh.
10. Kwestan Ftoohi.
11. Khadija Mazur.
12. Golaleh Sharafkandi.
13. Kawe Ahangari.
14. Said Baigzadeh.
15. Nasrin Hadad.
16. Ibrahim Ibrahimi (Zewayy).
17. Rahman Piroti.
18. Khalid Wanawsha.
19. Karim Mahdawi (Saqqizi).
20. Hassan Sheikhani.
21. Abdullah Bahrami.

The members of the Politburo were:

1. Khalid Azizi.
2. Mustafa Mawloudi.

3. Mustafa Shalmashi.

4. Qadir Wirya.

5. Kamal Karimi.

6. Hassan Qadirzadeh.

7. Omar Balaki.

The alternate members of the Central Committee included:

1. Soran Nouri.

2. Kourosh Nosrati.

3. Isma'il Sharafi.

4. Ibrahim Choukali.

5. Omar Shadab.

6. Sohaila Qadri.

7. Muhammad Rasoul Karimi.

8. Mawloud Sowara.

9. Hassan Hatami.

10. Siamak Qawi Panjeh.

11. Hassan Abrouzani.

12. Hashim Azizi.

13. Massoud Rawandoust.

The consultant members of the Central Committee were:

1. Mansour Mirwati.

2. Hajir Abdullah Pour.

3. Khidir (Bag) Pakdaman.

4. Ali Bidaghi.

5. Rahim Muhammadzadeh.

6. Khalid Hassanpour. (Naqshi, 2015, April 16; Hatami, Personal Communication, May 6, 2017).

In addition, according to Hatami, the Politburo with the approval of the CC selected the followings as the consultant members of the Politburo:

1. Abdullah Hassanzadeh.

2. Jalil Gadani.

3. Hassan Rastgar.

4. Hossein Madani (Hatami, Personal Communication, May 6, 2017; "Kurdistan Democratic," 2011).

***

The 15th Congress of the PDKI

The 15th Congress of the PDKI was held in Koya, Iraq on 29 September-3 October 2012. Mustafa Hijri was selected as the General Secretary and Hassan Sharafi as the alternate General Secretary.

The Congress chose these people as the Central Committee:

1. Mustafa Hijri.

2. Hassan Sharafi.

3. Muhammad Nazif Qadiri.

4. Taimour Mostafayy

5. Rahman Rahimi (Chako).

6. Karim Parwizi.

7. Loqman Mehfar.

8. Tahir Mahmoudi.

9. Shaho Farazmand.

10. Kawa Bahrami.

11. Rostam Jahangiri.

12. Tahir Kasili.

13. Nahid Hosseini.

14. Sadiq Darweshi.

15. Miro Aliyar.

16. Omar Gholamali.

17. Kawa Jawanmard.
18. Muhammad Sahebi.
19. Rambod Lotf Pouri.
20. Dara Natiq.
21. Muhammad Salih Qadiri.
22. Shaho Husseini.
23. Mansour Azizi.
24. Luqman Ahmadi.
25. Hassan Shiwasali (as honorary member).

The members of the Politburo included:
1. Mustafa Hijri.
2. Hassan Sharafi.
3. Muhammad Nazif Qadiri.
4. Taimour Mostafayy.
5. Miro Aliyar.
6. Rostam Jahangiri.
7. Karim Parwizi.

The alternate members of the Central Committee were:
1. Sayyed Aziz Nikjouyan.
2. Fatih Salehi.
3. Rounak Fathi.
4. Mousa Babakhani.
5. Azad Azizi.
6. Parwana Haidari.
7. Ali Ashraf Moradi.
8. Khosraw Abdullahi.
9. Ilham Chaichi
10. Foad Khaki Baigi

11. Keyhan Yousefi (Kurdistan Media, 2012; T. Mahmoudi, personal communication, January 9, 2016).

The last three people in the list, as the heads of the Democratic Women's Union of Iranian Kurdistan, the Democratic Youth Union of Iranian Kurdistan, and the Democratic Student Union of Iranian Kurdistan, were automatically chose as the alternate members of the Central Committee. According to Mohayadin Palani, later these three people were replaced by:
1. Fatime Osmani (head of the Democratic Women's Union of Iranian Kurdistan)
2. Karwan Sharafi (head of the Democratic Youth Union of Iranian Kurdistan)
3. Jalal Rawangard (head of the Democratic Student Union of Iranian Kurdistan) (Personal communication, December 11, 2016).

***

The 16th Congress of the KDP

The 16th Congress of the KDP was held in Koya, Iraq from 6-11 February 2016. Khalid Azizi was selected as the General Secretary and Mustafa Mawloudi as the alternate General Secretary.

The 16th Congress approved to reselect all the previous leadership of the 15th Congress for this new Congress.

The Congress chose these people as the Central Committee:
1. Khalid Azizi.
2. Mustafa Mawloudi.
3. Mustafa Shalmashi.
4. Qadir Wirya.
5. Kamal Karimi.
6. Hassan Qadirzadeh.
7. Omar Balaki.
8. Aso Hassanzadeh.
9. Khadija Mazur.

10. Golaleh Sharafkandi.
11. Kawe Ahangari.
12. Said Baigzadeh.
13. Nasrin Hadad.
14. Ibrahim Ibrahimi (Zewayy).
15. Rahman Piroti.
16. Khalid Wanawsha.
17. Karim Mahdawi (Saqqizi).
18. Hassan Sheikhani.
19. Soran Nouri.
20. Kourosh Nosrati

The members of the Politburo included:
1. Khalid Azizi.
2. Mustafa Mawloudi.
3. Mustafa Shalmashi.
4. Qadir Wirya.
5. Kamal Karimi.
6. Hassan Qadirzadeh.
7. Omar Balaki.

The alternate members of the Central Committee were:
1. Isma'il Sharafi.
2. Ibrahim Choukali.
3. Sohaila Qadri.
4. Muhammad Rasoul Karimi.
5. Mawloud Sowara.
6. Hassan Hatami.
7. Siamak Qawi Panjeh.
8. Hassan Abrouzani.

9. Hashim Azizi.

The consultant members of the Central Committee were:

1. Mansour Mirwati.
2. Hajir Abdullah Pour.
3. Khidir (Bag) Pakdaman.
4. Ali Bidaghi.
5. Rahim Muhammadzadeh.
6. Khalid Hassanpour. (Hatami, Personal Communication, May 6, 2017)

Appendix 9: The Cabinet of the Kurdistan Republic of 1946

The Cabinet according to Homayoun:

1. The Prime Minister or the Chief of the National Board of Directors of Kurdistan -Haji Baba Sheikh Siadat
2. The Minister of Defence-Muhammad Hussein Khan Saifi Qazi
3. The Minister of Interior-Muhammad Amin Mo'ini
4. The Minister Economy-Ahmad Ilahi
5. The Minister of Post and Telegraph-Karim Ahmadin
6. The Minister of Culture-Manaf Karimi
7. The Minister of Propaganda-Seddiq Haidari
8. The Minister of Commerce-Haji Mustafa Dawoudi
9. The Minister of Labour-Khalil Khosrawi
10. The Minister of Agriculture-Mahmoud Walizadeh
11. The Minister of Roads Ismail Ilkhanizadeh
12. The Minister of Health-Sayyed Muhammad Ayyoubian
13. The Minister of Consultation-Abdul Rahman Ilkhanizadeh
14. The Minister of Justice-Mullah Hussein Majdi (Homayoun, 2004, p. 55)

The Cabinet according to Sardashti:

1. The Prime Minister-Haji Baba Sheikh Siadat
2. The Minister of War-Muhammad Hussein Khan Saifi Qazi
3. The Minister of Education-Manaf Karimi
4. The Minister of Interior-Muhammad Amin Mo'ini
5. The Minister of Health-Sayyed Muhammad Ayyoubian
6. The Minister of Consultation-Abdul Rahman Ilkhanizadeh
7. The Minister of Roads Ismail Ilkhanizadeh
8. The Minister Economy-Ahmad Ilahi
9. The Minister of Post-Karim Ahmadin
10. The Minister of Commerce-Haji Mustafa Dawoudi
11. The Minister of Justice-Mullah Hussein Majdi

12. The Minister of Agriculture-Mahmoud Walizadeh

13. The Minister of Propaganda-Seddiq Haidari

14. The Minister of Labour-Khalil Khosrawi (Sardashti, 2002b, pp. 138-139)

The Cabinet according to Eagleton:

1. The Prime Minister or the Chief of Supreme Court -Haji Baba Sheikh Siadat

2. The Minister of Defence and Assistant to President-Muhammad Hussein Khan Saifi Qazi

3. The Minister of Education and Assistant to President -Manaf Karimi

4. The Minister of Health-Sayyed Muhammad Ayyoubian

5. The Minister of Foreign Affairs-Abdul Rahman Ilkhanizadeh

6. The Minister of Roads-Isma'il Ilkhanizadeh

7. The Minister Economy-Ahmad Ilahi

8. The Minister of Labour-Khalil Khosrawi

9. The Minister of Posts, Telegraphs, and Telephones-Karim Ahmadain

10. The Minister of Commerce-Haji Mustafa Dawoudi

11. The Minister of Interior-Muhammad Amin Mo'ini

12. The Minister of Justice-Mullah Hussein Majdi

13. The Minister of Agriculture-Mahmoud Walizadeh (Eagleton, 1963, p. 134)

Homayoun (2004) adds Khalil Khosrawi as the Minister of Labour. In addition, according to Manaf Karimi, Abdul Rahman Ilkhanizadeh was the Minister of Foreign Affairs (Homayoun, 2004, p. 56). Eagleton (1963) adds Khalil Khosrawi as the Minister of Labour and Seddiq Haidari as the Director-General of Propaganda (p. 135).

According to Manaf Karimi, Abdul Rahman Ilkhanizadeh was the Minister of Foreign Affairs (Homayoun, 2004, p. 56). Eagleton (1963) writes that Seddiq Haidari was the Director-General of Propaganda (p. 135). The majority of the Cabinet were members of the CC of the KDP. According to Eagleton (1963), all the cabinet members (92.3 percent), with the exception of Mullah Hussein Majdi, were the KDP's CC members (p. 134). The majority of the Cabinet also were the previous members of the J.K. According to Manaf Karimi, 11 of 14 (78.6 percent) of the Cabinet members were formerly members of the J.K. (Homayoun, 2004, p. 56). Some other previous J.K. affective members and leaders were given prominent positions in the Kurdistan Republic. Eagleton (1963) maintains that the following were Inspectors during Kurdistan Republic: Qasim Ilkanizadeh, Rahman Zabihi, and Najmadin Tohidi (Eagleton, 1963, p. 135).

Appendix 10: Supreme Council of the KDP in May 1946

According to Eagleton, the members of the Supreme Council of the KDP which formed in May 1946 included:

1. Mullah Hussein Majdi
2. Karim Agha Bayazidi,
3. Aziz Abbasi
4. Sheikh Hassan Shams Borhan
5. Sayyed Ali Husseini
6. Ali Khan Nozari Mangur
7. Abdullah Qadiri Mamash
8. Qasim Ilkanizadeh (Dehbukri)
9. Rahman Zabihi
10. Najmadin Tohidi
11. Muhammad Amin Khatami
12. Hashem Yousefi (Eagleton, 1963, p. 134).

Appendix 11: The Friendship Treaty of Azerbaijan and Kurdistan on 23 April 1946

The friendship Treaty of Azerbaijan and Kurdistan on 23 April 1946 maintains that:

> in parts of Azerbaijan inhabited by Kurds, Kurds would take part in administrative work, and Azeris living in Kurdish areas would do the same; an economic commission would be formed to deal with economic problems of joint interest to both parties; military co-operation would be organised; any negotiation with Tehran should be undertaken only upon agreement between the two parts; Kurds in Azerbaijan and Azeris in Kurdistan would be given the opportunity to develop their language and culture; and both parts were committed to punish any party seeking to destroy the friendship of the two republics. (Yassin, 1995, pp. 173-174)

Appendix 12: The publications of the KDP

The KDP's publications, before and during the Kurdistan Republic, include:

1. *Govari Kurdistan* (magazine Kurdistan). Issue 1, was published under Sayyed Muhammad Hamidi on 6 December 1945 in Mahabad. It was the organ of the KDP. In all, 9 issues of the magazine Kurdistan were published. It was a Kurdish literary, social, and political magazine (Hussein, 2008, pp. 74-78).

2. *Rojnamay Kurdistan* (newspaper Kurdistan). The Issue 1, was published under Sayyed Muhammad Hamidi on 20 Bafranbar 1324 (10 [the correct is 11] January 1946) in Mahabad. It was the organ of the KDP. While at least and certainly 92 issues have been published, Kurdish researchers estimate the total issues of it between 110 and 116 (Hussein, 2008, pp. 82-83).

3. *Govari Hawari Nishtman* (magazine Shout of Homeland). Issue 1, was published under Seddiq Anjiri on 21 March 1946 in Mahabad. It was the organ of the *Yaketi Jawanani Demokrati Kurdistan* (Democratic Youth Union of Kurdistan). Including the covers, the total pages of this magazine reach to 43 (Hussein, 2008, pp. 106-107, 713-755).

4. *Rojnamay Hawari Nishtman* (newspaper Shout of Homeland). Issue 1 was published under Seddiq Anjiri on 9 May 1946 in Mahabad. It was the organ of the *Yaketi Jawanani Demokrati Kurdistan* (Democratic Youth Union of Kurdistan). In total, five issues were published (Saleh and Saleh, 2007, p. 337).

5. *Govari Halala* (magazine Buttercup). Issue 1, was published under Hassan Qizilji February-March, before 21 March 1946, in Bukan. Issue 3, was published in April-May, before 22 May 1946 (Hussein, 2008, pp. 97, 105, 759).

6. *Govari Grougali Mindalani Kurd* (magazine Babble of the Kurdish Children). Issue 1, was published under Qadir Modarresi in April 1946 in Mahabad. Three Issues of this magazine were published (Hussein, 2008, pp. 117, 120).

Coinciding with the Kurdistan Republic events, Kurdish journalists in Tehran, Sanandaj, Kermanshah, and other parts of Iran were following the events of Kurdistan, Azerbaijan, and Iran. Some newspapers and magazines were published in Persian, while some parts of them were allocated to Kurdish writings. In addition, the Iranian government published *rojnamay Zagros* (the newspaper Zagros) in Sanandaj against the Kurdistan Republic's journalism. Some of the newspapers and magazines were: the *Namay Kurdistan* (Kurdistan's Letter), *Peik-e Kurd* (Kurd's Courier), *Derafsh* (Flag), *Didaniha* (Watchables or Attractions), *Ariz*, *Aria* (Aryan), *Enghqelab-e Kaveh* (Kaveh's Revolution), *Iran Jawan* (Young Iran), and *Tohfeh* (Gift). The most long-lasting one was the *Nameh-ye Haftehgi-ye Kouhestan* (Weekly Letter of Mountain or Letter of Mountain) under Dr. Ismail Ardalan (Hussein, 2008, pp. 123-124, 128). Regarding this last newspaper, Hussein (2008) also calls it as a weekly *Nameh-ye Kouhestan* (Letter of Mountain), and states that it was published in Persian language in Tehran with the permission of the Iranian government (Hussein, 2008, p. 12). Finally, according to Penaw (pseudonym for Hassan Qizilji) in the first issue of *Rega* (Way), the magazine *Ravej* (Consultation) was published in Sanandaj during the Kurdistan Republic (Karmi, 1999, p. 628).

Appendix 13: The Court Martial Charges against Qazi Muhammad

The court martial charges against Qazi Muhammad were:

1. Dealing and trading oil with Russia at the rate of 51 percent for the Russian government and 49 percent for Kurdistan.
2. Changing Iran's map and separating the five areas of Urmiya, Kermanshah, Sanandaj, Tabriz, and Ilam.
3. Making Kurdistan's map which has hammer and sickle symbols like the Soviet's flag.
4. Striking coins which has Qazi Muhammad's picture similar to Russian rupee, for the central government.
5. Making the Greater Kurdistan map for the four parts of Kurdistan of Iran, Iraq, Turkey, and Syria.
6. Bringing the foreigners like Mullah Mustafa Barzani and giving them some part of Iran's land.
7. Threatening the Shah of Iran, Iran's government, declaring war with Iran, and encouraging people to be enemies of the Shah.
8. Making a treaty with the Russia against Iran and cooperating with Russia in occupying Iran's soil.
9. Declaring Kurdistan's Government and occupying of Iran's land in name of Kurdistan.
10. Coming and going to Russia, having meetings with its leaders and with Baqirov, the leader of Azerbaijan of Russia.
11. Making commercial and political treaties with the foreigners and enemies of Iran without Iran's permission.
12. Arresting and killing government employees, especially non-Kurdish employees, destroying their homes, and burning their properties. (Saleh, 2003, pp. 6-9)

Appendix 14: List of People Who Were Executed After the Fall of the Kurdistan Republic

After the death of Qazis on 31 March 1947, on 7 April 1947 the government hung Hamid Mazouji, Rasoul Naqadehey, Abdullah Rowshanfekr, and Muhammad Nazemi in Mahabad. In addition, during the Qazis' trial, a simultaneous formal court was held in Saqqiz which resulted in execution of the following on 14 February 1947: Ahmad Khan Farouqi, Abdullah Khan Matin, Muhammad Khan Daneshwar, Hassan Khan Faizollah Baigi, Qalandar, Ahmad Khan Shaji'i Faizollah Baigi (Kiltga), Ali Jawanmardi, Rasoul Jawanmardi, Sheikh Seddiq As'adi, Sheikh Amin As'adi. Moreover, simultaneously, Ali Baig Shirzad was executed in Bukan. In total, 18 people were executed in Kurdistan. Khoshhali provides slightly different names (Homayoun, 2004, pp. 109-110; Khoshhali, 2001, p. 269).

Appendix 15: List of the members of the Reconstructing Committee who were prevented to attend in the 2nd Congress

According to Peshnimaz, 14 members of the Reconstructing Committee were prevented by the gunmen of Tawfiq to participate in the 2nd Congress. They only allowed Mirza Khidir Marasana to attend in the Congress.

The list included:

1. Hassan Rastgar.
2. Muhammad Amin Siraji,
3. Isma'il Sharifzadeh.
4. Salar Haidari.
5. Mirza Khidir Muhammadi Marasana.
6. Osman Azizian.
7. Qadir Qazi.
8. Rashid Smel.
9. Faqe Rasouli Zinwe.
10. Khalil Shawbash.
11. Hussein Aghay Siser.
12. Sayyed Fatah Nizami.
13. Abdullah Khayati Sardashti (known as Nawroz).
14. Rasoul Peshnimaz (Peshnimaz, 2012, p. 167).

Appendix 16: The Declaration of Cooperation between the Revolutionary Committee and the Tudeh Party of Iran

On 9 February 1968, a meeting was held in Baghdad between Radmanesh and Ghassemlou from the Tudeh Party and Siraji, Mo'ini, and Hisami from the Revolutionary Committee. They signed a declaration that stated that there was no difference between the Tudeh Party and the KDP in their main policies. Both parties recognized the Kurdish movement in Iran as part of the Iranian movement against imperialism, and the anti-democratic and anti-national regime of the Shah. They both agreed with Leninist principle of the right of self-determination of the nations by themselves including of the Kurdish nation in Iran. The KDP's national slogan was to guarantee the rights of the Kurdish nation in Iranian Kurdistan in the framework of Iran, in the form of a voluntary unity with the Iranian nations in a united federative state. In respect to the armed struggle in Kurdistan, both parties accepted that the struggle was due to the forcing of the Kurdish and the suppression of all types of national and democratic expression of the Iranian people. These parties considered this armed revolt as inevitable and a positive phenomenon, and praised the devoted friends who held the armed revolt. At the that time, the goal was to keep the revolt going, reinforce its political and organizational aspects, educate cadres, prepare people's mental conditions in Kurdistan and Iran for spreading the revolt to other parts of Kurdistan and Iran, creation of cells and party organizations in the cities, and gradually expand the armed struggle (Hisami, 2011, pp. 116-117).

In addition, these parties agreed to struggle in Kurdistan in the name of the KDP. They believed that all Marxist organizations in Iran should join the Tudeh Party. Likewise, the KDP should prepare itself for the political and organizational unification with the Tudeh Party. First and foremost, a Marxist leadership should be established in the KDP and then the party should gradually change into a Marxist party with a Marxist program. Moreover, the KDP's demands of the Tudeh Party included: the establishment of political courses (one to two months) in Kurdistan of Iraq and Iran for the training the KDP's cadres; sending some of the friends for military education abroad for three to four months; asking doctors and especially surgeons of the Tudeh Party to come to Kurdistan; sending about five

Kurdish students each year to be educated in socialist countries; sending Marxist books and publication in Persian and Kurdish to Iranian Kurdistan; providing typewriter and polycopier to the KDP; providing weapons and ammunitions to the revolt; the Radio *Peyk-e Iran* (Radio Iran Courier) to pay special attention to the Kurdish revolt, propagandize its goals and mottos; and providing an urgent financial aid to the KDP, while considering permanent salaries in future. Hisami maintains that after the declaration, Radmansh gave the funds to Siraji and Mo'ini (Hisami, 2011, pp. 116-119; Kaveh, 2005, pp. 82-83).

Appendix 17: The Scope of Wars between the Peshmergas and the Iranian Government

In order to realize the scope of the wars between the peshmergas and the Iranian government, some more important conflicts are briefly illustrated. During the following months, the Iranian forces in many places attacked the peshmergas. In Summer 1968 they attacked the group led by Abdullah Mo'ini in the village of Qalwe. While peshmergas killed an officer, a few gendarmes, and a jash, the Iranian forces killed Abullah Mo'ini and Mina Sham, and after wounding Hassan Khorkhorayy, they executed him in the military shooting range of Mahabad. In addition, on 16 August 1968, in a conflict between a group of peshmergas and the Iranian army, the commander of the army was killed and two soldiers were captured. They released the soldiers who were later executed on the orders of Lieutenant General Oveissi. In June 1968, in a battle, peshmergas under Qadir Sharif killed 15 gendarmes and a jash named Halmat Betoshi who was previously the party's peshmerga. In September 1968, some peshmergas under Sayyed Fatah Nizami were attacked on the Haji Kemi Mountain in the Akhtachi territory. After a heroic battle, they were killed. In the same month, two peshmergas in the Gawirk area fought a large group of the gendarmes. After they were killed, their bodies were paraded around in villages and were hung in Sardasht to create fear among the people. Finally, Morad Shirej and his friends fought many times with Iranian forces in the territory of Piranshahr and created fear among them. In one conflict, they killed a jash named Kowekha Karim Barkamran and wounded some others. Also, a peshmerga was wounded and sent to Mahabad to be cured. Some people in Mahabad who helped him t were imprisoned: Sayyed Muhammad Ishaqi, Muhammad Mamle, Abdullah Hakimzadeh, and Kak Ali Jandaran. On another occasion, Morad Shirej and his friends effectively fought with the Iranian forces on the Morad Rasouy Mountain in Lajan. At the end of Summer 1968, Morad Shirej and his friends were in the Bari Mergan Mountains when a large force of army, gendarmerie, and jash attacked them in the Kani Basi Mountain. They killed some Iranians, but Morad Shirej and some of his friends were also killed. Their bodies were hung in Piranshahr, Naqadeh, and Mahabad. After all of these events, killing many members of the Revolutionary Committee, and weakening the movement, the remaining peshmergas returned to the Kurdistan of Iraq (Gadani, 2008a, pp. 156-159).

In October 1968, the armed revolutionaries of the KDP in a declaration claimed that the armed struggle of the party is part of the struggle of the Kurdish and other Iranian nations against imperialism. The declaration revealed the conflict between the peshmergas and the Iranian forces. On 19 July 1968, in Sarshevi Aghlan, Sardasht, peshmergas attacked a group of gendarmes who were pursuing them. In an eight-hour battle, 15 jash and gendarmes including the leader of the jash, Halmat, were killed and six others wounded, and a helicopter was broken and its pilot was wounded. The KDP peshmergas gained 10 Brnos and an American rifle. In addition, on 6 August 1947, in the village of Shalmash, Sardasht, in an 11-hour standoff, the peshmergas attacked 500 armies, gendarmes, and jash forces. In this standoff, more than 40 Iranians were killed, 40 wounded, a helicopter was broken and the pilot was injured. Moreover, on 2 October 1968, on the Haji Kimi Mountain between the villages of Koka and Chowardiwar, Mahabad, the eight peshmergas engaged in a 12-hour war with 3500 Iranian armies, gendarmes, and jash, supported by six tanks, helicopters, and three planes. Some of the Iranian forces were killed and wounded, and a helicopter was taken down. In this conflict, peshmergas including Sayyed Fatah, Ali Gala, and Darvish Osman were killed. The government, to threaten people, hung the corpses in Mahabad (Sardashti, 2002a, pp. 77-79, 82).

Appendix 18: Organizations of the World Objected the Iranian Regime

After the publication of the declaration of the Tudeh Party, many organizations of the world objected the Iranian regime's suppression of the Kurds. The following organizations, without mentioning the names of the KDP-I or the Revolutionary Committee, protested the Iranian government: the Tudeh Party; the Iranian Kurdish Intellectual Organization Outside Iran; the newspaper *Shoaleh-ye Jonoub* (Southern Flame); the magazine *Peyman* (Promise), belonging to the International Confederation of Iranian Students, National Union (CISNU); the newsletter of the National Front; the Italian Communist Council; the New Movement of the Iranian Communists; the Executive Committee of the Confederation of Iranian Students, National Union (CISNU); the Association of Sympathy with and Help to the Peoples (Nations); the newspaper *Tariq* ash-*Shaab* (Path of the People) the organ of the Iraqi Communist Party; the newspaper *Alay Krekaran* (Workers' Flag), the publication of the Solaymaniya branch of the Iraqi Communist Party; the newspaper *Nib Sabbath Chak* the organ of the Hungarian Socialist Workers' Party; the Lebanese weekly newspaper *Al Akhbar*; the French newspaper *Le Monde* (16 November 1968); the *Morning Star*, the organ of the Communist Party of Britain; the journal *Problems of Peace and Socialism/World Marxist Review* (issue, 1, 1969); the newspaper *El Siglo*, the organ of the Communist Party of Chili (issue, 27, November 1968); the newspaper *L'Unità the* organ of the Italian Communist Party (26 October 1968); the Italian newspaper *Il Partito* (28 June 1969); and the newspaper *Regay Kurdistan* (Way of Kurdistan) the organ of the Committee of the Kurdistan Territory of the Iraqi Communist Party (5 November 1968) (Gadani, 2008a, pp. 163-164; Hisami, 2011, p. 123; Sardashti, 2002a, pp. 43-44).

Appendix 19: A Brief Biography of Abdul Rahman Ghassemlou.

Most sources reveal that Ghassemlou went to France to continue his education in 1948. Within 1948-1949, due to his political activates, France expelled him from studying economy in Sorbonne. In 1948, using the bursary of the Students International Union, he travelled to Prague where he received his Bachelor's degree in 1952. During Mosaddiq's government (1951-1953), he returned to Iran for political activities. In 1958, he went to Iraq where he, due to some political accusations and his supporting leftist ideas, was expelled and went to Prague in 1960. In Prague, in 1962, he continued his education and received his Doctorate in political economy and about Kurdish nationalism titled *Kurdistan and Kurd*. As an instructor, he taught capitalist and socialist economies and the theory of economic development in the Charles University in Prague until 1970. Later, he travelled to Iraq where he taught Kurdish history in the University of Baghdad and, at the same time, as an expert, worked with the Planning Ministry of Iraq on a 25-year project. In 1974, because of the political situation, he left to France where he taught in the section of Kurdish language and civilization at Sorbonne, between 1976-1978 (Ali Mahmood Shekhani, 2007, pp. 43-50, 95-96).

Appendix 20: Main Points of the Program and Constitution of the KDP (I)

The KDP (I), in its 3rd Congress in September 1973, developed a comprehensive and modern type of program and constitution. The general principles of the KDP (I) include: (1) The party is the vanguard party of the Kurdish people in Iranian Kurdistan. (2) Along with other progressive forces of the Iranian people, the party fights against imperialism and the reactionary monarchist regime for a free Iran and the Kurds' right to self-determination within Iranian Kurdistan. (3) The party supports the peace and freedom between the peoples and the liberating struggle of all countries against imperialism. (4) The final goal of the party is the establishment of a just socialist society. (5) The strategic slogan of the party is the formation of autonomy for Iranian Kurdistan within a democratic Iran (KDP (I)'s Program and Constitution, 1973, p. 17). The party approved that all minorities in Kurdistan have equal rights with the Kurds. In addition, their cultural rights will be fulfilled, their children will study in their mother language in elementary schools, and they can publish newspapers and books in their own languages (KDP (I)'s Program and Constitution, 1973, pp. 19-20). According to the party's program, women and men are equal in the family and in the society, and receive equal wages for equal work (KDP(I)'s Program and Constitution, 1973, p. 20). The program asserts that the autonomous government of Kurdistan grants the democratic freedoms, freedom of expressions and publications, and freedom of creating unions for all classes. Moreover, while the Kurdish government is separate from religion, it guarantees religious freedom, and the followers of different religions are equally treated, as racial and religious discriminations are condemned. According to the program, women and men are equal in the family and in the society and receive equal wages for equal work. The program upholds eight-hour workday and six-hour workday for laborious jobs; the workers are insured for work accidents, sickness, and seniority, and work for children under 14 years of age is illegal. The program also maintains that land belongs to s/he who works it, all the properties of the people's enemies will be distributed among landless peasants, and the instalment of the lands will be ended. Finally, the program affirms the Kurdistan autonomous government's assisting Kurds in other parts of Kurdistan and will accept patriotic Kurds as political refugees (KDP (I)'s Program and Constitution, 1973, pp. 20, 22, 25).

The constitution elaborates on all issues such as the name and essence of the party, membership, the duties and rights of the members, the conditions for acceptance of membership, the punishment of members, the structure of the party, the congresses and conferences conformances of the party, the CC, the Politburo, and finally the organizations and the finances of the party. Regarding the name and the essence of the party, the constitution of the KDP (I) states that the name of the party is *Hezb-e Demokrat-e Kurdistan* (Kurdistan Democratic Party [KDP (I)]), and recognizes itself as the revolutionary party of all Kurdish people in Iranian Kurdistan that organizes workers, peasants, and revolutionary intellectuals within its lines. The party uses the scientific evolutionary theory of society. The constitution maintains that the main principle of the party's structure is democratic centralism (KDP (I)'s Program and Constitution, 1973, pp. 26-34).

Appendix 21: Kurdish Political Organizations

Some of the most important political organizations, mainly established after the Iranian Revolution of 1979, include *Komalay Shorishgeri Zehmetkeshani Kurdistani Eran (Komala)* (Revolutionary Organization of the Toilers of Iranian Kurdistan [Komala]); the Communist Party of Iran (Komala [CPI]), *Komalay Zahmatkeshani Kurdistan* (Organization of the Toilers of Kurdistan), *Komalay Yaksaniy Kurdistan* (Kurdistan Equality Party) (KEP), or Kurdish Equality Association, *Sazmani Khabati Kurdistani Eran* (Organization of Iranian Kurdistan Struggle [Khabat]), *Parti Sarbakhoyy Kurdistan* (Independence Party of Kurdistan [PSK]), *Parti Azadi Kurdistan* (Kurdistan Freedom Party [PAK]), and *Partia Jiyana Azadi Kurdistan* (Party for Free Life in Kurdistan [PJAK]).

The second most influential Kurdish political party after the KDP (I), founded five days after the revolution, was *Komalay Shorishgeri Zehmetkeshani Kurdistani Eran (Komala)* (Revolutionary Organization of the Toilers of Iranian Kurdistan [Komala]). Abdullah Mohtadi, Secretary of the Komala, reveals that the first cells of a leftist political group, which later was called the Komala, were established on 27 October 1969 (Personal communication, September 17, 2012). Other Kurdish organizations include the Komala Kurdistan's Organization of the Communist Party of Iran (Komala [CPI]), *Komalay Zahmatkeshani Kurdistan* (Organization of the Toilers of Kurdistan), *Komalay Yaksaniy Kurdistan* (Kurdistan Equality Party) (KEP), *Sazmani Khabati Kurdistani Eran* (Organization of Iranian Kurdistan Struggle [Khabat]), *Parti Sarbakhoyy Kurdistan* (Independence Party of Kurdistan [PSK]), *Parti Azadi Kurdistan* (Kurdistan Freedom Party [PAK]), and *Partia Jiyana Azadi Kurdistan* (Party for Free Life in Kurdistan [PJAK]).

Abdullah Mohtadi states that Foad Mustafa Sultani, Muhammad Hussein Karimi, Mosleh Sheikh al-Islami, and Abdullah Mohtadi founded a group in Autumn 1969. Others who also joined them were Seddiq Kamangar, Iraj Farzad, Yadollah Baiglari, Saed Watan Doost, and Shoaib Zakariayy. Foad Mustafa Sultani was the group's leader. It was nine-

and-half years into the group's clandestine activity when the 1979 revolution occurred (Saedi, 2010, pp. 23-25, 41).

As for the ideological view of the Komala at that time, Ebrahim Alizadeh, the General Secretary of the Komala Kurdistan's Organization of the Communist Party of Iran (Komala [CPI]), and the executive member of the Communist Party of Iran (CPI), states that the Komala was mostly pro-Chinese but did not call itself a Maoist group. This tendency weakened as the group neared 1979 (Personal communication, September 13, 2012). According to Mohtadi, the 1st Congress of the Komal was held in Autumn 1978 in Sanandaj and Naqadeh (Saedi, 2010, p. 153). According to Malakeh Mustafa Sultani and Saed Watan Doost (2015), the leaders of the organization actually held a Plenum in 1978 but later it was called the 1st Congress of the Komala. In total, only 10 cadres participated in the Plenum which lasted 37 days (pp. 11-13). Alizadeh claims that at the beginning of the establishment of the Komala, under the influence of the Chinese revolution, they sought to launch a protracted struggle in Kurdistan and Iran. After the Iranian Revolution of 1979, they thought they could establish a liberated, "red" zone in Kurdistan and keep it for a long period, but they had not thought about passing the border and going to Iraq. They also had not considered a civil war in Kurdistan (Saedi, 2012, p. 30).

The Komala participated in the Iranian Revolution through organizing Kurdish people. Mohtadi claims that during 1978-1979, most of the demonstrations against the Iranian regime in Kurdistan were organized by the Komala. After the Komala became public, it attracted the majority of the Kurdish intellectuals and became one of the two major parties in Kurdistan (Saedi, 2010, p. 50). The Komala announced itself on 16 February 1979 (Saedi, 2010, p. 52). Since then, this organization has been one of the most influential organizations in Kurdistan. Along with some other organizations, the Komala held an armed struggle against the government. Since then, the Komala has gone through several merges and splits. Mohtadi believes that the Komala was most powerful party in Mukrian, including Mahabad (Saedi, 2010, p. 98).

The 3rd Congress of the Komala was held on 1 May 1982. It approved the shared program of the Komala and *Itihadi Mubarzani Komonist* (Unity of Communist Militants) (Saedi, 2010, p. 213). According to Alizadeh, the Communist Party of Iran was founded on 2 September 1983 in the Alan region in Sardasht (Saedi, 2012, p. 150). The Komala remained the Kurdistan organization of the Communist Party of Iran. Mohtadi claims that since the 6th Congress of the Komala, the views of the Komala were changed by Mansoor Hekmat (Zhoobin Razani). Before that, the Komala had named itself the leader of the Kurdish movement. However, since the 6th Congress it was argued that the leadership of the nationalist movement should be left to the nationalist parties, and of the socialist movement to the socialists, like the Communist Party of Iran (Saedi, 2010, p. 68-69). The Workers' Communist Party of Iran (WPI), under Mansoor Hikmat, had split from the Communist Party of Iran on 30 August 1991 (Saed, 2012, p. 170). Mohtadi maintains that the reason for the Workers' Communist Party (WPI) of Iran splitting from the Communist Party of Iran (CPI) in 1991 was that Hekmat had realized that the Communist Party of Iran (CPI) had come to a deadlock. Indeed, aside from the Komala, the party had failed to absorb the workers, students, and intellectuals, to the extent that the Communist Party's Tehran branch was organized by the Komala's cadres. The establishment of the Communist Party of Iran destroyed the relationship between the Komala and other Iranian leftist organizations. Mohtadi believes that the Communist Party of Iran would have never been able to mobilize a popular movement (Saedi, 2010, p. 78-84). Mohtadi states that the 9th Congress of Komala was held on 2000 when *Komalay Shorishgeri Zehmetkeshani Kurdistani Eran* (Komala) (Revolutionary Organization of the Toilers of Iranian Kurdistan [Komala] was separated from the Communist Party of Iran (Saedi, 2010, p. 88, 294). As observed, the separatists chose the original name of the Komala (where in fact it was officially established in 1979). As such, aside from its name in Kurdish, this organization chose the name *Hezb-e Komaleh-ye Kurdistan-e Iran* (Komala Party of Iranian Kurdistan) in Persian and the Komala Party of Iranian Kurdistan in English.

Alizadeh claims that the separatists after the 9th Congress took at most 20 percent of the forces of the Communist Party of Iran (Saedi, 2012, p. 208). According to Mohtadi, since the split from the Communist Party of Iran, the Komala did not recognize itself as a communist movement but simply as a leftist party. Its main goal was to combine Kurdish nationalism and leftist ideas. Mohtadi believes that the main problem of the Kurdish society is the national question (Saedi, 2010, p. 220). Mohtadi reveals that the Komala had applied to become a member of the Socialist International, but it ended up participating as a formal guest (Saedi, 2010, p. 324). Mohtadi believes that the Komala is a socialist party and recognizes itself as the leader of the national liberation in Kurdistan (Saedi, 2010, p. pp. 132-133).

At the present time, many of the Komala's members live in the Iraqi Kurdistan. Mohtadi points out that the Komala has kept its armed wing for two reasons. It has positively affected the morale of the Kurdish people in Kurdistan and had a positive impact on the equation of power between the Kurdish people and the Iranian government. If this force did not exist, the government could further supress the Kurds. However, the armed struggle is a mistake at the present: Since the Komala cannot overthrow the regime, armed struggle would only give excuse to the regime to widely attack political, social, cultural, and civilized movements (Saedi, 2010, pp. 380-381). Mohtadi states that the Komala, at the time of its armed clashes with the regime, had between 2,500 and 3,000 peshmergas and about 3,000 casualties (Saedi, 2010, p. 392). But the incomplete list of the Komala casualties, gathered by the CPI, has 1724 names in it (including cadres who died of natural causes or in accidents) (Albom-e Janbakhtegan, 2016, n.p.). One of the achievements of the Komala has been recruiting women and engaging them in political and military activities. Alizadeh claims that the Komala has more than 2,300 casualties from which exist more than 100 women. Alizadeh lists the names of 102 casualties from the Komala's women peshmergas (Saedi, 2012, pp. 91, 693-696).

In the 12th Congress of the Komala, held on 17 August 2007, a minority, under Ilkhanizadeh, refused to participate. Instead, in a declaration, this group announced the establishment of a minority faction within the Komala that aimed at reforming the party on 14 April 2007. This group later was named *Komalay Shorishgeri Zahmatkeshani*

Kurdistani Eran-Rawti Chaksazi w Gasha (Revolutionary Organization of the Toilers of Iranian Kurdistan-Path of Reform and Flourish) on 8 August 2007. A few months before the Congress, on 14 April 2007, in a declaration, this group announced the establishment of a minority faction within the Komala that aimed at reforming the party. This group later was named *Komalay Shorishgeri Zahmatkeshani Kurdistani Eran-Rawti Chaksazi w Gasha* (Revolutionary Organization of the Toilers of Iranian Kurdistan-Path of Reform and Flourish) on 8 August 2007. This faction officially split from the Komala on 20-27 September 2007. Later, the splinters, under Omar Ilkhanizadeh, chose *Komalay Zahmatkeshani Kurdistan* (Organization of the Toilers of Kurdistan) as the group's name. Mohtadi asserts that the separatist did not have different political views compared to those of the Komala. Their problems with the Komala were personal and pertained to their party ranks (Saedi, 2010, pp. 407-411; "Rawti Chaksazi", 2007, p. 1; "Rebarayati Komalay", 2007). Alizadeh confirms that no meaningful differences affirm the split and the programs and political strategies of the two groups under Mohtadi and Ilkhanizadeh are very similar. Their conflict was thus over organizational styles (Saedi, 2012, pp. 437-438). Ahmadzadeh and Stansfield (2010) state that the splinters that established the Organization of the Toilers of Kurdistan in October 2007 accused "the politburo of the Komala of being non-democratic" (p. 23). It should be noted that henceforth in this book, the term "Komala" designates the organization led by Mohtadi, unless noted otherwise.

The Komala passed through yet another split. The 2nd Plenum of the Komala was held on 9 November 2007, after which one of the members of the CC, Abdullah Konaposhi, resigned and later established *Komalay Shorshgeri Zahmatkeshani Kurdistani Eran-Rawti Yakgirtnawa* (Revolutionary Organization of Toilers of Iranian Kurdistan-Reunification Faction). Mohtadi claims that Konaposhi's problem was not organizational or political; instead, he had taken part in abhorrent activities (Saedi, 2010, pp. 422, 609). Ahmadzadeh and Stansfield (2010) use a slightly different name for this last splinter group: *Komalay Shorshgeri Zahmatkeshani Kurdistani Eran-Rewti Yekgrtnewe* (Revolutionary Organization of Toilers of Iranian Kurdistan-Reunification Faction), which was established on 29 April 2008. This faction accused "Abdullah Mohtadi of non-democratic management of the Komala and a policy of cooperation with Reza Pahlavi and the monarchists in Iran" (p. 23). Later Konaposhi joined the Organization of the Toilers of Kurdistan. Thereafter, nine members (eight of them, including Konaposhi, members of the CC), plus another previous CC member, announced the formation of a faction on on 30 March 2014 ("Bashek la komitay", 2014). The faction publically announced its formation on 18 April 2014. The announcement was signed by 10 members including Sabri Bahmani (Konaposhi's wife). The faction's main goals were the fulfilment of the resolutions of the 13th Congress, elimination of lack of financial clarity, as well as ending the transfer of internal conversations to outside of the organization ("Ragayandini fraksion", 2014). Finally, this faction, without issuing an announcement, separated from the Organization of the Toilers of Kurdistan and joined the Revolutionary Organization of the Toilers of Iranian Kurdistan (Komala) in 2014.

The communist Party has also witnessed its splits. It seems that, since the 12th Congress of the Komala Organization of the Communist Party of Iran, in June 2006, an opposition faction has existed including Saed Watan Doost, Mina (Muhammad Amin) Hisami, and Jafar Aminzadeh (Saedi, 2012, pp. 436, 442). Later this faction split from the Communist Party of Iran. Mohtadi claims that the *Rawti Sosialisti Komala* (Socialist Path of Komala) separated from the Communist Party of Iran (Saedi, 2010, p. 426). According to Hashem Ahmadzadeh and Gareth Stansfield (2010), this faction separated on 15 July 2009 from the CPI (p. 23).

With the splits within the Komala noted above, let us quickly address some other Kurdish political organizations.

Another Kurdish political organization is *Komalay Yaksaniy Kurdistan* (Kurdistan Equality Party or Kurdistan Equality Association) (KEP), which was established under the General Secretary Mamosta Sayyed Rashid Husseini and some of his friends, including Mamosta Abdullah Zaki (Mamosta Qandil), in Saqqiz on 21 March 1979. One year before that, some of the founders were conducting political activities under the name of *Binkay*

Boujanaway Farhangi Kurdi (Centre for Revival of Kurdish Culture) (Kurdistan Equality Party, 2013, n.p.).

The next Kurdish political organization is *Sazmani Khabati Kurdistani Eran* (Organization of Iranian Kurdistan Struggle [Khabat]). The Khabat is a Kurdish word for "struggle." According to Kamil Nuranifard, a leader of Khabat, *Sazmani Khabati Natawayati w Islami Kurdistani Eran* (the Organization of Iranian Kurdistan Nationalist and Islamic Struggle) was established under Sheikh Jalal al-Din Husseini, brother of Sheikh Izz al-Din Husseini, in Baneh on 27 August 1980. The Khabat was a nationalist and Islamic organization. Later, from the Khabat, *Sazmani Khabati Natawayati w Islami Kurdistani Eran* (the Organization of Iranian Kurdistan Nationalist and Islamic Revolutionary Struggle), under Mullah Khidir Abbasi, was split on 24 May 1987. The split is attributed to the splinters were hunger for power. Nuranifard maintains that in the 3rd Congress of the Khabat in 2005, the name of the organization changed to the Organization of Iranian Kurdistan Struggle [Khabat]. While previously the goal of the organization was the establishment of an Islamic government in Kurdistan, it changed its program to seeking a democratic and parliamentary government. In addition, Mr. Baba Sheikh Husseini was elected as the leader. Even though the Khabat believes in federalism and the right of self-determination for all nationalities in Iran, at the present it struggles for autonomy of Kurdistan in Iran (Personal communication, September 8, 2012). Many political activists have addressed the role of Zabihi in creation of the Khabat. For instance, Sheikh Izz al-Din Husseini asserts that Sheikh Jalal al-Din and Zabihi formed the Khabat Organization (Karimi, 1999, p. 357).

An additional Kurdish political origination is *Parti Sarbakhoyy Kurdistan* (Independence Party of Kurdistan [PSK]), which was established under Amir Qazi in Summer 1990. Originally the PSK was the transformation of *Baray Yakgirtouy Demokrati Kurdistan* (Democratic United Front of Kurdistan), which was formed in late Spring 1986. While many organizations took a friendly position regarding the establishment of the Front, the PDKI stood against it and disrupted all of its friendly and past relations with the members of the Front (Qazi, 2010, pp. 378, 382,385, 393). The Front believed that the struggle of the Kurdish nation for its liberation was democratic, progressive, pro-equality, anti-reactionary, and anti-exploitation, anti-dictatorship, anti-willfulness, anti-oppression, anti-terrorism, and anti-opportunism, just as it promoted the equality of nations and world peace. Based on these ideas, the Front published its organ, *Ala (Flag)* (Qazi, 2010, pp. 387-388). Before the formation of the Democratic United Front of Kurdistan, a discussion was going on among the Eastern Kurdistan's Kurdish activists. They were debating whether an organization should be established first or a newspaper in order to bring together Kurdish activists. Some activists started publishing a newspaper called *Serdemî Niwê* or *Serdama Nû (New Era)*. Soon, though, those in charge of this project, except Karim Hisami and some of his friends, stopped (Qazi, 2010, pp. 382-385). The first Issue of *New Era* was published on February 1986, in Stockholm, Sweden, and the Issue 54 (perhaps the last issue) was published on September 1990 (*Serdemî Niwê*, 1986; *Serdemî Niwê*, 1990). According to Mani Rahimi, *Parti Sarbasti Rojhalati Kurdistan* (the Eastern Kurdistan Independence Party [EKIP]) and the PSK unified on 23 April 2015, and continued their activities under PSK (Rahimi, 2016, January 4).

A further Kurdish political origination is *Parti Azadi Kurdistan* (the Kurdistan Freedom Party [PAK]), which was founded through its first Congress on 10-12 October 2006. Originally the name of the party was *Yaketi Shorishgerani Kurdistan* (Kurdistan Revolutionaries Unity), which was established in 1991 under Said Yazdanpanah. At present, the leader of the PAK is Ali Qazi, son of Qazi Muhammad, and its General Secretary is Hussein Yazdanpanah. The main slogan of the PAK is the reestablishment of the Kurdistan Republic Government (Kurdistan Freedom Manifesto, 2006).

The next Kurdish political origination is *Partia Jiyana Azadi Kurdistan* (the Party for Free Life in Kurdistan [PJAK]), which according to Azad Awraz, one of the leaders of this organization, was formed on 25 April 2004 in Kurdistan. The PJAK is a nationalist movement. This organization and the PKK follow the philosophy of Abdullah Ocalan (Personal communication, September 19, 2012). The leader of the PJAK is Abdul Rahman Haji Ahmadi. The PJAK has a strong relationship with *Partiya Karkerên Kurdistanê* (the Kurdistan Workers' Party [PKK]), a left-wing Kurdish organization in Turkish Kurdistan, which was founded by Ocalan on 27 November 1978. The PKK in 2002 changed its name to the Congress for Democracy and Freedom in Kurdistan (KADEK), and in 2003 it adopted the name of *Kongra-Gel* (People's Congress of Kurdistan (KGK). Amir Karimi, one of the leaders of this organization, states that, at the beginning, the goal of the PJAK was establishing a federal Iran, but now it has changed to a democratic confederalism in which the form of the government will be a democratic parliamentary system. He adds that the independence of confederalism is more than that of the federalism from the centre (Personal communication, November 29, 2012).

Although these organizations have different degrees of influence among the Kurdish people and have adopted various scales of leftism and democratic perspectives, they are also part of the Kurdish nationalist movement.

Appendix 22: The 8-Article Demands of the Kurds in February 1979

According to Ahmad Askandari (2015), the Kurdish representatives of some of the cities of Kurdistan included Sheikh Izz al-Din Husseini, Ghassemlou, Bolourian, Salah al-Din Mohtadi, and Foad Mustafa Sultani, and the Provisional Government delegation included Forouhar, Ibrahim Younesi, Dr. Ismail Ardalan, and Dr. Muhammad Mukri. The Kurdish delegation offered an 8-article list and then read it for larger numbers of representatives, including Sheikh Jalal al-Din Husseini from Baneh, Mullah Khidir Sardki from Sardasht, and Sanar Mamadi from Shapur in Western Azerbaijan Province (Askandari, 2015). The 8-article list of demands included: (1) the Kurdish people support the Iranian Revolution; (2) the Kurdish people, like the other Iranian people, ask for the removal of the national oppression and the right to self-determination in the form of a federative Iran, and they reject the accusation of being separatists; (3) toilers, workers, and peasants should participate in the revolutionary government; (4) Kurdistan demands the removal of economic oppression; (5) all garrisons in Kurdistan should be placed under a revolutionary council; (6) officers of the previous regime who had orders to shoot and kill demonstrators should be submitted to the people's court, and the army should purge counter-revolutionary elements; (7) all of the representative of the Kurdish cities in this meeting announce that Ayatollah Sayyed Izz al-Din Husseini is qualified to represent the Kurdish people in negotiations with the central government; and finally, (8) as Mullah Mustafa Barzani and the group of "Provisional Leadership [of the KDP [Iraq])" are agents of the CIA, SAVAK, and MIT (National Intelligence Organization of Turkey) and are hated by the all Kurdish people, the Provisional Government should cut all contacts with this group and to expel its leaders from Iran without harming the situations of the poor family refugees (Askandari, 2015).

Appendix 23: The Main Points of the 26-Article Plan

The main points of the 26-Article Plan were: Kurdistan includes the provinces of Ilam, Kermanshah, Kurdistan, and Western Azerbaijan; the sovereignty of the Kurdish nation in the Kurdistan of Iran would be in the form of autonomy in the framework of political, economic, and national unity of the Iranian territory; in the autonomous territory of Kurdistan, the Iranian government would (a) defend the borders against the foreign invaders, (b) deal with issues concerning the political and other foreign relations including the foreign consulates located in Kurdistan, (c) deal with foreign commerce and customs, (d) offer long term economic programs which need financial resources (all other issues would be under the authority of the offices of autonomous Kurdistan); the Kurdistan National Assembly of would be the highest source of authority in Kurdistan to be elected democratically every other year; the of Kurdistan National Assembly appoints the government of Kurdistan; the of Kurdistan National Assembly Kurdistan should provide the conditions for free and democratic activities of the social life including freedom of parties, meetings, publications, expression, writing, ideas, religion, democratic associations, and the right of strike in Kurdistan; Kurdish is the official language in the Kurdistan's offices while Persian will be the official language in Iran including Kurdistan; in the autonomous Kurdistan, education in all levels would be in the Kurdish language, while after the fourth elementary schools, reading the Persian language will be compulsory in all schools; the national minorities in Kurdistan would have the right to preserve and develop their cultures and traditions and study in their own languages in the schools; the autonomous government of Kurdistan establishes the peshmerga (military) forces for preserving the security and the discipline in Kurdistan; for empowering the unity of the Iranian people, in addition to sending Kurdistan's representatives to participate in the Iranian National Parliament, in proportion to the Kurdish populations, the Kurds will take part as Minsters and in the ministries; for guaranteeing the foundations of autonomy and protecting all Iranian nations, the Higher Council of Iranian Nations, comprised of three representatives of each nation within Iran, will be established; and all of the laws pertaining to the rights of the Iranian nations debated within the Iranian National Parliament must be discussed and approved by the Higher Council of Iranian Nations (Gadani, 2008a, pp. 249-255).

Appendix 24: The 6-Article Plan of the PDKI

The PDKI provided a shorter version of the 26-Article Plan named *Reous-e Kolli-ye Tarh-e Khod Mokhtari* (General Outline for Autonomy), known as the 6-Article Plan, on 1 March 1980. These Articles were:

> 1. The Kurdish nation, in the framework of an independent and united Islamic Republic of Iran, has its national rights in the form of self-determination while this right is embedded in the Constitution of Iran.
> 2. The geographic territory of Kurdistan is indicated based on the historical, geographical, economic conditions, and the will of the majority of the population in each area.
> 3. The autonomous Kurdistan, in free elections and through secret ballots, chooses the Kurdistan National Assembly.
> 4. The Kurdistan National Assembly appoints an executive board to deal with economic, cultural, administrative, and disciplinary issues.
> 5. Kurdish, along with Persian, is the official language in the autonomous Kurdistan in administrative relations and education.
> 6. All economic, administrative, social, cultural, and disciplinary issue are under the authority of the autonomous Kurdistan's organizations. (Gadani, 2008a, pp. 255-257)

Appendix 25: Democratic Visage

Baba Ali Mehrparwar, a former Politburo member, identifies the eight principles of Ghassemlou's *Simay Democrat* (Democratic Visage) in the 5th Congress:

> 1. A Democrat is to be independent and therefore, he/she prefers that his/her party without dependence will be completely free and independent of provisions that bind the party to certain supporters....
>
> 2. A Democrat is a supporter of pluralism, and has deep faith in the people's ability to judge for themselves. In practice and interaction with other political parties and people, always pursue this point....
>
> 3. A democratic regime will come to power in Iran on the basis of pluralism, and elections reflecting the multiple nations of Iran....
>
> 4. A democrat is not an insular nationalist. He/she respects the friendship between nations and respects the rights of all nations....
>
> 5. A democrat is a defender and protecter [protector] of the rights of workers and is against all exploitation of human beings....
>
> 6. A democrat is a supporter of the equal rights of women and men in family and society.
>
> 7. A democrat is a philanthropist and for friendship between people, without considering race and religion, and is against any kind of racism and fascism....
>
> 8. A democrat is against national oppression and struggles to abolish or neutralize it. (Monazzami, 2011, pp. 38-45)

Appendix 26: The 10-article Declaration of the PDKI-RL

The 10-Article Declaration of the PDKI-RL aimed in fulfilling the subsequent principles. (1) Creating the foundation of the anti-imperialist principles in the party, leaving the conservative policies of Sharafkandi-Ghassemlou Faction with the imperialist groups. (2) Striving for creating friendly relationships with the socialist and progressive countries and strengthening relationship with the progressive organizations and liberating patriotic movements. (3) Emphasizing and extending armed struggle and rejecting the politics of compromise and negotiation with the Islamic Republic. (4) Supporting the international efforts for ending the Iran-Iraq War based on the United Nations Security Council Resolution 598. (5) Trying to end convulsions among combatant, democratic, and revolutionary parties and organizations in Iran and Kurdistan; creating friendly relationships with the revolutionary Iranian opposition in order to strengthen the Kurdish national democratic movement and its relation with Iranian struggle for withdrawing from the Islamic Republic, and establishing a democratic regime in Iran. (6) Removing some deviational and reactionary subjects, which have been inserted in the Platform and Constitution of the Party by this Sharafkandi-Ghassemlou Faction. (7) Bringing back the democratic principles and ideas to the different organizations of the party, observing the members rights, and protecting their political and social prestige. Protecting democracy within and outside of the party. (8) Removing cult of personality, struggling against dictatorial tendencies and power concentration in the hands of an individual. (9) Enduring to reaccept the cadres, members, and peshmergas who have been expelled or became passive due to the policies of the Sharafkandi-Ghassemlou Faction. This principle does not include the traitors and criminals. (10) Protecting philanthropist values and considering the most ethical and social principles to establish sympathy and friendly correlations in all of the organizations of the party (Gadani, 2008b, pp. 26-27).

Appendix 27: The 6-Point Internal Memo of the Political-Military Commission of the PDKI

The Political-Military Commission of the PDKI distributed a 6-Point Internal Memo for the city and territorial committees which emphasized: (1) The 15 people who signed the declaration are traitors to the party and the nation; they are jash, and they will be treated as traitors and jash. (2) They should not be allowed to enter any of the PDKI's bases. (3) The PDKI's cadres, peshmergas, and supporters should boycott them, and encourage the Kurds in Iran and Iraq to boycott them, too. (4) The deceived cadres and peshmergas of PDKI-RL should be encouraged to return to the PDKI, and if they repented and honestly returned, they should be warmly accepted; the people who were with the *Ladar* (deviant) group and remained in the PDKI, can remain if they condemn the "deviant group" (i.e., PDKI-RL) as traitors and jash. However, if they pretend to condemn them by propagandizing for or working for them, they will be deemed as spies and will be treated as spies. (5) The people who are in charge of the city and territorial committees should, in their sessions (a) condemn the "deviant group" and the traitors to the party and nation as jash; (b) they should announce their support for the PDKI and send the announcements to the Iranian Kurdistan Voice Radio; (c) these committees should send the list of who have left the party, to the Political-Military Commission. In addition, the list should include the dates and the responsibilities of the people who have left, as well as the properties of the party which they have taken with them. The list should be received by the Political-Military Commission by 4 April 1988 (Gadani, 2008b, pp. 41-42).

Appendix 28: The Objectives and Internal Regulation of the PDKI in the 13th Congress

The general objectives of the PDKI in its 13th Congress include:

> 1- The PDKI is the vanguard party of the people of Iranian Kurdistan, and together with the progressive forces all over Iran, it struggles to safeguard Iran's independence, and establish a democratic regime in Iran to obtain the rights of the Kurdish people in Iranian Kurdistan for self-determination.
>
> 2- The long-term objective of PDKI is to establish a democratic socialist society.
>
> 3- The strategic objective of the PDKI is the establishment of a democratic federal Iran and the attainment of Kurdish national rights in Iranian Kurdistan.
>
> 4- The PDKI considers the oppressed nationalities of Iran as its strategic allies, and supports their national struggle to attain their national rights.
>
> 5- Support for the national-democratic struggle of Kurdish people in other parts of Kurdistan is the leading principle of the PDKI.
>
> 6- The PDKI supports the liberation struggle of all the people of the world, and supports peace and friendship of the people in all the countries. (Democratic Party of Iranian Kurdistan, 2004)

In addition, a change was made in the internal regulations of the PDKI in the 13th Congress. The internal regulation omitted the phrase "democratic centralism" which existed in previous internal regulations of the party but kept the principles of the democratic centralism. According to the internal regulation of the 13th Congress, Article VII: the Organizational Structure of the party is based on the following principles.

> 1. The fundamental organizational structure of the party will be guided by:
> - From top to bottom in the hierarchy, all party bodies are elected.
> - All the party organs regularly submit reports of their activities to their respective electorates and to the higher organs.

- Members are subject to the organization, and minority follows majority of members.

- Party disciplines apply to all the Party members equally, without any discrimination.

- A lower-level organ must carry out the decisions of a higher organ.

- From top to bottom in the hierarchy, decisions are made collectively.

- Self-centredness and egotism are condemned in the party. (Democratic Party of Iranian Kurdistan, 2004)

Appendix 29: The PDKI-RL's Three-Step Plan

In its plenum in Spring 1991, the PDKI-RL announced that the party was ready to unconditionally negotiate with the PDKI while suggesting a Three-Step Plan to solve their problems. Firstly, stopping the war: in shared or separate declarations, both parties condemn the internal armed conflict while promising to solve their problems in political ways. In addition, as separate political organizations, based on reciprocal respect, they have relationships with each other. Secondly, practical cooperation: conforming to real democracy based on respecting the ideas of communities of people in Kurdistan. Also, granting the multilateral activities of authentic forces and combatants in Kurdistan. Thirdly, unification: considering the fact that trampling on the constitution of the party and external democracy were the main reasons for the split, the following can provide the background for the unity: comprehensively condemning of the internal war within the movement; condemning the anti-people policy of the Islamic Republic of Iran, emphasizing on the withdrawn of this regime, and establishing a democratic government; leaving all kinds of incorrect and inimical relationships with the Iranian and Kurdish forces while trying to create a Kurdish and Iranian front; creating relationships with governments and social groups should be based on who is striving for the Kurdish rights; in a non-authoritarian way, trying to establish an all-inclusive Kurdish organization; with both organizations cooperating, trying seriously to establish the context for holding a shared congress; and, holding a shared congress for indicating the platform, constitution, and the organization of the party. This Three-Step Plan was rejected by the PDKI (Gadani, 2008b, pp. 79-83).

Appendix 30: The Main Organizations and Publications of the PDKI and the KDP

The main organizations of the PDKI include: *Yaketi Jinani Demokrati Kurdistani Eran* (Democratic Women's Union of Iranian Kurdistan), *Yaketi Lawani Demokrati Kurdistani Eran* (Democratic Youth Union of Iranian Kurdistan), *Yaketi Khowendkarani Demokrati Kurdistani Eran* (Democratic Student Union of Iranian Kurdistan), *Nawandi Nergiz* (Nergiz Centre) which is a centre for the children, and the PDKI Center for Strategic Research. In addition, the PDKI publishes the newspaper *Kurdistan*, the newspaper *Agri*, the magazine *Jinan* (Women), the magazine *Lawan* (Youth), the political and intellectual magazine *Tishk* (Ray), the magazine *Biri khowendkar* (Students Thought), and the children's magazine *Nergiz*.

Moreover, the party has an official website named Kurdistan Media (http://www.kurdistanmedia.com/), and the Democratic Party of Iranian Kurdistan (http://www.pdki.org/english/) in English. It also has some websites such the *Khaka Lewa* or Khakelewe (http://khakelewe.com/kurdi/), and *Peshmergakan* or Peshmergekan (http://peshmergekan.com/kurdish/), which are directed by its affiliates. Furthermore, the PDKI has an online radio channel named *Radio Dangi Kurdistani Eran* (Iranian Kurdistan Voice Radio), and a satellite TV channel named *Tishk* (Ray) TV. At the present time, both the radio and *Tishk* TV satellite stations are closed. However, the PDKI TV programs are broadcast online on Tishk News (https://www.youtube.com/user/TISHKTVNEWS/featured).

The major organizations of the KDP are *Yaketi Jinani Demokrati Kurdistan* (Democratic Women's Union of Kurdistan), *Yaketi Lawani Democrati Rojhalati Kurdistan* (Democratic Youth Union of Kurdistan), *Yaketi Natawayy Khowendkarani Kurd* (National Unity of Kurdish Students), which is not active now, *Nawandi Mindalparezi Rojhalati Kurdistan* (Eastern Kurdistan Centre for Child Protection), and *Anjoumani Bargiri la Zindaniya Siasiyakani Rojhalati Kurdistan* (Protection Council of Political Prisoners of Eastern Kurdistan). In addition, the KDP publishes the newspaper *Kurdistan*, the Magazine *Lawan*

(Youth), the magazine *Jinan* (Women), the political and intellectual magazine *Tishk* (Ray), which is not active now, and the magazine of children named *Dinyay Mindalan* (Children's World).

Moreover, the KDP has an official websites of *Kurdistan u Kurd* or Kurdistanukurd (http://www.kurdistanukurd.org/), the KDP Media (http://kdpmedia.org/index.php), and the KDP Press (http://archive.kurdistanukurd.com/en/english.php) in English. It also has some websites such as *Rojhalat Times* (http://rojhelattimes.net/), and or *Giareng* (http://www.giareng.com/), which are directed by its affiliates. Furthermore, the KDP has an online radio channel named *Radio Dangi Kurdistan* (Voice of Kurdistan Radio), and a satellite TV channel named *Kurd Kanal* (Kurd Channel). Additionally, the PDKI is one of the founders of the Congress of Nationalities for a Federal Iran (CNFI) (http://iran-federal.org/) which was established on 20 February 2005. This institution includes 12 Iranian political organizations from different Iranian nationalities and areas including Kurmanji Kurds of Khorasan, Baluchistan, Kurdistan, Azerbaijan, Ahwaz, Turkmenistan, and Bakhtiari and Lorestan. The CNFI struggles for the elimination of the Islamic Republic of Iran and the establishment of a Federal Republic in Iran. This Republic commits to the principles of democracy based on national and geographic standards as the only mechanism for fulfillment of the political will of all nationalities within a free Iran ("Congress of Nationalities," n.d.).

Both the PDKI and the KDP have also joined some international organizations. At present, the PDKI is a consultant member and the KDP is the full member of the Socialist International. Besides, the PDKI is a member of the Unrepresented Nations and Peoples Organization (UNPO).

Appendix 31: The Cooperation Agreement between the PDKI and the Komala

A concise account of the nine principles of the PDKI and the Komala agreement of 21 August 2012 includes:

1. Without overthrowing the Islamic Republic of Iran, the fulfilment of democracy and the rights of the Iranian nationalities especially the Kurdish nation will be realized. In addition, the PDKI and the Komala believe that the future political system in Iran will be secular, democratic, and federal.

2. The PDKI and the Komala strongly believe in free elections in Kurdistan.

3. Both parties believe in the separation of the institution of religion from the government.

4. Both parties believe in the equality of women and men in all political, social, economic, cultural, and familial aspects in society.

5. Both parties defend the freedom of expression, pen, publication, establishment of political organizations, and civil and guild organization such as workers, women, students, youth, teachers, and so on.

6. Both parties support social justice and protect Kurdistan's environmental life.

7. Both parties commit to solve the political problems between them through dialogue and far from any types of political violence. In addition, this form of solution is necessary for all political groups in Kurdistan.

8. Both parties choose the national-geographic federalism as their main slogan for removing national oppression in Kurdistan.

9. This agreement does not damage the political, organizational, diplomatic, and media independence of these parties. ("Hezb-e Demokrat-e Kurdistan-e", 2012)

Table 1

Population of the Kurds (Estimated)

Country	Number of Kurds	Percentage of the population
Turkey	13,700,000	24.1
Iran	6,600,000	12.4
Iraq	4,400,000	23.5
Syria	1,300,000	9.2
Europe [a]	700,000	
Former USSR [b]	400,000	
Total	27,100,000	

[a] McDowall (2000, pp. 3–4).

[b] Le Monde, 18 February 1999.

Source: Hassanpour, A., and Mojab, S. (2005). Kurdish Diaspora. In M. Ember, C. R. Ember, and I. Skoggard (Eds.) Encyclopaedia of Diasporas Immigrant and Refugee Cultures Around the World (pp. 214-224).

Table 2

The Size of Kurdish Diasporas

Region	Country	Number
Europe	Germany	500,000 [a]
	France	100,000–120,000 [b]
	Netherlands	70,000–80,000 [b]
	Switzerland	7,531 [c]
	Belgium	50,000–60,000 [b]
	Austria	50,000–60,000 [b]
	Sweden	25,000–30,000 [b]
	United Kingdom	20,000–25,000 [b]
	Greece	20,000–25,000 [b]
	Denmark	8,000–10,000 [b]
	Norway	4,000–5,000 [b]
	Italy	3,000–4,000 [b]
	Finland	3,916 [d]
	Russia	
	Siberia	35,000 [b] (30,000 in Vladivostok)
	Krasnodar	30,000 [b]
Central Asia	Kazakhstan	30,000 [e]
	Turkmenistan	50,000 [e]
	Kirghizia	20,000 [e]
	Uzbekistan	10,000 [e]

Region	Country	Number
	Tajikistan	3,000 [e]
	Armenia	75,000 [e]
Caucasia	Azerbaijan	12,000–30,000 [f]
	Georgia	40,000 [a]
Middle East	Lebanon	75,000–100,000 [g]
North America	Canada	7,140 [h]
	United States	15,000–20,000 [b]
Oceania	Australia	2,845 [i]
	New Zealand	603 [j]

[a] Estimate 2000, German parliament.

[b] Institut kurde de Paris (2003), estimate.

[c] Number of Kurdish speakers, Switzerland census 2000.

[d] Number of Kurdish speakers, Finland census 2002.

[e] Kurdish Human Rights Project (1996), estimate.

[f] Muller (2000, p.70).

[g] Meho (2001, p. 28).

[h] Number of Kurdish speakers, Canadian census 2001.

[i] Number of Kurdish speakers, Australian census 2001.

[j] Number of Kurdish speakers, New Zealand census 2001

Source: Hassanpour, A., and Mojab, S. (2005). Kurdish Diaspora. In M. Ember, C. R. Ember, and I. Skoggard (Eds.) Encyclopaedia of Diasporas Immigrant and Refugee Cultures Around the World (pp. 214-224).

Table 3

Women in the Leadership of the PDKI from 1945 to 2016

Congress	Total people in Leadership	Women in Leadership	Percentage of Women in Leadership	Percentage of Women in Central Committee	Percentage of Women in Politburo
1st Congress of the KDP. (1945)	20		0	0	0
2nd Congress of the KDP-I. (1964)	15		0	0	0
3rd Congress of the KDP (I). (1973)	17		0	0	0
4th Congress of the PDKI. (1980)	42		4.7	3.8	0
PDKI (FFC). (15 June 1980)	15		6.6	7.1	0
5th Congress of the PDKI. (1981)	40		0	0	0
6th Congress of the PDKI. (1984)	36		0	0	0
7th Congress of the PDKI. (1985)	38		0	0	0
8th Congress of the PDKI. (1988)	31		0	0	0
9th Congress of the PDKI-RL. (1990)	24		0	0	0
9th Congress of the PDKI. (1991)	32		0	0	0
10th Congress of the PDKI-RL. (1994)	26		0	0	0
10th Congress of the PDKI. (1995)	30		0	0	0
11th Congress of the PDKI. (1997)	35		2.8	0	0

12th Congress of the PDKI. (2000)	42		2.3	0	0
13th Congress of the PDKI. (2004)	39		2.5	0	0
14th Congress of the KDP. (2008)	35		14.2	14.2	0
14th Congress of the PDKI. (2008)	48		6.2	4	0
15th Congress of the KDP. (2011)	40		12.5	19	1
15th Congress of the PDKI. (2012)	35		11.4	4.1	0
16h Congress of the KDP. (2016)	35		11.4	15	0
Total			3.5	3.2	0

Notice 1. Leadership means the total of the CC, alternates, and consultants (see Appendix 8).

Notice 2. Percentage of women in CC = numbers of women in the CC divided by the total CC.

Figure 1

The PDKI Chart from 1945 to 2016

KDP	Kurdistan Democratic Party
KDP-I	Kurdistan Democratic Party-Iran
KDP (I)	Kurdistan Democratic Party (Iran)
PDKI	Democratic Party of Iranian Kurdistan
PDKI (FFC)	Democratic Party of Iranian Kurdistan (Followers of the Fourth Congress)
PDKI-RL	Democratic Party of Iranian Kurdistan-Revolutionary Leadership
KDP	Kurdistan Democratic Party

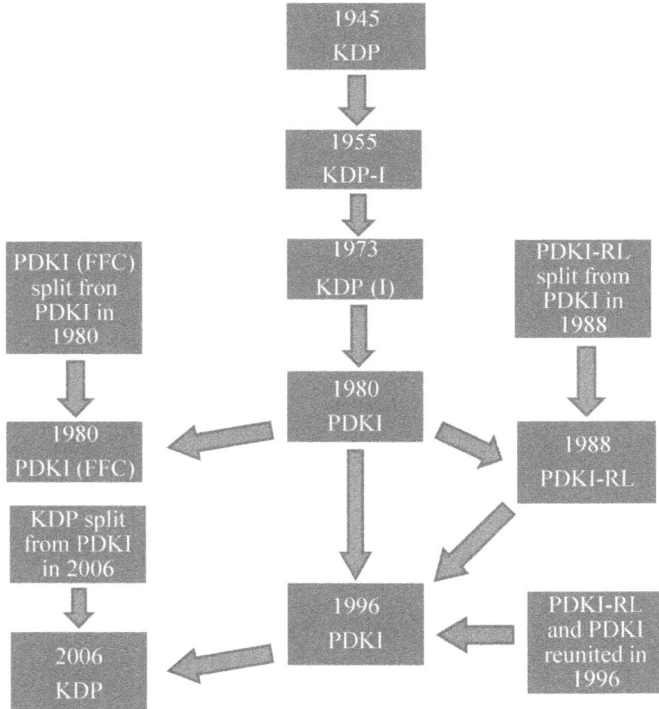

INDEX

Numbers

6-Article Plan named *Reous-e Kolli-ye Tarh-e Khod Mokhtari* (General Outline for Autonomy), 215, 457

7-Point Plan, 219-220, 221

8-Article Demand, 202, 226

10-article Declaration, 247, 398, 459

13-Point Platform, 250

17-point Proposal, 262, 265

20-Point Declaration, 262, 264

26-Article Plan (*Galalay 26 Madayy*), 214-215, 356, 455, 457

A

Abbas Agha Mosque in Mahabad, 137, 150, 347

Abbasi, Aziz, 430

Abbasi, Mullah Khidir, 451

Abbasi, Sadoun, 394

Abbasi, Sargord (Major) 203, 383

Abbas Khan Sardar Rashid, 72, 81-82

Abdali, Abdullah, xviii

Abd al-Karim Qasim, 40, 144, 351

Abd el-Rahman Pasha Baban, 29

Abdi, Ismat, 394, 398

Abdi, Qadir

Abdoli, Fatah, 254, 359, 392-393, 395-396, 403

Abdul Aziz, Ezat, 134

Abdul Fattah Ismail, 198

Abdul Karim Hawezi, Bakir, 133-135, 142-143, 312

Abdullah Bayazid Agha, 102

Abdullah Bayza Qinja, 173

Abdullah, T. A. J., 42, 312

Abdullahi, Mullah Abdullah (Mullah Sarbaz), 166, 352, 376

Abdullahi, Kamal, 96, 102-104, 107, 114, 312

Abdullahi, Rasoul (aka Faqe Ali Rasouy Alli), 240

Abdullah Pour, Hajar 421, 426,

Abdullah Pour, Qadir, 227

Abdullahzadeh, L., 126, 312

Abdul Rahman, Sami, 176, 187

Abaszadeh, Rzgar, xvii

Abrahamian, Ervand, 52, 54-56, 72, 312

Abrouzani, Hassan, 421, 426

Abu Ahmad, 220

Abu Ayad, 199

Abu Jamil, 211

Afandi, Seddiq, 171

Afkhami, I., 82-83, 312

Afsar, Azim, 389

Afshar, Houshmand (General), 93, 101

Afshin (Sarwan, Captain), 385, 217

Agahi, Abdul Hussein, 52, 58, 312

Agri newspaper, 464

Ahangari, Kawe, 298, 309, 312, 416, 420, 425

Ahmad, Ibrahim. *See* Ibrahim Ahmad

Ahmad (Ahmed) Khani, 47

Ahmad Tawfiq. *See* Ishaqi [later Ahmad Tawfiq], Abdullah

Ahmadi, As'ad, 407, 413, 417

Ahmadi, Luqman, 219, 423

Ahmadin [Ahmadain], Karim, 132, 371, 372, 427-428

Ahmad Shah, 55, 58

Ahmad Taqi, 69

Ahmadzadeh, Hashem, 76, 313, 449-450

Akbarov, 108

Al Akhbar newspaper, 441

Alakok (Falsify) (Hajar's Poem), 108, 131

Ala Rirzgari (Flag of Liberation), 36

Alawi, Bozorg, 22

Alay Krekaran (Workers' Flag) newspaper, 441

al-Bakr, Ahmad Hassan, 40

Alexander, G., 42, 317

Algerian war of liberation, 18

Algiers Agreement, of 5 March 1975, 197, 202, 225, 353

Al-Hakkari, Jamal al-Din, 72, 313

Ali Agha (Simko's brother), 67

Ali Agha (Simko's Grandfather), 78

Aliar Dehbukri, Ali Agha (Amir As'ad), 92, 94, 368

Aliar, Omar Agha (son of Amir As'ad), 94, 368

Aliar, Tahir, 389-390

Ali Gala, 440

Ali Gowe Rash, 173

Ali Hasaniani, 71

Ali Khan (son of Mohammad Sadeq Khan), 81

Ali Mahmood Shekhani, Hoshmand, 151-152, 174, 176, 194, 197-198, 233-234, 236, 242, 250-251, 253, 279, 313, 442

Aliyar, Miro (Dr.), 187, 196, 204, 238, 278, 280, 291, 313, 410, 412, 414, 418, 422-423

Alizadeh, Ebrahim, xvii, xviii, 242, 258, 282, 313, 446, 448-449

Allen, George, the United States Ambassador, 137, 140-141

Amanullah Khan, 82

Amer Khan (the Abdui Shikak leader), 74, 81

American Revolution of 1776, 11

Aminzadeh, Jafar, 450

Amnesty International, 37-38, 44, 313

Amuoghly. *See* Heidar Khan Amuoghly

Amu San, 71

Amouyy, Mohammad Ali, 213

Anayati, Muhammad Ali, 397, 403, 406, 409, 411

Anderson, Bebedict, 9, 14, 25, 287, 313

Anderson, L., 295, 314

Anjiri, Seddiq, xix, 126, 147, 157, 160, 162-165, 340, 374, 432

Anjomanakani ayalati wa wilayati (Provincial and District Assemblies), 60

Anjoman-e Melli-ye Kurdistan or *Hayat-i Raeisay Milli Kurdistan* (National Governing Assembly of Kurdistan), 17, 121-122

Anjoumani Bargiri la Zindaniya Siasiyakani Rojhalati Kurdistan (Protection Council of Political Prisoners of Eastern Kurdistan), 464

Anthias, Floya, 8

Aqal al-Tolab, Hashim [later Qadir Sharif], 151, 153, 159, 351, 373, 439

Arab Cordon Plan, 43

Ararat (Agri Dagh or Ağrı Dağı) Revolt (1928), 35-36

Ardalan, Homayoun, 254, 359, 389-390

Ardalan, Ismail (Dr.), 202, 354, 433, 454

Arfa, Hassan, 30, 48, 65-68, 78, 82, 92, 96, 98, 109, 129, 134, 314

Aria (Aryan), 433

Aria, Rahman (Mohandes, Engineer), 385. 388

Ariz, 433

As'adi Sheikh Amin, 435

As'adi Sheikh Seddiq, 435

Asadov, 118

Ashabi, Muhammad, 362

Ashti, Salahedin, xviii

Ashtiani, Eghbal, 29, 336

Askandari, Ahmad, 202, 314, 454

Asrary, Osman, 384

Assembly of Experts, 206

Association of Sympathy with and Help to the Peoples (Nations), 441

Assyrian Democratic Movement, 41.

Atakishiyev, a Soviet Union Army General, 113

Atatürk (Ataturk). *See* Mustafa Kemal Pasha (Atatürk)

Ataturkism, 38

Atayy, Rajab (Colonel), 141

Atiqi, Taha, 249, 384

Atri, Rahmat, 387

Awlay [Abdullah] Mina Khalandi, 101

Awraz, Azad, xvii, 314, 453

Ayatollah Khomeini, 196, 199, 205-206, 208, 210-211, 213-214, 216, 218, 221-222, 225, 229, 251, 327, 355

Ayatollah Khomeini (message to the people of Kurdistan on 17 November 1979), 213-214

Ayatollah Nouri, 202, 354

Ayoubzadeh, Hassan (Mamosta Goran), 277, 314, 392, 394

Ay Raqib (Lo the Enemy) anthem, 162, 201

Ayyoubi, Hussein (Dr.), 150

Ayyoubian Markazi, Ziba, 127

Ayyoubian, Sayyed Aziz, 150

Ayyoubian, Sayyed Muhammad, 371-372, 427-428

Ayyubian, Ubayd Allah, 104

Ayyubid Dynasty, 345

Ayyubids, 29

Axworthy, M., 55, 314

Azad, Hassan., 52, 314

Azerbaijan Democratic Party, 87, 88, 111-112, 117, 132, 136, 147, 151, 182, 193, 348

Azerbaijan Fadai force, 137

Azerbaijan National Government, 88, 117, 120, 125, 132, 144-145, 189, 348

Azerbaijan newspaper 132, 146

Azeri Committee of Naqadeh, 208
Azimi, Eshrat, 127
Azimi, Gholam Hussein (Colonel), 139
Azimi, Kobra 127
Azimi Kor, Hassan, xviii
Aziz Khan Kirmanj, 101, 347
Azizi, Ahmad, 383, 386
Azizi, Azad, 424
Azizi Gawirk, Bayazid Agha, 368
Azizi, Hashim, 421, 426
Azizi, Khalid, xvii, xix, 249, 264, 267-268, 271, 276, 338, 412-415, 419, 424-425
Azizi, Mansour, 423
Azizi, Mullah Karim, (Sardakosani), 375
Azizi, Mullah Khalid, 227
Azizi, Osman, 436
Azizi, Salam, 244, 393, 395-396, 403, 406-408

B

Ba'ath Party, 157, 283, 351
Baban, Zakiya 103
Babanzadeh, Salim, 382, 384-385
Babayov, 118

Babayy, Seddiq, 392-393, 396, 398-399
Babi Gawra village, 152
Bachimont, George H., 70
Badir Shikak, 400
Badkani, Ahmad, 404
Badr (Badir or Bedir) Khan Beg (Pasha), 30, 62, 345
Badr Khan, Abdul Razzaq, 48, 61-62
Badr Khan Beg. *See* Badr (Badir or Bedir) Khan Beg (Pasha)
Badr Khan Pasha. *See* Badr (Badir or Bedir) Khan Beg (Pasha)
Badr Khan, Jalalat 36, 346
Badrnia, Khalid, 227
Baghdadi, Rahim, 389, 392
Bahadiri (Harki), Zero Baig, 90, 142, 368, 372
Bahar, Malek al-Sho'ara, 58, 73, 314
Bahmani, Sabri, 450
Bahrami, Abdullah, 388, 391, 414-415, 420
Bahrami, Hammid, xviii
Bahrami, Kava, 6, 398, 404, 408, 411, 413, 417-418, 422

Bahrami, Khosraw, 410, 414, 418
Bahrami, Reza Khan's Secretary, 74
Baiglari, Yadollah, 445
Bidaghi, Ali, 421, 426
Baigzadeh, Hurko, 368
Baigzadeh, Nouri Baig, 113, 368
Baigzadeh, Said, 401, 405, 412, 414, 416, 420, 425
Bak, Sylvia, xviii
Bakhchi, Hosein, xviii, 120, 163, 212, 217-219, 221-229, 314, 387
Bakhtiar, Taymour (General), 154, 193
Balaki, Omar, 114, 130, 179, 262, 314, 404, 406, 411, 413, 415, 420, 425-426
Bali Maktabi Siasi (Political Bureau Wing) or the KDP (Iraq) Political Bureau, 160, 163, 172
Bani Sadr (President), 215
Bandi Ghassemlou (Ghassemlou's Gang), 222
Bapir Agha, 170
Baray Yakgirtouy Demokrati

Kurdistan (Democratic United Front of Kurdistan), 452
Baqirov, Mir Jafar (the leader of Azerbaijan of Russia), 113-114, 348, 434
Barda Sour village, 282
Barker, Ernest, 10
Baratoff (General), 63
Barzani, Idris, 172
Barzani, Masoud, 41, 156, 160, 174, 202, 275, 314
Barzani, Mullah Mustafa, xix, 39-41, 49, 103, 112, 129, 138-139, 142-144, 153-157, 160-161, 164-165, 168, 171-172, 175-176, 183, 190, 193, 196-198, 202-203, 226, 344, 350-351, 434, 454
Barzani, Sheikh Ahmad, 142
Barzanji, Sheikh Mahmoud, 39, 48, 66, 73-76, 80, 96, 146, 287
Bashiriyeh, H., 56, 315
Basij [Mobilization. The Organization for Mobilization of the Oppressed], 230
Bathayy, Taifour, 387
Bayat, Kaveh, 72, 315

Bayat, Prime Minister, 110
Bayazidi Hamza, 157
Bayazidi, Karim Agha, 430
Bazargan, Mehdi (Prime Minister), 206
Bazyar, Isma'il, xix, 407, 409, 411, 413
Bebash (Mamosta), 405
Behrouz, Sharif, 418
Benderly, Jill, 8, 315
Ben Bella, Ahmad (former President of Algeria), 251-252
Bentley, Livingston, 140
Beşikçi, Ismail, 33, 37
Besikci. *See* Beşikçi, Ismail
Be Soy-e Ayandeh (Toward Future), 147
Betoshi, Halmat, 439, 440
Bhabha, Homi, 8
Bidlici, M. S., 29, 315
Bilazad, Mazar (Mawzar), 127
Binayy, 110
Binkay Boujanaway Farhangi Kurdi (Centre for Revival of Kurdish Culture), 451

Biri khowendkar (Students Thought) magazine, 464
Bishku, M. B., 37, 315
Bitlîsiî, Prince Sharaf al-Dîn (Sharaf Khan). *See* Prince Sharaf al-Dîn Bitlîsiî (Sharaf Khan)
Blau, J., 26, 315
Bloody Nowruz in Sanandaj, 205
Bois, T., 29-30, 315
Bolouri, Iran, 127
Bolourian, Ghani, xix, 90-91, 95, 101-102, 105, 115, 125, 145-146-152, 155, 174-175, 201-207, 209, 212-216, 218-225, 228-229, 315, 331, 366, 373-374, 376, 379, 383, 385, 454
Bolourian, Wahab, 132, 372
Bolshevik Revolution, 65
Bolshevik Revolutionary Committee, 57
Borg, W. R., 5, 319
Borzooyy, M., 30, 48, 82-83, 315
Bourrie, Mark, 45, 315

Bowring, B, 28, 31, 35, 38, 315
Bozarslan, H., 29, 316
Brass, Paul, 8, 20, 288
Breuilly, John, 8, 20, 288
British Royal Air Force (RAF), 39
Bruinessen, M. V., 32-35, 61, 63, 72, 75-76, 316
Bukani, Muhammad, 381
Bulgarian Communist Party, 194
Bush, George, 42

C

Captain Nabavi, 141
Captain Namazaliov, the Soviet Union Town Commandant in Miandoab, 113
Carroll, William K., xvii
Castells, Manuel, 10
Chaichi, Ilham, 6, 419, 424
Chaldiran 1514, 29, 345
Chamran, Mostafa (Dr.), 210-212
Che Guevara, Ernesto, 8
Cherikhaye Fedai Khalgh. *See* Organization of Iranian People's Fedai Guerrillas (OIPFG)
Chia (Colonel), 217

Chicherin, Georgy Vasilyevich, 69
Children's Section, 5
Chinchilla, Norma Stoltz, 8, 316
Chira, Muhammad Amin, 228
Ciwata Azadi Kurd (Kurdish Freedom Society), later called the *Ciwata Kweseria Kurd* (Kurdish Independent Society) or *Azadi* (Freedom or Independence), 36
Chomsky, Noam, 34, 316
Chong, Aileen, xvii
Choukali, Ibrahim (Braym), xviii, 416, 421, 426
Christian Science Monitor, 160
CIA, 203, 454
Cinema in Mahabad (1946), 130
Colonel Arfa. *See* Arfa, Hassan
Comintern, 69
Committee of the Kurdistan Territory of the Iraqi Communist Party, 441

Communist Party of Britain, 441
Communist Party of Chili, 441
Communist Party of Iran (CPI), xx, 6, 240, 242, 244, 282, 445-448, 450
Congress for Democracy and Freedom in Kurdistan (KADEK), 37, 453
Congress of Nationalities for a Federal Iran (CNFI), 465
Connor, Walker, 10, 316
Constitutional Revolution of Iran (1905-1911), 51-53, 57, 59-60, 62, 83, 322, 331, 346
constitutive paradox, 3, 6, 22-23, 190, 286, 295, 307
Conversi, D., 34, 316
Council of Guardians, 216
Creswell, J. W., 5, 317
Cronin, S., 73, 315, 317
Cujol, French officer, 65

D

Dabaghi, Shahla, 280, 304, 317
Dabbaghi, Abdul Qadir, 102

Dabbaghi, Hawsat, 200
Dabbaghi, Kamal, 383, 388
Da'esh. See Islamic State of Iraq and Syria (ISIS) (*Da'esh*)
Dailami, P., 57, 317
Dangi Giti Taza (Voice of New World) journal, 101, 107
Daneshwar, Muhammad Khan, 435
Daniel, E. L., 52, 54, 56, 317
"*Daparyawa biparewa, napariyawa awa halita*" (if you pass to our side, so do it; otherwise, this is your condition), 264
Darvish Osman, 440
Darweshi, Sadiq, 417, 422
Darwija, Khalid, 419
Darwish, A., 42, 317
Dashti, Mahmoud, 394-395, 397, 403
Dasta guleki jowan u bon khosh la baghi nishtman parwari (*A beautiful and fragrant bouquet from the garden of patriotism*), 367

Davis, H. B., 8, 12-13, 317
Dawlati Jimhouryy Kurdistan (Kurdistan Republic Government), 119, 122, 453
Dawoudi, Abdullah (Mullah. Malay Hajoke), 362-363
Dawoudi, Amaneh, 127
Dawoudi, Haji Mustafa, 132, 371-372, 427-428
Dawoudi, Hassan (Dr.), 150
Dawoudzadeh, Khizir, 128
Dawoudzadeh, Saltanat, 127
Dayki Nishtman (*Mother of Homeland*), 105
Debrey, Régis, 8
de Crespigny, the British Air Vice-Marshal in Iraq, 94
Dehqan, Ali, 74, 317
Dehqan, Sayyed Rasoul, 151-152, 163, 200-201, 209, 350, 373, 375, 378, 381-383, 388
Dehqani, Behrouz, 167-168
Dehkurdi, Nouri, 254

Dekker, Karin, xviii
Deleuze, Gilles, 8
Democracy Party (DEP), 38, 359
democratic federal Iran, 261, 461
Democratic Federal System of Northern Syria, 44
Democratic-federative Iran, 291
Democratic Party of Iran, 136
Democratic Party of Iranian Kurdistan (Followers of the Fourth Congress) (PDKI- FFC), xx, 6, 191, 200, 218-219, 221-229, 232-233, 278, 280, 304, 356, 385-386, 470, 471
Democratic Party of Iranian Kurdistan (PDKI), xix, xx, 1-6, 22-24, 49, 88, 125, 187, 191, 200, 202-204, 206, 209, 215-236, 238-252, 254-271, 273-284, 286-287, 289-312, 314, 317-319, 321-324, 327-328, 331, 335-336, 340-341, 356-361, 382, 385-387,

390, 392, 394-398, 402, 404, 406, 408, 410, 412, 417, 422, 452, 457, 460-461, 464-466, 470-471
Democratic Party of Iranian Kurdistan-Revolutionary Leadership (PDKI-RL), xx, 160, 171, 191, 200, 233, 243, 247-251, 253-261, 266, 273, 278-279, 281-283, 358, 360, 398-401, 404-405, 459-460, 463, 470-471
Democratic Party of Iranian Kurdistan's Publication Commission, 31
Democratic Party of the Women, 127
democratic socialism, 195, 236-239
Democratic Student Union of Iranian Kurdistan, 270, 424, 464
Democratic Union Party (PYD), 44
Democratic Women's Union of Iranian Kurdistan, xix, 6, 267-268, 270, 302, 424, 464

Derafsh (Flag), 433
Derakhshan, the Assistant to the Interior Ministry, 208
Derrida, Jacques, 8
Deutsch, Karl, 19
Diari Komalay J.K. Bo Lawakani Kurd (*The Society of J.K.'s Gift for the Kurdish Youth*) or *Diari Komala* (*J.K.'s Gift*), 106, 367
Didaniha (Watchables or Attractions), 433
Dinyay Mindalan (Children's World), 465
Diroudgar, Sayyed Reza, 395, 397, 404, 408, 410-411, 413, 418
Disan Barzani (Again Barzani) newspaper, 156-157
Dolagrami, Mullah Khidir, 405
Dolatou village, 223, 230
Dooher, Gerald F. P., the Vice-Consul of the United States, in Tabriz, 124, 136, 140
"*doo layani Demokrat*" (two parts of Democrat)

or "*demokratakan*" (Democrats), 272
Doost Muhammad, 56
Dunsterville, Lionel (General) 53
Duverger, Maurice, 22

E

Eagleton, William, 67, 69, 72, 94, 96, 102, 109, 112-114, 118-119, 124, 129, 131-133, 139, 144, 159, 318, 363, 368, 371, 428-430
Education Commission, 4, 304
El Siglo newspaper, 441
Emami, Abdul Rahman, 362-363
Emami, Sayyed Hassan, 148
Ember, C. R., 467, 469
Ember, M., 467, 469
Emir Badr Khan, 30
Emir Faisal (Sharif of Mecca), 39
Engels, Friedrich, 8, 332
Enghqelab-e Kaveh (Kaveh's Revolution), 433
English Revolution (1649-1660), 11
Enloe, Cynthia, 8

Entessar, Nader, 3, 29, 35, 39-40, 60, 74, 82, 253, 255, 318
Erzurum Committee, 79
Esim, Sinan, 34, 38, 318
Eskandari, Muhammad Reza, 274, 318
Ettelaat (Information) newspaper, 123, 136, 213, 224
Evans, Christopher, xvii
Executions of 59 people of Mahabad, 235, 341, 357
Ezat, Mahmod Mola, 129, 135, 185, 318
Ezatpour, Abdullah, 390

F
Fadaian-e Khalgh. *See*, Organization of Iranian People's Fedai Guerrillas (OIPFG)
Fadaian (Majority). *See* Organization of Iranian People's Fadaian (Majority)
Fadaiyan. *See* Organization of Iranian People's Fedai Guerrillas (OIPFG)
Fadluyids. 29

Fahd, the General Secretary of the Iraqi Communist Party, 123
Fahimi, Khalil, 98, 110, 140
Faizollah Baigi, Hassan Khan, 435
Faizollah Baigi, Muhammad Amin, 368
Fakhrai, Ibrahim, 57-59, 318
Fakahi, Rashid (Rashay Qachaqchi), 155, 375
Falsafi, Mullah Abubakr, 159, 373
Fani, Enayat, BBC Persian anchor, 275-276
Fanon, Frantz, 18-19, 24-25, 285, 287, 318
Faqe Rasouli Zinwe, 434
Faraj, Bahiya, 103
Farazmand, Shaho, 412, 417, 422
Farhadi, Aziz, 95, 145
Farhadi, Hashem, 102
Farman (*Order*) (newspaper), 116, 122
Farokhian, Seddiq, 392
Farouqi Faizollah Baigi, Ahmad Khan, 142, 368, 435
Farzad, Iraj, 445
Fatah, R., 35, 318

Fatahi, Mansour, 395, 397, 403
Fatahi, Osman, 400
Fatemi, (Lieutenant), 143
Fathi, Rounak, 423
Fattahi Qazi, Shah Sultan Khanoum, 127
Federative Republic, 176
Fergay Siasi-Nizami (Political-Military Academy), 4
Fergay Siasi-Nizami Hizbi Demokrati Kurdistani Eran (Political-Military Academy of the Democratic Party of Iranian Kurdistan), 239
Ferqeh-ye Demokrat-e Azerbaijan. See Azerbaijan Democratic Party
Fevre, R., 8, 343
Fichte, Johann Gottlieb, 15
Firouz, Mozaffar (Colonel), 134-135
Firouzi, Seddiq, 397
Firouzi, Shapour, 384, 389, 391, 394, 399, 401
Firouz-Pishevari agreement (15-article Agreement), 135
First clash in Oramar, 241

Fiuzi (Colonel), 139
Free Syrian Army forces, 44
French Revolution of 1789, 11
French Socialist Party, 238
Forouhar, Dariush, 202, 354
Frouhar (Zeringaran, Zargari), Hussein, 89, 91, 96, 98, 101-102, 109, 151, 347, 362-363
Frouhar, Rana, 127
Ftoohi, Kwestan, 280, 282, 303-304, 318, 415, 420

G

Gadani, Ahmad, 106
Gadani, Ayshe Rash, 151
Gadani, Hawsat, 200
Gadani, Kwestan, 415
Gadani, Jalil, xviii, xix, 49, 88-89, 94, 105, 112, 113, 124, 129- 131, 145, 147-161, 163-164, 167, 170-177, 185-186, 191- 196, 198-201, 203-208, 210-218, 220, 222, 224, 226, 229-231, 233-236, 238-239, 242-251, 253- 258, 262-263, 265, 273, 278, 292, 297, 319, 358, 371-372, 374-378, 380- 382, 384-385, 387, 389- 392, 395-396, 398-402, 404-406, 408, 410, 422, 440-441, 457, 459-460, 463
Galawej, Ali, 146, 158, 197, 222
Galawej magazine, 88
Galawej School, 126, 131
Gall, J. P., 5, 319
Gall, M. D., 5, 319
Garcia, Alma M., 8, 319
Gellner, Ernest, 8, 13-14, 23-24,
    184-185, 287, 319
General Abd al-Karim Qasim. *See* Abd al-Karim Qasim
Ghafari (Colonel), 139
Ghamari-Tabrizi, Behrooz, xvii
Ghani, C., 55-56, 73, 319
Ghanipour, Ghani, 389
Ghassemlou, Abdol Rahman, xix, 24, 28, 80- 81, 88, 96, 147-148, 151-155, 158-159, 162- 163, 170, 172, 174-176, 182, 185, 190-192, 194- 198, 201-204, 206, 208- 209, 211, 214, 216-224, 228-231, 233-234, 236- 238, 244-254, 260, 273, 281-283, 288, 295-298, 303, 313, 319, 334, 337, 353-354, 356, 358, 369, 373, 377-380, 382-383, 387-388, 390-393, 395- 397, 402, 437, 442, 454, 458-459
Ghassemlou, Isma'il, 152- 153, 159
Ghazi, Ghasim, xviii
Ghazi, Hassan, xviii, 69, 313, 320, 342
Ghazi, Mohammad (translator), 335
Gheissari, A., 54, 56, 320
Gholamali, Omar, 414, 417, 423
Giddens, Anthony, 8, 20, 288
Girami, A., 125, 320
Giwargis, Ashor, 65-66, 320
Gohari, Hamid, 89, 91, 94, 96, 98-101, 103, 106- 108, 110, 113, 117, 121, 139, 147, 151-152, 180, 201-204, 211, 215, 222, 230, 235, 238-239, 278, 320, 364, 367
Goroupi Halwest (Position Group), 269, 273

Govari Awat, (magazine Wish), 367

Govari Grougali Mindalani Kurd (magazine Babble of the Kurdish Children), 432

Govari Halala (magazine Buttercup), 117, 432

Govari *Hawari Kurd* (magazine Shout of Kurd), 367

Govari Hawari Nishtman (magazine Shout of Homeland), 126, 432

Govari Kurdistan (magazine Kurdistan), 114, 117, 432

Govari Nishtman (magazine Homeland), xxii, 5, 96-99, 101, 104, 106, 177-179, 325, 366-367

Gracy, English captain, 65

Green, T. H., 8

Greenfield, Leah, 10

Green Movement, 270

Grosby, S., 9, 320

Guattari, Piere Felix, 8

Gudhart, Augusta, 60-70, 320

Guibernau, Montserrat, 8-9, 16, 287, 320

Gula Rehan, 151

Gulbjerek la diwani Haji Qadri Koyi blbli nishtmani Kurd (*A selected poems of Haji Qadir Koyi the Kurdistan homeland's nightingale*),367

Gulf War, 42, 359

Gunter, M. M., 26-27, 29-30, 36-38, 123, 314-316, 320-321, 330, 361

H

Habash, George, 199

Habiba, 151

Hadad, Karim, 192, 197, 380-381

Hadad, Nasrin, 420, 425

Hafidi, Morad, 402

Hafidi, Sirwan, 402, 405

Haidari, Khadijeh, 120, 127

Haidari, Parwana, 418, 424

Haidari, Salar, 157, 166, 352, 376, 436

Haidari (Farouqi), Seddiq, 115, 150, 362, 372, 427-429

Haji, Mullah Ismail, 380-381

Haji Ahmadi, Abdul Rahman, 384, 453

Haij Darwish, Hamid, 44

Haji Golawi, 402

Haji Ilkhani, 70

Haji Qadir Koyi, 48, 62, 180, 367

Haji Qasim Khayat, 149

Haj Rashidi, Nazakat, 127

Hakim Idris of Betlis, 29

Hakimzadeh, Abdullah, 105

Halabi, Jamileh, ii, xviii, xix

Halabi, Omar, xviii

Hallaj, Salahaddin, xviii

Hallaj, Setareh, xviii

Hamidi, Sayyed Muhammad, 367, 432

Hamidi, Jafar, 389, 391, 393, 395, 397

Hamza Abdullah, 39, 146, 366

Hamza Agha Mangur, 48

Hamza Agha Nalosi, 113

Hamza Bayazidi, 157

Hamzayy, Ghafour, 339, 391, 394-395, 397, 403,

Hamzeh-yy, Haji Kaka Muhammad Karim, 99

Haq Talab, Taha, 384

Hashemi Rafsanjani, Ali Akbar (President), 255, 249

Hashemov, 108, 110

Hashimi, Sayyed Hassan, 249, 384, 389
Hashimi, Sayyed Ibrahim, 404, 407, 409, 411, 413, 417
Hasil, Mirad, 165
Hassani, Amir, 196, 238, 279, 292, 297, 321
Hassaniani, Ali, 285
Hassanov, the Soviet Union Consul in Tabriz, 89, 106-107
Hassanpour, Amir, xviii, 26-29, 80, 97, 119, 177, 178, 180, 185, 321, 467, 469
Hassanpour, Khalid, 401, 405, 421, 426
Hassanpour, Mohammad, 410, 412, 414, 416
Hassanpour, Mohammad Rasoul, 380
Hassan Tilo Shikak, 368
Hasanwayhids, 29
Hassanzadeh, Abdullah, xix, 152-155, 157, 159, 161, 163-166, 169, 172-176, 191-192, 194-198, 201-202, 204-209, 212-216, 218-221, 223, 226, 229, 232-247, 249, 251-268, 272-273, 276, 292, 295, 298-299, 321-322, 324, 373-374-375, 377-380, 382-385, 388, 390-394, 396, 398, 402-404, 406-411, 422
Hassanzadeh, Aso, 415, 420, 425
Hatami, Hassan, xvii-xviii, xix, 228, 268, 271, 322, 421-422, 426
Hatefi, Rahman, 52-53, 322
Hawar (*Shout*), Hajar's poem, 178
Hawar (Shout) Play, 250
Hawar, Mohammad Rasoul, 48, 61-63, 65-67, 70-71, 73-75, 80, 322
Hawrami, A., 48, 63-64, 69, 78-79-80, 91, 101, 107-111, 113, 116, 121, 133-134, 136-137, 179-180, 184, 322
Hayat-i Raeisa" (Governing Council). *See Anjoman-e Melli-ye Kurdistan* or *Hayat-i Raeisay Milli Kurdistan* (National Governing Assembly of Kurdistan)
Hayat-i Raeisay Milli (National Governing Assembly) *See Anjoman-e Melli-ye Kurdistan* or *Hayat-i Raeisay Milli Kurdistan* (National Governing Assembly of Kurdistan)
Hayati Sikertariyay Hizibi Demokrati Kurdistan (Secretariat Board of the Kurdistan Democratic Party), 161
Haydarlou, Reza, xviii
Hechter, Michael, 19, 24, 287
Heidar Khan Amuoghly, 57-58
Hejab, Abdullah, 124, 279-280, 296, 323, 419
Hekmat, Mansoor (Zhoobin Razani), 447
Hela Gishtiyakani Rebazi Ema ("General Principles of Our Way"; aka "General Principles"), 265, 273, 328, 443
Hemin. *See* Mamosta Hemin (Sayyed Mohammad Amin Shaikholislami Mukri)
Hemmat (the first Iranian social democratic group), 52, 346

Herder, Gottfried, 8, 16
Hesam, Galawej, xviii
Hexalateral Commission (1987), 242-243
Hezb-e Demokrat-e Iran (Democratic Party of Iran), 58
Hezb-e Demokratik-e Mardom-e Iran (People's Democratic Party of Iran), 254
Hezb-e Komaleh-ye Kurdistan-e Iran (Komala Party of Iranian Kurdistan). *See Komalay Shorishgeri Zehmetkeshani Kurdistani Eran* (Komala) (Revolutionary Organization of the Toilers of Iranian Kurdistan. [Komala]). Also, in English called Komala Party of Iranian Kurdistan
Hezb-e Tudeh-ye Iran (Tudeh Party of Iran). *See* Tudeh Party of Iran
Hezi Parezgari (Protective Force), 263

Hezi Peshmergay Kurdistan (Kurdistan Peshmerga Forces), 142
Hezi Pishtiwan (Support Force), 49, 234
Hidayati, Abubakir, 383
Higher Council, 117
Higher Council of Iranian Nations, 455-456
Hijazi, Sayyed Ali, 143
Hijri, Mostafa, xvii, 6, 217, 246, 252, 254-263, 265-267, 269-273-276, 284, 298, 323, 383-385, 388-390, 392, 395-397, 402-403, 413, 418, 422-423
Hisami, Aziz, 146
Hisami, Karim, 80, 88, 90, 114-115, 146-155, 157-159, 165-166, 168-170, 172-177, 191-192, 194-199, 206, 208-209, 211-217, 220-224, 229, 235, 239, 323-324, 341, 377-381, 437-438, 441, 452
Hisami, Mina (Muhammad Amin), Hisami, 450
Hisami, Sa'adat, 151
Hiwa Party (Hope Party), of the Kurdistan of Iraq,

97-98, 103-104, 107, 119
Hizbi Azadikhowazi Kurd (Freedom-seekers of the Kurd Party), *See Hizbi Azadi Kurdistan* (Kurdistan Freedom Party)
Hizbi Azadikhowai Kurdistan (Freedom-seekers of Kurdistan Party). *See Hizbi Azadi Kurdistan* (Kurdistan Freedom Party)
Hizbi Azadi Kurdistan (Kurdistan Freedom Party), 6 87-91, 96
Hizbi Demokrati Jinani Kurdistan (Democratic Party of the Women of Kurdistan), 119, 127, 349
Hizbi Demokrati Kurdistan (Kurdistan Democratic Party [KDP]). *See* Kurdistan Democratic Party (KDP)
Hizbi Demokrati Kurdistani Eran (Democratic Party of

of Iranian Kurdistan [PDKI]). *See* Democratic Party of Iranian Kurdistan (PDKI)

Hizbi Demokrati Kurdistani Eran (Perawani Kongray Chowar) (Democratic Party of Iranian Kurdistan (Followers of the Fourth Congress). *See* Democratic Party of Iranian Kurdistan (Followers of the Fourth Congress) (PDKI-FFC)

Hizbi Demokrati Kurdistani Eran, Rebarayati Shorishger (Democratic Party of Iranian Kurdistan-Revolutionary Leadership) or PDKI-RL. *See* Democratic Party of Iranian Kurdistan-Revolutionary Leadership (PDKI-RL)

Hizbi Yayan (Ladies' Party), 127

Hobsbawm, Eric, 8, 13, 19, 288, 324

Homayoun, Said, 88, 91-94, 98, 101, 105, 114, 119-121, 127-128, 131, 133-135, 137, 139, 141, 144, 324, 370, 427, 429, 435

Homayouni (Major-General), 135, 138-140, 143, 349

Hook, Siney, 22

Hosseini, Nahid, 6, 417, 422

Houshmand, Ehsan, 263

Hroch, Miroslaw, 8

Human Rights Watch, 33, 41-42, 324, 332

Hungarian Socialist Workers' Party, 441

Hussein Aghay Siser. 436

Hussein Ali Khan Kolyayy, 81-82

Hussein, Himdadi., 95, 103, 105, 114-115, 117, 124-130, 132, 137, 178-179, 324, 367, 432-433

Hussein Khan, 56

Hussein Khan Reza, 81-82

Husseini, Baba Sheikh, xvii

Husseini, Mullah [Mamosta] Sayyed Rashid (Saqqizi), 165, 174, 191, 354, 374, 377, 451

Husseini, Rashad, 400

Husseini Sayyed Abdullah, 406, 416

Husseini, Sayyed Ahmad, 245, 397, 404, 407, 409

Husseini, Sayyed Ali, 430

Husseini, Sayyed Ezat, 418

Husseini, Shaho, 398, 403, 409, 413, 418, 423

Husseini, Sheikh Izz al-Din, 201-202, 205-206, 214, 354, 356-357, 451-452, 454

Husseinzadeh, Eran Khanim, 151

Husseinzadeh, Hashim 154

Hutchinson, John, 8-9, 15, 25, 316, 324-325, 334, 338, 340, 342

I

Ibrahim Ahmad, 98, 103, 105, 160, 174

Ibrahimi, Abdullah, 389, 397, 403

Ibrahimi, Hussein, 384

Ibrahimi (Zewayy), Ibrahim, 415, 420, 425

Ibrahimzadeh, Said, 114

Ihsannollah, 147

Ihsan Nuri, 36

Ilahi, Ahmad, 124, 371-372, 427-428
Ilkhanizadeh, Abdullah Agha, 182
Ilkhanizadeh, Abdul Rahman (Haji Rahman Aga), 99, 371-372, 427-429
Ilkhanizadeh, Ismail, 371-372, 427-428
Ilkhanizadeh, Kak Abubakr, 99
Ilkhanizadeh, Muhammad, (Koya) 156-157, 351
Ilkhanizadeh (Dehbukri), Qassem (Agha), 89, 96, 99, 113, 429-430
Ilmi, Ahmad, 363
Il Partito newspaper, 441
Imami (Hashimi), Sayyed Kamil, 374
Imami (Hashimi), Sayyed Tahir (son of Sayyed Kamil Hashimi), 375
Indirqash (Agrigash) village, 230
internal colonialism, 17, 19, 24, 84, 287
International Confederation of Iranian Students, 441
International Institute of Social History (Amsterdam), 5
Intezamat-e Ashayeri (Tribal Regiment), 102
IPFG, Iranian People's Fedai Guerrillas 242
Irandoust, Faysal, 400-401, 404
Iran-e Ma (Our Iran), 22
Iranian People's Fedai Guerrillas (Liberation Army of the Iranian Peoples [LAIP], 233, 242
Iran Jawan (Young Iran), 433
Iraqi Communist Party (ICP), 41, 103, 123, 154, 165, 167, 172, 211, 228, 258, 441
Iraqi Intelligence Service (*Mukhabrat*), 198, 220
Iraqi Kurdistan Front (IKF), 41
iron law of oligarchy, 6, 21-22-23, 198-190, 286, 295, 307
Ironside, William Edmond (General), 55
Ishaqi Abdullah [later Ahmad Tawfiq], 146, 148, 151-165, 169, 174-176, 190-193, 195, 297, 352, 374, 376, 436,
Ishaqi, Hassan, 165
Ishaqi, Mustafa (Qoula), 156, 375
Ishaqi, Sayyed Muhammad, 137, 439
Ishqi, M. M., 125
ISIS. *See* Islamic State of Iraq and Syria (ISIS)
Iskandari, Iraj, 169, 172, 176, 194, 197
Isma'il Agha Shikak (Simko), 2, 48, 51, 56, 59-81, 84-86, 93, 139, 287, 316, 322, 342
Ismail Faraji, Halab, 127
Islami, Hassan, 250
Islamic State of Iraq and Syria (ISIS) (*Da'esh*), 44
Isma'ili, Hawre, 418
Isma'ilzadeh, Jahangir, 225-226, 230, 386-387
Isma'ilzadeh, Kamal, 227
Italian Communist Council, 441
Italian Communist Party, 441
Itihadi Mubarzani Komonist (Unity of Communist Militants), 447

İttihat ve Terakki Cemiyeti (Committee of Union and Progress [CUP]), 30, 51
Ivanov, M. S., 52, 54-58, 325
Izadi, M. R., 26-27, 315, 325

J

Jafar Agha, 61, 77-78
Jafar Quli Khan Sardar As'ad, 56
Jafar San Lahun (Jafar Sultan Jaf or Jafer Sultan), 81
Jahanbani, Amanullah, 73
Jahangiri, Ebrahim, xviii, 227, 325
Jahangiri, Rashid Baig, 90, 372
Jahani Asl, Karim, xvii
Jahani Asl, Mohammad Nasser, i, 310, 325
Jahani Asl, Rojeh, ii, xvii-xviii, xix
Jahani Asl, Sherko, xviii
Jahani Asl, Shirin, xviii
Jalaeipour, H., 94-95, 325
Jalali, Amar Agha, 123
Jaldian Garrison, 209
Jalil, Jalil, 62-63, 325

"Jama'ati Sharafkandi" (the Sharafkandi's Band), 253
Jamiani, Kamram, 250
Jamil Pasha, 123
Jangali movement, 52, 57-58
Jangal Party (Ejtema'iyoun), 136
"*Jashakani 66*" (the 1966 traitors, meaning the KDP [Iraq] Politburo lead by Ibrahim Ahmad and Jalal Talabani), 173
jash Mujaheds, 249
Jawaher Khan (Simko's wife), 73
Jawanmard, Fowziyeh, 200
Jawanmard, Kawa, 423
Jawanmardi, Ali, 435
Jawanmardi, Rasoul, 435
Jawanmard Qazi, Rahim, 374-375
Jawhari, 147
Jawid, Salamullah (Dr.), Minister of Interior of Azerbaijan, 135, 137
Jawidfar, Ahmad (Hajar), 203, 387, 390

jawla (moving around a territory for military practice), 278
Jayawardena, Kumari, 8, 325
Jian, Aziz, 156
Jinan (Women) magazine, 464
J.K.. *See Komalay Jianaway Kurdistan (J.K.)* (Society for the Revival of Kurdistan [J.K.])
Jomhourikhahan-e Melli-ye Iran (National Republicans of Iran), 254
Junbalat, Kamal, 199
Jwaideh, Wadie 3, 30, 60, 116, 183, 325

K

KADEK. *See* Congress for Democracy and Freedom in Kurdistan
Kajehyy, Rahman, 384, 389
KAJIK (Party), 157
Kakagha or Kah Agha, 118, 129
Kalashi, Sulayman, 406, 408, 410

Kamali (Lieutenant), 143
Kamangar, Seddiq 445
Kambakhsh, Abdul Samad, 172
Kandiyoti, Deniz, 8, 325
Kaplan, Gisela, 8, 325
Karqashan, Sulayuman, 172
Karimi, Ali, xviii, 96-99, 103-104, 107, 119, 130, 140, 146, 177-180, 193, 325, 362, 366, 433, 452
Karimi, Amir, xvii, 326, 453
Karimi, Anwar, xviii
Karimi, Hashim, 198, 200-201, 379, 381-383, 388, 390-393, 396, 399, 401-402, 404-405
Karimi, Kamal, 223, 262, 282, 297, 326, 394, 398-399, 401, 405, 408, 410, 413, 415, 419-420, 425
Karimi, Manaf, 105, 113-114, 119, 131-132, 371, 372, 427-429
Karimi, Muhammad Hussein, 352, 445
Karimi, Muhammad Rasoul, 421, 426
Karimi, Rahman, 225-226, 230, 383, 386-387
Karimi, Raof, 339

Karimi, Sayyed Ibrahim, 399, 402, 405, 409, 412, 415
Karroubi, Ali, 223
Karroubi, Jafar, 223, 278
Karroubi, Mehdi, 270
Kars (the British Consul in Tabriz), 140
Kashghari, Ali, 28
Kashifpour, Ali, 388, 390, 393, 398-399
Kasili, Tahir, 412, 414, 417, 422
Kasnazani, Ali, 411
Kasravi, Ahmad, 61, 66, 74-75, 326
Kasrayy, Muhammad, 412, 414, 416
Kaveh (Kowestani), Said, xxiii, 154, 156, 165-166, 170, 208, 217, 248-249, 298, 326, 352, 376, 438
Kavianpur, N., 67, 69, 73, 326
Kawa, 36
Kawian, Ata, xvii, xviii
Kawian, Fatah, xviii, xix, 220, 385, 388-390, 392, 396, 398-402, 404-405, 408, 411
Kawkabi, Mullah Najmadin, 375

KDPI. *See* PDKI
KDP (Iraq), xxi, 44, 97, 142-143, 146-151, 155-156, 160, 163-164, 166, 169, 171-175, 187, 197-198, 202-203, 223, 225-226, 256, 259, 366, 445
KDP (I)'s Program and Constitution, 194, 196, 326, 443-444
KDP-Provisional Leadership, 41
Keddie, N. 54-56, 326
Kedourie, Elie, 8, 15-16, 25, 288, 326
Keegan, J., 5, 329
Keikhosrawi, Farouq, 222, 383, 386
Kellas, J. G., 8, 14, 19, 326
Kendal, Nezan, 36, 43, 326
KEP, *See Komalay Yaksaniy Kurdistan* (Kurdistan Equality Party) (KEP)
Kennion, R.L. (Lieutenant-Colonel), 60
Khadija, Karim Hadad's wife, 197
Khajeh-Nouri, I, 73, 326
Khaki Baigi, Foad, 419, 424

Khalid Baig Jibranli, 69, 79
Khalidi, Qadir (Mullah), 224, 226, 386
Khalighi, Hussein, xviii, xix, 187, 204, 223, 237-238, 241, 246-247, 253, 263, 277-282, 293, 297-299, 326-327, 390, 393, 395-396, 403
Khalkhali,Sadeq, 212
Khalu Qurban (Khalo Ghorban), 72-73
Khamenei, Ali (Ayatollah), 255

Kharazi, Rahim, 125
Khatami, Muhammad Amin, 430
Khatami, Seddiq, 146, 151
Khayat, Diyako, xviii
Khayati, Karim, 227
Khayati Sardashti, Abdullah (Nawroz), 436
Khizri, Babakir, 250
Khizri, Mohammad, xviii, 154, 157, 161-166, 168-169, 172-173, 187, 217, 249, 278, 281, 298, 327, 374-375
Khizirpour (Rabati), Saleh, 406

Khodayari, As'ad, 152, 154, 155, 157
khodgardani (self-governing), 213
khodmokhtari (self-determination), 213
Khomeini. *See* Ayatollah Khomeini
Khoshhali, Behzad, 93, 101, 102, 128, 135, 138, 140, 141, 327, 435
Khoshkalam, Nasser, 224, 227, 386
Khosh Nama, Qadir, 250
Khorshid (Simko's brother), 67
Khosrawi Ali, 118
Khosrawi, Khalil, 371-372, 427-429
Khosrawi, Motaleb (Dr.), 385
Khoybun (Independence), 36, 119, 346
Kiani, Abdul Rahman, 362
Kianouri, Noureddin, 194, 197, 220
Kinnane, Derk, 30, 48, 67, 69, 81, 92, 110, 129, 327
Kitabi, Ali, 389
Kitebkhanay Farhang (Culture Library), 131
Kohn, Hans, 15, 340

Komala Kurdistan's Organization of the Communist Party of Iran (Komala [CPI]), xx, 242, 282, 445-446, 450
Komalay Azadikhowazani Kurd (Association of Freedom-seekers of Kurd). *See Hizbi Azadi Kurdistan* (Kurdistan Freedom Party)
Komalay Azadikhowazi Kurdistan (Association of Freedom-seekers of Kurdistan). *See Hizbi Azadi Kurdistan* (Kurdistan Freedom Party)
Komalay Hiwa (Hope Party). *See* Hiwa Party (Hope Party), of the Kurdistan of Iraq
Komalay Jianaway Kurdistan (J.K.) (Society for the Revival of Kurdistan [J.K.]), xx, 1-3, 5-6, 48, 87, 89, 91, 94-112, 114-115, 119, 125-126, 157, 177-181, 188-189, 302, 312, 325, 339, 347, 362-364, 366-367, 429

Komalay Lawani Lade (Association of Village Youth), 147

Komalay Pewandiyakani Farhangi Soviet (Soviet Cultural Relations Society), 108, 110, 126, 348

Komalay Rizgari (*Kurdistan*) (Kurdistan Liberation Committee), 157

Komalay Shorishgeri Zehmetkeshani Kurdistani Eran (Komala) (Revolutionary Organization of the Toilers of Iranian Kurdistan. [Komala]). Also, in English called Komala Party of Iranian Kurdistan, xx, 2, 6, 199-200, 202, 205, 206, 214-215, 227, 233, 236, 239-245, 248, 268, 270, 277-283, 287, 290, 293, 299, 301-302, 308, 314, 323, 334, 338-339, 341, 352, 354, 356, 445-451, 466

Komalay Shorishgeri Zahmatkeshani Kurdistani Eran-Rawti Chaksazi w Gasha (Revolutionary Organization of the Toilers of Iranian Kurdistan-Path of Reform and Flourish), 338, 449

Komalay Shorshgeri Zahmatkeshani Kurdistani Eran-Rawti Yekgrtnawa (Revolutionary Organization of Toilers of Iranian Kurdistan-Reunification Faction), 450

Komalay Yaksaniy Kurdistan (Kurdistan Equality Party) (KEP), xx. 233, 354, 445, 451

Komalay Zahmatkeshani Kurdistan (Organization of the Toilers of Kurdistan) (Komala), xx, 337, 445, 449

Komali Istighlali Kurdistan (the Kurdish Independence Association), 69

Komeleh [Komala], 240-241

Komitay Barewabaryy Hizbi Dimokrati Kurdistan-Iran (Directing Committee of the Kurdistan Democratic Party-Iran), 156

Komitay Barewabari Katii Hizbi Demokrati Kurdistan-Eran (Temporary Directing Committee of the Kurdistan Democratic Party-Iran), 156, 351

Komitay Bazrasi (Inspection Committee), 217, 219, 384

Komitay Boujanaway Hizbi Demokrati Kurdistan (Committee for the Revival of the Kurdistan Democratic Party) or *Komitay Komonisti Kurdistan* (Communist Committee of Kurdistan [K.K.K.]), 146-147

Komitay Chawaderi Barz (Higher Inspection Committee), 161, 375

Komitay Hawkari Azerbaijan wa Kurdistan (Committee of

Azerbaijan and Kurdistan Cooperation, or KAK), 147-148, 151

Komitay Inqilabii Hizbi Demokrati Kurdistan-Eran (Revolutionary Committee of the Kurdistan Democratic Party-Iran or Revolutionary Committee), 111-112, 166-173, 186-187, 352, 375, 437, 440-441

Komitay Inqlabii Hizbi Demokrati Kurdistan (Revolutionary Committee of the Kurdistan Democratic Party or Revolutionary Committee). *See Komitay Inqilabii Hizbi Demokrati Kurdistan-Eran* (Revolutionary Committee of the Kurdistan Democratic Party-Iran or Revolutionary Committee)

Komitay Nawandi Kurdistan (Kurdistan's Region Committee), 79

Komitay Rabar (K-R) or Leadership Committee, 198, 353, 380

Komitay Sakh Karaway Hizbi Demokrati Kurdistan Kurdistan-Eran (Reconstructing Committee of the Kurdistan Democratic Party-Iran or Reconstruction Committee), 111, 158-164, 351, 373, 436

Komitay Sarkirdayati Katii Hzibi Dimokrati Kurdistan (Provisional Leadership Committee of the Kurdistan Democratic Party), also called Provisional CC or Provisional Leadership 175-176, 352, 377

Komitay Shorishger (Revolutionary Committee). *See Komitay Inqilabii Hizbi Demokrati Kurdistan-Eran* (Revolutionary Committee of the Kurdistan Democratic Party-Iran or Revolutionary Committee)

Komitay Siasy-Nizami (Sia-Mi) (Political-Military Committee or the Sia-Mi Committee), 198, 353, 380

Komitay Shoumal (North Committee), 225

Komitay Zagros (Zagros Committee), 201, 354, 382

Komiteh-ye Dehqanan-e Sarasari-ye Kurdistan (The Peasant Committee of throughout Kurdistan), 149

Komoni Sulaymaniyah (Sulaymaniyah's Commune), 153

Komsomol (Communist Union of Youth), 95

Konaposhi, Abdullah, 449-450

Kongra-Gel (KGK) (People's Congress of Kurdistan), 37, 453

Koohi-Kamali, Farideh, 3, 76-79, 328

Koohi-Kamali Dehkordi, 3. Also *see* Koohi-Kamali, Farideh

518

Kouhestan (Mountain), 136
Kowekha Karim Barkamran, 439
Kreulich, Helena (Ghassemlou's wife), 252
KRG. See Kurdistan Regional Government (KRG)
Kristeva, Julia, 8
Kuchgiri rebellion (1920), 35
Kulij village, 230
Kurd Ahmadi, Behrouz, 389-390
Kurdish Democratic Party of Syria, 44
Kurdish Institute (Stockholm), 5
Kurdish National Council (KNC), 44
Kurdish People's Democracy Party (HDP), 38
Kurdish Popular Protection, (YPG), 44
Kurdish Radio Program in Moscow, 108
Kurdish Radio station in Palestine, 101
Kurdish Socialist Party (Iraq) (PASOK), 41
Kurdish-Soviet Cultural Society (Kurdistan-Soviet Cultural Relations Society), 126
Kurdish Supreme Committee (KSC), 44
Kurdish Vanguard Workers Party (PPKK, also known as *Pesheng* or Vanguard), 36
Kurdistan (newspaper in Azerbaijan of the Soviet) 146
Kurdistan (newspaper in Prague 21 January 1965 to Spring 1970), 158
Kurdistan (newspaper in Tabriz in 1954), 151
Kurdistan (newspaper, of KDP since 2006), 464
Kurdistan (newspaper of KDP during the Kurdistan Republic), 104-105, 114, 116-118, 122, 125-128, 130-131, 135, 177-179, 192, 348-349, 367, 432
Kurdistan (newspaper, of PDKI), 239, 248, 464
Kurdistan (newspaper, of PDKI-RL), 250
Kurdistan (newspaper, the KDP-I resumed the publication in Iraq in Winter 1971), 176, 197
Kurdistan (newspaper, the PDKI (FFC) published in Iran between the Spring of 1980 and the Winter of 1983), 224, 226
Kurdistan Democratic Party-Iran (KDP-I), xx, 152-161, 163-164-169, 171-177, 186-187, 191, 194, 233, 265, 351-353, 355-356, 373-374, 376-377, 441, 470-471
Kurdistan Democratic Party (Iran) (KDP (I)), xx, 191-201, 203-214, 326, 359, 361, 378-382, 443-445, 470-471
Kurdistan Democratic Party (KDP), xix-xx, 1-2, 4-6, 40, 87-88, 92, 96, 104-105, 110-121, 124-126, 128, 130, 132-134, 136, 138, 142-143, 145-152, 159-162, 164, 165-167, 171-172, 174, 177-179, 184-186, 188-189, 191, 194, 200, 204, 223, 233, 261, 265-274, 276,

278-284, 289-290, 294-295, 298, 303-304, 306, 308-309-310, 347-348, 350, 361, 367, 370-371, 373, 414, 419, 424, 429-430, 432, 437-438, 440, 464-465, 470-471
Kurdistan Democratic Party of Syria, 97
Kurdistan Democratic Party of Turkey, 36
Kurdistan Media (website of PDKI), 464
Kurdistan Popular Democratic Party (KPDP), 41
Kurdistan Regional Government (KRG), 4, 45, 47, 255, 266-267, 275, 284, 287-288, 359
Kurdistan Republic, 6, 49-50, 77, 88, 94-95, 97, 104, 111, 116, 119-126, 128-134, 136, 138-139, 141-145, 162-163, 181-185, 188-189, 195, 288, 291, 295, 300, 320, 349-350, 366-367, 427, 429, 432-433, 435, 453
Kurdistan Republic Government. See Dawlati Jimhouryy

Kurdistan (Kurdistan Republic Government)
Kurdistan Socialist Party (KSP), 41
Kürdistan Teali Cemiyeti (Society for the Advancement of Kurdistan [SAK]), 30-31
Kurdistan u Kurd or Kurdistanukurd (website of KDP), 465
Kurd Kanal (Kurd Channel), satellite TV channel of KDP, 465
Kurdology Institute (Bonn), 5
Kürd Teavün ve Terakki Cemiyeti (Society for Mutual Aid and Progress of Kurdistan [SMPK]), 30-31
Kurta Basek La Sar Sosialism (*A Brief Discussion on Socialism*) (*Brief Discussion*), 236-238, 245
Kutschera, Chris, 33, 61, 68-69, 73, 78, 80, 91, 94, 105, 124, 129, 167, 185, 198, 214, 329, 353, 381
Kwiatkowski, Lynn M., 8, 329

Kymlicka, W., 8, 329

L

Labadi, Ahmad, xviii
Lachini, Mullah Qadir, 374
Ladar (Deviant) (i.e., PDKI-RL), 248-249, 460
Lahimi, Aziz, 389
Lahuti, Abolghasem (Major), 72-73
LAIP. See Iranian People's Fedai Guerrillas (Liberation Army of the Iranian Peoples [LAIP])
Lajani, Salih, 172-173
Lashai, Kourosh (Dr.), 167
Lausanne Treaty (24 July 1923), 25, 31, 35, 51
Lawan (Youth) magazine, 464-465
Lazarev, Mikhail Semenovich, 49, 63, 74, 81, 329
Lebanese Communist Labor Organization, 199
Lebanese Communist Party, 194, 199
LeClerk, Patrice, 8, 329
Legard, R., 5, 329

Lejnay Nowenarayati Gali Kurd, or the Delegation of the Kurdish People, 214, 355

Lemkin, Raphael, 31-32, 329

Le Monde newspaper, 441

Lenin, Vladimir. Ilych., 8, 12-13, 19, 24, 178, 194, 287, 329

Leonard, p., 8, 329, 337

Lesser, I. O., 38, 330

Lewis, J., 5, 329-330, 338, 342

Libraries, 4, 131

Listay Fix (Fixed List), 217, 237, 245-248, 263, 395-396

Llobera, 10

Lotf Pouri, Rambod, 238, 269, 280, 283, 291, 293, 330, 415, 423

Lowe, R., 43-44, 330

Löwy, Michael., 8, 13, 330

Lu, Zoe, xvii

L'Unità the newspaper, 441

Luxemburg, Rosa, 8

M

Madani, Hossein, xix, 26, 30, 48, 60, 72, 80, 83, 100, 136-137, 154, 157-159, 171, 183, 223, 238, 254, 279, 281, 283, 291, 330, 351, 373, 383, 388, 390, 392, 396, 398-401, 405, 408, 410, 422

Magazine *26 Sarmawaz* (17 December), 250

Mahabad [*Abiari*, now *Azadi*] Stadium, 104

Mahabad Garrison, 139, 203, 209

Mahabad Republic, 6, 183-184, 312, 333, 349

Mahabad's City Committee, 219

Mahdawi (Saqqizi), Karim, 408-409, 411, 415, 420, 425

Mahmoudi, Ali, 362

Mahmoudi, Tahir, xviii, 267-268, 330, 417, 419, 422, 424

Mahmoudian, Ghafour, 89, 124

Mahmud Khan (Agha) Kanisanani, 72, 81, 93

Mahmud Khan, Dezli, 72, 81-82

Mahmoudzadeh, Qadir, 95, 145

Maidani Chowar Chira (Four Light Square) in Mahabad, 141, 222, 350

Majdi, Mullah Hussein, 137, 140, 427-430

Majdi, Muhammad. 178

Majidian, Muhammad Amin, 391, 393

Major Abdullaov, the Russian officer in charge of Mahabad's security, 102, 108

Makki, H., 54-55, 72-74, 82, 330-331

Malekzadeh, M., 62, 331

Mamadi, Sanar, 143, 164-166, 193, 212, 224-226, 230, 331, 352, 375-376, 383, 387, 392, 454

Mamadi Shikak, Qoytas, 368

Mamasha War, 133-135

Mam Askandar, 173

Mamkan village, 215

Mamle, Aziz [jurist, Lawyer], 213-214, 239, 384, 387

Mamle, Muhammad. 439

Mamosta Abdullah Hassanzadeh. *See* Hassanzadeh, Abdullah

Mamosta Hajar. *See* Sharafkandi, Abdul Rahman (Mamosta Hajar),
Mamosta Hemin. *See* Shaikholislami Mukri, Sayyed Mohammad Amin (Mamosta Hemin)
Mandomi, Omid, 418
Mangaliso, Zengie A., 8, 331
Mangur Aghas, 60
Manguri, Jafar, 406
Manguri, Muhammad Amin, 112, 138-139-141, 143-144, 331
Manguri, Rahim, 414, 418
Mangur tribe, 82, 208-209
Manifesto of 11 March 1970, 40
Manifisti Azadiy Kurdistan: *Programi "Parti Azadiy Kurdistan"* (Kurdistan Freedom Manifesto), 329, 453
Mann, Michael, 8, 20, 288
Marasana, Mirza Khidir, 157, 161, 436
Marashi, Afshin, 14, 331
Mar Benyamin Shimun (Mar Shimun), 64-66, 70, 74

Ma'roufi, Mustafa, 415
Mardom, organ of the Tudeh Party of Iran, 224, 340
Marwanids, 29
Marx, Karl, 8, 331
Matin, Abdullah Khan, 435
Mawlawi, Abdullah, 375
Mawlawi, Ali (Dr.), 95, 373-374
Mawlawi, Amineh, Muhammad Mawlawi's daughter, 150
Mawlawi, Muhammad, 150
Mawloudi, Mustafa, 264, 267-268, 271, 397, 403, 407, 409-410, 413-416, 419-420, 424-425
Mawloudian, Muhammad, 142
Mawloudi Sabian, Abdul Aziz, xviii, 4, 118, 152, 180, 195, 234, 331
Mazouji, Hamed, 362, 435
Mazur, Khadija, 303, 331, 410, 412, 414-415, 420, 425,
McClintock, Anne, 8
McCrone, D., 8-9, 11, 13, 20-21, 331

McDowall, David, 28, 36, 39-40, 42-43, 59-60, 66, 68, 74, 207, 331-332, 467
McKenzie, Robert, 22
McKiernan, K., 41, 332
MED-TV, the MEDYA-TV, 360
Mehfar, Loqman, 404, 407, 409-410, 413, 417, 422
Meho, L. I., 43, 332, 469
Mehraban, Morad, 400
Mehrparwar, Baba Ali, 262, 388, 391, 393, 395-397, 403, 407-411, 413-414, 458
Meiselas, Susan, 69-70, 332
Mergasori, Isa, xviii
Mianali, Alireza, xviii, 111,125, 133, 332
Michels, Robert, 6, 21-22, 295, 332
Middle East Watch, 34, 332
Mikaeili, Hussein, 89
Milani, Abbas, 54, 332
Mill, John Stuart, 8, 332
Mina Khanim Qazi. *See* Qazi, Mina Khanim
Minahan, j., 26, 332
Mingol, village, 215

Minorsky, Vladimir, 27, 61, 68, 332, 333
Miradi, Nasir, 419
Mirawayy, Jalal (Mullah Osman), 381
Mir Haj (Colonel), 98, 105, 109, 363
Mir Mukri, Majid Khan, 368
Miro, Daham, 44
Mirwati, Mansour, 421, 426
Mirwati, Muhammad, 400, 402
Mirza Ali, 381
Mirza Awla (Abdullah), Muhammad, 165
Mirza Kuchek Khan, 52, 57-58, 67, 71, 73, 318
Mirza Saleh, Gholamhussein, 73, 333
MIT, 203, 454
Mitran, Faraydoun, 238-239, 384
Mitran, Mozafar, 399, 401
Mitterrand, François, (French President), 231
Mizgawti Sour (Red Mosque) in Mahabad, 138
Moazen, Jawad (Major), Ayatollah Taleqani's representative 208

Mobley, Richard A., 118, 120, 132-133, 136, 333
Modarresi, Mullah Abdullah, 137
Modarresi, (Mullah) Qadir, 96-99, 362-363, 367, 432
Mofti, Jafar, xviii
Mofizadeh, Ahmad, 205
Moghadam, Valentine, 8, 333
Mohammad Agha Shikak, 61, 78
Mohammad Ali Shah, 61
Mohammad Hussein Khan Zargham, 61
Mohammad Khan Baneh, 81
Mohammad Sadeq Khan, 81
Mohammadzadeh, Azad, xviii
Mohtadi, Abdullah, xvii, xviii, 240-241, 244, 281, 333, 339, 352, 445-450
Mohtadi, Muhammad, 379
Mohtadi, Salah al-Din, 156-157, 160, 187, 351, 454
Mo'ini, Abdullah, 163, 167, 170, 172, 375-376, 439

Mo'ini, Muhammad Amin, 124, 371-372, 427-428
Mo'ini, Nawid, 215, 228, 383, 386
Mo'ini, Sulayman (Fayq), xix, 151, 154, 156, 157, 160-166, 168-172, 174, 212, 374, 376, 437-438
Mojab, Shahrzad, 26-28, 103, 126-128, 321, 333, 467, 469
Mokhber al-Saltaneh, 59
Molotov (Soviet Union's Minister of Foreign Affairs), 89, 106, 123
Momeni, Hamid, 167-168, 333
Monazzami, Ali, 234, 237, 240-241, 333, 458
Moqtaderi, Ahmad, 227
Morad Rasouy Mountain, 439
Moradi, Ali Ashraf, 424
Moradi, Aziz, 129
Moradi, Golmorad, 92, 110, 118-119, 122, 183, 333
Morning Star newspaper, 441
Mosaddegh, Mohammad (Prime Minister), 83, 148-152, 188, 442

Mossad, 203
Mostafayy, Taymour, 263, 395, 397, 404, 406, 409, 411, 413, 417-418, 422-423
Mountain Turks, 36, 46
Movement of Azerbaijan, 52
Muhammad Agha Vosough Ghassemlou. *See* Vosogh Ghassemlou, Muhammad Agha
Muhammad Ali Mirza (Crown Prince), 67
Muhammad Amin Shikak, 368
Muhammad Amin Shirej, 173
Muhammad (Hama) Rashid Khan, 81, 92-93, 134
Muhammadi Marasana, Khidir. *See* Marasana, Mirza Khidir
Muhammad Pasha (known as Mir Kor), 30
Muhammadpour, Khidir, 406
Muhammadzadeh, Rahim, 388, 391, 394, 399, 416, 421, 426

Muhammadzadeh, Rasoul, 419
Mukri, Muhammad (Dr.), 202, 354, 454
Mukriani, Giw, 97
Mullah Ahmad Fawzi, 88
Mullah Awara. *See* Shalmashi, Mullah Ahmad (Mullah Awara)
Mullah Baqir, 153
Mullah Hassani, 208, 212, 230
Mullah Khalil (of Goramari, Goromari), 82-84, 227, 312
Mullah Mahmoud Rasoul, Fazil (Dr.), 251, 253, 358
Mullah Seddiq, 381
Muller, 469
Mustafa Amin, Nawshirwan, 29, 61, 67, 69, 75-76, 94, 97, 112, 114, 122, 128-129, 252, 333-334
Mustafa Kemal Pasha (Atatürk), 35, 75, 287
Mustafa Khoshnaw, Colonel 98, 109, 134, 362
Mustafa Pasha Yamulki, 70

Mustafa Sultani, Foad, 352, 445-446, 454
Mustafa Sultani, Malakeh., 334, 446
Muzaffar Al-Din Shah Qajar, 52
Mykonos Restaurant, 254-255, 359

N

Nabaz, Jamal, 89, 97, 180
Nabdel, Alireza, 167-168
Nabizadeh, Motalleb, 250
Nadir Ahmadi, Rahim, 228
Naghadehei, Hassan, 159, 374
Nahid, A., 52, 59, 337
Nahida Sheikh Salam, 103
Nahri, Abdullah, 105
Naima Khan, 103
Najatdari Kurdistan (Liberator of Kurdistan), 142
Najd al-Saltaneh, 58
Najib Pasha, 62
Namay Kurdistan (Kurdistan's Letter), 433
Nameh-ye Haftehgi-ye Kouhestan (Weekly Letter of Mountain or Letter of Mountain), 433

Nameh-ye Kouhestan (Letter of Mountain), 433
Nanavazadeh, Muhammad, 98, 362-363
Nanavazadeh, Pola 239
Narin, Tom, 8, 334
Naqadehey, Rasoul, 435
Naqadeh war, 205, 207-209, 355
Naqibzadeh, A, 68, 73-74, 82, 184, 334
Naqshbndi, Mahir, 419
Naqshi, Rahman, 267-268, 334, 372, 410, 412, 414, 416, 421
Nasab, A., 52, 334
Nasiri, Sayyed Mansour, 407, 409
Nasr, V., 54, 56, 320
Nasser al-Din Shah, 29
Nastani, Ahmad, 244, 398, 407
Natali, D., 3, 25, 31, 35, 39, 43, 334
National Council of Resistance of Iran (NCRI), 231, 239, 245
National Front, newsletter of, 441
National Liberation of Kurdistan (KUK), 36

Natiq, Dara, 419, 423
NATO (North Atlantic Treaty Organization), 38, 224, 318
Nawandi Mindalparezi Rojhalati Kurdistan (Eastern Kurdistan Centre for Child Protection), 464
Nawandi Nergiz (Nergiz Centre), 464
Nayeri, K., 52, 334
Nazdar, Hussein, xviii, 407, 412-413, 417
Nazdar, M., 44, 334
Nazemi, Muhammad, 435
Nehzati Mqawmat (Resistance Movement), 366
Nergiz magazine, 464
Nerwiy, Hawar Khalil Taher, 60, 80, 82, 106, 128, 132, 137, 184-185, 334
Neumann, Sigmund, 21-22
New Movement of the Iranian Communists, 441
Nezam al-Saltaneh, 61
Nib Sabbath Chak Newspaper, 441

Nikitin, B. (Russian Consul in Iran), 65, 81, 335
Nikjouyan, Sayyed Aziz, 423
Nikoozadeh, Reza (Colonel), 141
Nizami, Sayyed Fatah, 436, 439
Noorani, Mautasam, 244, 278, 293, 335, 407, 412
Norperforce (North Persia Force), 55, 59
Nosrati, Kourosh, 421, 425
Nouri, Soran, 421, 425
Novaya Frimya (Russian), 123
Nowrouzi, Sadiq Khan (Colonel), 74
Nozari Mangur, Ali Khan, 368, 430
Nuranifard, Kamil, xvii, 278, 335, 451

O

O'Ballance, Edgar, 30, 48, 129, 335
Ocalan, Abdullah, 37, 47, 354, 360, 453
O'Connor, W., 5, 338, 342

OIPFG. *See* Organization of Iranian People's Fedai Guerrillas (OIPFG)

Omar Ahmad Mihali, 227

Omary Shikak, Hassan, 368

Omarzadeh, Khidir (Mullah), 400, 402

Opozisioni Newkhoy Hizbi Demokrati Kurdistani Eran (Internal Opposition of the Democratic Party of Iranian Kurdistan), 264

Organization of Iranian Kurdistan Nationalist and Islamic Revolutionary Struggle) (Khabat). *See Sazmani Khabati Natawayati w Islami Kurdistani Eran* (Organization of Iranian Kurdistan Nationalist and Islamic Revolutionary Struggle) (Khabat)

Organization of Iranian Kurdistan Struggle [Khabat]). *See Sazmani Khabati Kurdistani Eran* (Organization of Iranian Kurdistan Struggle [Khabat])

Organization of Iranian People's Fedai Guerrillas (OIPFG), 22, 167, 186, 199-200, 202, 214, 215, 242, 353, 356

Organization of Iranian People's Fadaian (Majority), 200, 226-229, 233, 254, 278

Organization of Revolutionary Workers of Iran (Rah-e Kargar), 233, 242, 276

Organization of Struggle for the Emancipation of the Working Class or the Peykar, 233, 277-279, 287

Osmani, Fatime, 6, 302-303, 335, 424

Otroushi, Abdul Wahab, 173

Oveissi (Lieutenant General), 171, 173, 230, 439

Özoğlu, H., 30-31, 335

P

Pahlavi, Mohammad Reza Shah, 24, 55, 77, 87, 183, 285, 335, 354

Pahlavi, Reza Shah, 24, 35, 51, 54-56, 58, 68, 71-74-77, 81-84, 87, 96, 116-117, 189, 285, 287, 312, 315, 317, 319, 330-331, 333, 335, 339

Pahlavi, Reza (son of Mohammad Reza Shah), 450

Pahlavi Dynesti, 52, 55, 346

Pakdaman, Khidir (Bag), 421, 426

Paki, Morteza, xviii

Palani, Mohayadin, xvii, xix, 267-268, 335, 419, 424

Palestine Liberation Organization, 199

Panahian, Mahmoud (General Dr.), 192-193

Parastin, the security forces of the KDP (Iraq), 164

Parsa, Taha, 227

Parsa Benab, Y., 52, 111, 183, 335

Parsi Tabar (Colonel), 139

Partia Demokrat a Kurdistan—Suriye (Kurdistan Democratic Party—Syria (KDPS or KDP-S), 44

Partia Jiyana Azadi Kurdistan (Party for Free Life in Kurdistan [PJAK]), xxi, 6, 360, 445, 453

Partia Karkaren Kurdistan (*PKK*, Workers Party of Kurdistan). *See Partiya Karkerên Kurdistanê* (Kurdistan Workers' Party [PKK])

Parti Azadi Kurdistan (Kurdistan Freedom Party [PAK]), xxi, 329, 358, 360, 445, 453

Parti Dimokrati Kurdistan (Kurdistan Democratic Party) (KDP (Iraq)),

Parti Rizgari Kurdistan (Kurdistan Liberation Party), 103, 151

Parti Sarbakhoyy Kurdistan (Independence Party of Kurdistan [PSK]), xxi, 236, 280, 337, 358, 445, 452

Parti Sarbasti Rojhalati Kurdistan (the Eastern Kurdistan Independence Party [EKIP]), 452

Partiya Karkerên Kurdistanê (Kurdistan Workers' Party [PKK]), xxi, 37-38, 44-46, 287, 295, 302, 306, 354, 357, 453

Parvin, N., 58, 335

Parwizi, Karim, 417-418, 422-423

Pashayy, Naho (Bapir Shikak),163, 170, 374, 376

Patton, M. Q., 5, 335

Paymani Se Snour (Three-borders Pact), 103-104

PDKI and PDKI-RL Agreement, 257, 360

PDKI Center for Strategic Research, 464

PDKI's Program and Constitution, 236, 335

Peik-e Kurd (Kurd's Courier), 433

Peasants' Movement in 1952-1953, 149

Penaw (pseudonym for Hassan Qizilji), 433

People's Labour Party (HEP), 38

People's Mojahedin Organization of Iran (PMOI), 186, 231

People's Protection Units (YPG), 44

Père Lachaise Cemetery in Paris, 253

Pérez de Cuéllar, Javier, 251

Peshawa (*Pishwa*)(Leader), 94, *121, 141,* 371

Peshnimaz, Rasoul (Mullah), 154, 157-158-161, 164-166, 192, 197, 199, 204, 208-210 223, 249, 296, 335, 374, 378-379, 381, 384, 436

Pesyan, Mohammad Taqi Khan 52, 57-58, 72

Peykar newspaper, 277

Peymai, N., 56, 335

Peyman (Promise) magazine, 441

Pezeshkpour (Brigadier), 203

Pirani, Nasir, 406

Pirani, Reza, 278

Pirdi Sour (Red Bridge), 91

Pirnia, Hasan, 29, 335

Piroti, Rahman (Mullah), 225, 387, 420, 425

Pishevari, Jafar, 111, 113, 117-118, 120, 133-138, 348

527

PKK. See Partiya Karkerên Kurdistanê (Kurdistan Workers' Party [PKK])

Political-Military Commission of the PDKI, 234, 248, 460

Popular Front for the Liberation of Palestine, 199

Pour Azar, Muhammad, 385

Pourqobad, Karim, 203

Pouya, Arsalan, 152

President Ahmad Hassan al- Bakr. *See* Ahmad Hassan al-Bakr

President Georg Bush *See* Bush, George

"previous friends" (KDP), 268

Price, Massoume, 52, 336

Prince Salar al-Dowleh Qajar, 82

Prince Shakhovski, 79

Prince Sharaf al-Dîn Bitlîsiî (Sharaf Khan), 28, 315, 345

Problems of Peace and Socialism/World Marxist Review journal, 441

Progressive Socialist Party of Lebanon, 194, 199

Propaganda (*tablighat*) Commission, 5

Protection Council of Political Prisoners of Eastern Kurdistan, 4-5, 464

Provisional Committee, 159

Provisional Government, 204-205

Provisional Government emissaries (delegation) to Kurdistan, 202, 454

Prunhuber, Carol, 253, 336

Publication Commission, 4

Q

Qadir Chil Koch, 173

Qadiri, Abdullah, 358, 393, 395, 397

Qadiri, Amir, 400

Qadiri, Amir, 400

Qadiri, Iraj (Sarhang, Colonel), 203, 385, 394, 398-399, 401, 405

Qadiri Mamash, Kak Hamza, 368

Qadiri [Mamash], Abdullah (Visited Baku), 113, 430

Qadiri, Morad, 391, 392

Qadiri, Muhammad Nazif, 394, 395, 397, 403, 406, 408, 411-413, 417-418, 422-423

Qadiri, Muhammad Salih, 412- 413

Qadiri, Nabi, 388, 391, 393, 398-402, 405

Qadiri, Rahim, 262

Qadiri, Rouqya, 127

Qadiri Azar, Abdullah, 251, 253

Qadiri Qazi, Qasim, 104, 362-363

Qadiri, Qasim. *See* Qadiri Qazi, Qasim

Qadir Panira, 173

Qadir Sharif. *See* Aqal al-Tolab, Hashim [later Qadir Sharif]

Qadirzadeh, Hassan, 404, 407, 409, 411, 413, 415-416, 420, 425-426

Qadri Baig. *See* Qadri Jamil Pasha

Qadri Jamil Pasha, 63, 123

Qadri, Sohaila, 280, 282, 304, 336, 416, 421, 426

Qalandar, 435

Qalarashi, Faqe Abdullah, 381
Qalatan village, 230
Qandil Mountain, 4, 163, 174, 274, 352, 376
Qaragol village, 235
Qaragowezi (Warzer), Habib, 374
Qarani Agha Amir Ashayer, the Chief of Mamash Tribe. *See* Qarani Agha Zarza (Commander or Governor of Oshnavieh)
Qarani Agha Zarza (Commander or Governor of Oshnavieh), 109, 368
Qara saqal village, 274
Qarne village (massacre), 212, 230
Qavam al-Saltaneh, Prime Minister, 58, 133, 135-136, 181-183 58
Qawi Panjeh, Siamak, 416, 421, 426
Qawi Panjeh, Sirwan, xviii
Qawi Panjeh, Seddiq, 385
Qazani, Mullah Mahmoud, 381
Qazi, Ahmad, 215

Qazi Ali (Qazi Muhammad's father), 93
Qazi, Amir, xix, 88, 148-150, 153-154, 156-157, 160, 163-164, 168-169, 171-172, 174-175, 186, 195, 198, 202, 204, 207, 217, 226, 231, 235-237, 280, 337, 358, 375-380, 382, 384, 388, 402, 452
Qazi, Ali (Qazi Muhammad's son), 453
Qazi, Fawziyeh (Qazi Muhammad's daughter), 215, 382, 386
Qazi, Haji Abdullah, 88, 124-125, 131, 140, 170, 184, 337
Qazi, Ismat Khanim (Qazi Muhammad's daughter), 151
Qazi, Latif, 69-70
Qazi, Mina Khanim (Qazi Muhammad's wife), xix, 93, 126-127, 151, 349
Qazi Muhammad, xix, 88, 91-95, 98, 104-105, 108-118, 120-124, 126, 128, 131, 133-143, 151, 178, 182, 302, 325, 327, 337, 339, 346-350, 368, 371, 434, 435

Qazi, Qadir (Mamard), 159, 374, 436
Qazi, Qasim, xviii, 406
Qazi, Rahim, 3, 100-101, 111-112, 123, 137, 139-143, 146, 151, 182-183, 185-186, 224, 302, 337, 375, 383, 386-387
Qazi, Saad, xviii
Qazi, Sadr, 137, 139-141, 339, 350
Qazi, Salar, 149
Qazis (Qazi Muhammad, Muhammad Hussein Khan Saifi Qazi, Sadr Qazi), 139-141, 435
Qazi Wahab, 123
Queen Elizabeth, 14
Qiaday Mowaqati Parti (Provisional Leadership of the KDP [Iraq]), 202-203
Qizilji, (Mullah) Hassan, 146, 158, 172, 176 178, 197, 432-433
Qoliyov, Soviet Vice-Consul, N. K., 110 120
Qoreshi, Abdullah, 387
Qubadi (Major) Head of the Police Station in Mahabad, 101
Quli Khan Mamassani, 56

R

Rabiei, Sarhang (Colonel), 385

Rabinbach, A., 32, 337

Rad, Abubakir, 391, 393, 396, 398-399, 401, 405

Radio Dangi Kurdistani Eran (Iranian Kurdistan Voice Radio) of PDKI-RL, 250, 256

Radio Dangi Kurdistan (Voice of Kurdistan Radio) of KDP (since 1946, and of the later KDP), 130, 349, 465

Radio Serri (Secret Radio), 145

Radio Solh wa Taraqi (Peace and Progress), 228

Radioy Dangi Kurdistani Eran (Iranian Kurdistan Voice Radio) of KDP (I) and PDKI, 196, 229, 460, 464

Radioy Shoreshgerani Eran (Iranian Revolutionaries' Radio), 193

Radio Zahmatkeshan (Toilers), 228

Radmanesh, Reza, 166, 169-170, 172, 437

Rafigh Hilmi, 103

Rafsanjani's jash, 249

Rahbar (*Leader*) (newspaper), 116, 122

Rah-e Ettehad (Path to Unity), or in Kurdish, *Regay Yaketi*, 193

Rahimi, Ahmad (Mullah), 411, 417

Rahimi, M, 337, 452

Rahimi, Muhammad, 253

Rahimi, Osman, 238, 264, 393, 398-399, 401, 405, 408, 410

Rahimi, Rahman (Chako), 391, 394, 398, 403, 408-410, 413, 417, 422

Rahim Zadeh, Wahed, xviii

Rahmani, Sayyed Ali, 384

Rahnimoun, Erfan, 414, 417

Rains, Carole, xvii

Rais Dana (Captain), 143

Raisnia, R. 52, 59, 337

Rajai, Muhammad Ali (President), 225

Rajavi, Massoud, 231

Raouf Mullah Hassan (Wasta Raouf Khayat), 375

Rasan (Rising or Re-rising of the PDKI), 275-276, 294,

Rasha Ghachaghchi, 155

Rashid Baig Harki, 368

Rashid Smel, 434

Rashidi, Muhammad Amin, 405

Rashidi, Shahla, xviii

Rasoul, Fazil (Dr.). *See* Mullah Mahmoud Rasoul, Fazil (Dr.)

Rasoul Ali Laylan, Mirad, 165

Rasouli, Muhammad (Dilshad), 104, 131, 371-372

Rasouli Azar, Hussein, 230

Rastgar, Hassan, xviii, xix, 157-160, 163-165, 174, 192, 195, 204, 223, 238, 246, 250, 253, 256-257, 260, 262, 264-265, 281, 291, 297, 337-338, 351, 358, 373, 377-378, 381, 383, 388, 390-391, 393, 398-402, 404-405, 408-413, 415-416, 422, 436

Ratebi, Muhammad Amin, 89, 91, 151

Ravej (Consultation) magazine, 433
Rawandoust, Massoud, 416, 421
Rawti Reform (Reform Trend) within the PDKI, 269
Rawti Sosialisti Komala (Socialist Path of Komala), 450
Rayhani, Ali, 113
Razayy, Hakim, 384, 388, 391, 393
Razmavar, Morad [Aziz] (Captain), 193
Red Army, 54, 57, 91, 95, 114, 136-137, 178, 183, 346
Rega (Way), 146
Regay Kurdistan (Way of Kurdistan) newspaper, 441
Regay Yaketi. See, Rah-e Ettehad (Path to Unity), or in Kurdish, *Regay Yaketi Kurdistan* (Kurdistan Youth Organization)
Rekkhrawi Ganj u Lawani Kurdistan (Kurdistan Youth Organization), 204

Rekkhrawi Lawani Komalay J.K. (J.K. Youth Organization), 95
Renan, Ernest, 8, 13, 338
Rounak, Siraji's wife, 197
Revolutionary Democrats, 36
Revolutionary Organization of the Tudeh Party, 167
Reza Khan. *See* Pahlavi, Reza Shah
Reza Shah. *See* Pahlavi, Reza Shah
Rezaee, Mohsen, former Commander-in-Chief of the Revolutionary Guards, 275, 336
Razmara, Haj Ali (Major-General), 110, 134-135
Richard, Anna, ii
Ritchie, J., 5, 329-330, 338, 342
Rizgari (Liberation), 36
Rizwani, Yousef, 175, 377
Rocard, Michael, 238
Rojava, 45-47, 302, 306
Roji Kurd, 274-275, 338
Roji Kurd TV, 276, 338
Roji Kurd Shawi Ajam (Day of Kurd Naight of Ajam) or Roji Kurd (Day of Kurd) or Kurd newspaper, of Simko's time, 71, 80
Rojjimeri taybati Komala bo Sali 1322 (the J.K.'s calendar for the year (1943-1944), 367
Rojjimeri taybati Komala bo Sali 1323 (the J.K.'s calendar for the year (1944-1945). 367
Rojnamay Hawari Nishtman (newspaper Shout of Homeland), 126, 432
Rojnamay Kurdistan (newspaper Kurdistan), 432
Rojnamay Mirow (*Newspaper Human*), 367
Rojnamay Zagros (newspaper Zagros), 433
Roj (Sun) newspaper. 169
Roosevelt, A., Jr., 96 105, 113, 141, 338, 369
Rostami, Hashim, 402, 405
Rowangay Lawan (Youth View) magazine, 250
Rowshanfekr, Abdullah, 435

Russian Revolution (1905), 51

Russian Revolution (1917), 51, 64

S

Sabaghian, Hashem, 213, 215

Sabri, Osman, 44

Saddam Hussain, 42, 46, 220, 283, 317, 357

Sadiq Waziri, Sarm al-Din, 147-148, 214, 374-375

Sa'ed, Prime Minister, 110

Saedi, Bahman, 205, 214, 241-242, 244, 258, 281-282, 293, 339, 446-450

Safa, Ahmad, xviii, 225-226, 338, 387

Safai, I., 56, 339

Safari, Eqbal, 415, 420

Safari, Hamid, 228

Safiyeh Khan (Simko's daughter), 74

Sahabi, Ezzatollah, 213, 215

Sahafi, Ebrahim, xviii

Sahebi, Muhammad, 417, 423

Said Hama Qala Bostanchi, 97

Saif al-Qozat, 72, 179, 339

Saifi Qazi, Muhammad Hussein Khan, 113, 121-122, 132, 138-139, 141, 339, 349-350, 368, 371, 427-428

Saifi Qazi, Rahim. *See* Qazi, Rahim

Sajjadi, Ala-adin, 61, 71, 82, 339

Saladin [Ayyubi]. *See Salah al-Din* (*Saladin*), 29, 105, 345

Salah al-Din (*Saladin*) (Play), 105

Saleh, Badr al-Din, 139-141, 183, 339, 434

Saleh, Kiumarth (Captain), 139-141

Saleh, Rafiq, 104, 106, 115-116, 118, 120-122, 126-128, 130-131, 133, 135, 178, 369, 432

Saleh, Seddiq, 104, 106, 115-116, 118, 120-122, 126-128, 130-131, 133, 135, 178, 369, 432

Salehi, Fariba., 8, 339

Salehi, Fatih, 423

Salehian, Ahmad, 95

Salih Rad, Ibrahim (Ibraim Lajani), 394-395, 397, 404

Salihzadeh, Rahim, 400

Salim Rubai Ali, 198

Salimi, Muhammad, 362

Samadi, Sayyed Muhammad, xviii, 82-83, 91, 94, 96, 98-99, 124, 139-141, 339-340, 362, 366, 368

Samsam al-Saltaneh Bakhtiyari, 58

Sanandaj war, 205-206, 218

Sani, Khosrow, xviii

Sanjar Khan Miawaran, 81

Sarchinar village, 235

Sardakosani, Mullah Karim. *See* Azizi, Mullah Karim, (Sardakosani)

Sardke, Mullah Khidir, 454

Sardar Khorshid, 81

Sardar Nosrat, 67

Sardashti, Yasin, 89-93, 98, 101-102, 113, 121-124, 128-130, 133-135, 137-138, 143, 154, 156-157, 159-160, 163, 165-166, 171-173, 183-184,

340, 374, 427-428, 436, 440-441
Sari'al-Qalam, Mahabad's Governor, 92, 101-102
Sarokani village, 230
Sartip Khan (Shikak), 56, 368
SAVAK, the Iranian intelligence (The Organization for Intelligence and National Security), 152-155, 159, 163-165, 193, 350, 454
Sawzi village, 2325
Sayyad, Aso, 418
Sayyadian, Wilma, 120, 127
Sayyed Ahmadi, Sayyed Rasoul, 398, 404, 407, 409
Sayyed Haji Kalawe, 375
Sayyedi, Hemin, 414-415
Sayyed Muhammad Seddiq (Sheikh Pusho), 368
Sayyed Reza, 36
Sayyed (Sheikh) Abdullah Afandi [Gailani], 142, 182, 372
Sayyed Taha Shamzinan, 48, 60-61, 64, 66, 68-70, 75, 368

Sazman-e Kar-e Iran (Labour Party of Iran) or the Toufan, 233
Sazmani Jawanani Kurd (Kurdish Youth Organization), 95, 102, 125
Sazmani Khabati Kurdistani Eran (Organization of Iranian Kurdistan Struggle [Khabat]), xx, 233, 445, 451
Sazmani Khabati Natawayati w Islami Kurdistani Eran (Organization of Iranian Kurdistan Nationalist and Islamic Revolutionary Struggle) (Khabat), xx, 357
Schmidt, Dana Adams, 159-160
Schöpflin, George, 11, 15, 340
Schwarzkopf, Herbert Norman (General), 140
Secretariat Office, 5
Sedaqat (Honesty) Association, 60
Sedqi, Mullah Seddiq, 140
Seghatoleslam, 67
Seifi, the Governor of

Seljuq Sultan Sanjar, 28
Serdemî Niwê or *Serdama Nû* (*New Era*), 340, 452
Seton-Watson, Hug, 8, 340
Shabestari, Ali, 137
Shadab, Omar, 412, 421
Shaeirlar Majlisi (Poets' Sessions), 132
Shafaq (Aurora), magazine, 132
Shafe'I, Rahman, 102
Shafe'I, Rahmat, 102
Shafe'I, Sulayman, 156
Shafi'i [Nijnayy], Mullah Salam, 380
Shahabi, Qadir, 385
Shahandeh, Abbas, 116, 122
Shahbakhti, (Lieutenant General), 144
Shahbaz (Royal Falcon) Newspaper, 117, 147
Shahidian, 5, 340
Shah Sultan Khanoum Fattahi Qazi, 127
Shahidan (Martyrs) organization, 263
Shahin, Omar Mullah, 227
Shakiba [Shakib], [Muhammad Rashid], 213

533

Shahrawan, Muhammad, 404, 407, 409

Shaikholislami Mukri, Sayyed Mohammad Amin (Mamosta Hemin), xix, 48, 88, 91, 94, 108, 137, 149-150, 153, 174-175, 177-170, 195, 222-223, 323, 377-379, 383, 385-386

Shaji'i Faizollah Baigi (Kiltga), Ahmad Khan, 435

Shakir, Sadoun, 198

Shalmashi, Mullah Ahmad (Mullah Awara), xix, 157, 159, 166, 172, 352, 373, 376

Shalmashi, Mostafa, xix, 172, 195, 216, 223, 234, 237, 279, 281, 283, 341, 382, 384, 388-390, 415-416, 419-420, 425

Shaltouki, Mohammad Reza, 213

Shams, Said, 183, 279, 297, 341

Shams Borhan, Sheikh Hassan, 430

Shandri, Kazim, 144, 350

Shapasandi, Muhammad, 96, 102, 105-106, 109-110, 117, 145-146, 183, 193, 341, 362, 366-367

Sharafi, Hassan, xvii, 6, 260, 267, 270, 384, 388, 390-391, 393, 395- 397, 403, 406-413, 417-418, 422-423

Sharafi, Isma'il, 421, 426

Sharafi, Karwan, 424

Sharafi, Mohammad Amin, 102, 115, 363, 371-372

Sharaf Khan. *See* Prince Sharaf al-Dîn Bitlîsiî (Sharaf Khan)

Sharafkandi, Abdul Rahman (Mamosta Hajar), xix, 48, 104, 341, 374

Sharafkandi, Golaleh, xviii, xix, 304, 341, 416, 420, 425

Sharafkandi, Sadiq (Said Badal), xix, 30, 48, 66, 231-233, 236-237, 244-245, 247, 250, 252-255, 288, 297, 299, 341, 359, 383-385, 387-388, 390-393, 395-397, 402-403, 459

Sharafkandi-Ghassemlou faction, 247, 250, 254, 459

Shared Declaration of the PDKI and the Komala, 235, 341

Shariat, Taban, xviii

Shariati, Rahmat Allah, 373

Sharif (Captain), 139

Sharifi, Abdullah, 394-395, 397, 403

Sharifi, Ahmad, 105

Sharifi, M., 56, 341

Sharifi (Shikak), Omar Khan, 90, 93, 100, 136, 182, 372

Sharif Pasha (General), 30-31

Sharifzadeh, Isma'il (Mullah Aziz), xix, 157, 166-169, 172, 212, 352, 375- 376, 436

Sharifzadeh, Omar, 394, 399

Shahrikandi, Mullah Karim, 227

Sharwerani, Mustafa, 227

Shawbash, Khalil, 171, 436

Shed, American Consul, 65

Sheikh Abdul Ghadir of Shamzinan, 30, 79
Sheikh Abdul Rahman, 140
Sheikh Adil, 123
Sheikh al-Islami, Fatih, 156
Sheikh al-Islami, Mosleh, 445
Sheikhani, Hassan, 420, 425
Sheikh Kamil, 99
Sheikh Khaz'al, 53, 56, 68
Sheikh Mahmoud Barzanji. *See* Barzanji, Sheikh Mahmoud
Sheikh Muhammad Khiabani, 52, 54, 57-59, 67, 71, 78, 337
Sheikh Said, 35-36
Sheikh Qazi Fattah, 59-60
Sheikh Seraj al-Din, 72
Sheikh Ubayd Allah. *See* Sheikh Ubayd Allah Nehri
Sheikh Ubayd Allah of Nehri, 30, 48, 51, 59, 62, 75, 78, 142, 346
Sheikh Ubayd Allah Zinwe, 104
Sherzad, Ali Khan, 142-143

Sheyholislami, Jafar, 8, 16, 341
Shils, Edward, 9
Shirazi, Hashem, 96-98, 141, 148, 179, 341, 362
Shirej, Morad, 439
Shirkat-i Taraqi, or Progress Company. 124
Shirzad, Ali Baig, 435
Shitwi, Hassan (Dr.), 379
Shiwasali, (Mullah) Hassan, 201, 381-382, 389-390, 393, 395-396, 403, 418, 423
Shoaleh-ye Jonoub (Southern Flame) newspaper, 441
Shojai Fard, Shapour, 394, 399, 400
Short, D., 32, 341
Shumanov, Vasily, 65. 342
Siadat, Haji Baba Sheikh, 134, 138, 349, 368, 371, 427-428
Sidgi, Parvin, xviii
Silaman (Sulayman), 170
Simay Demokrat (Democratic Visage), 217, 234, 458
Simko. *See* Isma'il Agha Shikak (Simko)

Siraji, Muhammad Amin, 96-97, 99, 156-157, 165-167, 169-170, 172, 175, 191-193, 195, 197, 201, 208, 217, 220-222, 224, 228-229, 352, 375-382, 386-387, 436-438
Sir Percy Cox, 68
Sir Percy Loraine, 73
Sir Percy Sykes, 53
Sir Redder Bullard, British Ambassador to Tehran, 123
six freedom-seeking political parties, 136
six-year war (1984-1990) between the PDKI and the Komala, 243
Skoggard, I, 467, 469
Smith, Anthony D., 8-12, 35, 184, 288, 316, 324-325, 334, 338, 340, 342
Smith, Christopher, 35
SMPK. *See Kürd Tecvün ve Terakki Cemiyeti* (Society for Mutual Aid and Progress of Kurdistan [SMPK])
Socialist International, 245, 254, 291, 448, 465
Socialist Party, 136

Socialist Party of Turkish Kurdistan (SPTK), 36
Sofian village, 230
Solat al-Dowleh, 56
Solh Jou, Hussein (Captain), 141
Somanabad village, 215
Sontag, Monseigneur, 65
Soor, Kawa, xviii
sosializmi adilana (just socialism) (compatible socialism), 195
South Persia Rifles, 54, 55
Soviet Communist Party, 152
Soviet Cultural Relations Society. *See Komalay Pewandiyakani Farhangi Soviet* (Soviet Cultural Relations Society)
Soviet Madaniyat Evi (Soviet Cultural House; Soviet Cultural Society in Azerbaijan) in Tabriz, 132
Soviet Socialist Republic of Iran (Gilan), (1920-1921), 52, 54
Sowara, Mawloud, 416, 421, 426
Spivak, Gayatri Chakravorty, 8

Spencer, L., 5, 338, 342
Spencer, P., 9, 11-12, 20, 342
Sports Field [now Takhti Stadium], 207
Stalin, J., 8, 12-13, 19, 24, 141, 178, 287, 329
Stansfield, Gareth, 76, 313, 449-450
Stoel, Max van der, 34, 342
Student Union, 4
Sultani, Qasim, 153-154
Sultanian, Kolthum 127
Sultanian, Mustafa, 372
Sultanian, Rahim, 146-148
Sultanian, Said, 385
Sultan Selim I, 29
Supreme National Security Council (SNSC) of Iran, 272
Sutton, Lester, 140
Sutton, P. D., 4, 342
Sykes-Picot Agreement (Asia Minor Agreement), 25, 43, 346
Syrian Democratic Forces (SDF), 45

T

Tabai, Soheyla, xviii

Tabari, Ehsan, 52, 56, 68, 145, 343
Tabatabai, Sayyed Zia al-Din, 54-55, 58
Tabibi Ijbari (*Compulsory Doctor*). 105
Tabrizi, the Governor of Tabriz, 208
Tafazzoli, 22
Tagarani, Qala, 171
Taha Harki, 90, 368
Tahmasebi, 74
Talabani, Jalal, xix, 41-43, 49, 154, 160, 168, 172, 174, 211, 235, 251-252, 353
Talebpour, Zobaideh, 384
Tamaddon, 71
Tarh-e Khodgardani (Self-Governing Plan), 213, 222
Tarh-e Sargardani (Displacement Plan), 222
Taqmi Hassani Rastgar (Hassan Rastgar's Group), 265
Taqmi Hawt Kasi (Group of Seven People), 222
Tariq ash-Shaab (Path of the People) newspaper, 441
Tawfiq, Hoshang, 89

Taymour Khan (Governor of Khoy), 64
Tejel, Jordi, 44, 343
Tekoshar (Struggler), 192, 264
The New York Times, 159-160
The Quran, 99, 109, 121, 162, 178, 301
Peasants' Movement in 1952-1953, 149
Thompson, A., 8, 343
Three-Month War, 205, 209, 211-212, 355
Three-Step Plan, 254
Tikan Tapa, Sulayman, 200
Tilly, Charles, 8
Tishk News (TISHKTVNEWS) online TV of PDKI, 464
Tishk (Ray) magazine, of KDP, 465
Tishk (Ray) magazine, of PDKI, 464
Tishk (Ray) newspaper, of Revolutionary Committee, 169
Tishk (Ray) TV, of PDKI, xxii, 464

Tobacco Movement of 1891-1892, 52
Tohfeh (Gift), 433
Tohidi, Najmadin, 362, 429-430
Toiler Party, 41
Totagajy, Jina, xviii
Trask, Haunani-Kay, 8, 343
Treaty of Sevres (10 August 1920), 31, 35, 39
Tro, son of Sayyed Taha, 368
Tsar Nikolas II, 61
Tudeh Party. *See* Tudeh Party of Iran
Tudeh Party of Iran, 87-88, 95, 111, 116, 136, 140, 142-143, 145-150, 152-154, 158, 166, 169-170, 172-173, 175-176, 182, 193-195, 197, 199-200, 204, 212-213, 216-217, 219-229, 233, 235, 238, 245, 278, 323, 325, 343, 346, 337-338, 341
Tudeh Party's *Radio Peyk-e Iran* (Iran Courier), 158, 169, 438
Turjani (Turjanizadeh or Ghizilgi), Mullah Mohammad, 71, 72, 343

TV and Radio Section, 5

U

United Arab Republic (UAR), 43
United Nations, 32-34, 250-251, 342-343
United Nations Security Council Resolution 598, 560
Unrepresented Nations and Peoples Organization (UNPO), 465
Utamishi, Qasim, 124

V

Vafaee, Kamal, xviii
Vahabzadeh, Peyman, xvii, xviii, xix, 6, 22, 23, 167, 190, 285, 286, 343
Vali, Abbas, 3, 71, 80, 101, 112, 134, 321, 343
Vanly, I. S., 39-41, 343
Vosogh Ghassemlou, Muhammad Agha, 368
Vossugh al-Dowleh, 53, 54

W

Wahlbeck, O., 37, 343
Wakili, Siamak, 414-415
Wakil Jawanrood, 82

Walby, Sylvia, 8, 344
Walizadeh, Mahmoud, 371-372, 427-428
Walizadeh, Rahman, 124
Wallerstein Immanuel, 25, 344
Wanawsha, Khalid, 406, 412, 416, 420, 425,
Ward, K., 5, 329
War Ministry or *Wazarati Hezi Dimokrati Kurdistan* (Ministry of Kurdistan Democratic Force), 122
Washington Kurdish Institute (WKI), 40
Watamishi, Sultan (Dr.), 379
Watan Doost, Saed, 334, 445-446, 450
Watan Yolinda (For the Homeland's Sake), 122, 132366
Wender, Andrew, xvii
West, Lois A., 8, 315-316, 319, 325, 329, 331, 333, 343-344
Weysi, Karim, 146, 148
White, Emily, ii
Wilkinson, R., 32, 344
Wilson, Woodrow (United States President), 30, 39, 66, 68

Wirdi, Mullah Rahim, 163, 173, 374
Wirya, Qadir, xvii, xix, 171, 223, 237, 264, 281, 283, 292, 296, 344, 406, 408, 411, 415-416, 419-420, 425
Wollman, H., 8, 9, 11-12, 20, 342
Women's Protection Units (YPJ), 44
Workers' Communist Party of Iran (WPI), 447

X
Xenophon, 28, 345

Y
Yahou, Karim, 89
Yahou, Muhammad, 115, 362-363, 367
Yaketi Jawanani Demokrati Kurdistan (Democratic Youth Union of Kurdistan), 119, 125-126, 432
Yaketi Jinani Demokrati Kurdistan (Democratic Women's Union of Kurdistan), xix, 304, 464

Yaket Jinani Demokrati Kurdistani Eran (Democratic Women's Union of Iranian Kurdistan), xix, 4, 6, 267-268, 270, 302, 304, 424, 464
Yaketi Jinani Kurdistan (Women's Union of Kurdistan) (of KDP [Iraq]), 103
Yaketi Jinani Mahabad (Mahabad Women's Union), 202
Yaketi Khowendkarani Demokrati Kurdistani Eran (Democratic Student Union of Iranian Kurdistan), 270, 424, 464
Yaketi Lawani Demokrati Kurdistani Eran (Democratic Youth Union of Iranian Kurdistan), 270, 312, 424, 464
Yaketi Lawani Democrati Rojhalati Kurdistan (Democratic Youth Union of Kurdistan), xxii, 5, 327, 464
Yaketi Lawani Hizbi Demokrat (Youth Union

of the Democratic Party), 219
Yaketi Lawani Mahabad (Mahabad Youth Union), 202
Yaketi Natawayy Khowendkarani Kurd (National Unity of Kurdish Students), 464
Yaketi Nishtimani Kurdistan (Patriotic Union of Kurdistan (PUK), xxi, 41-42, 49, 234-235, 241, 251-252, 256, 258-259, 295, 354, 359
Yaketi Shorishgerani Kurdistan (Kurdistan Revolutionaries Unity), 259, 358, 361, 453
Yaqoubi (Lieutenant), 143
Yaşar (Yashar) Kemal, 38
Yassin, B. A., 3, 75, 81, 98, 114, 344, 364, 369, 431
Yazdanfar Halimeh, xviii
Yazdanfar Khalid, xviii
Yazdanpanah, Hussein, xvii
Yazdi, 110
Yildiz, Karim, 28, 34, 37, 42, 344

Younesi, Ibrahim, 329, 454
Young Turk Revolution of 1908, 30, 51
Young Turks. *See İttihat ve Terakki Cemiyeti* (Committee of Union and Progress [CUP])
Yousefi, Asaad, xviii
Yousefi, Aziz, xviii, xix, 146, 148, 151-152-153, 174-175, 200, 212, 373-374, 376, 379
Yousefi, Hashem, 430
Yousefi, Keyhan, 424
Yousefi, Qadir, 151
Youth Organization of PDKI, 219
Youth Union, 4
Yuval-Davis, Nira., 8, 344

Z

Zabihi, Abdul Rahman (Rahman), xix, 89, 96-98, 104, 106-107, 109, 119, 146, 177, 191, 193, 326, 362-363, 366-367, 371-372, 429-430, 452
Zafar al-Dowleh, 77
Zahir Nejad (Brigadier), 108
Zakariayy, Shoaib, 445

Zaki, Mamosta Abdullah (Mamosta Qandil), 328, 354, 451
Zamani, Arash, 165
Zenab, 151
Zand, Farideh, 127
Zandi, Aziz (aka, Almani, the German Aziz), 89, 91, 363
Zanganeh, Mozaffar (Major-General, Colonel), 104, 149
Zankoy Siasi-Nizami (Political-Military College), 339
Zarbakht, M., 144, 344
Zare', Khidir, 250
Zarza, Sadiq, 418
Zaza, Nureddin, 44
Zarza tribe, 209
Zerin, 151
Zibakalam, Sadeq, 213
Zinar Silopi, 63
Zinn, Maxine Baca, 5, 344
Zor Asna, Najmadin, 400
Zulfo, 81

www.ingramcontent.com/pod-product-compliance
Lightning Source LLC
Chambersburg PA
CBHW040003040426
42337CB00033B/5206